Andhra Pradesh Development

Economic Reforms and Challenges Ahead

The Centre for Economic and Social Studies (CESS), Hyderabad was set up in 1980 by Government of Andhra Pradesh as an autonomous research institution (registered under the Societies Act) with the objective of undertaking mutually supportive and interrelated research, training and documentation activities in the field of economic and social development in general and the state of Andhra Pradesh in particular. The Centre was accorded the status of a national institute in 1986 by the Indian Council of Social Science Research (ICSSR), New Delhi and was included in its network of institutions for grant support. It is located in a 5-acre area of the Nizamiah Observatory Campus, near Punjagutta, in the heart of Hyderabad city. The management of the Centre is vested in two bodies viz., Board of Governors and Executive Council.

The Centre's current research areas are mainly related to rural development and poverty; agriculture and food security; irrigation and water management; public finance; demography and health; environment and other studies. The Centre also conducts M.Phil/Ph.D Programme in collaboration with Dr. B. R. Ambedkar Open University. It is a part-time programme that enables the faculty of colleges, research organisations, NGOs etc., to pursue research without having to take long leave from their regular work. The Centre is also recognised as an institute for advanced research in social sciences by the University of Hyderabad and Osmania University.

The Centre receives financial support in the form of grants-in-aid from the ICSSR and the Government of Andhra Pradesh. The major source of funding, however, has been the research studies sponsored by several national and international organisations. The Centre's library has a collection of over 21,500 books and other volumes, and receives about 150 Indian and foreign periodicals.

Andhra Pradesh Development

Economic Reforms and Challenges Ahead

Edited by

C.H. Hanumantha Rao

S. Mahendra Dev

Centre for Economic and Social Studies

Hyderabad

Published by

Centre for Economic and Social Studies
Nizamiah Observatory Campus
Begumpet, Hyderabad – 500 016, India.
Tel: 040-23402789, 23416780 Fax: 23406808
E-mail: postmaster@cess.ac.in
Website: www.cess.ac.in

Distributed by

Manohar Publishers and Distributors
4753/23, Ansari Road
Daryaganj, New Delhi, India.
Tel: 011-23262796, 23289100 Fax: 23265126
E-mail: manbooks@vsnl.com
Website: www.manbooks.com

First Published, 2003

ISBN 81-88793-00-0

Typesetting and Printed at:

Sairam Printers
Saifabad, Hyderabad-500 004.
Tel: 23232316, 23237598

To

Shri B. P. R. Vithal garu

Founder of the CESS
on the occasion of his

75th Birth Anniversary

Contents

Preface

Andhra Pradesh has been vigorously pursuing economic reforms since the mid-1990s for stepping up economic growth and alleviating poverty, while protecting environment. There has been a significant fiscal correction in the last seven years. Reforms are underway in the power and irrigation sectors for expanding their capacity by improving efficiency and cost recovery. There is a breakthrough in the introduction of information technology. Significant strides have been made in respect of participatory management of land, water and forest resources. Women's self-help groups are a success story in the state and have formed a central element in the strategy for poverty eradication through social mobilization, community empowerment and capacity building. These initiatives have earned a name for Andhra Pradesh as one in the forefront of economic reforms, raising high expectations within the country and abroad about its performance.

The papers in this volume examine the development experience of Andhra Pradesh in the wake of the on-going economic reforms and challenges ahead. The book highlights that there remain significant challenges in the economic and social sectors that the state needs to address if it is to derive full benefits from the reforms already launched and to make development more balanced, broad-based and sustainable. It is hoped that the analysis in this book would provoke a useful debate on the formulation of appropriate strategies for sector-specific interventions and to reach out to the poor and the disadvantaged sections and backward regions.

Most of the papers in the volume were prepared by the faculty members of the Centre for Economic and Social Studies (CESS). Dr. T. L. Sankar, former Principal, Administrative College of India, and Prof. J.V.M. Sarma of the University of Hyderabad also contributed papers to the volume. We are thankful to them for their contributions. The papers were first presented in a seminar organised by the CESS in November 2002. All the papers have been revised in the light of the discussions following each presentation. We are grateful to Dr. C. Rangarajan, the then Governor of Andhra Pradesh, for the suggestions in his inaugural address at the seminar. We thank Shri B. P. R. Vithal and Prof. R. Radhakrishna for their comments and suggestions on the overview of this volume. Thanks are due to the participants of the seminar, particularly Prof. K. L. Krishna and Prof. K. Krishnamurty for their comments on the papers. *Economic and Political Weekly* in a Special Issue (March 22-April 4, 2003) published 15 out of the 22 papers of this volume. We are thankful to the editor, Shri Krishna Raj and his team for publishing these papers.

The authors of the papers extended full cooperation in this joint effort by positively responding to our suggestions and promptly revising their papers. Dr. C. Ramachandraiah helped us in co-ordination by getting the papers at various stages, in organising the seminar, and in the publication of this volume. We are thankful to all of them.

Hyderabad
July 10, 2003.

C. H. Hanumantha Rao
S. Mahendra Dev

List of Contributors

From CESS

C. H. Hanumantha Rao

S. Mahendra Dev

P. Venkatramaiah

S. Subrahmanyam

V. Ratna Reddy

S. Galab

S. Sudhakar Reddy

K.V. Narayana

M. Gopinath Reddy

C. Ramachandraiah

K. S. James

C. Ravi

P. Padmanabha Rao

R. Nageswara Rao

Deepita Chakravarty

N. Sreedevi

N. Chandrasekhara Rao

Others

T. L. Sankar, former Principal, Administrative Staff College of India, Hyderabad.

J.V. M. Sarma, Department of Economics, University of Hyderabad.

L.G. Burange, Department of Economics, University of Mumbai.

S. Indrakant, Department of Economics, Osmania University, Hyderabad.

P. Satya Sekhar, Indian Institute of Health and Family Welfare, Hyderabad.

Vijay Mahajan, Director, BASIX, Hyderabad.

S.V. Subramanian, Department of Health and Social Behaviour, Harvard School of Public Health, Harvard University, Boston, USA

Bhagirath Behra, Ph.D student, ZEF Bonn, Germany.

1

Economic Reforms and Challenges Ahead: An Overview

C.H. Hanumantha Rao and
S. Mahendra Dev

1. MACROECONOMIC SCENE

Introduction

If the balance of payments crisis in 1991 triggered off economic reforms in the country, the year 1995-96, in many ways, proved to be a watershed for the macroeconomic scene in Andhra Pradesh. State's own tax revenues as per cent of Gross State Domestic Product (GSDP) dropped by nearly 3 percentage points between 1990-91 and 1995-96, due largely to the fall in revenues from state excise following the introduction of Prohibition. The subsidy on rice, which is untargeted, amounted to thrice the level at which the population below the poverty line could be provided. These together with the low rates for water and electricity for irrigation resulted in a huge revenue loss which was much beyond the capacity of a state like A.P. whose per capita income was below the national average. The state thus landed itself in a severe financial crisis, holding up much needed developmental expenditure.

The state government responded to this challenge boldly and imaginatively by undertaking measures to raise tax and non-tax revenues and by launching several reforms to restructure the institutions for the management of infrastructure, after holding wide-ranging discussions with experts and people at large. These initiatives have earned a name for Andhra Pradesh as one in the forefront of economic reforms, raising high expectations within the country and abroad about its performance.

However, the impact of economic reforms on development is not instantaneous. There are usually considerable time lags between the initiation of reforms and the outcomes in terms of various indicators of development. For a short period of a few years, some of the observed achievements and deficiencies may be traceable to policies and programmes initiated long ago, whereas quite a few of the results from the policy initiatives currently being undertaken can be expected only after a considerable lapse of time. Nevertheless, this need not deter one from forming judgements as to the intrinsic worth of reforms being undertaken or their likely consequences.

Growth

The GSDP growth in the 1980s in A.P., at a little over 5% p.a., was nearly the same or marginally higher than the GDP growth for the country. But in the 1990s whereas there was a clear step-up in the growth rate of GDP for the country to a little over 6%, there is no clear evidence of an improvement in the growth rate of GSDP in A.P. However, thanks to the rapid decline in the population growth rate in the state during the 1990s, there was an improvement in the per capita SDP growth from 3.3% to 4.0%, but was still lower than the per capita GDP growth in the country in the 1990s. The level of per capita income in the state has always been lower than all India, and the gap has widened somewhat in the 1990s between the state and All India as well as fast growing states, as is evident from the increasing divergence in these per capita growth rates.

It is interesting to note that the improved performance of the state in terms of per capita GSDP growth in the post-reform period of nineties is entirely due to the deceleration in population growth rate which has hardly anything to do with economic reforms launched in the state since mid-nineties. We shall discuss later the factors contributing to this rapid decline in fertility rate.

The improvement in the GDP growth in the country in the post-reform period is accounted wholly by the growth in the service sector (which reflects in part the recent rise in salaries), as the growth rates for agriculture & allied as well as industry showed a decline. A.P. experienced a deceleration in the growth of service sector and was well below the All India growth.

How does one explain the fact that whereas some states did experience significant rise in their SDP growth rates in the 1990s by benefiting from economic reforms and thereby pushed up the All India average growth rate, A.P. could not respond in a similar way? The answer lies partly in the initial or pre-reform level of social and economic infrastructure conducive to growth and partly in the rate of capital formation, physical as well as human, in the post-reform period.

Capital Formation

The index of Social and Economic Infrastructure for Andhra Pradesh was slightly below the All India average in 1995, and was a little above the average in the year 2000. Of the seven states ranking higher than A.P. in respect of GSDP growth, except Rajasthan, the remaining 6 states had a higher rank than A.P. in regard to Social and Economic Infrastructure in 1995 as well as in 2000. Similarly, out of the seven states whose GSDP growth rates were lower than that of A.P., except Punjab in 1995, and Punjab as well as Uttar Pradesh in 2000, the remaining states had a lower rank than that of A.P. in respect of Social and Economic Infrastructure[1]. Clearly, the states whose initial or pre-reform conditions were favourable in respect of infrastructure could benefit more from the opportunities opened up, especially in the service sector, by economic reforms and register higher growth rates in GSDP.

The states ranking higher than A.P. in respect of social and economic infrastructure could attract greater foreign direct investment (FDI). Between 1991 and 2001, the top five states in terms of attracting FDI, viz., Maharashtra, Delhi, Tamil Nadu, Karnataka and Gujarat, accounted for 52% of total FDI approvals in the country. Despite its reforms, A.P. could manage to attract only about 4.6% of total FDI in the country. Domestic private investment is similarly influenced by the availability of social and economic infrastructure. For example, of the financial assistance disbursed by the All India financial institutions, the cumulative share of Andhra Pradesh upto March 1997 was 7.2% as against 13.5% for Gujarat and 21.0% for Maharashtra.

Thus there has been a deceleration in the growth rate of total gross fixed capital formation (public and private) in Andhra Pradesh from 6% in the 1980s to 3.6% in the 1990s.Despite this downtrend in the rate of capital formation, if there is no marked decline in the GSDP growth rate between the eighties and the nineties, it could well be due to some improvement in the efficiency of resource use, including possible changes in the composition of growth towards less capital-intensive activities.

Income Poverty and Human Development

The official poverty ratios, based on the Lakdawala Committee methodology, show very low levels of rural poverty (11%) and high levels of urban poverty (26.6%) for A.P. as compared to all India (27% and 23.6% respectively) for 1999-2000. Thus the official estimates of poverty ratio for urban areas in A.P. are more than double those for rural areas in the 1990s. This is quite contrary to what one would expect on the basis of the rural-urban differences in per capita income and wages. However, alternative estimates by reputed scholars like Angus Deaton and Jean Dreze show that the poverty ratios in A.P. were closer to the all India pattern i.e., 26% for rural areas and 12% for urban areas. The very low level of official rural poverty ratios in A.P. were due to its base year poverty line in

1973-74 being the lowest among all the major states in India. This in turn was due to low level of Consumer Price Index for Agricultural Labour (CPIAL) for A.P. The estimates by Deaton and Dreze, on the other hand, are based on the more realistic poverty line arrived at on the basis of the consumer prices computed from the National Sample Survey data.

Notwithstanding these differences regarding the levels of poverty, both the official estimates and those from Deaton and Dreze show a significant decline in the incidence of poverty in A.P. between the eighties and the nineties in line with the All India trends. It is, nevertheless, a matter of concern that the decline in rural poverty in A.P. was much slower than for All India and the growth of mean consumption for the rural A.P. was the lowest among southern states in the 1990s (between 1993-94 and 19999-00).

At one stage the A.P. Government had questioned the official estimates and protested against their use by the central government for the allocation of resources in respect of poverty alleviation programmes, as the state was losing significant amount of resources on this account. However, the position of the A.P. government on this issue has been inconsistent or at best ambivalent. For, the state government has not hesitated to take credit on certain occasions for bringing down rural poverty to a very low level! Needless to say, it would be necessary to adopt a consistent approach which is scientific and objective. The acceptance of the official estimates may lead to complacency and, as such, to ineffective policy initiatives for the alleviation of rural poverty, while at the same time creating unwarranted scare in respect of urban poverty.

The social sector expenditures as per cent of GSDP and total public expenditure were lower in the 1990s as compared to those of the 1980s.However, these ratios having deteriorated by the mid-nineties, recovered by 2000-01 to the levels obtaining in 1990-01. The human development Index across states shows that the relative position of A.P. has marginally declined in 2001 as compared to earlier two decades. Although there have been improvements in health and education, the levels are still low compared to many other states, particularly other South Indian states.

Fiscal Management

Reforms undertaken following the financial crisis of 1995-96 led to improvement in several indicators of fiscal management. State's own tax revenues, which had fallen to around 5% of GSDP in 1995-96, rose steadily to about 8% in 2000-01 - nearly the level obtaining in the early nineties. State's own non-tax revenues fell from around 2.4% of GSDP in the early nineties to around 2% of GSDP in 1995-96 and fell further in the three subsequent years, but recovered by 2000-01 to the level obtaining in 1995-96.

However, the expenditure rose at a higher rate than revenues during this period, leading to a rise in fiscal deficit from 3% of GSDP in 1995-96 to 4.5.% in 2001-02. It must be noted, however, that the rise in fiscal deficit was common to all the states as well as the Centre in this period. Indeed, the performance of Andhra Pradesh relative to other states was commendable. For 2001-02, there are indications that A.P.'s fiscal deficit as a ratio to its GSDP was lower than that for several major states and the All-states' average.

There has been a distinct improvement in the composition or quality of public expenditure in A.P. in the post-reform period, especially when compared to other states. Revenue deficit came down from around 31% of fiscal deficit in 1995-96 to 25% in 1999-00 - lower than the level for the other three southern states as well as for all states put together. Although the ratio deteriorated in the subsequent years, it continued to be well below that for the southern states and the All-states' average. Capital outlay improved to 40% of fiscal deficit and further to 50% in 2001-02, which was much higher than for Karnataka, Kerala, Tamil Nadu and the All-states' average. Expenditure on establishment came down from 29.6% of total expenditure in 1995-96 to 25% in 2000-01, while subsidies dropped from 27% of total revenue expenditure to 14% (excluding power subsidy), and 21% (including power subsidy) over the same period. Capital expenditure, including lending for developmental activities, which had declined to 2.1% of GSDP in 1995-96 rose to around 2.6% in 2001-02.

However, consequent to the steady rise in fiscal deficit, there has been a big rise in public debt after the crisis year of 1995-96. Debt raised was used mostly for repayment purposes. Whereas in 1990-91 nearly 20% of public debt raised was spent towards repayments, in 2000-01 as much as 71% of the public debt raised was spent for repayment purposes. However, despite rising indebtedness, outstanding public debt for A.P. at 25.9% of GSDP in 2000-01 was lower than for all the major states, the All-states average being 30.69%. Even so, the steep rise in the A.P.'s debt-GSDP ratio in the last five years which is expected to touch the level of 31% of GSDP is a matter of concern, as this can be sustained only with a rise in the growth rate of GSDP and state's revenues.

There is a justification for looking at the management of A.P. finances in a comparative perspective, that is, in relation to the position among all other states. This is because, in the wake of a substantial increase in the share of services sector in GDP in the nineties, there has been a significant decline in the tax-GDP ratio for the Centre as well as for states, as many of these services are not taxed. Second, due to the reduction in tax rates by the Center in the post-reform period, in the absence of necessary reforms to widen the tax base or to improve compliance, the growth of tax revenues has decelerated adversely affecting the revenues of the Centre as well as the states. Consequently, revenues from the Centre as a proportion of A.P.'s total revenue receipts declined significantly during this period. On the expenditure side, the rise in expenditure on salaries following the recommendations of the Fifth Pay Commission was the single most important factor affecting the finances of the Centre as well as the states. A comparative picture alone would reveal how different states have responded to the emerging fiscal stress. Looked at from this angle, the performance of Andhra Pradesh is not bad.

However, there is considerable scope for raising revenues in A.P., especially from non-tax sources. For example, successful implementation of reforms for the participatory management of the distribution systems for rural electricity and irrigation water can raise the revenues through higher user charges. Similarly, there is a scope for raising tax revenues from sales tax, motor vehicle tax, stamp duty and registration fee and profession tax through the necessary reforms and effective implementation. Needless to say, there is a significant potential for achieving economy in expenditure. These measures for augmenting resources need to be combined with refocusing expenditure towards greater capital outlays for building up infrastructure.

2 INFRSTRUCTURE

Andhra Pradesh has taken major initiatives in the mid-nineties to introduce reforms in the management of infrastructure in critical areas like power and irrigation, besides achieving a breakthrough in introducing Information Technology which has far reaching consequences for the economy and society. We propose to review in this Section the progress of reforms in these three major sectors in the state.

Power

Power sector in the state experienced a sharp deterioration in the nineties. The A.P. State Electricity Board (APSEB) has been the most well performing institution among the State Electricity Boards in the country upto 1990. It has passed through three distinct phases in the last three decades: Period of rise (1970-90); Period of fall (1990-96); and Period of reform (1996-2000).

The first period is characterized by the high rate of growth of capacity addition, rapid increases in the sale of energy and sound financial performance. Till 1980, industrial consumption accounted for nearly two-thirds of the total sales and contributed to the high average realization of revenue in spite of greatly subsidized tariff for agriculture which was compensated by relentlessly increasing the tariff for industries. During the first period industrial tariff increased by 7 times while agricultural tariff decreased. From 1982 onwards, APSEB adopted a non-metered flat rate for agriculture. Among other factors, this lenient tariff extended by the Rural Electrification Corporation led to rapid rise in the agricultural consumption and consequently, around 1990, agriculture occupied a space almost equal to industries. In addition, this cross-subsidization against industry played an important role in the rise of captive generation plants and consequently the reduction in the share of industry in consumption.

The rate of growth of generation capacity noticeably slowed down during 1990 to 1996. However, APSEB kept on increasing supply to agriculture by purchasing power at high cost from other sources. Moreover, due to several unavoidable factors cost of electricity generation increased significantly since 1994-95. For example, of the additional capacity set up during this period, nearly 85% was Thermal (coal and gas). During the period up to 1994-95 the tariff rose in step with consumer price index. Later the tariff was not revised and consequently APSEB started incurring losses. Tariff revision was undertaken in 1995-96 which led to an improved position of revenue collection in the following two years but declined very sharply from 1998-99 onwards. The revision was resorted to again only in January 1999. A big increase in tariff did push up the tariff to HT and commercial consumers, but it did not have significant positive revenue effect, because additional sales to these categories was insignificant!

It became clear that financial problems of APSEB were primarily due to: (i) irrational tariff setting, especially for agriculture, which rendered the system unviable; and (ii) increasing Transmission and Distribution (T&D) losses which were camouflaged by "treating" most of it as agricultural consumption. This was becoming clearly unsustainable. In response to the emerging crisis, the state government came forward with reforms through a forward-looking legislation.

In 1998, Andhra Pradesh Electricity Reform Act was enacted and Andhra Pradesh Electricity Reform Rules were issued in 1999. Andhra Pradesh Electricity Regulatory Commission (APERC) was set up and APSEB was restructured in 1999 into APGENCO, which was entrusted with all the generation related assets and APTRANSCO with transmission and distribution related assets. The generation function was thus separated from the transmission and distribution functions. This was a major step in the right direction based on the international experience, but much remains to be done to increase competition at the generation level as well as at the distribution end through decentralisation.

Power sector reforms in the state are stuck up on the core issue of tariff setting for agricultural uses and not much headway can be made without bringing about a measure of consensus by adopting innovative approaches to achieve the goals of higher revenue, greater equity, conservation of resources, e.g., power and ground water, and accountability of management to the consumers. The present debate on tariff centres round the goals of revenue and equity often by counter-posing the two. The other two issues, viz., conserving ground water and electricity, and accountability to the consumers are hardly brought into the picture. Yet, overexploitation of ground water on account of flat rate for power where the marginal cost of pumping water is zero, is a matter of serious concern. This issue has to be brought into the forefront of debate on electricity tariff for agriculture.It may be noted, in this context, that the heavy implied subsidy in the water rates for assured sources of irrigation is seen by the farmers under lift irrigation as a justification for a corresponding subsidy for them. Therefore, rationalization of surface irrigation rates has also to be looked at simultaneously.

A viable solution would be to combine subsidy on power with metering of pump sets within a decentralised system of distribution through the participation of user-farmers. A reasonable subsidy on a certain number of units sufficient to pump water for one or two hectares can be given to all the farmers where there are no assured sources of surface irrigation. Coupons can be issued to the farmers sufficient to cover the cost of subsidised electricity which they can use for payment of bills, while paying on their own for the excess electricity consumed. This system would have the merit of inducing economy on the use of electricity beyond the subsidised units by the middle and large farmers who are in fact the bulk consumers, while providing relief to the small and marginal farmers. Since all the farmers are provided subsidy uniformly at a flat rate, the scheme can become politically feasible, even as the effective incidence of electricity rate would be progressive, because the proportion of subsidised consumption would decline as the size of holding increases. Under the system of decentralised participatory management, the latter would be accountable to the farmers for the promised quantity of supply well as for the quality of services.

It should be possible to take steps, that are overdue, for improving business management and corporate governance under the public ownership. Urgent action is needed to tighten the internal control procedures and introduce innovative rewards and penalties with assigned accountability at all levels. The regulatory commission must have a policy on how cross subsidization would be dealt within their commercial tariff fixation. The tariff should be based on costs that are competitive assuming minimal losses on account of T&D and theft of power. Finally, reforms should be projected as the means to provide adequate power of acceptable quality at affordable prices to all consumers.

Irrigation

Andhra Pradesh has been a leading participant in Green Revolution in the country, especially for rice. This has been greatly facilitated by the availability of good irrigation infrastructure. However, the existing systems have deteriorated over time and addition to the capacity has been negligible due to the decline in public investment. According to the Planning Commission, nearly 35% of the ultimate potential from Major & Medium irrigation projects in the state is yet to be exploited. In the case of minor irrigation, about 40% of the ultimate potential remains unutilised.

In Telangana and Rayalaseema regions, well irrigation has become the dominant source replacing tanks. Tanks, which used to be traditionally managed by the village communities were being managed now by the irrigation department. With the neglect of maintenance and encroachment of tank beds by resourceful farmers, most of them became dysfunctional. In the absence of ground water replenishment, mainly through tanks, failure of wells has become common. Recent cotton farmer suicides in the state are attributed, among other factors, to well failure.

Major problems in irrigation sector in the state are: Inadequate allocation for Operation and Maintenance (O&M), inequitable distribution of water, lack of incentives for saving water and low recovery of water rates. Neglect of O&M is attributable to low recovery of water charges. This problem is compounded on account of water rate being in the nature of a tax collected by the revenue department, robbing the irrigation systems of a sense of ownership.

Andhra Pradesh is the first state in the country to enact in 1997 the Andhra Pradesh Farmers Management of Irrigation Systems Act,1997,(APFMIS Act) making the formation of Water Users' Associations (WUAs) mandatory for the management of irrigation. This is designed to bring greater accountability in irrigation department as well as a sense of ownership of the management systems among farmers. More than 10,000 Water Users' Associations (WUAs) have been formed, of which about 80%

are in minor irrigation sector. However, bulk of the area covered is under canal irrigation.

The impact of WUAs has been encouraging in these areas, especially in terms of providing irrigation to tail end farmers. This has been made possible by cleaning of canals and water courses and monitoring of water losses by the WUAs. Area under paddy is reported to have increased significantly following reforms. However, much of the reported increase could be statistical because of underreporting of irrigated area before reform , as this meant lesser payment of water tax to revenue department. Paddy yields are reported to have increased by 40%.

Irrigation charges were increased by more than three times from 1997. Even so, the surface water rates will at best cover maintenance charges, whereas in the case of lift irrigation the farmer also bears the full capital cost of the well or bore. However, despite a significant rise in irrigation charges, the farmers' support for reforms in respect of surface irrigation is visible. This is because the launching of these reforms was preceded by widespread consultation and awareness building among farmers about the benefits from reforms. Consequently, increased water tax is seen by farmers as supplementing the resources of WUAs for maintenance of irrigation systems. Even so, the effective rate of collection remains low at around 64%.The reason could be that WUAs have not yet been made fully responsible for collection of water charges, making the process fully democratic and accountable. Another notable development was that the works were executed by WUAs themselves at lesser cost instead of getting them done by contractors. But the vested interests lost no time in adjusting to the new situation by presidents of the WUAs acting as contractors. This and other malpractices invited the wrath of farmers who in several cases used the provision in the Act for recall of the presidents. The only long-term solution to this is awareness building and promoting participatory monitoring and evaluation. Unlike in the case of canal irrigation, WUAs are not found to be effective in respect of tank irrigation due to insufficient allocations.

Further reforms contemplated in the immediate future are to ensure greater share in water tax to the WUAs, ranging from 50% in the case of major irrigation to 90% in the case of minor irrigation where the costs of rehabilitation are high and management problems more complex.

It is proposed that, in the medium term, WUAs should move towards volumetric pricing so as to induce efficient use of water, including shifts in cropping pattern, after the delivery systems are technically upgraded by installing measuring devices for this purpose. WUAs seem to be willing to collect water charges on a volumetric basis. However, successful implementation requires, in addition to improved awareness of the benefits e.g. conservation of water, capacity building through training to the lower level officials as well as the functionaries of the WUAs.

There has been a major progress towards bringing ground water under the purview of community management through Watershed Development. We shall discuss this below when we take up the issue of environmental degradation. While reforms for rehabilitating the existing systems through WUAs and measures for conserving rain water through watershed development have inspired the farmers and won their support, there is, as yet, not enough clarity in official pronouncements on the efficient management of rural electricity systems and the expansion of irrigated area from assured sources. The controversy on these issues has acquired sharper overtones because backward regions like Rayalaseema and Telangana are heavily dependent on electricity for pumping water and, at the same time, the unexploited potential from major irrigation projects is greater for these regions. Clarity in official policy and credible steps to reduce regional imbalances in respect of assured sources of irrigation can alone win wider support of the farmers for reforms in irrigation sector.

Information Technology

The IT industry has an immense potential for growth in Andhra Pradesh on account of a large pool of scientific manpower and a strong commitment of the state government to promote this industry. In A.P., especially in the city of Hyderabad, a great thrust has been given in the nineties to the growth of software industry. This is evidenced by the impressive growth of software exports from the state from Rs.0.20 million to nearly Rs.37 billion during 1991-92 to 2002-03. The state stood fourth in the country with nearly 10% of exports made by STP units in 2002-03.The bulk of software exports from Hyderabad went to the USA and Canada (59%).The IT-enabled services accounted for 39% of the software exports in 20002-03 and are playing a significant role in the creation of employment opportunities in this sector.

An area of about 52 sq. km near the 'Hi-Tec City' has been carved out as Cyberabad. Efforts seem to be on to ensure broad based development of this sector, as in Tamil Nadu, by shifting the focus of software development to the other important urban centres in the state. Indian software industry has so far been basically engaged in meeting the export demand as a low cost supplier. But it must now venture into high-end products and services moving up the value chain and cater to demand from Indian industry, agriculture and consumers at large. From this angle, some of the recent developments in A.P. are encouraging.

Among the several 'e-government' initiatives that the government of A.P has undertaken, e-Seva seems to be getting popular in Hyderabad. It is planned for expansion to 56 other towns with a total of 146 centres. These are basically collection centers for various bills/fees (like telephone, electricity, trade license fee etc.) and other services for the citizens and are integrated with several departments. Apart from e-Seva, some of the 'e-government' projects in the state are Computer Aided Registration Department(CARD), Fully Automated Services of Transport(FAST), Andhra Pradesh State Wide Area Network(APSWAN), Andhra Pradesh Development Monitoring System(APDMS) and Secretariat Knowledge and Information System(SKIMS).

In addition to such services, priority should be given for IT applications that directly benefit industry, agriculture and rural areas in general for reducing poverty. Rural people should be convinced that IT solutions would help them to improve their incomes and livelihoods. It is heartening that the National Institute of Agricultural Extension Management (MANAGE), Hyderabad, is taking up measures towards this end by selecting some villages in Rangareddy district. These villages had successful Mutually Aided Co-operative Thrift and Credit Societies(MACTCS). Multimedia CDs are distributed to these groups on several aspects of Agriculture, Rural Development, Health and Education etc. They have been using the Internet for browsing the websites for government programmes and schemes, weather forecasts, market prices, job opportunities, news etc. regularly. MANAGE is planning to connect over 350 blocks in 28 districts in the country on Internet in the near future.

There is a need, on the above lines, for a greater thrust in the policy framework in A.P. towards making IT an enabler in development and equaliser of opportunities. With the spread of education and decentralisation of governance, IT can become a powerful tool in the hands of people at large for their socio-economic betterment and overall empowerment.

3. SECTORAL DEVELOPMENT - PRODUCTION SECTORS

Agriculture

Andhra Pradesh was among the very few states in the country which heralded green revolution, especially in respect of rice, in the 1970s. Agriculture & Allied sector in the state registered a growth rate of 2.21% in the eighties and its performance was only marginally better in the post-reform period of nineties (2.47%). There was a deceleration in the growth of this sector in the country as a whole in the nineties to 2.73%. Thus agricultural growth of A.P. in the post-reform period is below the low All India growth rate and significantly lower than 3.7% projected by the 'A.P. Vision 2020' document for the period 1995-2000. The available data shows that the state experienced a decline in capital formation in agriculture sector in the post-reform period, even in absolute terms, basically on account of a decline in capital formation by the private sector, at a time when there was a significant increase in the private sector capital formation in this sector for the country as a whole. This aspect needs further investigation.

The growth rate of crop output in the state decelerated from 3.4% in the eighties to 2.3 per cent in the nineties. The growth rate of total factor productivity in the crop sector declined from 1.58 per cent to 1.05 per cent over the same period. As a result, the state has slided down in its competitiveness in respect of several crops. For example, in the case of rice, the cost of production per unit of output in A.P. is now higher than in major rice growing states of Punjab and Uttar Pradesh. Cost of production of cotton is also higher as compared to Maharashtra. The resulting unremunerativeness of crop production probably explains the increase in fallow land noticed in some districts of Telangana and Rayalaseema. Given viable strategies, such lands could have been used for water-saving enterprises like fodder cultivation for dairy development, animal husbandry and horticulture.

Growth rate in Agriculture & Allied sectors has been maintained during the nineties in the state roughly at the eighties level, despite a significant reduction in the growth of crop output, because of diversification of agriculture into enterprises like dairying, animal husbandry, poultry etc., which contribute more than 20 per cent to the state domestic product from agriculture. The demand for these products has been favourable on account of the rise in per capita income and high income elasticity of demand for such products. Thus the nineties witnessed a revival in milk production with an annual growth rate rising to 5.7 per cent per annum, with a prospect of further growth in its demand to about six per cent per annum during the current decade. Development of dairying has received a special impetus with the shift from cattle to buffalo on account of a significant reduction in animal power consequent to mechanisation, and adoption of cow where buffalo is not suitable. Further, there has been a steep increase in the demand for mutton since the eighties. Therefore, the population of small ruminants, particularly goats, has been increasing at a fast rate, especially in resource poor areas. Andhra Pradesh specializes in poultry production, contributing as high as 20 per cent of the total eggs produced in the country.

Despite encouraging trends in some of these sectors, the overall performance of agriculture in the last two decades has remained poor and much below its potential. It is surprising that even in the post-reform period, government regulations that inhibit private investment and enterprise in agriculture, e.g., restrictions on the movement of foodgrains, levy on millers and other restrictions on marketing and processing are, by and large, intact. Such restrictions together with declining public investment in irrigation, rural infrastructure, and agricultural research explain the steep decline in private investment. Increase in concealed tenancy with insecurity of tenure and continued rural unrest and extremist violence may also be inhibiting private investment.

Area under public sources of irrigation, e.g., canals declined in the nineties due to deceleration in public investment. As such, the entire increase in the irrigated area in the nineties is due to well irrigation which has become highly erratic in most areas on account of a steep fall in water table. Growth rate of public expenditure on research and education declined from 6.6 per cent in the eighties to 3.9 per cent in the nineties. The intensity of government investment in agricultural research and education in the state at 0.26% of its agriculture GDP during 1992-94, was lower than for the other three southern states and was just around half of that for All India (0.49%),i.e., for the Centre and states together. Public expenditure on extension, which is borne by the state government, declined in absolute terms in the nineties. It constituted a mere 0.02% of state's Ag GDP during 1992-94, as against the All States average of 0.15%.

Several studies show that small and marginal farmers in A.P. still depend on informal or non-institutional sources of credit, particularly money-lenders, for 60 to 80 per cent of their credit requirements. Consequently, the rates of interest charged are also quite high. This has had an adverse fall-out in the context of the emerging high-input, high-risk agriculture. With the virtual breakdown of the extension machinery and lack of access to institutional credit, small and marginal farmers are becoming increasingly dependent upon the private trade for credit and extension services. In the absence of public regulation of such services, the resource-poor and gullible farmers are becoming victims of exploitation by the unscrupulous traders and moneylenders interested in selling spurious materials like pesticides. The cases of suicide by the farmers in the state relate basically to small and marginal farmers and tenants, and are traceable to such deprivation and malpractices, and so highlight the immediate need for revamping the extension and credit delivery systems in the state.

Despite its poor performance in the last two decades, agriculture in the state has the potential for achieving a minimum growth rate of 4 per cent per annum. In fact, the average growth rate of agriculture for the state projected by the Vision-2020 document of the government of A.P. is over 6% p.a. for the period 2000-2020. Andhra Pradesh has a special advantage of being centrally located in the country with a long coast line. It has varied agro-climatic conditions conducive to diversified agriculture in tune with the emerging demand. The farmers in the state are known for their enterprise and willingness to take risk. High agricultural growth would step up the rural demand for non-cereal items of food including dairy products, as well as non-farm products, as income elasticities of demand for them are quite high in rural areas. This can provide an impetus to the growth of rural non-farm sector in the state and would contribute to eradicating rural poverty by absorbing the labour force released from agriculture.

The Vision-2020 document focuses on critical areas of importance for agriculture in A.P. taking into account state's comparative advantage, opportunities being opened up in the country and globally, and the development experience in other countries. The document emphasises a critical role both for public and private investments, and releasing of private initiative and enterprise by liberalising the regulatory framework. Within this framework, the Vision-2020 document advocates full exploitation of the available irrigation potential, development of rural roads and marketing infrastructure, evolution and application of cost reducing technologies, especially biotechnology focusing on dry land crops and enterprises, and strengthening the small farm sector through the consolidation of holdings and supply of institutional credit. It also advocates contractual arrangements between the private sector engaged in agro-processing etc., and the small farmers with a view to ensuring for them easy access to technology, inputs and credit and for minimising risk by guaranteeing remunerative prices for their produce.

It is clear that the role of the government is critical by way of stepping up investments as well as creating the policy environment conducive to private investment and enterprise, and for ensuring full participation of the resource-poor farmers and the lagging regions in agricultural development. The initiatives of the state government in this direction so far fall very much short of the requirements and expectations. The government, therefore, needs to set its priorities right by placing agriculture development high on its agenda.

Industry

There has been some slow down in the growth rate of GSDP from industry in the state from 7.36% to 6.2% between the eighties and the post-liberalisation period (1993-94 to 2000-01). Though the share of the industrial sector in the state domestic product has increased somewhat in the nineties, this has not been accompanied by the increase in its share in employment. During the last three decades AP economy has been experiencing a slow but significant structural shift from agriculture to mainly services sector both in terms of output and employment. To sustain the growth of the services sector, which now accounts for 50% of GSDP, the commodity sectors, especially industry, need to grow at a sufficiently rapid rate to generate adequate demand for the services.

The slow down in industrial growth in the post-liberalisation period is accounted by the deceleration in the growth of registered manufacturing sector. Construction and the non-agro based industries have shown a higher growth in this period. The annual growth rate of chemical and chemical products, of which drugs and pharmaceuticals is an important component, has more than doubled. The transport equipment and parts has also shown a phenomenal growth in the post liberalization period.

In its 1992 'New Industrial Policy Statement' the government of AP identified the agro-based industries as one of the most potential industrial activities and suggested a number of incentives for this sector. Despite this, the growth rate of agro-industries declined, though marginally, with the exception of textile products and cotton textiles. There is an indication of a rise in the input prices of agro-based industries compared to those of metal and chemical-based ones. Among the agro-based industries food processing sector is given most importance. But it is difficult to judge the impact of the policy effort to boost this industry in the 90s. While there is probably a positive impact of emphasis on export promotion on the textile product sector in the state, some of the industries have performed unsatisfactorily in the post-reform period. The other industrial sector which has got specific emphasis in the 'New Industrial Policy' of 1992 is the electronic and software-based industries. The data show a considerable decline in the organized sector of this industry during 1994-95 to 1997-98.However, the considerable increase in the software exports from the state in the recent years points to the possibility of much of this activity taking place in the unregistered sector.

There is a fear that the liberalized regime in the Indian context may lead to jobless growth. However, employment in the registered manufacturing sector in A.P. has grown at a higher rate in the post-liberalization period when compared to the earlier years. The agro-based industries of textile products, food products and synthetic fiber textiles have mainly contributed to this rise, while employment growth rate in the non agro-based industries is nearly the same in both the periods. The rate of growth of real wages was lower in the nineties when compared with the pre-liberalization period. Disaggregated data show a similar trend for the agro-based industries. However, the growth of wages in the non agro-based industries is higher in the nineties where growth rate of employment is lower. It appears that in the liberalised regime growth in employment has been higher in sectors where the wage rates have risen slowly. There is a general improvement in the labour productivity in almost all the industrial categories, but, in general, this increase in labour productivity has not been associated with the increase in the rate of growth of employment due to slow down in industrial growth. In comparison with industrially developed states of India, labour productivity is significantly low in the small-scale industrial activities in A.P. Non-availability of credit facilities and acute shortage of infrastructure, mainly power, may account for inefficient technology in small units. However, export promotion parks taken up by the government in the recent years may improve some of the small scale sector activities in the state.

The Vision-2020 document for A.P. has recognized that investment needed for the proposed growth rate of 11% is not possible with internal savings only. There is evidence of a slow rate of growth of investment in the state in the 1990s. According to the CII study, AP has the 8th rank among states in respect of investment attractiveness. Together with a number of incentives, government is trying to assure sufficient infrastructural support to the new industrial ventures as well as make the process less bureaucratic and hazard-free, for example, through its special emphasis on the 'single window' procedure. In order to reduce the investment gap, the government hopes to get external investments both from domestic and foreign sources by making the state an attractive destination for investments. However, it is very unlikely that the level of funding available would be such as to raise levels of living by nine times as envisaged in the Vision- 2020 document.

Of the growth engines identified by the Vision-2020 document, knowledge-intensive industries have, by and large, shown a high growth. I.T. sector and Chemical and Chemical products belong to this category. Barring construction, other resource-intensive and labour-intensive industries, for which there is a large potential for growth in the state, have not performed equally well. Agro- industries including food processing, leather products, and mining belong to this group. Some of these, e.g., garments and leather products, have a large potential for exports as well as employment generation.

Unlike in agriculture, A.P. does not have a strong background and tradition of industrial development, like the neighbouring state of Tamil

Nadu, in terms of entrepreneurship, technical skills, infrastructure and the orientation of bureaucracy. Besides, new challenges have been thrown up in this sector in the post-liberalisation era: Industry is exposed now to greater domestic as well as external competition. Also, a consensus is emerging now among the states to desist from unhealthy competition among themselves to attract industries by providing undue tax concessions and such other incentives. In this new context, therefore, growth of industry in A.P. depends crucially on the internal capabilities at the state level such as the availability of physical infrastructure like power, water and transport, skilled manpower, credit and absence of regulatory constraints that inhibit investment and growth. These requirements are even more critical for small and medium industries including agro-industries lacking in resources and influence.

One of the major constraints on the growth rate is ensuring timely availability of adequate credit at reasonable cost from institutional sources to the small and medium enterprises, especially to those located in rural areas. The other is good governance for ensuring growth-promoting regulatory environment by cutting down delays in clearances and corruption.

4. SECTORAL DEVELOPMENT: SOCIAL SECTOR

Demography

After high growth in population for four decades between 1951-91, there was a rapid decline in population growth in the last decade (1991-2001). The Sample Registration System shows that the total fertility rate (TFR) has fallen from nearly 4.6 children per women in the early 1970s to 2.5 children by 1997, a decline to the tune of 2 children per woman during the 26-year period. The National Family Health Survey (NFHS) estimate of TFR is 2.25 during 1996-98 period with rural areas having slightly higher fertility (2.32) than urban areas (2.07). The state, thus, would achieve a replacement level of fertility in the very near future. The decline in fertility was largely attained through the contraceptive use and particularly through female sterilization. It is worth noting here that the fertility reduction has embraced all sections of the society in all the regions irrespective of economic, social, religious or cultural differences.

It is interesting that fertility reduction in A.P. defies conventional theories and beliefs, which thought that fertility reduction needed considerable improvement either in economic or social development. The experience of Kerala state indicates that female education and health improvement (e.g. reduction in infant mortality) were responsible for decline in fertility levels. In the case of A.P., female illiteracy and infant mortality are relatively high but fertility decline has been faster. The existing fertility levels, however, are higher among the illiterate and low-income groups, and in backward or less-developed districts.

The policies and programmes followed in the state during 1980s and 1990s could be responsible for the fertility decline. The rapid decline began in the state by the second half of 1980s and accelerated in the 1990s. In the 1980s, welfare programmes like Public Distribution System (PDS) and Integrated Child Development services (ICDS)), women's movement (DWCRA groups) and expansion of health services could be responsible for fertility decline by providing social security, raising awareness of women and empowering them. The family planning programme received further boost in the 1990s through concrete policies and action. In order to have decentralized decision making, district population stabilization societies were formed and funds devolved to local levels. In the 1990s, the women's self help group movement is an undoubted success story. Such groups not only helped women to earn additional income but also would have imparted progressive outlook on issues such as small family size and contraceptive use.

Hence the success of the state in controlling the population problem partly lies in better governance of both family planning related and welfare oriented programmes including women's self help groups.

Regarding mortality levels, although the overall mortality level is low the present level of infant mortality is comparatively high. A major part of infant mortality is now explained by neonatal mortality (28 days). Oddly, neonatal mortality has not recorded any marked decline even with dramatic decline in fertility level. The main causes of neonatal deaths are usually associated with mother specific factors. Given the poor social and health indicators of women in the state, major strides in infant mortality is unlikely to be achieved without addressing the overall socio-economic and health status of the women particularly the nutritional levels, and access to health care in the critical post delivery period.

The population projections show that state has to face two challenges in future. First, there is going to be considerable increase in the working age population primarily due to the high fertility in the past. This would create severe pressure on employment by the year 2020. This can also be an opportunity as, for example, the faster increase in working population was found to be a blessing for the economic boom in East Asian countries. Second, old age population may double between 1991-2016. At the same time, the younger population will be declining in numbers. This would result in a greying population and the state has to prepare for old age security measures.

Health

Health indicators such as life expectancy and infant mortality show that the performance of the state is lower as compared to the rest of the southern states. Surveys on medical facilities in the state indicate the predominance of private sector in health care and its rapid growth. The NSS data indicate that the private sector was predominant in AP even during the 1980s. It accounted for about 70 percent of inpatient care in rural areas and 62 percent in urban areas, which was highest in the country. By mid 1990s, its share further increased to 77.5 percent in the rural areas and marginally increased in the urban areas. The role of private sector was much higher in the developed districts.

The government hospitals have their limitations in terms of inadequate funding, overcrowding, corruption, lack of cleanliness etc., but the private hospitals need regulation. They indulge in overcharging, excess medication/testing, unnecessary treatment etc., which are more harmful to the patients physically and financially. The poor suffer much more than the rich because of these unethical practices.

The private sector in medical care has outgrown the size of public sector through the direct and indirect incentives given by the state. Public policy should focus on mechanisms to enforce the provision of providing free care to the poor by private hospitals who utilized the financial incentives, land grants, etc. Otherwise the role of the state should be confined to regulation of quality and pricing of medical care. Instead of direct regulation, the state should create independent regulatory institutions with representations to all stakeholders like consumer societies, NGOs, government officials, private medical establishments, etc. to ensure basic standards in the quality and pricing of medical care.

Due to lack of adequate resources, there was stagnation in the size and degeneration in the quality of care at the public hospitals. There is overcrowding and more than full capacity utilization of public hospitals, particularly at the secondary and the tertiary levels. There is still widespread unmet demand for medical care among the poor and the government should expand facilities in the public sector to meet this demand. The recent investments in the secondary level hospitals and perceptible improvement in the quality of care attracted more and more patients particularly from the poorer sections. Thus public hospitals at present are self-targeted, i.e., used mostly by the poor. It is not very clear whether increase in user charges would improve the performance of public hospitals.

Major weakness in public health care system is poor performance of the primary health centres, mainly due to staff absenteeism. Hospital

Advisory Committees (HACs) have been created, but they are not effective. There is a need to involve Panchayati Raj Institutions (PRIs) in health sector at local level. State should encourage community participation to improve the functioning of the public health care system.

In the case of health sector, three issues have to be addressed to improve the performance. First, public expenditure on health sector has to be increased. Public expenditure on health is now only around 1 per cent of GSDP. The expenditure on primary health is at a meagre 0.1 per cent of GSDP. These percentages have been stagnant in the 1990s and there is a need to allocate more resources to the sector. However, along with this the efficiency of public spending has to be improved. More resources should be spent on preventive care, as the poor benefit more from this. Primary health care services should be accountable to the local governments and ensure better services for the money spent. The second issue is how to make the private sector accountable. The share of private sector in the total health care sector is high and has increased over time. One can not ignore, therefore, the role of private sector in the state. Government should promote institutions to regulate the private sector. Third, there is a need to promote community health insurance schemes (e.g. SEWA's scheme) in order to provide health services at low cost to poor.

Education

Literacy rate in Andhra Pradesh has been much below the all India level during the last four decades. However, the gap between the two has narrowed down during the 1990s, as the rate of increase in literacy rate during this period in the state is one of the highest in the country. Literacy rates across regions show highest rural-urban as well as social disparities in Telangana while Rayalaseema reflects highest gender disparities. Between 1971 and 2001, regional disparities in literacy rates have come down substantially. Enrolment ratio has increased substantially but dropouts continue to be a problem despite declining trend, especially in backward regions.

The RBI data shows that the ratio of public expenditure on education to GSDP in A.P. declined from 3.3% in 1985-86 to 2.1% in 1995-96. It then started increasing and reached the ratio of 2.9% in 2000-01.As compared to other South Indian states, the share of public expenditure on education in GSDP and budget was lower in A.P. Primary education gets low priority within education. As a result, quality of education suffers (per student expenditures are much lower in AP).

While the demand factors are important in influencing the extent of literacy and dropout rates, access or supply or quality factors influence enrolment rates. Poverty in backward regions and rising demand for labour in developed regions are the most important reasons for dropouts. Indirect cost of education (Uniform, transport etc.) is substantial and hence dampens the demand for education.

There is a need for an integrated approach in order to bring children to school and retain them. The Vision 2020 document rightly identifies demand and supply factors like low literacy of parents, poverty, lack of access to school and poor infrastructure facilities as the main causes of low literacy rates. The 93rd amendment of the Indian Constitution to provide universal provision of school education to all the children in the age group 6-14 years will now require the state governments to improve supply side factors like access to schools, increase in the number of teachers, infrastructure etc. Andhra Pradesh government is preparing for provision of universal education to all children. A.P. is the first state to consider all the non-school going children as child labourers. The state feels that such a definition would put pressure on government, parents and civil society to achieve universal provision of school education. From the demand side, generation of productive employment and minimum wages would go a long way in reducing the household's dependence on children. Specific policies are required to address the gender and social disparities.

Similar to health, there are three issues that the state has to address in improving literacy and primary education in the state. First, more resources have to be allocated to education, particularly to primary education, from the budget. Second, the quality of education in terms of curriculum, better infrastructure and teaching has to be improved. Third, retaining children in the schools is more difficult than enrolling them. The A.P. government has designed schemes such as 'Mabadi' (our school), 'Chaduvkundam' (back to school) and akshara sankranti to improve access to children, women and disadvantaged communities. The focus of these programmes being more on enrolment this may result in more dropouts later. Retaining of children in the schools needs social mobilization of the community against child labour and for education and intensive institutional arrangements. Such attempts are very successful at the micro level as demonstrated by NGOs like the MV Foundation. Also, there is a need to involve PRIs in primary education at local level.

5. EMPLOYMENT, POVERTY AND INEQUALITY

Faster growth through economic reforms is not always accompanied by a faster rate of poverty reduction. Poverty can be reduced if growth increases employment potential (quantity and quality). Similarly, the extent to which the working poor are able to integrate into the economic process also determines the impact of growth on poverty. For example, if there is a mismatch between the opportunities available due to economic reforms and skills of the workers, the poor will not be able to take advantage of such opportunities and gain from the reforms.

Employment

Employment in A.P. is largely unorganized, rural and non-industrial. The work participation rates declined significantly in both rural and urban areas in the 1990s. The employment growth recorded a drastic decline during 1993-94 to 1999-2000 as compared to the period 1983-84 to 1993-94. Thus the expectations of increasing employment opportunities due to economic reforms have not materialized.

Only around 6 per cent of the total work force is in the organized sector in A.P. The growth of employment in the organized sector has declined over time. In the post-reform period, the growth of public sector employment declined drastically while that of private sector employment increased. However, the growth of private sector employment has not been able to compensate for the loss of jobs in the public sector.

The share of non-farm employment in rural areas has been stagnant since 1983. The diversification of employment has been slower in A.P. as compared to all India in the 1990s. There is no sign of increase in the usual status unemployment rates. However, the daily status unemployment recorded significant increase in the 1990s. This is a matter of concern for the state. The problem of unemployment is more severe for the educated and the youth. Casualization has been increasing over time. Rural A.P. has the second highest percentage of casual labourers in the country. Labour productivity showed high growth in agriculture and manufacturing in the 1990s. In spite of this, the growth of real wages in rural areas declined significantly in the 1990s. Around 91 per cent of the rural workers in A.P. are either illiterate or have been educated only up to primary level.

Some macro projections show that to focus on agriculture & allied and services would be the most desirable option from the point of view of increasing employment, while reducing poverty and income disparity significantly. There are some constraints for private sector participation.

Failures in labour, credit, and product markets are some such constraints. Low infrastructure is another important constraint.

Given the problem of unemployment and underemployment for the masses and unemployment for educated, there is a need to have twin strategies for improving the livelihoods. The first sub-strategy should aim at rural and urban masses that are illiterate/semi-literate, unskilled, and semi-literate/skilled. The second sub-strategy has to address the educated unemployed. The policy goal should be to improve economic growth in rural areas with emphasis on employment generation for the poor, and shift workers from agriculture to non-agriculture activities, particularly services in rural areas. To achieve this goal, it is necessary to focus on selected growth engines and clusters: In order to have a focused intervention, the Vision 2020 had suggested 18 "growth engines" for vertical (e.g. leaf to cloth) sub-sectoral interventions. However, these may not be adequate to generate near full employment. As such, the number of growth engines in agriculture, industry and services may have to be increased to between 30 to 40 for that purpose.

The task of generating employment (quantity and quality) is an urgent and crucial one for reducing poverty. It needs a range of concerted actions from the government, donors, banks, and the private sector and from civil society institutions.

Poverty

We already looked at the measurement issues and the trends in official and alternative estimates of poverty in the state. Here we propose to examine the determinants of poverty and poverty alleviation programmes.

A multivariate analysis using wages and agriculture output as independent variables shows that in the post-green revolution period (1970s to1990s) increase in real wages played a more important role than the growth of agricultural output. On the other hand, the effect of real wages was low in the pre-green revolution period. It is possible that the gains from agricultural growth were shared more widely in the pre-green revolution period. Also, poverty in the post-green revolution period is concentrated more among the wage labour.

Regarding poverty alleviation programmes, an evaluation shows that the entry of non-poor into the Integrated Rural Development Programme (IRDP) is around 26 percent across the selected districts viz., Anantapur, Nalgonda, and Vizianagaram in the late 1990s. The income gains are more pronounced in the developed districts and among the relatively better off among the poor. Under the Jawahar Rozgar Yojana (JRY), employment generated per person per year, on an average, is around

40 days across the sample villages of selected districts in 2001. The employment created is not adequate to influence the wage rates in labour market.

The government's strategy paper on poverty eradication recognizes that long- term investment in core sectors such as agriculture, health and education will accelerate the pace of poverty reduction. The government would like to build on the successful lessons learnt from the self-help and group approach towards empowerment of the poor for poverty reduction. There are also some innovative programmes such as Janmabhoomi and Deepam (LPG scheme), which help the poor. The rural poverty reduction strategies thus will be multi-pronged and multi-sectoral. They can be broadly classified under three categories: (a) intensive poverty reduction initiatives through a strategy of social mobilization, (b) aggressively promoting agricultural growth and (c) provision of basic minimum services.

After experimenting with several poverty alleviation programmes, Government of A.P. has settled for two important programmes. One is self-help group programme and the other is watershed based approach. The Government's basic strategy for removal of rural poverty in A.P. would revolve around social mobilization and empowerment of the poor. The ongoing mobilization of the rural poor women into self-help groups is a major element of this strategy. The ongoing District Rural Poverty Initiative (DPIP) project in 6 backward districts and the proposed A.P. Rural Poverty Reduction project (APRPRP) are based on the strategy of social mobilization and the empowerment of the rural poor. Considering the inadequacies in the past developmental strategies, these two projects are mandated to focus on the poorest of the poor, who have been left out of various development initiatives. The impact of these programmes is yet to be evaluated. Another important component for improving livelihoods is micro watershed approach. The objectives of natural resource management, growth in rainfed agricultural productivity and growth in employment and incomes for the poor are sought to be achieved in a participatory manner using the micro watershed as the basis for planning.

Andhra Pradesh has taken bold steps to demonstrate that a convergence of conservation and development objectives can be achieved through Joint Forest Management (JFM). Formation of JFM Committees in Andhra Pradesh has successfully targeted remote and under-served communities, in particular tribal populations. Women and landless members of the community are specifically identified as they are much more likely to be directly dependent on forests for income and to meet their daily needs for fuel and fodder.

Presently, there are more than 25 poverty alleviation and welfare schemes in the state. There is a need to have a re-look at some of these programmes because welfare and poverty alleviation programmes that are not cost-effective crowd out long-term investments.

Providing productive employment in agriculture and rural non-farm sector is important for reduction in poverty. Access to land (as owners or tenants) and credit are important for the poor in agriculture. In order to develop the rural non-farm sector, there is a need to look at issues such as rural-urban linkages, infrastructure, markets, technology, and training in skills.

Poverty alleviation depends on both macroeconomic policies and poverty alleviation programmes. The economic reforms open up opportunities for some groups and adversely affect some others. The key strategy for reducing poverty lies in creating productive employment for the poor through labour-intensive pattern of growth and better implementation of poverty alleviation programmes.

Women's Groups

Another important social change taking place in A.P. relates to women's empowerment (social and economic) through self-help groups. As mentioned above, women's self help group (SHGs) approach has formed a central element in the state's social mobilization and community empowerment strategy for poverty reduction. We look here at the contribution of these groups to poverty alleviation and empowerment.

Groups formed under Development of Women and Children in Rural Areas (DWCRA), South Asia Poverty Alleviation Programme (SAPAP) and Cooperative Development Foundation (CDF) are considered here. The basic assumption of all the models is that social capital contributes to poverty alleviation. The groups consist of only the poor as members except in CDF. While there are internal and external funds in DWCRA and SAPAP, there are only internal funds in CDF.

DWCRA is the main model with large number of groups. Out of the total existing SHGs of 4.28 lakhs in September 2002, around 1.90 lakhs are covered under DWCRA with a membership of around 25 lakhs. The thrift and revolving fund of these groups add up to Rs.1000 crores. SAPAP created 5,201 groups in 20 mandals covering 34,600 women and CDF formed 45,605 women into 200 woman thrift co-operatives (WTCs). In terms of functioning of DWCRA groups, only 18 per cent of the groups are of 'A' grade, 63 per cent of 'B' grade, and 19 per cent are of 'C' grade. In case of SAPAP, 47.6 per cent of groups are of 'A' grade.

Weaker sections of the society viz., SCs, STs, BCs are emphatically targeted in DWCRA and SAPAP and to some extent in WTCs. However, the participation of the poorest of the poor is very less in these models. The entry of non-poor was found to be 16.65% in DWCRA and 28% in SAPAP. The membership of groups is fairly long lived viz., 10 years or more and drop outs are very low (less than 4%). The single most important benefit from the groups is that they improved access to credit for the women members. As they provide both production and consumption loans, the members are relieved from the clutches of money lenders. As a result, the interest rate in the informal credit market declined sharply. A main strength of the DWCRA groups lies in the fact that these women groups have managed to receive credit from banks. The repayment rate is high, i.e., more than 85% across all the models.

It was found that these groups had a perceptible impact on alleviation of poverty. The additional income accrued to the members from the activities undertaken in DWCRA varied between Rs.10-30 per day, on an average. In SAPAP, poverty was reduced for 69% of the members but reduction in poverty was less for Dalits and women headed households. Though gender poverty did not decline significantly, food security improved marginally. These group-based activities enabled the near poor to cross the poverty line. The activities undertaken are mostly traditional, utilizing the existing skills of the members. These activities provided full employment to the members as well as their male counterparts. In many cases, the quality of employment improved as a result of shift from wage employment to self-employment.

There were also non-economic impacts of the groups such as on literacy, health, housing, and empowerment. The drive for literacy is a common feature in all the models. The expenditure on health of the members improved and infant mortality rate declined in DWCRA and SAPAP. It was found that the women have taken up non-farm (service and small business) activities and are venturing into non-traditional tasks and enterprises, to some extent. Besides, the role of women in decision-making in the family improved slightly. Some of them contested local body elections also.

The findings show that the poorest of the poor are not participating in the existing self-help groups. The repayment schedule suitable to the poorest of the poor should be adopted. The improvement in skill base, given the other asset base, can also be a solution to tackle the problems of the poorest. Proper livelihood planning, bulk purchases of inputs and collective marketing of outputs help the poorest of the poor to organize their economic activity effectively. Thus micro-credit alone cannot address the problems of the poorest. Interventions in commodity markets are also needed. The second issue is how to make the existing groups sustainable over time. The low growth of the economy and existing class relations are posing constraints for the relatively better off among the poor in improving their well-being. The process of empowerment of women can not be sustained unless their livelihood concerns are aptly addressed. There is a need to undertake viable economic activities which can improve incomes much faster.

Food Security

The state is considered as food grain surplus and food secure at macro level. However, there is food insecurity at the household level. Around one fourth of the state's population still suffers from chronic food insecurity and around 40 per cent of the children suffer from malnutrition.

The consumption data indicate declining per capita monthly consumption of cereals across all the income groups in rural and urban areas of Andhra Pradesh. Within cereals rice, which is a staple food in AP, shows mixed trends. In the case of the poorest 30 per cent in rural areas, rice consumption increased at 2 per cent per annum, while for their counterparts in the urban areas it fluctuated without any significant trend. For the top group, both rural and urban, the rice consumption declined considerably. High rate of decline in coarse cereal consumption is visible across all the three income groups.

The implications of these trends for the cost of energy and energy intake levels are adverse. The declining cereal consumption and within this the declining coarse cereal consumption raised the cost of calories derived from food expenditure considerably. The calorie-rupee ratio (the ratio of calorie intake and food real expenditure) is declining for all the income groups. It is of great concern that it is declining faster among the poor compared to that of the richer groups. Given these trends, any price rise in food items will further erode the calorie content of the food expenditure for the poor.

To understand the factors responsible for these changes, the trends in total expenditures and prices have been examined. In rural areas, with the exception of 1999-2000, the growth rate of real expenditure is positive for all the years. In urban areas also, the real expenditures show positive growth rates. For the entire period, the trend growth rate for rural areas is faster compared to that for urban areas. The relative price indices for cereals in rural areas show a declining trend over the past three decades. However, the rate of decline is coming down gradually in each of the last two decades. In urban sector, the relative price index declined in the seventies and eighties, but increased in the nineties. Though these trends do not indicate anything adverse as of now, the trend, if it continues, may have adverse impact on the poor who derive substantial portion of their energy intake in the form of cereals. The shift in the consumption patterns inspite of favourable price and income movements is attributed to the changes in tastes and preferences, associated with increasing modernization and urbanization of rural areas. Given the existing patterns of consumption, ensuring adequate food security for the poor is possible only by raising their purchasing power and by subsidizing their consumption.

The performance of state in the PDS is better than in the country as a whole. However, it is still lagging behind southern states. The income gains through the PDS in 1999-00 forms 6.57 per cent of the rural poor's total expenditure. PDS reduced rural poverty by about 7 percentage points in 1999-00. Covering about 70 per cent of the households, the rice scheme of Andhra Pradesh is highly cost ineffective. The estimates indicate that the cost of transferring a rupee to the poor through PDS is about Rs.10.85, on account of ineffective targeting.

The projected demand estimates indicate that an additional 30 to 40 lakh tones of rice will be required by 2020 depending on the growth rate of total expenditures. Given the problem of poverty and malnutrition, there is a need for direct interventions like PDS and ICDS. The rice scheme in AP can be modified to make it cost-effective so that the poor can be protected without straining investments in other sectors of human development.

Regional Disparities

Andhra Pradesh is conventionally classified into three broad regions,viz., Coastal Andhra, Rayalaseema and Telangana for comparisons of the levels of development. However, there is significant heterogeneity within the Coastal Andhra and Telangana regions. Therefore, in addition to the conventional classification into three regions, it is found useful to disaggregate them into six regions, viz., North Coastal Andhra, South Coastal Andhra, Rayalaseema, North Telangana, South Telangana and Hyderabad.This is done on the basis of agro-climatic conditions, level of urbanisation and industrial development.

Whether one follows the conventional or the more disaggregated classification, the regional disparities in the levels of socio-economic development in the state have come down over the last 50 years.There has been a significant decline in disparity in the levels of agricultural development, measured as the value of crop output per hectare, between Coastal Andhra and Telangana, especially between South Coastal Andhra and North Telangana. This is because area under irrigation, including from canals, expanded at a faster rate in Telangana and green revolution technologies have been adopted widely.

Agriculturally developed regions in the state like South Coastal Andhra had a low level of industrialisation in the initial period.Also, industrial development has been faster in the agriculturally backward regions like South Telangana, Rayalaseema and North Coastal Andhra. As a result, the regional disparities in per capita domestic product, consisting of income from agriculture as well as non-agricultural sources, are now lower than when income from agriculture alone is considered.

Social development, e.g.,education and health are basically dependent on public investment, the impact of which is quicker and widely spread compared to investment in physical infrastructure.Consequently, the regional disparities in literacy, primary education and health facilities are not as marked as in other sectors.These disparities, particularly in the case of literacy and education, have come down substantially because of the special programmes launched by the government during the 1980s and the 1990s. The regional differences in the incidence of rural poverty have also been reduced significantly.The Information Technology(I.T.) sector which was initially concentrated in Hyderabad is now spreading to other big urban centres in different regions of the state.

These favourable trends notwithstanding, the regional disparities in the levels of development are still significant in the state.For example, South Coastal Andhra, because it tops in respect of assured sources of irrigation, continues to occupy the top position in regard to agricultural output per hectare, followed by North Telangana and North Coastal Andhra. Rayalaseema and South Telangana are at the bottom because of insufficient irrigation coupled with low and erratic rainfall. Moreover, well irrigation is predominant in Telangana and Rayalaseema, entailing high cost of power for pumping water, besides exposing them to weather shocks and shortages of drinking water.

The index of average per capita Gross Domestic Product for the period 1995-2000 (with state average as 100) ranged from 91 for North Telangana to around 106 for South Coastal Andhra and 122 for Hyderabad & Ranga Reddy.The incidence of rural poverty in North Coastal Andhra in 1993-94 was way above that for North Telangana. The literacy rates for Telangana (excluding Hyerabad) and North Coastal Andhra were well below that for South Coastal Andhra.The drop-out rates at primary education in 2000-01 for boys and girls were quite high in Telangana, especially for S.C.s and S.T.s.In respect of health care, private sector is concentrated mainly in the developed districts, so that the state policy aimed at encouraging privatisation has benefited the developed districts accentuating the regional inequalities in the availability of medical facilities.The Child mortality rates are quite high in North Coastal Andhra, Rayalaseema and South Telangana.

The develpment experience of A.P. clearly brings out that stepping up public investment in physical and social infrastructure has an immense potential for reducing regional disparities in the levels of development. The gap between the ultimate irrigation potential from major and medium irrigation projects, which can be undertaken only through public investment, and the potential actually created so far is quite high for the drought prone regions of Rayalaseema and Telangana.Public investments for undertaking the remaining projects and for the speedy completion of the on-going ones together with rehabilitation of existing tanks by involving Water Users' Associations holds a great promise for further development and for mitigating the severity of droughts in these regions.Public expenditure on health and education needs to be stepped up substantially focusing on the less developed areas.

Small and marginal farmers being preponderant in these regions require special public support towards the provision of cheaper power, better access to quality inputs and institutional credit. Further, the overall working of the women's Self-Help Groups and Panchayati Raj institutions is found to be relatively better in the developed regions. The less developed regions, therefore, need special attention for empowering the weaker sections and the community institutions.

6. ENVIRONMENT

Environmental concerns are among the policy priorities in A.P. Here we briefly look at the status and strategies relating to environment in four areas viz., land and water management, mining, industrial pollution and urban environment.

It is estimated that the cost of soil degradation alone is about 1.2 per cent of its GSDP. That is, by checking degradation of soil the level of GSDP can be raised by 1.2 per cent. The state's experiments with watershed development programme to promote dry-land agriculture and the irrigation development programme are the most innovative in the country. Watershed development under the new guidelines, in general, has an overall positive impact on environment. However, groundwater tables are depleting at an alarming rate. The de facto privatization of groundwater and subsidized power supply are the main culprits. There has been a neglect of minor irrigation sources like tanks. Shortage of drinking water has accentuated and quality of water has declined over time.

About 19% of cultivated area is degraded. There is no relation between development and degradation across districts. However, incidence of degradation seems to be more in less irrigated areas. Composition of livestock is shifting in favour of small ruminants. The declining number of cattle means lower ratios of organic to inorganic input (fertilizer) and higher dependence on tractors for cultivation. Both these practices would have an adverse impact on the environment. In A.P. about 38% of forest area is degraded, as against 25% for All India. Overexploitation of fish rendered fishing unsustainable and aquaculture created serious environmental problems.

Mining could lead to irreversible damages if follow-up action is not taken after the mining activity is completed. The Vision document proposes to issue the safety bonds for the future mining activity. In industrial sector, most polluting industries have attracted highest investments. Water bodies are the worst affected. The estimated annual loss per household affected is about Rs.36000. The main reasons for industrial pollution include weak institutions (implementing agencies), lack of cost effective technologies, political interference, nexus between industry, bureaucracy and politicians, absence of awareness and weak bargaining power of the victims. In urban areas, water supply shortage is around 36%. Among the regions, Rayalaseema has the highest shortage (43%) of water supply. Sewerage facilities are too little to meet the demand.

An integrated approach is needed for water resources management in the state. An appropriate strategy should integrate institutional approaches with market principles. Since institutional innovation (Water user associations) is already in place for canal irrigation, it is time now to implement volumetric pricing. There is a need to de-link water rights from land rights in order to ensure equity and sustainability.

In the case of land and forestry, watershed approach and Joint Forest Management are crucial for protecting the environment. The critical issue is sustainability of these programmes. Although watersheds have shown positive economic impact, the social issues are missing. More participatory approach and involvement of women would lead to sustainability of watershed development approach. In the case of JFM, the department is focusing on high income areas like timber. Low value products constituting sources of livelihoods for the poor have low priority. Customary rights of the tribals on podu (shifting cultivation) have to be recognised.

Industrial pollution can be reduced by awareness building and promotion of environment friendly technologies through proper (dis)incentive structures. Rekindling the rural industrialization process would go a long way in addressing the problem of urban congestion.

Demand management of urban amenities such as drinking water should be given top priority. Efficient provision of services fostered with appropriate pricing would result in their efficient use. Solid waste management is another area of importance. Appropriate institutional arrangements need to be worked out to collect, recycle and dispose the waste.

Awareness and involvement of the civil society is a precondition for checking environmental degradation. Environmental movements would have a discerning impact in this regard.

7. DECENTRALISATION

Keeping in view the main objectives of the 73rd Constitutional Amendment Act, the Government of A.P. has passed the A.P. Panchayat Raj Act 1994. The actual performance so far in terms of genuine decentralization / devolution to the local bodies is far from satisfactory. In the functional domain, the present status in AP shows that it transferred functions in respect of 16 subjects of which 5 subjects with funds and only 2 subjects with functionaries are transferred to the local bodies. The performance of AP in this respect is much lower than that of Karnataka, Kerala and West Bengal. Moreover, a majority of the line departments in AP have not been brought under the control of PR bodies. Only the relatively less important functions have been transferred to the local bodies. The District Rural Development Agency (DRDA), which commands sizeable resources, functions independently of the PR bodies. Similarly, Corporations, like AP Scheduled Castes Corporation, AP Backward Caste Corporation, AP Women Development Corporation work independently of PR bodies in the state.

The panchayats have no financial autonomy either in raising financial resources or in deciding on the allocation of funds across different sectors. Funds for centrally sponsored public works schemes like JRY form the bulk of the panchayat's budgets. The allocations to different activities are generally decided by the central/state governments. The devolution of funds to panchayats in A.P. is much less than in Kerala where around 40% of state plan funds are allocated to local bodies.

There are some structural aspects of AP PR system, which impede the local bodies from functioning effectively. The State Government, the Commissioner and the District Collector have been given powers under various sections of the Act to control PR institutions at all the three levels.

Besides, the AP Act does not provide for the constitution of District Planning Committee (DPC), which is a glaring omission.

Another feature which undermines the PRIs in A.P. is a practice of diverting the funds of the PRIs for special programmes to be implemented by functionaries of other government departments. One example of this is the contentious issue relating to the promotion of parallel institutions in the form of a number of Community Based Organisations (CBOs), such as Janmabhoomi programme etc., which are entrusted with numerous functions bypassing PRIs. These initiatives have evoked keen interest all over the country as experiments in direct democracy, but they undermine representative institutions. The State Government's claim of integrating CBOs with Panchayats has not been translated so far into a reality.

8. CONCLUSION

Andhra Pradesh has been pursuing economic reforms for stepping up the GSDP growth rate and alleviating poverty, while protecting the environment. There has been a significant fiscal correction in the last seven years. Reforms are underway in the power and irrigation sectors for expanding their capacity by improving efficiency and cost-recovery. There is a breakthrough in the introduction of Information Technology. Significant strides have been made in respect of participatory management of land, water and forest resources through the Watershed Development Committees, Water Users' Associations and Joint Forest Management. Women's Self-Help Groups are a success story in the state and have formed a central element in the strategy for poverty eradication through social mobilization, community empowerment and capacity building.

These reforms can be expected to yield significant results in course of time. However, there are some major areas of concern which need to be addressed for deriving full benefits from the reforms already launched and, indeed, for making development more balanced, broad-based and sustainable. First, A.P. has not been able to step up its GSDP growth rate in the post-reform period in the same way as the fast growing states and its distance from such fast growing states has widened on account of the weak social and economic infrastructure. Therefore, the state has to increase capital outlays substantially to build up infrastructure.

Second, agriculture has been an area of strength for A.P. but has not received adequate priority in the last two decades. Stepping up agricultural growth and raising rural demand is essential for raising the growth rate in GSDP and for reducing poverty through the expansion of rural non-farm sector to absorb the large labour force still engaged in agriculture. This calls for a high priority to irrigation, agricultural research, especially in biotechnology focused on dry land farming, extension services by using Information Technology and ensuring adequate access to institutional credit for the resource-poor farmers.

The third major area of concern is slow industrial growth. Strengthening infrastructure e.g., power, roads and ports, expansion of institutional credit for small-scale and rural industries, and good governance by cutting down delays in giving clearances and reducing corruption stand out prominently as areas urgently in need of reform for attracting private investment, domestic as well as foreign.

Fourth, in social sectors like health and education, insufficient allocations, especially in the post-reform period, poor quality of services, inadequate access for the poorer sections, and lack of accountability of the systems to the community have emerged as major problem areas. In particular, it is necessary to ensure the expansion of public services for the poor at a low cost, effective public regulation of private services like health care, and accountability of these systems, public as well as private, to the local communities.

Fifth, the current strategy of social mobilization for watershed development can be sustained in the long-run only through capacity building and by making land use more remunerative through the new dry land technologies and the development of infrastructure. Similarly, poverty eradication through community empowerment can become sustainable only if productive assets of the poor are augmented and employment is generated through labour-intensive growth. These self-help groups need better technical and marketing assistance and training for availing of the emerging income-earning opportunities.

Sixth, conservation of surface and ground water has become imperative. This is best achieved when water and power are priced according to the volume of consumption. Involvement of rural communities is essential in setting the user charges as well as for assessing the individual consumption. A subsidy, say, on power, for all the farmers for a fixed number of units, irrespective of the size of holding, combined with volumetric rate for extra consumption could be a feasible solution, as it would provide greater relief to the small users while providing incentives to conserve the resources.

Seventh, there is a significant scope for reducing further the regional disparities in development by stepping up public investment substantially for completing speedily the on-going major and medium irrigation projects, rehabilitation of existing tanks and on health and education, focusing on the less developed regions.

Finally, the experience so far from the working of Panchayati Raj Institutions in the state has brought out the need for greater devolution of functions, finances and powers, along with capacity building of the functionaries, for ensuring the relevance and quality of works designed as well as for their effective implementation. Andhra Pradesh needs to make a significant progress towards financially and administratively strengthening these institutions making them self-sustaining.

Notes

1 The rank correlation coefficients between per capita GSDP growth rate and the index of Social and Economic Infrastructure for both the years (0.41 and 0.43) are statistically significant at 10% level.

PART - I
MACRO-ECONOMIC SCENARIO

2

Macro-economic Scene: Performance and Policies

S. Mahendra Dev and
C. Ravi

1. INTRODUCTION

The state of A.P. was formed by combining regions with widely different endowments, historical legacies and institutional arrangements. The challenge of development policy in the period subsequent to the formation of the state was to integrate these diverse units into a single economic entity and to accelerate the growth of its productive sectors along with the promotion of adequate opportunities to ensure broad based participation by all sections of society[1]. The performance of the economy in the subsequent years reveals that the response of the Governments to this challenge has not been very satisfactory. The focus of the government policy in the 1960s and 1970s was on infrastructure like irrigation and power. The historical advantage that coastal regions enjoyed in terms of government investment in canal irrigation was reinforced with the advent of the green revolution, which benefited crops grown under irrigated conditions. The industrial growth also concentrated in the irrigated regions and in around the capital city. The government in the 1980s concentrated more on welfare policies. 'Two Rupees a Kilo Scheme' supplied under public distribution system was one of the important welfare schemes in the 1980s. The 1990s witnessed liberalization of economic policies in the country. By the end of 1990s, Andhra Pradesh has earned a reputation as the state at the forefront of many reforms in India as several fiscal, governance and sectoral reform initiatives are underway to accelerate economic development and reduce poverty. These and other reforms have been articulated in a broad vision of economic, political and social development, known as 'Andhra Pradesh - Vision 2020'. The document is the guiding force for many policies of the Government in recent years. It also states that " by 2020, every individual of AP will be able to lead a comfortable life, filled with opportunities to learn and develop skills". Thus, the experience of Andhra Pradesh raises several far-reaching issues regarding the development strategies to be followed in India and other developing countries.

The objective of this chapter is to examine the macro economic performance and policies in terms of economic growth and human development in Andhra Pradesh (A.P.). We evaluate the macroeconomic performance in the last two decades with emphasis on the 1990s. The analysis is done in two ways: (a) how did A.P. perform over time? (b) What is the performance and status of A.P. compared to other major states and all India? The specific objectives of the study are the following.

(a) What has been the growth experience in the economy and in different sectors? (Section 2).

(b) Has there been a significant growth in capital formation in the economy? How developed is the physical and economic infrastructure in the state? (Section 3).

(c) What has been the rate of growth of inflation? What is the status of A.P. in fiscal performance across states? (Section 4)

(d) What has been the experience of the state in reducing income poverty?(Section 5).

(e) What is the status of A.P. as compared to other states in raising social or human development? (Section 6)

(e) What are the recent economic and institutional reforms in the state? What should be done to improve them? (Section 7)

2. ECONOMIC GROWTH

Higher economic growth is important for several reasons. More resources will be available for further investments and social development. It will also create better opportunities for the population if the growth is labour intensive. In this sub-section, we examine the trends in economic growth of A.P. in the last two decades in comparison with all India and other states.GSDP (gross state domestic product) is used for this purpose. The data base for GSDP figures is Directorate of Economics and Statistics, Hyderabad[2]. The data on GSDP for other states is obtained from their respective Directorates of Economics and Statistics (DES). DES of state governments usually make the GSDP estimates with guidance of Central Statistical Organization (CSO). Although, the guidelines and methodologies of CSO are uniform across all the states, the GSDP estimates are not strictly comparable mainly for two reasons.

First, GSDP series of each state are not fully consistent with the national accounts estimates of GSDP. The GSDP estimates are compiled by the respective state government following broad guidelines and methodologies of CSO. There are differences in methods of estimating the SDP in different states and therefore statistically not comparable with each other.

Secondly, since the CSO no longer releases comparable estimates of GSDP series, the data has to be compiled from different sources. With frequent revisions and multiplicity of data sources, the 'growth rates' estimated in different plan documents and by researchers are not consistent. However, as shown below our aim is mainly to examine changes in distance between AP and all India (or fast growing states) over the last two decades.

The growth performance over the last two decades is summarized as follows.

(1) *Growth of GSDP in A.P.*: Table 1 provides trend rate of growth[3] for GSDP (Gross State Domestic Product) for A.P. for two periods viz., 1980/81 to 1990/91 (1980s) and 1993/94 to 2000/01 (1990s). It shows that the growth rate in the 1980s for A.P. was 5.5 per cent per annum. As compared to the 1980s, the GSDP for A.P. recorded more or less similar growth rate in the 1990s (5.31 per cent per annum)[4]. In other words, there is no significant difference between the growth rate of GSDP in the 1990s as compared to that of 1980s for A.P[5]. Our statistical tests also proved this point[6]. The mid-term appraisal of 9th Five Year Plan (GOI, 2000) provides estimates of growth rates of GSDP at state level for two periods viz., 1980-81 to 1990-91 and 1991-92 to 1997-98. Our growth rates for 1980s are similar to those of the Mid Term Appraisal. In other words, data used by us and mid-term appraisal are similar for 1980s. Ahluwalia (2000) provides similar estimates for the 1980s. The Tenth Five Year Plan document also gives growth rates for two periods viz., 1980-81 to 90-91 and 1993-94 to 1998-99. However, in the case of growth rates of GSDP for the 1980s, there are significant differences between the estimates of mid-term appraisal and Tenth Five Year Plan. In the case of A.P., mid-term appraisal shows 5.65 per cent growth rate while the 10th Five Year Plan shows 4.3 per cent per annum. We stick to our estimates for the 1980s in A.P. which are similar to those of mid-term appraisal for 9th Five Year Plan and Ahluwalia (2000). However, in order to see the impact of reforms on A.P., better test would be to examine the changes in the distance between A.P. and all India over the two decades.

(2) *Per capita GSDP Growth in A.P.*: Per capita GSDP in the 1980s in A.P. was 3.33 per cent per annum (Table 1). In the 1990s, it significantly increased to 4.04 per cent[7]. The increase in per capita growth in the 1990s was due to lower population growth. Welfare programmes in the last two decades and women s' empowerment might have contributed to lower population growth in the 1990s.

(3) *Comparison of A.P. with all India* : Table 1 also provides growth rates for all India. A comparison of A.P. with all India reveal that while the GSDP growth in 1980s was marginally higher (by 0.13 percentage point) than all India, in the period 1993-94 to 2000-01 the performance of A.P. was lower than that of all India. The growth rate of GSDP in the 1990s for A.P. was 5.31 per cent as compared to 6.13 per cent for all India.

Economic Survey of Andhra Pradesh for the year 2001-02 (GoAP, 2002) provides the annual growth rates of GSDP of A.P. with 1993-94 as base. The average annual growth rate for the period 1994-95 to 1999-00 comes 5.50 per cent. The national average for this period is 6 per cent

(Rangarajan, 2002). Thus, even if we take the average annual growth rate for the last six years of the 1990s, the performance of A.P. was lower than all India.

The per capita SDP growth shows that the growth rate in A.P. was similar to all India in the 1980s. In the 1990s, however, it was slightly lower than all India. The Estimates based on Economic Survey of Andhra Pradesh (GOI, 2002) show that in per capita terms, the average annual growth rate for A.P. during 1994-95 to 1999-00 was 4.1 per cent as against the national average of 4.5 per cent (Rangarajan, 2002). These numbers also indicate that A.P. performed well during the 1990s in terms of per capita income but it was slightly lower than all India.

The gap between per capita income of A.P. and all India (Table 2) shows that there were significant fluctuations in the 1980s – the gap increasing in the mid-80s and declining in the late 1980s (Fig 1). The gap seems to have widened in the 1990s. It showed a widening a gap till 1997-98 and narrowed down in the last two or three years.

Table 1. Growth Rates in GSDP : A.P. and All India

Period	GSDP Growth (%)		Per capita GSDP Growth (%)	
	A.P.	All India	A.P.	All India
1980/81-1990/91	5.50	5.37	3.33	3.24
1993/94-2000/01	5.31	6.13	4.04	4.38

Source: Based on the data from Directorate of Economics and Statistics, Hyderabad; 2000-01 data refer to quick estimates.

Fig.1 Percentage of per capita GSDP of A.P. to All India: 1980-81 to 2000-01 (at 1993-94 prices)

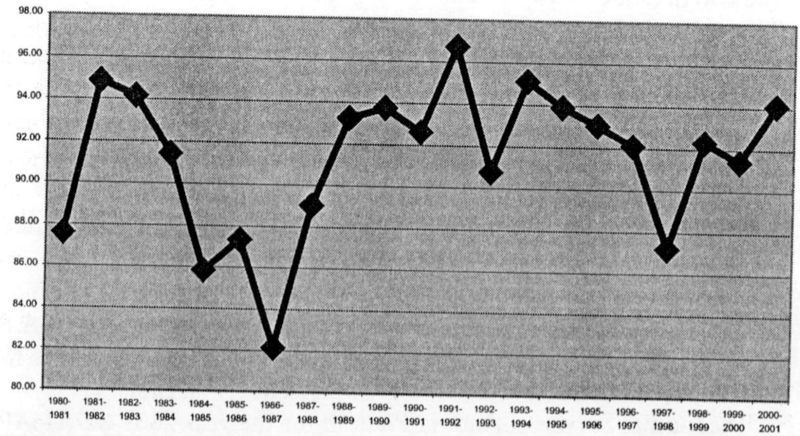

Table 2. Distance between Per capita GSDP of A.P. and All India (at 1993-94 prices)

Year	GDP		Ratio
	Andhra Pradesh	All India	
1980-1981	5175.88	5907.63	87.61
1981-1982	5828.15	6142.67	94.88
1982-1983	5827.33	6187.56	94.18
1983-1984	5965.62	6524.79	91.43
1984-1985	5716.89	6658.69	85.86
1985-1986	5947.36	6807.81	87.36
1986-1987	5714.18	6955.34	82.16
1987-1988	6292.19	7065.71	89.05
1988-1989	7125.57	7640.97	93.25
1989-1990	7487.70	7984.56	93.78
1990-1991	7650.03	8258.30	92.63
1991-1992	7931.54	8199.33	96.73
1992-1993	7679.96	8460.92	90.77
1993-1994	8341.98	8769.30	95.13
1994-1995	8667.64	9229.42	93.91
1995-1996	9031.87	9704.02	93.07
1996-1997	9474.69	10287.20	92.10
1997-1998	9241.87	10597.14	87.21
1998-1999	10249.55	11102.25	92.32
1999-2000	10591.37	11589.30	91.39
2000-2001	11154.14	11853.14	94.10

Source: Same as Table 1.

(4) *Comparison with Other States:* Table 3 provides growth rates of GSDP and per capita GSDP for 15 major states. It shows that in the 1980s, A.P. was one of the top performing states in terms of GSDP growth. Only three states viz., Rajasthan, Haryana, and Maharashtra showed higher growth than A.P. in the 1980s. However, in the 1990s, A.P.'s rank in terms of GSDP growth was eight. Seven states showed higher growth than AP in the 1990s. Apart from the above three states , four more states viz., Gujarat, Karnataka, Tamil Nadu and West Bengal recorded higher growth than A.P. in the 1990s. Similar trends can be seen for the growth of per capita income in the1990s across states. A.P.'s rank in per capita growth was lower in the 1990s as compared to that of the1980s (see Table 3).

(5) *Changes in Distance in growth rates between A.P. and Others from different Sources:* As mentioned above, there are different estimates of growth rates from different sources. However, our main aim is to see whether the distance between A.P. and all India (and fast growing states)

Table 3. Growth Rates of GSDP and Per capita GSDP (%) and Ranks for Major 15 states

State	G.r. in GSDP (%)		G.r. in per capita GSDP (%)		Rank for g.r. in GSDP		Rank for g.r. in per capita GSDP	
	1980-81to 1990-91	1993-94 to2000-01	1980-81to 1990-91	1993-94 to 2000-01	1980-81to 1990-91	1993-94 to 2000-01	1980-81to 1990-91	1993-94 to 2000-01
A.P.	5.50	5.31	3.33	4.04	4	8	5	8
Assam	3.51	2.59	1.37	0.98	14	15	15	15
Bihar	4.55	4.50	2.42	2.81	11	12	10	12
Gujarat	4.96	5.98	3.00	4.39	8	5	8	4
Haryana	6.23	5.57	3.81	3.68	2	7	2	9
Karnataka	5.16	7.92	3.20	6.41	7	1	7	1
Kerala	3.51	5.17	2.13	4.05	14	10	13	7
M.P.	4.46	4.33	2.10	2.36	12	13	14	13
Maharashtra	5.85	5.75	3.56	4.30	3	6	4	5
Orissa	4.20	3.22	2.39	2.00	13	14	12	14
Punjab	5.18	4.96	3.30	3.01	6	11	6	11
Rajasthan	6.39	6.26	3.84	4.22	1	3	1	6
Tamil Nadu	5.24	6.04	3.80	4.99	5	4	3	3
U.P.	4.83	5.26	2.54	3.10	9	9	9	10
WestBengal	4.60	6.88	2.41	5.32	10	2	11	2
All India	5.37	6.13	3.24	4.38	--	--	--	--

Note: 1.For Bihar, Madhya Pradesh and Uttar Pradesh the data are for the years prior to the reorganization of these states- 1993-94 and 1998-99.
2. For the above three states growth rates are available after reorganization also. The growth rates of GSDP for the reorganized states of Bihar , M.P. and U.P. during 1993-94 to 2000-01 were 5.30 per cent, 4.20 per cent and 4.17 per cent respectively.
Source: See Note 2.

has been increasing or declining. Table 3a provides our estimates along with 9th plan (mid-term) and 10th plan estimates. Irrespective of the source, the estimates show that distance between A.P. and all India has increased in the 1990s as compared to 1980s. Similarly, all the sources have shown that the distance between A.P. and fast growing states such as Gujarat, Maharashtra, Karnataka and Tamil Nadu has increased significantly in the 1990s as compared to 1990s.

(6) *Comparison of Sectoral Growth with All India:* Table 4 gives growth rates for three major sectors for A.P. and all India. In the case of A.P., the growth rate for agriculture& allied sector increased by 0.26 percentage point in the 1990s. However, in the case of industry and services, the growth rate in A.P. declined by one percentage point. As compared to all India, growth in agriculture& allied was lower while it was higher in industry and services sectors in the 1980s. In the 1990s, the growth rates of agriculture& allied sector in A.P. was lower by 0.26 percentage point in relation to all India. A.P.'s growth rate in industry in the 1990s was similar to all India However, in the case of services, the growth rate of A.P. was

Table 3a. Growth Rates from Different Sources and the Distance Between A.P. and Fast Growing States: 1980-91 and 1993-2001

State	Our estimates		Tenth Five Year Plan		Mid-term Appraisal of Ninth Plan	
Period	1980-91	1993-2001	1980-91	1993-99	1980-91	1990-98
			Growth Rates			
Andhra Pradesh	5.50	5.31	4.30	4.90	5.65	5.03
Gujarath	4.96	5.98	5.10	8.00	5.08	9.57
Karnataka	5.16	7.92	5.40	8.20	5.29	5.29
Maharashtra	5.85	5.75	6.00	7.10	6.02	8.01
West Bengal	5.24	6.04	4.80	6.80	4.71	6.91
Rajasthan	6.39	6.26	5.90	7.70	6.60	6.54
Tamilnadu	5.24	6.04	5.40	6.80	5.38	6.22
All India	5.37	6.31	5.60	6.80	5.55	6.89
Distance in terms of differences in growth rates between AP and others						
Andhra Pradesh	0.00	0.00	0.00	0.00	0.00	0.00
Gujarath	0.54	-0.67	-0.80	-3.10	0.57	-4.54
Karnataka	0.34	-2.61	-1.10	-3.30	0.36	-0.26
Maharashtra	-0.35	-0.44	-1.70	-2.20	-0.37	-2.98
West Bengal	0.26	-0.73	-0.50	-1.90	0.94	-1.88
Rajasthan	-0.89	-0.95	-1.60	-2.80	-0.95	-1.51
Tamilnadu	0.26	-0.73	-1.10	-1.90	0.27	-1.19
All India	0.13	-1.00	-1.30	-1.90	0.10	-1.86

lower by 1.42 percent. Thus, the main reason for the lower GSDP growth in A.P. as compared to all India in the 1990s seems to be the lower performance of service sector in A.P.

Growth rates of GSDP for important sub-sectors are given in Table 5. It shows the growth rate declined in the 1990s for A.P. in manufacturing, trade, hotels & restaurants. On the other hand, it increased in transport & communications and public services. As compared to all India, the growth rate in agriculture & allied activities was lower in both the decades –the difference being much higher in the 1980s. In the 1990s, the growth rate for trade, hotels & restaurants was much lower for A.P. as compared to all India and *vice versa* for transport & communications. In the case of public services, A.P.' growth was lower than all India.

Table 4. Growth Rates of AP GSDP and All India GDP in Three Major Sectors

Period	Agriculture& allied	Industry	Services
	Andhra Pradesh		
1980/81-1990/91	2.21	7.36	7.69
1993/94-2000/01	2.47	6.20	6.71
	All India		
1980/81-1990/91	3.12	6.60	6.48
1993/94-2000/01	2.73	6.25	8.13

Source: Same as Table 1.

Table 5. Growth Rates of AP GSDP and All India GDP in Important Sectors

Period	Manufacturing	Trade, Hotels& Restaurents	Transport & Communications	Public Services
	Andhra Pradesh			
1980/81-1990/91	8.39	8.66	5.16	5.68
1993/94-2000/01	6.20	5.15	7.86	7.34
	All India			
1980/81-1990/91	6.95	5.89	7.08	7.4
1993/94-2000/01	6.47	8.11	5.40	8.1

Source: Same as Table 1.

(7) *Comparison of Sectoral Growth with Other States:* In the 1980s, A.P.'s growth rate in agriculture & allied was one of the lowest in the country (Table 6). The rank of A.P. in agriculture growth was 11 (Table 7). On the other hand, the growth rates for industry and services were quite high in the 1980s with ranks of 5 and 2 respectively. In the 1990s, there was only a marginal increase in the growth of agriculture & allied sector in A.P. However, the rank of A.P. was high at 5 because there was a significant decline in the growth rate of agriculture sector for majority of states during 1993-94 to 2000-01. Another important conclusion from our state level analysis is that there was a decline in the rank of industry and a very significant decline in the rank of services for A.P. in the 1990s. The rank for industry in A.P. declined from 5 to 9 while for services it declined from 2 to 12. In other words, Andhra Pradesh is lagging behind some of the states in the growth of industry and in services. Particularly in services the growth rate was lagging behind many other states. The growth rate of agriculture & allied in A.P. in the last two decades is less than 2.5 per cent per annum.

The conclusion is that Andhra Pradesh made significant progress in terms of economic growth in the 1980s and 1990s. However, the growth is not enough and it has to grow much faster in all the three sectors in order to catch up with some of the high growing states.

Table 6. Statewise Sectoral GSDP growth rates in the 1980s and 1990s

States	1980/81-1990/91				1993/94-2000/01			
	Agriculture & Allied	Industry	Services	Total	Agriculture & allied	Industry	Services	Total
Andhra Pradesh	2.21	7.36	7.69	5.50	2.47	6.20	6.71	5.31
Assam	2.21	4.10	4.59	3.51	1.05	3.10	3.18	2.59
Bihar	2.93	5.90	5.42	4.55	-0.66	6.56	7.42	4.50
Gujarat	-0.53	7.48	7.01	4.96	-1.34	7.57	7.88	5.98
Haryana	4.21	8.97	7.42	6.23	1.61	6.65	9.00	5.57
Karnataka	2.36	6.52	7.30	5.16	4.73	8.51	9.94	7.92
Kerala	1.99	2.88	5.10	3.51	1.36	5.47	7.08	5.17
Madhya Pradesh	2.22	6.24	6.33	4.46	1.58	5.21	6.19	4.33
Maharashtra	3.60	6.25	6.83	5.85	0.17	6.51	7.04	5.75
Orissa	1.36	7.38	5.93	4.20	-0.43	2.49	7.02	3.22
Punjab	4.67	7.10	4.59	5.18	2.19	7.04	6.98	4.96
Rajasthan	4.34	7.48	8.57	6.39	2.72	7.48	7.79	6.26
Tamil Nadu	3.51	5.07	6.36	5.24	1.42	5.35	8.69	6.04
Uttar Pradesh	2.62	7.60	6.17	4.83	2.66	7.95	6.06	5.26
West Bengal	5.37	3.62	4.78	4.60	3.06	6.14	9.60	6.88
All India	3.12	6.60	6.48	5.37	2.73	6.25	8.13	6.13

Notes: 1. Agriculture and Allied includes Agriculture and Livestock, Forestry and Logging and Fishing.

2. Industry includes manufacturing, mining and quarrying electricity and gas, and construction.

3. Services includes all the remaining sectors.

4. For Bihar, Madhya Pradesh and Uttar Pradesh the data are for the years prior to the reorganization of these states- 1993-94 and 1998-99.

5. Data for 2000-01 are quick estimates.

Source: See Note 2 .

The above trends relate to the past performance. The Vision 2020 document provides projections up to the year 2020. It has ambitious vision of achieving high growth rates for the entire economy and in each major sector of the economy. The average per capita income is projected to increase nine times (9.4% per annum) during the 25 year period. The overall GSDP is expected to grow at the rate of 10.3 per cent per annum, on an average, during 1995-2020. The corresponding projected growth rates for agriculture, industry and services respectively are 6%, 11% and 12% per cent per annum during 1995-2020. The projections of average

Table 7. Ranking of State wise Sectoral Growth Rates of GSDP

States	1980/81-1990/91				1993/94-2000/01			
	Agriculture & Allied	Industry	Services	Total	Agriculture & Allied	Industry	Services	Total
Andhra Pradesh	11	5	2	4	5	9	12	8
Assam	11	12	14	14	11	14	15	15
Bihar	7	10	11	11	14	7	7	12
Gujarat	14	3	5	8	15	3	5	5
Haryana	4	1	3	2	7	6	3	7
Karnataka	9	7	4	7	1	1	1	1
Kerala	12	14	12	14	10	11	8	10
Madhya Pradesh	10	9	8	12	8	13	13	13
Maharashtra	5	8	6	3	12	8	9	6
Orissa	13	4	10	13	13	15	10	14
Punjab	2	6	14	6	6	5	11	11
Rajasthan	3	3	1	1	3	4	6	3
Tamil Nadu	6	11	7	5	9	12	4	4
Uttar Pradesh	8	2	9	9	4	2	14	9
West Bengal	1	13	13	10	2	10	2	2

annual growth rates for five years each up to 2020 are given in Table 8. The projections of growth rates look very ambitious and achieving them may be difficult. Particularly, the growth rate of 6 per cent per annum for agriculture sector looks very high given the past record of the state. It is true of other sectors.

The Economic Survey of the Government (GOAP, 2002), however, claims that "during the first five years of 25 years of Vision, the performance of the State economy is satisfactory, despite bad years due to failure of both monsoons". It seems the average annual growth rate in GSDP during first five years of the vision (1995-00)works out to 5.50 per cent per annum as against the average annual growth rate of 5.7 per cent per annum (Table 8) given in the Vision 2020. The shortfall is mainly due to lower growth in agriculture while industry and services achieved the targeted growth rates. It may be noted, however, that the targets for the next five years (2000-05) are on the higher trajectory with an average annual growth rate of 8.6 per cent per annum in GSDP. In the subsequent five-year periods, the targeted growth rates look much higher. Achievement of these targets looks difficult unless some drastic changes occur in investments, efficiency, institutions, governance etc.

Table 8. Vision 2020 Document's Projections of Average Annual Growth Rates

Year	GSDP	Per capita	Agriculture	Industry	Services
1995-00	5.7	4.4	3.7	5.3	7.0
2000-05	8.6	7.6	6.1	9.7	9.5
2005-10	10.9	10.1	6.9	11.6	12.6
2010-15	12.4	11.7	6.3	13.8	14.0
2015-20	14.0	13.4	5.7	14.6	15.5
Overall Annual Growth Rate	10.3	9.4	6.0	11.0	12.0

Source: Vision 2020 Document, GOAP.

3. CAPITAL FORMATION AND INFRASTRUCTURE

Gross Fixed Capital Formation

Capital formation is important for economic growth. Here we look at fixed capital formation in different sectors of A.P.[8].The trend growth rates for two decades in Table 9 shows that 1980s recorded a high growth rate of 6.0 per cent per annum for the total economy but in the 1990s it declined to 3.6 per cent per annum. Similar declines can be seen for public and private sectors. Interestingly, decline in growth rate of private sector was higher than that for public sector in the 1990s. Fixed capital in agriculture recorded high growth in the 1980s but in the 1990s it declined in absolute sense as shown by the negative growth. Similarly, secondary and tertiary sectors showed 5 to 6 per cent growth in the 1980s. In the 1990s the capital formation in these two sectors declined but it was above 4 per cent per annum. The decline in private investment in agriculture for A.P. is in contrast to that of all India where private sector increased in the 1990s[9]. This needs further investigation.

Foreign Direct Investment

A look at the foreign direct investment (FDI) during August 1991 to June 2002 shows that the top five states in terms of attracting FDI are Maharashtra, Delhi, Tamil Nadu, Karnataka and Gujarat (Table 10). Top five states account for 52 per cent of total FDI approvals in the country. Maharashtra topped in attracting the inflow of FDI ever since 1991 when the country opened its doors to foreign capital. It attracted Rs.48,722 crores and has about 17 per cent share in the total FDI of the country. Despite its reforms, A.P. could manage to attract only Rs.13,092 crores of FDI which works out to 4.65 per cent of total FDI in the country. Tamil Nadu and Karnataka have done better than A.P. in terms of attracting foreign direct investment.

Table 9. Sectoral Growth Rates of Gross Fixed Capital Formation (At 1980-81 Prices) in A.P.

Years	Sectors					
	Agriculture	Manufacturing	Primary	Secondary	Tertiary	Total
			Public			
1980/90	8.5	19.3	8.9	8.6	4.9	7.2
1990/00	1.4	0.8	-2.4	4.5	5.9	5.6
			Private			
1980/90	4.7	5.2	4.7	3.4	7.2	5.1
1990/00	-3.8	2.3	-3.3	4.0	3.7	1.9
			Total			
1980/90	6.6	6.4	7.2	5.1	6.1	6.0
1990/00	-1.1	2.1	-2.7	4.2	4.7	3.6

Table 10. Foreign Direct Investment Approvals (Aug 1991-June 2002)

States	Total No. of Approvals	Amount (Rs. In crores)	% to Total
Maharashtra	4002	48722.4	17.32
Delhi	1990	33806.6	12.02
Tamil Nadu	2165	23470.3	8.34
Karnataka	1973	21945.0	7.80
Gujarat	1050	18453.2	6.56
Andhra Pradesh	1017	13092.2	4.65
Madhya Pradesh	225	9227.3	3.28
West Bengal	594	8808.3	3.13
Orissa	136	8229.0	2.92
Rest of the states and approvals in which states are not indicated	8932	95579.3	33.98
Total	22084	281333.6	100.0

Source: Financial Express, December 23, 2002.

Infrastructure

Physical and social infrastructures are important for economic growth and higher human development. The Report of 10th and 11th Finance Commissions provide Index of social and economic infrastructure for major Indian states. The index for each state is estimated in relation to all India. The index for 1995 for A.P. was almost close to all India with a rank of 10 out of 15 major states (Table 11). In 2000, the index and rank of A.P. increased to 103 and 9 respectively. Punjab, Kerala, Tamil Nadu, Haryana and Gujarat have much higher levels of infrastructure than A.P. in the year 2000. The CMIE index of infrastructure and per capita NSDP for major states in the year 1993-94 are plotted in Fig. 2. It shows that the per capita income in A.P. was less and infrastructure was marginally higher than all India. Kerala has slightly higher per capita income than A.P. but its infrastructure is much higher because of social development. CMIE index also shows that Tamil Nadu, Punjab, Haryana, Gujarat have higher infrastructure index than A.P.

Table 11. Index of Social and Economic Infrastructure

States	Index		Rank	
	1995	2000	1995	2000
Andhra Pradesh	99.19	103.3	10	9
Assam	81.94	77.72	12	13
Bihar	92.04	81.33	11	11
Gujarat	123.01	124.31	6	5
Haryana	158.89	137.54	3	4
Karnataka	101.2	104.88	9	8
Kerala	205.41	178.68	2	2
Madhya Pradesh	65.92	76.79	14	14
Maharashtra	121.7	112.8	7	6
Orissa	74.46	81	13	12
Punjab	219.19	187.57	1	1
Rajasthan	70.46	75.86	15	15
Tamil Nadu	149.86	149.1	4	3
Uttar Pradesh	111.8	101.23	8	10
West Bengal	131.67	111.25	5	7
All India	100	100	-	-

Source: GOI, 1995, 2000.

4. INFLATION AND FISCAL PERFORMANCE

Inflation

We look at here the inflation rates in A.P. as compared to all India and other states. The macro level inflation can be captured with implicit deflators from National Accounts Statistics (see Appendix 2 for details). The implicit deflator, however, does not reveal the rate of inflation for consumers. The consumer price index for agricultural labour (CPIAL) gives some idea about the inflation in rural areas particularly for the poor. Similarly CPIIW reveals in urban areas. The CPIAL and their growth rates for three decades in A.P. and All India are given in Table 12 . The indices for the mid-60s show that the index for A.P. was lower by about 20 per cent as compared to all India. In the 80s and 90s also the general index for A.P. was lower by 10 to 15 per cent. The index for food for A.P. was lower than all India till early 1990s. From mid-90s it was closer to all India. In fact, it was higher than all India in the last two years of the 1990s. Regarding growth rates, the rate of growth for general index for A.P. increased over time from about 6.6 per cent in the 1970s to 9.1 per cent in the 1990s. The index for food also showed similar growth rates except in the 1980s. The lower growth rate for food in the 1980s could be due to Rs. 2 per kg rice scheme, which was introduced in 1983. The growth rate of general index for A.P. was higher than that for all India in all the decades. In the case of food index also the rate of growth in A.P. was higher than all India except in the 1980s. We will discuss further about the rate of growth of CPIAL in the next section on poverty. The consumer price index for Industrial workers (CPIIW) for A.P. was closer to that of all India (Table 12a). The growth rate of CPIIW increased over time in A.P. and all India over time. However, the growth rates in A.P. were slightly lower than that for all India in all the decades.

Fiscal Performance

There has been a deterioration in state finances particularly in the 1990s. Andhra Pradesh is not an exception in this context. The Report on Currency and Finance 2000/01 of RBI has cautioned about the deteriorating performance. It says "the low and declining buoyancies in both tax and non-tax receipts, constraints on internal resource mobilization due to losses incurred by state PSUs, electricity boards and decelerating resource transfers from the Centre have resulted in the rising fiscal deficits of State Governments, with an accompanying surge in the outstanding stock of debt" (p.34). Most of the states are having high levels of fiscal deficits, interest payments and high ratio of public debt to GDP ratio (see Table 13). These fiscal problems increased significantly for A.P. along with other states in the later half of the 1990s. As compared to A.P.'s past performance, there has been significant decline in its performance in the 1990s (see Appendix Figures A1 to A3). Table 14 shows that A.P.'s relative ranking has slightly worsened in the 1990s. However, A.P.'s ranking in the 1990s as compared to other states is not bad. In the 1990s, it has a rank of six in the case of public debt as per cent of SDP and five for fiscal deficit as per cent of SDP while it has 7th rank in the case of interest burden. In other words, only five to six states have performed better than A.P. in terms of main fiscal indicators. Excluding the borrowings from Small savings and Provident fund, the debt-SDP ratio increased from 21 percent in 1998-99 to 25 percent in 2000-01 (Fig A2 in Appendix).

Fig 2. Index of Economic and Social Infrastructure and Per Capita Income

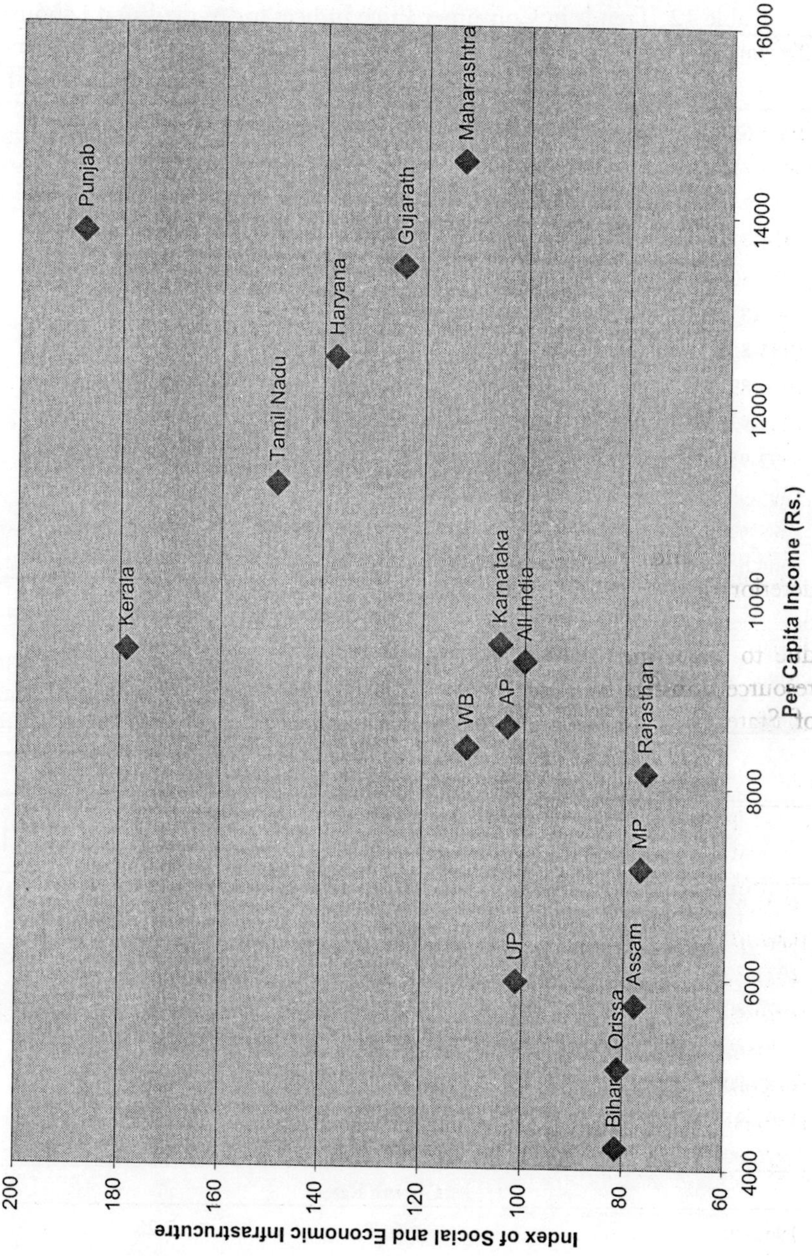

Table 12. Trends in Consumer Price Indices for Agricultural Labour

Triennium	Andhra Pradesh		All India		Price Differential	
	General	Food	General	Food	General	Food
1965-68	149	156	180	197	83	79
1968-71	170	179	190	206	89	87
1971-74	202	215	225	246	90	88
1974-77	296	316	329	361	90	88
1977-80	295	309	329	355	90	87
1980-83	351	414	435	477	81	87
1983-86	448	472	529	576	85	82
1986-89	535	562	636	691	84	81
1989-92	679	710	836	909	81	78
1992-95	983	1041	1146	1252	86	83
1995-98	1259	1326	1481	1392	85	95
1998-99	1496	1617	1726	1546	87	105
1999-00	1539	1668	1802	1592	85	105
	Growth Rates					
1970s	6.62	6.55	6.61	6.50		
1980s	7.11	5.59	6.55	6.44		
1990s	9.14	9.46	8.63	8.95		

Table 12a . Trends in Consumer Prices for Industrial Workers

Period	Andhra Pradesh	All India	AP as % of All India
1961-65	113.2	116.6	97.1
1966-70	162.4	171.8	94.5
1971-75	245.0	250.6	97.8
1976-80	330.8	337.2	98.1
1981-85	504.0	526.4	95.7
1986-90	740.6	785.6	94.3
1991-95	1203.6	1267.6	95.0
1996-00	1812.8	1934.4	93.7
	Growth Rates		
1961-70	6.79	7.28	-
1971-80	7.20	7.31	-
1981-90	7.72	8.10	-
1991-00	8.15	8.41	-

Table 13. Selected Fiscal Indicators for the 15 major States

State	Public Debt as % to SDP		Interest Burden (IP/RR)		Gross Fiscal Deficit as % to SDP	
	1990-95	1995-00	1990-95	1995-00	1990-91	1998-99
Andhra Pradesh	22.0	23.2	12.1	16.9	3.2	5.5
Assam	37.6	32.8	13.8	15.0	-	-
Bihar	41.6	41.1	20.5	20.2	7.0	4.1
Gujarat	22.4	18.6	15.4	17.4	7.4	6.3
Haryana	22.2	23.9	12.4	15.7	2.6	5.9
Karnataka	20.7	20.4	11.4	13.6	2.7	4.1
Kerala	33.3	27.9	16.5	19.5	6.6	5.3
Madhya Pradesh	23.9	22.5	12.1	14.8	3.8	5.2
Maharashtra	15.5	17.0	11.5	15.1	2.8	5.8
Orissa	44.2	48.1	19.7	26.1	6.4	9.8
Punjab	39.9	41.4	19.3	32.6	7.4	7.9
Rajasthan	30.6	33.4	15.2	22.9	3.0	8.9
Tamil Nadu	19.3	18.3	10.1	13.8	4.1	4.5
Uttar Pradesh	30.2	31.3	18.2	27.2	6.2	7.8
West Bengal	24.3	25.8	18.1	28.9	5.2	6.7
Average of 15 states	28.5	28.4	15.1	20.0	4.9	6.3

Table 14. Relative Ranking of States by the Fiscal Indicators

State	Public Debt as % to SDP		Interest Burden (IP/RR)		Gross Fiscal Deficit	
	1990-95	1995-00	1990-95	1995-00	1990-91	1998-99
Andhra Pradesh	4	6	4	7	5	5
Assam	12	11	6	4	-	-
Bihar	14	13	14	10	12	1
Gujarat	6	3	8	8	13	8
Haryana	5	7	5	6	1	7
Karnataka	3	4	2	1	2	1
Kerala	11	9	9	9	11	4
Madhya Pradesh	7	5	4	3	6	3
Maharashtra	1	1	3	5	3	6
Orissa	15	15	13	12	10	13
Punjab	13	14	12	15	13	11
Rajasthan	10	12	7	11	4	12
Tamil Nadu	2	2	1	2	7	2
Uttar Pradesh	9	10	11	13	9	10
West Bengal	8	8	10	14	8	9

5. INCOME POVERTY AND HUMAN DEVELOPMENT

The concept of poverty is multi-dimensional (viz., income poverty and non-income poverty). It covers not only levels of income and consumption, but also health and education, vulnerability and risk; and marginalisation and exclusion of the poor from the mainstream of society[10]. Here we look at performance of A.P. in both income poverty and human development.

Income Poverty

The National Sample Survey (NSS) data on consumer expenditure is generally used for estimating poverty in India. NSS has both annual surveys and quinquennial surveys. We concentrate on the estimates based on the latter as they provide reliable estimates at the state level. The estimates based on expert group method and approved by the Planning Commission are presented in Table 15 . It shows that there has been significant reduction in rural poverty of Andhra Pradesh from 48.4 per cent in 1973-74 to 11.05 in 1999-00. The rural poverty level in A.P was less than half of that of all India in 1999-00. On the other hand, the rate of decline in urban poverty has been slower in the state up to 1993-94. Urban poverty declined faster between 1993-94 and 1999-00. Inspite of this decline the level is still high at around 27 per cent in 1999-00 and this level is higher than all India. In fact the absolute number of urban poor (6.1 million) was higher than the rural poor (5.8 million) because of the higher poverty ratio of the former. The changes in rural poverty are given in Table 16. If we take long term from 1973-74 to 1999-00, rural poverty declined faster in A.P. (37 percentage points) as compared to all India (29 percentage points) while the reverse was true in the case of urban poverty. The short term changes between quinquennial rounds can be seen from Table 16.

Table 15. Poverty in A.P. and All India (Head Count Ratio): Official Estimates

Year	Andhra Pradesh			All India		
	Rural	Urban	Combined	Rural	Urban	Combined
1973-74	48.41	50.61	48.86	56.44	49.01	54.88
1977-78	38.11	42.55	39.31	53.07	45.24	51.22
1983	26.53	38.30	28.81	45.65	40.79	44.48
1987-88	20.92	40.11	25.60	39.09	38.20	38.85
1993-94	15.92	38.33	22.19	37.27	32.36	35.97
1999-00	11.05	26.63	15.57	27.09	23.62	26.10

Source: GOAP(2002).

Alternative Estimates of Income Poverty

There is a controversy regarding the poverty ratios of Andhra Pradesh. The official estimates for rural poverty have been much lower than those of

Table 16. Changes in Poverty: A.P. and All India : Official estimates (percentage points)

Year	A.P.		All India	
	Rural	Urban	Rural	Urban
1977-78 over 1973-74	10.3	8.1	3.4	3.8
1983 over 1977-78	11.6	4.3	7.4	4.5
1987-88 over 1983	5.6	-1.8	6.6	2.6
1993-94 over 1987-88	5.0	1.8	1.8	5.9
1999-00 over 1993-94	4.9	11.7	10.2	8.7

alternative estimates made by independent researchers. Deaton (2000, 2001) estimates unit prices for different states for the years 1987-88,1993-94 and 1999-00 using the NSS data. The study shows that rural poverty line for A.P is more or less similar to all India (Table 17). On the other hand, official poverty lines for rural A.P. are much lower than those for rural India. In a recent study, Deaton and Dreze (2002) provide alternative estimates of poverty using Deaton's methodology in estimating prices[11]. According to their estimates, A.P.'s rural and urban poverty ratios have been closer to those of All India (Table 18). In 1999-00, alternative estimates show that rural poverty was 26.2 per cent while the official ratio was 11 per cent. On the other hand, alternative estimate of urban poverty was 10.8 per cent for A.P. while the official estimate was 26.6 per cent in 1999-00 (Table 19). The rank for rural poverty in A.P. was lower for alternative estimate as compared to official estimates and *vice versa* for urban poverty.

Table 17. Poverty Lines: Official and Alternative for 1999-00, A.P. and All India

Poverty Line	A.P.		All India	
	Rural	Urban	Rural	Urban
Official	262.94	457.40	327.56	454.11
Alternative	309.62	344.76	303.52	349.22

Source: Deaton (2001).

Table 18. Alternative Estimates : 1987-88 to 1999-00, A.P. and All India

Year	Rural		Urban	
	A.P.	All India	A.P.	All India
1987-88	35.0	39.0	23.4	22.5
1993-94	29.2	33.0	17.8	17.8
1999-00	26.2	26.3	10.8	12.0

Source: Deaton and Dreze (2002).

Why Official Rural Poverty Line for A.P. has been much lower than that of All India?

Let us first examine the methodology used by the Report of the Expert Group (known as Lakdawala Committee) for estimating the base line (1973-74) poverty line for all India and states (GOI, 1993). Expert group wanted to have consumer price index for middle rural population (CPIMR) to derive poverty line. Since it is not readily available, they have used consumer price index for agricultural labourers (CPIAL) for estimating CPIMR. The CPIAL index for food is already available. Non-food index for CPIAL was derived from the general index and the weighing diagram[12]. Having obtained food and non-food consumer price indices of agricultural labourers for each state, a combined price index is then obtained using the consumption pattern of the people around the poverty line in rural areas at the national level for 1973-74.

Table 19. Alternative Estimates on Incidence of Poverty: 1999-2000

States	Rural				Urban			
	Official		Alternative		Official		Alternative	
	Povery Ratio	Rank	Poverty Ratio	Rank	Poverty Ratio	Rank	Poverty Ratio	Rank
A.P	11.05	4	26.2	9	26.63	10	10.8	5
Assam	40.04	13	35.5	13	7.47	2	11.8	7
Bihar	44.30	14	41.1	14	32.91	13	24.7	12
Gujarat	13.17	5	20.0	5	15.59	5	6.4	3
Haryana	8.27	2	5.7	2	9.99	3	4.6	2
Karnataka	17.38	7	30.7	10	25.25	9	10.8	5
Kerala	9.38	3	10.0	3	20.27	7	9.6	4
M.P.	37.06	12	31.3	11	38.44	14	13.9	9
Maharashtra	23.72	9	31.9	12	26.81	11	12.0	8
Orissa	48.01	15	43.0	15	42.83	15	15.6	10
Punjab	6.35	1	2.4	1	5.75	1	3.4	1
Rajasthan	13.74	6	17.3	4	19.85	6	10.8	5
Tamil Nadu	20.55	8	24.3	8	22.11	8	11.3	6
U.P.	31.22	10	21.5	6	30.89	12	17.3	11
W. Bengal	31.85	11	21.9	7	14.86	4	11.3	6
India	27.09	--	26.3	--	23.62	--	12.0	--

Source: Economic Survey 2001-02, Government of India and Deaton and Dreze (2002).

Once we get the all India poverty line, we have to take care of price differentials across states. In order to get the specific poverty lines the all India poverty line needs to be adjusted for (a) inter-state price differentials in the base year and (b) differential movements of prices in the states from the base year onwards. The methodology used by expert group for obtaining state specific poverty lines is given in Appendix 3. It shows that the base year inter-state-price adjusted consumer price index was 15 per cent lower in A.P. as compared to all India.

The rate of growth in prices in A.P. are not significantly different from those of India (Appendix 3). Table 20 shows that only in the 1980s particularly between 1977-78 and 1983, the rate of change in price indices for A.P. was lower as compared to all India. In other cases it was either closer or higher than all India. The slightly lower rate of change in the 1980s could be due to the impact of Rs.2 a kg. Rice scheme under PDS[13]. We have seen above that the growth rate of CPIAL for food in the 1980s in A.P. was lower than all India. However, this alone can not explain the lower poverty line in A.P. from 1973-74 to 1999-00. Table 21 shows that except in 1977-78, the poverty line in A.P. was 15 to 20 per cent lower than that of all India.

The above discussion including the methodology given in Appendix 3 is summarized as follows.

(a) The base year price index (CPIMR) in 1973-74 was much lower for A.P. as compared to all India. CPIAL was used to derive the CPIMR price index. There could be some problem in the construction of CPIAL for A.P. As a result of lower CPIMR, the poverty line in A.P. in the base year was the lowest among all the major states in India. This could be the major reason for the lower levels of poverty in A.P.

(b) The rate of change in price indices over long term shows that the growth rates for A.P. were not significantly different from all India. In the 1980s, the rate of change in the price indices in A.P. was lower than all India. This could be due to the depressing impact of Rs. 2 a kg rice scheme under PDS on overall prices. However, this does not explain the lower poverty lines in A.P. for different periods from 1973-74 to 1999-00.

(c) There is a need for further research on the issue of lower levels of rural consumer prices represented by CPIAL in A.P.

Table 20. Inflation Rates of Implicit Poverty Deflators

State/All India	Growth Rates of Implicit Poverty Line Deflators				
	1973/78	1977/83	1983/88	1988/93	1993/2000
Andhra Pradesh	22.0	42.8	26.5	77.3	61.3
All India	14.5	57.4	29.0	78.3	59.2

Table 21. Ratio of poverty line of A.P. to all India

Years	Ratio
1973-74	85.1
1977-78	92.0
1983	82.8
1987-88	81.6
1993-94	79.2
1999-00	80.2

Mean Per Capita Consumption

Another way of looking at the trends in the levels of living is to look at changes in consumption directly. NSS data indicate that growth in mean per capita consumption in rural Andhra Pradesh was slower than other South Indian states and all India during 1993-94 to 1999-00. It indirectly indicates that progress at poverty reduction in A.P. in the 1990s may have been slower than in many other states.

Table 22. Mean Per capita Monthly Consumption: Rural Areas, 1993-94 and 1999-00

States	1993-94 (Rs.)	1999-00 (Rs.)	% Change between 1993-94 and 1999-00
A.P.	289	454	57
Karnataka	269	500	86
Tamil Nadu	294	514	75
Kerala	390	766	96
All India	281	486	73

Source: Computed from NSS Rounds.

Employment and Wages

Another indirect way of looking at the income poverty is to examine trends in employment and wages. The chapter on employment and unemployment in this volume looks at these trends. The trends show that employment growth in A.P.declined drastically in the 1990s as compared to the decade of 1983 to 1993-94. In rural A.P., it declined from 2.40 per cent per annum during 1983 to 1993-94 to 0.29 per cent during 1993-94 to 1999-2000. The corresponding number for urban areas were 4.28 per cent and 0.01 respectively. Similar decline can be noticed for all India. But, the decline was higher for A.P. as compared to all India. Regarding real wage, it increased in the 1980s, but growth rate was low in the 1990s for both men and women. The trend rate of growth for males declined from 5.74 % in the 1980s to 1.53 % in the 1990s. Similarly for women, the trend rate of growth in real wages has declined from 4.76 % in the 1980s to 1.94 % in the 1990s. Growing rural wages in real terms was one of the key determinants of poverty reduction in India in the 1980s. The trend in Andhra Pradesh is therefore worrying (more on this see chapter on employment and unemployment in this volume).

Social Sector and Human Development

As mentioned above, poverty is a broader concept, which includes non-income poverty like human development. In this sub-section, we look at social sector expenditures and indicators relating to human development.

Social Sector Expenditures

Here we examine the trends in social sector expenditures in A.P. Our focus is on the social sector, which we define as the total of expenditure on 'Social Services' and ' Rural Development' as given in Central and State budgets. The head 'Social Services' includes, among other things, education, health & family welfare, water supply and sanitation. The expenditure under the head 'Rural Development' (which is listed under 'Economic Services' in the budget classification) relates mostly to anti-poverty programmes. Table 23 gives an overview of social sector expenditure a) as percentage of GDP, and b) as percentage of aggregate expenditure for the period 1980-81 to 2000-01. A.P. spent around 6 to 11 per cent of its GSDP on the social sector in the last two decades (col.4). In 1980-81, the share in GSDP was 7.5 per cent and increased to 11 per cent in 1986-87. It started declining from late 1980s. The shares were lower in the 1990s as compared to 1980s. Similar trends can be seen for social services and rural development.

As per cent of aggregate expenditure, A.P. spent between 36 to 48 per cent on the social sector during 1980-81 to 2000-01. Here also the percentages in, general, were lower for social services and rural development in the 1990s than in the1980s.

Table 23. Social Sector Expenditure as % of GSDP and Total Public Expenditures: A.P., 1980-81 to 2001-02

Years	As percentage of GSDP			As percentage of Total Public Exp.		
	Social Services	Rural Develop-ment	Total Social Sector (col.2 +col.3)	Social Services	Rural Develop-ment	Total Social Sector (col.5 + col.6)
1	2	3	4	5	6	7
1980-81	6.4	1.1	7.5	37.4	6.4	43.8
1981-82	6.0	1.4	7.4	36.7	8.3	45.0
1982-83	6.3	1.1	7.4	39.2	6.8	46.0
1983-84	7.8	1.3	9.0	41.6	6.8	48.4
1984-85	7.9	1.7	9.6	38.0	8.0	46.0
1985-86	7.8	1.6	9.4	37.9	7.5	45.4
1986-87	8.9	2.1	11.0	39.2	9.1	48.4
1987-88	7.8	1.6	9.3	39.4	8.1	47.5
1988-89	6.7	1.5	8.2	35.0	7.7	42.8
1989-90	7.0	1.1	8.1	38.5	6.0	44.4
1990-91	6.5	1.4	7.9	36.2	7.9	44.1
1991-92	5.9	1.4	7.3	35.2	8.0	43.2
1992-93	6.3	1.6	7.9	34.9	8.9	43.8
1993-94	5.2	1.3	6.5	32.0	7.8	39.8
1994-95	5.1	0.9	5.9	30.5	5.2	35.6
1995-96	5.9	0.7	6.6	36.2	4.5	40.7
1996-97	5.9	0.8	6.7	36.4	5.0	41.5
1997-98	5.8	1.0	6.8	35.5	6.3	41.8
1998-99	6.3	1.3	7.5	39.2	8.1	47.3
1999-00	6.1	0.9	7.0	37.6	5.3	42.9
2000-01	6.0	0.7	6.9	32.1	3.6	35.7

Note: All the numbers are actual expenditures.
Source: Budget documents of Government of A.P.

The conclusion is that social sector expenditures as per cent of GDP and total public expenditures were lower in the 1990s as compared to those of the 1980s. It may be however, noted that the impact on the outcomes in social sector depends on both expenditures and on the effective utilization of these expenditures. We have not looked at the question of efficient utilization of expenditures in this paper.

Human Development Indicators

The National Human Development Report (2002) provides human development index at the state level over time. The index shows that A.P.'s index was lower than all India in the last two decades. A.P.'s rank is 8 in 1981 and declined marginally in 1991 and 2001 (Table 24). In other words, the relative position of A.P. in terms of human development has not increased over time. On the other hand, states like Tamil Nadu, M.P. and Rajasthan have improved their relative position. The numbers in Table 24 show that a lot of effort is needed to improve the levels of human development in A.P.

Table 24. Human Development Index for India – Combined (Rural +Urban)

States/UTs	1981 Value	1981 Rank	1991 Value	1991 Rank	2001 Value	2001 Rank
Andhra Pradesh	0.298	8	0.377	9	0.416	10
Assam	0.272	9	0.348	10	0.386	14
Bihar	0.237	14	0.308	15	0.367	15
Gujarat	0.360	4	0.431	6	0.479	6
Haryana	0.360	4	0.443	5	0.509	5
Karnataka	0.346	5	0.412	7	0.478	7
Kerala	0.500	1	0.591	1	0.638	1
Madhya Pradesh	0.245	13	0.328	13	0.394	12
Maharashtra	0.363	3	0.452	4	0.523	4
Orissa	0.267	10	0.345	12	0.404	11
Punjab	0.411	2	0.475	2	0.537	2
Rajasthan	0.256	11	0.347	11	0.424	9
Tamil Nadu	0.343	6	0.466	3	0.531	3
Uttar Pradesh	0.255	12	0.314	14	0.388	13
West Bengal	0.305	7	0.404	8	0.472	8
All India	0.302		0.381		0.472	

Source: GOI (2002).

Selected indicators of human development (Table 25) show a mixed picture. Literacy levels are still below the level of all India. The levels of life expectancy and infant mortality are marginally better than all India levels. In the case of maternal mortality, A.P. is much better than many other states. A.P. lags behind in human development indicators particularly in literacy, schooling and infant mortality as compared to other southern states.

Table 25. Selected Indicators of Human Development

States/UTs	Literacy 2001 Male	Female	Total	Life Expectancy at birth (1993-97)	Infant mortality per 1000 live births 1999	Maternal mortality per 1 lakh live births 1998
Andhra Pradesh	70.85	51.17	61.11	62.4	66	159
Assam	71.93	56.03	64.28	56.7	76	409
Bihar	60.32	33.57	47.53	59.6	63	452
Gujarat	80.50	58.60	69.97	61.9	63	28
Haryana	79.25	56.31	68.59	64.1	68	103
Karnataka	76.29	57.45	67.04	63.3	58	195
Kerala	94.20	87.86	90.92	73.3	14	198
Madhya	76.80	50.28	64.11	55.5	90	498
Pradesh	86.27	67.51	77.27	65.5	48	135
Maharashtra	75.95	50.97	63.61	57.2	97	367
Orissa	75.63	63.55	69.95	67.7	53	199
Punjab	76.46	44.34	61.03	60.0	81	670
Rajasthan	82.33	61.46	69.68	64.1	52	79
Tamil Nadu	70.23	42.98	57.36	57.6	84	707
Uttar Pradesh	77.58	60.22	69.22	62.8	52	266
West Bengal						
All India	75.85	54.16	65.38	61.1	70	407

Source: Census of India, 2001.

Some related indicators on women and children based on NFHS data are given in Table 26. It shows that in A.P. more than 50 per cent of women and more than 70 per cent of children have anemia while around 38 per cent of the children are undernourished. Only in the case of undernourished children, the percentage was lower for A.P. than all India while it was closer to all India regarding anemia for children and women.

The National Commission on population has ranked all the districts in India based on composite indicators of socio-economic and demographic indicators (Table 27). The districts of A.P. figured neither in the top 100 districts nor in bottom groups (300-400 and 401-569). They were concentrated in the middle groups i.e. between 100-300. Efforts have to be made to improve the ranks of A.P. districts particularly in the 200-300 group.

Table 26. Percentage of Women and Children with Anaemia and Percentage of Children Undernourished : 1998-99

States	Percentage of Women with any anaemia	Percentage of children with anaemia	Percentage of children undernourished*
Andhra Pradesh	49.8	72.3	37.7
Assam	69.7	63.2	36.0
Bihar	63.4	81.3	54.4
Gujarat	46.3	74.5	45.1
Haryana	47.0	83.9	34.6
Karnataka	42.4	70.6	43.9
Kerala	22.7	43.9	26.9
Madhya Pradesh	54.3	75.0	55.1
Maharashtra	48.5	76.0	49.6
Orissa	63.0	72.3	54.4
Punjab	41.4	80.0	28.7
Rajasthan	48.5	82.3	50.6
Tamil Nadu	56.5	69.0	36.7
Uttar Pradesh	48.7	73.9	51.7
West Bengal	62.7	78.3	48.7
India	51.8	74.3	47.0

*weight for age

Source: National Family Health Survey (NFHS-2, 1998-99).

Table 27. Percentage Distribution of Districts Ranked on the Basis of Composite Index of Socio-Economic Demographic Indicators

State	Total No. of districts	0-100	101-200	201-300	301-400	401-569	All
Group-I							
1. Andhra Pradesh	23	8.7	47.8	39.1	4.3	0.0	100.0
2. Gujarat	25	8.0	60.0	16.0	12.0	4.0	100.0
3. Haryana	19	21.1	57.9	21.1	0.0	0.0	100.0
4. Karnataka	27	48.1	29.6	18.5	0.0	0.0	100.0
5. Kerala	14	92.9	7.1	0.0	0.0	0.0	100.0
6. Maharashtra	35	17.1	40.0	31.4	11.4	0.0	100.0
7. Punjab	17	70.6	29.4	0.0	0.0	0.0	100.0
8. Tamil Nadu	30	93.3	6.7	0.0	0.0	0.0	100.0
Sub-total (1 to 8)	190	42.1	35.3	17.4	4.7	0.5	100.0
Group-II							
9. Assam	20	10.0	5.0	35.0	30.0	20.0	100.0
10. Bihar	55	0.0	0.0	0.0	7.3	92.7	100.0
11. M.P.	61	0.0	6.6	32.8	24.6	36.1	100.0
12. Orissa	30	0.0	6.7	46.7	43.3	3.3	100.0
13. Rajasthan	32	0.0	0.0	0.0	28.1	71.9	100.0
14. Uttar Pradesh	83	0.0	6.0	10.8	27.7	55.4	100.0
15. West Bengal	18	11.1	22.2	33.3	27.8	5.6	100.0
Sub-total (9 to 15)	29	1.3	5.3	18.7	25.1	49.5	100.0
Total	489	17.2	17.0	18.2	17.2	30.5	100.0

Source of basic data: Districtwise Social Economic Demographic Indicators, National Commission on Population, Government of India 2001.

6. POLICIES FOR ECONOMIC GROWTH AND POVERTY REDUCTION

Economic and Institutional Reforms

As mentioned above, the document 'Andhra Pradesh - Vision 2020' is the guiding force for many policies of the Government in recent years. The GOAP has established a number of Cabinet Sub-committees to develop approach papers for the delivery of the various elements of the vision. A number of Task Forces were constituted to consider rural poverty alleviation, Urban Poverty Alleviation, Women's empowerment and Governance. The GOAP has also adopted a mission approach for promoting development. Missions have been set up for poverty alleviation, employment generation, Women's empowerment, Water conservation and literacy.

A.P. undertook many reforms in the last six years. They are: fiscal reforms, power reforms, governance reforms and institutional reforms.

Fiscal Reforms

The major reforms for government expenditure restructuring are aimed at improving the developmental impact of the expenditure, and reducing unproductive expenditure resulting from mis-targeted welfare programs and subsidies. It also includes public enterprise reforms. A number of reforms for budgetary accounting were initiated. Zero-based budgeting was adopted as an important policy tool to bring fiscal discipline in all the departments. The government has compiled a list of performance indicators with inputs from departments. These indicators would subsequently be applied by each department through the entire government but on a test basis, and progressively improved based on feedback. The revenue side measures basically aim for a comprehensive reform of the structure and administration of the state's main taxes such as sales tax, stamp duties, and the profession tax. The government is now preparing to introduce the state level value added tax system by April 2003. In addition, the government has embarked on a Medium Term Fiscal Framework to help plan fiscal policies following the passing of Fiscal Responsibility and Budget Management Act, 2000 at Centre.

Power Reforms

The government of A.P. has taken several policy and implementation initiatives to accomplish the reform process. The electricity supply is reorganised by creating separate corporations for transmission (APTRANSCO) and generation (APGENCO). Power subsidy will be phased out over time. The state has taken strong measures to halt theft, regularize connections, stiffen penalties with the establishment of special tribunals, monitor and effectively enforce supply regulation policy for agricultural consumers, improve customer service, undertake full census of agriculture pump sets and in implementing tariff rulings of the independent state regulatory agency.

Governance Reforms

The basic thrust of the vision document is to bring to the people of Andhra Pradesh SMART government i.e. Government which is Simple, Moral, Accountable, Responsive and Transparent and can transform AP into a state 'where poverty is totally eradicated'. The Task Force on Good Governance recommended many governance reforms. The government launched several initiatives like AP State Wide Area Network (APSWAN), Twin Cities' Information Network System (TWINS) and Computer-aided Administration of Registration Department (CARD) to introduce information technology in citizen services.

The Task Force on Good Governance, after interacting with various sections of society, made certain recommendations on governance[14]. One of the important recommendations of the Task Force on Good Governance was the setting up of a Centre for Good Governance, which would drive government's reform program. Government accepted this recommendation. A Centre for Good Governance, in collaboration with DFID, UK was set up at Hyderabad. The CGG will guide and coordinate the reform activities and support implementation of reforms and change management to achieve government's goals and priorities.

Institutional Reforms

Participatory democracy was initiated in the state. The state is recognized for its strong emphasis on rural development, community empowerment, and support for women's' groups. Self Help Groups like women's thrift and credit societies, water user associations, watershed committees, school education committees, mother's committees, vana samrakshna Samitis (VSS, Joint forest management) were introduced. Janmabhoomi programme is also a participatory programme. Recently there were efforts to link Panchayati Raj Institutions (PRIs) with the self help groups. The issue of how to integrate them is still being debated.

Select Growth Engines

To achieve the 9-10 per cent growth targeted, the Vision 2020 document recommends focus on specific sectors that offer high growth opportunities. These will be the growth engines of the economy: dynamic and fast growing agricultural, services and manufacturing enterprises. They will be the primary growth engines of the economy because they will contribute a sizeable part of the state's GSDP (gross state domestic product) and employment.

A.P. Vision 2020 provides 19 primary growth engines:
(a) Six in agriculture: Rice, poultry, dairy, horticulture, agro-industry and fisheries
(b) Six in industry: construction, mining-based industries, labour intensive export oriented, pharmaceuticals, small scale industry and infrastructure industry
(c) Seven in services: basic information technology, services, knowledge based services, logistics, tourism, small scale services, health care and education in services

The vision2020 document tries to answer the following questions. How were the growth engines identified? How will they create economic growth? What does the State government need to do to facilitate the development of the growth engines.

Strategies for Poverty Removal

The government's strategy for poverty eradication recognises that long term investment in core sectors such as agriculture, health and education will accelerate the pace of poverty reduction in the state. The government would like to build on the successful lessons learnt from the self-help and group approach towards empowerment of the poor for poverty reduction. The rural poverty reduction strategies thus will be multi-pronged and multi-sectoral. They can be broadly classified under three categories: (a) intensive poverty reduction initiatives through a strategy of social mobilization, (b) aggressively promoting agricultural growth and (c) provision of basic minimum services.

Concentrating on Two approaches for Poverty Reduction

After experimenting with several poverty alleviation programmes, Government of A.P. has settled for two important programmes. One is self help group programme and the other is watershed based approach.
(i) Self help groups and social mobilization: The basic strategy for removal of rural poverty in A.P. would revolve around social mobilization and empowerment of the poor. The ongoing mobilization of the rural poor women into self-help groups is a major element of this strategy. The ongoing District Rural Poverty Initiative (DPIP) project in 6 backward districts and the proposed A.P. Rural Poverty Reduction project (APRPRP) are based on the strategy of social mobilization and the empowerment of the rural poor. Considering the inadequacies in the past developmental strategies, these two projects are mandated to focus on the poorest of the poor, who have been left out of various development initiatives.
(b)Micro Watershed Development with Equity: Another important component for improving livelihoods is micro watershed approach. The objectives of natural resource management, growth in rainfed agricultural productivity and growth in employment and incomes for the poor are

sought to be achieved in a participatory manner using the micro watershed as the basis for planning.

This initiative is proposed on following grounds:

(i) To protect the poor communities from adverse climatic conditions. Even though adverse climatic conditions affect everybody, the poor who have the lowest capacity to absorb the shock have to bear the brunt of it. Micro watershed works would contribute to ecology development as well as insulate communities against climatic shock such as droughts, erratic distribution of rainfall and excess rainfall. In the long term, this intervention itself will provide for greater crop assurance because of the reliability of the water supply on account of the improvement in surface water supply and the ground water-table level.

(ii) water scarcity is a serious constraint for the poor and has a major impact on the productivity of their meager resources.

(iii) Enhance employment opportunities: This will enhance opportunities for work, for the poor and particularly the poorest – directly, during the execution of the works and indirectly afterwards, as there will be optimum use of land and water and therefore the need for extra manpower. It would also expand the scope of employment and income by way of the engagement of people in allied agricultural activities such as dairy, fisheries, poultry and sericulture where feasible. An important concern in watershed development is the equitable distribution of the benefits of land and water resources development and the consequent biomass production.

Lastly, a few words about the political environment, donors and administration.

Political

Leadership is very important for appropriate policies. The present Chief Minister who came to power in 1996 has been supporting the economic reforms followed in the country. He has been focusing on the development of the state even during the election time. However, there have been two criticisms on the present leadership. The first one relates to the impact of his policies on the common man. The criticism is that he is emphasizing more on information technology, which would not help the common man. The second criticism is that he is encouraging parallel groups like self help groups without linking them with panchayats.

External Donors

External development agencies play a substantial role in AP in financial terms. The World Bank is the largest with annual disbursement of around Rs 1225 crores ($266.23 million) in 1999-2000 (inclusive of disbursements made under its own multi-state programs). Under DPIP and APRPRP programmes, World Bank is expected to give more than Rs.3,000 crores[15].

DFID is the next largest with current commitments of around Rs 1500 crores (230 million Pound Sterling) spread over three to four years. These numbers should be compared with the annual state revenue of Rs 16143 crores and total borrowings of Rs 29,771 crores by 1999-2000. In terms of strategies, they (particularly the World Bank) play important role in Andhra Pradesh. Since the Government of AP has been following reform oriented policies, the donors are also taking lot of interest in the policies.

Administration and NGOs

The bureaucracy in A.P. is considered to be better than many other states. Similarly, there are good NGOs in several parts of the state.

Suggestions for Higher Growth and Poverty Reduction

The strategies of the GOAP mentioned above are in the right direction. But, further improvements in the policies and implementation are needed if the state wants to achieve higher economic growth and reduce poverty.

Policies for Economic Growth

The growth engines given in Vision 2020 are too broad and there is a need to look at much disaggregate level. The constraints and possible solutions for higher growth can be given more easily at a disaggregate level. The policies have to be framed in keeping with changes in domestic and external environment. Competition is the buzzword. Within the country, there is increasing competition among states to attract private sector participation. The process of liberalization is also forcing external competition. State governments, which recognize these domestic and external developments and adopt suitable policies and initiate reform efforts will top as the key destination for fresh investments across sectors. On external front, removal of all quantitative restrictions and WTO regulations pose challenges and opportunities to the state.

At the aggregate level for agriculture, the following policies are required for higher growth: (a) Augmenting the investment in agriculture and rural infrastructure; (b) Improving the quality and reach of technology dissemination, particularly in rain-fed areas (c) Re-examine the legal framework for land-leasing to ensure adequate safeguard for both the tenants and the landowner, as this is likely promote greater investment in agriculture; (d)Provision of enabling environment to facilitate the farmers to benefit from the emerging opportunities thrown up by the liberalization and globalisation; (e)Aggressively pursue diversification in agriculture to optimise income and employment (f)Focus on non-farm employment opportunities, by promoting appropriate agro based processing industries; (g) Promotion of rapid rural growth in drought-prone and rainfed areas of the state poses special problems. In these areas, horticulture, forestry and livestock will play a larger role.

With states agreeing to have sales tax floor rates and doing away with fiscal incentives to new industries, the availability of physical infrastructure and human capital in a state will be a key determinant for industrial location. As a result of the phasing out of QRs on imports in 2001 and of the MFA by 2005, and further expected reduction in import tariff, the state must ready itself to face greater external competition and provide a conducive policy environment and infrastructure that will facilitate the competitiveness of local businesses. As part of its WTO commitments, India has phased-out all quantitative restrictions (QRs) on imports (except those imposed on strategic or environmental grounds) resulting in Indian firms facing increasing import competition, from countries where infrastructure and policy environment are better. Given the relatively weak manufacturing base vis-à-vis states like Tamil Nadu, Karnataka, Maharashtra and Gujarat, GoAP's two-pronged strategy for industrial development could involve (i) developing high-technology oriented sunrise industries such as information technology (IT), IT-enabled services, pharmaceuticals and biotechnology, etc - (ii) develop select traditional industries based on available resources, locational merits and employment generation potential, such as garments, leather, agro-processing, mining and cement. The credibility of any state commitment to additional infrastructure spending, to be marketed as an alternative to tax relief, has to be rapidly established. Under current arrangements, prospective investors enjoy the comfort of the legislated status of tax privileges and the knowledge that Andhra Pradesh is locked in tax competition with other states. However in the absence of sales tax based incentives, the focus of investors will now shift to the quality of physical infrastructure and human capital available in a particular location vis-à-vis other competing locations in India.

The share of service sector in GSDP has increased significantly over time. The growth of this sector has to be increased further in order to raise the overall growth of the economy. The quality of service sector has to be improved in order to attract investments. This sector has also good employment potential both in organized and unorganized sector.

Fiscal Policy

As mentioned above, the past performance shows some positive signs and concerns during 1995-96 to 2000-01. On positive side, capital expenditure as per cent of GSDP increased marginally over time. Own revenue mobilization as per cent of GSDP increased from 6.32 per cent in 1995-96 to 9.84 per cent in 2000-01. The concerns are: (a) increase in revenue and fiscal deficits; (b) increase in interest payments as per cent of GSDP; (c) increase in the share of unproductive or non-developmental expenditure (establishment costs and subsidies); (d) Significant increase in the ratio of total debt to GSDP from about 19 per cent in 1995-96 to 29 per cent in 2000-01 (see Fig A2 in Appendix).

The medium term fiscal framework (2001-07) indicates that the government tries to reduce fiscal deficit and debt stock to a sustainable level in the next few years. The core elements of fiscal reform strategy are fiscal stabilization, restructuring expenditure, revenue mobilization and power sector reforms. All these measures are in the right direction. It may be noted, however, the medium term fiscal reform strategy is based on projections regarding revenues, expenditures, deficit, debt etc. One has to have a strategy but it can go wrong any time. For example, the central government transfers are expected to be around 5 per cent of GSDP per annum during next five years. The way the central finances are deteriorating, we expect that this optimism may not materialize in future.

Most of the fiscal problems of state governments are due to power subsidies. If the government can take care of this single biggest problem, more than half of the fiscal problems would be solved. But it depends on many assumptions like increase in efficiency, cut in transmission and distribution losses etc. For improvements in overall finances of the economy, increase in tax to GSDP ratio is important. Reduction in subsidies is also needed. In Section 3, we have seen that the growth of capital formation has declined in all the sectors in 1990s. It is important to improve the investment to raise growth in the economy. Restructuring expenditure from non-developmental and low priority areas to priority areas like primary health and education, operation and maintenance and public investment in infrastructure should be given top priority.

Institutions

The institutional reforms in rural and urban areas are in the right direction. The success of these institutions depend on the degree of participation by the local population and the stake holders. Top down approach may be useful to scale up the successful programmes. However, scaling up of programmes may have the danger of concentrating on fulfilling some physical targets and ignoring social mobilization and peoples' participation. The examples are water users associations and watershed development programmes and other self help groups. Institutions are needed even in the case of health and education. For example, Government regulation of health sector needs to be carefully designed. It is evident from studies (see the chapter on health in this volume) that the role of private sector in health care has increased over time. With increasing investments in private sector, as happening in A.P., there is bound to be enhanced pressure on clients to spend more on sophisticated procedure and investigations, which may not be necessary always. When clients are ignorant, such provider induced demand for services would escalate the healthcare costs unless there is an independent regulatory institution.

Governance

In recent years it has been shown that governance is the key factor for raising economic growth and human development. In this respect, A.P. has introduced many governance reforms given above to improve the administration and delivery systems. These reforms, including e-governance, have yielded some results. But, general impression is that inspite of reforms, improvements at ground level are not visible. Change in the mind set of bureaucracy, involving good NGOs in local development programmes, convergence of line departments with Panchayats are some of the measures needed to improve the governance in the state.

7. CONCLUSION

This chapter examined trends in macro economic status of A.P. and discussed some policy issues for raising economic growth and human development. Two comparisons are made. First, A.P.'s performance was examined over time. Second, the performance of A.P. was compared with all India and other states. The analysis shows that the performance of A.P. improved in many indicators while it worsened in some other indicators particularly fiscal matters. Comparison with other states shows that the rank of A.P. has been somewhere in the middle (neither top nor bottom) in both growth and human development. The ranks for many indicators are in the range of 7 to 9 among 15 major states. The performance in general has been closer or marginally below to that of all India.

To be specific, the SDP growth in the 1980s in A.P. was marginally higher than in all India but in the 1990s it was 0.82 percentage point lower than all India. The distance in growth rates of GSDP between A.P. and all India (and fast growing states) has increased in the 1990s as compared to 1980s. The per capita GSDP was, however, lower by only 0.32 percentage point than in all India because of lower population growth in A.P. in the 1990s. The level of per capita income has always been lower than all India but the gap seems to have widened slightly in the 1990s. The trends in investments show that the growth rates declined in the 1990s particularly in agriculture. There were some marginal improvements in the relative ranking of infrastructure index in the later half of the 1990s. But, the infrastructure index has been closer to all India. Regarding inflation, the growth rates of implicit deflator in A.P. were closer to all India while the growth rates of CPIAL were marginally higher than all India in the last three decades. Fiscal indicators show that similar to other states, fiscal situation worsened in terms of revenue and fiscal deficits, interest payments and public debt. However, if we compare with other states, A.P.'s performance is not bad.

The official poverty ratios show very low levels of rural poverty and high levels of urban poverty for A.P. as compared to all India. Some alternative estimates, however, show that the poverty ratios in A.P. were closer to all India. The low level of official rural poverty ratios in A.P. were due to the low base year poverty line in 1973-74. This in turn was due to low level of CPIAL for A.P. The growth of mean consumption for the rural A.P. was the lowest among southern states in the 1990s (between 1993-94 and 19999-00). This is a matter of concern. The social sector expenditures as per cent of GSDP and total public expenditure were lower in the 1990s as compared to those of the 1980s. The human development Index across states shows that the relative position of A.P. has marginally declined in 2001 as compared to earlier decades. Although there have been improvements in health and education, the levels are still low compared to many other states particularly other South Indian states.

A.P. undertook many reforms in the last six years. They are: fiscal reforms, power reforms, governance reforms and institutional reforms. The paper provides details of these reforms and also strategies adopted by the government for poverty removal. Then the paper makes some suggestions for higher growth and poverty reduction.

The analysis in this study shows that initial conditions such as physical and human infrastructure in A.P. were not favourable to fully make use of the benefits of economic reforms in the 1990s. Better infrastructure and other favourable conditions are needed in order to catch up with some of the faster growing states in the country. The development challenges for the state, therefore, are to accelerate economic growth and improve human or social development. The reforms relating to fiscal policy, power sector, governance and institutions have to be continued further to achieve these goals of development. The borrowed funds should be used for productive purposes (to improve physical and social infrastructure) rather than for current expenditures. It may be noted, however, that economic growth alone can not reduce poverty as the experience of 1990s showed that growth can not guarantee creation of employment. The labour intensive pattern of growth coupled with direct initiatives by the government to generate employment are needed. Agricultural growth is important for reduction in poverty. In other words we have to aim to achieve growth with equity in order to spread the benefits of growth widely. Here the role of government and civil society are important to help the socially disadvantaged groups like Scheduled Castes and Scheduled Tribes and vulnerable groups such as old age population, widows, destitute, disabled and child labour. Regional disparities in economic growth and human development are high in A.P. Government has to invest more in relatively backward regions such as some parts of Telangana, North Coastal

Andhra and some parts of Rayalaseema. To conclude, drastic changes in efficiency, investment, governance, institutions, and measures towards equity are needed in order to come anywhere closer to the targets envisaged in Vision 2020 document.

[The authors thank C. Rangarajan, C.H. Hanumanta Rao, K.L. Krishna and K.Krishnamurty for comments and suggestions on an earlier draft]

Notes

1 See Rao et al, 1998. Some useful references on the historical factors and developments in A.P. in the earlier decades see Mukund (1990), Radhakrishna (1990), Parthasarathy (1995), Vithal (1998).

2 For 1980-91, the data are take from data base of *www.circonindia.com.*
For 1993-94 to 2000-01 the data are obtained from respective Directorates of Economics and Statistics.

3 All the growth rates of GSDP in the paper are based on time series data and estimated using semi-log function.

4 The growth rates of NSDP (net state domestic product) for four decades in A.P. shows that the growth rate was 1.52 per cent per annum in the 1960s and has barely kept pace with population growth. In the decade of 1970s (1970-71 to 1979-80) the growth rate of NSDP was 3.17 per cent per annum. On the other hand, the growth rate of NSDP for the 1980s and 1990s show more than 5 per cent per annum.

5 We have also estimated growth rates for GSDP in A.P. for the periods 1980-81 to 1989-90, 1990-91 to 99-00, 1990-91to 2000-01 and 1993-94 to 1999-00. These trend growth rates show that there are minor fluctuations depending on the years chosen for a period. For example, the growth rate of GSDP in A.P. for the period 1980-81 to 1989-90 was 5.2 per cent while it was 5.5 per cent for the period 1980-81 to 90-91. The estimates also show that sometimes 1990s record marginally higher growth than 1980s and *vice versa* depending on the years chosen. Therefore, one can say that growth rates have not shown any significant differences between 1980s and 1990s in A.P.

6 We examined whether 1990s growth rate is *statistically* different from 1980s in A.P.

7 The estimates for NSDP per capita for four decades show that growth rate was negative in the 1960s (-0.36%) and around 1 per cent per annum in the 1970s. The decade of 1990s showed the highest growth rate of per capita NSDP.

8 The estimates of gross fixed capital formation in the state are published by the Directorate of Economics and Statistics. There are several gaps in the coverage of these estimates. Therefore, the estimates can be taken only as indicative.

9 See Appendix 1 for ratio of sector-wise gross fixed capital formation to sectoral GSDP in A.P.

10 "There has been much debate about how exactly poverty should be defined. In popular understanding, poverty is identified with lowness of income, which prevents a family from obtaining and enjoying the basic necessities of life, including a minimum of food, clothing, shelter and water. This concept is defined as income poverty. For a comprehensive picture of poverty those other deprivations, such as in relation to health, education, sanitation and insurance against mishaps, must be taken into account" (Chellaiah and Sudarshan, 1999), p.xiii.

11 Essentially, the alternative procedure involves three major departures from the official estimates. First, an attempt is made to 'adjust' the 55th Round estimates to achieve comparability with the earlier rounds. Second, they use improved price indexes to

update the 'poverty line' over time, and to derive state-specific poverty lines from the all India poverty line. Third, a similar procedure is used to derive an explicit estimate of the appropriate gap between rural and urban poverty lines (in contrast with the often implausible rural-urban gaps that are implicit in the official estimates) (Deaton and Dreze, 2002).

12 See GOI (1993).

13 Rs.2 a kg. Rice scheme was introduced in 1983.

14 They include: Setting up a Centre for Good Governance: Transparent Public Policy; Right to Information: Fiscal management and social audit; Awareness building for qualitative policy framework; E-Governance & IT as instruments of Good Governance; Participatory Management; Citizen charter; Civil Service Reform; Publication of government information; Streamline transfer policy; Legal and Judicial Reform; Prevention of corruption; Human resources development.

15 DPIP and APRPRP refer to District Poverty Initiative Project and Andhra Pradesh Rural Poverty Reduction Programme respectively.

References

Chelliah, R.J. and R..Sudarshan (1998), *Income Poverty and Beyond: Human Development in India*, Social Science Press, New Delhi.

Deaton, A. A. Tarozzi (2000), "Prices and Poverty in India", Princeton, NJ, Research Program in Development Studies, processed

Deaton, A. (2001), "Computing prices and poverty rates in India, 1999-2000", Princeton, NJ, Research Program in Development Studies, First Draft

Deaton, A and Jean Dreze (2002), " Poverty and Inequality in India: A Re-examination", *Economic and Political Weekly*, Vo.37, No.36.

GOAP (1999), *Andhra Pradesh Vision 2020*, Document prepared by Government of Andhra Pradesh and Mckinsey & company, January 1999.

GOI (1993), *Report of the Expert Group on Estimation of Proportion and Number of Poor*, Perspective Planning Division, Government of India, New Delhi, July, 1993.

GOI (1995), *Report of 10th Finance Commission*, Government of India.

GOI (2000), *Report of the 11th Finance Commission*, Government of India.

Mukund, K. (ed., 1990), *Andhra Pradesh Economy in Transition*, Centre for Economic and Social Studies and Book Links, Hyderabad.

Parthasarathy, G. (1995), "Public Intervention and Rural Poverty: Case of Non Sustainable Reduction in Andhra Pradesh', *Economic and Political Weekly*, Vol.30, No.15

Radhakrishna, R., 1990, "Poverty in Andhra Pradesh, Underpinnings and Policy Intervention', in Mukund (1990), op.cit.

Rangarajan, C. (2002), "Inaugural Address at the Two-day Seminar on Andhra Pradesh Development Report", organized by Centre for Economic and Social Studies (CESS), Hyderabad, November 30, 2002.

Rao, Hanumantha V., N.K. Acharya and M.C. Swaminathan (eds.), (1998), *Andhra Pradesh at 50: A Data Based Analysis*, A Data News Features Publication, Hyderabad.

Vithal, B.P.R. (1998), 'An Overview', in Rao et al (1998), op.cit.

World Bank (1996), "Andhra Pradesh: Agenda for Economic Reforms, Report no. 15901-IN", World Bank, Washington, D.C.

Appendix 1. Sector-wise Gross Fixed Capital Formation

The sector-wise gross fixed capital to sectoral GSDP (Table A1) also shows that the ratios have not increased in the 1990s. Only in the case of manufacturing and secondary sectors, the ratios were slightly higher during 1989-90 to 1992-93. This trend reflected in the ratios for the overall economy.

Table A1. Ratio of Sector-wise Gross Fixed Capital Formation to Sectoral GSDP in A.P.

Year	Total (Public and Private)						Total Public Investment
	Agriculture	Manufac-turing	Primary	Secondary	Tertiary	Total	
1980-81	6.2	40.6	7.1	38.2	25.4	19.0	9.45
1981-82	5.0	34.7	5.8	33.3	17.6	14.6	5.98
1982-83	8.0	40.3	9.2	36.2	17.9	17.4	7.53
1983-84	6.2	46.1	7.6	38.2	19.9	17.5	7.49
1984-85	8.4	38.6	8.8	32.4	21.1	17.9	7.99
1985-86	9.4	34.0	10.3	29.6	18.3	17.3	7.63
1986-87	11.8	35.5	13.1	27.9	20.0	19.0	9.15
1987-88	9.5	34.4	11.2	27.9	17.8	17.2	8.07
1988-89	8.1	29.5	9.4	24.2	16.0	14.8	6.92
1989-90	7.0	44.0	9.4	46.2	20.3	21.2	10.48
1990-91	7.0	60.3	9.0	51.7	18.2	22.2	7.74
1991-92	7.2	44.2	8.5	49.8	16.9	20.5	8.81
1992-93	6.9	41.7	8.8	40.2	21.6	20.4	10.49
1993-94	6.1	36.9	7.1	33.5	20.6	17.9	9.20
1994-95	5.4	49.0	7.5	44.1	18.9	19.8	10.15
1995-96	4.6	49.2	5.4	45.2	18.3	19.0	9.16
1996-97	4.1	51.3	4.7	45.9	17.0	18.3	7.58
1997-98	5.9	29.3	6.3	35.4	17.2	17.4	7.76
1998-99	4.9	36.6	5.5	40.4	17.4	17.3	7.56
1999-00	6.6	32.0	6.8	37.2	16.8	17.4	Na

Appendix 2. Inflation at all India and states

The macro level inflation can be captured with implicit deflators (obtained from SDP data in current and constant prices). The inflation rate in A.P was around 6 per cent in the 1970s (Table A2). It increased to more than 7 per cent in the 1980s and 1990s. As compared to all India, the inflation rate for A.P. was much lower in the 1970s. On the other hand, it was closer to that of all India in the 1980s and 1990s.

Table A2. Implicit SDP Deflator for all India and States

State	Implicit SDP Deflator (% per annum)		
	70s	80s	90s
Andhra Pradesh	6.3	7.6	7.5
Assam	8.4	9.7	6.0
Bihar	7.1	8.0	6.1
Gujarat	7.4	7.0	5.9
Haryana	7.4	6.6	7.6
Karnataka	6.3	7.5	6.6
Kerala	8.8	8.8	11.9
Madhya Pradesh	8.0	8.7	6.5
Maharashtra	7.8	7.3	3.3
Orissa	6.5	6.7	8.4
Punjab	7.2	7.6	7.4
Rajasthan	7.2	7.0	7.2
Tamil Nadu	6.4	8.3	7.5
Uttar Pradesh	7.7	7.4	7.2
West Bengal	7.1	7.4	8.4
15 States	7.7	9.5	6.5
All India	8.0	7.4	7.5

Appendix 3. Why the poverty line in A.P has been lower than all India

The Expert group has adopted the following procedure for obtaining state specific poverty line in the base year.

Chatterjee and Bhattacharya (1974) constructed state-specific relative (Fisher's) indices for various quintile groups of rural population for 1963-64. For this purpose, Expert Group considered state-specific relative indices relating to purchasers of consumers who were around the poverty line (Col.2 in Table 18). They were assumed to be same in 1960-61 and were carried forward to 1973-74 by using state-specific price indices for the middle group of population, with 1960-61=100. Table 18 provides the state specific price indices (relative to all India) for middle rural population as worked out by Chatterjee and Bhattacharya along with the adjusted indices for 1973-74, and the specific poverty lines.

The Fisher index for 1960-61 in col.2 of Table A3 shows that there was not much difference between A.P. and all India. However, the CPIMR in 1973-74 (col.3) shows that the price index for A.P. was 244.54 while for all India it was 289.90. The CPIMR was used to get the Fisher index in 1973-74 (col.4) for states in relation to all India. It shows that the level of

Table A3. Inter-state Price Differentials and Poverty Lines in Rural Areas

State	Fisher's Index 1960-61	CPIMR 1973-74 (1960-61=100)	Fisher's Index 1973-74	Rural Poverty Lines 1973-74	1977-78	1983	1987-88	1993	1999-00
1	2	3	4	5	6	7	8	9	10
AP	100.90	244.54	85.11	41.71	50.88	72.66	91.94	163.09	262.74
Assam	110.80	266.01	101.67	49.82	60.29	98.32	127.44	232.16	365.43
Bihar	102.00	334.55	117.71	57.68	58.93	97.48	120.36	212.26	333.07
Gujarat	112.10	248.56	96.11	47.10	54.70	83.29	115.00	202.06	318.94
Haryana	104.70	282.23	101.93	49.95	59.37	88.57	122.90	233.77	362.81
HP	104.70	282.23	101.93	49.95	59.37	88.57	122.90	233.77	367.45
Karnataka	98.60	283.46	96.41	47.24	51.95	83.31	104.46	186.60	309.59
Kerala	106.60	286.85	105.48	51.68	58.88	99.35	130.61	243.93	374.79
MP	93.80	316.62	102.45	50.20	56.26	83.59	107.00	193.27	311.34
Maharashtra	105.50	283.01	102.99	50.47	58.07	88.24	115.61	194.81	318.63
Orissa	97.90	283.27	95.66	46.87	58.89	106.28	121.42	194.04	323.92
Punjab	104.70	282.23	101.93	49.95	59.37	88.57	122.90	233.77	362.68
Rajasthan	103.30	291.86	104.00	50.96	57.54	80.24	117.52	216.07	344.03
Tamil Nadu	108.20	246.57	92.03	45.09	56.62	96.15	118.23	196.59	307.64
UP	94.60	305.93	99.83	48.92	54.21	83.85	114.57	212.80	336.88
WB	116.0	277.92	111.21	54.49	63.34	105.55	129.21	220.68	350.17
All India	100.0	289.90	100.00	49.00	55.29	87.77	112.67	205.96	327.56

Note: 1. State specific price indices (relative to all India) for middle population given in Column (2) are the fisher's indices constructed by Chatterjee & Bhattacharya.

2. Column (4) is obtained on multiplying column (2) with column (3) and dividing with 289.90.

3. Column (5) is obtained on multiplying column (4) with 49.00 (All India Poverty line for rural areas at 1973-74 prices.

4. Columns 6 to 10 are obtained by updating the poverty line of 1973-74 with CPIMR index in respective years.

Source: GOI (1993) for Columns 2 to 8; Planning Commission for columns 9 and 10.

Fisher Index in A.P. was only 85 per cent of all India in 1973-74. The Fisher Index for A.P. (in relation to all India) was the lowest across states in 1973-74. It may be noted CPIAL was used to get CPIMR, which in turn was used to get Fisher Index in 1973-74. It looks like something is wrong with the construction of CPIAL in A.P. It needs further research. As a result of the lower Fisher Index in A.P. the poverty line was only Rs. 41.71 as compared to Rs. 49.00 for All India in 1973-74 (col.5).

Let us examine whether rate of growth in prices are responsible for the lower poverty line in A.P. Table A4 shows that the price deflator increased from 100 in 1973-74 to 630 in 1999-00. The corresponding figures for all India were 100 and 660 respectively. The growth rates over the long period also show that they were no significant difference between A.P. and all India. However, there are fluctuations over short periods.

Table A4. State-Specific Price Deflators Used for Updating the Poverty Lines

Sl No.	State	Poverty Line (1973-74)	Price Deflator						Annualized Growth Rate
			1973-74	1977-78	1983	1987-88	1993-94	1999-00	
1	Andhra Pradesh	41.71	100	122	174	220	391	630	7.03
2	Assam	49.82	100	121	197	256	466	734	7.78
3	Bihar	57.68	100	102	169	209	368	577	7.02
4	Gujarat	47.10	100	116	177	244	429	677	7.48
5	Haryana	49.95	100	119	177	246	468	726	7.77
6	Himachal Pradesh	49.95	100	119	177	246	468	736	7.80
7	Karnataka	47.24	100	110	176	221	395	655	7.35
8	Kerala	51.68	100	114	192	253	472	725	7.88
9	Madhya Pradesh	50.20	100	112	167	214	385	620	7.11
10	Maharashtra	50.47	100	115	175	229	386	631	7.14
11	Orissa	46.87	100	126	227	259	414	691	7.40
12	Punjab	49.95	100	119	177	246	468	726	7.76
13	Rajasthan	50.96	100	113	157	231	424	675	7.47
14	Tamil Nadu	45.09	100	126	213	262	436	682	7.43
15	Uttar Pradesh	48.92	100	111	171	234	435	689	7.63
16	West Bengal	54.49	100	116	194	237	405	643	7.27
	All India	49.00	100	115	180	233	415	660	7.38

Fig A1.

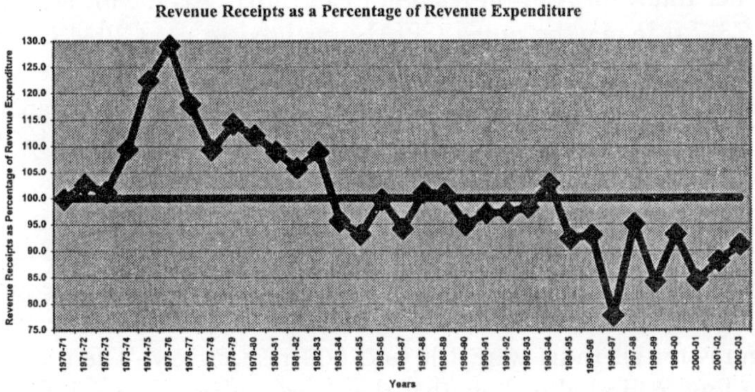

Fig A2.

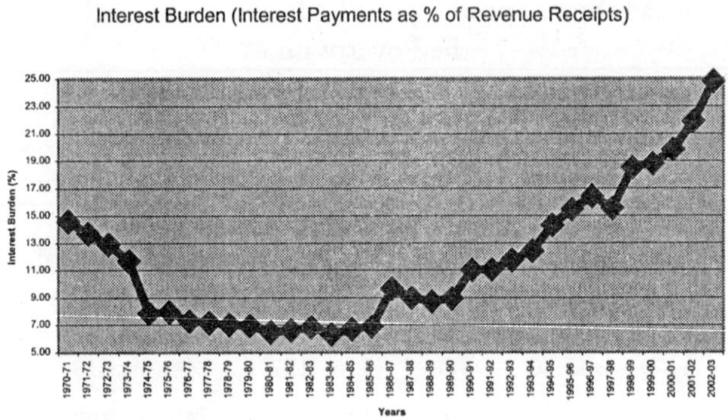

Fig A3.

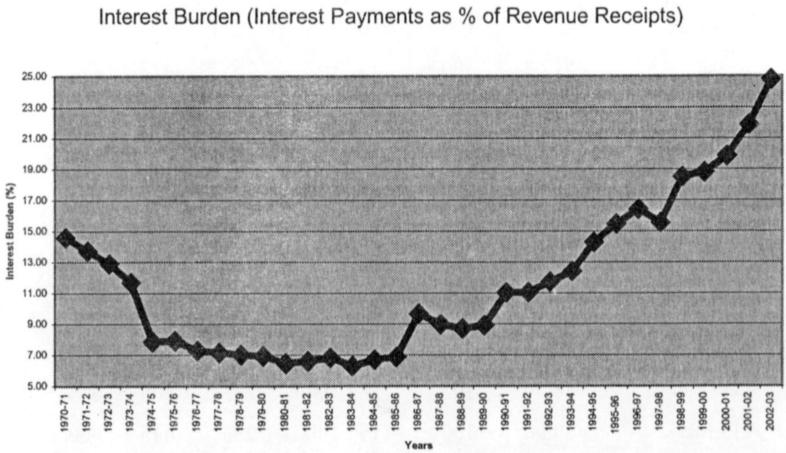

3

Fiscal Management: A Review

J.V.M. Sarma

1. ANDHRA PRADESH STATE FINANCES: BROADER ISSUES

Andhra Pradesh is one of the pioneering States to earnestly initiate economic and fiscal reform at the States' level in the country. When the reform program was started sometime around 1995-96, the State's budgetary position was under severe stress like in many States in India. The development of the State was below potential and not commensurate with its natural resource endowments. The growth rate was lower than the country's average of 5.2 percent per annum. The reduction of poverty was slower than in other States. The development of human resources also lagged behind the national average, particularly the female literacy. The provision of infrastructure was grossly inadequate. The expenditure allocation for roads, for example, was just 50 percent of that in other States, operation and maintenance (O&M) allocation was 60 percent less, and irrigation network was poorly maintained. If the provision of essential public services was substantially below the State's needs, the mobilization of resources also did not keep pace with the expenditure requirements. Consequently, the fiscal deficit steadily deteriorated and led to higher debt-financing resulting in interest payments eating up over 15 percent of the government revenue.

Beginning from 1996-97, several steps were initiated as part of the over all economic reforms in the State. The rice subsidy scheme that put tremendous burden on the State's fiscal position was moderated. Power tariff rates were substantially revised *albeit* moderated later. The power sector was revamped and private initiatives were encouraged. The policy of prohibition of alcoholic liquor was reviewed in an attempt to safeguard the excise revenue.

Nevertheless, these measures, although constituted a good beginning, appear to be inadequate. During the last few years the State has witnessed not only slowing down of the pace of fiscal reforms but also a proliferation of counter-reform measures, thus bringing back the fiscal stress. The fiscal deficit that appeared to be under reasonable control till 1998-99 suddenly began to deteriorate and is threatening to touch 5.4 percent of the Gross State Domestic Product (GSDP) by the end of the fiscal year 2001-02. Also, there has been a steady rise in the revenue and primary deficits. Consequently, the stock of outstanding debt is expected to touch the level of 30 percent of GSDP, which might soon prove unsustainable given the meager growth of GSDP.

All this suggests that it is time to make an informed assessment of the progress of the fiscal reform in the State with a view to identify appropriate measures and formulate strategies for further fiscal correction. This study is an attempt in this direction. In section II we give a brief assessment of the fiscal situation in Andhra Pradesh prior to the 1996 reforms and look into the factors leading to the reform movement in the State. In section III, we examine some of the remedial measures suggested in the recent past. In section IV we look into some of the important steps taken by the government as part of the reform process and review the progress. Finally, in section V an attempt is made to indicate what remains to be pursued and identify strategies for further fiscal correction.

2. FISCAL SITUATION IN ANDHRA PRADESH PRIOR TO 1996 REFORMS

Growth of Government Expenditure[1]

Before assessing the progress of the fiscal reform process, it is useful to understand the circumstances that called for the reform options. As in several States, the pre-1996 fiscal situation in Andhra Pradesh was basically characterized by growth of unproductive government expenditure without commensurate revenue augmentation, leading to high fiscal and revenue imbalances[2].

Although total expenditure grew at an average 15.7 percent per annum during the decade 1985-86 to 1995-96 (from Rs 3,271 crore to Rs 14,150 crore), the growth did not match the GSDP growth at over 18.6 percent and the resultant developmental needs[3]. This is evident from the falling trend in the expenditure-GSDP[4] ratio notwithstanding the sporadic humps in 1986-87 and 1992-93 (Figure 1). The trend (from 21.3 percent in 1985-86 to 17.7 percent in 1995-96) in the expenditure-GSDP ratio is somewhat indicative of the inadequate provision of public goods and services commensurate with the growing needs. Clearly, there was a need for reprioritization towards specific areas, particularly, the social sectors and infrastructure – both in terms of creation of assets and maintenance. A look at the functional and economic classifications brings this out.

Functional Classification

Between 1985-86 and 1995-96, the expenditure on general services mainly comprising debt servicing, grew at a faster rate of 18.5 percent per annum while that of social services and economic services were just 13.4 percent and 12.6 percent per annum respectively. This pattern is also evident from the notable decline in the expenditure-GSDP ratios of functional components relating to social and economic services (Table 1

Table 1. Andhra Pradesh: Trends in the government expenditure during 1985-86 to 2002-03 (Percent to GSDP)

	1985-86	1990-91	1995-96	1996-97	1997-98	1998-99	1999-00	2000-01	2001-02r	2002-03b
Current expenditure	17.2	15.5	13.3	16.0	15.2	15.0	16.6	17.5	17.8	18.6
General Services	4.2	4.3	4.5	4.6	4.9	5.0	5.9	6.5	6.7	7.5
Interest payments	1.2	1.7	1.9	2.0	2.2	2.3	2.7	3.0	3.4	4.2
Others	3.0	2.6	2.6	2.5	2.7	2.6	3.2	3.6	3.3	3.3
Social and Community Services	7.1	6.0	5.9	5.8	5.7	6.2	6.4	6.1	6.1	6.2
Education	3.3	2.8	2.1	2.2	2.3	2.5	2.8	2.9	2.8	3.0
Medical and public health	1.1	0.9	0.8	0.9	0.9	0.9	1.0	1.0	1.0	1.0
Water Supply, Sanitation, Housing and Urban Development	0.8	0.5	0.3	0.5	0.6	0.7	0.3	0.3	0.5	0.5
Information and Publicity	0.0	0.0	0.0	0.0	0.0	0.0	0.1	0.0	0.0	0.0
Welfare of SC, ST and OBCs	1.3	1.0	0.7	0.6	0.7	0.7	0.6	0.7	0.8	0.8
Labour and Labour Welfare	0.1	0.1	0.1	0.1	0.1	0.0	0.0	0.1	0.1	0.1
Social Welfare and Nutrition	0.4	0.2	0.2	1.4	1.1	1.1	1.2	1.2	0.8	0.8
Other	0.2	0.4	1.7	0.1	0.1	0.1	0.3	0.0	0.0	0.0
Economic Services	5.6	5.2	2.9	5.5	4.4	3.6	4.1	4.8	4.9	4.7
Agriculture and Allied Activities	1.1	0.8	0.6	0.6	0.6	0.6	0.5	0.6	0.6	0.6
Rural Development	1.5	1.3	0.7	0.8	1.0	1.3	0.9	0.6	0.7	0.7
Irrigation and Flood Control	1.3	1.2	1.1	1.0	1.1	1.1	1.3	1.1	1.2	1.3
Energy	0.2	0.2	0.0	2.5	1.0	0.1	0.1	1.8	1.6	1.2
Industry and Minerals	0.3	0.2	0.2	0.2	0.2	0.1	0.1	0.1	0.1	0.1
Transport	0.4	0.3	0.2	0.3	0.3	0.3	0.5	0.3	0.4	0.4
Science, Technology and Environment	0.0	0.0	0.0	0.0	0.0	0.0	0.0	0.0	0.0	0.0
General Economic Services	0.9	1.1	0.1	0.1	0.1	0.1	0.1	0.3	0.2	0.2
Grants in aid to Local bodies	0.3	0.1	0.1	0.1	0.1	0.1	0.2	0.1	0.2	0.2

	1985-86	1989-90	1990-91	1995-96	1996-97	1997-98	1998-99	1999-00	2000-01	2001-02r	2002-03b
Capital disbursements	3.9	3.5	3.1	4.6	2.1	3.3	4.4	3.4	3.5	3.0	3.4
Capital expenditure	2.3	1.5	1.3	3.0	0.1	1.1	1.2	2.0	1.8	2.1	2.4
General Services	0.1	0.0	0.0	0.0	0.0	0.0	0.0	0.0	0.0	0.1	0.2
Social Services	0.3	0.1	0.1	0.1	0.1	0.1	0.1	0.4	0.2	0.4	0.3
Economic Services	2.0	1.3	1.2	1.1	1.0	1.0	1.1	1.5	1.5	1.6	1.8
Loans and advances	0.7	1.2	1.1	1.1	1.0	1.7	1.8	0.8	1.1	0.9	1.0

Source: RBI Bulletin, various issues.

and Figure 1). The ratio went down from 3.5 to 2.2 percent in the case of education; from 1.2 to 0.7 percent in the case of medical welfare; from 0.8 to 0.6 percent in the case of water supply, sanitation etc, and from 1.4 to

0.6 percent in the case of welfare of weaker sections. The descent was even steeper in the case of economic services, which came down from about 6 percent of GSDP in 1985-86 to as low as 3.1 percent by 2001-02, mainly due to low allocations for agriculture, rural development, irrigation, industry and transport. The decline was more noticeable in the case of agriculture and allied activities, rural development, and industry and minerals.

In contrast, there has been a marked growth in the expenditure on general services, particularly, the interest and debt-servicing component (22 percent per annum). The sectoral (functional) distribution of government spending also shows that, over the years, The ratio of interest and debt-servicing to GSDP has gone up from 1.2 percent in 1985-86 to over 2.0 percent by 1996-97.

Economic Composition[5]

A major cause for the imbalance was the relative neglect of capital expenditure, basically infrastructure, thereby affecting the developmental impact of the government expenditure. While current expenditure grew at over 14.5 percent per annum in the pre-1996 period, the average growth rate of capital component was just 12.6 percent. It was only after the 1991 reforms at the national level, did capital expenditure receive some importance in the State as is evident from the slight rise in its ratio to GSDP during the first half of the 90s. However, since 1995-96 again, current expenditure has been rising while capital expenditure ratio at best remaining the same (Figure 1)

The fast growing consumption items were establishment expenditure (at 15.7 percent per annum, owing mostly to pay revisions), and interest payments (at over 19 percent per annum). These trends are more clearly brought out in Table 2 in terms of the changing pattern of government spending. The share of current expenditure in total has gone up from about 70 percent in 1985-86 to 82 percent in 1996-97. The share of establishment expenditure went up from 22 percent to about 30 percent and that of interest payments went up from 11 percent to 22 percent. In contrast, the share of goods and services expenditure, which includes the operation, and maintenance of assets (O&M) declined from 9.2 percent to 8.6 percent.

One of the fast-growing components of government expenditure has been the salaries and wages. Till 1995-96, employment in the government grew by about 3.7 percent a year. As a result, the salary and pension bill accounted for nearly 50 percent of the current expenditure and over 80 percent of the state's own revenue every year prior to 1995-96.

Interest payments and debt servicing accounted for about 22 percent of the current expenditure. The rising stock of debt over the years carried

Table 2. Andhra Pradesh: Trends in the structure of economic components of government expenditure 1985-86 to 2001-02.

(Percent of total expenditure)

	1985-86	1990-91	1995-96	1996-97	1997-98	1998-99	1999-00	2000-01R	2001-02B
Current Expenditure	69.7	74.1	81.9	82.1	81.7	80.3	80.3	79.3	76.5
Consumption Expenditure (net)	30.8	31.6	38.0	38.5	38.2	37.1	36.7	35.8	34.3
Establishment	22.0	24.0	29.6	29.9	29.4	28.0	26.8	25.1	22.6
Goods & Services	9.2	7.9	8.4	8.6	8.8	9.1	9.9	10.8	11.9
Interest on general debt	11.0	13.8	20.3	21.8	22.8	23.2	23.8	23.8	23.0
Subsidies	5.2	7.0	3.3	1.9	1.2	0.8	0.6	0.5	0.4
Transfers	22.7	21.6	20.3	19.9	19.6	19.2	19.3	19.2	18.7
Gross capital formation	16.7	10.3	11.2	11.9	12.8	14.5	14.3	14.5	15.3
Capital transfers	11.1	9.2	4.0	3.1	2.5	2.1	1.8	1.6	1.3
Loans & Advances	2.5	6.4	2.9	2.9	3.0	3.1	3.6	4.7	6.9

Source: *Economic & Functional Classification of the Budgetary data* by the Bureau of Economics and Statistics, various issues.

Figure 1. Andhra Pradesh: Major trends in government expenditure during 1985-86 to 2001-02

(Percent to GSDP)

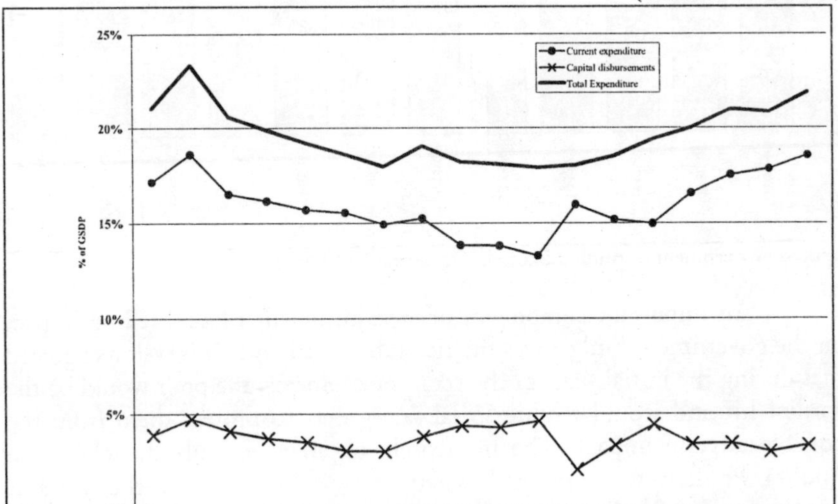

	1985-86	1986-87	1987-88	1988-89	1989-90	1990-91	1991-92	1992-93	1993-94	1994-95	1995-96	1996-97	1997-98	1998-99	1999-00	2000-01	2001-02r	2002-03b
Current expenditure	17.2%	18.6%	16.5%	16.2%	15.7%	15.5%	14.9%	15.2%	13.9%	13.8%	13.3%	16.0%	15.2%	15.0%	16.6%	17.5%	17.8%	18.6%
Capital disbursements	3.9%	4.7%	4.1%	3.7%	3.5%	3.1%	3.0%	3.8%	4.4%	4.3%	4.6%	2.1%	3.3%	4.4%	3.4%	3.5%	3.0%	3.4%
Total Expenditure	21.1%	23.4%	20.6%	19.9%	19.2%	18.6%	18.0%	19.1%	18.2%	18.1%	17.9%	18.0%	18.5%	19.4%	20.0%	21.0%	20.9%	21.9%

Sources: same as Table 1.

with it the high cost of borrowing firstly due to changing pattern of borrowing. As will be seen later, the dependence on interest bearing Central and market borrowings went up as the availability of cheaper sources such as the public account funds (government employees' provident fund, gratuity etc) declined. Secondly, the new borrowings contracted – either for rolling over the older debt or for financing additional fiscal deficit – became costlier with the rising interest rates. The average effective interest rate nearly doubled during 1985-86 to 1995-96. All this resulted in higher interest and debt servicing expenditure.

Figure 2. Andhra Pradesh: Expenditure on Wages and Salaries 1985-86 to 2001-2002

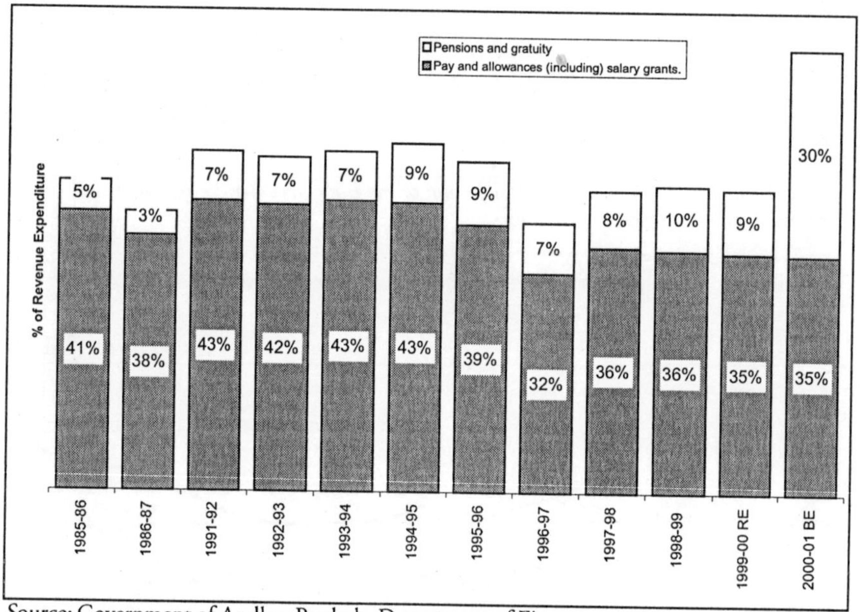

Source: Government of Andhra Pradesh, Department of Finance.

An important component of expenditure that had a telling impact on the government budget was the rice subsidy scheme. It is well recognized that during the initial years of the economic reforms, the poor would be the hardest hit and would require social safety nets to protect them from the possible adverse impact. The immensely popular rice subsidy scheme in Andhra Pradesh was one such safety net. However, over the years it aggravated the fiscal deterioration. The expenditure on the scheme was larger than the combined allocations for health and family welfare. The burden steadily went up from 3.6 percent of the current expenditure in 1992-93 reaching a peak of 11.3 percent in 1995-96 (Figure 4). Despite this large fiscal burden, only a small proportion of the rice subsidy reached the truly vulnerable segments of the population.

In contrast, the share of expenditure on public investment in total non-interest expenditure declined over the past 10 years from 27 percent to 22 percent. This has created a large infrastructure gap in the state and has become a serious obstacle for economic and social development. Also, the low and declining share of expenditure on O&M in total public expenditure has substantially reduced the efficiency of the public assets in physical and social infrastructure. Inadequate O&M spending has

Figure 3. Andhra Pradesh: Growth of stock of debt and average effective interest rate: 1985-86 to 2001-02

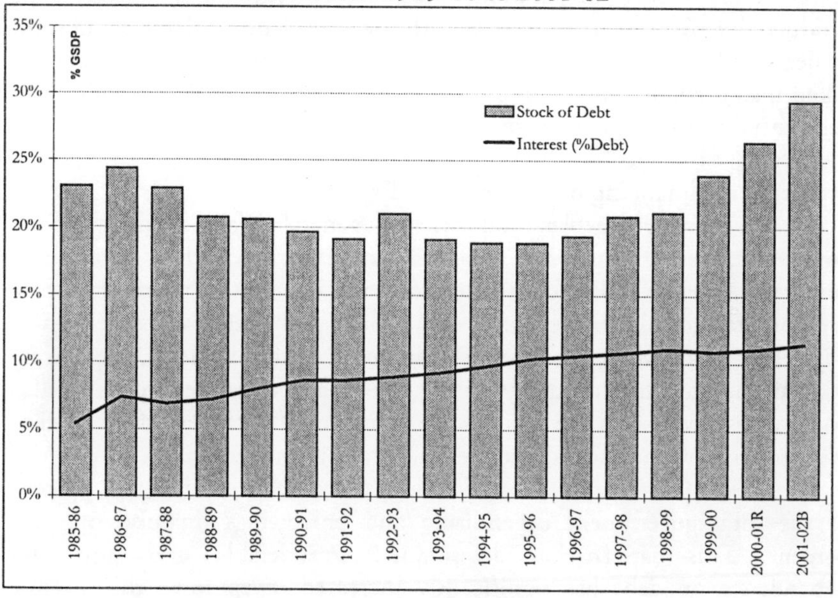

Figure 4. Andhra Pradesh: Expenditure on Rice Subsidy, 1985-86 to 2000-01

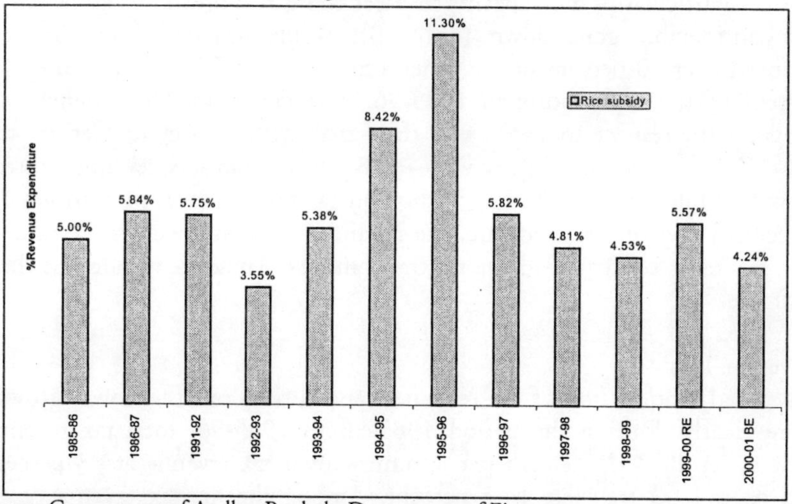

Source: Government of Andhra Pradesh, Department of Finance.

been a common problem in all sectors but particularly acute in irrigation and roads. Actual O&M allocations are far short of the norms. Moreover, a large proportion of these funds is spent on salaries.

The above trends clearly bring out the misplaced priorities marking the expenditure allocations during the pre-96 reform period. Also, the management of government expenditure left a lot to be desired. The incremental budget preparations with short-term focus affected the productivity. Besides, resources were thinly spread over a large number of projects and the recurrent cost implications of starting new schemes are not taken into account thus leading to large time and cost overrun resulting in substantial expenditure inefficiency.

Structure of Financing of Government Expenditure

A plausible explanation for the generally falling trend in the government expenditure till 1996-97 could be in terms of resource constraint. The revenue raising effort concentrated only on tax revenue, and the potential for higher non-tax revenues through better-cost recoveries was neglected. Also, while tax revenues reached a saturation level, there were institutional constraints in improving the non-tax user recoveries as also borrowings. Even with the reforms the major revenue raising efforts such as introduction of value added tax, are yet to take a concrete shape.

Till 1985-86 non-debt revenue sources financed about 87 percent of the total government expenditure and borrowings financed only 13 percent. This pattern has deteriorated considerably over time and dependence on debt has significantly increased. Even now, the revenue sources finance only a little over 73 percent of the total expenditure, while borrowings finance as much as 27 percent (Figure 5).

Particularly, the capacity to meet the expenditure by tax revenues has considerably gone down (Table 3). While revenues from taxation financed over 60 percent of the expenditure in 1985-86, they met only 50 percent of the expenditure in 1995-96. The fall in the dependence was steeper with respect to own taxes than that with respect to Central tax share. The pattern was similar with respect to the non-tax revenue sources as well. While the contribution of the non-tax revenues was just around 20 percent of the total expenditure, the reliance has been lower in the case of own nontaxes compared to the central transfers. These trends are less than desirable.

Revenue Trends

A detailed examination of the revenue trends brings out the slower growth more clearly. During the period 1985-86 to 1995-96, total tax revenue grew at hardly 13.5 percent per annum – own tax revenue at 13 percent and central tax transfers 14.3 percent. Among the nontax revenue, own nontax revenue grew at 15 percent and grants in aid from Centre, at 16.5

Figure 5. Andhra Pradesh: Broad trends in financing government expenditure through revenues and borrowings 1985-86 to 2001-02

(Percent to total expenditure)

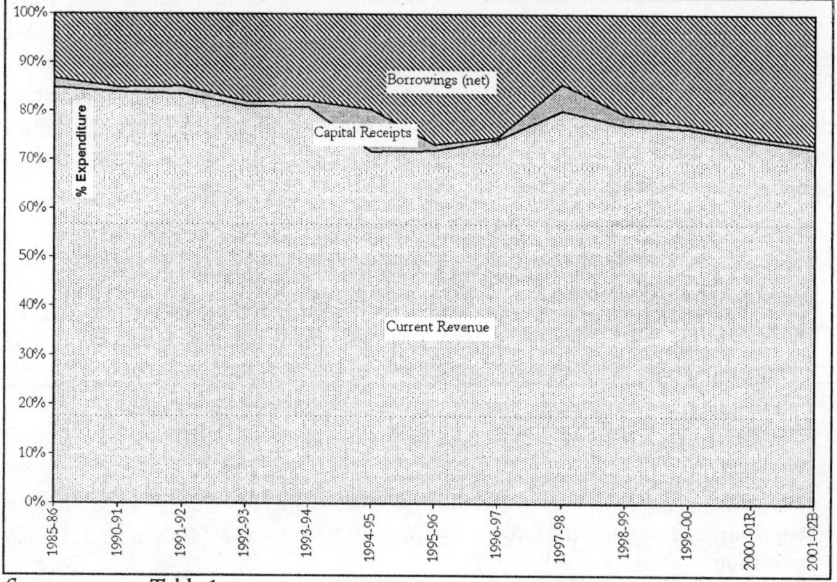

Source: same as Table 1.

Table 3. Andhra Pradesh: Pattern of financing government expenditure during 1980-99

(Percent total expenditure)

	1985 -86	1989 -90	1990 -91	1995 -96	1996 -97	1997 -98	1998 -99	1999 -00	2000 -01	2001 -02R	2002 -03B
Current Revenue	81.2	77.6	81.1	69.1	68.8	78.0	64.9	69.0	70.8	73.0	73.6
Tax receipts	59.2	57.0	57.6	46.7	48.1	59.3	50.0	50.7	52.8	53.4	54.3
States's own taxes	42.1	41.3	40.2	28.8	30.0	40.1	36.3	37.0	38.4	39.7	40.5
Share in Central taxes	17.0	15.6	17.4	17.9	18.1	19.2	13.7	13.7	14.5	13.8	13.8
Non-tax receipts	22.1	20.6	23.6	22.3	20.7	18.7	15.0	18.3	18.0	19.6	19.3
Own NTR	11.4	12.4	11.8	11.2	10.0	10.1	8.4	10.0	10.0	10.1	10.6
Grants from Centre	10.6	8.2	11.8	11.1	10.7	8.6	6.6	8.3	8.0	9.5	8.7
Capital Receipts	1.8	1.1	0.9	11.2	8.6	5.4	1.8	0.4	0.4	2.0	2.4
Borrowings (net)	16.9	21.3	18.0	19.7	22.5	16.6	33.3	30.5	28.8	25.0	24.0
Centre	9.5	10.8	10.3	10.4	13.2	9.2	11.1	15.0	6.3	11.3	12.1
Domestic Loans	4.3	6.5	4.3	6.0	9.1	4.8	10.2	12.0	17.4	11.4	9.7
Public Accounts	3.0	4.0	3.4	3.4	0.2	2.6	11.9	3.6	5.1	2.3	2.2

Source: same as Table 1.

percent. Nevertheless, all these growth rates were much below the 18 percent growth rate of GSDP thereby indicating their low-income buoyancies. Consequently, there was a noticeable decline in the ratios of the revenue components to the GSDP (Table 4). The total revenue to GSDP ratio had come down by 5.2 percent points – own tax revenues by 3.1 percent points. Among the own taxes, sales tax, the main source declined by 0.5 percent points of the GSDP, while the other major own tax, State excise fell by as much as 2.6 percent. Clearly, the rise in the current (revenue) deficit was more due to the steeper decline in the revenues as compared to the fall in the current expenditure.

Table 4. Andhra Pradesh: Pattern of Tax Revenue Components during 1985-86 2001-02

(Percent to GSDP)

	1985 -86	1989 -90	1990 -91	1995 -96	1996 -97	1997 -98	1998 -99	1999 -00	2000 -01	2001 -02r	2002 -03b
Current Revenue	17.1	14.9	15.1	12.4	12.4	14.5	12.6	13.8	14.9	15.2	16.1
Tax receipts	12.5	10.9	10.7	8.4	8.7	11.0	9.7	10.1	11.1	11.1	11.9
States's own taxes	8.9	7.9	7.5	5.2	5.4	7.4	7.0	7.4	8.1	8.3	8.9
Sales tax	4.7	4.1	4.0	3.7	3.9	4.9	4.6	5.1	5.6	5.6	5.8
Stamp duty and registration	0.4	0.4	0.4	0.4	0.5	0.5	0.4	0.5	0.5	0.5	0.5
Motor Vehicles tax	0.7	0.6	0.5	0.6	0.6	0.7	0.6	0.6	0.6	0.7	0.7
Electricity duty	0.0	0.1	0.1	0.1	0.0	0.1	0.1	0.1	0.1	0.1	0.3
Land revenue	0.1	0.1	0.1	0.1	0.1	0.1	0.1	0.1	0.1	0.1	0.1
State excise duty	2.6	2.2	2.1	0.1	0.1	0.9	0.8	0.9	0.9	1.2	1.2
Other taxes	0.3	0.3	0.3	0.2	0.3	0.3	0.3	0.2	0.2	0.2	0.2
Share in Central taxes	3.6	3.0	3.2	3.2	3.3	3.6	2.7	2.7	3.0	2.9	3.0
Income tax	0.9	1.0	1.0	1.2	1.3	1.9	1.1	1.2	3.0	2.9	3.0
Union excise duties	2.7	2.0	2.3	2.0	2.0	1.7	1.6	1.6	0.0	0.0	0.0

The revenue growth relative to the GSDP also shows similar trends. The buoyancy coefficient of total tax revenue at 0.77 was much below unity, and that of own tax revenue was even lower at 0.75. As for the individual taxes, the major tax sources, have been the sales tax (51.1 percent of own tax revenue), the State excise duties (24.8 percent), the motor vehicles taxes (8.2 percent) the stamp duties and registration fees (6.2 percent and the entertainment tax (2.9 percent). These five sources together account for 93.2 percent of the aggregate tax revenues. Other indirect taxes contribute about 2.9 percent. Direct taxes on income and property, namely, land revenue, agricultural income and urban land tax together account for the rest. Incidentally, the dependence on taxes on commodities and services is higher in Andhra Pradesh (93.2 percent) as compared to other major States.

Table 5. Andhra Pradesh: Pattern of Non-tax Revenue Components during 1985-86 to 2001-02

(Percent to GSDP)

	1985-86	1989-90	1990-91	1995-96	1996-97	1997-98	1998-99	1999-00	2000-01	2001-02r	2002-03b
Non-tax receipts (NTR)	4.6	4.0	4.4	4.0	3.7	3.5	2.9	3.7	3.8	4.1	4.2
Own NTR	2.4	2.4	2.2	2.0	1.8	1.9	1.6	2.0	2.1	2.1	2.3
Interest receipts	1.1	1.3	1.3	0.9	0.9	0.9	1.0	1.2	1.1	1.1	1.2
Dividends	0.0	0.0	0.0	0.0	0.0	0.0	0.0	0.0	0.0	0.0	0.0
General Services	0.2	0.1	0.1	0.1	0.1	0.1	0.1	0.1	0.1	0.1	0.3
Social and Community Serves	0.2	0.1	0.1	0.1	0.1	0.1	0.1	0.2	0.1	0.1	0.1
Economic Services	0.9	0.8	0.7	0.9	0.7	0.7	0.5	0.5	0.7	0.8	0.8
Grants from Centre	2.2	1.6	2.2	2.0	1.9	1.6	1.3	1.7	1.7	2.0	1.9

Table 6. Andhra Pradesh: Buoyancy Coefficients of the Tax Receipts with Respect to GSDP.

	Buoyancy coefficients with respect to GSDP	
	1985-86 to 1995-96	1985-86 to 2001-02
Current Revenue	0.80	0.87
Tax receipts	0.77	0.88
State's own taxes	0.75	0.87
Sales tax	0.91	1.02
Stamp duty and registration	1.02	1.05
Motor Vehicles tax	0.77	0.92
Electricity duty	1.03	0.62
Land revenue	0.92	0.88
State excise duty	-0.13	0.18
Other taxes	0.60	0.78
Share in Central taxes	0.82	0.89
Income tax	1.00	1.04
Union excise duties	0.68	0.89
Non-tax receipts	0.87	0.84
Own non-tax receipts	0.84	0.81
Grants from Centre	0.91	0.87

The single most important tax that was responsible for the revenue sluggishness was the excise loss on account of partial and full prohibition and the sloth characterizing the minor taxes. The buoyancy estimates show by and large similar trends. Stamps and registration fees has been the most buoyant (1.02) followed by sales tax (0.91), while the other taxes (excluding electricity duty) buoyancy was much below.

Own nontax revenues constituted 16.5 percent of the State's total revenues. Out of this, half of the nontax revenues came from the interest receipts and the other half comprised of the administrative receipts. However, the revenue from forestry and wildlife, major and minor irrigation, mines and minerals, power as well as civil supplies, is negligible due to low cost recovery policies.

Fiscal Balances

Between 1986-87 to 1995-96, the fiscal deficit deteriorated from 2.6 percent to 3.5 percent of GSDP. It further slipped to 4.8 percent during 1995-96 basically due to increased spending on the social and community services expenditure (particularly, education) without a corresponding rise in the revenue receipts. Given the constraints on borrowing ability of States, the burden of adjusting to the imbalance has generally tended to fall mainly on capital and maintenance expenditures with adverse implications in terms of infrastructural constraints, declining productivity of public sector investment and deceleration in long-term growth of the economy. Since the States do not have independent power to borrow from the market unlike the Centre, nor can they take recourse to borrowing from the central bank because of the regulation of the overdrafts, the main concern is the current balance.

Figure 6. Andhra Pradesh: Trends in the fiscal balances during 1985-86 to2001-02

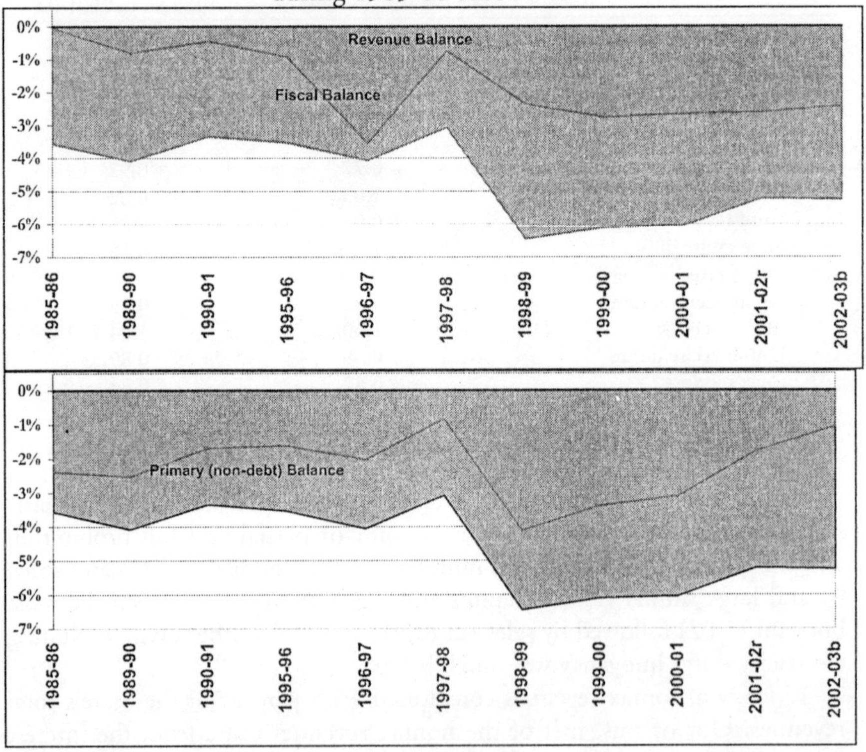

Debt Management

There is a considerable change in the pattern of financing of the fiscal deficit. The dependence on public account balances, State provident funds and small savings, has declined in favor of more and more market sources thus raising the interest costs. Earlier, long-term loans from the Central government and internal debt sources used to finance over 80 percent of the fiscal deficit. Over the years, while the borrowings from the central government remained at 50 to 55 percent of the total, the share of domestic borrowings has considerably increased (from about 25 percent to over 40 percent).

Table 7. Andhra Pradesh: Trends in the Pattern of Government Borrowing 1985-86 to 2001-02

(Percent to total)

	1985-86	1990-91	1995-96	1996-97	1997-98	1998-99	1999-00	2000-01	2001-02R	2002-03B
Loans from the Centre	56.4	57.3	52.7	58.7	55.2	33.5	49.0	21.7	45.2	50.3
Domestic Loans	25.7	24.0	30.2	40.4	29.2	30.6	39.3	60.6	45.5	40.4
Public Accounts	18.0	18.7	17.1	0.8	15.7	35.9	11.7	17.6	9.3	9.4

Figure 7. Andhra Pradesh: Pattern of financing the fiscal deficit during 1985-86 to 2001-02

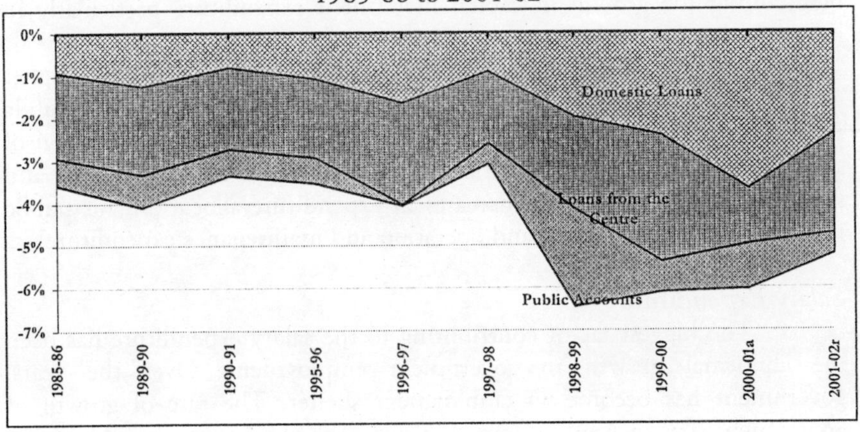

To sum up, like many States, prior to the 1996 reforms, Andhra Pradesh was facing deteriorating budgetary positions, with serious implications on its developmental efforts. Insufficient revenue sources and uncontrolled growth of current expenditures were the major sources of the imbalance. Further, the constraints on States' borrowings made the burden of adjustment to fall mainly on capital and maintenance expenditures with adverse implications on infrastructural development leading to declining productivity of public sector investment and deceleration in long-term growth of the economy.

3. SUGGESTED FISCAL REFORMS

The studies and reports that have looked into its fiscal decadence in Andhra Pradesh came up with detailed remedial measures with appropriate phasing. Particularly the Chelliah Committee (1994), Sarma (1995) and World Bank (1995) and more recently, the Vision 2020 documents.

Measures needed on the Expenditure side

Capital and infrastructure

All the above studies reiterated the need for progressive reduction of the debt-servicing component over time. This will be possible by restructuring the expenditure towards more capital investments particularly, in infrastructure. Higher expenditure on infrastructure will also be conducive for private investment and in the long run, will automatically yield higher revenues to the exchequer. The World Bank (1995) has observed that Andhra Pradesh's development potential was below potential basically due to inadequate provision of infrastructure. The Vision 2020 document put the required investment in power, roads, irrigation, and ports at about Rs.11000 crore a year while the budgetary allocation for capital is a meagre 15 percent of this amount. Thus, the importance of maintaining the growth in capital investment expenditure particularly in infrastructure cannot be overemphasized.

To bring fiscal balances to sustainable levels and achieve higher growth, there is need to increase the developmental impact of public expenditure. The measures that are needed in this respect are reduction of salary expenditure, discontinuation of mis-targeted welfare programs and subsidies with simultaneous increases in expenditure allocations for public infrastructure, social sectors and operation and maintenance expenditure.

Salary Expenditure

The biggest factor contributing to the salary expenditure has been the abnormal growth in government employment. Over the years, government has become an employment shelter. The rate of growth of government staff in Andhra Pradesh is one of the highest among the States. It is important to arrest the steep rise in employment while simultaneously improving the skills and productivity of the remaining staff to support economic and social development. Also, in the long run, with larger private investment coming forth in response to the higher infrastructure development by the government, the unemployment problem will be taken care of.

The World Bank recommendation in this regard was to reduce staffing in the public sector by 1 percent a year till 2001-02. The Vision 2020 document however, favored reduction by only 0.5 percent a year even while allowing for some increase in employment in the primary education and health sectors. It was also recommended that the Government could also offer the option of voluntary retirement scheme (VRS) in some departments where redundancy is more pronounced. The savings from this reform was estimated at about Rs.60 crore in the first year of reform, reaching about Rs.400 crore per year after five years from 1998-99.

Welfare Schemes and Subsidies

As regards subsidies given under the welfare schemes, they did make the task of budget balancing difficult. In the case of Andhra Pradesh, the rice subsidy scheme was an important factor aggravating the budgetary crisis. Therefore there is no doubt that scheme should be downsized to cover only the poor that constitute about 35 percent of the people. Simultaneously, the World Bank suggested that the subsidized price should be maintained at 50 percent of the cost. As regards fertilizer subsidy, Hanumantha Rao, a well-known economist, has come out with a suggestion that the fertiliser subsidy should be given to farmers for certain amount, which would be sufficient for small farmers leaving the big farmers to buy the additional quantity at market price if they need more[6].

Allocations for operation and maintenance (O&M) works

The main suggestion in this respect was that the Government should bifurcate the O&M budget into works and salary component and raise the works component to the required norms to enable efficient utilization of public investment.

Allocation for education and health

The reform program should include substantial increase in allocations for education and health with particular emphasis on achieving universal primary education and strengthening primary health care services. This endeavor should be supported by policy reforms in both sectors aimed at increasing the quality, reach and effectiveness of the service.

Industrial Incentives

As regards the industrial incentives, the response to the schemes appeared to be lukewarm, partly due to the cumbersome procedures involved in availing them. Also there was little evidence if these incentive schemes had any appreciable impact on the industrialization of the State. In view of this, it was strongly recommended to do away with them. Instead, provision of essential infrastructure, particularly, power supply, marketing and financial help, could be more effective.

Expenditure Management

Apart from expenditure restructuring, the World Bank as well as others have emphasized the need to strengthen the management of government expenditure. The present practice of incremental budgeting with short-term focus and thinly spreading the resources over a large number of projects leads to large time and cost overrun and substantial expenditure inefficiency. Introduction of zero-budgeting and continuous assessment of performance, efficiency and priorities could help address this problem. Besides, often the expenditure budget is prepared without adequate reference to resource availability, leading to large gaps between projected and actual expenditure leading to recurrent demands for supplementary budgetary allocations. These extra-budgetary allocations erodes not only the credibility of the budget, but also incentives for efficient financial planning and management. Budget formulation needs to start with a realistic estimate of the revenues from all sources, including borrowing. Explicit budget ceilings for each department at the beginning of the budget preparation would encourage prioritization of programs and minimize the need for supplementary budget allocations. Further, there is need to switch over to computerization of account, which will facilitate easy verification and reduce costs.

Measures needed on the Revenue side

As seen above, the deceleration of the revenues can be largely attributable to the sluggishness in the State's own sources. The revenue growth had a set back mainly due to the excise losses on account of prohibition. Although the other taxes showed impressive growth, they could not make up for the excise loss. Mobilizing resources for infrastructure and social services requires considerable improvement in State's finances and sector policies.

Sales tax

The rationalization of the sales tax system - combining the different components, reducing the number of rates, and abolishing the tax-on-tax practice – was long overdue and therefore is welcome. An important impediment for improving the tax revenue has been the lack of mutual trust between the tax collecting authorities and the taxpayers. As a result, the procedures of tax collection, the forms to be filled, and the rules to be followed tend to become complex and not easy to comply with. Therefore, along with the tax laws, there is also a need to simplify the procedures. The tax reform strategy should concentrate on systemic changes (simplification, base broadening, and more effective administration/based on information technology) rather than rate increases.

The main suggestions in this respect have been to replace the existent scheme with a broad based 'trade margin' VAT for larger dealers, abolition of the turnover tax, improving the tax administration and phasing out sales tax concessions. Eventually, the VAT system that is being contemplated should also include the services sector comprising transportation, communications, and financial services as the value added from it forms a sizable component of the domestic product.

Other Taxes

At the time of starting the reforms, Stamps and Registration fee was already under the process of restructuring. Although, there appears to be not much scope for upward revision of the rates as there is a persistent attempt to understate the value of the property. Clearly growth in revenues can only be secured through better implementation of the market value scheme and procedural improvements. The rationalization of the procedures determining the market value system did yield expected results. Nevertheless, care must be taken to see that this will not result in more loopholes. As regards the motor vehicles taxation, it was suggested that the life tax system be extended to small commercial vehicles apart from the non-transport private vehicles. The turnover basis at 15 percent is applicable to the RTC carriages - can be converted to seating capacity basis and should be uniformly applied to private carriages. Among the other taxes, there was a need to step up the administrative efforts to collect profession tax from self-employed professionals.

Non-taxes

On the non-taxes side, the broad consensus has been to improve user charges and cost recovery in a range of government services. Further, the irrigation charges were to be merged with the present water taxes.

Public Enterprise Reform

Total budgetary subsidies (explicit and implicit) to the 39 public enterprises was estimated at over Rs.650 crore per a year. To reduce their cost to the budget and to the economy, an effective disinvestment program is an urgent imperative. It was suggested that government should retain investment only in those enterprises, which are of strategic importance or whose deliverables have a public good or merit good character. All other units should either be closed down or privatized. The government could consider setting up an autonomous Privatization Commission to plan and implement public enterprise reforms and also establish a State Renewal Fund to finance rehabilitation and retraining of the affected work force.

Sectoral Policies

Power sector

In the power sector, the finances of Andhra Pradesh State Electricity Board (APSEB) were under severe strain since 1989-90, as the cost of its operations have vastly outstretched the revenues from sales of energy. APSEB has struggled but could not achieve the expected 3 percent rate of return on their value of net fixed assets. Steps like converting of government's loans to equity, writing off of long term government loans were resorted to but they did not address the underlying causes of the problems leading to severe cash crunch. These daunting financial problems have made difficult for APSEB to mobilize the resources needed to bring in capacity additions in generation, transmission & distribution commensurate with the growth in demand.

The World Bank has suggested to raise the power rate to farmers to 50 paise kWh or higher, continuously adjust tariffs to cover costs, reduce cross-subsidies and, improve the quality of service delivery. Further, it recommended suitable legislation to enable gradual privatization of distribution, establishment of an independent regulatory body, and corporatization and privatization of power utilities.

Irrigation sector

Construction and maintenance of surface irrigation networks is expensive. Thus it was clear that unless the costs of delivering irrigation services to farmers are fully recovered, the Government will not be able to maintain and operate the existing network effectively and expand the system to take advantage of the substantial unused irrigation potential in the state. It was suggested that the Government should allocate adequate funds to meet the O&M requirements in the public canal irrigation network and improve the quality of service delivery.

In addition the World Bank has suggested several other reforms such as, improving the efficiency of the public canal irrigation network, improving maintenance and upgradation of roads, speeding up private sector participation in the port sector, implementing universal primary schooling, and improving public health services. Besides, the Vision 2020 document also indicates a strategy for phasing these reforms and its impact through a macro-fiscal model.

Given the bleak fiscal situation, what, in fact, required is not a quantum reduction in the of public expenditure, but a radical compositional shift towards infrastructure, operation and maintenance and social sectors and reducing the shares of interest payments, untargeted subsidies and salary bill. There is also a clear need for better expenditure management to improve the developmental impact of the expenditure and revenue augmentation.

4. PROGRESS IN THE FISCAL REFORM PROCESS: 1995-2000

The suggestions and recommendations made by the expert bodies like the World Bank formed the basis of the reform process that began in 1995-96 with the publication of White Papers on State Finances[7] and other aspects. A summary of the fiscal reforms undertaken by the government during 1995-2000 is given in Table. While assessing the progress of the fiscal reforms, it should be kept in mind that given the institutional and socio-political constraints, the implementation of the fiscal reforms cannot be hurried nor the impact can be expected to be instantaneous. Nevertheless, our objective is to see if the reform measures are in the right direction and adequate.

Expenditure Restructuring

The major reforms for government expenditure restructuring are aimed at improving the developmental impact of the expenditure, and reducing unproductive expenditure resulting from mis-targeted welfare programs and subsidies. In practical terms it implies reduction of the salary bill by pruning government employment, revamping of the welfare schemes, chalking out more targeted poverty alleviation strategies, reform of the public enterprises. It also implies simultaneous increases in infrastructure, social sectors and maintenance expenditure.

Government staff size

As for the reduction of the salary bill by pruning government employment, since 1996-97, there has been a clear-cut change and improvement. The growth in the government employees averages to less than one percent per annum after 1996-97 as compared to the 3.4 percent per annum, prior to the reform. This is after protecting the needs of the human resource sectors like education, medical and health and police departments. Fresh recruitment is minimized leading to the reduction of the overall size of the government employees by 2.6 percent by way of attrition. Even in the government-aided institutions, staff reduction of 2.4 percent was achieved. Consequently, the salary component of the expenditure has come down from 42.5 percent of the revenue expenditure to just over 32.3 percent (Figure 2). However, the pension bill has gone up. According to the recent White Paper, there are nearly 4 lakh pensioners in Andhra Pradesh and the number has grown rapidly in the recent past due to the extension of the pension scheme to employees of local bodies and aided institutions. Coupled with the recommendation of Fifth Central Pay Commission to give proportionate increase to the pensioners, including dearness allowance, the pension bill has rapidly climbed up from Rs. 1139 crores in 1997-98, to Rs. 1382 crores in 1998-99, to Rs. 1657 crores in 1999-2000, and is expected to go up to Rs. 2176 crores in 2001-02.

Rice subsidy

The rice subsidy that proved to be a burden on the government budget was partially pruned. The issue price of subsidized rice was raised from Rs 2 to Rs. 3.50 per kg. Consequently, the expenditure share on rice certainly came down (Table 4) but for the revised estimate of the fiscal year 1999-00.

Operation and Maintenance Expenditure

Expenditure on O&M has improved considerably and expenditure on goods and services has gone up from 8.4 percent of GSDP in 1985-86 to around 12 percent in 2001-02 (Table 2).

Allocation for education and health

Social development indicators of AP, especially in education, were far below the national average. Allocations, particularly for teaching and health material, were substantially below the required norms. The reforms called for substantial increase in allocations for education and health with particular emphasis on achieving universal primary education and strengthening primary health care services. Consequently, the expenditure on education has increased from 2.2 percent of GSDP to 2.7 percent in 2001-02 (Table 1).

Capital investment

The declining share of expenditure on public investment in total non-interest expenditure has created large infrastructure gaps that became serious obstacle for economic and social development. Raising capital budget sharply was imperative and it is clear that the public funds alone are not sufficient to meet the needs. Accordingly, efforts are on to encourage private investment. Expenditure allocation for capital has improved considerably from 11.2 percent of total expenditure in 1995-96 to 15.3 percent 2001-02 (Table 2).

Public Enterprise Reform

Total budgetary subsidies (explicit and implicit) to the 39 public enterprises is estimated at over Rs.650 crore per a year. To reduce their cost to the budget and to the economy, an effective disinvestment program was needed. Government seeks to close down or privatize the loss-making enterprises and retain investment only those that are of strategic importance or whose deliverables have a public good or merit good character. The Government set up an autonomous Commission to plan and implement public enterprise reforms and also establish a State Renewal Fund to finance rehabilitation and retraining of the affected work force and necessary steps were taken to privatize State enterprises. Over 5000 surplus employees were retrenched through voluntary retirement (VRS) scheme.

Infrastructural Reform

There was significant increase in the Capital expenditure-GSDP ratio in 1995-96 because of the reform initiatives. Also, realizing that inadequate infrastructure is the biggest bottleneck in the path to the industrial and economic development, the Government has come out with a comprehensive Infrastructure Policy. An Infrastructure Development

Enabling Act (IDEA) is also under preparation. The focus of the Government in all these initiatives has been to play a facilitating and enabling role in infrastructure development.

Power Sector Reform

The government of Andhra Pradesh has taken several policy and implementation initiatives to accomplish the reform process. On the recommendations of the Hiten Bhaiya Committee and in accordance with the new reforms policy, the Government enacted the AP Electricity Reform Act 1998 that provided for the creation of an independent regulatory commission to be called AP Electricity Regulatory Commission. The electricity supply is reorganized by creating separate corporations for transmission (APTRANSCO) and generation (APGENCO). The regulatory commission is made to be solely responsible in the state to issue electricity transmission and supply licenses and regulate tariffs for transmission and supply of electricity. The commission is expected to fix and enforce standards of performance and quality of supply for the licensees duly taking into account the financial viability of the licensees and the legitimate interests of the consumers. Despite revisions in power rates, agricultural tariffs are still 9 percent of the average cost of power production. The power deficit itself had increased from four per cent in 1994 to 22 per cent in 1997. Therefore, it was clear that unless all tariffs, and particularly agricultural tariffs, are further adjusted to fully recover costs, the Andhra Pradesh State Electricity Board (APSEB) losses could not be contained and the creditworthiness of the power sector turned out to be not sufficient to attract private investment.

As a result of the expenditure reforms, the revenue component of the expenditure could be contained around 14.15 percent of GSDP for the last three years while capital outlay has shown improvement from 2.1 percent in 1995-96 to 3.04 percent in 1999-2000. Since 1997-98 most of the expenditure indicators have been moving in the right direction and can be considered broadly on track. Interest on public debt was contained at 2.52 percent of GSDP in 1999-2000 and so was revenue deficit brought down to below 1 percent in 1999-2000.

Strengthening the Expenditure Management

A number of reforms for budgetary accounting were initiated. Several similar schemes were merged and their budget heads of accounts were integrated to provide greater flexibility. Zero-based budgeting was adopted as an important policy tool to bring fiscal discipline in all the departments. Under this concept every department was required to justify its budget need for projected performance starting from scratch. All the existing schemes and projects were to be scrutinized thoroughly and made subject to an in-depth questioning to evaluate its relevance to the development and welfare of the people of the State. Thereon, the resources available, including manpower, were utilized effectively on the evaluated schemes. Every department was asked to evaluate each scheme under select 'Performance Indicators' and all future financial allocations and releases are linked to the performance and its impact. Computerization of public offices

Table 8. Andhra Pradesh: Chronological progress of the fiscal reforms 1995-2000

1996-97	Prohibition was partially rolled back. Issue price of subsidized rice was raised to Rs. 3.50 per kg . Fresh recruitment and unnecessary expenditure were minimized. The first large public enterprise, Hyderabad Allwyn, was privatized.
1997-98	Irrigation rates were raised by five times. Self-help groups were encouraged under major irrigation commands as water users' associations. Women and the poor were organized under DWACRA. Joint forest management and watershed management. The government also appointed a staff review committee and a committee for restructuring public enterprises.
1998-99	Peoples' participation was extended to cover the management of village schools, hospitals, youth groups and nutrition program. Power tariff was hiked by 9 percent and AP Electricity Regulatory Commission was set up. The government launched several initiatives like AP State Wide Area Network (APSWAN), Twin Cities' Information Network System (TWINS) and Computer-aided Administration of Registration Department (CARD) to introduce information technology in citizen services. The government also succeeded in attracting private investment from prestigious business houses in India and abroad in its projects of Hi-Tech City, Indian School of Business (ISB) and Indian Institute of Information Technology (IIIT).
1999-2000	In January, the state's long-term goals were enunciated in VISION 2020 that would determine future strategies of social and economic development in Andhra Pradesh. The state government collaborated with the Union and other state governments to introduce uniform floor rates of sales tax and withdrawal of tax-based incentives to industries throughout the country. The concept of cost recovery by public agencies through levy and retention of user charges was introduced in several departments. The Water User Associations were permitted to plough back water rates for maintenance. APSRTC was permitted to raise bus fares to offset petrol and diesel price hike. The Municipal Corporation of Hyderabad was allowed to levy an impact fee to capture unearned capital appreciation on account of public investment in road development. Hospitals were permitted to charge for diagnostic services and retain the proceeds for hospital development.

Source: Government of Andhra Pradesh (2001) White Paper on Fiscal Reforms Strategy, Hyderabad.

was expanded. The government also took steps to computerize the administration under Andhra Pradesh State Wide Area Network

(APSWAN), Twin Cities' Information Network (TWINS), Computer-aided Administration of Registration Department (CARD).

In addition, peoples' active participation in the creation and supply of public goods is being encouraged. In 1998-99, peoples' participation in the management of village schools, hospitals, youth groups under 'Janmabhoomi' scheme was organized[8].

Revenue Augmentation

The revenue side measures basically aim for a comprehensive reform of the structure and administration of the State's main taxes such as sales tax, stamp duties, and the profession tax.

Sales Tax

In this regard, the Chelliah Committee (1994) had recommended several reforms pertaining to the sales tax. They include streamlining and consolidation of the sales tax, surcharge and turnover tax into a single tax with value added tax for trade margins; reduction of the number of rates to no more than five; improving tax audit procedures; abolition of internal checkposts; relax the self-assessment conditions; and computerization.

The government responded to the Chelliah Committee recommendations by abolishing the turnover tax, additional tax, and the surcharge, and introduced the trade margin VAT for dealers engaged in the second and subsequent points of sale of 19 groups of commodities. The government is also in the process of computerization. In 1999-2000, the government collaborated with the Union and other State governments to introduce uniform floor rates of sales tax and withdrawal of tax incentives to industries. However, the reintroduction of the turnover tax in 1996 was a regressive step. The government also retained the internal checkposts. Thus, the government did not seem to pursue the tax reform at right pace.

Nevertheless, the sales tax rationalization embarked in 2000 did improve the tax collections in the medium term. New slabs of rates were introduced for different commodity groups in line with the consensus reached on the floor rates. The government is now preparing to introduce the state level Value Added Tax system by April 2002. Much depends upon the strategies for overcoming several obstacles like administrative difficulties.

State Excise

As regards State excise, in 1996-97 prohibition was partially rolled back with a view to improve the excise revenue. The reform efforts need to concentrate more on systemic changes, simplification, administrative improvements and base broadening rather than rate increases. The right option for the sales tax reform would be to widen the VAT coverage on the lines suggested by the NIPFP and the Committee of Finance Ministers.

The Government of Andhra Pradesh is pursuing a policy of maintaining a judicious balance between ban on production, sale and consumption of arrack on the one hand, and containing the menace of illicit distillation and smuggling of liquor on the other by making available IML made out of Extra Neutral Alcohol (ENA) to cater to the needs of relatively better off consumers. The present policy is thus a blend of temperance with regulated access to better quality liquor.

Stamp Duties and Registration fees

In stamp duties, the rate structure is simplified, several concessions were removed, administration improved by introduction of computers and the composition method in lieu of affixing stamps to individual documents. After introduction of CARD project, a Citizens Charter, prescribing time frames for each and every item of work is being implemented. The CARD Project has improved the service levels enormously besides ensuring accuracy and tamper free preservation of the registered documents. The public has appreciated this measure and Andhra Pradesh has given a lead in this regard to other States to emulate.

Non-Tax Revenues

Although there is scope for improving user charges and cost recovery in a range of government services, the government has decided to permit the concerned departments and administrative units to retain the additional revenues as an incentive. This is done in recognition of the fact that to mobilize fees, beneficiaries will expect to receive improved services. Retention of user fees is also related to existing initiatives to allow more revenues to be utilized directly by beneficiaries.

The concept of cost recovery by public agencies through levy and retention of user charges was introduced in several departments. In the fields of water management, transport, and hospitals, the concerned authorities were allowed to hike the user charges and plough-back the extra earnings. Power tariff was hiked by 9 percent. In 1997-98 irrigation rates were raised by five times. Improving the efficiency of irrigation system, maintenance of the upgraded forests is the key idea behind the formation of water user associations or *vana samrakshan samithis*, which are empowered with authority over the use of a share of fees collected for water charges or minor forest produce.

Consequent to these reforms, the fiscal position does shows some improvement. The State's own revenue receipts rose from 6.32 percent in 1995-96 to 8.49 per cent of GSDP in 1997-98. Although it came down to 7.82 per cent in 1998-99, it recovered to 8.75 per cent of GSDP during the next year and is likely to further increase during 2000-01. The share of own revenue in total has improved from 59.54 percent in 1997-98 to 63.84 per cent in 1999-00 and is likely to be around 65 percent in 2000-01.

A Medium Term Fiscal Framework

In addition, the government is embarking on a Medium Term Fiscal Framework (MTFF) to help plan fiscal policies following the passing of Fiscal Responsibility and Budget Management Act, 2000 at the Centre. There are two main objectives of formulating the MTFF in Andhra Pradesh according to the Government White Paper (2001). The first is to ensure that public expenditure is stable and sustainable and not prone to fiscal crises. The second is to improve the efficiency of allocation decisions and protect high priority public expenditures such as on social services, recurring non-wage expenditure requirements (operations and maintenance), and infrastructure investments. The MTFF is a tool for establishing the overall affordability of government spending within reasonable revenue forecasts, while identifying a broad path for expenditures that protects expenditure priorities. It aims to identify key fiscal policies needed to reverse the State's growing debt problem.

On the whole, the progress made in implementing the fiscal reforms appears to be in the right direction. In the first two years of the reform, 1996-97 and 1997-98, there were some encouraging results. The total expenditure – GSDP ratio has increased from 16.8 percent to 18 percent basically due to conscious efforts to raise infrastructure through capital outlay allocations and net lending. The revenue – GSDP has also shot up from 12.5 percent to 15.4 percent, presumably due to significant improvement in the sales tax and to some extent the lifting of prohibition being shown up as higher excise revenue. Although the transfers from the Centre have declined, the rise in the own revenue has more than compensated for the decline. Consequently, the fiscal deficit was under control being below 3 percent and revenue deficit near zero 0.8 percent. However, since 1998-99 there are signs of recurring fiscal laxity.

5. TASKS AHEAD

However, as can be seen, the revival in the fiscal situation could not be sustained. Since 1998-99, there has been a consistent deterioration in the fiscal balance from 2.6 percent to 5.4 percent, which is worse than the all-State average of 4.9 percent[9]. Even the stock of debt at 30 percent (Figure 3) is considered to be high as the all-States average is just about 22 percent.

Containment of current expenditure

A major factor seems to be the inability to contain the current expenditure and improve expenditure management. Most of the current expenditure is either fully 'committed' like debt servicing or 'semi-committed' like salaries and establishment expenditure that is well protected[10]. Only a strong political will and committed bureaucracy can bring about the required change in the expenditure management. While the burden of power subsidy continues despite the power sector reforms, the rising debt has been causing fresh increases in the current expenditure. This is further aggravated by the proliferation of the welfare schemes. Several new schemes have started with fresh financial commitments (Table). The rice subsidy still needs to be properly targeted. The scheme still covers about 78 percent of the population, while the population below the poverty line - the intended target group - is estimated to be just around 30 percent. As regards the O&M, more adjustments are needed if the revenue from water charges fully cover the O&M costs. Also, government should also gradually transfer the management of irrigation systems to the recently formed Water Users Associations.

Better expenditure control and management

The expenditure control and management systems also need to be further improved. In the efforts to control the fiscal deficit, often governments end up spending more money for controlling expenditure, since the processes have become so cumbersome. "Anyone who deals with the central or state government would know that this is because everyone is controlling everyone else's expenditure. A file on expenditure probably moves through 180 people today, because governments have no money or the money is committed. The control system that has come into being is more crucial to the quality of expenditure than the allocations, etc that economists analyze." (Jalan, 2001).

Infrastructure

The development of infrastructure services requires sustained long-term investment and more importantly involves reforms of processes. It requires a strong partnership of the private and public sector, which alone can commit large amount long-term capital, with long pay back period and uncertain returns.

Power Sector

As for the power sector, although the required legislative framework has been created, the reform process will need closer cooperation between the government, the APSEB, its employees, consumers and various other stakeholders and the financial institutions. Also, the State was far behind Punjab, Haryana, Gujarat, Tamil Nadu, Karnataka and Kerala with regard to attracting investments. It is hoped that the creditworthiness of the government in this respect will be restored soon to be passed on to the customers by way of improved quality and reliability of supply at reasonable tariffs.

Revenue Growth

What is needed to catch the revenue growth with that of the expenditure rise is to improve the tax administration and tax compliance. In the words of Chelliah "Simple tax laws with only a few rates for each tax and with few exemptions would considerably reduce the scope for the exercise of discretionary power of the tax officers. Correspondingly, the

Table 9. Welfare Schemes launched during 1995-2000

Scheme	Estimated cost (Rs Crore)
Janmabhoomi programme was launched on January 1, 1997 as 'a people-centred development process aimed at achieving overall growth and improving the quality of life.' An amount of Rs 1,018 crore has been spent on this scheme till the end of 11th round.	1500
Chief Minister's Empowerment of Youth Programme, launched in December 1996, was initially taken up for implementation in two villages per mandal all over the state. It was subsequently extended to all rural as well as urban areas in the state. Till the end of 1999, as many as 51,517 CMEY groups were formed all over the state.	400
Adarana programme was launched in 1998 for providing improved hand tools, power tools and other equipment to backward class artisans. Under the Adarana programme, over 518,000 beneficiaries were supplied various tools worth Rs 121.72 crore till December 1999.	300
Girl child protection scheme was launched in 1996. As many as 146,498 girl children were benefited under the scheme till end of 1999.	75
Integrated Girl Child Labour Rehabilitation project was introduced for bringing attitudinal change in the society towards education of girl child.	1
Back to School programme for Scheduled Castes working children was started in 1997 as a pilot project to prepare children (who have either never attended schools or have been drop-outs) for admission into schools.	300
Deepam scheme was launched in 1999 to provide 15 lakh cooking gas connections to women below the poverty line in the state. The outlay on this programme is Rs 150 crore and Rs 60 crore has been spent so far.	150
Mundadugu is an integrated package of the programmes for the economic and social development of Scheduled Castes. The consolidated programme was re-launched in 1998. AP Scheduled Caste Cooperative Finance Corporation evolved an action plan to assist two lakh SC families at an outlay of Rs 210 crore during 1999-2000.	250
Roshni is the name of the integrated package of schemes for the economic development and welfare of the minorities.	55

extent of collusion between the erring taxpayers and the errant officers would be reduced. The reform of the tax structure is moving in the direction of simple laws. However, in spite of the reduction in the rates of tax, tax evasion by substantial sections of taxpayers and corruption indulged in by tax officers is wide spread. Government has been content with taking sporadic action against tax evaders, large or small, and against corrupt officers. Only planned and determined deterrent action would serve to cut down evasion and corruption. Computerization and strong deterrent action against tax evaders and corrupt taxmen are the two most important steps to be taken to increase revenues in the existing situation" (Chelliah and Rao, 2001). In this respect the steps contemplated by the government of Andhra Pradesh are worth noting. "The government is fully committed to improve the orientation of all the revenue earning departments and make them into modern, efficient and user-friendly agencies that are capable of scientific and accurate analysis of the revenue potential in their respective fields. At the same time their enforcement capabilities will be enhanced to ensure effective compliance of tax laws. For this, the State government will provide resources for computerization, on line connectivity, mobility and streamlined administration through upgrading the technical skills and organizational structures. The departmental officers will also be made more accountable for their performance" (Government of Andhra Pradesh White Paper, 2001).

However, there remains the need to further improve the nontax revenue through appropriate pricing of power, and enhanced cost recovery in irrigation, water supply, public transportation, higher education, hospital care at the secondary and tertiary levels and housing loans.

Implementation Strategy

The steady deterioration in the last three years indicates that the fiscal reform is not as effective as expected. To some extent this can be attributed to lack of a viable implementation strategy. The implementation strategy should involve fixing of viable targets for each expenditure component at the departmental level, rationalization of institutional arrangements and devising a macro fiscal framework[11].

In this context, some of the fiscal management rules specified in the Fiscal Responsibility Bill are worth adopting, particularly those relating to ensuring reasonable transparency. The State government should take suitable measures to ensure greater transparency in fiscal operations and to minimize, as far as practicable in public interest, secrecy in the preparation of any review of the trends in receipts and expenditures in relation to the budget by the Finance Minister and placing the outcome of such reviews before both Houses of Parliament. It should cut expenditure authorizations in a proportionate manner, while protecting the "charged" expenditure, whenever there is a shortfall of revenue or excess of expenditure over specified targets. Further, the Finance Minister to make a statement in the legislature explaining any deviation in meeting the obligations cast on the State Government and the remedial measures the Government proposes to take. Also, necessary statements should be made regarding any relaxation from deficit reduction targets to deal with unforeseen demands on the finances of the Government on account of natural calamities.

Fiscal Responsibility Rules at the State Level

Kopits (2001), in his assessment of the adoption of fiscal policy rules for India has also suggested to establish a mechanism to ensure adoption of fiscal rules at the States levels. This might entail infusion of strong incentives for expenditure reduction and revenue raising at lower tiers of government without sacrificing regional or local autonomy. In particular, those pertaining to fiscal balances can be recast as follows.

- Reduce revenue deficit by an amount equivalent to one-half percent, or more of the estimated gross domestic product at the end of each financial year beginning on the 1st day of April, 2002;
- Reduce revenue deficit to nil within a period of five financial years beginning from the initial financial year on the 1st day of April 2002 and ending on the 31st day of March 2007;
- Build up surplus amount of revenue and utilize such amount for discharging liabilities in excess of assets;
- Reduce fiscal deficit by an amount equivalent to one-half percent or more of the estimated gross domestic product at the end of each financial year beginning on the 1st day of April 2002;
- Reduce fiscal deficit for a financial year to not more than two percent of the reduce fiscal deficit for a financial year to not more than two percent of the estimated gross domestic product for that year, within a period of five financial years beginning from the initial financial year on the 1st day of April, 2002 and ending on the 31st day of March 2007;
- Not give guarantee for any amount exceeding one-half per cent of the estimated gross domestic product in any financial year and;
- Ensure within a period of ten financial years, beginning from the initial financial year on the 1st day of April, 2001, and ending on the 31st day of March, 2011, that the total liabilities (including external debt at current exchange rate) at the end of a financial year, do not exceed fifty per cent of the estimated gross domestic product for that year.

6. CONCLUSION

Apparently, the government has been rather cautious in the implementation of fiscal reforms as it is not easy to enlist public support for some of the reform programs such as tax reforms, subsidy cuts, power tariff restructuring and user fee hikes[12]. One of the basic purposes of the action plan called 'Vision 2020' is to build public awareness of the reform strategy and process. Macro-management of the State's economy cannot succeed unless adequate fiscal correction takes place. One can only hope that the State's economy is still in transition and the fruits of reform will ripen with collective hard work and passage of time.

Notes

1 Several studies have examined the fiscal crisis in the State and tried to identify the factors responsible for it. Notable among them are Sarma and Sreedevi (1994), Chelliah Committee (1994), Sarma et al (1995), and World Bank (1996) based on the background study by Sarma (1996). Much of the analysis here of the pre-1996 reform situation is broadly supportive of the conclusions drawn by these and other studies.

2 The fiscal analysis is primarily based on the budgetary data supplemented with compositional information reported in the Andhra Pradesh Economic & Functional Classification of the Budget.

3 Although, the fall in the ratio of government expenditure to GSDP can also be viewed as reflective of its productivity, this relation cannot be easily identified as testified by the huge empirical literature on causality between government expenditure and GSDP. In the absence of convincing evidence on the developmental impact of aggregate government expenditure on GSDP we follow the conventional demand side determination that assumes a uni-directional causality from GSDP to government expenditure.

4 The ratios of fiscal variables to GSDP reported here may not tally with those of earlier studies because of revised GSDP estimates. The Central Statistical Organization (CSO) has revised its National Accounting Statistics in February 1999 by changing the base year from 1980-81 to 1993-94. At the State level also, attempts are made for estimating the State Domestic Product as per the guidelines of Central Statistical Organization. The new series, at present available from the year 1993-94 onwards, has sought to improve the coverage by including several new activities along with several conceptual changes. The new series show higher level of output than the old series. For instance the GSDP (at factor cost) in the base year 1993-94 now stands at Rs. 58,227 crore instead of Rs. 54,487 crore under the old series (an increase of 6.86 percent). Nevertheless, while the real GSDP growth for 1994-95 is 5.6 percent per annum as against 4.8 in the old series, growth rates pertaining to 1995-96, and 1996-97 have declined from 6.91 percent (old series) to 5.5 percent. Again, the growth rate during 1997-98 was also slightly lower under the new series than under the old series. In so far as the impact on sectoral composition of real GSDP is concerned, the share of services and industrial activities is higher with the new series.

5 While the major thrust of government expenditure can be seen from the trends in its functional pattern, its efficiency and productivity can be better assessed from its economic composition.

6 Hanumantha Rao, Ch, former Member of Planning and Finance Commissions at a Seminar on 'AP State Economic Situation: Problems and Solutions' organized by the Chandra Rajeswara Rao Foundation for Social Progress, Hyderabad June 2000.

7 The objectives stated in the White Paper are:

- To augment revenues,
- To redirect government expenditure away from less productive schemes,
- To invest in people to improve their quality of life and strengthen their social and economic assets through improved health, education and other social services,
- To create an environment conducive for private sector participation in the development process, and,
- To strengthen O&M expenditure to maintain productivity levels of existing infrastructure.

See Government of Andhra Pradesh White Paper (2001).

8 'Janmabhoomi' is a people oriented development process launched in in January 1997. This process has evolved out of the experience gained through the implementation of 'Prajala Vaddaku Paalana' (taking administration to the doorsteps of people) launched in November 1995 and 'Sramadanam' (contribution of labor) launched in January 1996. It aims at establishing people's participation for enhanced quality of life with social justice. It focuses on five core areas: 1) Community Works, 2) Primary Education, 3) Primary Health and Family Welfare, 4) Environment Conservation, and, 5) Responsive Governance. So far, approximately, Rs 1800 crore worth of community works have been started, about 12 lakh children were enrolled for primary education, special medical camps were set up and several environmental protection schemes were initiated.

9 In 1998-99 fiscal deficit (FD) of all States taken together measured 4.2 percent of Gross Domestic Product (GDP), an all-time high and rose further to 4.9 percent in 1999-00 (RBI, 2000). While the intensity of the stress varies across States, none has remained unaffected. In 1998-99, in as many as 8 out of the then 25 States, FD exceeded 7 percent of their Gross State Domestic Product (GSDP). See Anand *et al* (2001).

10 To quote from a recent speech of Bimal Jalan, the RBI Governor - "It is a fact that we have liberated the public servant, but imprisoned the public. ... Now all expenditure is committed expenditure on either paying interest on past debt, or paying government servants who provide no public services".

11 Some progress seems to have already been made in this respect. The government has identified 312 development indicators that need to be monitored to assess the progress Of these 32 indicators are considered 'Core Indicators' that directly contribute to the social, economic and infrastructural development of the state. The remaining are termed as 'functional' indicators that are important from the point of view of the delivery of developmental, technical, welfare, social and economic services by individual departments. Vision 2020 has identified five-year targets that have now been broken into annual targets that would be monitored at the state, district and mandal /municipality levels. These would be reviewed with suitable periodicity. Each government department is being asked to prepare their SIP clearly highlighting their goals, strategy, policy and program content, and budgetary allocations to leverage private sector participation and encourage community contributions. This activity is likely to be completed by all the departments by the end of the current financial year. (Government of Andhra Pradesh White Paper, 2001).

12 "All expenditure benefits those who receive the money – it may not be the public – either a government servant, a contractor, a lender – you're taking away something from somewhere. Thus there will be plenty of opposition to transparency by lobbying groups, and the public that may back you is widely dispersed. The problem with reducing government expenditure is that you get opposition, and you don't get support from a very large number of people who don't benefit form the expenditure. One way to do this perhaps is to institute changes at the margin" (Jalan, 2001).

References

Ahluwalia, M.S. (1999), "Economic Performance of States in Post-Reforms Period", *Economic & Political Weekly*, May 6.

Anand, M, A. Bagchi and T. Sen (2001), "Fiscal Discipline at the State Level: Perverse Incentives and Paths to Reform", Paper presented at the *Conference on Fiscal Policies to Accelerate Economic Growth*, May 21-22, New Delhi.

Government of Andhra Pradesh (1994), *Interim Report of the Expert Committee on Tax Reforms in Andhra Pradesh*, Hyderabad.

Government of Andhra Pradesh (1992), "New Comprehensive Scheme of State Incentives", Department of Industries, Hyderabad.

Government of Andhra Pradesh (1994), "Note on the Finances of the State", Finance and Planning Department, Hyderabad.

Government of Andhra Pradesh, *Memorandum Submitted to the Tenth Finance Commission*, Finance and Planning Department, Hyderabad.

Government of Andhra Pradesh, *Economic-cum-Functional Classification of the Budgetary Transactions*, (various volumes) Directorate of Economics & Statistics, Hyderabad.

Government of India (1994), *Report of the Tenth Finance Commission*, New Delhi.

Government of India (1995), *Report of the Committee of State Finance Ministers on Sales Tax Reform*, National Institute of Public Finance & Policy, June.

Government of Andhra Pradesh (2001), "Strategy Paper on Fiscal Reform", Finance Department, Hyderabad.

Harshe, R and C. Srinivas (2000), "Andhra Pradesh: Dilemmas of Development", *Economic & Political Weekly*, June 3.

Kopits, G. (2001), "Fiscal Responsibility Rules for India", *Economic & Political Weekly*, March 3.

Kurian N J (1999), "State Government Finances A Survey of Recent Trends", *Economic & Political Weekly*, May 8.

Jalan, B. (2001), Closing speech at the *Conference on Fiscal Policies to Accelerate Economic Growth*, May 21-22, New Delhi.

Premchand, A. and S. Chattopadhyaya (2001), "Fiscal Adjustment and Expenditure Management", *Conference on Fiscal Policies to Accelerate Economic Growth*, May 21-22, New Delhi.

Reserve Bank of India (2000), *State Finances A Study of Budgets of 2000-2001*, Mumbai.

RV (1999), "Sweet Dreams: Andhra Pradesh Vision 2020", *Economic & Political Weekly*, February 13.

Sarma, J.V.M and S. Mehta (1988), *Study of Sales Tax in Andhra Pradesh (Revenue Forecasting and Target Fixation)*, National Institute of Public Finance & Policy, New Delhi.

Sarma, J.V.M, S. Mehta, and A.Bagchi (1989), *Sales Tax System in Andhra Pradesh*, National Institute of Public Finance & Policy, New Delhi.

Sarma, J.V.M and N. Sreedevi (1994), "Fiscal Imbalances in Andhra Pradesh", *The Asian Economic Review*, vol. xxxvi, No 2, August.

Sarma, J.V.M, N.Sreedevi and Usha Nori (1994), "Scope for Reforming the Taxation of Services in Andhra Pradesh - Stamp Duties and Motor Vehicles Tax", *CESS Working Paper*, Centre for Economic & Social Studies, Hyderabad.

Sarma, J.V.M. (1995), "Resource Mobilization for the New Welfare Programs in Andhra Pradesh", *Economic & Political Weekly*, March 4.

———, "Tax Rationalization in Andhra Pradesh: Reasons for Introducing VAT" and "How to get a VAT System Working", *Business Line*, June 21-22.

——— (1996), *Fiscal Situation in Andhra Pradesh,* Report submitted to the World Bank, March.

Sarma, J.V.M, N.Sreedevi, Usha Nori and M.Lakshmi (1995), *Tax Reforms in Andhra Pradesh (Background Studies for the Expert Committee on Andhra Pradesh Tax Reform)*, Centre for Economic & Social Studies, March.

The World Bank (1996), *Andhra Pradesh: Agenda for Economic Reforms,* Country Operations, Industry & Finance Division, Report No 15901-IN, November.

4

State Finances: Comparative Scenario and Reforms Required

N. Sreedevi

1. INTRODUCTION

The state has been experiencing fiscal imbalances for the last two decades. This is reflected in the abnormal rise in fiscal deficit. In the first phase, the deterioration of fiscal performance showed in the increasing revenue deficits. This compelled the state to divert the resources meant for capital expenditure, which are mostly borrowings, to fill the revenue deficits. This resulted in a massive rise in interest burden accentuating the revenue deficit, and low overall productivity of government expenditure has kept the base for raising resources, that is NSDP, low. In the second phase, the borrowings were spent not only to fill the revenue deficit but also to repay the loan component. In 90-91, nearly 20% of the public debt raised was spent towards repayments. This proportion has increased to 64% by 1999-2000 (See Appendix I) and further increased to 71% during 2000-01. The remaining portion of the public debt raised i.e., net public debt and other sources (Public Account) are financing the fiscal deficit (Appendix II). Moreover, the revenue deficit component in fiscal deficit has been increasing while the component of capital expenditure showing a declining trend. The fiscal reforms at the state level assume importance in this context.

This paper presents an analysis of the fiscal position of government of Andhra Pradesh (AP). The study is divided into five sections. In Section II an attempt is made to compare the financial position of the AP with other States. A comparison of fiscal situation of AP with Southern States, other major States and also at 'all States' level is done. Section III briefs the views of World Bank (WB) and the suggestions to reach the targets set for AP. This section also examines whether AP has reached the targets set, by WB, for second half of 90s. The aspirations of AP, Vision 2020, to overcome the existing crisis are also mentioned briefly. Section IV discusses whether any desirable improvement is achieved in the developmental activities, both social (especially on crucial areas such as primary education, primary health and water supply) and economic activities (energy, irrigation and roads). An attempt is made to explore the possibility to increase the revenue receipts (both tax and non-tax) and reduce the expenditure. As each component of either receipts or expenditure requires a separate and a thorough study, here an attempt is made to mention only a few important issues. The externally aided projects for restructuring purposes are also briefly mentioned. Section V gives the summary of the paper.

Sources of Data and Methodology

The main sources of data for AP are Explanatory memoranda and budget in brief. For comparative picture, data from various issues of RBI bulletins are taken. State-wise average annual growth rates of major fiscal indicators calculated by RBI are borrowed to compare AP's major fiscal indicators with other southern States, and 'all States'.

2. FISCAL SITUATION IN AP: A COMPARATIVE PICTURE

The own tax- SDP ratio of AP was better than many other states during 90-00 (Table 1). However, the implementation of prohibition on the sale of alcohol affected the revenue of AP during 94-97. Even after the partial withdrawal of ban on consumption of alcohol, the ratio of

Table 1. Fiscal Indicators: Comparative Analysis (%)

State Own Tax Revenue / NSDP				State Own Revenue / Aggregate Expenditure				Interest Payments / Revenue Expenditure				Interest Payments/ Revenue Receipts			
90-95		95-00		90-95		95-00		90-95		99-00		90-95		95-00	
KER	10.4	TN	9.5	HAR	69.4	HAR	62.7	ORI	18.4	PUN	25.9	BIH	20.5	PUN	32.6
KAR	10.2	KAR	9.4	MAH	62.6	MAH	60.6	BIH	18.1	UP	22.8	ORI	19.7	WB	28.9
TN	10.2	GUJ	8.5	GUJ	59.2	KAR	58.4	UP	16.4	WB	21.4	PUN	19.3	UP	27.2
GUJ	9.3	KER	8.3	KAR	56.6	GUJ	58.0	PUN	16.0	RAJ	21.0	UP	18.2	ORI	26.1
HAR	8.6	MAH	7.8	PUN	53.9	TN	57.3	WB	15.8	HAR	19.5	WB	18.1	RAJ	22.9
MAH	8.2	HAR	7.7	TN	52.8	PUN	55.7	RAJ	14.9	BIH	17.7	KER	16.5	BIH	20.2
PUN	7.9					KER	51.4	KER	14.8			GUJ	15.4	KER	19.5
						MP	46.4	GUJ	14.5			RAJ	15.2	GUJ	17.4
								HAR	12.3			HAR	12.4		
								MP	11.9						
AP	7.8	AP	7.3	AP	49.8	AP	45.0	AP	11.8	AP	17.2	AP	12.1	AP	16.9
RAJ	6.8	PUN	7.1	KER	49.7	RAJ	40.1	MAH	11.3	KER	16.9	MP	12.1	HAR	15.7
WB	6.6	RAJ	6.4	MP	46.9	WB	34.0	KAR	11.1	MAH	16.5	MAH	11.5	MAH	15.1
MP	6.4	MP	6.1	RAJ	42.1	UP	33.0	TN	9.0	GUJ	16.0	KAR	11.4	MP	14.8
UP	6.1	UP	5.9	WB	41.8	BIH	30.4			ORI	14.6	TN	10.1	TN	13.8
ORI	5.5	ORI	5.2	UP	33.4	ORI	27.3			MP	13.3			KAR	13.6
BIH	5.1	WB	5.0	BIH	30.4					KAR	13.2				
		BIH	5.0	ORI	28.7					TN	13.1				

Source: RBI Bulletin, Jan 2002.

tax/NSDP has not reached its earlier position. During 90-95 nearly 50 per cent of the AP state's aggregate expenditure was met from the state's own revenues – keeping the state in a better position than the middle-income states of Kerala and West Bengal and all the low income states. In the second half of 90s its situation was better than only low-income states.

During 90-95 in many of the major states the ratio of interest payments to revenue expenditure was higher than for AP. During 95-00 the ratio has increased in all these states, but the position of AP was still comparatively lower (Table 1). The proportion of interest payments in revenue receipts of AP also shows a similar trend.

Own Tax-SDP ratios are calculated taking data for tax revenue and NSDP figures from various issues of RBI bulletins and Indian Public Finance Statistics respectively.

The proportion of debt servicing in gross transfers during 1990-95 (Table 2) shows that in the case of AP it is only about 20% - much less than that for the major states except UP (17.7%). In 99-00 its debt servicing ratio was higher than that for Bihar, MP and Orissa only. The debt-income ratio at 22% in 90-95 was higher than that for three states only but has increased to 23% in 95-00 which was higher than that for five states (See also Appendix III).

The average annual growth rate of public debt of AP (17.5%) for the period 90-99 is higher than all States' average (15.4%). In all these cases the rate of growth of public debt is higher than the rate of growth of revenue (Table 3). With the growth rate of debt exceeding the revenue growth and the interest rates on borrowings going up, it is obvious that the burden of interest payments on the revenue budget will keep going up. This reflects upon the sustainability of debt accumulation.

Gross Fiscal Deficit: Major Fiscal Indicator

Fiscal deficit is the gap between the total revenue (revenue receipts inclusive of loan recoveries) and total expenditure (includes expenditure on revenue and capital accounts and loans advanced). In other words, fiscal deficit is the sum of revenue surplus/deficit, capital expenditure and net lending. (Most of the net lending, excluding housing loans, goes for developmental activities. Hence net lending can be considered as developmental expenditure.)

The proportion of gross fiscal deficit in net state domestic product (NSDP) in AP has increased over a period of time from 3.2% in 90-91 to 5.5% in 98-99 and declined to 4.5% in 99-00. The relative position of AP (Table 4) in this regard is much better than many major states. (See also Appendix IV).

However, it may be argued that the size of fiscal deficit is not important regardless of the purpose for which it is resorted to. Huge fiscal deficit on account of heavy interest payments, however, is not desirable as this is at the cost of prudent fiscal management. Hence it is necessary to look at the composition of fiscal deficit.

Table 2. Fiscal Indicators: Comparative Analysis (%)

Primary Deficit / NSDP				Debt-NSDP Ratio				Debt Servicing/ Gross Transfers				Capital Outlay / Gross Fiscal Deficit			
90-95		95-00		90-95		95-00		90-95		99-00		90-95		1999-00	
PUN	3.3	ORI	3.7	ORI	44.2	ORI	48.1	GUJ	42.1	PUN	125.1	KAR	85.9	KAR	41.6
UP	2.3	RAJ	3.1	BIH	41.6	PUN	41.4	PUN	38.9	MAH	79.4	RAJ	83.4	HAR	41.9
ORI	2.2	WB	3.1	PUN	39.9	BIH	41.1	HAR	34.6	HAR	60.0	MP	77.5		
GUJ	1.9	UP	2.3	KER	33.3	RAJ	33.4	MAH	34.3	GUJ	58.5	MAH	75.7		
TN	1.8	MAH	2.3	RAJ	30.6	UP	31.3	WB	27.8	WB	57.6	ORI	71.9		
KER	1.8	HAR	1.8	UP	30.2	KER	27.9	KER	26.6	RAJ	39.1	GUJ	70.3		
KAR	1.6	KER	1.8	WB	24.3	WB	25.8	KAR	24.3	TN	36.3				
		GUJ	1.8	MP	23.9	HAR	23.9	RAJ	22.2	UP	35.8				
				GUJ	22.4			ORI	21.5	KER	35.0				
				HAR	22.2			BIH	20.6	KAR	33.5				
								TN	20.2						
								MP	20.1						
AP	1.5	AP	1.5	AP	22.0	AP	23.2	AP	19.9	AP	31	AP	58.5	AP	40.0
RAJ	1.4	KAR	1.4	KAR	20.7	MP	22.5	UP	17.7	BIH	24.7	HAR	48.1	GUJ	39.7
WB	1.3	TN	1.3	TN	19.3	KAR	20.4			MP	24.3	KER	36.9	MAH	32.1
BIH	1.2	MP	1.2	MAH	15.5	GUJ	18.6			ORI	14.1	BIH	31.2	BIH	31.2
MAH	1.0	PUN	0.9			TN	18.3					UP	30.3	RAJ	28.3
MP	0.9	BIH	0.7			MAH	17.0					TN	29.1	MP	24.3
HAR	0.5											WB	27.8	UP	22.8
												PUN	27.3	ORI	21.3
														KER	14.3
														PUN	13.7
														TN	12.0
														WB	8.6

Source: RBI Bulletin January, 2002.

Table 3. Growth Rates in Public Debt and Revenue: AP, Southern States and all India for 1990-99 (%)

States	Public debt	Revenue Receipts
Andhra Pradesh	17.5	15.0
Karnataka	16.2	15.5
Kerala	17.7	16.6
Tamil Nadu	17.5	14.6
All States	15.4	14.4

Source: State Finances: A Study of Budget of 1999-2000, RBI Bulletin, January 2000, p.20.

Table 4. Gross Fiscal Deficit as a Ratio of NSDP (%)

	90-91	95-96	97-98	98-99	99-00
Andhra Pradesh	3.2	3.4	2.8	5.5	4.5
Bihar	7.0	4.1	1.9	4.1	9.7
Goa	9.4	3.5	3.5	6.6	-
Gujarat	7.4	2.8	4.1	6.3	7.6
Haryana	3.2	3.8	3.3	5.9	5.0
Karnataka	2.7	2.9	2.5	4.1	5.0
Kerala	6.6	3.7	3.2	5.9	7.7
Madhya Pradesh	3.8	2.5	2.1	5.2	4.5
Maharashtra	2.8	2.9	3.8	4.0	5.5
Orissa	6.4	6.0	6.6	9.8	11.4
Punjab	7.4	4.0	5.8	7.9	5.8
Rajasthan	3.0	6.2	4.5	7.9	8.0
Tamilnadu	4.1	1.8	2.3	4.5	4.6
Uttar Pradesh	6.2	4.3	5.8	7.8	6.7
West Bengal	5.2	4.0	4.5	6.7	9.5

Source: RBI Bulletin, January 2003.

Decomposition of Gross Fiscal Deficit (GFD)

At the sub-national level, deficit on revenue account is taken as a main indicator to study the financial status of a particular state. The decomposition of fiscal deficit shows that AP is relatively better than other States with lower proportion of revenue deficit (except in 96-97). However, this proportion has been continuously going up in AP compared to its own past performance (Table 5).

Table 5. Decomposition of Fiscal Deficit – A Comparison

(As percentage of gross fiscal deficit)

	90-95	95-96	96-97	97-98	98-99	99-00	2000-01	2001-02 (RE)
Revenue deficit								
Andhra Pradesh	11.50	30.60	113.80	29.00	47.00	24.80	49.20	40.80
Karnataka	11.20	-4.30	29.80	17.20	39.00	54.40	44.10	58.40
Kerala	44.00	30.90	41.70	46.50	67.40	79.90	81.20	67.10
Tamilnadu	72.30	24.80	45.10	64.30	71.90	81.80	67.70	59.80
All States	24.60	26.10	43.30	37.00	58.80	58.80	59.80	56.80
Capital Outlay								
Andhra Pradesh	58.50	100.20	4.70	44.70	24.30	40.00	37.30	50.00
Karnataka	85.90	85.10	59.30	75.20	56.00	41.60	46.10	34.50
Kerala	36.90	43.30	40.40	30.60	21.60	14.30	14.90	28.60
Tamilnadu	29.10	47.10	37.60	69.20	24.10	12.00	30.50	34.10
All States	55.30	58.90	47.10	51.60	31.10	27.90	34.80	36.00

Table 5 Contd....

Table 5 contd...

	90-95	95-96	96-97	97-98	98-99	99-00	2000-01	2001-02 (RE)
Net lending								
Andhra Pradesh	30.00	-30.80	-18.50	26.30	28.70	35.20	13.50	9.20
Karnataka	2.90	19.10	11.00	7.60	4.90	4.00	9.70	7.20
Kerala	19.00	25.80	18.00	22.90	11.00	5.80	4.00	4.30
Tamilnadu	-1.40	28.20	17.20	-33.50	3.90	6.30	1.80	6.10
All States	20.00	15.20	10.20	11.50	10.80	13.30	5.40	7.20

Note: '-' indicates loan recoveries were higher than loans advanced.
Source: Various issues of RBI Bulletins.

The proportion of capital outlay of AP to its GFD was lower than all states' average during 96-99 and better than Kerala during 97-99. However, during 1999-2000, the proportion of capital outlay in gross fiscal deficit was higher than in southern states and all states' average. The low percentage of capital outlay in Kerala and Tamil Nadu and the high percentages in AP and Karnataka are partly due to the heavy investments on irrigation projects in the latter. In this context the percentage of capital outlay to GFD in AP falling compared to Karnataka continuously since 1996-97 is disturbing. It has improved in 2000-01 and 2001-02.

The proportion of net lending in GFD of AP is higher than that for southern States and all States average throughout 90's except in 95-96 and 96-97.

However, if we compare the position of AP with other States in the entire nineties the relative position of the State has not worsened.

3. WB TARGETS VS AP'S ACTUAL FINANCIAL POSITION

In order to reverse the State's past poor record in growth and human resources development, World Bank has suggested an 'Adjustment Scenario' and the strategy relevant to strengthening AP finances which are based on

1. Significant change in the composition of expenditure from unproductive to growth enhancive expenditure.
2. Strong cost recovery efforts to raise adequate revenue to cover the necessary O&M needs and improve efficiency of resource use.
3. An improvement in tax system that broadens the revenue base and increases buoyancy through simplification and other administrative measures.

WB suggested a few reforms which would, if implemented, strengthen the State's exchequer. Here, it is examined whether AP has reached the targets set by WB.

For achieving a strong fiscal situation, any government has to set targets both on receipts and expenditure side. As Vision 2020 document has not given such targets, one can look at the targets set by the World Bank and see whether Andhra Pradesh has reached those targets.

The proportion of total revenue in GSDP for 96-97 as set by WB (Table 6) was 14% while the accounts show only 12%. In 97-98, 98-99 and 99-00 also AP could not achieve the targets set by WB. However, total revenue includes central shared taxes, the fluctuations in which affect total revenue of the State government.

Table 6. Targets set by World Bank and the Actuals Achieved by AP in Finances

(Percentage of GSDP)

Item	1996-97		1997-98		1998-99		1999-2000	
	WB projections	Actuals	WB projections	Actuals	WB projections	Actuals	WB projections	Actuals
Total Revenue	14.20	12.42	16.20	14.45	16.80	12.41	17.00	13.58
Own Revenue	8.30	7.22	10.40	9.29	11.00	8.53	11.20	9.25
Own Tax Revenue	6.90	5.42	8.90	7.43	9.40	6.93	9.40	7.28
Own Non-tax revenue	1.40	1.80	1.50	1.87	1.60	1.61	1.70	1.97
Total Expenditure	17.50	16.11	19.50	16.32	19.60	15.95	19.70	16.19
Revenue Expenditure	15.10	15.97	14.90	15.18	15.10	14.74	15.00	14.58
Capital Expenditure	2.40	0.15	4.60	1.13	4.50	1.21	4.60	1.61
Fiscal deficit	3.30	3.12	3.30	2.53	2.80	4.96	2.70	4.02
Primary deficit	0.90	1.08	0.70	0.29	0.20	2.66	0.10	1.47
Interest payments	2.50	2.04	2.60	2.25	2.60	2.30	2.60	2.56
Debt outstanding	27.10	16.94	27.10	18.54	26.70	18.74	26.30	21.10

Source: World Bank document (1997).
Calculated from AP budget documents.
For the year 1999-2000, Table 4, Annual Fiscal Framework for 2002-03, 29th January 2002, Finance Department, Government of AP.

Even if we take own revenue, AP could not achieve the targets set by WB. Decomposition of own revenue into own tax and own non-tax revenue shows that actuals of own non-tax revenue has crossed the targets set in all the four years 96-00. This is mainly because of interest receipts and dividends. The proportion of receipts from economic and social services show a declining trend. AP has to increase its receipts from social and economic sectors at least to meet maintenance charges. Own tax revenue targets could not be achieved in any one of the 4 years mainly because of the continuing prohibition policy. Even after the withdrawal of prohibition policy, the target could not be achieved. The proportion of own tax revenue to GSDP in 98-99 was 6.93% - the target fixed for the year 96-97.

As for the proportion of capital expenditure in GSDP, it is very negligible and far short of targets set. This would affect the growth of the economy, inflow of investments which would in turn affect the revenues of the State (though the economy is opened up and private participation invited). It projects a gloomy picture of the State economy. These targets are set by WB assuming that the economy would open up and invite private or people's participation in the economic activities. Hence care should be taken by the State government to step up capital expenditure.

As far as revenue expenditure is concerned, though its proportion to GSDP was more than the targets set for 96-97 and 97-98, it was brought down and is less than the target set by WB in 98-99 and 99-00 – an appreciable trend set by AP. If this were continued, AP would achieve revenue surplus and a substantial increase in the funds for capital expenditure and lessen fiscal deficit, borrowings and interest payments in future.

Vision 2020

The government of AP has taken various steps to restore the health of its economy. These include reforming the tax structure, rationalising subsidies, restructuring expenditure, improving expenditure management, inviting private sector participation in the infrastructure sector and framing growth-enhancing policies. However, the Vision document has not mentioned targets for tax, non-tax and other resources.

4. FISCAL REFORMS IN ANDHRA PRADESH AND MAJOR SUGGESTIONS

Fiscal reforms comprise reforms on the revenue side and also on the expenditure side. Reforms on the revenue side include reforms in tax revenue and non-tax revenue components. The main classification of expenditure includes revenue and capital components. Under each of this classification, the expenditure is categorized, on the basis of functions, into general, social and economic services. This section deals with the reforms implemented by the State government and analyzes the direction of reforms and suggests what more is to be done. As each component of either receipts or expenditure requires a separate and a thorough study, here an attempt is made to mention only a few important issues.

Tax Reforms in Andhra Pradesh

The ratio of State's own tax revenue (SOTR) to Gross State Domestic Product (GSDP) has declined from 7.94% in 1990-91 to 5.16% in 1995-96 (Table 7) mainly due to implementation of prohibition on the consumption of liquor. As the decline of Tax-NSDP ratio is the feature not only of AP but also of other states, the decline in these ratios may also be attributed to the increase in the component of service sector in state income, which is not taxed. However, after partial withdrawal of prohibition, the ratio has increased to 7.28% and 7.70% in 1999-2000 and 2001-02 respectively but not reached the level of 1990-91. Hence, it is necessary to explore what has been done so far and also the possibility to increase this ratio through other sources of tax revenue. The steps to be taken in this direction are to be looked at.

The remaining major state taxes, besides State Excise, are
Sales tax
Motor Vehicle Tax and tax on goods and passengers
Stamp duty and Registration Fee
Taxes on professions, trading and callings
Other taxes and duties
a. Entertainment Tax
b. Luxury and Betting Tax
c. Tax on Electricity

Sales Tax: Reforms towards VAT

For revenue receipts from any tax, the determinants are mainly tax rate, tax base and number of transactions, urbanization and administration and other factors. Sales tax rate structure, multi point tax structure, range of tax rates, concessions, exemptions and tax administration became, over a period of time, very complex, not only in AP but in all states. With the intention of making the Indian tax system more effective, broad-based and elastic, the GOI constituted the Raja Chellaiah Committee on tax reforms in 1991. Important among the recommendations regarding Commodity tax was implementation of Value Added Tax (VAT) and streamlining the tax administration.

Andhra Pradesh introduced a limited form of VAT on 19 commodities in April 1995 by adding a separate schedule to APGST Act. In December 1995, the Committee of State Finance Ministers, constituted by GOI, had drawn a programme for the reform of State Sales Tax in order to move towards a harmonized system of VAT laying floor-rates for major commodity groups, minimizing tax competition among the states and eliminating concessions and exemptions and evolving common assessment procedures.

Some State governments opposed the implementation of VAT expressing the fear of loss of revenue as one major reason while states like Maharashtra and Andhra Pradesh which expressed their willingness to implement VAT are postponing the same because they fear that introduction of VAT in some states only may not be beneficial.

Table 7. State's Own Tax Revenue as % of GSDP (%)

	90-91	91-92	92-93	93-94	94-95	95-96	96-97	97-98	98-99	99-00	2000-01	2001-02	2002-03(RE)
A. States own Tax Revenue (1+2+3)	7.94	7.51	7.63	6.62	6.13	5.16	5.42	7.43	6.93	7.28	7.67	7.70	7.78
1. Taxes on Income	0.08	0.08	0.08	0.07	0.06	0.05	0.08	0.08	0.11	0.10	0.10	0.10	0.10
Taxes on Professions, Trades, callings & employment	0.08	0.08	0.08	0.07	0.06	0.05	0.08	0.08	0.11	0.10	0.10	0.10	0.10
2. Taxes on Property and Capital Transactions	0.54	0.50	0.56	0.50	0.56	0.50	0.58	0.56	0.53	0.58	0.58	0.55	0.63
Land Revenue	0.09	0.07	0.15	0.11	0.09	0.07	0.08	0.08	0.09	0.09	0.08	0.01	0.06
Stamps and Registration Fees	0.44	0.42	0.40	0.39	0.45	0.41	0.48	0.47	0.43	0.48	0.49	0.54	0.57
Urban Immovable Property Tax	0.01	0.01	0.01	0.01	0.02	0.02	0.02	0.02	0.01	0.01	0.01	0.00	0.00
3. Taxes on Commodities and Services (1 to 7)	7.32	6.94	7.00	6.06	5.51	4.61	4.75	6.79	6.29	6.60	6.99	7.05	7.05
1. Sales Tax	4.28	4.12	4.17	4.02	4.10	3.70	3.91	4.94	4.57	4.99	5.31	5.16	5.13
2. State excise	2.18	2.00	2.08	1.31	0.64	0.10	0.07	0.93	0.80	0.84	0.90	1.10	1.16
3. Taxes on Vehicles	0.56	0.50	0.50	0.52	0.52	0.58	0.61	0.66	0.60	0.59	0.61	0.63	0.60
4. Taxes on Goods & Passengers	0.00	0.00	0.00	0.00	0.00	0.00	0.00	0.00	0.00	0.00	0.00	0.00	0.01
5. Taxes &Duties on Electricity	0.12	0.19	0.10	0.08	0.12	0.09	0.00	0.08	0.14	0.07	0.08	0.07	0.06
6. Entertainment Tax	0.11	0.09	0.09	0.07	0.08	0.08	0.07	0.08	0.07	0.07	0.04	0.04	0.05
7. Other Taxes and Duties	0.06	0.04	0.06	0.05	0.05	0.06	0.08	0.10	0.10	0.04	0.05	0.04	0.04

Source: Budget Documents of Andhra Pradesh and Economic survey, Government of Andhra Pradesh.

However, the exercise for introducing VAT in AP was taken up with the assistance of the Department of International Development (DFID), Government of United Kingdom and the preliminary work commenced in April 1999. A detailed implementation plan, which included two years' preparation and one-year assistance after the implementation, was drawn up. In the meanwhile, the Chief Ministers' Conference at New Delhi, in November 1999, decided to implement VAT in all States from April 2001. However, this deadline has been postponed by one year since majority of the states pleaded for time. As the second deadline came nearer, the states pleaded for some more time and again the deadline was postponed. Finally at the Chief Ministers' meeting in New Delhi, headed by the Prime Minister, on 18th October 2002 it was decided to implement VAT system from April 2003. But it has been postponed again and discussions are continued.

In a seminar organized by the CII, Montek Singh Ahluwalia said that once VAT is implemented it becomes easier to attract investments and the loss of revenue, feared by the states, can be compensated by this increased investment. This not only creates a source of additional revenue for the states but also meets the employment targets. The implementation will also ensure that free flow of trade between the states takes place and will have a decisive influence in the transfer of resources. Also, VAT would widen the tax base, add buoyancy to revenue collections and improve compliance as it covers a wider range of products and services (Chandra Sekhar, 2002).

International experience suggests that the development activity is fuelled by a transparent taxation system. More than 110 countries had moved to VAT and much of the success is directly attributable to this move. For India to attain such a pinnacle, it is imperative to implement VAT. The additional time given should be used to simplify and harmonize the sales tax system and move towards the VAT. It is important to ensure that the VAT that is actually implemented is conceptually sound and simple to put it in practice (Chandra Sekhar, 2002).

Motor Vehicle Tax and Tax on Goods and Passengers

Revenue receipts are determined mainly by the number of vehicles, tax base (types of vehicles and tariff or seating capacity) and administration and, at times, other factors.

The ratio of revenue from motor vehicles to GSDP of AP, though declined below 0.56% in the early 90s, picked up in 1995-96 and increased subsequently to 0.66% in 1997-98. It again declined to 0.63% in 2001-02 but was higher than in 1990-91.

The decline in the early 90s may be partially attributed to the Supreme Court decision. Till the early nineties, transport authorities used permits to control the number of commercial vehicles on different routes while considering applications and assessing traffic requirements. In practice, quotas did not operate for goods vehicles. After the Supreme Court decision in a particular case of Uttar Pradesh in 1992, however, permits have to be issued to all the applicants after collecting prescribed fees. Now, permits only specify design and operational parameters for transport vehicles and the market determines the vehicle operation. But violation of permit conditions can be effectively punished by taking a transport vehicle off the road through suspension or revocation of the permit without using extreme measures like cancellation of registration (Government of Karnataka, 2001). Private operation of passenger transport would result in market determined service levels and fares, tax payment at normal rates and observance of comfort and safety parameters.

This resulted in extensive operation of private passenger services. The tax rates for State Transport Undertakings were different and higher than for private carriages. MVT on Private carriages is levied as certain amount per seat while it is levied as a percentage of traffic revenue on RTC. The studies show that this rate on RTC works out to be much higher than that for private vehicles.[1] The owners of the private vehicles who have registered their passenger vehicles as contract carriages started operating their vehicles as stage carriages. The differential motor vehicle tax rates and unlawful operations of private contract carriages hit the revenue from this source. With this the revenue from motor vehicle tax schedule has been substantially distorted. Thus the tax base and tax rate of this source of revenue have become ineffective and consequently resulted in not adding revenue to the exchequer.

The concessions and exemptions, though a social welfare measure, eat away a considerable amount of revenue. Karnataka Tax Reforms Commission felt that concessional tax rates for school and collage buses are sometimes not passed on to users. If the tax concession is not fully reflected in commuter prices, institutions become the true beneficiaries. If similar concessions are given in Andhra Pradesh to buses run by educational institutions whose charges are higher than those of government institutions, they should either be taxed or concessions removed. The rationale of exemptions and concessions need to be focused.

Hence strict measures, which are so far absent, should be taken to check the clandestine operations of the private transport which would benefit the exchequer and also arrest the misuse of concessions and exemptions provided to the vehicles run by the institutions.

Stamp Duties and Registration Fee (S&R)

While the objective of Stamp Act is to collect revenue, that of Registration Act is to prevent people being duped by the seller / person who does not own it at the time of transaction. Thus there is a public policy that differentiates the principles that govern the interpretation of these two Acts.

Stamp Duties are of two types – judicial and non-judicial.[2] The bulk of the stamp duty is contributed by non-judicial stamp duty. Of the total revenue form Stamp duty and Registration fee, 90% comes from stamp duty and 10% from Registration fee. Nearly 80% of the stamp duty is realized from non-judicial stamp duty. Stamp duty on various documents is also categorized into specific and ad valorem. For transactions linked with the transfer of immovable property ad valorem rates are the norm while specific duties may be levied on documents related to the primary or final stages of a deal like an agreement of sale or the surrender of a lease. Avoidance techniques adopted by the public are usually tackled by shifting from specific to ad valorem duties.

Revenue from S&R is one of the important sources of revenue to AP, as in other states, next to sales tax and state excise. Revenue from this source assumes crucial importance in the present context of resource crunch. The proportion of revenue from stamp duty and registration fee in GSDP of AP was 0.44% in 90-91. Though declined in the first half of 90s, it increased to 0.48% in 1996-97 and was 0.54% in 2001-02.

If we observe the Budget Estimates and actuals for the period of 90s, we find that during 1996-2001 the actuals were nearer to budget estimates and at times more than that of budget estimates. Errors in estimation were negligible during the second half of 90s. This shows that the revenue from this source is upto the estimations and expectations of the department and also the government. However, in the presence of severe resource crunch, this department is looked upon as revenue raising branch. Hence it is necessary to look into the factors influencing this source of revenue. Three important determinants of revenue from S&R are: tax rate structure, tax base and the number and type of documents registered.

As far as tax rate structure (stamp duty structure) is concerned, there was no revision since 1986. Of all the instruments (Documents) conveyance (sale of immovable property) has higher tax rate, higher tax base and also higher number of transactions and (Sreedevi Venkatramaiah, 1998). The stamp duty on a sale deed, existing since 1985-86, is 6% for rural, 7% for municipalities and 8% for urban areas. Market Value scheme (this determines the value of the tax base of the S&R i.e., the value of movable/immovable property sold, mortgaged, leased or gifted), which was implemented with effect from 16/8/1975, revised at irregular intervals, determined the value of the tax base till 1995. Recently, i.e., in 1997, the periodicity of the revision of market value for urban areas is fixed every year with effect from first August and for rural areas every alternate year with effect from first April.

The general tendency of the registering public is to opt for other modes of transactions such as General Power of Attorney (GPAs), whenever the tax base is revised upwards for immovable property. The revision of market value guidelines in 1995-96 not only increased the market value for sale registrations but also broadened the tax base by fixing the rate of General Power of Attorney (GPAs) at 5% from a nominal amount of Rs.50/- and thus tackled the avoidance techniques of the registering public.

Regarding the number and type of documents registered, sale documents formed the most important instrument and with a relatively higher tax base and tax rate than for other instruments, followed by mortgages, leases and others.

Higher stamp duty and revision of market values on higher side at irregular intervals led to large-scale evasion of registration.[3] Besides this, the Registration fee, which is also ad valorem in nature, is an added burden to the registrants. Considering this, the Registration fee, which was 1% till recently, is reduced to 0.5%. This reduction is done mainly to lessen the burden on the registering public and also attract more registrations, which are kept away from registrations even after the execution of the documents.

In the context of liberalization, the Centre has taken the initiative of probing the stamp duty schedule as a whole and making suggestions for reform. This was done for removing fiscal disincentives and impediments to normal commercial activity. The NIPFP undertook a study of the stamp duty and registration structure in 1995. Subsequently a committee of State Ministers, headed by Dr. Raja Chelliah, was constituted which made extensive recommendations. Both studies covered the whole range of duties under State and Central Acts. A model Stamp Act has been circulated to states setting down tax slabs, categories and rates for both categories of instruments. Given the large proportion of revenues from conveyance in budgetary inflows from stamp duties and the high level of evasion, the Chelliah Committee of State Finance Ministers on Stamp Duty Reform recommended that the duties of all states should be brought within a narrow range of 5% to 10% to be lowered over a period of time to 6% - 8%.

AP has already introduced the computerization of the process of the registration of documents (CARD System) to minimize the delays in registration process and in returning documents. Fixation of photographs of both the purchaser and the seller on the sale documents with effect from 1st May 2002 is another important step taken by the department to control bogus registrations.

Some of the suggestions given by a Study in 1998 were followed by the Registration Department (Sreedevi and Venkatramaiah). Other important suggestions given by the Study, which are still valid for implementation to improve the revenue through this source, are:

The stamp duty on other major instruments like lease, certificate of sale, gift, exchange, mortgage etc is low in AP at 5% while in other states the duty is as per conveyance (Sale). It can be suggested that stamp duty can be levied on long leases as per sale conveyance.

In AP the number of slabs governing the levy of stamp duty on lease can be reduced from 8 to 4. Duty on perpetual leases can be considered as per conveyance like other southern states for two reasons: one to increase the revenue and secondly to discourage the tendency to opt for perpetual lease agreements which do not result in any income tax/ wealth tax problems.

Property transactions contribute a large part of the revenue of the department. With increasing commercialization and developments in the financial market the sources like leases are likely to grow in importance. Effort should be made to tap revenues from the lease agreements. It should be made obligatory on the part of the implementing authorities entering into leases like the municipalities, banks etc to recover adequate stamp duty. The discussions with the officials reveal that the revenue from stamp duty on leases in the Vijayawada area can go up to Rs. 5 crores as against the present Rs. 1 crore if effectively implemented.

The factor that blocks the flow of revenues is the restriction that no document shall be registered by the registering authority unless pattadar passbook relating to such land is produced before registering authority. Due to inherent defects in the records of rights the issuance of pattadar passbooks to all the landholders is not going to be easy. Due to pressing financial needs land transfers are taking place in significant numbers without registration even when passbooks are not available. This results in not only the government losing revenue but would make the land records incomplete and unrealistic. There are many landholders enjoying the defacto ownership on the basis of agreements, oral agreements, will and partitions etc. In these cases issuing passbooks is not going to be easy. In a field visit to Krishna District we have observed that there is a 40% fall in registrations due to insistence on passbooks and title deeds. It is recommended that the sub-registrar after satisfying that if the requisite forms are filled with the revenue authorities under acknowledgement, the registration may be completed and details may be informed to Mandal Revenue Officer for incorporating the same in the passbook to be issued.

Important Suggestions Relevant for the Present Situation

In continuation to the above point it is necessary to mention that updating of the land records is essential. It may be realized that in AP as much as 65% of the revenue comes from the registration of agricultural lands. Most of the ignorant public (includes illiterates, literates and few educated) after registering their purchased land/plot/site feel that their bought property is safe and do not know the fact that they should give for mutation regarding their transaction in Mandal Revenue Office concerned and see that their names and details of their property holdings are entered in the land records – not a hassle-free transfer. The ignorance of the purchasers regarding these procedures gives an opportunity for the old land-owner (as per the land records) to resale the same property to another ignorant 'would be purchaser'. Though ignorance of these rules is not an excuse, considering the level of illiteracy and also the levels of awareness in the public, the department should give much publicity in this regard and also extend their services by improving the inter-departmental services to the required levels. The inter-departmental coordination between

Registration Department and Mandal Revenue Office generates updating of land records, automatically tackles the problem of maintaining the land records and also increases the number of registrations augmenting the revenue resources to the exchequer. This step benefits the public, administration and the exchequer at high speed. This is not a difficult task in this E-networked State. This improves the efficiency of the administration in rendering services to the registering public and also attracts more revenue through registrations.

The village sarpanch should play his role very carefully while endorsing the land for purposes of sale of plots especially when a layout is modified and brought twice/thrice for endorsement purpose. This is to avoid further complications both at administration level and from public interest point of view. The role of village Secretary is also very crucial in protecting the layout of the land of the both public and private parties.

To safeguard the property purchasers, as most of the public (includes rural, urban, illiterates and literates) are ignorant of the rules of transactions, the State government/Registration Department should give much publicity or create an awareness among the public regarding the documents for which registration is compulsory, effect of non-registration of documents required to be registered and the procedures to be followed and the validity of the period of time. Educating the public regarding the legal matters such as Transfer of Property Act, Evidence Act and Limitation Act with respect to stamp duty and registration of documents is equally important to achieve the triple objective i.e., the interest of public, increase revenue through increasing the registrations under this source and efficiency in administration.

The problem of already existing improper land records, which arose because of some historical events, is getting further complicated because of the ignorance of the purchasers on one hand and insincerity of the local bodies (sarpanchs, village secretaries and MROs) on the other. Resurveying, though a difficult task, is not an impossible issue. Settling the disputed properties, resurveying the land[4] and the introduction of Torrens system facilitates the administration as well as benefits the public.

Taxes on Professions, Trading and Callings

States can levy a tax on professions, trades, callings and employments under Entry 60 List II (the State List) of the Seventh Schedule to the Constitution. The last revision of ceiling on profession tax was done in 1988, when it was raised from Rs. 250 (fixed in 1949) to Rs.2500/- p.a. through an amendment in clause (2) of Article 276 of the Constitution.

The main problem with the profession tax is that it is collected mainly from the employees in the formal or organized sector via deduction at source. For the self-employed, collection is weak. The government increased the rates tenfold in August 1996 – a step towards revenue augmentation. However, measures need to be taken to strengthen the administration to collect this tax from the self-employed professionals.

At present there are 20 categories of professions, which come under the Profession tax Act. Some of these categories are with sub categories. The tax rates also vary with slabs under each category. In view of the large number slabs, verification is also required to ensure that those who have escalated to upper slab are taxed suitably. Reducing the number of slabs may moderate the labour involved for this purpose. If tax base is widened covering the professionals extending information technology services and other upcoming professionals, the tax potential will increase and also the requirements of the local bodies are met.

The great number of taxpayers, nonexistence of computerization and the revenue unimportance of the tax is the existing feature, which needs to be dealt with. For example the cumulative number of legal practitioners (advocates) registered under Bar Council of Andhra Pradesh during 1991-2000 was 25047 and the tax amount, which the government failed to collect from them, amounted to roughly Rs. 2.5 crores for the year 1999-2000.[5]

In Andhra Pradesh, 95% of the profession tax revenue, after collection at the state level, is allocated to local bodies on the basis of origin principle. Increase of revenue through this source improves the financial position of the local bodies.

Reforms in Own Non-Tax Revenue

More than 50 percent of the own non-tax revenue comes from interest receipts (Table 8) from Departmental Commercial Undertakings, Public Sector Undertakings (PSUs) and other Undertakings and Co-operative Societies and dividends from Public Undertakings.

The economic reforms initiated in the early part of the present decade with a focus on private participation in the areas, so far treated as exclusive area of the state, had raised the issue of the relevance of the public enterprises.

A P State Electricity Board (APSEB)

Financial deterioration of APSEB began in 1991. The AP government felt that the tremendous drain on government resources was caused by subsidization of power sector. In 1998, after having discussions with the cross-section of people, the state cabinet moved forward with legislation approving the AP Electricity Reform Act of 1998 and was passed by the legislative assembly. Then the government moved forward to implement its key elements viz., restructuring APSEB into two independent corporations - AP Transco and AP Genco – in February 1999 and formation of an independent AP Electricity Regulatory Commission

Table 8. State Own Non-Tax Revenue (SONTR) as % GSDP

	90-91	91-92	92-93	93-94	94-95	95-96	96-97	97-98	98-99	99-00	2000-01	2001-02	2002-03 (RE)
C. SONTR	2.33	2.41	2.43	2.34	2.22	2.01	1.80	1.87	1.61	1.97	1.99	1.94	1.96
1. Interest Receipts	1.38	1.57	1.30	1.22	1.11	0.90	0.91	0.94	1.00	1.15	1.07	1.03	1.03
2. Dividends and Profits	0.01	0.00	0.00	0.00	0.01	0.01	0.01	0.01	0.01	0.00	0.00	0.00	0.00
3. General Services	0.13	0.14	0.12	0.09	0.11	0.13	0.12	0.10	0.08	0.08	0.11	0.12	0.10
4. Social Services	0.13	0.12	0.12	0.12	0.09	0.08	0.08	0.08	0.06	0.23	0.14	0.14	0.11
6. Economic Services	0.69	0.58	0.89	0.90	0.90	0.90	0.68	0.75	0.46	0.51	0.68	0.65	0.75
Major & Medium Irrigation Projects	0.15	0.03	0.15	0.13	0.15	0.12	0.07	0.01	0.00	0.00	0.01	0.01	0.01
Minor Irrigation	0.01	0.01	0.02	0.02	0.01	0.01	0.01	0.00	0.00	0.00	0.00	0.00	0.00
Power Projects	0.09	0.10	0.04	0.03	0.03	0.02	0.00	0.02	0.04	0.02	0.03	0.03	0.02
Road Transport	0.01	0.01	0.02	0.00	0.02	0.02	0.02	0.02	0.02	0.02	0.03	0.03	0.03

Source: As per table 7.

(APERC) in March 1999. In April 2000, AP Transco projected large losses in the coming year and proposed to cover 22% through tariff hikes, 14% through efficiency gains and 63% through government subsidies.[6] In July 2000 the government proposed a new law to curb theft of electricity. In one month, about 2 million connections were regularized (GoAP, 2002).

A P State Road Transport Corporation (APSRTC)

APSRTC, another PSU, is often viewed as loss making public sector. Main factors for this loss, as viewed by the government, are inefficiency of the PSU and excessive staff strength. At this juncture the Corporation is preparing grounds to implement Voluntary Retirement Scheme (VRS) to RTC employees.

So far RTC was bound to take the approval of the State government whenever the issue of hike in bus fare arose. To minimize the losses in this sector, the government has decided to give the authorization to RTC to increase the bus fares autonomously whenever fiscal emergency arises.[7] This concept is already implemented in Maharastra. However, checking unlawful operations of the private passenger vehicles would increase the revenue through motor vehicle tax and also improves the revenue position of the Corporation. But it seems that the government is making a move towards privatizing this sector.

Privatization of Public Units

The first phase of measures was quite extensive. As a first step, government had identified 19 small and medium size Public and Cooperative Enterprises for restructuring, downsizing, privatization or closure. Under the first phase of reform process, which was handled by Implementation Committee, an independent body overseeing the reform process, 4 Co-operative units were privatized, 4 units (corporations and co-operatives together) were closed. The process of downsizing or restructuring took place in 3 key corporations such as AP State Irrigation Development Corporation, AP State Agro Industries Development Corporation and Andhra Pradesh Meat Development Corporation[8], which are potentially of great significance even in terms of assisting private sector development and small-scale employment-intensive industry.

The Andhra Pradesh Government proposes to take up as part of the second phase of reforms of the public sector undertakings, about 68 enterprises including 10 co-operative sugar mills and two spinning mills. The State government has made its intentions clear in a "Strategy Paper on State PSUs" (GoAP, 2001), in which it declares that, since the return on investments made by the State is negligible, there is a huge loss of opportunity in terms of revenue that could be generated on such investment. Therefore, it proposes

- *To privatize all manufacturing and trading companies* (emphasize added) where private sector has requisite expertise, resources and managerial skills to turn around the companies and operate in a competitive market.
- Encourage market forces (private sector) to play in the areas, which are considered socially relevant but in which private sector does not have any interest as of now.

Thus the second phase of reforms would take up the remaining units. These include the APSRTC and AP Seeds Development Corporation. A large number of cooperative societies are also scheduled to be closed. The basic perspective of the state government is that " as against the declining efficiency of PSUs, private sector operations have emerged as an alternative force to reckon with, and there is no business that the private sector cannot operate", presumably better than the public sector. There is no ambiguity that with a profit motive, private sector may run the units efficiently but it is also obvious that it would concentrate less on the economic and social welfare. Privatizing/closing down of public units such as AP Seeds and APSRTC can have very negative effects on a cultivating and economically weaker community. A large number of cooperative societies, both producer and finance cooperatives, are also slated to be done away with, despite the fact that some of these have actually rendered important services to rural communities which are unlikely to be substituted by other private companies.

The resources released by privatization, the strategy paper claims, would be utilized for poverty alleviation, education, health and development of infrastructure and technology. But these resources would not last long.

Revenue Expenditure on Social and Economic Activities

Of the increased expenditure in 80s, the proportion allocated to crucial areas of education and health, that are necessary for economic growth in the long run, declined but the share for social welfare programmes increased. This trend has continued even in the reform period of 90s.

The proportion of revenue expenditure to GSDP, basically a recurring expenditure towards salaries, wages and maintenance, showed a declining trend from 16.51% in 1990-91 to 13.29% in 95-96. However, it increased to 15.97% in 96-97. Though it again started declining during 1997-00 increased in the subsequent years. The ratio of revenue expenditure on primary education to total revenue expenditure has declined from 7.64% in 90-91 to 6.69% in 2001-02 (Table 9) and the revised estimate for 2002-03 for this sector was 7.37% - higher than the 90-91 position.

The ratio of revenue expenditure on water supply and sanitation to total revenue expenditure increased from 1.86% in 90-91 to 3.24% in 94-95 but declined in subsequent three years. Though its proportion has reached 3.99% in 98-99, it declined drastically (i.e., below one percent) in subsequent years.

The ratio of revenue expenditure on primary health in total revenue expenditure has not shown consistency during 90s. It was 0.73% in 91-92 and then started declining reaching 0.62% in 96-97. It rose to 0.63% in 2001-02 (Table 9). The expenditure on key sectors of social development such as primary health and water supply and sanitation has not shown impressive trends.

Expenditure on developmental activities which include expenditure on nutrition, health, and education, is relatively productive not only because of its direct influence on welfare of the people but also because it is an investment in the development of human capital. Further, these non-profit oriented programmes are financed mainly through taxation - a non-market instrument. When resources are scarce, productivity of expenditure should be of prime importance to any State government. The effectiveness of these programs requires an appropriate combination of inputs taking into account the complementarities as well as substitutability between nutrition, health, and education programs.

Productivity of expenditure declines because of many factors such as uncertainties, lack of a well-trained staff, deficient or ineffective checks and balances in political and budgetary process. Inaccurate valuation of input prices and under-utilisation of existing facilities also indicate expenditure inefficiency IMF, 1995.

Table 9. Trends in Revenue Expenditure in Crucial Social Sectors

(%)

Year	As % of Revenue Expenditure			As % of GSDP			
	Primary Education	Primary Health	Water supply & Sanitation	Primary Education	Primary Health	Water supply & Sanitation	Total Rev Exp
1990-91	7.64	0.68	1.86	1.26	0.11	0.31	16.51
1991-92	6.99	0.73	1.83	1.11	0.12	0.29	15.87
1992-93	7.17	0.72	2.18	1.16	0.12	0.35	16.20
1993-94	0.00	0.00	2.16	0.00	0.00	0.30	13.86
1994-95	7.10	0.71	3.24	0.98	0.10	0.45	13.80
1995-96	6.46	0.73	2.34	0.86	0.10	0.31	13.29
1996-97	5.27	0.62	2.13	0.84	0.10	0.34	15.97
1997-98	5.90	0.70	2.76	0.90	0.11	0.42	15.18
1998-99	5.50	0.68	3.99	0.81	0.10	0.59	14.74
1999-00	6.65	0.78	2.20	0.97	0.11	0.32	14.58
2000-01	6.00	0.68	0.98	0.99	0.11	0.16	16.54
2001-02	6.69	0.63	0.70	1.10	0.10	0.12	16.48
2002-03(RE)	7.37	0.94	0.96	1.22	0.16	0.16	16.55

Source: As per Table 7.

To enhance expenditure productivity, the State government must utilise the inputs or resources (including human capital) fully with cost-effectiveness. Further, given their prices, inputs should be combined optimally - a technical as well as an economic issue. For instance, a shortage of medicine or nurses relative to doctors indicates inefficient health expenditure. Insufficiency of textbooks relative to teachers is an evidence of ineffective education programmes. High teacher-student ratio in the absence of high educational attainment also indicates inefficiency.

Because of the difficulties involved in valuing public sector outputs and measuring the efficiency of their production, the empirical analysis of public expenditures often assumes that changes in the composition of functional expenditure suggest changes in the public sector output mix. A change in the 'expenditure composition' is not synonymous with a change in the 'output mix of public programs' with increased productivity and a reduction in cost, but not output (IMF, 1995).

Capital Expenditure

The capital expenditure /GSDP ratio showed a decline from 1.39% in 90-91 to 1.21% in 98-99 barring the period 93-96 when the proportion ranged between 2 to 3 per cent. The sector-wise details show that the proportion of Capital expenditure on roads and bridges to GSDP showed some consistency while the corresponding proportion on irrigation, though increased in the first half of 90s, started declining thereafter and did not reach the 90-91 level of 0.92 per cent. The position of Energy also shows a similar picture (Table 10).

Major and Medium Irrigation

Performance of existing irrigation system in AP has caused concern, particularly in the case of major and medium irrigation schemes. Despite massive investments in the irrigation sector, irrigated area, particularly in tail-end, declined in several major commands, due to insufficient maintenance of irrigation schemes, poor recovery of water charges, limited user involvement, low quality of agriculture extension etc., resulting in a ayacut gap of 11.80 lakh acres (GOAP, 2001b).

Government of AP, in 1996, has evolved a three-fold strategy namely; (i) to achieve maximum irrigation by completing on-going irrigation projects; (ii) to rehabilitate and modernise existing irrigation schemes to bridge the gap ayacut in tail-end area; and (iii) to hand over the management and maintenance of all irrigation schemes in the state to farmers' organisations to ensure reliable and timely supply of water.

Energy/Power

The sector enjoyed a reasonably comfortable position till 1991-92 by meeting the operating expenditure from out of its revenues and state government was assisting the erstwhile APSEB only to the extent of providing the 3% return on net fixed assets as prescribed in the Electricity Supply Act. The decline since 1992-93 in its financial position was due to various reasons such as adverse change in hydro thermal mix, steep increase in cost of supply due to hike in cost of inputs, higher growth in consumption of subsidised categories like agriculture and domestic when compared to the categories like industries, stagnant growth in industrial consumption from the grid and shift to captive generation and high level of T&D losses. Till 1994, there was no direct cash infusion into the sector by the State Government while the assistance was mostly through a variety of accounting adjustments. It was only from 1995 onwards that either cash or cash equivalent assistance was extended to the erstwhile APSEB by the State Government in the form of write-off of loans, sanction of cash assistance and infusion of cash by issuing Government guaranteed Bonds.[9]

As envisaged in the April 1998 Act, as part of the reform process, the vertically integrated monolithic APSEB has been unbundled into two separate companies viz., A P Transmission Corporation Limited (APTRANSCO) and A P Generation Corporation Limited (APGENCO) and have become operational effective from 1st February 1999. With effect from 1st April 2000, Distribution business has been segregated from the

Transmission Corporation. Apart from the unbundling of the organisation, long-term improvements in their structures, processes and systems are initiated as a part of the reform process. An independent statutory Regulatory Commission was set up on 31st March 1999 to balance the interests of the various stakeholders and the utility (GOAP, 2001c).[10]

Table 10. Trends in Capital Expenditure On Core Sectors of Infrastructure

Year	As % of Capital Expenditure			As % of GSDP			
	Energy	Irrigation & Flood Control	Roads & Bridges	Energy	Irrigation & Flood Control	Roads & Bridges	Capital Expenditure
1990-91	2.24	66.19	6.92	0.03	0.92	0.10	1.39
1991-92	-25.98	88.96	8.47	-0.27	0.92	0.09	1.03
1992-93	1.47	63.42	12.75	0.03	1.15	0.23	1.81
1993-94	3.63	57.30	11.56	0.09	1.35	0.27	2.36
1994-95	49.81	38.41	5.26	1.39	1.07	0.15	2.79
1995-96	57.77	26.21	3.73	1.75	0.80	0.11	3.03
1996-97	-690.64	483.65	66.43	-1.01	0.70	0.10	0.15
1997-98	2.91	67.90	9.18	0.03	0.77	0.10	1.13
1998-99	1.28	58.03	19.08	0.02	0.70	0.23	1.21
1999-00	8.88	54.13	18.03	0.14	0.87	0.29	1.61
2000-01	1.95	47.32	33.57	0.03	0.80	0.57	1.69
2001-02	0.72	36.99	24.54	0.01	0.76	0.51	2.06
2002-03(RE)	0.52	38.56	24.65	0.01	0.85	0.54	2.20

Source: As per Table 7.

Roads

The sector-wise details show that the proportion of Capital expenditure on roads and bridges in GSDP showed an increase in the initial years of 90s and declined in subsequent years till 97-98. Again it started increasing in last years of 90s. The state government has conducted Strategic Option Study in 1994 (GOAP, 2001d) to identify the deficiencies in the road network and also to prepare plans to improve the road network in a phased manner on scientific basis. Based on this report, Road development plans were prepared to improve the main arterial network and also the high priority roads in the first phase. The funds required are proposed to be raised in many ways including through budget provision.

Externally Aided Projects

Presently there are 19 externally aided projects being implemented in Andhra Pradesh – a pioneer in state level fiscal reforms. Ten projects out of nineteen projects are financed by the World Bank. These projects cover health, forestry, agriculture, irrigation, power and roads sectors. The total cost of the ongoing projects is Rs. 16865.62 crores, of which the state's share is Rs. 3988.96 crores. As credit closing dates for some projects are in 2003, outcome of these projects has to be studied in future (Table 11).

Table 11. Status of World Bank Assisted Projects in Andhra Pradesh

Sl.no	Name of External Funding Agency	No. of Funding Projects	Share of the Funding Agency (Rs. Cr)	State's Share (Rs. Cr)	Total (Rs. Cr)
1	World Bank	10	7961.73	2919.98	10881.71
2	International Fund for Agl. Dev	1	149.25	36.25	185.50
3	Department of International Development	3	1392.19		1392.19
4	Overseas Economic Cooperation Fund	3	3178.08	994.44	4172.52
5	Netherlands	2	195.41	38.29	233.70
	Total	19	12876.66	3988.96	16865.62

Source: downloaded from various sources.

5. SUMMARY

Increased expenditure did not lead to an increase in the proportion of expenditure in crucial areas such as education and health, which are necessary for economic and social development. Instead, much is spent on welfare schemes resulting in revenue deficit, which, though moderate in early 90s, magnified in subsequent years. Consequently, capital expenditure was cut down which in turn narrowed the base for raising revenue. This resulted in diversion of borrowings to meet the revenue expenditure, interest payments and also debt repayments.

This feature is not specific to AP state alone. However, if we compare the position of AP with other states in the entire 90s, the relative position of AP has not worsened, though its position has definitely worsened over its own past performance.

While the state has taken a few steps to increase the tax and non-tax revenues, much needs to be done in a right way to augment the resources. The concept of reforming Public Sector Units has unfortunately meant either privatisation or closure. The government should probe other alternative measures to strengthen the units. The government should concentrate, in order to minimise wasteful expenditure, on effective checks and balances in political and budgetary process. The efficiency of the government programmes also requires appropriate combination of inputs for relevant programmes taking into account the complementarities, as well as substitutability, between the programmes.

Notes

1 Ramachandraiah and Patnaik, 2002
2 Judicial stamp duties are collected under Court Fee Act. The receipts under this mainly are court fee realized in the form of stamps, fines and penalties and miscellaneous receipts. Under the Constitution, powers to levy non-judicial stamp duties are distributed between Central and State governments. Entry 91 of the Central list empowers the Center to determine rates of stamp duties for the documents regularly used for commercial, banking and industrial transactions, for which rate uniformity is desirable. In Entry 63 of List II, States have been given exclusive powers to fix rates of stamp duty for all other documents.
3 The additional burden on the purchaser in AP is payment of transfer duty of 5%, which, though collected by the Registration Department, goes to local bodies.
4 AP is the only State in the country which has opened up Cadastral Surveys and building up accurate, fully computerized Land Information System. This will help to arrive at a viable, speedy, economical and accurate procedure for rebuilding uptodate Cadastral records on a large scale, in ready to maintain Digital Format. Government in their G.O. Ms.No.626 Rev(SS)Dept Dt. 24/8/98 have accorded administrative approval for a total cost of Rs. 68.7 lakhs for conducting Experimental Resurvey in 3 districts of Karimnagar, Guntur and Chittor. Subsequently the cost of the project was worked out to be Rs. 102.55 lakhs. This includes the cost of Resurvey, computerization and providing outputs by the private agencies and procurement of hardware and software for the 3 selected Mandals. This is a state scheme. The work began in Nov. 2001.
5 The number of legal practitioners is calculated from the Electoral role, Bar Council of the State of AP, Hyderabad 2000. Levy of tax is taken from Profession Tax Act.
6 The World Bank Group: 'India: Power Sector Reform in Andhra Pradesh', participation in macro economic policies case studies, accessed from http://www.worldbank.org/participation/web/webfiles/indiapower.htm.
7 *Eeenadu* daily newspaper, 17th September, 2002.
8 *The Economic Times* daily dated 1st Nov 2002.
9 Government of Andhra Pradesh (2001): "Strategy Paper on Power", p.1.
10 *Ibid*, p.7.

Reference

Bar Council of Andhra Pradesh (2002), *Electoral Roll*, Hyderabad.

Chandra Sekhar, Y. (2002), "Sales Tax Reform: Towards Transparency", *Analyst*, March.

GoAP (1999), *Vision 2020*, Government of Andhra Pradesh, Hyderabad.

————(2001a), "Strategy Paper on Public Sector Reform and Privatisation of State Owned Enterprises in Andhra Pradesh", Department of Public Enterprises, Government of Andhra Pradesh, Hyderabad.

———— (2001b), "Strategy Paper on Irrigation Development", Irrigation and C.A.D. Department, Government of Andhra Pradesh, Hyderabad.

——— (2001c), "Strategy Paper on Power", Energy Department, Government of Andhra Pradesh, Hyderabad.

——— (2001d), "Strategy Paper on Infrastructure", Government of Andhra Pradesh, Hyderabad.

——— (2002), "Annual Fiscal Framework 2002-03", Finance Department, Government of Andhra Pradesh, Hyderabad.

Government of Karnataka (2001), "Motor Vehicle Tax", in *Tax Reforms Commission*', (Report I).

International Monetary Fund (1995), *Unproductive Public Expenditure: A Pragmatic Approach to Policy Analysis,* Fiscal Affairs Department, Pamphlet Series No.48, Washington, D.C.

Ramachandraiah, C and A.K.Patnaik (2002), "Making the Public Sector Crumble: The Case of APSRTC", in Jos Mooij (ed), *Politics of Economic Reforms in India (forthcoming).*

Reserve Bank of India (2000), *State Finances: A Study of Budgets of 1999-2000,* Mumbai.

———(2002), *State Finances: A Study of Budgets of 2001-02,* Mumbai.

———(2003), *State Finances: A Study of Budgets of 2002-03,* Mumbai.

Sreedevi, N.and P.Venkatramaiah (1998), "Revenue from Stamp Duty and Registration Fee in Andhra Pradesh: A Report", (submitted to the Department of Registration and Stamps) Centre For Economic and Social Studies, Hyderabad.

The World Bank Group (no date), "India: Power Sector Reform in Andhra Pradesh", participation in macro economic policies case studies. Accessed from www.worldbank.org/participation/web/webfiles/indiapower.htm.

The World Bank (1997), *Andhra Pradesh: Agenda for Economic Reforms,* Country Operations, Industry & Finance Division, Report No. 15901-IN, January 16.

APPENDIX - I

Public Debt of Andhra Pradesh

Year	Debt Raised (Cr)	Debt Repaid (Cr)	Net Debt (Cr)	Repayment/ Debt Raised (%)	GSDP (Cr)	Debt Raised /GSDP (%)	Repayment/ GSDP (%)
90-91	1069.93	217.88	852.05	20.36	33336.22	3.21	0.65
91-92	1441.97	394.45	1047.52	27.35	40659.40	3.55	0.97
92-93	1412.74	256.73	1156.01	18.17	44395.14	3.18	0.58
93-94	1956.16	329.41	1626.75	16.84	57867.00	3.38	0.57
94-95	2461.90	746.68	1715.22	30.33	68923.00	3.57	1.08
95-96	3650.45	1756.42	1894.03	48.12	79854.00	4.57	2.20
96-97	4429.08	2616.17	1812.91	59.07	90147.00	4.91	2.90
97-98	6232.40	3824.21	2408.19	61.36	95782.00	6.51	3.99
98-99	9875.30	6273.63	3601.67	63.53	114937.00	8.59	5.46
99-00	13165.11	8449.57	4715.54	64.18	123719.00	10.64	6.83
2000-01	15097.55	10773.18	4324.37	71.36	137602.00	10.97	7.83
2001-02	18608.19	13232.63	5375.56	71.11	150050.00	12.40	8.82
2002-03(RE)	12069.15	6876.67	5192.48	56.98	164742.00	7.33	4.17

Note: all figures are actuals;
Source: As per Table 7.

APPENDIX - II

Direction of Public Debt Spent - Andhra Pradesh

(Rs.Cr)

Year	Public debt		Revenue Deficit	Capital Expenditure	Net Lending	Fiscal Deficit (3+4+5)	Debt repaid +Fiscal Deficit (col 2+col 6)
	Raised	Repaid					
	1	2	3	4	5	6	7
90-91	1069.93	217.88	157.60	461.91	347.56	967.07	1184.95
	(100.00)	(20.36)	(14.73)	(43.17)	(32.48)	(90.39)	(110.75)
91-92	1441.97	394.45	169.57	419.21	546.53	1135.32	1529.77
	(100.00)	(27.35)	(11.76)	(29.07)	(37.90)	(78.73)	(106.09)
92-93	1412.74	256.73	123.81	802.95	642.54	1569.30	1826.03
	(100.00)	(18.17)	(8.76)	(56.84)	(45.48)	(111.08)	(129.25)
93-94	1956.16	329.42	-232.28	1365.96	699.51	1833.19	2162.61
	(100.00)	(16.84)	(-11.87)	(69.83)	(35.76)	(93.71)	(110.55)
94-95	2461.90	746.69	727.74	1921.61	-300.83	2348.52	3095.21
	(100.00)	(30.33)	(29.56)	(78.05)	(-12.22)	(95.39)	(125.72)
95-96	3650.45	1756.42	738.79	2422.20	-744.17	2416.81	4173.23
	(100.00)	(48.12)	(20.24)	(66.35)	(-20.39)	(66.21)	(114.32)
96-97	4429.08	2616.16	3199.05	131.38	-518.90	2811.53	5427.69
	(100.00)	(59.07)	(72.23)	(2.97)	(-11.72)	(63.48)	(122.55)
97-98	6232.40	3824.21	703.19	1086.00	638.56	2427.76	6251.97
	(100.00)	(61.36)	(11.28)	(17.43)	(10.25)	(38.95)	(100.31)
98-99	9875.30	6273.61	2684.05	1385.23	1636.28	5705.57	11979.18
	(100.00)	(63.53)	(27.18)	(14.03)	(16.57)	(57.78)	(121.30)
99-00	13165.11	8449.57	1233.25	1992.23	1750.92	4976.40	13425.97
	(100.00)	(64.18)	(9.37)	(15.13)	(13.30)	(37.80)	(101.98)
2000-01	15097.56	10773.18	3595.12	2319.62	987.20	6901.94	17675.12
	(100.00)	(71.36)	(23.81)	(15.36)	(6.54)	(45.72)	(117.07)
2001-02	18608.19	13232.63	2881.28	3090.96	750.88	6723.12	19955.75
	(100.00)	(71.11)	(15.48)	(16.61)	(4.04)	(36.13)	(107.24)
2002-03 (RE)	12069.15	6876.67	3165.67	3627.06	548.65	7341.38	14218.05
	(100.00)	(56.98)	(26.23)	(30.05)	(4.55)	(60.83)	(117.80)

Note: The amount (column 7) over and above debt raised (column 1) is financed through Public Account.

'-' sign indicates revenue surplus in column 3 and loan recoveries column 5.

Figures in the parentheses are percentages to the public debt raised.

Source: Budget Documents of Andhra Pradesh.

APPENDIX – III

Outstanding Public Debt/GSDP Ratio (%)

States	1995-96	1996-97	1997-98	1998-99	1999-2000	2000-01
Andhra Pradesh	18.99	18.74	20.85	20.80	23.25	25.62
Assam	28.13	27.65	27.24	26.75	30.32	34.00
Bihar	67.67	55.88	59.90	59.66	66.94	73.11
Gujarat	15.48	14.89	16.57	17.81	21.60	26.58
Haryana	19.40	18.29	19.74	21.81	23.94	24.50
Karnataka	17.60	17.41	18.05	17.59	19.65	21.14
Kerala	26.09	25.69	26.00	27.91	32.27	34.64
Madhya Pradesh	25.75	25.83	26.71	27.84	29.68	35.92
Maharastra	11.58	12.13	13.32	14.56	15.75	18.70
Orissa	35.32	40.99	39.15	44.16	50.46	60.50
Punjab	35.30	35.02	35.35	37.43	37.94	40.66
Rajasthan	25.74	24.82	25.66	28.93	35.84	40.09
Tamil Nadu	15.99	15.85	15.71	16.45	18.71	20.89
Uttar Pradesh	28.21	26.70	29.25	31.50	35.24	36.70
West Bengal	20.85	22.14	22.50	24.77	28.93	33.69
All 15 States	22.05	21.79	22.90	24.30	27.33	30.69

Source: 1. *State Finances: A Study of Budgets*, RBI Bulletin, (Various Issues).
2. *State Domestic Product of Andhra Pradesh (1993-94 to 2001-02)*, Directorate of Economics and Statistics, Government of Andhra Pradesh, Hyderabad.

APPENDIX – IV

Gross Fiscal Deficit/GSDP Ratios of the State Governments (%)

States	1995-96	1996-97	1997-98	1998-99	1999-2000	2000-01
Andhra Pradesh	3.03	3.12	2.53	4.96	3.97	5.25
Assam	3.36	0.35	0.62	1.32	5.68	5.13
Bihar	6.42	2.74	2.92	6.12	14.42	10.56
Gujarat	2.43	2.75	3.49	5.39	6.38	7.13
Haryana	3.31	3.08	2.92	5.15	4.42	4.21
Karnataka	2.59	2.98	2.24	3.54	4.49	4.03
Kerala	3.36	3.47	4.88	5.36	7.26	5.62
Madhya Pradesh	3.41	3.50	3.03	5.96	5.03	3.71
Maharastra	2.63	2.76	3.32	3.49	4.81	3.76
Orissa	5.25	6.16	5.69	8.55	10.32	9.14
Punjab	3.53	3.31	5.09	6.78	5.12	5.70
Rajasthan	5.44	4.36	3.99	7.06	7.20	5.64
Tamil Nadu	1.60	2.73	2.05	4.01	4.22	3.70
Uttar Pradesh	4.12	4.64	5.54	7.54	6.52	5.63
West Bengal	3.65	4.14	4.09	6.15	9.12	7.79
All 15 States	3.03	3.10	3.35	4.87	5.71	4.92

Source: Same as Appendix III.

PART - II

INFRASTRUCTURE

5

Power Sector: The Rise, Fall and Reform

T.L. Sankar

1. INTRODUCTION

"Andhra Pradesh State Electricity Board (APSEB) has achieved a certain celebrity status as the only State Electricity Board (SEB) in India which has been maintaining steadily a profitable profile with a surplus after meeting its costs over the last 10 years. This has been achieved under the same environmental conditions under which other SEBs function and which have made it difficult for them to avoid large losses over the years. APSEB has achieved this while maintaining a rate of growth of sales of about 10% per year during a decade.

The main contributory factors for the good performance of the APSEB which merit attention are:

- The lean staffing in the generating stations and contracting out of several services including maintenance.
- Effective management through single phasing of the rural system during certain hours of the day and rostering of agricultural load in order to flatten the load curve.
- Modernisation of the work through extensive computerisation in power stations both for process control and general management. In distribution system planning computers are also extensively used for commercial land establishment applications in the Head Office.
- Setting up of Consumer Service Cell to improve consumer service.
- A system of almost annual revision of the tariff to catch-up with the increasing costs.
- Attention to human resource development and training for staff at all levels in job related skills and modern technical and analytical skills and computers right from induction level and all levels.
- Striving always to ensure that water in its hydel stations is not spilled and that the thermal generation is not backed down except in rare unavoidable situations like high grid frequency etc.
- Finally, more purposeful pursuit of power generation to augment the needs for the nineties including active enlistment of private sector participation for meeting the growing power needs of the state. (The

first such project in the country after the central government liberalising steps were announced had been set up by APSEB jointly with some of its bulk consumers)."

The above paragraphs are extracts from a review made by the Administrative Staff College of India (ASCI) in 1993 on the working of APSEB. But by the year 2000, the APSEB has slid to the last position among SEBs in financial management. It has recorded the highest losses among all the SEBs in the last three years.

This paper attempts to examine how this horrendous deterioration happened and what factors contributed to this. To study this, we have periodised the history of Andhra Pradesh electricity sector into three periods: period of rise: 1970-90; period of fall: 1990-96 and period of reform: 1996-2000.

2. RISING PERIOD (1970-90)

The high rate of capacity addition, rapid increase in sale of energy and good financial results characterise this period. The period could be 1970-90 (Table 1).

Table 1. APSEB Financial Results 1970-90

Sl No	Item	1969	1980	1990
1	Generation capacity	615	1888	4542
1a	% increase per year in the intervening period	12.5	10.9	11.5
2	Energy generated (MU)	2277	6493	15024
2a	% increase per year in the intervening period	11.3	10	8.8
3	Energy purchase (MU)	28	104	4047
3a	Energy purchase as % availability	1.2	1.5	21.2
4	Available energy (MU) (2+3)	2305	6597	19071
4a	% increase per year of available energy	14.5	10.1	11.2
5	Energy Sales (MU)	1638	4870	14628
6	Energy loss %	28.9	26.2	23.3
7	Total income by power sale (Rs. crores)	28.2	174.9	1016.0
8	Total Expenditure (Rs. crores)	28.8	174.9	1013.5
9	Surplus (+) / Deficit (-) (Rs. crores)	(-) 0.6	--	2.5

MU : Million Kwh

It is noteworthy that roughly around the middle (1975) when many SEBs started incurring losses, APSEB was financially comfortable upto 1990 and for even a year beyond. During the period (1970-90) the expenditure rose at the rate of 18.5 per cent, while income by sale of power increased by 18.6 per cent. During this period, the Consumer Price Index (CPI) rose by 18.8%. This record was maintained by adopting good commercial practices and keeping a high level of efficiency in generation, transmission and distribution.

It is interesting to see the changes in the composition of the consumers in the Table 2.

Table 2. Consumer Composition, APSEB: 1970-90

(MU %)

Consumer category	1969	1980	1990
Domestic	179 (8.2)	546 (10.3)	2079 (12.9)
Commercial	127 (5.8)	216 (4.1)	513 (3.2)
Agricultural	394 (18.7)	915 (17.3)	6294 (39.1)
Industrial (LT + HT)	1289 (59.0)	3556 (67.1)	7042 (43.8)
Others	197 (9.0)	64 (1.2)	165 (1.3)

Note: Figures in parenthesis indicate % share of the category in the total sales.

Up to 1980, industrial consumption accounted for nearly two-thirds of the total sales and contributed to the high average realisation inspite of highly subsidised tariff for agriculture which was compensated by relentlessly increasing the tariff for industries. This is because for the last four decades the principle of pricing power was based on a very rough approximation to "the ability to pay" principle. By 1990, agriculture became a very important sector among consumers and occupied a space almost equal to industries. What happened as a consequence is traced in the next section. In the event, however, APSEB was financially comfortable upto 1985 and from then on a small gap emerged between average cost of supply and average tariff and the small difference was made up by non-tariff income (Table 3).

Table 3. Cost of Supply and Tariff : 1960-90

Sl	Item	1960	1975	1980	1985	1990
1.	Average cost of supply P/Kwh	17.6	30.0	37.8	53.3	78.7
2.	Average Tariff P/Kwh	17.2	30.1	37.3	50.0	74.5
3.	Operating profit over cost P/Kwh	(-) 0.4	0.1	(-) 0.5	(-) 0.3	(-) 4.2

From 1st November 1982, APSEB adopted a non-metered flat rate for agriculture and the flat rate was Rs.50 per horsepower per annum for the irrigation pumps. This led to agricultural consumption increasing rapidly, which was aided by the generous financial assistance extended by Rural Electrification Corporation (REC) and due to high subsidisation. It can be traced by examining the relative share of agricultural consumption and tariff for agriculture & industry (Table 4).

Table 4. Statement of Gap Between Cost and Revenue

Sl No	Item	1975	1980	1982	1985	1987	1989	1990
1.	Share of Agricultural Consumption (%)	20.8	17.9	19.6	24.9	34.1	36.6	43.8
2.	Average cost of energy P/Kwh	26.3	37.8	44.2	53.3	62.0	70.2	78.0
3.	Average Revenue P/Kwh	30.1	37.3	44.0	50.0	59.3	70.4	74.0
4.	Agricultural Tariff	16 P/U	16 P/U	Rs.50/ HP/Yr	Rs.50/ HP/Yr	Rs.50/ HP/Yr	Rs.50/ HP/Yr	Upto 5 HP : Rs.50/HP/Yr 5 HP to 10HP: Rs.100/HP/Yr Above 10HP: 50 Ps/Unit (metered)
5.	Industrial Tariff P/Kwh	15-21 Paise	24-30 Paise	32-33 Paise	40 Paise	48 Paise	95 Paise	115 Paise

From 1980 the average revenue was lower than the average cost of supply. But the loss on account of this was corrected by having recourse to frequent tariff increases which essentially led to tariff increase to industries. During the period 1975-1990 the industrial tariff increased seven fold while agricultural tariff decreased. In other words, the increasing share of agriculture and supply at highly subsidised rate was not seen as needing government subsidy but was considered as capable of financing through cross subsidy from industrial consumers whose tariff was increased without any relation to the cost of supply. An abstract of the indices of average tariff for agriculture, domestic and industrial tariff is provided in Table 5.

Table 5. Indices of Tariff of Different Consumer Groups

Year	CPI	Average Revenue		Domestic		Agricultural		Industrial	
		Ps/Kwh	Index	Ps/Kwh	Index	Ps/Kwh	Index	Ps/Kwh	Index
1971-72	100	18	100	34	100	15	100	13	100
1975-76	154	30	166	41	120	28	186	22	169
1980-81	205	36	200	46	135	20	133	35	269
1982-83	247	43	238	47	138	15	100	47	361
1985-86	318	50	277	47	138	6	40	65	500
1988-89	404	61	338	54	158	4	26	102	784
1990-91	478	75	416	73	214	3	20	139	1069
1991-92	543	88	488	78	229	3	20	155	1192

The table shows that upto 1990 the index of average tariff was moving up slower than the index of consuming price index CPI i.e., the average price of electricity did not even increase as fast as inflation and the APSEB was not incurring any loss! A signal achievement.

After 1975-76, while the cost of power increased, agriculture consumers were made to pay less than even what they were paying in 1970-71. The trend of increasing supplies to agriculture and pricing power to agriculture at levels far below the cost of supply started in 1975. However, up to 1990 it was possible to some extent to meet the resultant deficit by cross subsidization by charging the industrial consumer a lot more than the cost of supply.

Technical Efficiency During the Period of Rise

During this period of rapid growth, the generation was not planned with reference to the needs as seen from the seasonal load profile. As agricultural consumption grew a heavy seasonal demand is exerted on the grid during the non-monsoon months from December to June or roughly the first half of each calendar year. During the non-monsoon season, hydel generation was carefully regulated with reference to the water available in the reservoir at the end of the rainy season so that the peak hours demand could be met from hydroelectric projects. This increased the operating levels of thermal plants which worked as base load stations. The Table 6 gives the hydel and thermal generation and power purchased in the two seasons of two years.

In the period January - June of a year, the demand for agriculture is more but the supply from state projects is limited because of the restricted generation from hydel stations. This led to increased power purchases during this period. Inspite of this, supplies were inadequate and this led to power restrictions. Load shedding started in 1977-78 itself in a small way but it kept increasing. In some years for over 3 to 5 months during January - June period, restrictions to large industrial consumers was as high as 60%. It is noteworthy that power restrictions were imposed in consultation with HT consumers who accepted it stoically (see Annexure 6).

Table 6. Seasonal Consumption of Energy

(MU)

Category	1 st half 1989	2 nd half 1989	1 st half 1990	2 nd half 1990
Thermal (Coal)	4139	2833	4626	3576
Hydel	2339	5485	2461	6379
Power purchased	2260	1535	2189	954
Total	8738	9853	9276	10909

The hydrothermal mix (Table 7) was the result of power sector aligning to the irrigation sector in planning and installing hydel power capacity, without paying adequate attention to the development of thermal power especially taking advantage of the coal reserves in Andhra Pradesh.

Table 7. Generation Capacity

Year	Thermal MW	Hydel MW	Share of Thermal Power in total power %
1970-71	237	268	46.9
1975-76	620	383	61.8
1980-81	1260	1038	54.8
1985-86	1193	2173	35.4
1989-90	1403	2422	36.6

On the operations side, APSEB made a name for itself in thermal generation. In the eighties the plant load factor (PLF) of thermal plants exceeded 60% and in several successive years APSEB was commended for achieving the highest PLF among SEBs and reaching close to 70%. APSEB also out-performed other SEBs in several other technical parameters during this period.

Summing up, this was a period of rapid growth of demand and supply and was characterised by shortages in most summers, but the finances were well managed by regular increases in tariff to catch up with the increasing average cost of power. Technical performance was of a high standard.

3. THE PERIOD OF FALL (1990-96)

The details of operational performance during 1990-91 to 1999-2000 are summarised in Tables 8, 9 and 10 below.

The period 1990-91 to 1995-96 was characterised by low growth of generation capacity. This increased slightly at less than 5% but energy availability increased by 8% as the additions during this period were mostly thermal with high plant load factor. Of the 1262 MW of additional capacity set up during this five year period, only 200 MW was hydel and the rest were thermal (coal and gas). As a result the cost of power increased sharply from 1994-95 onwards when the new thermal stations with relative higher fuel costs were commissioned. During the period upto 1994-95 the tariff rose in step with Consumer Price Index (urban middle class). Later, the tariff was not revised and the gap between revenue collection and revenue required suddenly widened and APSEB started incurring losses.

The Table 8 reveals how the finances were hit by not revising the tariff regularly as it was the practice in APSEB earlier. During the 1991-96 period, the tariff revision was effected on 01-11-1990, 01-01-1991 and 01-12-1992 which brought the tariff levels high enough to just meet the costs. But the next revision was in 02-08-95 i.e., after 3 years. During this period costs went up due to increased share of thermal power in the total available units, increasing fuel costs, and due to increased depreciation and interest charges (see Annexure 2).

Table 8. Relative Increase of Average Revenue and CPI

Sl No	Item	1990-91	1991-92	1992-93	1993-94	1994-95	1995-96
1.	Capacity including central station (MU)	4893	4973	5080	5926	6111	6155
2.	Energy available including purchases (MU)	21103	23508	25374	27865	29985	30924
3.	Total Expenditure (Rs. crores)	1148	1504	1921	2265	3049	3651
4.	Total Revenue by sale of power (Rs. crores)	1210	1531	1887	2173	2145	2288
5.	Total sale (MU)	16093	17750	19927	21186	22935	23400
6.	Cost per Rs/Kwh	0.71	0.85	0.96	1.07	1.33	1.56
7.	Revenue per unit Rs/Kwh	0.75	0.86	0.98	1.03	0.94	0.98
8.	Index of Average Rev/unit	100	115	131	137	125	131
9.	Index of CPI (urban middle class)	100	114	125	134	147	161

During this period, the employee cost and administration cost appears to have increased rapidly as the overall expenditure was Rs. 248 crores in 1990-91 which doubled to Rs. 451 crores in 1995-96. In effect, the costs increased at a rate far in excess of the inflation rate upto 1992-93, the revenue by sale of power was less than the expenditure increase. As a result, the deficit became Rs. 856 crores in 1994-95 and Rs. 1128 crores in 1995-96. Government of Andhra Pradesh chose to meet the deficit by subsidy instead of raising tariff. That was the beginning of the woes of APSEB. The tariff revision was not taken up in these years, because certain local level elections were to be held and during this period there were changes in the government at the state level.

During the period 1991-96, the consumption pattern also changed further in "favour" of the subsidized sectors of agriculture and domestic, while the share of subsidising sector industries declined (Table 9).

It is seen that upto 1993-94 the share of HT & LT industries was maintained but after 1993-94, this share as well as the quantity consumed by this category declined. Part of the reason lies in the tariff revision in December 1992 which increased the HT rates to very high levels. The Table 10 sets out the tariff as on 01-6-89 (which were corrected to some extent in 1-11-1990) and the real "revision" came in 1994-95.

Table 9. Category-wise Consumption of Power: 1990-95

Sector	Consumption (MU)			% share		
	1990-91	1993-94	1995-96	1990-91	1993-94	1995-96
Domestic	2079	3187	3276	12.9	15.0	14.0
Commercial	513	673	704	3.7	3.2	3.0
Industrial (LT+HT)	6285	8093	7798	39.1	38.2	33.3
Agricultural	7042	9022	11399	43.8	42.6	48.7
Others	174	211	223	1.1	1.0	1.0
Total	16093	21186	23400	100	100	100

Table 10. Revision of Power Tariff in AP: 1989-95

Paise/Kwh

Sector	As revised on 01-06-89	As revised on 01-12-92	As revised on 01-08-95
Domestic	60-70	70-145	70-245
Commercial	130	175-200	230-250
HT	100-115	190-200	245-255
Agriculture	Rs.50/HP/Yr	Rs.75/HP/Yr upto 5 HP Rs.250/HP/Yr above 5 HP	Rs.50/HP/Yr upto 75 HP

Source: The respective tariff revision orders as extracted in "Power Development in Andhra Pradesh (Statistics) 1999-2000" - Transmission Corporation of AP Ltd. publication in 2001.

It is noticed that the trend at every revision was to increase the HT tariff steeply, marginally change the domestic tariff, but reduce the agricultural tariff. A minor upward revision for agriculture was attempted by increasing the flat rate per horsepower from Rs.50/HP to Rs.75/HP but it was "corrected" due to the "political will" in 1995 to be back to where it was in 1989 ! No correction was made even for inflation !

During the period the actual metered sales decreased and unmetered supply (which is the sum of agricultural consumption and T&D losses) has increased (Table 11).

Table 11. Energy Available, Metered Sales and Unmetered Supply

Year	Total Energy Available (MU)	Metered Sales	Unmetered sales (Agri & T&D losses)	Unmetered supplies as % of availability
1990-91	20233	9808	10425	51.5
1993-94	26863	12164	14699	54.7
1995-96	29457	12001	17456	59.3

As the share of unmetered supplies increased it became easy for the SEB officials to "allocate" the share of agricultural consumption and the T&D losses as it suited their purposes. They "maintained" the level of

T&D losses at a reasonable level and the rest was booked under agricultural consumption.

Taking note of the rising criticism of the quality of supply to agriculture and the possible misreporting of the quantity of power consumed by the agricultural pumpsets, APSEB set up an internal taskforce of experts to make a proper sample survey of agricultural consumption. This taskforce came out with a finding that suggested that agricultural pumpsets consumed approximately 1500 Kwh per horsepower of connected load. APSEB itself corrected its data in the year 1996-97. By this, the consumption in agricultural sector which was reported to be 11399 MU in 1995-96 was corrected to 7835 MU in 1996-97. If that correction was made to the agricultural consumption in all the years from 1990 to 1995, the figures reported are gross over statements in the years from 1992 and by 1995-96, agricultural consumption is overstated by 3000 million units and consequently T&D losses understated by 6% (Table 12).

Table 12. Agriculture Consumption – T&D Loss Correction

Item	1990-91	1991-92	1992-93	1993-94	1994-95	1995-96
Officially declared % T&D loss	23.8	24.5	24.3	24.0	23.5	24.3
No. of Agricultural Pumpsets (lakhs)	11.93	12.74	13.98	15.05	16.06	16.43
Connected load (MW)	3760	4013	4414	4756	5077	5553
Agricultural consumption (MU)	6285	6972	7895	9022	10922	11399
Index of no. pumps electrified	100	107	117	126	135	138
Index of consumer load	100	107	117	126	135	148
Index of agricultural consumers	100	111	126	144	174	181
Corrected agricultural consumption (MU)	5640	6019	6621	7134	7616	8330
Corrected T&D loss %	22.8	24.7	25.8	27.5	31.4	30.4

During this period, distribution efficiency deteriorated not only on the technical side but also on the commercial side. The arrears of collection of the amounts billed arose especially in respect of the arrears from live connection. This reveals that the distribution staff had become lax in their collection which is normally made by using the powers to disconnect. It appears possible that some of the employees of APSEB colluded with the consumers and allowed the arrears to increase. The Table 13 provides the details.

As a result of such "comprehensive mismanagement" of the commercial aspects, APSEB which was a proud, profit making concern was made to become an organisation incurring the maximum losses and had to depend on the government to subsidise the power sector to the extent of Rs.1260 crores in 1995-96. The Table 14 illustrates the APSEB's financial deterioration.

Table 13. Arrears of Revenue in APSEB: 1990-95

Item	1990-91	1992-93	1995-96
LT	107	129	262
HT	260	277	329
Total	367	406	591
Debts pending in courts	204	189	176
Amounts due from live services	89	126	211
Amounts due for disconnected services	46	47	96

Table 14. Financial Results of APSEB: 1990-95

Item	1990-91	1991-92	1992-93	1993-94	1994-95	1995-96
Energy sold (MU)	16254	18198	19737	21746	23383	23905
Energy purchased	2984 (18.36)	5266 (28.94)	7502 (38.01)	8593 (39.52)	9456 (40.44)	9159 (38.31)
Purchase price P/Kwh			82.2	90.1	103.0	112.5
Cost of power P/Kwh	71	85	96	107	133	156
Revenue per unit P/Kwh	75	86	98	103	94	98
Commercial profit/loss (Rs. crores)			- 4	- 23	- 981	- 1255
Subsidy (Rs. crores)	39	70	0	0	944	1259

Note: Figures in the parentheses indicate the energy purchased as a percentage of energy sold.

In sum, during the period of fall, APSEB kept on increasing supply to agriculture and purchased power at high cost from all possible sources, which resulted in an increase in the average cost of purchased power as well as the share of purchased power in total supply. All this was done without any strategy to bridge the power supply-demand gap and retrieve the financial performance. During this period, inspite of increased availability; the HT consumers were subjected to severe power restrictions, as indicated in the Annex table.

As power tariff to HT consumers was increased rapidly (see Annexure 6) the HT consumers were forced to go in for captive generation. It is also likely that during this period, the theft by even HT consumers might have increased with the connivance of some of the delingnent staff of APSEB. Subsidy to APSEB was not paid in cash by the Government of AP but by adjustments such as conversion of debt into equity and this led to very severe cash flow problems and increase in payment defaults for the power and fuel supplies received.

The precipitous fall in the efficiency of managing demand-supply position and pursuing a policy of placating the vocal agricultural consumers without a well conceived strategy for correcting the situation, led to increasing financial losses which continued in the next period 1995-96 to 1999-2000.

4. PERIOD OF REFORM (1996-2000)

By 1995, the government became concerned at the fast deteriorating financial and overall performance of APSEB and setup a high power committee to report on Reform & Restructuring of APSEB under the chairmanship of Dr Hiten Bhayya and with only Indian experts*. This Committee gave its report within 4 months. The recommendations of the Committee inter alia suggested :

a) the demand should be made on a realistic basis and supply arranged on rational basis.
b) APSEB should be restructured into a Generation Corporation (Genco), a Transmission Corporation (Transco) and four or five distribution companies.

The Government of Andhra Pradesh accepted in principle all the recommendations but decided to seek World Bank (WB) assistance for designing the reform and restructuring of APSEB. The WB in turn engaged a large number of foreign consultants to advise on various aspects and the total technical advisory services through expatriate advisers is reported to have cost over Rs.130 crores, though a major part of which would be treated as a grant. The design was not very different from the recommendations of the Hiten Bhayya report. But these high cost consultancies resulted in the reform being delayed and it was only in 1998 that the Andhra Pradesh Electricity Reform Act was enacted and the Andhra Pradesh Electricity Reform Rules were issued in 1999. Andhra Pradesh Electricity Regulatory Commission (APERC) was set up with the appointment of the first chairman in 1999. APSEB was restructured on 1.2.1999 into APGENCO, which was entrusted with all the generation related assets and APTRANSCO which got all the rest of the assets which related to transmission and distribution. On 1.4.2000 the distribution function was separated from the transmission function.

In the wasted years from 1996 to 1999, there was a state of uncertainty in the APSEB. Workers were posed to oppose every move towards reform and the government adopted a policy of appeasement towards the employees. Employee morale and efficiency deteriorated steadily. The developments could be seen from an examination of the finances of APSEB and its successor organisations.

While expenditure increased rapidly, tariff revision was undertaken in August 1995 and August 1996, which led to an improved position of revenue collection by sale of power in 1996-97 and 1997-98 but declined very steeply in 1998-99 onwards. The Government for non-economic reasons delayed the revision again and resorted to it only in January 1999, just a few days before the appointment of the APERC Chairman.

When the reform process was initiated it was clear that the financial problems of APSEB were primarily due to –

(i) Increasing T&D losses which were camouflaged by "treating" most of it as agricultural consumption.
(ii) Irrational tariff setting which did not fully cover the cost of supply. The inadequacy of the revenue that could be collected on the projected revisions from time to time was sourght to be justified by pointing out distribution losses and poor quality of service.

The reform efforts should have first tried to correct these, or atleast map out a strategy for correcting these shortcomings according to a schedule. The efforts however, appear to have been directed in two directions as follows :

(i) To discuss with the workers the proposed reforms and to buy peace through softening all managerial controls and distribute largesse through pay increase.
(ii) To keep increasing the supply of energy into the system without concern for the deterioration such poorly regulated supplies were bringing to APSEB.

This could be analysed with reference to the changing composition of the consumer categories in the consumer profile of APSEB, (Table 15 and 16).

Table 15. Consumer Composition: 1995-2000

(MU)

Category	1995-96	1996-97	1997-98	1998-99	1999-2000
Domestic	3276	3801	4535	5090	5486
Commercial	704	795	927	1060	1142
Industrial	1194	1293	1382	1519	1603
Agricultural	11399	7835	9336	7969	10632
Others	223	285	374	472	525
Total LT	16796	14009	16554	16110	19388
HT	6604	6914	7216	7136	6824
Gross Total	23400	20923	23770	23246	26212

The details for the year 1995-96 is a corrupted version as the agricultural consumption has been over stated and was "corrected" in 1996-97. It is seen that from 1996-97 to 1999-2000, the three years when reform efforts were in full swing, the share of HT consumption got reduced from 33% to 26%, though the actual quantity consumed by HT consumers

Table 16. Percent Share of Different Categories of Consumers

Category	1995-96	1996-97	1997-98	1998-99	1999-2000
Domestic	14.0	18.2	19.1	21.9	20.9
Commercial	3.0	3.8	3.9	4.6	4.4
Industrial	5.1	6.2	5.8	6.5	6.1
Agricultural	48.7	37.4	39.3	34.3	40.6
Others	1.0	1.4	1.6	2.0	2.0
Total LT	71.8	67.0	69.7	69.3	74.0
HT	28.2	33.0	30.3	30.7	26.0
Gross Total	100.0	100.0	100.0	100.0	100.0

got reduced only in 1999-2000. This was not due to lack of supply. During these three years energy available increased from 33.6 billion units to 45.8 billion units i.e., by 36% (Table 17).

Table 17. Cost and Price in Andhra Pradesh Electricity Companies: 1995-99

Item	1995-96	1996-97	1997-98	1998-99	1999-2000
Energy generated (MU)	21765	24690	26265	27022	29632
Energy purchased (MU)	9159	8993	11881	13550	16137
Energy available (MU)	30924	33683	38146	40573	45769
T&D losses as reported	24.3	37.9	37.7	42.8	42.8
Total expenditure (Rs. crores)	3651	4197	5429	7054	7583
Total revenue by sale of power (Rs. crores)	2288	3286	3990	4169	4520
% revenue by sale of power to total expenditure	62.7	78.3	73.5	59.1	59.6

What really happened to all the extra energy pumped into the system needs some analysis. While availability of energy increased by 36%, the sales increased from 20.9 billion units to 26.2 billion units (a mere 25% increase) and the T&D losses increased. (There seems to be an attempt again in 1999-2000, to 'book' more energy consumption by agricultural sector). Inspite of it, it is seen that the marginal T&D loss, i.e., loss out of the incremental supply of energy in 1996-97 to 1999-2000 period is 56.2% as follows :

$$\text{Marginal T\&D loss} = \left[1 - \frac{\text{Incremental Sales}}{\text{Incremental Available Energy}}\right] \times 100$$

$$= \left[1 - \frac{5289}{12086}\right] \times 100 = 56.2\%$$

Of the sales, agriculture got the lions share of 52.9% and domestic 31.8% while HT lost 1.8% (Table 18). The sales were essentially to consumers who pay far below the cost of power while the share of paying consumers was very meagre in most categories and negative in the HT category. It is not surprising that in three years, the expenditure increased by Rs. 3835.8 crores, while the income increased only by Rs. 1233.9 crores. In these years, for every one rupee spent additionally APSEB (and later the successive organizations) got only 32 paise and lost 68 paise. This, in spite of a whacking big increase in tariff with effect from 1.1.1999 which did push the tariff to HT and commercial consumers. It did not have significant positive revenue effect, because additional sales to these categories was insignificant!

Table 18. Share of Incremental Sales 1996-97 to 1999-2000

Item	1996-97	1999-2000	Difference	% of Total
Domestic	3801	5486	1685	31.8
Non-Domestic	795	1142	347	6.7
Industrial	1293	1603	310	5.9
Agricultural	7835	10632	2797	52.9
Others	285	525	240	4.5
Total LT	14009	19388	5379	101.8
HT	6914	6824	-90	-1.8
Grand Total (LT+HT)	20923	26212	5289	100.0

The officials of the Andhra Pradesh power corporations (Transco and Discoms) plead that the years from 1996-97 were years of great turmoil in APSEB and that led to the deterioration. But from the consumers point of view hardly anything changed in the power sector as they had the same set of power bureaucrats interacting with them and apart from the change in the name of the organization in the bill received by them, there was no change in the officials dealing with them nor in their attitude towards them.

5. THE ROAD AHEAD

Given the background discussed above, privatisation seems to have become a distant goal. In 2002 end, it is clear that privatization would not happen till the completion of the general elections in 2004. The importance of sound business management and good corporate governance at the corporate level, inspite of a hostile political environment, should be accepted. The management of any commercial organization has to keep a tight rein on the normal operations of the organization and should not allow the external environment to unduly affect its working. APSEB, from the time the reform was initiated, appears to have paid decreasing attention to the normal maintenance and commercial functions. The morale of staff has been allowed to deteriorate. Urgent action is therefore, needed to tighten the internal control procedures and introduce a system of innovative rewards and penalties with assigned accountability at all levels. Introducing professionals laterally in Genco and Transco may prove to be difficult. Special efforts should be made to send selected officials at different levels to short-term and long-term training programmes to equip them with the requisite management skills.

The next vexed questions are the T&D loss, its verification and arranging cross-subsidisation. These are interrelated. The cross-subsidy question and subsidy for agriculture will continue to remain a sore issue as long as subsidy and higher tariff for industrial/commercial consumers is arranged through the distribution company. It can be remedied only by making such subsidies directly payable through coupons given to consumers. This needs some explanation. Currently each agricultural pumpset is subsidised annually to the extent of Rs.11,000/-. This subsidy is financed partly by cross-subsidisation from industry/commercial consumers and partly by subvention given to the government. The extent of cross-subsidy from industries and subvention from government is calculated ex-ante each year on the report (tariff filing) by the distribution companies. There is no check on how much the farmers really get.

Therefore metering of agricultural supplies at the pump level is essential both in the interests of ensuring that the farmers get their entitlement and also to ensure that the distribution companies are able to plan the supply according to the needs in each area and improve the distribution system infrastructure. But farmers are reluctant to get meters fixed because of the fear that the fixing of meters is only a prelude to increasing the tariffs. If, on socio-economic considerations, we decide that agriculture, especially the small and marginal farmers and farmers in drought prone areas, are to get supplies at subsidised rates, we should announce a 10 year tariff profile for such farmers and a slightly higher (but still subsidised rate) for other farmers and announce it. With this they could be persuaded to get meters fixed. Further, the empowerment will carry conviction, if, for all metered supply, the farmers are given in advance coupons to the extent of the entitled quantity. If 20 paise is the rate for the first, say, 1000 units and 30 paise for the 1000 to 3000 units coupons could be sold to the farmers at this rate so that they could use this to make payment. These are for units consumed and not subsidised as far as the supplier is concerned. As coupons are issued in public to only those who have an agreement for regular agricultural supply and have fixed a meter, the misuse can be totally avoided. Coupons purchased from others cannot be misused under this scheme. These coupons should be encashable at any bank by the distribution companies for the value fixed by the regulator. Then the farmer can insist on getting good service as he is paying for the metered supply. It is also possible that by reducing the T&D loss and operating expenses gradually the cost of power can come down.

The misunderstandings about the "subsidy" to agriculture should also be removed. Agricultural supply is not made during the peak hours. Therefore there is a good case for their cost-to-serve completely excluding the fixed cost. Further more, agricultural supplies are interruptible supplies, that is, supplies which are interrupted at any time by the distribution companies with reference to their technical and administrative convenience and not with reference to the farmers convenience. Such interruptible supplies are given hardly 50% of the normal rates. Therefore, even the correct "cost-to-serve" of agriculture, calculated on objective economic considerations would give a tariff which is almost half of the average cost of supply. With reference to this if the element of subsidy to be given is calculated, it would be for less than what is now claimed.

On the general issue of governance at the distribution level there is need to rethink the restructuring arrangements made by forming four distribution companies in AP. The distribution companies which have been formed are too large and unwieldy. They should be made much smaller. Each Discom should not exceed more than about 10 lakh consumers or a turnover of Rs.1000 crore. This would make the new Discoms, size-wise, equal to most of the distribution companies in the world. Even these small Discoms should arrange for the distribution function to be separated from the supply functions. The supply functions i.e., billing, collection and routine maintenance, can be handed over to specified consumer groups or consumer approved entities like companies, cooperatives or societies. They would be in charge of maintenance below 11 kv, (without undertaking capital works) and billing and collection, fuse call attendance and extension of line with material drawn from DISCOMs.

The Transco/Discom executives and workers should be trained to become electricity entrepreneurs to take out partial ownership and management of small Discoms and supply companies. The state government and financing institutions should contribute funds and technical assistance to set up "incubation companies" on the lines of the IT industry, to bring about this change among electricity executives and make them entrepreneurs.

The government has declared the policy to achieve universal electrification by a definite date, i.e., 2012 A.D. They should involve workers, executives, panchayats, civil society and NGOs in working out the details. Reform should be projected as the means to provide adequate power of acceptable quality at affordable prices to all consumers and not as one of privatisation alone! Talk of reform should not result in the neglect of normal functions. The road to "power for all" is a long one, but Andhra Pradesh can do it provided, the emphasis of reforms is changed form finance to people.

Annexure-1
Details of Expenditure

Sl No	Item	1990-91	1991-92	1992-93	1993-94	1994-95	1995-96	1996-97	1997-98	1998-99	1999-2000
1.	Total Expenditure (Rs.Crores)	1148	1504	1921	2265	3049	3651	4197	5429	7056	7583
2.	Energy available (MU)	20233	22550	24415	26863	28847	29457	32092	36358	37268	40804
3.	Cost of Av. Power (Rs./Kwh)	0.567	0.666	0.787	0.843	1.057	1.239	1.308	1.493	1.893	1.858
4.	Expenditure	1196	1575	2055	2433	3223	3869	4457	5763	7170	7813
	a) General Exp. as %	26.0	25.2	24.6	26.1	23.1	28.9	30.6	29.4	40.8	45.4
	b) Purchases Exp. as %	18.5	25.2	28.8	30.5	29.0	25.4	23.5	30.7	29.0	30.9
	c) Repair of Ma Exp. as %	4.8	4.6	3.9	4.0	3.3	2.9	3.5	2.9	1.6	1.8
	d) Employee Cost Exp. as %	16.6	15.0	13.0	12.2	11.9	10.4	10.1	9.0	7.7	8.5
	e) Admn. & General Exp. as % Expenditure	3.6	3.4	3.1	3.1	3.9	2.1	3.5	3.2	5.9	2.9
	f) Depreciation Exp. as %	7.9	7.3	7.2	7.1	8.9	9.0	9.4	7.6	3.8	3.9
5.	Int. of Fin. Exp. as %	22.6	19.2	19.3	76.9	20.6	21.2	19.6	17.3	11.2	6.5

Annexure-2
Andhra Pradesh Power Sector

Sl No	Item	1956	1961	1969	1980	1990	1995	2000
1	Total Generating Capacity / MW	99	213	615	1888	4542	5111	5657
	1.a. Thermal		89	342	1050	1403	2453	2955
	1.b. Hydel		124	273	838	2422	2658	2672
2	Generation Total (MU)	239	784	2277	6493	15024	20529	29632
	2.a. Thermal		174	1218	3268	7222	10842	21499
	2.b. Hydel		610	1059	3225	7802	9687	8133
3	Purchase Power	--	--	28	104	4047	9456	16137
	3.a. NTPC/Central Power Co.		--	--	--	3550	8449	7897
	3.b. Others		--	28	104	497	1007	8240
4	Energy Sales Total MKwh	186	601	1638	4870	14628	23383	27604
	4.a. LT (MKwh)				2050	8701	16172	19387
	4.b. HT (MKwh)				2820*	5927*	7211*	8217*
5	a. Losses MKwh				1326	3714	5464	16143
	b. % of available				21.40	20.25	18.94	36.90
	HT Sales within the state				2502*	5734*	6763*	6824*
6	Available power (2 + 3)	239	784	2305	6597	19071	29985	45769
7	4 ÷ 6 (%)	78	77	71	74	76	78	60
8	Sales % per increase		25	13	11.5	11.5	9.8	3.5
9	Available % of income		25	14.2	10.0	11.2	9.5	9.0

Annexure-3
Agricultural Consumption Correction

Sl No	Item	1990-91	1991-92	1992-93	1993-94	1994-95	1995-96	1996-97	1997-98	1998-99	1999-2000
1	Energy available (MU)	20233	22550	24415	26863	28847	29457	32092	36358	37268	40804
2	Energy Sales (MU)	16247	17932	19386	21346	23095	23562	23067	23944	23198	25747
3	Agri Connected Load (MW)*	3760	4013	4414	4756	5077	5553	5999	6117	6315	6418
4	No. of consumers ('000)	1135	1211	1332	1434	1530	1563	1706	1736	1792	1821
5	Av. Connected load (KW)	3.3	3.3	3.3	3.3	3.3	3.6	3.5	3.5	3.5	3.5
6	a) Total energy consumption (MU)	6285	6972	7895	9022	10922	11399	7835	9336	7969	10632
7	Consumption per KW (MU)	1672	1737	1789	1897	2151	2052	1306	1526	1261	1657
8	Consumption at 1500 units per MW (MU)	5460	6019	6621	7134	7616	8330	8999	9176	9472	9627
9	Difference (6 – 8) (MU)	645	953	1274	1888	3306	3069	-1164	160	-1503	1005
10	Corrected energy sales (MU)	16892	18885	20660	23234	26401	26631	21903	24104	21695	26747
11	Difference (2 – 9) (MU)	15602	16979	18112	19458	19789	20493	22231	23784	24701	24742
12	Corrected T&D loss	22.8	24.7	25.8	27.5	31.4	30.4	30.7	34.5	33.7	39.4
13	Addl. Availability (MU)	2317	1865	2448							
14	Addl. Sales @ (MU)	1685	1454	1960							
15	Addl. Sales ÷ Addl. Availability	72.7%	78.0%	80.0%							

* (7 + 9)

Annexure - 4
APSEB/APTRANSCO Working Results

Sl No	Item	1990-91	1993-94	1996-97	1997-98	1998-99	1999-2000
1	Quantity Generated (MU)	16529	17748	23099	24476	25127	27394
2	Quantity Purchased (MU)	3704	9115	8993	11882	12141	13410
3	Quantity purchased as % of total available [2÷(1+2)]	18.3	33.9	28.0	32.7	32.6	32.9
4	Cost of Generation Rs/Kwh	0.33	0.55	0.91	1.03	1.16	1.29
5	Cost of Purchased Power Rs/Kwh	0.60	0.81	1.17	1.49	1.71	1.80
6	Cost of Power Purchased	221.56	742.75	1049.40	1767.48	2081.00	2418.10
7	Repairs & Maintenance (crores)	57.15	96.51	143.08	168.57	116.24	137.86
8	Employee and Administration Cost (crores)	241.38	374.41	605.69	700.56	971.29	894.28
9	Depreciation (crores)	94.44	172.97	420.37	435.28	271.22	307.25
10	Interest and Financial charges (crores)	269.97	411.68	872.51	994.88	804.79	504.88
11	Total Expenditure (crores)	1147.75	2264.59	4196.86	5429.09	7054.57	7583.27
12	6 ÷ 11 (%)	19.3	28.04	25.0	32.5	29.5	31.89
13	7 ÷ 11 (%)	4.97	4.26	3.41	3.10	1.65	1.81
14	8 ÷ 11 (%)	21.00	16.50	14.43	12.90	13.77	11.79
15	10 ÷ 11 (%)	23.50	18.18	20.79	18.32	11.40	6.60
16	Total Energy Average (MU)	20233	26863	32092	36358	37268	40804
17	Total Energy Sold (MU)	16247	21346	21067	23944	23198	25747
18	Energy Sold/Energy Available	80.30	79.46	65.60	65.86	62.25	63.10
19	Revenue Realised (crores)	1207.24	2121.28	3441.15	4167.87	4175.52	4875.40
20	Revenue Received /Total Expenditure	105.18	93.67	82.00	76.77	59.19	64.29
21	Total revenue realizable if T&D loss was 20%	1202.73	2135.70	4196.52	5062.27	5366.13	6181.00
22	Hypothetical revenue realizable/Total expenditure	104.79	94.31	99.99	93.25	76.07	81.51

Annexure-5
APSEB : Revenue Account

Sl No	Description	1990-91	1991-92	1992-93	1993-94	1994-95	1995-96	1996-97	1997-98	1998-99	1999-2000
I	Revenue										
1	Energy Sales (MU)	16247	17932	19386	21346	23095	23562	23067	23944	23198	25747
2	a) Energy Generated (MU)	16529	16605	16259	17748	18907	19768	23099	24476	25127	27394
	b) Purchases (MU)	3704	5945	8156	9115	9940	9689	8993	11882	12141	13410
	Total (a + b)	20233	22550	24415	26863	28847	29457	32092	36358	37268	40804
	T&D Losses (as declared)	19.7	20.5	20.6	20.5	19.9	20.0	34.4	34.1	37.8	36.9
3	Revenue (Rs.crores)										
i)	a) Revenue from sale of power	1243.68	1530.98	1886.85	2172.78	2232.87	2462.92	3509.28	4241.54	4175.52	4875.4
	b) Less State Electricity Duty	36.44	40.02	42.13	51.5	65.23	59.66	68.13	73.67	--	--
	[a – b]	1207.24	1490.96	1844.72	2121.28	2167.64	2403.26	3441.15	4167.87	--	--
ii)	Miscellaneous Revenue	19.26	32.83	48.58	130.24	43.3	-19.73	49.2	121.76	398.15	407.9
iii)	Total (i + ii)	1226.5	1523.79	1893.3	2351.52	2210.94	2383.53	3490.35	4289.66	4573.67	5283.3
II	Expenditure (Rs. Crores)										
1	Generation of Power	311.18	397.2	506.35	635.08	746.29	1121.81	1365.51	1696.7	2925	3550.73
2	Purchase of Power	221.56	397.59	591.46	742.75	940.29	982.69	1049.4	1767.48	2081	2418.1
3	Repairs & Maintenance	57.15	73.03	80.37	96.51	107.6	113.36	143.08	168.57	116.24	137.86
4	Employees Cost	198.35	235.96	267.64	298.1	353.32	399.98	448.34	517.35	548.64	666.2
5	Adm. & Gen. Expenses	43.03	53.21	64.44	76.31	126.71	81.4	157.35	183.21	422.65	228.08
6	Depreciation & Related Expenses	94.44	115.25	147.52	172.97	288.3	349.37	420.37	435.28	271.22	307.25
7	Interest and Finance Charges	269.97	302.56	397.09	411.68	660.31	821.33	872.51	994.88	804.79	504.88
	Sub-total (1+2+3+.........+7)	1195.68	1574.8	2054.87	2433.4	3222.82	3869.94	4456.56	5763.47	7169.61	7813.1
8	Less: Expenses Capitalised	90.17	92.08	135.3	170.96	195.4	220.83	279.86	337.1	115.04	229.83
9	Other Debts & Extra-ordinary items	42.24	21.04	1.01	2.15	21.6	1.8	20.16	2.72	--	
	Sub-total (8-9)										
	Total Expenditure	1147.75	1503.76	1920.58	2264.59	3049.02	3650.91	4196.86	542.06	7054.57	7583.27

Annex. 5 contd...

Annex. 5 contd…

10	Profit/Loss	78.75	20.03	-27.28	-13.07	-838.08	-	-706.51	-	-2480.9	-2299
							1267.38		1139.43		
11	Revenue subsidies and grants	38.76	69.57	0.07	0.13	944.28	1259.17	850.46	1256.01	2629.01	2200
12	Profit/Loss with Revenue subsidies & grants	117.51	89.6	-27.21	-12.94	106.2	-8.21	143.95	116.58	48.11	-99.97
13	Net prior period credits/charges	-36.52	-5.16	106.66	99.93	-18.95	138.8	-14.75	4.97	--	--
14	Surplus/Deficit	80.99	84.44	79.45	86.99	87.25	130.59	129.2	121.55	--	--
15	Surplus as a percentage of the value of fixed assets of the Board in service at the beginning of the year.	4.71%	3.74%	3.26%	3.19%	3.00%	3.00%	3.00%	3.00%	--	--
16	Cumulative retained earnings at the end of the period									838.62	738
17	Subsidy receivables									1246.13	--
18	Gross receivables (Days of Sales)									139.25	135.92
19	Payables (Days of Purchase)									95.78	47.97

Annexure-6
Power Restrictions (1977-2000)

Year	Period	Consumers with CMD (KVA)											
		Upto 200		201 to 500		501 to 1000		1001 to 2000		2001 to 10000		Above 10000	
		Energy	Demand	Energy	Demand	Energy	Demand	Energy	Demand	Energy	Demand	Energy	Demand
(1)	(2)	(3)	(4)	(5)	(6)	(7)	(8)	(9)	(10)	(11)	(12)	(13)	(14)
1977-78	1.4.77 to 14.8.77	30	30	30	30	30	30	30	30	30	30	30	30
1977-78	25.4.77 to 14.8.77 (Textile Units)	20	20	20	20	20	20	20	20	20	20	20	20
No Power Restrictions from 15.8.78 to 4.9.79													
1979-80	5.9.79 to 31.7.80	30	30	30	30	30	30	30	30	30	30	30	30
1980-81													
No Power Restrictions from 1.8.80 to 26.1.84													
1983-84	27.1.84 to 30.4.84	25	25	25	25	25	25	25	25	25	25	25	25
1984-85													
No Power Restrictions from 1.5.84 to 14.4.87													
1987-88	15.4.87 to 6.6.87	15	15	15	15	15	15	60	60	60	60	60	60
	7.60.87 to 30.6.87	-	-	-	-	-	-	60	60	60	60	60	60
1987-88	1.7.87 to 9.7.87	-	-	-	-	-	-	60	60	60	60	60	60
	10.7.87 to 14.7.87	-	-	-	-	-	-	30	30	30	30	30	30
	16.11.87 to 19.1.87	-	-	-	-	-	-	35	35	35	35	40	40
	20.11.87 to 31.01.87	15	15	15	15	15	15	35	35	50	50	40	40
	1.2.88 to 13.3.88	15	15	15	15	15	15	35	35	50	50	60	60
1988-89	4.3.88 to 30.6.88	15	15	15	15	15	15	35	35	50	50	80	60
	1.7.88 to 29.7.88	15	15	15	15	15	15	35	35	30	25	80	60
	28.11.88 to 31.12.88	30	-	30	25	30	25	30	25	30	25	30	60

Annex. 6 contd...

Annes. 6 contd…

1989-90	1.1.89 to 14.4.88	15	-	30	25	30	25	40	30	50	40	60	50
	15.4.89 to 30.6.88	15	-	30	25	30	25	40	30	50	40	60	50
	1.7.89 to 31.7.89	15	-	30	25	30	25	40	30	50	40	60	50
	1.8.89 to 31.8.89	-	-	20	10	20	10	30	20	40	30	40	30
	1.9.89 to 30.6.89	-	-	-	-	-	-	20	-	20	-	20	-
	23.12.89 to 22.2.90	-	-	-	-	40	35	40	35	40	35	40	35
	23.2.89 to 7.5.90	-	-	-	-	40	35	40	35	40	35	60	55
	8.5.90 to 22.5.90	-	-	-	-	60	55	60	55	60	55	80	75
	23.5.90 to 15.6.90	-	-	-	-	40	35	40	35	40	35	60	55
	16.6.90 to 30.6.90	-	-	-	-	40	20	20	20	20	20	20	20
1990-91	1.7.90 to 31.7.90	-	-	-	-	20	20	20	20	20	20	20	20
	8.1.91 to 30.4.91	-	-	-	-	30	25	30	25	40	35	40	35
	1.5.91 to 13.6.91	-	-	-	-	40	35	40	35	60	55	40	35
	14.8.91 to 23.6.91	-	-	-	-	30	25	30	25	40	35	40	35
	24.6.91 to 30.6.91	-	-	-	-	-	-	-	-	40	35	40	35
1991-92	1.7.91 to 10.7.91	-	-	-	-	-	-	-	-	20	20	20	20
	11.7.91 to 13.8.91	-	-	-	-	-	-	-	-	-	20	-	20
	6.1.92 to 22.5.92	-	-	-	-	30	25	30	25	40	35	40	35
	23.5.92 to 30.6.92	-	-	-	-	40	35	40	35	60	55	60	55
1992-93	1.7.92 to 15.8.92	-	-	-	-	40	35	40	35	60	55	60	55
	16.8.92 to 5.9.92	-	-	-	-	30	25	30	25	40	35	40	35
	23.1.92 to 30.6.92	-	-	-	-	60	25	30	25	40	35	40	35
1993-94	1.7.93 to 22.8.93	-	-	-	-	30	25	30	25	40	35	40	35
	1.2.94 to 22.4.94	-	-	-	-	30	25	30	25	40	35	40	35

Annex. 6 contd…

Annex. 6 contd...

	23.4.94 to 30.6.94	-	-	-	-	60	60	60	60	60	60	60	60
1994-95	1.7.94 to 7.7.94	-	-	-	-	60	60	60	60	60	60	60	60
	8.7.94 to 22.7.94	-	-	-	-	30	25	30	25	40	35	40	35
	23.1.95 to 22.2.95	-	-	-	-	-	-	30	25	40	35	40	35
	23.2.95 to 30.6.95	-	-	-	-	30	25	30	25	40	35	40	35
1995-96	1.4.95 to 28.12.95	-	-	-	-	30	25	30	25	40	35	40	35
	29.12.95 to 31.3.96	40	-	40	-	50	45	50	45	60	55	60	55
1996-97	1.4.96 to 17.6.96	40	Nil	40	Nil	50	45	50	45	60	55	60	55
	18.6.96 to 6.9.96	Nil	Nil	Nil	Nil	30	25	30	25	40	35	40	35
	7.9.96 to 27.9.96	Nil	Nil	Nil	Nil	Nil	Nil	Nil	Nil	20	20	20	20
	28.9.96 to 10.2.97	Nil	Nil	Nil	Nil	Nil	Nil	Nil	Nil	-	-	20	20
	11.2.97 to 31.3.97	Nil	Nil	Nil	Nil	30	25	30	25	40	35	20	35
1997-98	1.4.97 to 9.5.97	-	-	-	-	30	25	30	25	40	35	40	35
	10.5.97 to 31.3.97	Nil	Nil	Nil	Nil	Nil	Nil	Nil	Nil	20	20	20	20
1998-99	1.4.98 to 2.5.98	Nil	Nil	Nil	Nil	Nil	Nil	Nil	Nil	20	20	20	20
	3.5.98 onwards	Nil	Nil	Nil	Nil	Nil	Nil	Nil	Nil	Nil	20	20	20
1999-2000	No Power cuts during this year	-	-	-	-	-	-	-	-	-	-	-	-

6

Irrigation: Development and Reforms

V. Ratna Reddy

1. INTRODUCTION

Andhra Pradesh is emerging as first among equals as far as agricultural sector reforms are concerned. The state's experiments with watershed and irrigation development programmes are among the most ambitious in the country. Perhaps for the first time participatory approach is being implemented from above. Participatory irrigation management has been taken up in a big way. More than 10, 000 water user associations (WUAs) have been formed, of which about 80 per cent are in minor irrigation sector i.e., tanks (Raju, 2000). The main objective is to rehabilitate the existing systems. Huge amounts of loans from World Bank and other international agencies are taken for this purpose. It is apprehended that their sustainability is in danger once the funds dry up. In this context it is necessary to examine the allocation and utilisation of funds in the irrigation sector. Productive utilisation of these funds (borrowed) would ensure sustainability in the long run.

Irrigation expenditure is the single largest expenditure item (about 10 per cent) in the state budget (1999-2000). However, this huge expenditure does not seem to reflect in the effective area irrigated. In other words, at the moment the economic returns to irrigation do not appear to be attractive due to long gestation periods and time over-runs. This could be due to various reasons. The most important ones are: a) higher costs of major and medium irrigation due to the location of the projects in increasingly difficult terrains, as the propitious locations are exhausted, b) escalation of unproductive expenses such as salaries, interest charges, etc., during the recent years, c) overemphasis on major irrigation to the neglect of medium and minor irrigation, and d) continuation of the supply side approach to the neglect of demand management of water resources. Given the magnitude of the budget expenditure it is necessary to examine the allocative and technical efficiency in the irrigation sector. Major issues in this regard include the rationale for continued focus on major irrigation *vis a vis* medium and minor irrigation; cost effectiveness in terms of capital costs and working costs; distributional, inter as well as intra regional, aspects (costs and benefits), role of supply side as well as demand side approaches in addressing the efficiency and equity issues, etc. In order to understand some of these aspects an attempt is made here to examine the trends in irrigation expenditure and area under irrigation in detail during the recent years in Andhra Pradesh (Details are presented in Appendix I). This would help in identifying the areas where efficiency can be improved. Besides, based on our discussions with irrigation officials and other experts, an attempt is made to understand the philosophy towards irrigation development in the state.

2. STATUS AND POTENTIAL OF WATER RESOURCES IN ANDHRA PRADESH

Of late there has been great emphasis at the policy level (macro) on the judicious management of water. Market (pricing) and institutional (user participation) approaches are suggested to overcome the strident problems. However, these policy measures have mostly remained on paper while much deserves to be done at the implementation level. This is mainly due to the ineffective institutional arrangements existing at the operation and maintenance (irrigation department) level and also due to lack of political will (Reddy, 1998). In order to correct these anomalies the government of Andhra Pradesh has embarked on an ambitious programme of irrigation sector reforms. In fact, Andhra Pradesh is the first state to bring out the Water User Association (WUA) act, making the formation of WUAs mandatory for the management of irrigation. However, this legislation covers only the surface irrigation leaving another major source of irrigation i.e., groundwater, outside its preview. Groundwater is the single largest source of irrigation and it covers most of the rain-fed regions (covering 2/3 of the total cropped area). In the absence of any effective policy measures groundwater regions are plagued with water scarcity, inequitable distribution of water and environmental degradation.

Land use pattern determines the economic efficiency of the resource use. Besides, it determines the ecological sustainability of land resources in the long run. There have been marginal changes in land utilization in Andhra Pradesh between 1960-61 and 2000-01 (for details see Reddy and Behera in this volume). Land use pattern is more or less stable over the period. Net sown area remained more or less stagnant at 11 million hectares from 1955-56 onwards. However, area under irrigation and cropping intensity continued to increase during 1980s and 90s. Cropping intensity increased from 110 per cent in 1960-61 to 123 per cent in 1999-00. This is mainly due to the increase in area under irrigation, which has grown from 2.90 million hectares in 1960-61 to 4.29 million hectares in 1999-00.

Along with the area under irrigation the composition of irrigation has changed over the period especially in the recent years (Figure 1). The proportion of area under Canal and Tank irrigation has declined while the importance of well irrigation has gone up substantially. This may be attributed to the decline in public investment in agriculture in the recent

Figure 1

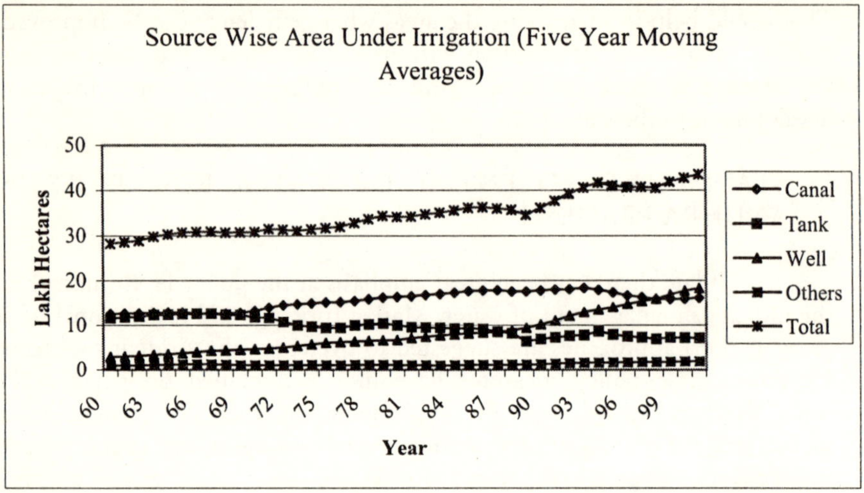

years. These changes have environmental consequences. The increase in area under well irrigation coupled with the decline in tank irrigation invariably results in over exploitation of groundwater resulting in environmental problems such as desertification in the fragile resource regions. Across the regions, Telangana and Rayalaseema have experienced drastic shifts in the composition of irrigation. By 1980s well irrigation has become the dominant source of irrigation replacing Tank irrigation in Telangana and Rayalaseema regions. Though Canal irrigation still dominates in the Coastal Andhra region, well irrigation replaced Tank irrigation for the second place. Let us examine the present status and development of these three sources of irrigation in the state.

Canal Irrigation

While huge expenditures on the major and medium projects were incurred, there was no proportionate allocation for the maintenance and infrastructure, which, interalia resulted in poor utilisation. Thus, after fifty years and an investment of over Rs.7000 crores, additional area irrigated under major and medium irrigation in Andhra Pradesh was 17.87 lakh hectares at a cost of Rs. 42000 per hectare. Besides, the additional area brought under well irrigation is marginal in these regions. Interestingly, despite huge investments, the area under canal irrigation after recording a positive growth till 1990 started declining during the 1990s. The evolution of novel institutional arrangements like WUAs during the late 1990s does not seem to have helped in altering the trend (Fig. 1)1. The total potential created in major and medium irrigation sector is slightly more than the 13.313 lakh hectares potential bequeathed to the State at the beginning of the planning era (prior to 1950-51). There are gaps in potential contemplated, created and utilized (Fig. 2). These gaps are wider in the case of medium irrigation when compared to major irrigation projects. Capacity utilisation in medium projects is 65 per cent against 83 per cent in the case of major irrigation projects. More importantly there is wide gap between capacity contemplated and actually created. Actually created irrigation is as low as 26 per cent of capacity contemplated in the case of medium projects and 66 per cent in the case of major projects (Fig. 2).

Figure 2.

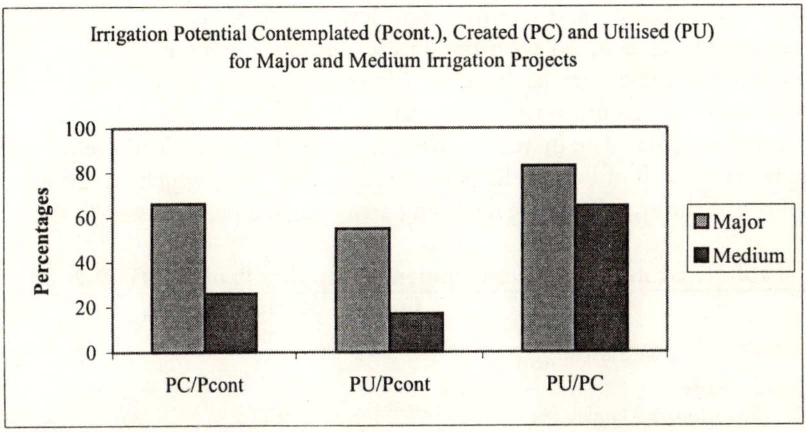

Ground Water

Groundwater development in Andhra Pradesh is about 42 per cent of the potential leaving apparently a large potential for future development2. At present there are 22.23 lakh wells in the state, of which 13.36 lakhs are in Telangana, 4.71 lakhs in Rayalaseema and 4.16 lakhs in Coastal Andhra regions. Further, 11.46 lakh wells are estimated to be feasible with a distribution of 3.89, 1.38 and 6.19 lakh wells in the respective regions (with ground water development of 85 per cent). It is clear that the potential for well irrigation is limited in Rayalaseema, as groundwater development in this region has crossed 50 per cent of the potential. Similarly, Telangana has also limited potential. Between 1975 and 1999 well population increased from 8.20 lakhs to 22.22 lakhs, while the area increased from 10 lakh hectares to 26.44 lakh hectares. Despite the advent of new technologies in water lifting in recent years area irrigated per well has gone down marginally from 1.22 acres to 1.19 acres indicating declining water yields (Fig. 3). Decline in area per well is higher in Rayalaseema followed by Coastal Andhra region whereas Telangana recorded an increase in the area irrigated per well. Problem seems to be more serious at the local level. For, 62 per cent of the villages in 9 dark mandals in Rayalaseema region fall under dark category due to over exploitation of groundwater (Table 1). But the latest reports (based on official estimates) on groundwater situation are alarming. In the entire state 336 mandals are identified as problematic. In 79 mandals water table has gone down by 20 meters. Between November 2000 and February 2001 the decline in water table ranged from 2.28 meters in Telangana and 1.52 meters in Rayalaseema regions. In both Rayalseema and Telangana regions majority of the wells are of 10-20 meter depth. This is reflected in the growth in tube wells in these regions. Well population is increasing at the rate of 56000 wells per year of which 60 per cent is in the Telangana region alone. Given the present low irrigation levels in these regions (Rayalaseema and Telangana) coupled with the absence of any potential canal irrigation possibilities, these regions have to depend more on tank irrigation and improving the groundwater potential through rain water harvesting and percolation tanks. The increased stress on groundwater is clearly reflected in the faster growth of bore wells (compared to dug wells, which are drying up in most of the areas) and the declining area irrigated per well.

Table 1. Groundwater Development in Andhra Pradesh (1999-2000)

		Coastal	Rayala-seema	Telangana	Total
1.	Level of GW development (% of Potential)	34	51	49	42
2.	No. of Dark Mandals (% villages)	2 (2)	9 (62)	4 (35)	15 (45)
3.	No. of wells with depth of				
	a) 0-2 meters	10	0	2	12
	b) 2-5 meters	28	11	5	44
	c) 5-10 meters	67	31	25	123
	d) 10-20 meters	30	50	58	138
	e) above 20 meters	16	12	18	46
4.	% of locations recording GW				
	a) Rising	13	5	10	8
	b) Falling	87	95	90	92
5.	No. of Existing wells	416234	470750	1335523	2222507
6.	No. of Feasible (additional) wells	618683	137774	389190	1145647

Source: Water Conservation Mission, GoAP, 2000.

Tank Irrigation

There are about 70 thousand tanks in the state, of which Telangana has 44 per cent followed by Andhra (38 per cent) and Rayalaseema (18 per cent) regions. Interestingly, the region with highest dependence on groundwater (Rayalaseema) has the lowest number of tanks. A more serious problem is regarding the functioning of tanks. At the state level 69 per cent of the tanks are under repair, which account for 82 per cent of the area irrigated by tanks. Effectively only 18 per cent of the tank *ayacut* (command area) is being irrigated. The decline, quantitative as well as qualitative, in tank irrigation may explain the low groundwater development in Rayalaseema and Telangana regions. Whereas, the situation is different in Andhra region due to perennial river basins like Krishna, Godawari, etc. Given the high complementarity between well and tank irrigation, it is necessary to strengthen the tank systems in Rayalaseema and Telangana regions. A better option would be to convert the existing tanks into percolation tanks so that groundwater potential would improve.

Figure 3

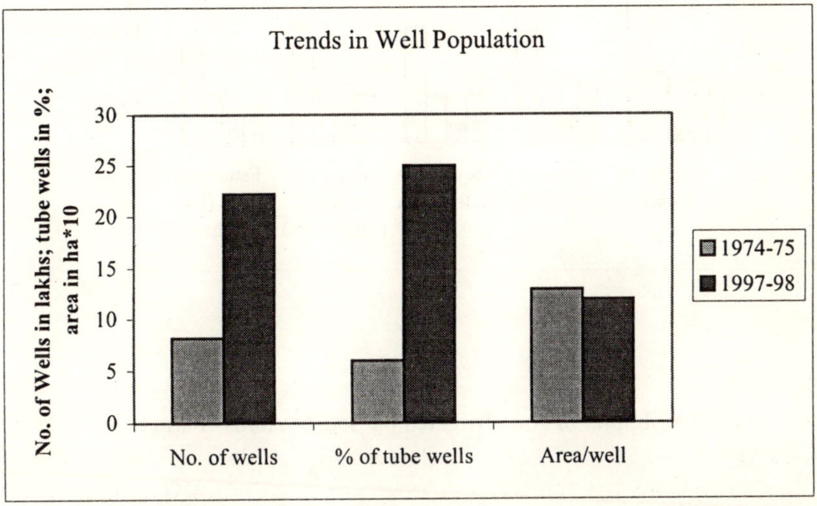

The changes in the distribution of irrigation across regions have two important repercussions as far as distributional aspects are concerned. Firstly, well irrigation is concentrated in the fragile resource regions. More importantly, private people mostly finance well irrigation, while canal and tank irrigation are financed by the state. This has resulted in aggravation of regional inequalities. Secondly, development of well irrigation is less favourable to small and marginal farmers when compared to canal and tank irrigation due to the high capital intensive and lumpy nature of the former (Figure 5). In most of the regions, especially fragile resource regions, groundwater irrigation has become privy to large farmers, denying the genuine right to small and marginal farmers in the common pool resources. Due to the high capital-intensive nature of extraction, groundwater is being treated as private property. Unless ground water is made a common pool resource in the real sense of the term, it is difficult to ensure equity in its distribution. This could be done either through legislation or making the technology cost neutral. Interestingly, our recent field visits to Telangana region indicated that bore well technology is becoming size neutral due to the declining costs consequent to the entry of local manufacturers (for details see Reddy, 2002).

Figure 4

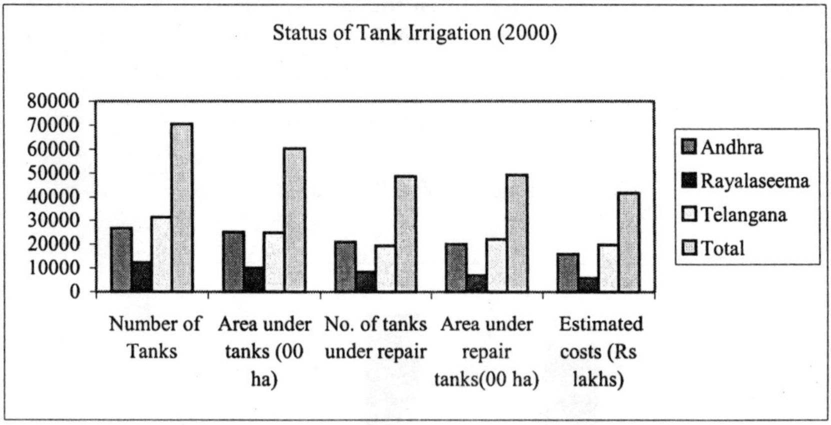

Figure 5

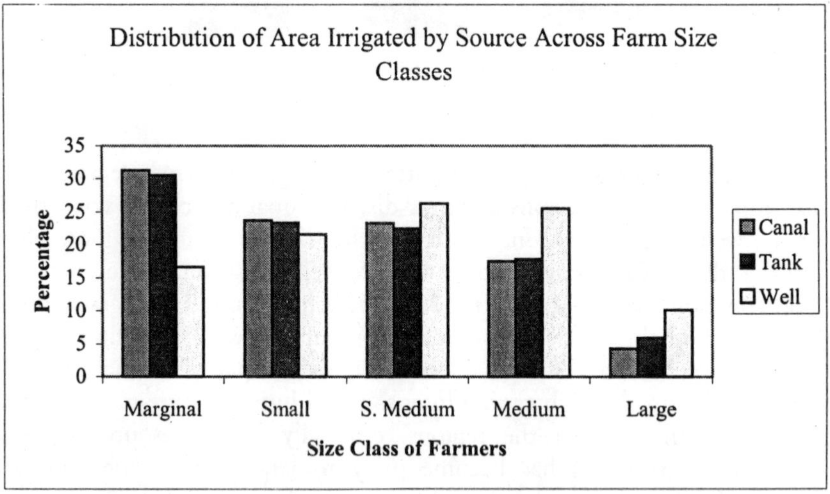

Irrigation Potential and Achievement

The ultimate irrigation potential of major and medium irrigation in the state is 5 million hectares and the potential of minor irrigation is 6.2 million hectare (Table 2). The potential of minor irrigation sources (mostly groundwater) has been revised upwards3 between 1992 and 1997, while the potential of major and medium irrigation sources (mostly canal) remained same. About 65 per cent and 49 per cent of the potential from major and medium and minor sources respectively has been tapped so far. In terms of actual achievement (actual area under irrigation) these figures are 64 and 45 percent respectively for major & medium and minor irrigation respectively. These estimates from the plan documents, however, seem to differ from the state level data (GoAP, Economic Survey, 2000-2001).

Table 2. Ultimate Irrigation Potential and Achievement by Source in Andhra Pradesh (area in '000 ha)

		Major&Medium	Minor
1.	Ultimate potential	5000.00	6260.00
2.	Potential Created till 2000 March	3254.22	3045.00
3.	% Potential Created to ultimate	65.00	48.60
4.	Actual utilisation till 2000 March	3206.22	2831.16
5.	% Achieved to the ultimate potential	64.00	45.20
6.	Number of New proposed projects*	20	4948
7.	Expected New potential to be created	349.78	139.00
8.	Expected total potential	3604.00	3184.00
9.	% Expected potential to the Ultimate	72.00	51.00
10.	Estimated Costs (Rs. In crores)*	2582	226
11.	Cost per hectare (in Rs. In constant prices)	73818	16258

Source: Government of India, Planning Commission, Ninth Five-Year Plan, 1997-2002.

* These are taken from Government of Andhra Pradesh, Irrigation and CADA department, Strategy Paper on Irrigation, 2002. Ninth Plan does not give figures in this regard. But according to eighth plan there are 34 on going major and medium projects in Andhra Pradesh (Rao, 1994). However, no project was completed during the eighth plan period.

As per the Economic Survey of Andhra Pradesh (2001-02) the total (major, medium, minor and others) area under irrigation never crossed 45.39 lakh hectares (1998-99) during the last 45 years (GoAP, 2000-01), though it is shown in the plan documents that 61.90 lakh hectares of area was actually brought under major, medium and minor irrigation (achievement) by the end of March 2000 (Table 2). Economic Survey does not provide the break up for major and medium and minor irrigation to examine which source is responsible for this gap. Given these discrepancies the proportion of potential actually achieved might be still lower in major and medium as well as minor irrigation. Further expansion in area under irrigation, especially major and medium, is expected from the new (20) projects4. But there is no time frame specified for completion of these projects. Speedy completion of these projects will ensure achievement of the full potential of major and medium sources. On the other hand, the gap between potential and achievement is more in minor irrigation. Even without considering the expansion of minor irrigation potential, the ultimate irrigation potential in the state, when materialized as per the present plans, will cover about 60 per cent of the existing net sown area.

Therefore, the focus should be on expanding and strengthening the minor irrigation sources and completion of the on going major and medium projects rather than starting new projects. This point has also been highlighted by the recent report by the World Commission on Dams (Parasuraman and Sengupta, 2001).

3. RECENT TRENDS IN IRRIGATION EXPENDITURE IN ANDHRA PRADESH

Irrigation accounts for a significant share in the total budget allocations. It is as high as 10 per cent during 1999-00. Even otherwise it hovers between 10 and 15 per cent of the total budget (Fig. 6). Its share in plan expenditure is very high compared to the non-plan expenditure. During the recent years the average share of plan irrigation expenditure in the total plan expenditure is about 30 per cent, while the non-plan share is below 10 per cent in all the years. This indicates that more emphasis is placed on new projects rather than maintaining the old systems. This is clearly reflected in the increasing trend in the irrigation, especially plan, expenditure during the last five years (Fig. 7). This is not in tune with the objectives of the irrigation reforms.

Figure 6

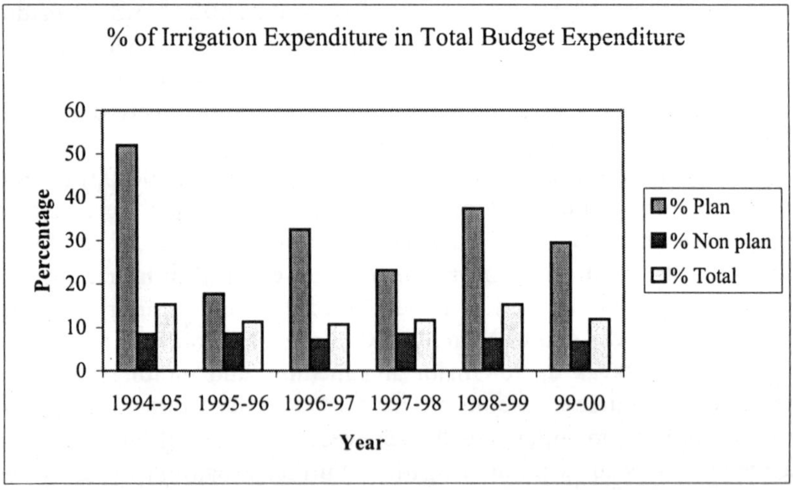

Within the irrigation sector the share of major and medium irrigation is above 80 per cent and it has risen considerably during the last six years (Figure 8). In fact, its share is above 90 per cent during1999-00. Of this major irrigation accounts for more than 90 per cent leaving little scope for medium irrigation. Despite the enhanced emphasis on major and medium irrigation area under canal irrigation has not shown any improvement. On the contrary it has saturated, if not declined, during the recent years. Moreover, it has slipped to second position during the 1990s, while well irrigation gained in importance. Despite the emphasis on plan expenditure there is stagnation in area under canal irrigation, as major projects have longer gestation periods. For, there would be a time gap, usually long, before the new investments fructify in the case of major and medium irrigation works. However, the substantial decline in canal irrigation in some areas needs further probing. Area under canal irrigation is observed to decline in all the three regions of the state.

Figure 7

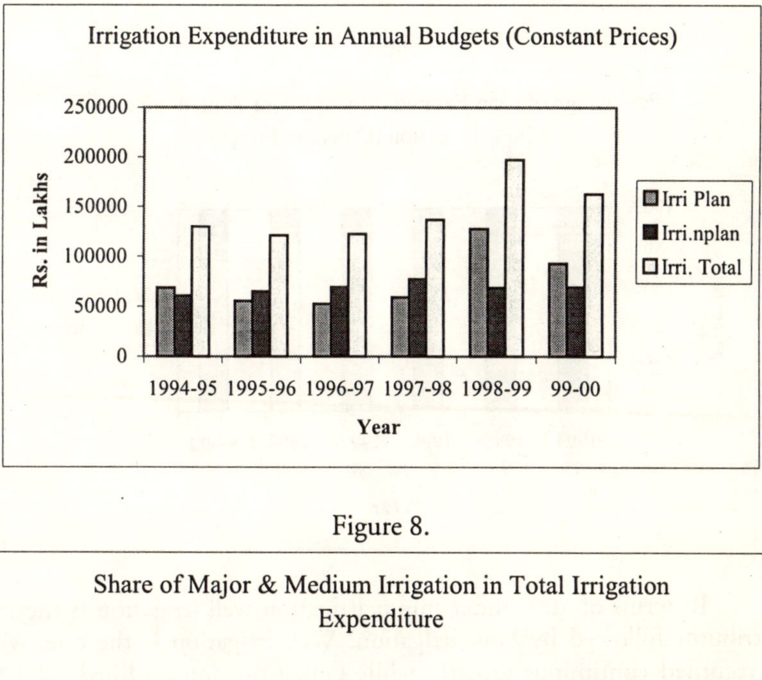

Figure 8.

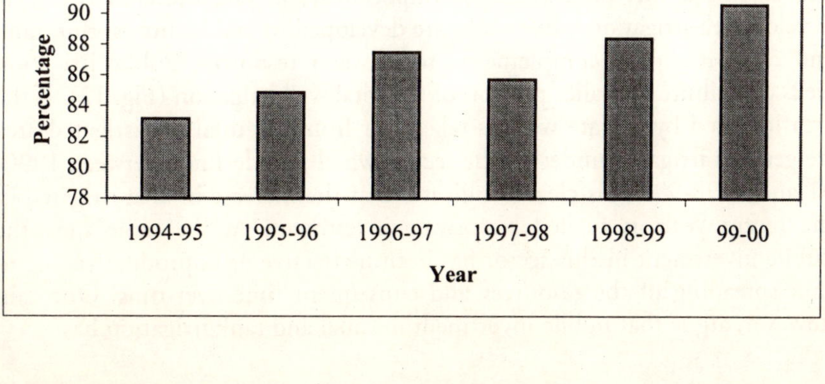

As far as minor irrigation is concerned it has been receiving low priority over the years. It accounts for only about 10 per cent of the total plan expenditure on irrigation, which is more or less stagnant during last five years (Fig. 9). Its share in the non-plan expenditure is much lower and declined during the recent years (Fig. 10). The actual expenditure on minor irrigation by plan and non-plan clearly reflects this (Fig. 11). This indicates, as in the case of major and medium irrigation, new schemes are given more importance over rehabilitating (maintenance) the old ones. This would affect mainly the minor tank and lift irrigation schemes, as the state has ceased to promote well (community) irrigation after 1995-96. Perpetuation of this trend would adversely affect not only tank irrigation but also the growing well irrigation in the private sector.

Figure 9

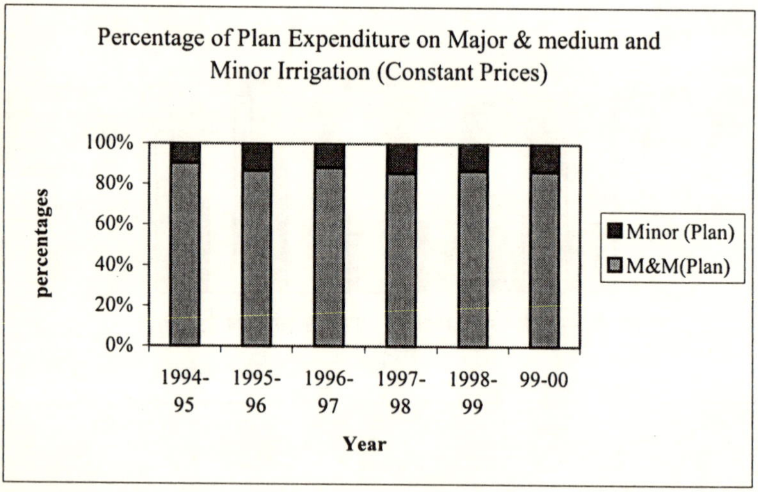

In terms of area under minor irrigation well irrigation is the main contributor followed by tank irrigation. Well irrigation is the one, which has recorded continuous growth, while tank irrigation declined till 1990s and stabilised thereafter (Fig. 1). Importantly, private individuals mostly develop well irrigation while tanks are developed by public funds. But, tank and canal irrigation complement groundwater resources. Public irrigation wells contribute a smaller portion of the total well irrigation (Fig. 12). If the area irrigated by private wells is taken out from the total net irrigated area we get area irrigated under public sector, which has declined between 1990-91 and 1998-99. This clearly indicates that the increase in area irrigated in the recent years is fuelled by private investment. At the same time the public investment in this sector has been ineffective or unproductive due to thin spreading of the resources and consequent time over-runs. One can, however, argue that public investment in canal and tank irrigation has

Figure 10

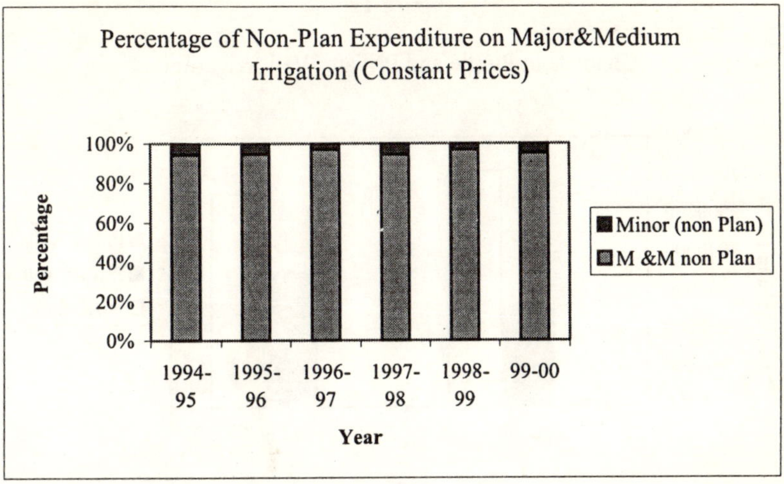

Figure 11

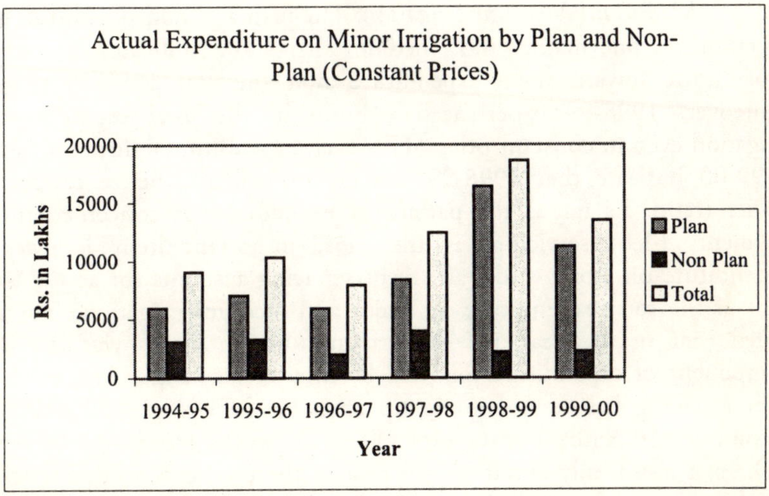

indirectly helped the private investment in groundwater exploitation through improvement in groundwater tables. This needs to be examined in terms of establishing the link between investments in canal and tank irrigation and well irrigation across the regions. Public investment in power is also a major factor promoting groundwater development. In what follows we examine the ways in which public funds on irrigation sector are spent.

Figure 12

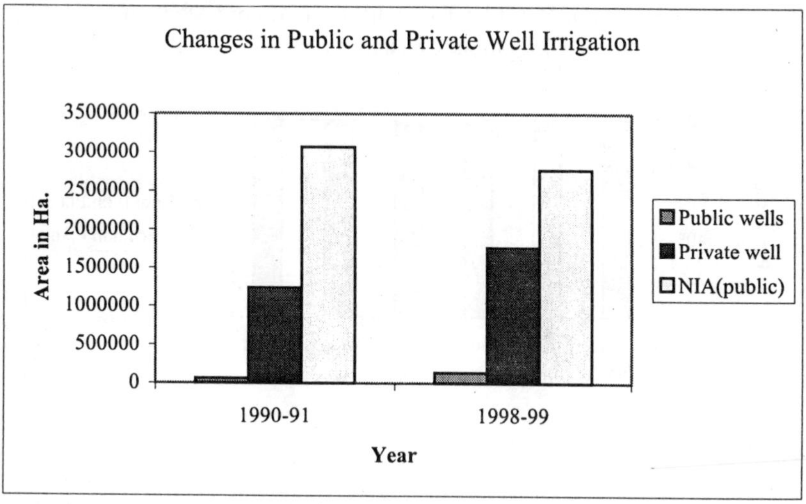

Note: NIA= Net Irrigated Area.

Pattern of Public Expenditure

Major and Medium Irrigation: The plan and non-plan break up of expenditure on major and medium irrigation indicates a shift in expenditure towards plan expenditure after the year 1998-99 (Fig. 7). Moreover, 1998-99 experienced a jump in the total expenditure on irrigation even in constant prices. However, expenditure figures for the year 1999-00 indicate that 1998-99 was exceptional and hence reverses the earlier trend. As far as the pattern of expenditure is concerned interest payments (debt servicing) is the most important item followed by expenditure on works and staff. Debt servicing accounts for about 50 per cent of the total expenditure on major and medium irrigation. It may be noted that in the year 1994-95 expenditure on works was the major component of expenditure followed by interest payments. The burden of debt servicing has started going up after 1994-95 (Fig. 13). Staff costs account for 50 per cent of the expenditure on 'works' (construction, repairs, etc). As a result only about 30 per cent of the total expenditure is left for 'works'. Given the declining quality of works in the recent years, the productive work carried out could be limited.

Sub-head wise break up of plan and non-plan expenditure reveals that entire interest burden is put in the non-plan, which is usual practice. Unfortunately in the recent years most of the borrowed money is going for interest payments. Very little is left for works after interest payments and staff expenditure (Fig.15). The department seems to have got in to a debt trap. It is forced to borrow more to repay the old debts rather than utilising it for productive purposes. When the borrowings are substantial (over and

Figure 13

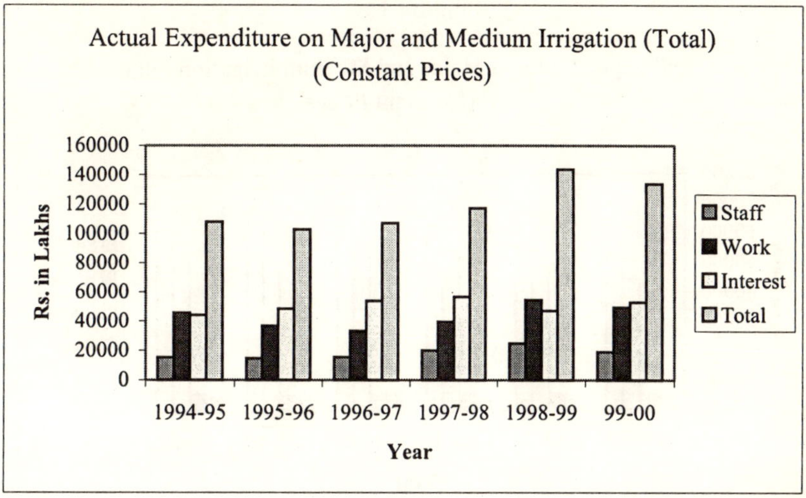

Figure 14

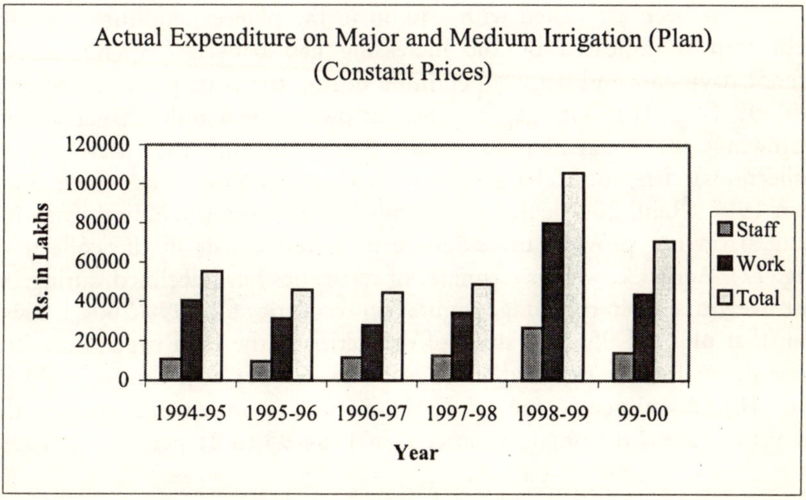

Figure 15

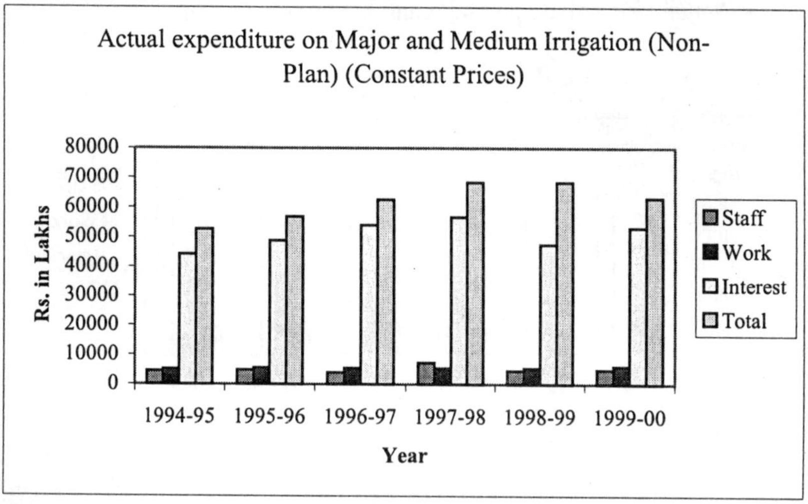

above the interest charges and staff expenditure) then there is scope for expenditure on works (as the case could be in 1998-99). But, the impact of these borrowings is reflected in terms of catching up of interest payments from the year 1999-00. The impact of substantial borrowing during 1998-99 has been associated with a jump in the plan expenditure (Fig.14). Debt trap is indicated by the increasing gap between expenditure on interest payments and work expenditure during the years prior to and after 1998-99 (Fig. 16). The gap can be narrowed down only through more borrowings or repayment of loans by increasing the user charges (collections). Irrigation charges were increased by more than three times from 1997 (Raju, 2000). But, the trends in recoveries (including irrigation charges) do not provide any evidence of improvement in the collections (Fig. 17). Actual as well as estimates of recoveries have declined during the past five years. Even the budget figures on recoveries for 1999-2000 is lower than that of 1994-95. The share of recoveries in the total expenditure has come down from 4 per cent in 1994-95 to 1.5 per cent during 1999-00 (Fig. 18). As a percentage to operation and maintenance charges the recoveries have slid from 135 per cent in 1994-95 to 21 per cent in 1999-00.

Figure 16

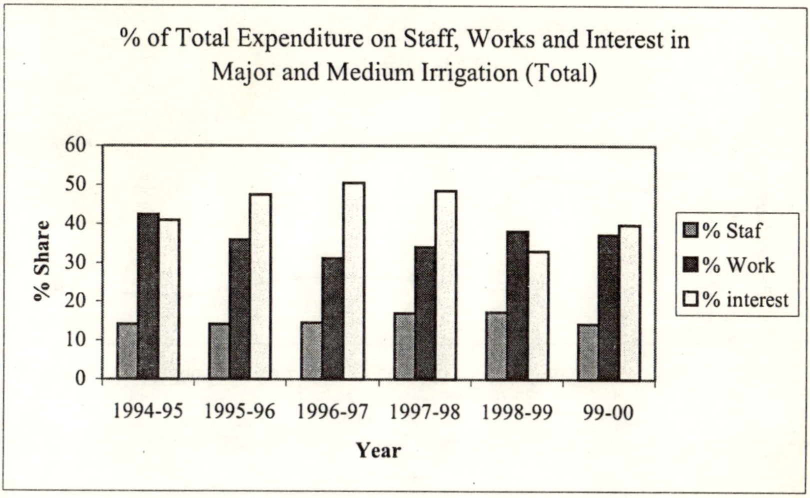

Figure 17

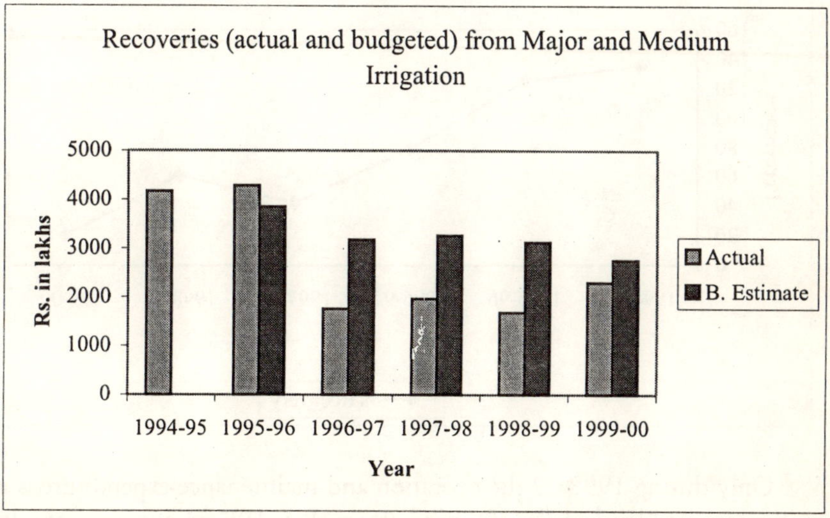

Figure 18

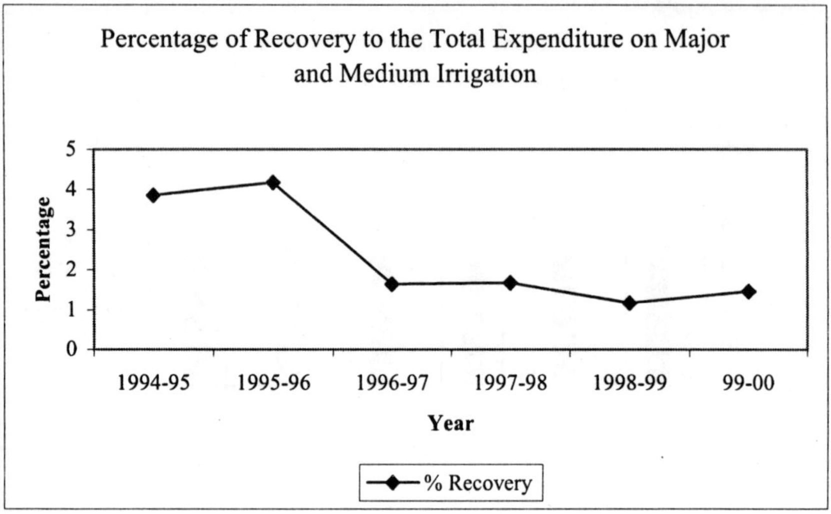

Figure 18a

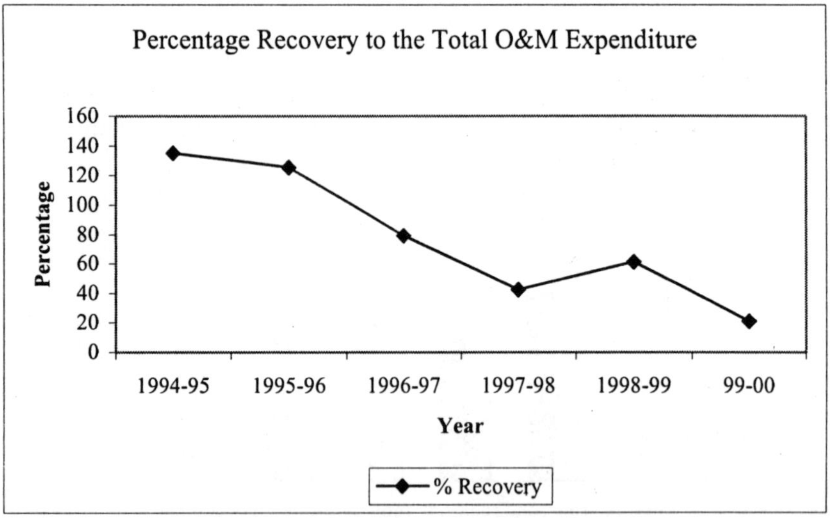

Only during 1998-99 the operation and maintenance expenditure is up to the required level of Rs. 300 per hectare (Fig. 19)[5]. However, more data on this front, especially on borrowings and recoveries from water charges, is essential to substantiate the argument. Another interesting feature of post 1997-98 irrigation expenditure is the significant jump in 'others' category, which has risen multi-fold. This has occurred mainly in the non-plan expenditure accounting for 15 per cent of the expenditure. In fact, the expenditure under this item was negative during the preceding three years. 'Others' include professional charges like lawyer fee, etc.

Figure 19

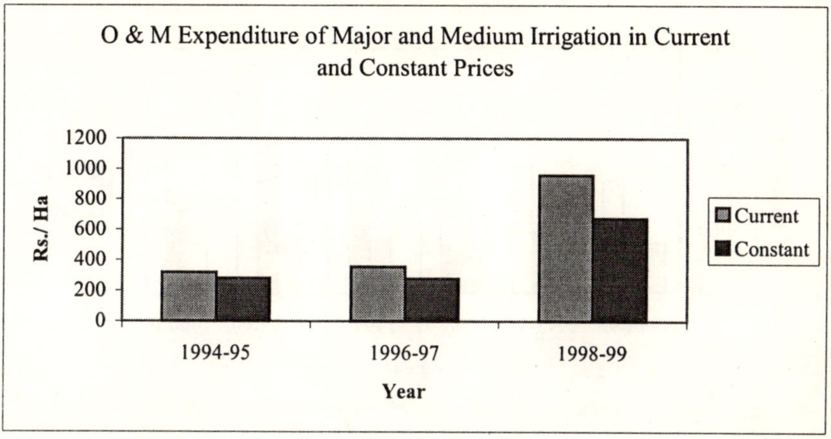

Minor Irrigation

Pattern of expenditure in minor irrigation is more or less on the same lines as major and medium irrigation except for the fact that minor irrigation does not have the interest payment component. Apparently, minor irrigation is totally funded through internal sources. The emphasis on new works to the neglect of existing ones is more conspicuous in the case of minor irrigation. While total expenditure along with plan expenditure has recorded an increase during the last five years the non-plan expenditure has declined substantially during 1998-99 and 1999-00 (Figs. 20-22). Another important feature is that staff costs account for more than 50 per cent of the work expenditure in all the years except 1998-99. In the case of non-plan expenditure staff costs are more than work expenditure in all the years except 1997-98 (Fig. 23). The low priority accorded to maintenance is reflected in the number of tanks (69 per cent) requiring repairs and defunct lift irrigation schemes.

Poor maintenance of minor irrigation systems like tanks will have two important repercussions, especially in the fragile resource regions. One is the direct decline in area irrigated by tanks, which is already conspicuous, and the other is the indirect impact on well irrigation. In the absence of groundwater replenishment (mainly through tanks) well failure has become a common phenomenon in some regions. In fact, the recent cotton farmer suicides in the state are attributed mainly to well failure. In the larger social interest minor irrigation needs to be protected, maintained and enhanced. Maintaining minor systems also makes economic sense, as the operation and maintenance costs of minor irrigation are half that of major and

Figure 20

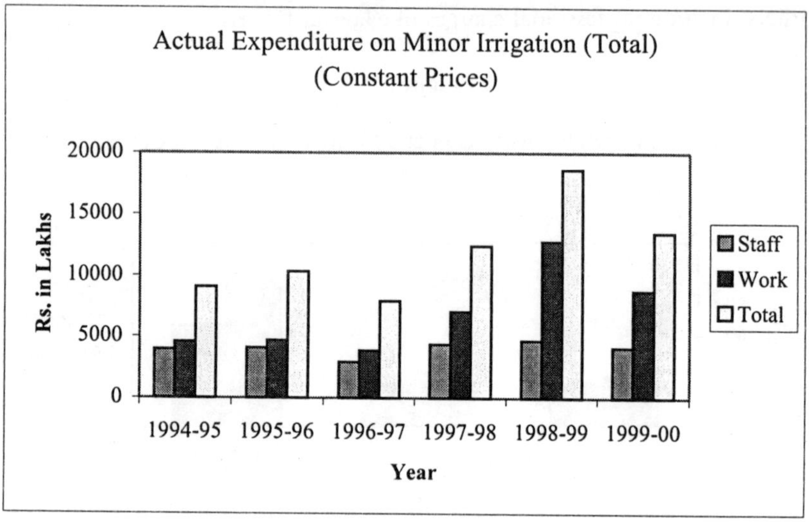

Figure 21

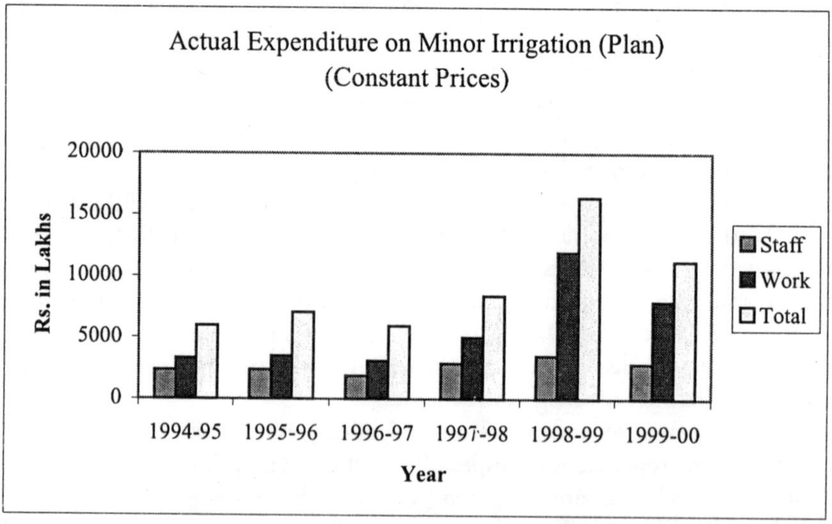

medium irrigation (Figs. 20 and 23). However, we hasten to add that minor irrigation is not a substitute for major and medium irrigation. But at the same time the latter is not a panacea for all geographical and geological locations. There are regions where promotion of minor irrigation would be more effective, economically, ecologically and socially.

Figure 22

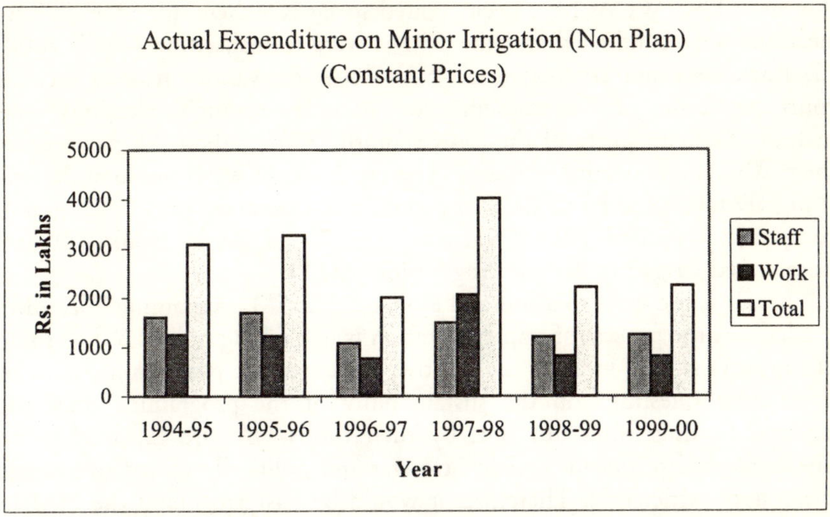

Figure 23

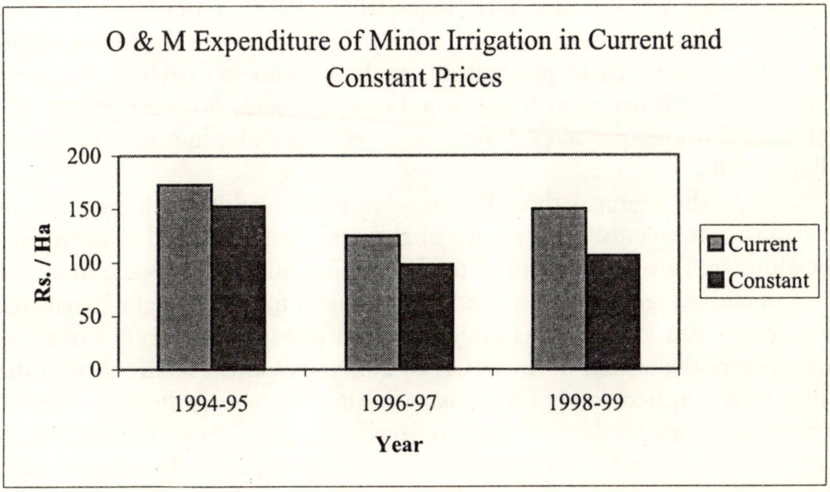

4. NEW INITIATIVES IN IRRIGATION MANAGEMENT

Andhra Pradesh is the first state in India to initiate large-scale institutional reforms in irrigation management. In 1997 the state has brought in the legislation to create Water User Associations (WUAs) under the Andhra Pradesh Farmer Managed Irrigation Systems Act. The main objectives include i) realising the maximum irrigation potential, ii) improving the efficiency of the existing irrigation network and iii) managing water resources better through stakeholder participation. Under this act 10292 WUAs have been created so far. Of these, for 9800 WUAs elections were conducted and the WUAs were formalised by March 2000. Elections were not conducted in 492 WUAs for various reasons such as court stay order or Government stay order. Interestingly, elections were unanimous in majority of the cases (Jairath, 2001). About 80 per cent of these WUAs are in minor systems. The evolution of water user associations is mainly facilitated by the A. P. Economic restructuring project (irrigation component) funded (Rs.4994 crores) by World Bank, NABARD and Accelerated Irrigation Benefit Programme (AIBP).

It is too early to assess and evaluate the PIM programme in Andhra Pradesh, as the process of implementation is just falling in line. While some of the early studies indicate the positive aspects of the programme, most of them raise questions on the sustainability of the programme once the external funding dries up. But, by then the WUAs are expected to be financially self sufficient, socially stronger and politically united to manage the systems efficiently. Therefore, it would be hasty to brand the PIM in Andhra as a success or failure6. The impact appears to differ between canal WUAs and tank WUAs. The impact of canal WUAs has been positive, especially in terms of providing irrigation to tail end farmers who were not getting water for the fast 5-10 years (Raju, 2000; Jairath, 2001). The tangible benefits include: a) area under irrigation has increased mainly in the tail reaches by 10-15 per cent due to the increase in carrying capacity of canals by 20-30 per cent; b) increase in paddy yields from 2.5 tonnes per acre to 3.5 tonnes per acre; c) increase in revenue collections by 20 per cent (Raju, 2000).

At the moment these WUAs seem to be working well especially in the canal commands. In majority of the cases it is observed that tail-end locations are getting sufficient water for the first time in five years. In one of the tail end villages we have visited in the Nagarjuna Sagar Right Canal area it was observed that the area under irrigated paddy has gone up from 500 acres before the advent of the WUA to 2000 acres after its advent. And the area under irrigated paddy is increasing steadily. However, these benefits are not reflected in the data at the state level or regional level. As reflected in our analysis, the reform process initiated in irrigation sector in particular does not seem, as yet, to have made any dent in increasing the area under irrigation or increase in revenue collection or an increase in paddy production. Apart from this the success of WUAs is attributed mainly to the availability of external funding and the sustainability of the programme is critically linked with the availability of resources (Raju, 2000). Besides, investments may not bear any fruit, as this money is not productively invested in terms of social capital development. This, in turn, blocked the hard decisions envisaged in the reforms, such as implementation of user charges effectively.

On the other hand, evolution of Water User Associations (WUAs) is focused on operation and maintenance of the existing systems. Success of WUAs is linked with the funding, as little effort is being made to make them self-sufficient or financially independent. Our discussions with some of the WUA members revealed that the formation of WUAs helped in taking water to tail end areas. Beyond this they achieved little. They could not even reduce the under reporting of area irrigated. For the official figures on area under canal irrigation show a decline, while most of the tail-end locations are reporting substantial improvement in the availability of water after the advent of WUAs. There seems to be a nexus between farmers and the officials (who collects the area statistics). It is indicated that often 60 per cent of the irrigated area is reported for the collection of water charges and the officials take the charges on 20 per cent of the area. Effectively the farmer will be paying for 80 per cent of area irrigated by him. This is a mutually beneficial arrangement. These arrangements are widespread in the regions where WUAs are not strong. In fact, it was observed that in some cases the irrigation department has not yet revealed the details of command area under each WUA. There is widespread feeling that the department is not keen in strengthening the WUAs, as their continuation will go against the department's interests. In some regions WUAs have turned into mere political entities. Moreover, in majority of the cases contractors have turned into WUA presidents. As a result, WUA's have become money making ventures.

The approach at the policy level seems to be to sustain WUAs through injecting more funds (borrowed). This is in the interest of policy makers and political entrepreneurs. For, it perpetuates rent-seeking activity as well as populism. User contribution has not really materialised, as it goes against political interests. As a result, economic efficiency gets least priority though talking about it is in vogue. Political compulsions are the hackneyed excuse. This approach is myopic at its best, as it would fail to achieve economic as well as political gains in the long run. Supporting the WUAs is rewarding to political entrepreneurs as well as policy makers in the short run i.e., as long as funds are available. The sustainability of WUAs is in danger once the funds dry up. Approach of the state is not to build social capital by making the best use of the available resources, but to dilute it by giving political colour. Consequently, neither the bureaucracy nor the beneficiaries are motivated enough to sustain these institutions. Though it is not feasible to make these institutions totally apolitical, an integrated approach would have been more rewarding.

Hitherto the active participation of people is ensured through proper flow of funds. Further, groundwater irrigation is not integrated with other sources of irrigation. Groundwater is the single largest source of irrigation and highly dependent on surface water sources like tanks. In the absence of any institutional arrangements for managing groundwater, its sustainability is uncertain. For all practical purposes groundwater is treated as a private source and hence none of the numerous regulations on the use of groundwater was effective. Unless groundwater is brought under the purview of community management, it would be impossible to ensure sustainability (ecological) and equity in its distribution. However, of late, there appears to be some progress in this direction under the guidance of water conservation mission established in the state.

Another important dimension of WUA's is the emphasis on elections. Elections are fought on the party basis, which makes people insensitive to common good. Besides, the WUA election is one among the five such committees electing their office bearers every two to three years. Party politics have already made a dent in the village unity. The frequent elections to the newly created institutions would aggravate the situation. The indications are already there, especially in the case of watershed committees. This goes against the basic philosophy of participatory development and management. For, these institutions in their present form tend to dilute the social capital rather than strengthening it.

Despite these shortcomings, the pioneering effort of the Government of Andhra Pradesh in irrigation reforms is unprecedented. In fact, these reforms are ranked very high even at the global level and expected to be a future model in irrigation management. The state has shown the way that political will is the main ingredient for such initiatives. The most interesting feature of these reforms is that they are 'top down' with a 'bottoms up' approach. It has the advantage of greater reach (possible under 'top down') and intensity through involvement of the community (possible under 'bottoms up'). These reforms under the guidance of some committed officials at the state level have taken off in good spirit and received good support at the farmer level. Though, one may argue that flow of funds is the main factor in generating such response, it is necessary to support the ailing systems in order to generate trust among beneficiaries. For, over the years farmers have lost the trust in the government and in no position to respond to false promises. Therefore, the initial boost is necessary to regain the lost credibility and build the trust. Once this is in place institutional reforms from top becomes smooth and easier. But it is necessary to understand the direction in which the reforms are progressing. This direction would ultimately determine the strength and sustainability of the reforms. In what follows we discuss briefly some pointers for strengthening and sustaining this important policy initiative.

1. There is an immediate need to bring the balance between minor, major and medium irrigation systems through judicious fund allocations.
2. Minor irrigation sources of tanks and groundwater should be treated in an integrated fashion. For this groundwater needs to be brought under the purview of the reforms. This calls for major initiatives in legal and legislative reforms to address the rights on groundwater. The experience

of South Africa would help in understanding the issues of de-linking water rights from land. In fact, South Africa has effectively abolished the riparian rights.

3. In the present context, provision of equal rights on water for all sections of the community is essential. Though this would amount to huge transaction costs, it is necessary that the reform process be in this direction in order to achieve the objective in the long run.
4. The reforms should initiate the process to convert water in to an economic good through introduction of volumetric pricing at least in the canal commands to start with. Effective reforms require integration of market and institutional dimensions. Though short run political interests may go against this, it would have multiplier effect on the long run political and economic gains. At the same time proper devolution of powers to local level institutions would help in addressing the political bottlenecks effectively.
5. Transfer of powers and responsibilities to the WUAs at the local level should be done in an effective and phased manner. Hitherto, WUAs are entrusted with responsibilities without any rights.
6. There is need for exploring the possibility of integrating the *Panchayati Raj* institutions into the reform process for sustaining the reforms in the long run. For, these local bodies are totally bypassed by the new initiatives.
7. Similarly, integration of tank restoration with watershed development would not only strengthens the ecological base but also gets the community support as it would enhances benefits from both these programmes (Reddy, 2001).

5. POLITICAL ECONOMY OF IRRIGATION REFORMS:

To recapitulate the preceding analysis:

- A secular increasing trend is observed in the irrigation expenditure during the last five years even in constant prices. There is a spurt in the expenditure during the year 1998-99 in major and medium as well as minor irrigation. This spurt is mainly due to the increase in plan expenditure. But the year 1999-00 reverses this spurt, as the expenditure is more in line with the earlier years.
- A significant share of the irrigation expenditure goes towards major projects (about 80 per cent) followed by medium and minor irrigation schemes.
- Emphasis is more on new works rather than on rehabilitation of old ones, as the plan expenditure takes the major share in the increased budget expenditure. Plan expenditure has gone up in 1998-99 in terms of work as well as staff expenditure. While the increase in staff expenditure could be due to the implementation of pay commission's

recommendations of higher scales to all state government employees, the increase in work expenditure could be due to the new projects, on going or initiated.

- Despite the huge investments in major and medium irrigation, area under canal irrigation is either stagnant or declining. This is due to thin spreading of resources and the consequent time and cost over-runs. Often new projects are pushed more due to political reasons rather than economic reasons.
- Work expenditure is stagnant while interest charges are rising in the major and Medium irrigation in all the years except 1998-99. On the whole interest charges account for about 50 per cent of the total expenditure. Expenditure on staff accounts for more than 50 per cent of the work expenditure in most of the years.
- Most of the borrowed money goes for interest payments (debt servicing). In most of the years interest charges account for about 80 per cent of the non-plan expenditure except in 1998-99. If this trend continues there is a danger of irrigation department falling into a debt trap. For, the recoveries are on the decline despite the increase (three times) in irrigation charges in 1997. As a result irrigation reforms are dependent more on borrowed funds, especially for rehabilitation and maintenance.
- Plan expenditure on minor irrigation has gone up while the non-plan expenditure has gone down during the last 6 years. Except in the year 1998-99, expenditure on staff accounts for more than 50 per cent of the plan expenditure on minor irrigation.
- The neglect of operation and maintenance is more conspicuous in the case of minor irrigation despite the fact that operation and maintenance costs of minor irrigation are half that of major and medium irrigation.
- Completion of on-going projects rather than starting new ones will ensure bringing substantial area under irrigation. Minor irrigation has more than 50 per cent of unexploited potential. Therefore, there is a case for bringing the balance between major & medium and minor irrigation. This strategy would be more sustainable, economically as well as ecologically.

The present status and trends in irrigation reforms in the state can be better understood in the political economy framework. For, the attitude, philosophy and ideology of the policy makers are crucial in determining the development path. The core philosophy of the policy makers dealing with water has not changed despite the process of economic reforms for a decade in the country. The philosophy of water resource management continues to be supply sided to the neglect of demand side management. Supply side approach aims at supplying water at any cost to meet the demands through expansion of supply sources. In this approach emphasis is more on creating new sources of water. Efficiencies are improved through supply regulation in the supply side management by creating scarcity conditions. This, however, is not a long run sustainable solution, as the costs of supply keep rising and supplies dwindling. Besides, resource (financial) constraints would further aggravate supply regulat!on and hence shortages. The spiralling affect of this would result in acute shortages, as it happened in the case of drinking water (Reddy, 1999). Unfortunately, the approach of the irrigation policy makers continues to be tuned to this line of thinking.

On the contrary, demand side approach stresses on improving the efficiency of water use with the given amount of water. This is possible through reducing the wastage, adoption of technologies that would increase water use efficiency, etc. Since agriculture is the largest consumer of water saving a small fraction in this sector would release large quantities for other needs or irrigation itself. According to one estimate raising irrigation efficiencies by 10 per cent would save enough water to supply all global residential water needs (Postel, 1984). The efficiency of irrigation systems worldwide is estimated to average only 37 per cent (Postel, 1985). Apart from the distribution losses, which account for 30-40 per cent, there are no pricing policies or institutions to conserve and use water judiciously at the farm level. The absence of demand management resulted not only in inefficient allocation of water but also in unequal distribution of water within canal commands.

The main factors that determine irrigation water demand can be grouped as economic, technological and institutional. It was observed that in most of the Southeast Asian countries, except Philippines, the revenue from irrigation does not even cover the operation and maintenance costs. Though there is plethora of literature on irrigation pricing (for reviews, see Jhonson III 1990; Eason, 1979), only a few studies deal with the specific aspect of the impact of price on water demand. In a study of Mexico it was found that where charges increased with the amount of water used, irrigation efficiencies increased by 20 per cent on average when compared to the earlier situation where farmers paid a fixed fee unrelated to their usage (quoted in Postel, 1985). In another study of Indonesia Jhonson III (1990) observed that direct water charges ($ 0.40 /100 m3) would lead to a 9 per cent saving in water use but reduces crop value by 4 per cent. In the case of United States also price is observed to be a very practical demand management tool (quoted in Reddy, 1996).

On the technology front, though there are water efficient techniques available, the area covered by these techniques is still negligible. They include sprinkler and drip irrigation systems. Sprinkler irrigation, for instance, uses 20-25 per cent less water while drip irrigation consumes 40-60 per cent less water when compared to traditional gravity system (Postel, 1985). However, the main constraints for adopting these technologies are: i) at present these technologies are mostly used on horticultural crops; and ii) these technologies are capital intensive at the farm level. But the ongoing research efforts for bringing more crops under these techniques and reducing per unit costs may help in wider adoption in the coming years.

Institutional factors are considered as the key for improving the efficiency of irrigation systems. It is often argued that the reason for the ills of irrigation management is the alienation of farmers / beneficiaries from the process of planning and implementation. Maintenance and management of irrigation systems through user societies and participatory process is expected to bring inefficient and equal distribution of water resources. It was observed in Philippines that the participatory units obtained improvements over non-participatory units in terms of irrigation fee collections and thus improving the viability of the system (Sengupta, 1991). In the case of Japan the Land Improvement Districts (LIDs), which are nothing but farmers organisations carry out comprehensive land and water management programme in order to improve agricultural productivity. These institutions are not only engaged in the operation, maintenance and smooth distribution of water but also conceive new ideas, new schemes to be implemented through construction activities (Mitra, 1992).

The new initiatives in irrigation management in Anadhra Pradesh are a step in this direction. However, these institutional arrangements (WUAs) need to be made autonomous and strengthened in terms of finances and administration. In the short run, the WUAs should be made responsible for collection water charges, making them democratic and transparent as well as accountable. To complement this investment in agriculture should be enhanced. In the long run, WUAs should move towards volumetric pricing and efficient use of water, including shifts in cropping pattern.

Notes

1 Our discussions with the irrigation department officials and other experts in the field revealed that the decline in canal irrigation could be due to underreporting of area, as there were no breakdowns in any of the ongoing projects. The problem of underreporting was expected to be nullified with the advent of WUAs (see last section). Latest data (1999-2000) do not indicate any correction in this regard. However, it is felt that the correction would, at the most, give a picture of stagnation in the area under canal irrigation rather than resulting in an increase.

2 It may be noted that all this potential is not utilizable as it includes groundwater resources in inaccessible areas like forest and hilly regions. Further, reliability of these estimates is questionable, as they do not reflect the ground realities in many areas.

3 As mentioned earlier reliability of groundwater estimates is questionable.

4 As per the data provided in strategy paper by the irrigation department the estimated potential to be created under the on-going 20 major & medium projects is about 3.49 lakh hectares while it is about 1.39 lakh hectare from the rehabilitation of 4948 minor irrigation tanks (GoAP, Strategy Paper on Irrigation and CADA, 2002).

5 We do not have break up of area under major and medium irrigation for the year 1999-00.
6 To capture divergent views see Pangare (2002), Jairath, (2001), Raju (2000), Reddy (1999) and Peter, and Pingle (1999).

References

Eason, V. S (1979), "Irrigation Water Pricing: A Critical Review", paper presented at the Indian Econometric Conference, Srinagar, May.

GoAP (various years), *Appendices to the Budget Estimates.* Vol. XI/2, Department of Finance and Planning, Government of Andhra Pradesh, Hyderabad.

GoAP (various years), *Budget Estimates: Irrigation and Command Area Development,* Vol. XII/13, Finance and Planning Department, Government of Andhra Pradesh, Hyderabad.

GoAP (various years), *Statistical Abstract of Andhra Pradesh,* Finance and Planning Department, Government of Andhra Pradesh, Hyderabad.

GoAP (2001), *Economic Survey 2000-2001,* Planning Department, Government of Andhra Pradesh, Hyderabad.

Jairath, Jasveen (2001), *Water User Associations in Andhra Pradesh-Initial Feedback,* Concept Publishing Company, New Delhi.

Johnson III, Sam H. (1990), "Impact of Indonesian Public Water Pricing Policy on Crop Mix and Irrigation Practices in Java", in R. K. Sampath and Robert A. Young (Eds.), *Social, Economic and Industrial Issues in Third world Irrigation Management: Studies in Water Policy and Management,* No. 15, West view Press, Boulder, Sanfrancisco and Oxford.

Mitra, Ashok K. (1992), "Joint Management of Irrigation Systems in India", *Economic and Political weekly,* Vol. 27, No. 26, June 27.

Moore, Mick (1991), "Rent-Seeking and Market Surrogates: The case of Irrigation Policy", in Ch. Colclough and J. Manor (Eds.), *State or Markets? Neo-liberalism and the Development policy Debate,* Oxford, London.

Pagare, Ganesh (2002), Scalling up Participatory Irrigation Management in India: Lessons Learnt from the Andhra Pradesh Model and Future Strategies", Working paper/ monograph Series 5, Indian Network on Participatory Irrigation Management, New Delhi.

Peter, J. Raymond and Pingle, G. (1999), "Participatory Irrigation Management in Andhra Pradesh: Big Bang, Consolidation, Extension", I & CADD, Hyderabad.

Postel, Sandra (1984), "Water: Rethinking Management in the Age of Scarcity", *World Watch Paper 62,* December.

Postel, Sandra (1985), "Conserving Water: The Untapped Alternative", *World Watch Paper 67,* September.

Parasuraman, S. and Sohini Sengupta (2001), "World Commission on Dams: Democratic Means for Sustainable Ends", *Economic and Political Weekly,* Vol. XXXVI, No. 21, May 26.

Raju, K. V. (2000), "Participatory Irrigation Management in Andhra Pradesh: Promise, Practice and a Way Forward", Working Paper 65, Institute for Social and Economic Change, Bangalore.

Rao, C. H. Hanunumantha (1994), "Policy Issues Relating to Irrigation and Rural Credit in India", G. S. Bhalla (Ed.), *Economic Liberalisation and Indian Agriculture*, Institute for Industrial development, New Delhi.

Reddy, V. Ratna (1996), *Urban Water Crisis: Rationale for Pricing*, Rawat Publishers, Jaipur.

Reddy, V. Ratna (1998), "Institutional Imperatives and Co production Strategies for Large Irrigation Systems in India", *Indian Journal of Agricultural Economics*, Vol. 53, No. 3, July-September.

Reddy, V. Ratna (1999), "Quenching the Thirst: Means and Costs of Water in fragile Environments", *Development and Change*, Vol. 30, No.1, January 1999.

Reddy, V. Ratna (2000), "Watershed Development in AP", *Deccan Chronical*, June 23.

Reddy, V. Ratna (2002), Environmental Degradation: Market, Institutional and Policy Failure (A Case of Water Resources in Andhra Prades), Project Report, Center for Economic and Social Studies, Hyderabad.

Sengupta, Nirmal (1991), *Managing Common Property: Irrigation in India and Philippines*, Sage Publications, New Delhi.

Wade, Robert (1988a), "The Management of Irrigation systems: How to evoke Trust and Avoid Prisoner's Dilemma", *World Development*, Vol. 16, No. 4, April.

Wade, Robert (1988b), *Village Republics: Economic Conditions of Collective Action in India*, Cambridge University Press, Cambridge.

Appendix I: Details on Data

For this purpose we have used the data from the annual budget accounts of the state. The analysis is carried out for the past six years i.e., 1994-95 till 1999-2000. The year 1996-97 roughly represents the advent of irrigation sector reforms in the state and hence making 1994-95 as a starting point would bring out the difference, if any, between pre and post reform periods. Data were analysed on the basis of major components and heads such as plan and non-plan, estimated and actual, and by staff, work, interest, etc. Besides, we have used the data from other secondary sources such as Economic Survey of Government of Andhra Pradesh, Statistical Abstract of Andhra Pradesh, etc. The budgetary data provides 55 sub-heads under which expenditure is classified for major and medium irrigation, minor irrigation, Command Area Development (CAD) and flood control. For the sake of pointed analysis and clarity we have grouped the 53 sub-heads under staff, works, interest, others and total. Further, we restrict our analysis to major and medium and minor irrigation components. It would have been helpful if the details on major and medium irrigation were given separately.

Staff component includes salaries, office expenses, pensions, professional fee and petrol, etc., works component includes work expenditure, machinery, equipment, investment and materials and the 'others' component is an uncategorized item (details are presented below). We have estimated the operation and maintenance expenditure by adding the staff and works expenditure minus the expenditure on establishment expenditure under non-plan category. The analysis is carried out by plan and non-plan as well as budgeted and actual expenditure. We have also converted the expenditure figures into constant prices with the help of wholesale price index for all commodities with the base year of 1993-94 (GoAP, 2000). Moving averages of 3 and 5 years are used to iron out year on year fluctuations.

Budget sub-heads

The following 53 budget sub-heads are used to group the major expenditure items i.e., staff, work, interest, etc. These are available for Major & Medium Projects, Minor Irrigation, Flood Control and Command Area Development separately. Budget codes are given in brackets.

I Salaries (010)

1) Pay of Officers (011); 2) Pay of Establishment (012); 3) House Rent Allowance (013); 4) Other Allowances (014); 5) Encashment of Earned Leave (015); 6) Ex-gratia/Ad-hoc Payment, ESI Allowance/Tiffin Charges and Overtime Allowance (016, 018 & 019); 7) Leave Travel Concession (017).

II Wages (020)

1) Daily wages (021); 2) Contingent Employees (022).

III Dearness Allowance (030)

IV Travel Expenses (040)

1) Traveling Allowance (041); 2) Fixed Traveling Allowance (042); 3) Conveyance Allowance and Bus Warrants (043 & 044); 4) Transfer Traveling Allowance (045).

V Office Expenses (050)

1) Service postage and Telegram Charges (051); 2) Telephone Charges (052); 3) Water Charges (053); 4) Electricity Charges (054); 5) Purchase of Motor Vehicles (055); 6) Other office Expenses (056); 7) maintenance of office Vehicles (057).

VI Rents, Rates and Taxes (060)

VII Publications (070)

VIII Advertising and Publicity (080)

IX Grants-in-aid (090)

1) Towards Salaries (091); 2) Other Grants-in-aid and Obsequies Charges (092 & 093).
X Subsidies (110)
XI Scholarships and Stipends (120)
XII Secret Service Expenditure (150)
XIII Major Works (160)
XIV Minor works (170)
XV Maintenance (180)
1) Ordinary Repairs, Flood Repairs and Pumping schemes (181, 182 & 183); 2) Work Charged Establishment (184).
XVI Machinery and Equipment (190)
1) Purchases (191); 2) Renewals & Replacements, Recoveries towards depreciation & sale, deduct-receipts & recoveries towards maintenance (192, 193 & 195); 3) Maintenance (194).
XVII Motor Vehicles (210)
1) Purchases (211); 2) Maintenance of Functional Vehicles (212)
XVIII Investments (220)
XIX Materials and Supplies (240)
XX Interest (250)
XXI Pensions/Gratuities (270&280)
XXII Suspense (320)
XXIII Payments for Professional & Special services (330)
1) Pleaders Fee and other Payments (331, 334); 2) Payments to Home Guards (332); 3) Payments to Anganwadi Workers (333)
XXIV Other Charges (340)
XXV Arms and Ammunitions (440)
XXVI Petrol, Oil and Lubricants (450)
XXVII Diet Charges (660)
XXVIII Drugs and Medicines (670)
XXIX Others (-)

Appendix II : Basic Budget Data on Irrigation Expenditure (Constant Prices)

Major & Medium actual Expenditure (Plan) (Rupees in lakhs)							
	Staff	Work	Total	% Staf	% Work	% interest	
1994-95	10745.5	40606.03	55280.81	19.43804	73.45412	0	
1995-96	9698.541	31304.39	45807.57	21.17235	68.3389	0	
1996-97	11630.87	27932.02	44497.88	26.13802	62.77158	0	
1997-98	12634.43	34323.07	48779.91	25.90089	70.36312	0	
1998-99	26683.91	79948.11	105815.4	25.21742	75.55435	0	
99-00	14130.12	43690.07	70719.68	19.98047	61.77922	0	

Contd....

Contd....

Major& Medium Actual Expenditure (Non-plan) (Rupees in lakhs)							
	Staff	Work	Interest	Total	% Staf	% Work	% interest
1994-95	4553.752	5208.894	44193.88	52641.38	8.650518	9.895055	83.95275
1995-96	4838.918	5571.377	48730.64	56820.59	8.516135	9.805208	85.76229
1996-97	3964.281	5466.398	54052.81	62522.23	6.340595	8.743128	86.45375
1997-98	7307.328	5539.978	56795.18	68389.16	10.68492	8.100666	83.04704
1998-99	4658.239	5544.085	47431.36	68333.37	6.816932	8.11329	69.41171
1999-00	4943.692	6144.815	53191.23	63147.19	7.828839	9.73094	84.23373
Major& Medium Grand Total Actual Expenditure (plan+non-plan)							
	Staff	Work	Interest	Total	% Staf	% Work	% interest
1994-95	15299.26	45814.92	44193.88	107922.2	14.17619	42.45181	40.94977
1995-96	14537.46	36875.77	48730.64	102628.2	14.16517	35.93143	47.48272
1996-97	15595.15	33398.42	54052.82	107020.1	14.57217	31.20761	50.50716
1997-98	19941.76	39863.04	56795.18	117169.1	17.01965	34.02181	48.47284
1998-99	24977.15	54804.25	47431.36	143879.8	17.35974	38.0903	32.96596
99-00	19073.82	49834.88	53191.23	133866.9	14.24835	37.2272	39.73443
Minor Irrigation Expenditure (plan) (Rupees in lakhs)							
	Staff	Work	Total	% Staf	% Work		
1994-95	2332.31	3301.434	5975.381	39.03199	55.2506		
1995-96	2373.23	3466.877	7053.721	33.64507	49.14962		
1996-97	1854.758	3095.906	5935.156	31.25036	52.16217		
1997-98	2882.187	5021.925	8406.388	34.28567	59.7394		
1998-99	3490.028	11955.3	16418.09	21.25721	72.81782		
1999-00	2862.144	7968.979	11230.34	25.48581	70.95936		
Minor Irrigation Expenditure (Non Plan) (Rupees in lakhs)							
	Staff	Work	Total	% Staf	% Work		
1994-95	1608.257	1260.646	3094.885	51.96499	40.73321		
1995-96	1699.844	1229.434	3272.27	51.94694	37.5713		
1996-97	1082.047	773.75	2004.945	53.9689	38.59208		
1997-98	1495.888	2066.022	4021.201	37.20003	51.37824		
1998-99	1215.479	822.662	2215.254	54.86861	37.13624		
1999-00	1254.685	817.5616	2251.096	55.73663	36.31838		
Minor Irrigation Grand Total Actual Expenditure (plan+non-plan)							
	Staff	Work	Total	% Staf	% Work		
1994-95	3940.566	4562.08	9070.265	43.44488	50.29709		
1995-96	4073.074	4696.311	10325.99	39.44487	45.48049		
1996-97	2936.805	3869.656	7940.102	36.98699	48.7356		
1997-98	4378.075	7087.948	12427.59	35.22867	57.03397		
1998-99	4705.507	12777.96	18633.35	25.25315	68.57576		
1999-00	4116.829	8786.541	13481.44	30.53701	65.1751		

7

Information Technology and Social Development

C. Ramachandraiah

1. INTRODUCTION

In the last decade, the information and communication technology (ICT) sector has grown rapidly in India and made a significant impact on setting priorities and organisational development in different sectors. Several state governments have taken lead and were ahead of the Government of India in formulating their own policies to attract multinational companies, especially from the United States. The southern states of Andhra Pradesh, Tamil Nadu and Karnataka and the western state of Maharashtra have been literally in competition in this sector. In the present paper an attempt his made to analyse the growth of IT sector in terms of software units and exports, government policy measures etc., and the application of ICTs for rural development. The role of ICTs vis-a-vis social development has been discussed briefly.

2. GROWTH OF 'IT' IN INDIA

Characterised as 'an island of competitiveness', this industry's comparative advantage was drawn from the technical base of India's higher education as exemplified by the Indian Institutes of Technology (IITs) and regional engineering colleges. It was further observed that this export-driven industry was born as a by-product of import substitution policies whereas its export success was due to open trade policies targeted specifically at this sector (Patibandla et al, 2000). By the year 2000, 19 of the 26 state governments had already come out with their own IT policies. The Government of India has formulated a national IT policy in 1998 and also set up a National Task Force on Information Technology and Software Development with the objective of making India an 'IT superpower'. The policy aims to raise Indian IT industry turnover to US$ 85 billion by 2008. It is proposed to set up an Indian Institute of Information Technology (IIIT) in every state. English medium education and a strong stream of science and mathematics at school and college level have been the major advantages for the southern states of Andhra Pradesh, Karnataka and Tamil Nadu (with Hyderabad, Bangalore and Chennai as capital cities respectively) in accelerating the growth of this industry.

The number of Internet users in the country is estimated to have reached 7 million by September 2002 (www.nua.ie). The actual number of users with ready access to Internet is estimated at about 5.7 million. Since Internet is equated with power and not just another means of communication, it is felt that India urgently needs at least 150 to 200 million telephone and Internet connections. While access to the Internet can enable people in all kinds of ways, a lack of it would put people at a tremendous disadvantage. Therefore, widespread access should be provided to telecom and Internet facilities in the country. Otherwise, there would be accentuation of differences between countries who have provided widespread access and those who have not, and between haves and have-nots within countries (Jhunjhunwala, 2000).

As per the National Association of Software and Services Companies (Nasscom), the software industry currently accounts for about 2 per cent of India's Gross Domestic Product which is expected to rise to about 8 percent by 2008. The software exports from the units set up with the Software Technology Parks of India (STPI) have reached Rs. 46,100 crore (US$ 9.5 billion) in 2002-03 recording a 26.3 per cent growth over the previous year. The growth rate of software exports has slightly declined from 29 per cent in 2001-02 and an earlier high of 65 per cent in 2000-01 in the country. Much of this decline may be attributed to the aftermath of September 11, 2001, apart from the very high growth in the earlier years. Software exports from India accounted for about 20.4 per cent of total exports of the country in 2002-03. This share has increased from only about 5 per cent in 1997 to 13.8 per cent in 2000-01 and 16.5 per cent in 2001-02. This sector is estimated to contribute about 35 percent of the total exports by 2008.

The United States has been the largest export destination from India for more than a decade. The share of exports of the Americas, including Latin America, went up to 71 per cent in 2002-03 from 67 per cent in the previous year. The UK is the next main destination with a share of 14 per cent followed by Europe, excluding the UK (9 per cent). The share of exports to the UK increased slightly while there is a decline to the rest of Europe over the previous year. It seems that India is spending about 60 per cent of its software earnings (60 cents out of every dollar earned) on procuring software from abroad because only through imports can the demand for standard products be met. It was observed that instead of remaining as 'low-cost suppliers of software to meet routine demand abroad', the Indian software companies must 'venture into high-end products and services', 'move up the value chain', and 'cater to the demands of Indian industry itself'.[1]

IT Enabled Services (ITES) or "remote processing" are considered as the major technology driven services industry in the coming years. The ITES sector, together with Business Process Outsourcing (BPO), with a revenue of Rs. 11,300 crore or US$ 2.3 billion, has registered a high growth of 59 per cent during 2002-03 (as against 73 per cent in 2001-02) whereas the software sector grew by only 18.3 per cent. This sector accounted for about 25 per cent of the software exports and has given a major hope to the IT industry in the last couple of years. It is expected to grow by about 50 per cent during 2003-04 and account for about 29 per cent of the exports. This sector includes functions and services delivered over telecommunications or data networks from a country different from the one where end products are delivered. The most important of them in India are customer interaction services like call centres, back office operations and content development and animation services.[2] India has several advantages like nearly a 12-hour time-zone difference with the USA, a huge pool of English-speaking computer literate graduates and low cost of personnel.[3] This sector is also receiving a lot of support from the central and state governments with incentives like income tax holiday until 2010, special policy for call centres, and several other incentives relating to infrastructure etc. Apart from generating incomes, this sector seems to have a high potential for generating employment opportunities on a large scale for the average educated persons. By the end of March 2002, about 102,000 people were estimated to be employed in IT-enabled services and this number is projected to reach 11 lakhs by 2008 (www.nasscom.org).

Here is an example to illustrate how IT-enabled service can create gainful employment without having to move from their homes. An enterprise in Bangalore receives a few hundred engineering journals on science and technology. It distributes them to educated ladies in their homes. Their job is to go through the contents in the journals and prepare extracts or synopsis so that a search over them would enable a seeker to get the entire text. With dumb terminals in their homes, they dial and gain access to a computer into which the information text is typed and the whole thing is sent out over telecom links from Bangalore to a worldwide web in the US. They are paid handsome amounts based on the number of words constituting an abstract. Similar tasks can be performed from small towns or villages as well (Chowdary, 1998).

3. 'ICTs' FOR RURAL DEVELOPMENT

The rural people should be convinced that IT solutions would help them in improving their incomes and lives by concrete experiments.[4] This is well exemplified in the case of dairy cooperatives of Anand in Gujarat where automatic milk collection system (AMCS) allows the reading of quality and quantity of fat content, and maintains daily record of milk societies at village level. In Dhar district of Madhya Pradesh a programme of administration known as Gyandoot, meaning "ambassador of knowledge", that was launched in January 2000, was awarded Stockholm

Challenge Award for public service and democracy.[5] In five blocks of this district, 26 major centers are connected through an intranet network. With each centre connecting to about 15 gram panchayats and 25-30 villages, the benefits are supposed to be reaching out to over half a million people in more than 600 villages. This model seems to be under replication in 44 other districts in Madhya Pradesh (Srivastava, 2002). It is, however, known that the original Gyandoot project has been closed, which brings into question the issue of sustainability of ICT projects in rural areas.

A Delhi-based non-governmental organisation, Development Alternatives, has set up seventeen rural cybercafes or IT centres known as TARAkendras in September 2000 – five in Uttar Pradesh, four in Madhya Pradesh and eight in Bhatinda district of Punjab. More such kendras were planned for in the coming months. All of them are connected to a portal, TARAhaat.com and through it to the Internet. This site seems to have collected a lot of information on issues of concern to villagers: health, education, government services, commodity prices, local news and a host of other matters. This is claimed as the first Mother Portal for rural areas in the Third World (Khosla and Rana, 2000). Two years after the launch, TARAkendras seem to have become popular with more products and rising awareness levels about IT are creating more jobs to rural youth and are generating good incomes to their owners in the Bundelkhand region. The main portal, TARAhaat.com was given the Stockholm Challenge Award for 2001 (Rana, 2002). However, it has also been observed that some of the older TARAkendras have 'been performing badly in terms of student enrolment and user turn out making them economically unviable' and hence have been 'either closed down or disenfranchised' (Sreekumar, 2002). A number of enterprises that will create jobs can be located in small towns. For example, about 15 years ago, an entire trunk exchange work was removed from Stockholm in Sweden and all the trunk call booking and operations were put in one village near a small town, 150 km away, for the entire country. Operators work in that village commuting the least distance (Chowdary, 1998).

In recent years, a number of efforts are being made by both governmental and non-governmental agencies in reaching the IT to rural areas and enable the rural people to take advantage of IT services either in communicating their demands/grievances to the concerned officials or knowing the information related to markets and services for their products. The National Institute of Agricultural Extension Management (MANAGE), Hyderabad has taken-up a number of what are called "Cyber Extension" initiatives in the country. It has established Internet connectivity in 24 districts in 7 States, namely Andhra Pradesh, Bihar, Himachal Pradesh, Jharkhand, Maharashtra, Orissa and Punjab under National Agricultural Technology Project (NATP). Ten villages in Rangareddy district of Andhra Pradesh were selected to test the efficacy of the experiments. These villages had successful Mutually Aided Co-operative Thrift and Credit Societies (MACTCS). Multimedia CDs are distributed to these groups on several aspects of agriculture, rural development, health and education etc. (the Interactive self learning package on watershed management, the Vyavasaya Panchangam - Encyclopedia of Agricultural Practices, cultivation of paddy, cotton, mango and coconut etc.). The experiences of these groups have shown that they have been using the Internet for browsing websites for government programmes and schemes, weather forecasts, market prices, job opportunities, news etc., regularly. It seems that they have also started charging nominal amounts for some of these services selectively. MANAGE is planning to connect over 350 blocks in 28 districts on Internet in the near future (www.manage.gov.in). There is a need to assess the impact of these interventions on the quality of life in those villages. The other notable experiments in applying IT to rural livelihoods are being carried out by the Chennai-based (Tamil Nadu) M.S. Swaminathan Research Foundation in about 8 villages around Pondicherry in which information on fisheries, agriculture, buses, healthcare, jobs etc., is received by coastal people through the network that is all wireless and driven by solar power.

A multitude of factors such as 'limited local participation, lack of availability of local resources, fractured relationship with the state agencies, limited integration with local organisations and the exogenous social and economic environment' are identified as some of the factors for the inability of the ICT projects to deliver their full range of outputs in rural areas. These factors are often overlooked while projecting the promises of the projects (Sreekumar, 2002). Indian industry and scientists would have to come together to provide the resources and drive to design and deploy low cost technology that best caters to Indian conditions. The n-Logue Communications, set up by the Chennai-based TeNet group realised that the key to success is not just the connectivity but the availability of relevant content for rural people in Internet. Further, efforts are needed to incorporate local language and local content in Internet in a massive way. Having to use keyboard by everyone may limit the use of Internet. There is a need to develop voice-enabled Internet service (with Indian languages) soon. Ultimately, to be successful in India, Internet requires Indian applications – applications that emerge from the Indian way of life (Jhunjhunwala, 2000, 2002).

4. 'IT' IN ANDHRA PRADESH

In Andhra Pradesh, especially in its capital city of Hyderabad, a great thrust has been given in nineties to the growth of software industry. The state accounts for about 23 per cent of software professionals from India in the United States as per Nasscom's survey in 1998. The *Vision-*

2020 Document of the Government of Andhra Pradesh (1999) states 'Andhra Pradesh will leverage information technology to attain a position of leadership and excellence in the information age and to transform itself into a knowledge society' (p. 276). The *Document* outlines a five-pronged strategy towards achieving this goal (p. 278):

- Developing world-class IT infrastructure, including broadband digital connectivity,
- Making Andhra Pradesh a hub for developing electronic government applications,
- Promoting Andhra Pradesh as the premier location for world class IT companies,
- Developing education and research institutions to make Andhra Pradesh a premier IT education centre in India, and
- Bringing IT into the service of the people in all parts of the state.

Some of the important objectives of the IT Policy of the Government of Andhra Pradesh are centred on using IT for economic development by different means, human resource development, and electronic governance etc.

The Software Technology Parks (STP) of India, Hyderabad unit was set up in 1991-92. The value of software exports from Hyderabad has increased from Rs. 0.20 million to Rs. 36.68 billion in 2002-03 (Table 1). They have grown at a rate of over 100 per cent annually till 1998-99, by 84 per cent in 1999-00, by 90 per cent in 2000-01, by 45 per cent in 2001-02 and by 26 per cent in 2002-03. This sharp decline in the growth rate of software exports in the last two years may have to do, at least to some extent, with the events relating to September 2001 in the USA and the general slow down in the IT industry, apart from the very high growth achieved in earlier years. The top two exporters from Hyderabad during 2002-03 were Satyam Computers (12.61 per cent) and Wipro (12.24 per cent). The GE Capital has emerged as an important software exporter in the last year with 9.32 per cent. The bulk of software exports from Hyderabad have gone to the USA and Canada (59 per cent) in 2002-03 as against 61.69 per cent in 2001-02, 69.15 per cent in 2000-01 and 73.15 per cent in 1999-00. This indicates that the software markets for STP units in Hyderabad have expanded beyond North America in the last couple of years. Europe is the next major destination with 23.74 per cent (including 5.02 per cent to Netherlands) followed by 15.2 per cent to the Middle East & Asia (including 3.79 per cent to Japan). The share of software exports from Hyderabad to North America has declined whereas it has gone up in the case of all-India figures. The number of exporting units registered with the STP has crossed one thousand mark in 2000-01 and now stands at

1401 by March 2003. The operating units are, however, only 57 per cent (820).

Table 1. Growth of Software Units and Exports from Hyderabad: 1991-2003

Year	Software Units (Nos.)		Software Exports (Rs. million)	Growth rate of Exports
	Registered	Operating		
1991-92	7	--	0.2	--
1992-93	15	--	42	--
1993-94	24	--	98	137
1994-95	44	--	218	122
1995-96	60	31	604	177
1996-97	88	46	1334	122
1997-98	112	70	2835	112
1998-99	194	106	5741	102
1999-00	977	359	10590	84
2000-01	1206	674	20070	90
2001-02	1320	755	29070	45
2002-03	1401	820	36680	26

Source: 1. STPI, Hyderabad.

Fig.1: Software Exports from STP, Hyderabad (Rs. million)

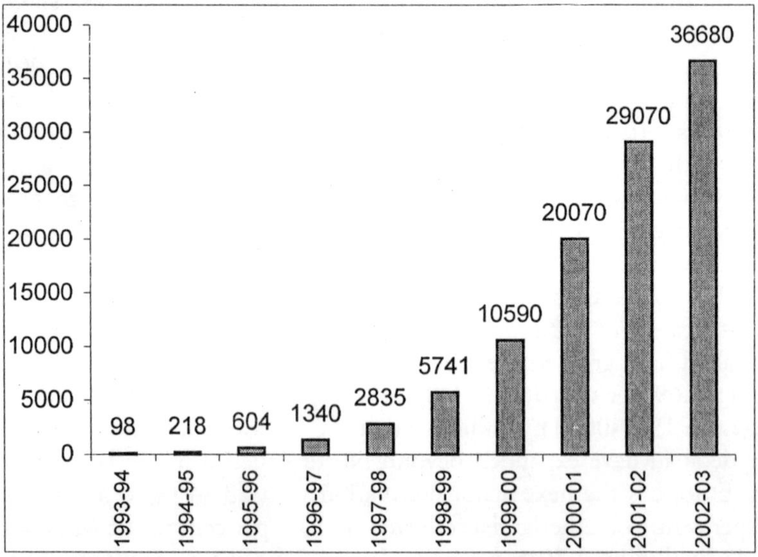

The share of STP units in Hyderabad has increased only very marginally to 7.96 per cent in the all-India software exports in 2002-03 from that of 7.82 per cent in 2001-02. Based on figures of software exports available for 1999-00 (in US dollar terms) for different states, Andhra

Pradesh stood sixth in the country with 7.21 per cent. It is interesting to note that Uttar Pradesh (U.P), with 7.33 per cent, was ahead and Haryana was closely following Andhra Pradesh.[6] About half of the total software exports from India were going from only two states - Karnataka (25.12 per cent) and Delhi (23.11 per cent). The eastern region is totally lagging behind in this sector (Sambandan, 2001). However, the data available from Nasscom for software exports by STP units for 2002-03 indicates that Andhra Pradesh stands fourth with 9.79 per cent of the total exports.[7] The top three states in the country are Karnataka (33.32 per cent), Tamil Nadu (16.96 per cent) and Maharashtra (14.82 per cent). Delhi is in the 7th position with 5.55 per cent behind Haryana (7.35 per cent) and Uttar Pradesh (6.76 per cent). In all the states, the capital cities have become the hubs of this industry because of the requirements of teleconnectivity and other associated infrastructure, apart from administrative and political factors.

In the ITES-BPO sector, Hyderabad appears to be emerging as one of the fastest growing centers in the country. From a mere 0.34 per cent in 1999-2000, the share of this sector has increased to 39.16 per cent of the total software exports from Hyderabad in 2002-03. In the previous two years its share was 24.11 per cent in 2001-02 and 8.15 per cent in 2000-01. The big companies like GE Capital from the United States and HSBC (a leading British bank) have set up facilities in Hyderabad for providing back-office services. Several other companies are providing medical transcription services to the United States. A leading Indian financial service company, Karvy, has also entered into this rector. With a large pool of English-speaking manpower, there are immense possibilities for securing jobs in IT-enabled services in the state in the coming years. About 20,000 professionals are estimated to be working in this sector. The high attrition rate of about 40 per cent in this sector seems to be posing problems for the companies to retain their staff. They are planning to work out a code for employers in this regard.[8]

Cyberabad

A 'Hi-Tec City' (Hyderabad Information Technology and Engineering Consultancy City) has been under construction in an area of about 158 acres (65 hectares). It is a joint venture (public-private) of A.P. Industrial Infrastructure Corporation (APIIC) and Larsen & Toubro Ltd. to create about 1.4 million square-feet (sft) of top class IT space. Phase I of this project, known as 'Cyber Towers' with about 0.55 million sft, was completed in December 1998 and the total space has been occupied. Some of the leading software companies have shifted into this 'Towers'. The Phase II of this project, known as 'Cyber Gateway', has also been completed with about 0.87 million sft of IT space in four blocks.[9] Several companies have also started their own offices around the 'Hi-Tec City'. By the end of

March 2003, software-exporting industry is estimated to be employing about 64,295 persons, with 7150 supporting staff. Employment in the previous year was 58000 with 6000 supporting staff. This indicates that only about 6000 new professional jobs were created as against the target of 17000 in the STP units during 2002-03 in Hyderabad. There are about 287 registered cyber cafes in Hyderabad. An Indian Institute of Information Technology (IIIT) was started in 1998. It is closely associated with the Carnegie Mellon University in the United States. It is more or less like a private university. Software giants like Metamor, IBM, Signaltree, Oracle and Satyam have started their Schools in the IIIT. Microsoft is helping to establish a faculty chair in this institute. Motorola has a School affiliated to the IIIT. For Microsoft, Hyderabad is the second software development centre outside the United States.

An area of about 52 sq.km around this 'Hi-Tec City' has recently been carved out and named as Cyberabad, the name supposed to be in conjunction with the existing twin cities of Hyderabad and Secunderabad. The difference, however, is that the nomenclature of the twin cities is based on their historical past whereas the latest one has no such roots. This new township includes the IIIT, Indian School of Business, University of Hyderabad, a golf course (planned), sports complex, Durgam Cheruvu (a lake) etc., and is proposed for development on international standards. A separate Cyberabad Development Authority has been constituted for this purpose. Future prospects of IT industry in Hyderabad are seen in new entrants, expansion of the existing units and diversifying into new areas. The state government and the STP, Hyderabad are planning to dedicate an earth station (of STPI) exclusively for Internet gateway for IT-enabled services.

The software industry is spreading to other urban centers in the state. Visakhapatnam (Vizag), with 39 software units by the end of March 2003, had an export turnover of Rs. 1174.4 million as against Rs. 161.5 million in 2001-02. An international gateway was inaugurated at Vizag in December 2000. There are plans to install a 2,500 km submarine cable connectivity between Vizag and Singapore, and also construct a mini 'Hi-Tec City'. Vizag is thus emerging as another important software center in the state. 10 international gateways are planned for installation, 6 of them in Hyderabad and one each in Vizag, Vijayawada, Warangal and Tirupati. Apart from Hyderabad and Vizag, 31 STP units are located in Vijayawada (16), Guntur (10), Tirupati (3) and Warangal (2). They have contributed exports worth Rs. 61.7 million in 2002-03.[10]

The public sector Bharat Sanchar Nigam Ltd. has laid about 22,000 km of fibre-optic network, making it the most extensive network in any state in the country. From the corporate sector, Reliance is establishing a "high-speed digital backbone" of about 2,300 km that will support data speeds ranging from one terabit to one petabit per second in the state. In the later phases, Reliance intends to add further 5,500 km to this network. Bharati Telecom (2,500 km) and Tata Teleservices (1,750 km) are also taking up laying high-speed optical fibre network in the state (Sudan, 2001).

'e-Government' Initiatives

Some measures are being initiated through ICTs in Andhra Pradesh to make the governance more electronic. The *ICT Policy 2002-05* provides several incentives, some of which are already existing, to this sector.[11] Some of the 'e-government'[12] projects that are now at different stages in the state are APSWAN (Andhra Pradesh State Wide Area Network), CARD (Computer Aided Registration Department), e-Seva, FAST (Fully Automated Services of Transport), APDMS (Andhra Pradesh Development Monitoring System), SKIMS (Secretariat Knowledge and Information System) and MPHS (Multipurpose Household Survey Project). The efficacy and transparency achieved through these projects needs to be scrutinised more thoroughly based on the experience gained so far. Under APSWAN, 25 towns including 23 district headquarters are connected with the state secretariat. Eventually all the towns and 1107 mandal headquarters in the state will be covered in this project. The project envisages simultaneous communication of vast amounts of data, voice and video transmission. The Chief Minister, ministers and other higher officials in Hyderabad can hold statewide conferences, and district officials can hold interactive sessions with other officials at short notices and access vast quantities of information simultaneously, which will save time and money by avoiding travel and related expenses. Already, video conferencing from Hyderabad with district officials and teleconferencing from district headquarters with mandal offices has become quite a routine practice in the state in recent months. While this practice is allowing instant interaction and saving time, there are apprehensions of the decision-making power getting concentrated at higher levels.

Among all the 'e-government' initiatives, the e-Seva has become more popular with the urban middle class in Hyderabad. It is planned for expansion to 56 other towns with a total of 146 centers. These are basically collection centres for various bills/fees (like telephone, electricity, trade license fee etc.) and applications from the citizens and are integrated (though partly as of now) with several departments.[13] It began (initially as TWINS) with certain services limited to a few localities but expanded significantly towards the end of 2001 and early 2002, both in terms of number of centres across Hyderabad and also in terms of number of departments to which payments could be made.

What is lacking so far in the state is a system of IT applications that would directly benefit the agricultural sector and reduce rural poverty. The state is also lacking in the kind of projects that have been initiated in

Madhya Pradesh, Tamil Nadu and Uttar Pradesh for rural development as discussed earlier. The state's approach on 'IT and poverty reduction' has no focussed agenda. The stress seems to be on several sectors which, if developed, are going to have an indirect impact on poverty reduction. For example, the statement 'use of information technology for enhancing agricultural production and productivity could have an immediate impact on the poverty reduction' (Sudan, 2001) may mean nothing in the absence of a concrete and workable policy in this direction. While several hundred primary health centres do not have doctors, the approach talks about 'use of telemedicine for making available medical expertise in remote locations'. The approach elaborates more on the possibilities rather than what is happening currently and touches upon diverse areas from women's Self-help Groups (SHGs) to Water Users Associations (WUAs). It is opined that 'in the absence of a broad attack on poverty and illiteracy', the A.P. government's strategy is forced to rely on the 'trickle-down effects' of ICT (DN, 2001).

As the IT infrastructure expands towards district headquarters, the state has natural advantages of attracting large numbers of youth coming out of English medium education. Along with Tamil Nadu and Karnataka, the school education is strong in Mathematics and Science disciplines in the state. As the evidence from developed countries suggests, it is imperative to develop the services sector that has been the engine of growth in those countries. Knowledge-based services are going to play a major role in increasing the role of the service sector in the economy. In a survey conducted for 53 countries, India came first in IT sector but last in infrastructure (Bajpai and Radjou, 2000). Development of basic infrastructure facilities is key to the growth of service sector. In the Global Competitiveness Report of the World Economic Forum, India has been ranked last or last but one among 53 countries in recent years for its low quality of infrastructure like roads, power and telecommunications. The service sector contributes about 45 per cent of the SDP in Andhra Pradesh (Quick Estimates for 1997-98). About 73 per cent of population in the state is living in rural areas, which are characterised by low productivity. This is reflected in the low share of primary sector (26 per cent).

It is, however, also argued that the vision of India as a knowledge-based economy can be realised only when it is based on the foundation of a robust industrial economy. The 'greatest source of productivity and growth attributed to the knowledge economy derives not from the knowledge economy itself, but from its effects on the industrial economy.' The "leapfrogging" argument, whereby India skips heavy infrastructure building and transforms directly into a knowledge economy, is therefore suspect. In this context, it is worthwhile to note what the noted economist Paul Krugman said, "A country is not a company!" (Konana and Balasubramanian, 2002). The governments of Andhra Pradesh and

Karnataka are projecting Hyderabad and Bangalore respectively as the future hubs of software technology in Asia. Certain areas in these cities are being exclusively developed as "hubs of IT industry" with "world class" and "high tech" facilities. These cities are claiming Singapore to be their role model. However, certain extraordinary positive qualities of that city, like public transport, housing and environmental planning etc., have been ignored in these upcoming software capitals.

5. 'ICTs' AND SOCIAL DEVELOPMENT

It requires a lot of overt resources to access and use the ICTs like a telecommunications infrastructure, an electrical infrastructure, money and literary skills which the poor do not have. Experience suggests that where the approach to development has switched to technical factors, and away from the underlying political, economic and social factors, the 'development' enables 'those with political, economic and social power to reinforce their position at the expense of those without such power' (Heeks, 1999). Since the existence of cable networks, transmitters, and receivers etc., are essential for communication technology, 'access to information will depend upon location with respect to the network'. Though a 'world without distance has become a reality' in certain respects, 'telemobility' in itself cannot create a world without distance (Chapman, 1979). Highly advanced technologies are introduced chiefly to reduce delivery-time costs with the concern for time overriding that of distance thus drastically altering the space/time relationship. This whole process is widening the gap between areas that are regarded as economically 'viable' and those that are not (Wackermann, 1997). Drawing from experiences of social exclusion, Castells (1998) argues that not only individuals but entire places and communities can get bypassed by the networks of communication.

The experience of IT-led growth has shown an over-emphasis on urban areas and certain regions. There are apprehensions that the IT-led economic growth may contribute to widening of rural-urban disparities, as the evidence shows both within and outside (Bajpai and Radjou, 2000). The Hsinchu Park in Taiwan has failed to establish linkages with surrounding areas. The IT parks in Tamil Nadu are basically satellite towns of Chennai with which they would like to be linked culturally and administratively. The international reputation of Bangalore has not affected the overall picture of the state including high incidence of rural poverty. Further, rampant wage-inflation in Bangalore was largely because of foreign high-tech companies (cited from several sources in Bajpai and Dokeniya, 1999). Wealth inequalities have risen in Bangalore. This is because of 'participation in the information-intensive global economy by a core elite, and non participation by the masses' and further that 'the recent internationalization' of that city had a 'negative impact on the poor'

(Madon, 1998). As Raza (1991) put it so tellingly, Indian cities appear to be geared to attract 'the tourist but not the neighbouring peasant'. Wealth creation in future may depend not on knowledge per se but in the application of knowledge and more importantly on 'control over knowledge'. With these trends, the global disparities may widen since in the past wealth creation depended on equipment and natural resources (Thurow, 1999 as cited in Bajpai and Radjou, 2000).

Equitable development through the application of ICTs depends, firstly, upon the capabilities of the people in general to take advantage of these technologies. The literacy rate (61.11 per cent) in Andhra Pradesh is below the national average of 65.38 per cent, and is also lower than that of the four southern states of Tamil Nadu, Karnataka and Kerala as per 2001 census. The female literacy is only 51.17 per cent.[14] In the city of Hyderabad itself the condition of many of the government schools is very poor. Dilapidated buildings, lack of drinking water, lack of sanitation, lack of power, holding classes under trees in the open, very few teachers etc., are some of the common problems afflicting them. Thousands of children from poor families are enrolled in such schools.[15] While it is a fact that millions of Indians are getting connected to the Internet it should also be noted that 'millions more aren't connected to fresh water'. While India accounts for about 30 per cent of the world's software engineers, about 25 per cent of the world's malnourished are also in India.[16] Secondly, unless adequate priority is given simultaneously to social development and poverty eradication, exclusive dependence on ICTs may lead to the accentuation of the existing social and economic inequalities.

6. CONCLUSION

The IT industry in Andhra Pradesh has several advantages for growth with a large pool of scientific manpower and a proactive state government. The software exports have grown impressively in the last decade. The IT-enabled services may play a significant role in creation of employment opportunities in the coming period. Heeks (2002) argues that ICTs offer genuine possibilities in achieving development objectives, and that what is required is a right approach towards ICTs. To achieve this, he emphasizes that 'we need to move away from concepts of 'electronic development' that places ICTs centre-stage'. Instead, the approach 'must be information-centred, integral to its environment, integrated with development objectives, intermediated, interconnected, and indigenised. Above all, it must be intelligent. Our development priority for the future must therefore be 'i-development, not e-development'. As the knowledge-based economy has a tendency to reverse the sources of equality (Thurow, 2000), the basic challenges lie in improving the social sectors like education, health, poverty etc., and develop infrastructure. If these problems are not tackled on a priority basis, the fast-growing IT sector will leave majority of the population behind which may lead to a more iniquitous and polarised society. Thus, there is a need for a greater thrust in the policy framework in Andhra Pradesh towards making IT an enabler and equaliser in opportunities and developpent.

Notes

1 Editorial entitled "IT and the Economy", *Economic and Political Weekly*, April 21, 2001.

2 Some of these are Call Centres, Medical Transcription, Data Digitisation, Legal Databases, Revenue Accounting, Data Processing, Back Office Operations, Web Content Development, Animation, Insurance Claims Processing, Payroll, Logistics Management, Remote Network Management, Specialised Knowledge Services, Help Desks etc. Some of the Western companies obtaining such services from India are Bechtel (from New Delhi), GE Capital (from Gurgaon, New Delhi and Hyderabad), US Hospitals (from Bangalore), HSBC (from Hyderabad), British Airways, 3 Com etc.

3 It is estimated that a clerk carrying out routine back office operations might cost around US $ 36,000/- per year in the US or UK. In India the cost would be less than $ 10,000/- per year (based on personal discussions).

4 For more details on the impact of IT in rural areas, see Yadav, 2001; Biswas, 2001; and several other websites like www.tenet.res.in , www.tarahaat.com , www.mssrf.org etc.

5 In a little over a year since the Gyandoot was launched, about 6000 e-mail complaints have been sent to the district administration making the slothful administration more accountable (Biswas, 2001).

6 The location of software industry in NOIDA and Gurgaon, which are administratively in Uttar Pradesh and Haryana respectively but located on the outskirts of Delhi, is accounting for these states.

7 Source: www.nasscom.org accessed on 6th June 2003. (Data obtained from the presentation by S.N. Zindal, Director General, STPI).

8 *Times of India*, June 10, 2003, Hyderabad.

9 Discussions with the concern official (in November 2002) in 'L & T Infocity' revealed that about 85 per cent of the space in the Phase II was already occupied. However, the website of the State Government shows that about 57 per cent of the space in the Phase II is available for occupation (www.ap-it.com accessed on 11th June 2003).

10 Source: Software Technology Park, Hyderabad.

11 Some of the incentives extended to IT companies in this Policy include:

- Exemption from purview of AP Pollution Control Act, except in power generation sets.
- Self certification and exemption from inspections under Factories Act, Maternity Benefit Act, AP Shops & Establishments Act, Contract Labour Act, Payment of Wages Act, Minimum Wages Act, Employment Exchanges Act.
- Permission to run a three-shift operation.
- Concessional power tariff - Under this scheme, IT units will be eligible for a 25% rebate in power tariff for a period of 3 years from the date of commencement of commercial operation.
- Reimbursement of stamp duty - A 50% reimbursement of the stamp duty, transfer duty and registration fee will be allowed to ICT companies.
- Exemption from zoning regulations.

• Rebate in cost of land.
• Capital investment subsidy.
• Special provision for mega IT projects - with an investment of Rs. 50 crores and above.
• The government has also established an IT-enabled single window system for providing a smooth interface between industrial and business units and the regulatory agencies of the government.

Andhra Pradesh is the first state to promote 'free right of way" telecommunication along highways, thus supporting increased PC and internet penetration and teledensity leading to broad band. Andhra Pradesh is the 'ideal ICT destination' with the conducive business environment that it fosters, and the various incentives given and the initiatives taken to foster an environment to promote quality management, promote businesses and enhance citizen services through e-Governance (source: www.ap-it.com accessed on September 12, 2002).

12 The objective of e-government is not in the technical sense but good governance as reflected in 'SMART' government. SMART is the acronym for Simple, Moral, Accountable, Responsive and Transparent (Sudan, 2000).

13 Citizens are fed up of standing in long queues for making payments at several departments and lose valuable time and energy during working hours. This *e-Seva* facility enables multiple payments at one counter. The issue of tokens on first-come-first basis avoids the need for standing in queues. This is a big relief for citizens. For the departments participating in the e-Seva network,. the bill collection charges are estimated to have come down to 0.45 per cent of their operating cost. This facility is thus benefiting both the institutions and citizens that are reflected in its growing popularity. (Based on personal observation Aniket Alam, 'e-Seva spreading fast and wide', *The Hindu*, 16th May 2002, Hyderabad).

14 About 7189 habitations (12 per cent) do not have a primary school within one km radius, and about 21762 (34 per cent) do not have upper primary school within 3 km radius in the state (Sudan, 2001).

15 'Many Government schools in dilapidated buildings: MCH', *The Hindu,* 4th August 2002, Hyderabad; Similar news items in *Vaartha* (Telugu Daily), 2nd August 2002; *The New Indian Express,* 12th September 2002.

16 Speech by Bill Clinton, President of the United States, to the Hyderabad business community at 'Hi-Tec City' on 24th March 2000 (Source: www.andhrapradesh.com accessed in April, 2000).

References

Bajpai, Nirupama and Navi Radjou (2000), "Rising Global Competitiveness of Tamil Nadu's IT Industry", *Economic and Political Weekly,* Vol. 35, No. 6.

Bajpai, Nirupama and Anupama Dokeniya (1999), "Information Technology-Led Growth Policies: A Case Study of Tamil Nadu", Development Discussion Paper No. 729, Harvard Institute for International Development, Harvard University, the U.S.

Biswas, Soutik (2001), "Digital Empowerment – Seeds of E-volution", *Outlook* (A Weekly Newsmagazine), April 9, New Delhi.

Castelles, M. (1998), "Information Technology, Globalisation and Social Development", Paper prepared for the UNRISD Conference on Information Technologies and Social Development, Geneva, 22-24 June.

Census of India (2001), *Provisional Population Totals, Paper 1 of 2001*, Series-29: Andhra Pradesh.

Chapman, Keith. (1979), *People, Pattern and Process: An Introduction to Human Geography*, Arnold-Heineman, London.

Chowdary, T.H. (1998), "Information Technology and Village Development", *Journal of the Centre for Telecom Management and Studies*, Vol. 7, No. 9.

DN (2001), "ICTs in Rural Poverty Alleviation", *Economic and Political Weekly*, Vol. 36, No. 11.

Government of Andhra Pradesh (2002), *ICT Policy 2002-05*, Hyderabad.

Government of Andhra Pradesh (2000), *IT Policy-2000*, Hyderabad.

Government of Andhra Pradesh (1999), G.O. Ms. No. 114 dated 25-05-1999 – Orders on Incentives for Promotion of IT Industry and IT Enabled Services in the State, Hyderabad.

Government of Andhra Pradesh (1999), The *Vision-2020 Document*, Hyderabad.

Heeks, Richard (2002), "I-Development not e-Development: Special Issue on ICTs and Development", *Journal of International Development*, Vol. 14, No. 1.

Heeks, Richard (1999), "Information and Communication Technologies, Poverty and Development", Development Informatics Working Paper Series No. 5, Institute for Development Policy and Management, University of Manchester, UK.

Jhunjhunwala, Ashok (2002), "Challenges in Rural Connectivity for India", *ASCI Journal of Management*, Vol. 31, Nos. 1&2.

Jhunjhunwala, Ashok (2000), "Unleashing Telecom and Internet in India", Paper presented at India Telecom Conference at the Asia/Pacific Research Centre, Stanford University, November (downloaded from www.tenet.res.in)

Khosla, Ashok and Surender Rana (2000), "TARAhaat has arrived: Connecting Rural India to the Global Village", *Development Alternatives Newsletter*, Vol. 10, No. 12, December.

Konana, Prabhudev and Sridhar Balasubramanian (2002), "India as a knowledge Economy: Aspirations versus Reality", *Frontline*, January 19 - February 01.

Madon, S. (1998), "Information-based Global Economy and Socio-economic Development: The Case of Bangalore", *The Information Society*, Vol. 13.

Patibandla, Murali, Deepak Kapur and Bent Petersen (2000), "Import Substitution with Free Trade: Case of India's Software Industry", *Economic and Political Weekly*, Vol. 35, No. 15.

Rana, Surender (2002), "TARAhaat: Changing Realities in Field (Jhansi)", *Development Alternatives Newsletter*, Vol. 12, No. 5, May.

Raza, Moonis. (1991), "On the Nature of Rural Urban Interactions in the Indian Context", *IASSI Quarterly*, Vol. 10, No. 1.

Sambandan, V.S. (2001), "Regional Divide in Software Exports", *The Hindu*, 29 March, Hyderabad.

Sreekumar, T.T. (2002), "Civil Society and ICT-based Models of Rural Change: History, Rhetoric and Practice", Paper presented in the International Seminar on *ICTs and Indian Development: Processes, Prognoses and Policies*, 9-11 December, Bangalore.

Srivastava, Anil (2002), "ICT-Human Development Interface: Charting the Growth path in Madhya Pradesh", *ASCI Journal of Management*, Vol. 31, Nos. 1&2.

Sudan, Randeep (2001), "Use of Information Technology for Poverty Reduction: A Focus on Andhra Pradesh"', Paper presented at ADB's Asia and the Pacific Forum on Poverty, February 5-9, Manila.

Thurow, Lester (1999), *Building Wealth*, Harpercollins, New York.

Thurow, Lester (2000), "Globalisation: The Product of a Knowledge-based Economy", *Annals of the American Academy of Political and Social Science*, Vol. 570.

Wackermann, Gabriel. (1997), "Transport, Trade, Tourism and the World Economic System" *International Social Science Journal*, No. 151.

Yadav, Kushal Pal Singh (2001), "Rural Infotech: Virtually There", *Down To Earth*, Vol. 9, No. 18.

PART - III
SECTORAL STUDIES

8

Agricultural Growth: Pattern and Prospects

S. Subrahmanyam and
P. Satya Sekhar

1. INTRODUCTION

Agricultural growth is necessary not only for attaining high overall growth but also for eradication of poverty. The Ninth Five Year Plan of India (1997-2002) aimed at a growth rate of 4.5 per cent per annum for the agricultural sector. The Government of Andhra Pradesh, in its Vision 2020 document, envisaged a still higher growth rate of 6.0 per cent per annum in the first decade of this century (Government of Andhra Pradesh, 1999). The Working Paper prepared subsequently identified three sources of accelerating growth of Andhra Pradesh agriculture (Government of Andhra Pradesh, 2001). The first source is improvement of yields of rice, groundnut, cotton, maize and pulses. For each crop, a separate approach is suggested for raising the yield. The second source identified for attaining high agricultural growth is improving cropping intensity, as the present level of 130 per cent is too low for the irrigation ratio of 43 per cent attained in the state. The third source identified is improving the input use efficiency in order to withstand global competition. The Working Paper does not provide comprehensive picture of trends in Andhra Pradesh agriculture in terms of growth of output and inputs of various crops. The possibility of attaining this growth has not been worked out in a consistent framework.

The objective of this paper is to examine the pattern of development of Andhra Pradesh agriculture and suggest a perspective for its development in the first decade of 21st century. The growth performance since mid-fifties is reviewed in Section 2 by considering growth of production, total factor productivity, expansion of irrigation, investment in agriculture and growth in fertiliser. Section 3 focuses on growth potential of the sector by examining the scope for increasing net area sown and yields of various crops. The strategy needed in different agro-climatic regions is also examined in this section. A brief summary of conclusions is presented in Section 4.

2. REVIEW OF PAST PERFORMANCE

Growth performance of the agricultural sector of Andhra Pradesh is examined for the long period of 44 years (1955-56 to 1998-99) with a break up into four sub-periods. The first sub-period extending from 1955-56 to 1969-70 is the pre-green revolution period. The second and third sub-periods, covering seventies and eighties, represent first and second phases of green revolution. The fourth sub-period of nineties is the period of economic liberalization. Growth rates of production, area and yield of important crops are estimated from a single log-linear trend equation with dummies for separating the growth rate of each sub-period. The details of the methodology are discussed in Appendix 1.

Agricultural Growth

Indian agricultural growth in the post-independence period can be distinguished into four distinct phases – pre-green revolution phase, first phase of green revolution, second phase of green revolution and liberalization phase. The decade of eighties is treated, as the second phase of green revolution and the decade of nineties as the liberalization period. The first phase of green revolution maintained the growth rate of output achieved in the pre-green revolution period, despite deceleration in the growth rate of area. In other words, this period could maintain the growth rate of the pre-green revolution period by achieving significant improvement in crop yields. This can be seen from the fact that the growth rate of aggregate output improved, though marginally from 2.8 per cent to 3.0 per cent, despite decline in the growth rate of gross cropped area from 1.2 per cent to 0.6 per cent. Similarly, the growth rate of food grain production accelerated marginally from 2.5 to 2.8 per cent, despite deceleration in the growth rate of area under food-grains from 1.0 to 0.4 per cent (Rao and Deshpande, 1986). While this is the positive side of the green revolution, on the negative side, the first phase witnessed accentuation of inter-regional and inter- crop imbalances because of the restriction of HYV seeds for only rice and wheat in the initial years and the adoption of these varieties only in the well-endowed regions (Rao, 1994). The second phase of green revolution (1980s) appears to be the best period for Indian agriculture with significant acceleration in output growth and reduction in regional inequalities because of the introduction of HYVs for other crops, spread of green revolution to eastern region and emphasis on watershed programmes in dry areas. For instance, the growth rate of aggregate output accelerated from 2.5 per cent in the first phase to 2.9 per cent in the second phase. Similarly, the growth rates of pulses accelerated from 0.3 and 2.3 per cent and the growth rate of oilseeds accelerated from 2.3 to 2.9 percent. The early nineties also experienced continuation of the trends observed in the eighties. The output index of all crops increased at

3.4 per cent per annum in the eighties as well as in the early nineties. The net domestic product from agriculture grew at 3.2 per cent (Sawant, 1997). However, when the entire period of nineties is considered, there is clear evidence of deceleration in agricultural growth. The growth rate of GDP from agriculture declined from 4.2 per cent in the eighties to 3.7 per cent per annum in the nineties. The growth rate of crop output decelerated steeply from 3.4 to 2.2 percent. Barring wheat, which maintained a stable growth of 3.6 per cent per annum in both the periods, all other crops experienced deceleration in growth (Government of India, 2001).

Given this all India scenario, what is the experience of Andhra Pradesh? Has the first decade of green revolution experienced accentuation of regional inequalities without much improvement in output growth? Has the eighties experienced accelerated and balanced growth across regions? Has the nineties maintained the trends observed in the previous decade in terms of growth and regional inequalities?

The results on growth rates of output for all the major crops in different periods are shown in Table 1. The growth rates of area and yield

GRAPH-1: DIVISIA INDEX OF TOTAL CROP OUTPUT IN ANDHRA PRADESH: 1955-56 TO 1998-99

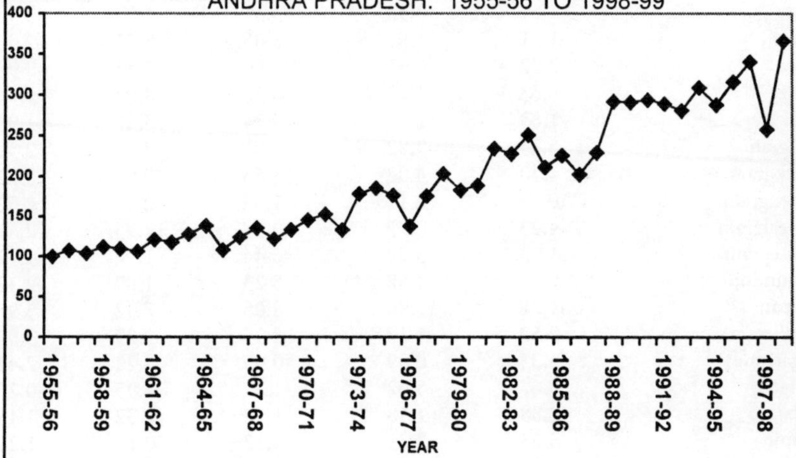

of major crops in different periods are presented in Table 2. Changes in cropping pattern are shown in Table 3. The results indicate that, in contrast to the experience at the national level, Andhra Pradesh attained significant acceleration in agricultural growth in the first phase of green revolution over the pre green revolution period. The growth rate of aggregate output accelerated dramatically from 1.9 per cent in the pre-green revolution period to 3.5 per cent per annum in the first phase of post-green revolution period (Graph-1). This high acceleration is not merely due to rice, the main beneficiary of green revolution in the initial phase, but due to the good performance of all food grain crops. For instance, while rice output grew at 3.6 per cent, pulses attained growth rates ranging between 3.2 to 8.1 per cent and millets attained growth rates ranging between 1.8 to 7.1 per cent per annum. These high growth rates of unirrigated crops resulted in a broad-based growth and reduction in regional inequalities in contrast to the experience at all-India level. While food grains attained high growth, the performance of non-food grain crops, except cotton, is not satisfactory. However, the high growth rate of cotton enabled the output of non-food grains to maintain a stable growth at 2.8 per cent in both the periods. Though rice attained higher growth rate of output than all other cereals, except maize, the growth rate of yield is lower than that of pulses, except red gram. Among the non-food grains, cotton, chillies and tobacco exhibited high growth rates of yield. The remaining non-food grain crops experienced decline in yield and output growth was contributed by area expansion.

Table 1. Growth Rates of Output of Selected Crops in Different Periods

Crop	Triennium Ending				
	1957-58 to 1969-70	1970-71 to 1979-80	1980-81 to 1989-90	1990-91 to 1998-99	1957-58 to 1998-99
Rice	1.61	3.58	3.31	1.57	2.48
Jowar	-1.71	1.81	-3.05	-5.77	-2.04
Bajra	-2.22	2.62	-5.66	-7.45	-2.98
Maize	6.63	7.14	0.36	8.02	5.54
Ragi	-1.83	2.67	-5.34	-3.47	-1.94
Redgram	5.25	-7.92	8.07	3.97	2.50
Blackgram	4.72	4.02	13.63	0.08	5.72
Greengram	0.75	8.11	1.82	-0.44	2.52
Bengalgram	-4.23	0.77	-0.38	17.25	2.41
Horsegram	-1.73	3.24	-6.44	-1.97	-1.72
Groundnut	0.94	1.58	5.23	1.89	2.32
Cotton	-1.28	11.90	8.05	7.42	5.95
Chillies	2.52	1.17	8.95	3.29	3.90
Sugarcane	5.33	0.39	-0.95	4.28	2.42
Gingelly	0.67	-5.02	-1.21	4.95	-0.25
Tobacco	2.88	1.48	-1.14	2.32	1.46
Castor	3.33	-3.21	4.12	-0.18	1.21
Onions	-3.84	-2.49	7.49	7.90	1.67
A. Cereals	1.05	3.64	2.17	1.40	2.01
B. Pulses	1.78	2.97	6.72	1.49	3.19
C. Food grains	1.10	3.61	2.47	1.50	2.12
D. Non-foodgrains	2.85	2.82	4.96	3.20	3.41
E. All Crops	1.94	3.46	3.41	2.30	2.73
F. NSDPAG	0.73	2.72	2.91	1.32	1.94

Note: Growth Rates are computed for Triennium Averages.
NSDPAG: Net State Domestic Product from Agriculture.

The results indicate accelerated and broad based growth of Andhra Pradesh agriculture in the first phase of green revolution since growth of rice output is due to area expansion and growth of millets is due to yield expansion. Thus, in contrast to the all-India experience, the first phase of green revolution witnessed significant acceleration in growth of output and reduction in regional inequalities as the growth was broad based covering both irrigated as well as dry crops.

Table 2. Growth Rates of Area and Yield of Selected Crops in Different Periods

Crop	1957-58 to 1969-70		1970-71 to 1979-80		1980-81 to 1989-90		1990-91 to 1998-99	
	Area	Yield	Area	Yield	Area	Yield	Area	Yield
Rice	0.81	0.80	1.04	2.50	0.27	3.05	0.27	1.30
Jowar	0.06	-1.77	-0.64	2.45	-1.69	1.36	-4.28	1.49
Bajra	-0.97	-1.25	0.21	2.42	-5.99	0.33	-11.31	3.86
Maize	1.95	4.68	3.48	3.65	-0.77	1.12	1.71	6.29
Ragi	-0.72	-1.10	-0.52	3.19	-4.64	-0.69	-5.32	1.86
Redgram	1.73	3.51	0.68	-8.60	4.56	3.51	0.86	3.12
Blackgram	4.43	0.28	-1.17	5.19	7.89	5.75	3.68	-3.60
Greengram	2.23	-1.48	1.02	7.09	0.09	1.73	-0.91	0.47
Bengalgram	-3.50	-0.73	-1.49	2.26	-3.09	2.72	11.07	6.18
Horsegram	-1.22	-0.50	-0.74	3.97	-7.50	1.07	-5.0	3.03
Groundnut	3.08	-2.11	-0.30	1.89	4.88	0.36	1.19	0.71
Cotton	-0.89	-0.35	1.33	10.57	4.58	3.43	6.04	1.39
Chillies	4.22	-1.70	-2.07	3.24	2.96	5.99	1.08	2.21
Sugarcane	5.89	-0.56	0.42	-0.03	0.82	-1.77	3.24	1.04
Gingelly	0.58	0.10	-3.95	-1.07	-0.47	-0.73	1.29	3.66
Tobacco	4.16	-1.28	-0.89	2.36	-3.31	2.16	1.10	1.21
Castor	0.58	2.77	-1.40	-1.79	1.89	2.23	-3.31	3.16
Onions	-0.32	-3.52	-1.11	-1.38	3.11	4.38	2.54	5.36

Table 3. Changes in Cropping Pattern

(% to GCA)

Crop	Triennium Ending				
	1958-59	1968-69	1978-79	1988-89	1998-99
Rice	24.0	25.2	29.9	30.4	30.5
Jowar	21.2	20.5	17.9	13.1	6.1
Bajra	5.1	4.8	4.5	2.6	0.9
Maize	1.6	1.8	2.4	2.5	3.0
Ragi	2.6	2.6	2.6	1.5	0.8
Cereals	54.5	55.0	57.3	50.2	41.2
Redgram	1.3	1.4	1.6	2.6	2.7
Blackgram	1.1	1.5	1.5	3.3	3.7
Bengalgram	0.9	0.6	0.5	0.4	1.0
Greengram	3.1	3.7	4.0	4.1	3.6
Horsegram	3.8	3.2	2.7	1.5	0.9
Pulses	10.1	10.5	10.3	12.0	12.0
Groundnut	9.8	10.0	9.1	16.2	15.3
Gingelly	2.1	1.9	1.2	1.4	1.3
Castor	2.4	2.2	2.1	2.6	1.6
Sunflower	-	-	-	0.7	2.6
Oilseeds	14.2	14.1	12.4	20.8	20.7
Sugarcane	0.6	1.0	1.2	1.2	1.6
Cotton	2.9	2.5	2.9	4.5	8.2
Tobacco	1.3	1.7	1.8	1.1	1.4
Chillies	1.1	1.5	1.1	1.6	1.7
Onion	0.2	0.1	0.1	0.2	0.2
Other Crops	6.0	6.7	7.2	8.6	13.1
All Crops	84.9	86.2	87.1	91.5	87.0
Gross Cropped Area (hectares)	121.8	126.4	125.1	119.2	130.6

The second phase of green revolution maintained the growth rate attained in the first phase in contrast to acceleration at the national level. Even this achievement is not due to continuation of growth in yield of various crops attained in the previous period, but due to shift in the cropping pattern from low-valued coarse cereals to high-valued crops like oilseeds, cotton and pulses. The share of millets in gross cropped area declined from 27 per cent during 1978-79 to 20 per cent. On the other hand, the share of oilseeds increased from 12 to 21 per cent and that of cotton increased from 3 to 4.5 per cent. Because of these shifts in area from food grains to commercial crops, the growth rate of cereal output decelerated from 3.6 to 2.2 percent per annum while growth rate of non-food grain output accelerated from 2.8 to 5.0 per cent. But the yield performance of both groundnut and cotton was very poor. The growth rate of groundnut yield decelerated from 1.89 per cent to 0.36 per cent in the eighties and that of cotton from 10.57 per cent to 3.43 per cent. Even the growth rates of millets, declined steeply. Only rice experienced acceleration in the growth rate of yield from 2.50 per cent to 3.05 per cent. But the slow down in growth of rice area led to deceleration in output growth from 3.58 per cent in seventies to 3.31 per cent per annum in the eighties. Regions with dominance of rice and regions that have shifted from coarse cereals to groundnut or cotton attained a higher growth rate of aggregate output than other regions. Thus, the decade of eighties is not a period of accelerated and broad-based growth for Andhra Pradesh as in the case of all-India. It is a period of shifts in cropping pattern from low value crops to high valued crops.

In the nineties, the State experienced steep deceleration in growth as the nation. The growth rate of aggregate output index declined from 3.4 to 2.3 percent. The growth rate of rice output declined from 3.3 to 1.6 percent per annum. The growth rate of groundnut output decelerated from 5.2 to 1.9 percent. The growth rate of cotton declined from 8.1 to 7.4 percent. This decline is mainly caused by deceleration in the growth rates of yields of all the important crops. The growth rate of rice yield declined steeply from 3.1 to 1.3 per cent and that of cotton from 3.4 to 1.4 percent. The growth rate of groundnut yield remained low at 0.7 per cent. Sugarcane also experienced a significant decline in the growth rate of yield from 3.2 to 1.0 percent per annum. It is significant to note that output growth in the nineties decelerated steeply, despite significant growth in the gross cropped area at 0.6 per cent per annum on account of increase in the cropping intensity from 117 to 123 per cent. Expansion of area could not offset the decline in the growth rates of yield.

The growth rates of net state domestic product from agriculture at 1980-81 prices are also computed for the above periods. These growth rates are far below the corresponding rates based on Divisia index. For instance, the growth rate of net state domestic product from agriculture in the nineties is found to be as low as 1.3 percent per annum at 1980-81 prices as compared to the growth rate of 2.3 per cent based on Divisia output index. While Divisia index is based on changing weights, the index of state domestic product from agriculture at constant prices is based on base year weights, which may not reflect the values of the commodities at a later period.

What are the factors that contributed for the observed growth pattern of Andhra Pradesh agriculture? In other words, how could the sector attain high growth in the first phase of green revolution? Why has the decade of nineties turned to be a period of steep deceleration in the growth rate of aggregate output? Since area under cultivation is an important determinant of agricultural output, it is necessary to examine as to what extent area under cultivation is responsible for the slow down in agricultural growth in Andhra Pradesh. Changes in area under cultivation and fallow land are shown in Table 4. The area under cultivation increased marginally in the pre-green revolution period from 111.5 to 112.1 lakh hectares, but declined continuously in the 70s and 80s and came down to 105.1 lakh hectares. However, it recovered marginally in the nineties to 105.5 lakh hectares. The cumulative decline in net area sown since the beginning of seventies is as high as 6.6 lakh hectares. This decline is the result of increase in the fallow land by 11.5 lakh hectares. Only in the nineties the extent of fallow land started declining along with increase in net area sown. The eighties witnessed highest increase in the extent of fallow land by 9.7 lakh hectares. Thus, area under cultivation is not the factor responsible for deceleration of agricultural growth in the nineties. Even cropping intensity is not responsible for this deceleration as cropping intensity increased steeply in the nineties from 117 percent in TE 1988-89 to 123 percent TE 1998-99. Only deceleration in the growth rates of yield of several crops is responsible for deceleration in the agricultural growth of Andhra Pradesh in the nineties.

Table 4. Changes in Area Under Cultivation and Fallow Lands

(Lakh hectares)

Year (T.E)	Net Area Sown		Fallows		Gross Cropped Area		Cropping Intensity
	Actual	Growth Rate	Actual	Growth Rate	Actual	Growth Rate	
1958-59	111.46	-	28.38	-	121.78	-	109
1968-69	112.10	0.06	31.43	1.03	126.42	0.04	113
1978-79	109.56	-0.23	35.84	1.32	125.07	-0.11	114
1988-89	105.11	-0.41	45.56	2.43	123.33	-0.14	117
1998-99	105.53	0.04	42.87	-0.61	130.57	0.57	123

Note: T.E. stands for triennium ending.

Investment in Agriculture

As information on investment in agriculture at State level is available only from the eighties, expansion of irrigated area could serve as an indicator of investment for long-term analysis. Gross irrigated area is a better indicator of investment than net irrigated area since investment in some of the delta modernization schemes is intended to increase intensity of irrigation rather than spread of irrigation to new areas. Data on the extent of irrigated area in Andhra Pradesh is shown in Table 5 and data on source-wise irrigated area is presented in Table 6. Gross irrigated area expanded at a high rate of 1.5 per cent per annum in the seventies and the growth decelerated to 0.6 per cent in the eighties. But the nineties witnessed all time highest growth of 1.9 per cent per annum (Table 5). If there is a time lag between investment and expansion of irrigated area, this high growth in irrigated area in the nineties must be partly the result of investment in the eighties. Similarly, the low growth of irrigated area in the eighties may be the result of low investment in the seventies. The lag between investment and expansion of irrigated area depends on the source of irrigation. Investment in canal irrigation involves time lag whereas tank irrigation schemes can be completed in the same year. Ground water exploitation does not involve much time lag. The high growth in irrigated area in the seventies was contributed by both canal and ground water sources. Canal irrigation projects taken up in the pre-green revolution period and private investment in ground water exploitation in the first phase of green revolution resulted in balanced growth of surface and ground water sources in the seventies. The slow down in public investment in irrigation in the seventies might have resulted in slow growth of canal area in the eighties. While 3.2 lakh hectares of canal irrigated area is added in the seventies, only 1.1 lakh hectares have been added in the eighties. On the other hand, ground water irrigation expanded by 3.2 lakh hectares in the eighties as against 2.2 lakh hectares in the seventies. As a result, the ratio of surface to ground water declined steeply from 4.1 in 1978-79 to 2.7 in 1988-89. In the nineties, there is a decline in the area under canal irrigation and phenomenal increase of 7.6 lakh hectares in area under ground water irrigation. As a result, the ratio of surface to ground water irrigation came down to 1.4 by 1998-99. The trends in irrigated area indicate that public investment in irrigation started declining and private investment started growing at an accelerated rate from mid-seventies.

Table 5. Changes in Irrigated Area

(Lakh hectares)

Year (T.E)	Net Irrigated Area		Gross Irrigated Area		% Of		Irrigation Intensity
	Actual	Growth Rate	Actual	Growth Rate	NIA to NAS	GIA to GCA	
1958-59	28.16	-	34.19	-	25.3	28.1	121.4
1968-69	29.59	0.50	38.04	1.07	26.4	30.1	128.6
1978-79	34.83	1.64	44.10	1.49	31.8	35.3	126.6
1988-89	37.26	0.68	46.99	0.64	35.4	38.1	126.1
1998-99	42.93	1.43	56.77	1.91	40.3	43.5	132.2

Table 6. Changes in Net Irrigated Area by Source

(Lakh hectares)

Year (T.E.)	Canal		Tank		Other Sources		Ground Water		Surface	
	Actual	Increase	Actual	Increase	Actual	Increase	Actual	Increase	Actual	Increase
1958-59	12.57	-	11.61	-	0.93	-	3.06	-	25.11	-
1968-69	13.16	0.59	10.84	-0.77	0.97	0.04	4.62	1.56	24.97	-0.14
1978-79	16.40	3.24	10.47	-0.37	1.14	0.17	6.82	2.20	28.01	3.04
1988-89	17.48	1.08	8.48	-1.99	1.27	0.13	10.03	3.21	27.23	-0.78
1998-99	16.00	-1.48	7.39	-1.09	1.86	0.59	17.67	7.64	25.25	-1.98

The data on investment in agriculture at State level is available from 1980 onwards. Investment in agriculture became an important aspect in recent times. Three issues are considered in this context. Firstly, what is the type of relationship between public and private investment? Some studies show complementary relationship and others show that they are not related except in the case of canal irrigation. Secondly, what are the factors that induce private investment in agriculture? Some studies show that terms of trade play a significant role in inducing private investment and others show that technology is more important than price factor. Thirdly, what is the relationship between public investment and agricultural growth? Gulati (2001) shows that the elasticity of GDP from agriculture with respect to public cumulative investment in agriculture is 0.32 while the elasticity with respect to terms of trade is 1.8, indicating that price has a greater impact than public investment. His results also show that the elasticity of private investment with respect to canal irrigation is high, but terms of trade is found to be the most powerful variable influencing private investment in agriculture. Dhawan and Yadav (1995) found complementary relationship between public and private investment using All India Debt and Investment Survey data for 1981-82.

The data on gross fixed capital formation in Andhra Pradesh and all India are analysed for eighties and nineties. While the nation experienced trend decline in investment in agriculture till 1987-88 and increase in the subsequent period, Andhra Pradesh showed the opposite trend of higher growth in the eighties than in the nineties. Gross total investment in agriculture declined in the eighties at 0.8 percent at the national level and increased at 6.0 percent per annum in Andhra Pradesh in the eighties (Table 7). On the other hand, the nation experienced revival of investment in the nineties with a growth rate of 7.7 per cent, but Andhra Pradesh attained a very low growth rate of 1.5 percent per annum in the nineties. Thus, the nineties is a period of high growth of ground water irrigation and very low growth of total investment (public plus private) in agriculture.

Table 7. Logarithmic Trend Equations of Gross Fixed Capital Formation in Agriculture at Constant Prices: 1980-81 to 1996-97

	Andhra Pradesh	India
Constant	5.06	8.43
Coefficient of time	0.0597	-0.0079
	(4.25)	(-1.65)
Coefficient of time dummy	-0.0442	0.0852
	(1.81)	(8.53)
R^2	0.68	0.95
Growth Rate during 80's	5.97	-0.79
Growth Rate during 90's	1.54	7.73

Note: Figures in parentheses are t values.

Growth of Total Factor Productivity

Agricultural growth has to be attained by increasing productivity so that cost of production is reduced. A number of studies have examined the contribution of total factor productivity for the growth of output in different phases of agricultural growth. Most of the studies show that the contribution of total factor productivity was quite low in the pre-green revolution period. But the conclusions for the first and second phases of green revolution are not unanimous. Dholakia and Dholakia (1993) found that the second phase of green revolution witnessed acceleration in the growth of output as well as increase in the contribution of total factor productivity to output growth. On the other hand, Shenggen Fan and Peter Hazell (1997) found marginal decline in the contribution of total factor productivity in the decade of eighties over seventies.

Our results for Andhra Pradesh show that total factor productivity was declining in the pre-green revolution period, as aggregate input growth was higher than aggregate output growth (Table 8). This was due to slow growth of aggregate output at 1.94 percent and rapid growth of aggregate input at 3.96 percent per annum during the period. In the first decade of green revolution, total factor productivity grew at 1.13 per cent per annum and contributed one-third to the growth of output. The second decade of green revolution experienced a further increase in the productivity growth to 1.58 per cent per annum and the contribution of total factor productivity to output growth increased to 46 percent. This is a significant achievement in view of the fact that the output growth was more or less the same as in the first phase. Thus, the second decade of green revolution attained a significant improvement in resource use efficiency as compared to the first decade. In the nineties, the growth rate of output declined from 3.42 to 2.30 per cent per annum, but the growth rate of aggregate input also declined from 1.84 to 1.25 per cent. As a result, the productivity

Table 8. Growth Rates of Output, Input and Total Factor Productivity Indices in Different Periods

Period	Output Index	Input Index	Total Factor Productivity Index
1957-58 to 1969-70	1.94 (100.0)	3.96 (204.1)	-2.02 (-104.1)
1970-71 to 1979-80	3.46 (100.0)	2.33 (67.3)	1.13 (32.7)
1980-81 to 1989-90	3.42 (100.0)	1.84 (53.8)	1.58 (46.2)
1990-91 to 1998-99	2.30 (100.0)	1.25 (54.3)	1.05 (45.7)
1957-58 to 1998-99	2.74 (100.0)	2.49 (90.9)	0.25 (9.1)

Note: Figures in brackets are percentage contributions of input and productivity to output growth.

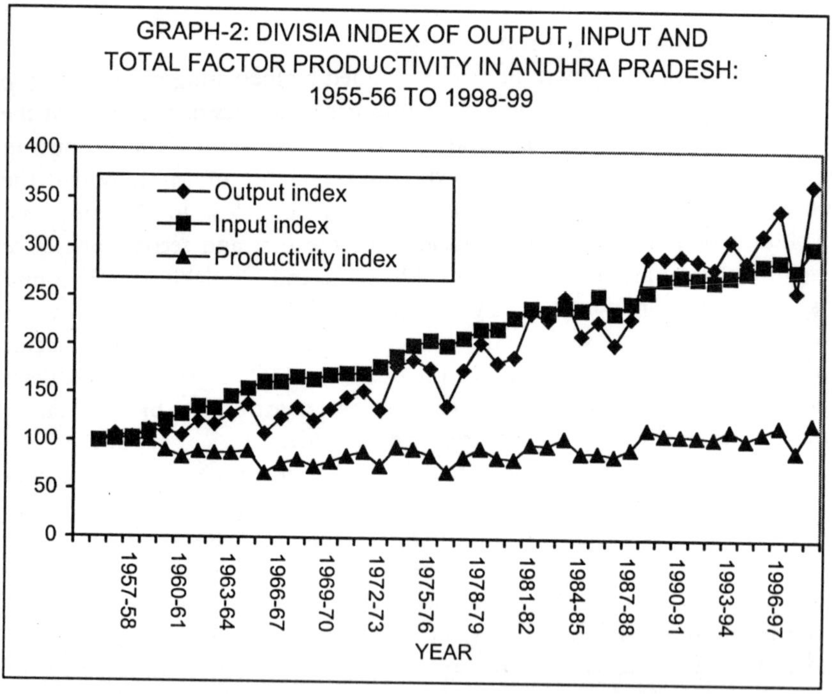

growth declined from 1.58 to 1.05 percent per annum. However, the contribution of total factor productivity remained the same as in the eighties (Graph 2).

Fertiliser Consumption

Andhra Pradesh is one of the States with heavy consumption of chemical fertilisers. While the average intake at all-India level is 90 kg per hectare during 1997-2000, the intake at the State level is as high as 140 Kg per hectare. Only two States in India viz., Punjab and Tamilnadu have a higher level of fertiliser intake than Andhra Pradesh. The level of application is found to be higher than the recommended level for most of the crops. For instance, the application is higher by 48 per cent for paddy and about 17 per cent for groundnut as well as cotton (Table 9). There is a shortfall in the fertiliser use for sunflower, jowar and sugarcane.

Table 9. Fertiliser Use for Selected Crops: 1997-98

(Kgs/hect)

Crop	Application	Recommended Level	% of Excess
Paddy	237	160	48.1
Groundnut	142	120	18.3
Cotton	281	240	17.0
Chillies	241	240	-
Sugarcane	138	300	-54.0
Sunflower	89	130	-31.5
Jowar	62	130	-52.3

Note: Negative sign indicates deficiency.
Source: Subrahmanyam *et. al* (1998).

Using requirement norms for each crop, the requirement per hectare of gross cropped area is estimated for each of the six agro-climatic zones and it is compared with total fertiliser distributed in the zone. At the State level, there is not much shortfall from the recommended level (Table 10). Two agro-climatic zones namely, North Coastal Zone and Scanty Rainfall Zone exhibit significant shortfall of 52 and 31 per cent respectively. The North Coastal Zone, comprising of Srikakulam, Vizianagaram and Visakhapatnam districts, receives high rainfall and has moderate irrigation. But tank is the major source of irrigation and most of the tanks in the district are rainfed. The Scanty Rainfall Zone, comprising of Kurnool, Anantapur and Cuddapah districts, receives less than 75 cm of rainfall and it has the lowest irrigation ratio in the state (17 per cent). Groundnut is the major crop in this zone. Both these agro-climatic zones require strengthening of irrigation through watershed development and minor irrigation programs in order to increase fertiliser consumption to the desired level. The North Coastal Zone can benefit by improvement of tanks and the Scanty Rainfall Zone by watershed programmes. Thus, the data on fertiliser use indicates that there is not much scope for attaining growth through increasing fertiliser use except in selected pockets of the state with the existing technology and irrigation levels.

In order to find the response of output to fertiliser use, Divisia index of output is regressed on fertiliser use. The results show that there is no decline in the elasticity of output with respect to fertiliser use in the

Table 10. Fertiliser Consumption Per Hectare of Gross Cropped Area (Kgs)

Zone	Triennium Ending				
	1975-78	1988-91	1996-99	Requirement	Gap (%)
North Coastal	20	68	69	145	52.4
Godavari- Krishna	70	213	203	157	-
Southern	27	113	139	150	7.3
Scanty Rainfall	19	64	87	126	31.0
South Telangana	17	72	140	138	-
North Telangana	36	126	153	155	-
Andhra Pradesh	33	118	139	146	4.8

nineties. The elasticity remained around 0.4 at the State level, which is in the economical range (Table 11). Among agro-climatic zones, South Telangana has the lowest elasticity (0.27) and North Telangana has the highest elasticity (0.55). The Scanty Rainfall zone, with a substantial shortfall in fertiliser use from the recommended level, has high elasticity of output with respect to fertiliser use, indicating the feasibility of increasing output through higher fertiliser use. Only when soil moisture conditions improve, farmers can increase the application of chemical fertiliser. The Southern zone also showed a low response to fertiliser use in the early period, but it has improved significantly in the recent period.

Table 11: Regression Equations of Logarithm of Divisia Output Index on Logarithm of Fertiliser

	1975-76 to 1989-90			1975-76 to 1998-99		
Zone	Constant	Reg. Coeff.	R^2	Constant	Reg. Coeff.	R^2
North Coastal	34.11	0.45 (4.09)	0.55	0.67	0.42 (7.00)	0.69
Godavari- Krishna	-0.46	0.46 (5.75)	0.73	-0.53	0.47 (10.15)	0.82
Southern	3.42	0.17 (2.83)	0.34	2.17	0.29 (5.80)	0.63
Scanty Rainfall	-1.48	0.57 (5.18)	0.64	-0.86	0.52 (7.43)	0.73
South Telangana	3.12	0.21 (2.33)	0.31	2.45	0.27 (6.75)	0.63
North Telangana	0.52	0.44 (5.50)	0.72	-0.76	0.55 (13.75)	0.84
Andhra Pradesh	-0.11	0.41 (6.8)	0.76	-0.4	0.43 (10.75)	0.86

3. PROSPECTS FOR AGRICULTURAL GROWTH

The potential growth rate of the agricultural sector is worked out under three assumptions- expansion of net area sown by bringing down the extent of fallow land to the level observed at the beginning of seventies, increase in cropping intensity by expansion of irrigation and increase in crop yields to the levels presently observed in the states with highest yield for each crop.

If the extent of fallow land is brought down to the level as observed in the beginning of seventies, there will be an addition of 12.87 lakh hectares to the net area sown, so that it reaches 119.29 lakh hectares by the terminal year i.e., 2010. However, it raises the question of desirability from ecological angle. It is found that these are the dry areas with low irrigation as well as rainfall and farmers leave the land as fallow due to various constraints. These constraints have to be identified and solutions have to be found. If the irrigation ratio is raised from 40 to 50 per cent, net area irrigated reaches 59.65 lakh hectares by the terminal year. Irrigation intensity is assumed to rise from 132.2 to 135.0 per cent. Cropping intensity (CI) is projected from the following estimated regression equation of cropping intensity (CI) on irrigation intensity (II) for the period 1980-81 to 1998-99:

$$CI_t = 59.71 + 0.56\ II_t \qquad R^2 = 0.48$$
$$\text{t value} = \qquad (3.73)$$

The projected cropping intensity is found to be 135.3 per cent. Given the net area sown of 119.29 lakh hectares, and the above cropping intensity, gross cropped area is projected to be 155.73 lakh hectares (Table 12).

Table 12. Particulars of Cropped and Irrigated Area in the Base (T.E: 1998-99) and Terminal (2010-11) Years

(Lakh hect)

S.No	Item	TE 1998-99	2010-11
1	Fallow Land	42.87	30.00
2	Net Area Sown	106.42	119.29
3	Net Area Irrigated	42.93	59.65
4	Surface Irrigation	25.26	37.28
5	Ground water Irrigation	17.67	22.37
6	Intensity of Irrigation (%)	132.20	135.00
7	Gross Irrigated Area	56.75	80.53
8	Intensity of Cropping (%)	122.70	135.30
9	Gross Cropped Area	130.57	155.73

The yields of major crops in Andhra Pradesh, Tamil Nadu, Karnataka and the state with the highest yield are presented in Table 13. There is a wide gap between the yield level attained in Andhra Pradesh and the highest yield level. For instance, yield of rice is 2.6 tonnes in Andhra Pradesh as compared to 3.3 tonnes in Punjab indicating a gap of 27.8 per cent. Similar gap is observed for jowar and bajra also. The yield of groundnut is only 8.89 quintals per hectare as against 16.19 quintals in

Tamil Nadu. The performance of Sunflower also very poor in Andhra Pradesh with a yield of 6 quintals per hectare as against 16 quintals in Haryana and 10 quintals in Tamil Nadu. Cotton also shows a poor performance with a yield of 2.5 quintals as compared to 3.67 quintals in Punjab.

It is quite reasonable to assume that the State can attain the present highest yield level in a period of ten years. The present cropping pattern is used in the projection of area under different crops as no assumptions could be made about the relative prices of various crops. Using the projected gross cropped area, present cropping pattern and the assumed yield levels, production levels of major eighteen crops are projected for the year 2010. The value of aggregate output is calculated at 1998-99 prices from which the annual growth rate of potential output is derived (Table 14). The annual growth rate of projected output is found to be 4.63 per cent per annum.

Table 13. Yield of Selected Crops in Andhra Pradesh and Selected States: Triennium Ending 1998-99

(Kg/hect)

Crop	Andhra Pradesh	Tamil Nadu	Karnataka	State with Highest Yield		Gap (%)
				State	*Yield*	
Rice	2606	2784	2391	Punjab	3331	27.8
Jowar	695	836	892	U.P	892	28.3
Bajra	867	1156	593	Gujarat	1185	33.3
Maize	3076	1622	3074	-	-	-
Ragi	1121	1880	1504	-	-	67.7
Bengalgram	698	680	460	H.P	1072	-
Redgram	341	771	406	Bihar	1065	126
Other Pulses	484	344	346	U.P	786	-
Sugarcane (Quintals)	744	1038	871	-	-	39.5
Chillies	2168	462	724	-	-	-
Groundnut	889	1619	863	-	-	82.1
Sunflower	598	1042	399	Haryana	1643	74.2
Gingelly	189	424	406	Assam	488	124
Castor	250	311	1156	Gujarat	1847	362
Tobacco	1132	1488	835	Gujarat	1715	31.4
Cotton (lint)	251	240	258	Punjab	367	2.8
Onions (quintals)	174	94	57	Gujarat	264	-

Note: Gap is calculated taking the yield in the other two Southern States.

Since constraints for yield improvement vary across agro-climatic zones, an understanding of the regional profiles is needed for formulating policies for agricultural growth. A detailed study of each region is needed for such an explanation. However, available information indicates three location specific problems. Fallow land, which is identified as an important source of growth, is concentrated in the four districts of South Telangana.

These four districts account for as high as one-third of the total wasteland in the State. On the other hand, the extent of fallow land is negligible in the North Coastal and the Krishna-Godavari Zones. These seven districts account for only 8 per cent of the wasteland in the State. Among the remaining districts, Anantapur, Kurnool, Karimnagar, and Adilabad have a significant extent of wasteland. Factors responsible for keeping land idle in these districts have to be identified and policies have to be initiated for bringing them under cultivation. Thus, the problem of fallow lands needs attention in eight districts namely, Anantapur, Kurnool, Mahabubnagar, Nalgonda, Rangareddy, Medak, Karimnagar and Adilabad.

Table 14. Projections of Agricultural Output

Crop	Output 1999 (Tonnes)	Output 2010 (Tonnes)	Price (1998-99) (Rs. Per tonne)	Value of Output (1998-99) Rs. Lakhs	Value of Output 2010 Rs. Lakhs
Rice	10357970	15817500	8960	928074	1417248
Jowar	554881	845500	6807	37771	57553
Bajra	102665	167200	5303	5444	8867
Maize	1218909	1436000	4852	59141	69675
Ragi	119844	235000	4698	5630	11040
Redgram	121932	447300	17070	20814	76354
Blackgram	268071	452200	16235	43521	73415
Bengalgram	92699	166900	14890	13803	24851
Greengram	193959	440400	16663	32319	73384
Horsegram	42835	109900	6022	2580	6618
Groundnut	1785323	3884000	13054	233056	507017
Gingelly	31107	99000	18337	5704	18154
Castor	51146	460700	13951	7135	64272
Sunflower	200384	664200	17843	35755	118513
Sugarcane	1504137	1750270	10087	151722	176550
Cotton (Lint)	267513	472500	62940	168373	297392
Tobacco	210649	373900	30599	64456	114410
Chillies	475173	574500	39861	189409	229001
Onions	392111	818400	4428	17363	36239
Total				2022071	3380553

Note: Output in tonnes and value in Rs. Lakh.

The low average yield levels of several crops are mainly due to very poor performance of certain zones. The crops whose yield levels are less than 30 per cent as compared to the yield level in the zone with highest yield are identified for each zone (Table 15). It is significant to note that South Telangana is the most backward zone in the State with as many as eight low yield crops which together account for 49 per cent of the gross cropped area in the zone. Improvements in yields of these crops will contribute to significant increase in output growth. Next to South

Telangana, North Coastal is found to be backward. The performance of rice that accounts for one-third of the gross cropped area of the zone is very poor with a low yield of 1.7 tonnes per hectare. Black gram and sugarcane also reveal poor performance in this zone. It is significant to note that the zone receives high rainfall and has moderate irrigation ratio. North Telangana zone exhibits poor performance in cotton, which is an important crop in the zone occupying 17.6 per cent of the gross cropped area, and jowar occupying 9.4 per cent of the gross cropped area. The yield levels of these two crops fall short by 40 and 49 per cent respectively. The remaining three crops with shortfall in yield together account for only 5 per cent of the gross cropped area. The performance of the Scanty Rainfall zone is also very poor because the yields of groundnut and cotton, which account for 54 per cent of the gross cropped area are very low. Thus, out of the six agro-climatic zones in the State, three zones viz., Scanty Rainfall, South Telangana and North Coastal are agriculturally backward. The North Telangana zone deserves attention mainly in cotton and jowar.

Table 15. Agro-Climatic Zones With Low Yields and Extent of Shortfall during T.E. 1998-99

Zone	Crop	Yield (Kg/hect)	Shortfall from best Performance Zone (%)	Percentage to GCA
South Telangana	Jowar	604	57.1	17.1
	Maize	2779	35.6	4.3
	Redgram	266	130.8	5.0
	Blackgram	259	137.1	2.0
	Bengalgram	279	356.6	1.2
	Groundnut	751	53.7	9.5
	Cotton	197	71.2	8.2
	Sunflower	508	29.5	2.1
North Coastal Andhra	Rice	1718	47.8	33.0
	Maize	2102	79.2	0.7
	Redgram	338	81.6	0.7
	Blackgram	467	31.5	3.8
	Sugarcane (Gur)	5317	71.9	4.4
North Telangana	Jowar	672	49.2	9.4
	Redgram	299	105.4	3.4
	Blackgram	461	33.2	1.6
	Bengalgram	280	355.0	0.3
	Cotton	241	40.1	17.6
Scanty Rainfall	Redgram	341	80.0	2.3
	Bengalgram	778	63.7	3.4
	Groundnut	780	47.9	47.9
	Cotton	205	64.7	6.3
Southern	Redgram	351	74.9	3.6

Since irrigation is the major factor influencing crop yield, the poor performance of a zone has to be related to the level and quality of irrigation. North Coastal receives highest rainfall and has moderate irrigation ratio (Table 16).

South Telangana receives moderate rainfall and has moderate irrigation ratio. But the sources of irrigation differ between these two zones. While canal and tank are the major sources in North Coastal Andhra, well is the main source in South Telangana. Scanty Rainfall zone suffers from severe scarcity of water with low rainfall and irrigation. Further, the share of tank irrigation is negligible at 7.8 per cent and the districts receive very low rainfall of 62 cm per annum. Thus, the poor yield levels in North Coastal as well as South Telangana are not entirely due to low irrigation level. The quality of irrigation appears to be poor in these zones. On the other hand, scanty rainfall zone suffers from low irrigation.

Table 16. Changes in Groundwater to Surface Irrigation Ratio

Zone	Rainfall	Ratio of Groundwater to Surface Irrigation		% of Irrigated Area
		T.E: 1976-77	T.E: 1998-99	T.E: 1998-99
North Coastal	High	0.03	0.11	38.8
Godavari-Krishna	High	0.09	0.22	62.4
Southern	Moderate	0.45	0.75	50.2
Scanty Rainfall	Low	0.53	1.41	23.1
South Telangana	Moderate	0.35	2.01	33.5
North Telangana	High	0.31	1.35	48.0
State	-	0.23	0.64	43.5

High: > 1000 mm; Moderate: 750 mm to 1000 mm; Low: <750 mm

In order to see the role of irrigation for the poor yield performance of a crop, the share of irrigated crop in the zone during triennium ending 1998-99 is examined. The poor yield of rice and sugarcane in the North Coastal zone is partly due to a substantial proportion of area under rain-fed conditions (16.3 and 23.4 per cent). Secondly, 50 per cent of the rice area is under tank irrigation. If tanks are not maintained properly, the yields suffer both due to inadequate water and low fertiliser use consequent to risk of crop damage. The poor yield of maize in both North Coastal and South Telangana zones is due to predominantly rain-fed nature of the crop. The yield of cotton appears to be affected by soil conditions rather than irrigation conditions. In the Godavari-Krishna zone with highest yield of cotton, only 9 per cent of the area is under irrigated cotton. On the other hand, North Telangana and Scanty Rainfall Zones with significant shortfall in yield, have a high proportion of 21 per cent and 29 per cent under irrigated cotton. Similarly, the low yield of groundnut in the South

Telangana zone is not related to irrigation. While 39 per cent of the area under the crop is irrigated in the South Telangana zone, only 24 per cent of the crop is irrigated in the Southern zone with highest yield. Thus, while soil and climate appear to be responsible for low yields of cotton and groundnut, irrigation in terms of quality and quantity are responsible for low yields of rice and sugarcane.

4. DOMESTIC COMPETITIVENESS OF ANDHRA PRADESH AGRICULTURE

In an environment of trade liberalization, a region has to establish its competitiveness in domestic and international markets to benefit from trade in the surplus commodities. Presently, the state has clear surplus in rice, groundnut and cotton. These three crops together account for 55 per cent of the gross cropped area. The competitiveness of these crops in the domestic market is examined by comparing the cost of production in the major producing States. The data on cost of production is taken from the reports of the Commission for Agricultural Costs and Prices under its Comprehensive Scheme for Cost of Cultivation of Principal Crops. Cost C2 is used as it covers all the costs of production.

Rice is grown in 30 per cent of the gross cropped area. The State supplied 54.9 lakh tonnes to the Food Corporation of India and got back 19.9 lakh tonnes for public distribution system during 1999-2000, indicating a net out flow of 35.0 lakh tonnes. As there is no possibility of rice coming into the State from other States, it can be taken as surplus in Andhra Pradesh. However, the data on production and consumption reveal a smaller quantity (about 8 lakh tonnes) of surplus, which is an underestimate. Since the quantity is procured by the FCI at a uniform price, there is no consideration for competitiveness. Once FCI withdraws from procurement operations, the question of competitiveness of the State vis-a vis other States arises. Cost of production has been higher than in Punjab and Uttar Pradesh by 10 to 18 per cent (Table 17).

Table 17. Cost of Production (Cost C2) of Paddy in Selected States

(Rs.Per Qtl)

Year	Andhra Pradesh	Punjab	Madhya Pradesh	Utter Pradesh	% of Excess over Punjab
1974-75	77.06	91.63	83.45	-	-15.9
1981-82	112.47	102.31	101.06	117.40	9.9
1982-83	121.27	103.87	116.86	124.74	16.8
1983-84	141.53	122.32	102.93	118.95	15.7
1990-91	216.13	194.69	230.54	203.13	11.0
1994-95	341.74	290.36	331.09	NA	17.7
1995-96	363.60	330.81	327.45	NA	9.9
1996-97	405.82	344.81	389.44	39.20	17.7

The cost of production of groundnut in Andhra Pradesh is higher than in Madhya Pradesh by more than 26 per cent in the early seventies. However, the data for the subsequent years shows improvement in the relative position of the state. Given the rainfed nature of the crop, no definite conclusion can be drawn on the basis of data for one or two years (Table 18).

Table 18. Cost of Production (Cost C2) of Groundnut in Selected States

(Rs. Per Qtl)

Year	Andhra Pradesh	Madhya Pradesh	Tamil Nadu	Gujarat	% of Excess over Madhya Pradesh
1981-82	343.45	NA	245.29	331.52	-
1982-83	349.67	NA	326.70	444.80	-
1983-84	393.55	NA	294.49	411.04	-
1990-91	701.26	649.14	NA	NA	8.0
1992-93	835.98	661.19	NA	832.09	26.4
1994-95	1248.93	988.50	863.43	788.74	26.3
1995-96	1073.93	1046.30	1020.33	1209.38	2.6
1996-97	1244.85	1219.72	NA	903.46	2.1

Cotton is produced at very high cost in Andhra Pradesh as compared to Maharastra and Tamil Nadu. The position of this crop in the State is worse than that of rice and groundnut in seventies with cost of production being higher by more than 65 per cent. However, after the mid-nineties the variation declined to less than 18 per cent (Table 19). The results indicate that the major three crops in Andhra Pradesh are not competitive in the domestic market. This State with a large surplus of rice has been losing its competitiveness over time. Groundnut and cotton reveal improvement over time in their relative position in cost of production.

Table 19. Cost of Production (Cost C2) of Cotton in Selected States

(Rs. Per Qtl)

Year	Andhra Pradesh	Maharastra	Tamil Nadu	% of Excess over Maharastra
1975-76	537.88	276.97	265.99	94.2
1976-77	463.20	279.54	373.21	65.7
1977-78	491.35	221.89	349.55	121.4
1978-79	409.46	312.52	356.47	31.0
1994-95	1424.00	1293.15	1253.63	10.1
1996-97	1832.91	1548.81	2008.97	18.3

Expenditure on agricultural research and extension is an important source for accelerating agricultural growth. Agricultural research is partly funded by the Union Government and partly by the state governments. Extension system is completely with the state governments. At the national level the intensity of investment in research and education increased from 0.21 per cent in the sixties to 0.49 per cent in the early nineties (Pal and Singh, 1997). But investment by the Government of Andhra Pradesh accounts for 0.23 per cent of net state domestic product from agriculture. While the share increased in the eighties marginally, it remained constant in the nineties (Table 20). Since the expenditure includes education, even this small increase does not indicate increase in expenditure on research. The growth of expenditure on research and education decelerated from 6.6 per cent in the eighties to 3.9 per cent in the nineties. Expenditure on extension which is completely under the purview of the state government has declined in the nineties.

Table 20. Expenditure on Agricultural Research, Education and Extension

(Rs. In Crores at 1993-94 Prices)

Year	Expenditure in Rs. Crores		% to NSDP from Agriculture	
	Research & Education	Extension	Research & Education	Extension
1980-81	17.18	2.10	0.18	0.022
1990-91	33.93	3.00	0.22	0.020
1994-95	39.81	2.83*	0.23	0.017
Growth Rate (1980-81 to 1989-90)	6.59*	3.06*		
Growth Rate (1990-91 to 1994-95)	3.86**	0.01		

* Relates to 1993-94.

5. SUMMARY AND CONCLUSIONS

After a good growth performance of 3.5 per cent per annum for two decades, the agricultural sector of Andhra Pradesh witnessed steep deceleration in output growth in the nineties with the growth rate slipping to 2.3 per cent per annum. The seventies was a period of broad-based growth across regions and crops and the eighties was a period of shifts in cropping pattern from low-valued to high-valued crops. The decade of nineties witnessed deceleration in the growth rates of yields of all the major crops like rice, cotton, chillies, tobacco, blackgram and greengram.

The deceleration in output growth has to be attributed to slow growth of public investment in agriculture. It is significant to note that, in contrast to the all-India experience, the growth rate of investment in agriculture in the State decelerated from 6 per cent in the eighties to 1.5 per cent in the nineties. This decline in the growth rate of investment was the result of slow growth of public investment. As a result, area under surface irrigation declined by 2 lakh hectares during the nineties. Apparently, the high expansion of groundwater irrigation could not compensate this decline in the surface irrigation. The areas where groundwater irrigation has been expanding have low surface irrigation leading to depletion of groundwater.

The slowing down of yield- raising technological changes may be another important factor, as there is deceleration in the growth of total factor productivity.

The State has potential for achieving a growth rate of 4.6 per cent per annum in the next ten years. The sources of growth identified for attaining this growth are: increasing the irrigation ratio from the existing 40 per cent to 50 per cent, bridging the yield gaps and development of fallow land for crop cultivation or fodder development.

In order to improve the yield levels, regional approach in the identification of problems and their solutions is needed. Among the six agro-climatic zones in the State, South Telangana is most backward with as many as eight crops, accounting for nearly half of the gross cropped area, exhibiting high yield gap. Similarly, North Coastal zone, despite its high rainfall and moderate irrigation, exhibits very low yield for rice and sugarcane. Tank being the major source of irrigation in this zone, it appears that poor maintenance of tanks appears to be major reason for the low yields of rice and sugarcane. These two zones require special attention for accelerating agricultural growth. North Telangana exhibits poor performance in cotton and jowar and scanty rainfall zone is lagging in the yields of groundnut and cotton. While soil and climatic conditions appear to be the major factors for low yields of cotton and groundnut, irrigation in terms of quantity and quality are responsible for low yields of rice and sugarcane. The high rate of groundwater exploitation without sufficient measures for recharge has been resulting in decline in water table. Public investment in watershed programmes has to be complementary to private investment in groundwater exploitation.

Application of chemical fertiliser and pesticides is very high in the State. Though some shortfall from the recommended doses exists, it is only due to insufficient moisture conditions. Improvement in the soil moisture conditions through watershed programmes, proper maintenance of irrigation infrastructure, and raising yield potential through agricultural research and extension should be the focus of agricultural development in the state. Expenditure on agricultural research and extension is found to be almost stagnant in the nineties.

References

Dhawan, B. D. and S. S. Yadav (1997), "Public Investment in Indian Agriculture: Trends and Determinants", *Economic and Political Weekly*, Vol. 32, No. 14, April 5-11.

Dholakia, R. H. and B. H. Dholakia (1993), "Growth of Total Factor Productivity in Indian Agriculture", *Indian Economic Review*, Vol. 28, No.1.

Government of Andhra Pradesh (1999), *Andhra Pradesh: Vision 2020*, State Secretariat, Hyderabad.

Government of Andhra Pradesh (2001), *Working Paper on Agriculture*, Department of Agriculture.

Government of India (2001), *Economic Survey: 2000-2001,* Ministry of Finance Economic Division, New Delhi, p. 152.

Gulati, A. and Seema Bhati (2001), "Capital Formation in Indian Agriculture: Revisiting the Debate", *Economic and Political Weekly*, Vol. 36, May 19.

Pal, Suresh and Alka Singh (1997), "Agricultural Research and Extension in India: Institutional Structure and Investments", Policy Paper 7, National Centre for Agricultural Economics and Policy Research, New Delhi.

Rao, V. M. and R. S. Deshpande (1986), "Agricultural Production: Pace and Pattern of Growth" in Dantwala, M.L (ed), *Indian Agricultural Development Since Independence: A Collection of Essays*, Oxford and IBH, New Delhi.

Rao, C. H. H. (1994), *Agricultural Growth, Rural Poverty and Environmental Degradation in India,* Studies in Economic Development and Planning, No. 59, Oxford University Press, Delhi.

Sawant, S. D. (1997), "Regional Variations in Agricultural Performance", *Indian Journal of Agricultural Economics,* Vol. 52, No.3, July-September.

Shenggen Fan and Peter Hazell (1997), "Should India Invest More in Less-Favoured Areas?" *EPTD Discussion Paper No. 25*, Environment and Production Technology Division, International Food Policy Research Institute, Washington, D.C.

Subrahmanyam S, R. N. Rao and G. K. Mitra (1998), "Economics of Bovine Production in Andhra Pradesh (mimeo)", Centre For Economic and Social Studies, Hyderabad.

Appendix 1: A Note on Methodology

The functional form of the estimated equation is as follows:

$$\text{Ln } Yt = \alpha + \beta 1t + \beta_2 (t-t_1) D_1 + \beta_3 (t-t_2) D_2 + \beta_4 (t-t_3) D_3$$

Where Yt refers to production or area or yield; t_1, t_2 and t_3 are break points at 1969-70, 1979-80 and 1989-90 and D_1, D_2, D_3 refer to dummies taking zero for years prior to the corresponding break point and unity for subsequent years. In this specification the growth rates for the four sub-periods are β_1, $\beta_1+\beta_2$, $\beta_1+\beta_2+\beta_3$ and $\beta_1+\beta_2+\beta_3+\beta_4$ respectively. The growth rate for the entire period is calculated as the weighted average of growth rates of the four periods with number of years as the weight for each sub-period. Because of year-to-year fluctuations in agricultural output, the growth rates are affected by extreme observations and sometimes even numerically high growth rates become statistically insignificant. Further, the growth rates of area and productivity will not add up to the growth rate of output if the fluctuations are wide. To overcome some of these problems, three-year moving averages are used in estimating the trend equations. The values of R^2 are found to be very high and statistically significant at less than 1 per cent level of significance. As dummy variables are used to distinguish the time periods, the significance of the marginal coefficients of each sub-period is not tested because they may turn out to be statistically insignificant due to multi-collinearity. Growth rates are also computed for groups of crops by using the Divisia index with of output with the Tornquist approximation defined as follows:

$$I_t = \Pi \exp (\Sigma\, 0.5\, (w_{it}+w_{it-1})\, I_{it} \qquad i = 1 \text{ to } 18$$

Where w_{it} is the share of ith crop in the value of aggregate output in year t at current prices and I_{it} is the output index of ith crop in relation to output of the previous year. Divisia index of output is computed by chaining the above indices. The indices are computed for four broad groups of crops viz., cereals, pulses, food grains and non-food grains. Divisia index of aggregate input is computed by aggregating five inputs viz., human labour, bullock labour, pump sets, chemical fertilisers and net area sown. To incorporate the effect of changes in quality of land due to investment in irrigation, each unit of irrigated land is counted as two units of dry land on the assumption that output from irrigated land is twice the output from dry land. The indices of these factors are aggregated using cost shares as weights. The relevant data are taken from the reports of the Commission for Agricultural Costs and Prices. For the crops not covered in the survey, weights relating to a crop in the same sub-group are used. All the major 18 crops are considered in the analysis. Intra-State analysis focuses on the six agro-climatic zones in the state. The classification of districts into agro-climatic zones is shown below:

Zone	Districts
North Coastal	Srikakulam, Vizianagaram, Visakhapatnam
Godavari-Krishna	East Godavari, West Godavari, Krishna, Guntur
Southern	Prakasam, Nellore, Chittoor
Scanty Rainfall	Kurnool, Cuddapah, Anantapur
South Telangana	Ranga Reddy, Medak, Mahabubnagar, Nalgonda
North Telangana	Warangal, Khammam, Karimnagar, Adilabad, Nizamabad

9

Livestock Development

S. Subrahmanyam

1. INTRODUCTION

Livestock sector consisting mainly of bovines, small ruminants and poultry has been gaining importance in recent times because of the high income elasticity of demand for milk, meat and egg. The sector contributes more than 20 per cent to the net state domestic product from agriculture. The bovine sector has a dual role of producing milk and supplying draught animal power to agriculture. Given the poor availability of fodder, there is a conflict between the two goals and supply of draught animal services becomes the primary goal. When the requirement of animal power is reduced through mechanization, the fodder resources can be used for milk production. An understanding of the changes taking place in the agricultural sector and their impact on dairying is necessary for introducing the needed policy interventions. In resource poor region, where bovine sector faces severe constraints, small ruminants production becomes important. Poultry sector has become an important activity in the state. The state accounts for 20 per cent of the eggs produced in the country. This paper focuses on the dynamic changes that are taking place in the livestock sector and its potential for development. Section 2 deals with the bovine sector and considers milk production and consumption. It also examines the trends in the work animal population and the factors responsible for such changes. Section 3 deals with the poultry sector and examines growth of egg production, consumption of poultry products and basic problems confronting the sector. The trends in the sheep and goat population and the agro-climatic factors associated with the growth of small ruminants are examined in Section 4. The major conclusions of the paper are brought together in Section 5.

2. BOVINE SECTOR

Size and Composition

Changes in the size and composition of bovine population indicate changing priorities in the livestock sector. The size and composition of the livestock population in Andhra Pradesh has undergone significant changes after mid-eighties. The increasing trend of the bovine population was reversed and the male bovine stock stared to decline since mid-eighties. Bovine population grew at 0.5 per cent per annum till 1987 and declined at

0.4 per cent in the later period (Table 1). The increase in the bovine population in the earlier period was contributed by buffaloes as cattle population remained constant and the decrease in the subsequent period was contributed by cattle as the population of buffaloes continued to grow. Though cattle population remained stable in the earlier period, the population of cows was declining even during this period. The population of young stock increased showing improvement in the ratio of young stock to cows. Either the calving efficiency must have increased or unproductive old cows must have been reduced during the period. In the second period besides cows the population of male cattle also declined. Animal draught power is being replaced by mechanical power and consequently the cow population needed to replace the work animals is also reduced. The population of cattle declined at a high rate of 1.3 per cent per annum.

The increase in the buffaloes in both the periods is due to increase of female buffaloes. Male buffaloes declined at a high rate of 2.2 per cent in the earlier period and 3.1 per cent per annum in the subsequent period. The trends in the two periods indicate that the earlier period is the period of mixed farming, in which milk production was taking place without reduction in the dependence of agriculture on animal draught power and the second period is the period, in which dairying was growing by substituting draught animal power with mechanical power.

There was a debate in the late sixties and seventies regarding the existence of surplus cattle in India. It was argued that 30 to 40 per cent of the cows are surplus and it is the result of the Hindu religious veneration of cow and the taboo against cow slaughter (Dandekar,1969; Mishra, 1979; National Commission on Agriculture, 1976). Contradicting this view, a number of studies showed that there was no surplus of cattle and farmers adjust the number and type of bovines to their requirements who operate under constraints which may appear as irrational behaviour (Raj, 1971; Rao, 1969; Vaidyanathan, 1988). The steady decline in the cow population since mid-seventies indicates that farmers adjust the size and composition of the livestock to the agro-climatic conditions. Availability of common grazing land and low demand for milk may be responsible for maintaining a larger number of cows in the earlier period. But with increase in the demand for milk and decline in the common grazing lands, farmers have reduced the population of cows and increased the buffaloes. Though number of cows was higher than the social optimum, it coincided with private optimum and hence cannot be treated as surplus cattle.

Animal Draught Power

The requirement of work animals is determined by several factors like mechanization, irrigation, size of land holding and cropping pattern. Though mechanization is expected to reduce the requirement of animal power, there is no empirical evidence. The NSS data for 26th and 37th

rounds pertaining to 1972-73 and 1982-83 revealed that mechanization had not reduced the draught animal requirement (Nair and Dhas, 1989). The reduction in work animals in some states, like Tamil Nadu was attributed to development of dairying rather than increase in farm mechanization (Dhas, 1989). A village study in Uttar Pradesh revealed that each tractor replaced only four draught animals as against the ideal replacement of 12 to 16 animals (Sharma, 1989). It is argued that tractors are not suitable for carrying out certain operations like inter-cultivation and

Table 1. Size and Composition of Bovine Population

(Lakh)

Category	1966	1977	1987	1993	1999	Growth Rate (%)	
						1966-87	1987-99
Cattle							
Adult Males	54.12	54.01	54.20	52.48	49.02	0.0	-0.8
Adult Females	41.51	41.13	35.64	30.26	29.30	-0.6	-1.9
Young Stock	27.81	25.26	33.90	26.72	27.38	0.9	-1.8
Total	123.41	120.41	123.74	109.47	105.71	0.0	-1.3
Buffaloes							
Adult Males	14.63	12.75	9.22	6.56	6.32	-2.2	-3.1
Adult Females	32.24	36.68	44.75	48.23	51.99	1.6	1.2
Young Stock	21.11	22.20	33.60	36.74	38.07	2.2	1.0
Total	67.91	71.63	87.57	91.53	96.39	1.2	0.8
Total Bovines							
Adult Males	68.75	66.76	63.41	59.04	55.34	-0.4	-1.1
Adult Females	73.75	77.81	80.41	78.49	81.29	0.4	0.1
Young Stock	48.92	47.46	67.50	63.46	65.45	1.5	-0.3
Total	191.32	192.04	211.31	201.00	202.10	0.5	-0.4

hence mechanization is not leading to replacement of animal power by mechanical power. The regression results based on inter-district data pertaining to the four southern states for the year 1972 indicated that there was no association between mechanization and work animal density (Vaidyanathan, 1988).

Among the crops, paddy was found to have high requirement of work animals (Mishra, 1990). Rainfall showed positive association, but irrigation ratio has not shown significant association with the density of work animals (Rao, 1994).

Farm size is found to have negative association with work animal density and positive association with the proportion of households owning work animals and it is interpreted as inability of small holdings and indivisibility of animals (Vaidyanathan, 1988). All the conclusions are based on data pertaining to 1982 or earlier period. The declining work animal density indicates that some of these relationships might have changed in recent times. Correlation coefficients between work animal density and the agro-climatic variables have been calculated using inter-district data for the years 1966, 1987 and 1999. The results clearly indicate that the relationships are completely changed by 1999. In 1966, irrigation, rainfall, percentage of area under paddy and percentage of marginal and small farmers had statistically significant positive association and density of tractors had no association with work animal density confirming earlier results. The strength of association with all the above variables declined in 1987 and further declined in 1993. For instance, the association with paddy area turned out to be negative. As paddy is the main crop in irrigated areas, the association with irrigation ratio also got weakened (Table 2). A village study in Andhra Pradesh showed that development of canal irrigation led to shift in cropping pattern from commercial crops to paddy and sugarcane and replacement of animal power with tractors (Subrahmanyam, 1996). Thus, wherever irrigation shifted the cropping pattern towards paddy, animal power is replaced by tractors. The strength of association with holding size is also reduced as the average size of holding declined rapidly in irrigated areas. On the other hand, the correlation with the density of tractors turned negative. By 1999, the negative association between work animals and tractors per hectare got further strengthened and the positive association with the proportion of marginal and small farmers further weakened, on account of mechanisation on these farms.

Table 2. Correlations between Work Animal Density and Agro-Climatic Variables

Variable	1966	1987	1999
Percentage of Irrigated Area	0.34***	-0.11	0.10
Normal Rainfall	0.62*	0.45**	0.35***
Cropping Intensity	0.20	-0.04	0.10
Value of Agricultural Output Per Hectare	0.24	-0.31	-0.04
No. of Tractors Per Hectare of Net Area Sown	0.07	-0.36***	-0.43**
Percentage of Marginal and Small Holdings	0.52*	0.39**	0.23
Percentage of Area under Rice	0.43**	-0.17	0.02

* Significance at 1 % level; ** at 5 % level and *** at 10 % level.

The situation of low replacement of animal power per tractor found in other states is also noticed in Andhra Pradesh till mid-eighties. The number of tractors increased from 21.5 thousand in 1983 to 32.5 thousand in 1987 with no decline in the size of work animal population. But a further increase of tractors to 56.89 thousand resulted in the decline of work animals from 63. 4 lakh in 1987 to 59.04 lakh in 1993, indicating the desired replacement of 12 animals per tractor. The rate of decline in work animal population was not uniform across districts. As against the average decline of 12.7 per cent at the state level during 1987-1999, four districts experienced a steep decline of more than 32 per cent and three districts experienced an increase of more than 10 per cent (Table 3).

Table 3. Districts classified by Change in Work Animals: 1987-99

Extent of Change	Districts
High Decline (>32.0%)	West Godavari, Krishna, Prakasam, Nellore
Moderate Decline (12.0-32.0%)	East Godavari, Guntur, Chittoor, Cuddapah, Kurnool, Rangareddy, Karimnagar
Small Decline (0.0-12.0%)	Vizianagaram, Visakhapatnam, Mahabubnagar, Medak, Nalgonda, Nizamabad, Warangal, Khammam
Increase	Srikakulum, Anantapur, Adilabad

The rate of decline of work animal population has systematic positive association with the density of tractors, irrigation ratio, mechanization, share of paddy in gross cropped area. In the districts with average density of 1053 tractors per lakh hectares, work animals declined by 38.9 per cent (Table 4). On the other hand, in the districts with a density of 393 tractors per lakh hectares, work animals declined by only 8.5 per cent. In the districts with the lowest density of 168 tractors per lakh hectares, work animals increased by 8.61 per cent. The areas of highest decline have distinctly high proportion of area under paddy (53.6%). But when the paddy area is less than 30 per cent, the impact of paddy is not felt because animal power has to be maintained for the other crops accounting for more than 70 per cent. The relation between the extent of decline in work animal density and irrigation ratio also shows interesting trend. While

Table 4. Rate of Decline of Work Animals and Agro - Climatic Characteristics

Rate of decline	Change (%)	Tractors per lakh ha of NAS	Bullocks per 100 ha of NAS	Rice area (%)	Irrigation ratio (net)
High decline	38.94	1053	23	52.6	68
Moderate decline	21.03	587	43	28.3	45
Small decline	8.50	393	70	31.2	45
Increase	8.61	168	51	22.0	27

high irrigation ratio is associated with high rate of decline and low irrigation ratio with low rate of decline of work animals, moderate irrigation has no clear association with the rate of decline. In areas with moderate irrigation ratio, mechanization is slow if cropping pattern is diversified because of the need for animal power to carry out inter-cultivation for certain crops. But in mono-crop areas of paddy and sugarcane all operations are mechanized and hence animal power is reduced.

The state consists of six agro-climatic zones based on soil, irrigation and rainfall characteristics. Godavari-Krishna zone, a highly developed zone with a high proportion of area under paddy, has the lowest density of 19 draught animals per 100 hectares (Table 5). Southern zone, which occupies second position in agricultural development, has a significantly higher density of 37 animals per 100 hectares. This is due to its highly diversified cropping pattern with groundnut as an important crop. However, the decline since mid-eighties is significant even in this zone. North Telangana and North Coastal Andhra have fairly high irrigation ratio and receive high rainfall. The former has attained high agricultural growth and the latter suffered stagnation. Both of them have very high density of more than 75 animals per 100 hectares and there is not much decline in the density. Scanty Rainfall zone and South Telangana are agriculturally backward with low rainfall and low irrigation ratio. The former has low density of 33 animals and the latter has high density of 63 animals per 100 hectares and the density remained constant in both these zones. The regional patterns of work animal density clearly indicate that paddy cultivation has clear effect of reducing work animal density and the effect of other factors is ambiguous and is linked to the cropping pattern.

Table 5. Work Animals per 100 Hectares of Net Area by Region

Region	1987	1993	1999
North Coastal Andhra	93.9	82.5	84.1
Godavari-Krishna	33.3	28.0	19.3
Southern	54.1	50.9	37.5
Scanty Rainfall	39.4	33.7	32.7
South Telangana	68.5	79.5	63.2
North Telangana	79.4	83.5	75.8
State	60.6	56.2	50.0

As cropping pattern is more important in determining the density of work animals than the size of landholding, the indivisibility problem has turned out to be less important in the present context. This is clearly revealed in the results of a survey of bovine holdings conducted in 1995-96 covering a sample of 600 holdings spread over different zones in the state (Table 6). The results indicate that mechanization is high even on marginal and small farms. Those who own animal power use it more for hiring out than for own. Further, employment of work animals on small holdings is as high as employment of animals on medium holdings. The proportion of marginal farmers owning work animals is low because of the differences in their willingness to hire out the animal services which requires supply of human labour services.

Table 6. Ownership of Work Animals and Use of Tractors

Category	Farmers Owning Bullocks (%)	Work Animals Per 100 ha	Days Employed per year	Percentage of Hired Out Days	Farmers Using Tractor (%)
Marginal	35.0	142	58	76.0	58.1
Small	72.8	112	74	51.6	59.6
Medium	83.2	84	61	33.6	62.7
Large	92.7	58	48	19.1	80.1
All Categories	67.6	104	86*	49.1	82.0

'All Categories' includes landless households who maintain bullocks for cart pulling.

The high work animal density is explained in terms of the vicious circle of low fodder availability resulting in low tillage capacity which leads to high requirement (Mishra, 1990). This has an implication that the requirement of work animals can be reduced through better feeding. While the relationship between feeding and breeding efficiency among cows is quite clear, the relationship between feeding and tillage capacity among bullocks is not so straight forward. The capacity required in tillage depends on the soil conditions. Farmers, in general, maintain animals as per their requirements. A strong animal is needed for tillage in black soils and for certain operations like puddling and cart pulling.

Production and Consumption of Milk

The state is backward in production as well as consumption of milk. With a total production of 49.5 lakh tonnes during 1999-2000, the per capita production of milk is only 160 grams per day as compared to 190 grams at the national level.

Table 7. Trends in Milk Production in Andhra Pradesh

Year	Milk Production (lakh tonnes)	Annual Compound Growth Rate (%)
1976-77	14.30	-
1985-86	27.81	7.67
1990-91	30.10	1.60
1999-00	49.51	5.69

After growing at a high rate of 7.67 per cent per annum for a decade from mid-seventies, the growth rate slipped to a very low level of 1.6 per cent during the late eighties. The growth again revived to 5.7 per cent in the nineties (Table 7).

Consumption of milk is also significantly lower in the state than the national average in both rural and urban areas. Rural consumption is 87 grams per day against 131 grams at the national level. Urban consumption is 131 grams per day against 163 grams at the national level. The gap between rural and urban consumption is wider in the state than at the national level. While rural consumption is 67 per cent of urban consumption in Andhra Pradesh, the ratio is as high as 81 per cent at the national level. (Table 8). The consumption patterns of Gujarat and Punjab indicate that as consumption levels rise, the gap between the rural and urban areas will be narrowed down. The experience of Punjab reveals that rural consumption may even exceed urban consumption.

Table 8. Average Daily Consumption of Milk: 1993 – 94

(Grams/Day)

State	Rural	Urban	Rural-urban Ratio
Andhra Pradesh	87	131	0.668
Gujarat	169	207	0.816
Punjab	478	323	1.477
All India	131	163	0.806

It is difficult to match the figures of consumption and production of milk as NSS data underestimates milk consumption. A significant proportion of milk is consumed in hotels. Milk is also consumed in the form of milk products. Because of these difficulties in estimating consumption of milk, the production of milk is found to be 39.5 lakh tones in 1993-94, whereas consumption is found to be only 30.5 lakh tones, indicating a gap of about 20 per cent between production and consumption. It is proper to use the estimates of base year production rather than base year consumption in demand projections.

Demand Projections

Demand projections need information on population projections, projections of income growth and income elasticity of demand. Income (expenditure) elasticity of demand is derived from the Engel functions estimated for the 50th round NSS data (1993-94) pertaining to Andhra Pradesh. The value of the elasticity is found to be ranging between 1.34 and 1.65 for rural areas and 1.17 and 1.39 for urban areas. Population projections are taken from the medium level projections made for Vision 2020 document of Andhra Pradesh (Government of Andhra Pradesh, 1999). The growth rate of per capita income is found to be 1.87 per cent per annum, which is quite low as compared to the growth performance at the national level. Since population growth rate declined to 1.3 per cent per annum in the nineties and the income growth target for the Tenth Five Year Plan period is kept at 8 per cent, it is assumed that per capita income of Andhra Pradesh grows at twice the rate observed in the earlier period. Growth rate of demand under the two variants of income growth are shown in Table 9.

Table 9. Annual Growth Rate of Demand for Milk in Andhra Pradesh

(Percentages)

Year	Population Growth Rate		Growth Rate of Demand: Low Projection			Growth Rate of Demand: High Projection		
	Rural	Urban	Rural	Urban	Over all	Rural	Urban	Over all
2000-05	0.58	2.80	3.05	4.92	3.73	5.52	7.05	6.07
2005-10	0.45	2.67	2.79	4.67	3.51	5.13	6.67	5.71
2010-15	0.29	2.26	2.49	4.12	3.15	4.70	5.98	5.20
2015-20	0.10	1.95	2.05	3.69	2.74	4.21	5.43	4.71

Growth rate of expenditure is taken as 1.67 for rural and 1.74 for urban for Low Projections and 3.34 for rural and 3.48 for urban for High Projections

The projections based on low growth rate of state income reveal that demand for milk increases at 3.73 per cent per annum during 2000-2005. As the growth rate of population is assumed to decline, the growth rate of demand comes down to 2.74 during 2015-2020. The projections based on high growth rate of per capita income reveal that the demand for milk grows at 6.07 per cent during 2001-2005 and the growth rate comes down to 4.71 per cent during 2015-2020. Using the base year production and these growth rates of demand, the total demand for milk is projected (Table 10). The demand for milk increases from 49.51 lakh tones in 2000-01 to 59.5 lakh tonnes in 2005-06 as per low projections and to 66.46 lakh tonnes as per high projections. In other words, milk production has to increase by 2.00 lakh tonnes as per low projection and 3.39 lakh tonnes per annum as per high projection during 2000-2005. The annual increase in

Table 10. Projected Demand for Milk in Andhra Pradesh

Year	Low Projection	High Projection
	Total Production (lakh tonnes)	
2005-06	59.45	66.48
2010-11	70.65	87.77
2015-16	82.50	113.12
2020-21	94.46	142.38
	Annual Increase (lakh tonnes)	
2001-06	2.00	3.39
2006-11	2.24	4.26
2011-16	2.37	5.07
2016-21	2.39	5.85

Note: Production in 1999-2000 is taken as 49.5 lakh tonnes.

production has to rise to 2.39 lakh tonnes per annum as per low projection and 5.85 lakh tonnes per annum as per high projection during 2015-2020.

The required increase in milk production has to be achieved by increasing the productivity of milch animals. Since milk yield of local cows is very low, they have to be replaced by crossbred cow or graded buffalo. Even after the implementation of the crossbreeding programme for more than two decades, the achievement is so low that only 8.5 per cent of the cows were crossbred and 12.6 per cent of the buffaloes were graded by 1993. Even this small achievement is because of the good performance of Godavari-Krishna zone for buffaloes and Southern Zone for cow with an achievement of 26 per cent and 31.7 per cent respectively (Table 11).

Table 11. Crossbred Cows and Graded Buffaloes: 1993

(Percentages)

Region	Crossbred Cows	Graded Buffaloes
North Coastal Andhra	6.75	6.40
Godavari-Krishna	6.52	26.10
Southern	31.70	2.40
Scanty Rainfall	3.02	4.08
South Telangana	3.27	7.10
North Telangana	1.11	3.80
State	8.51	12.6

While cow can adapt to any environment, buffalo is not suitable for dry areas and areas of hilly terrain. However, due to favourable demand and marketing conditions for buffalo milk, buffalo is replacing cow in all the regions. For instance, even in the Scanty Rainfall and South Telangana Zones, where surface irrigation is low, buffalo population has been growing (Table 12). Similarly, North Coastal Andhra and North Telangana zones with hilly terrain have also been experiencing growth of buffalo population. But they are mostly local buffaloes with low milk yield.

Table 12. Growth of Buffaloes Across Agro – Climatic Regions

Region	1966 (lakh)	1987 (lakh)	1999 (lakh)	Annual Growth Rate (%)		
				1966-87	1987-99	1966-99
North Coastal Andhra	2.23	3.56	4.05	2.2	1.1	1.8
Godavari-Krishna	10.89	13.02	15.12	0.9	1.2	1.0
Southern	4.23	7.65	8.64	2.8	1.0	2.2
Scanty Rainfall	5.71	6.71	6.86	0.8	0.2	0.6
South Telangana	4.30	6.03	7.67	1.6	2.0	1.8
North Telangana	4.80	7.67	9.54	2.2	1.8	2.1
State	32.19	44.75	51.99	1.6	1.2	1.5

Dairying is highly developed in five districts of Andhra Pradesh. Four of them belong to the canal irrigated Krishna – Godavari zone and the fifth (Chittoor) has low irrigation ratio. Buffalo is suitable for the former and cow for the latter. Because of this, buffalo replaced cow in the former and all the buffaloes have been graded up. In the other region buffalo replaced cow in the early stage, but because of the suitability of cow, buffalo is again replaced by crossbred cow. In Krishna-Godavari region, buffalo population increased at 0.85 per cent per annum between 1966-87 and 1.25 per cent per annum between 1987-99 and more than 25 per cent of the buffaloes were graded up by 1993 (Table 13). In Chittoor district buffalo population increased at 1.2 per cent and cow population declined at 0.77 per cent per annum during 1966-87, indicating replacement of cow by buffalo. But the subsequent period witnessed reversal of this trend. Cow population increased at 0.58 per cent and buffalo population declined at 0.56 per cent per annum and 32 per cent of the cows in the Southern zone to which the district belongs are crossbred. Dairying is highly developed in both these regions because of the adoption of environmentally suitable species as well as the reduction in the work animal population. If dairying has to be developed in other regions, they have to adopt cow because of its environmental suitability and also reduce the work animal population through mechanization of agriculture.

Table 13. Growth of Cow and Buffalo in Bovine Population in Intensive Dairy Areas

Category	Godavari Krishna Zone		Chittoor District	
	1966-87	1987-99	1966-87	1987-99
Adult Female Buffalo	0.85	1.25	1.21	-0.56
Adult Cow	-2.24	-2.48	-0.77	0.58
Male Cattle	-2.40	-2.88	-1.31	-1.76
Total Bovine	-0.42	-0.31	-0.08	-0.84

In order to understand the factors influencing the density of buffaloes per 100 persons and changes in the importance of these factors over time, correlation coefficients are estimated using inter-district data for 1966, 1987 and 1999. Rainfall, irrigation, work animals density, fodder availability, value of crop output per capita rural are considered in the analysis. Increase in the value of per capita agricultural output increases demand for milk and increase in fodder availability and reduction in the draught animal population increase supply of milk. Irrigation and rainfall are the environmental factors. Irrigation is expected have a positive influence and rainfall is expected to have a negative influence on the density of buffaloes became high rainfall areas are generally hilly areas.

The signs of correlation coefficients are proper and consistent in all the three years (Table14). Rainfall and work animal density have negative association and fodder availability, irrigation and value of per capita agricultural output have positive association with density of buffaloes. However, only per capita agricultural output and draught animal density have statistically significant correlations. In other words, one variable on the demand side and one on the supply side are found to be playing a significant role. Environmental suitability is not playing a significant role, indicating that buffalo is reared even in the areas where it is not considered suitable. Fodder availability is not playing an important role because of the use of common grazing lands. Thus, increase in the local demand for milk and reduction of work animals have a greater impact on milk production than other variables.

Table 14. Factors Influencing the Density of Buffaloes per 100 Persons

Variable	1966	1987	1999
Normal rainfall	-0.18	-0.28	-0.17
Work animals per 100 ha	-0.57	-0.51	-0.41
Fodder per 100 bovine units	-0.03	0.12	0.07
Irrigation	0.13	0.25	0.28
Agricultural output per capita rural	0.19	0.48	0.49

3. SMALL RUMINANT SECTOR

Small ruminants constituting sheep and goat are the major source of meat accounting for nearly 75 per cent of the total meat consumed. The consumer preference for this meat is much higher than that of poultry meat. Though the price of mutton increased at a faster rate than that of poultry meat, there is no decline in the consumption of mutton.

The population of small ruminants remained stagnant at 117.5 lakh for two decades, indicating a steep decline in the per capita availability of mutton (Table 15). But in the recent period, the population of small ruminants increased at an annual rate of 1.95 per cent, which is slightly more than the population growth rate. Given the high income elasticity of demand for mutton, this growth rate is not adequate to meet the growing demand. The gap between the demand for and supply of mutton is corrected by price increase. The trends in small ruminant population reveal two significant features. Firstly, during the period of growth of bovine population, the population of small ruminants remained stagnant and its growth picked up when the bovine population began to decline. Secondly, the composition of small ruminants has undergone significant change over time. The share of goats increased from 32 per cent in mid-sixties to 42 per cent in early eighties and the population of goats reached the all time high level of 54.59 lakh. This high growth of goat population is due to higher price of goat meat than sheep meat.

Table 15. Trends in Small Ruminants

Year	Sheep (Lakh)	Goats (Lakh)	Total (Lakh)
1966	80.06	37.62	117.68
	(68.03)	(31.97)	(100.00)
1983	75.18	54.59	129.77
	(57.93)	(42.07)	(100.00)
1987	68.71	48.76	117.47
	(58.49)	(41.51)	(100.00)
1993	77.87	43.29	121.16
	(64.27)	(35.73)	(100.00)
1999	96.43	51.64	148.07
	(65.12)	(34.88)	(100.00)
Growth Rate: 1966-87	-0.73	1.24	-0.01
Growth Rate: 1987-99	2.86	0.47	1.95
Growth Rate: 1966-99	0.56	0.96	0.70

Note: Figures in brackets indicate percentage share in total small ruminants.

Small ruminant production is predominant in resource poor areas and among resource poor farmers (Nadkarni,1987). Correlations based on inter-district data for 1999 also support this view (Table 16). Irrigation, rainfall, proportion of marginal and small holdings and per hectare value of agricultural output have negative association with density of small ruminants. However, the strength of association with irrigation and rainfall differs between sheep and goats. Density of goats has weak association with rainfall and strong association with irrigation, whereas the opposite is the case with sheep. Agricultural income per hectare also has negative association with the density of small ruminants, indicating that the activity

Table 16. Correlation between Small Ruminants per Lakh Population and Agro - Climatic Variables

Variable	Sheep	Goats	Small ruminants
Irrigation Ratio	-0.376***	-0.671*	-0.492*
Normal Rainfall	-0.733*	-0.486*	-0.738**
Marginal & Small Holdings (%)	-0.553**	-0.661*	-0.636**
Agricultural Output/Net Area Sown	-0.395**	-0.731*	-0.523*
Net Area Sown/Rural Population	0.493*	0.567**	0.561**
(Geographical Area-Net Area Sown)/Rural Population	0.265	0.603**	0.381***

* 1 % level ** 5 % level *** 10 % level

is concentrated in resource poor regions. Cultivated land per capita and uncultivated land per capita have positive association with density of small ruminants. Density of population on cultivated land and density of population on uncultivated land are higher in resource poor regions than in resource rich regions. These correlations indicate that when agricultural activity is intensive, dairy is developed and where resources for agriculture are poor, small ruminant production is taken up.

4. POULTRY SECTOR

Indian poultry sector has been transformed from traditional activity to commercial farming during the seventies and since then the sector has been growing at high rate of six per cent per annum. This high growth rate could be sustained for two decades because of high growth of internal as well as export demand. The growth of internal demand is mainly contributed by urbanization and export demand is restricted to a few countries. Future growth of this sector requires expansion of demand in the rural areas and entry into European markets. he former needs development of marketing network in the rural areas and the latter requires improvement in the quality of the products to meet the health standards prescribed by the developed countries.

Growth of Production

Andhra Pradesh occupies top position among Indian states in poultry production, with a share of 20 per cent of the eggs produced in the country. While the state produced 5751 million eggs in 1997-98, Tamil Nadu occupying second position produced only 3050 million eggs. Per capita availability of eggs is 77 in the state as against 30 at the national level. Egg production increased from less than 1166 million in 1982-83 to 2547 million in 1986-87, indicating phenomenal growth of 21.6 per cent per annum (Table 17). In the next ten years the growth rate decelerated to about 7 per cent.

Table 17. Trends in Egg Production

(Quantity)

Year	No. of Eggs (Millions)	Annual Growth Rate (per cent)
1982-83	1166	-
1986-87	2547	21.6
1992-93	3962	6.5
1997-98	5751	7.7

The high growth of the poultry sector is contributed by the breed improvement rather than growth in the number of birds. The growth rate of birds was highest at 6.65 per cent during 1977-83 and decelerated to 4 per cent in the nineties (Table 18). The productivity of birds is 51.3 per cent higher than at the national level.

Table 18. Trends in Poultry Population

Year	No of Birds (000)	Share in India	Growth Rate
1966	14715	12.75	-
1977	21609	15.60	3.50
1983	31841	15.32	6.65
1987	39048	14.18	5.23
1992	49884	16.25	5.00
1999	65531	-	4.00

Input and Output Prices

The trends in the prices of inputs and output are not favourable to the poultry sector. Prices of eggs and poultry meat increased at a lower rate than the price of the competing product (mutton) as well as the feed price. While the egg and poultry meat prices increased at about 5 per cent per annum during the eighties and nineties, the price of poultry feed increased at about 8.5 per cent per annum (Table 19).

Table 19. Index Numbers of Wholesale Prices: Meat, Egg, Mutton and Poultry Feed

(Base: 1981-82=100)

Item	1985-86	1990-91	1995-96	1999-00	Growth Rate	
					1980s	1990s
Egg Price	125.0	160.9	274.6	327.4	5.1	6.3
Poultry Meat Price	139.9	158.5	264.6	308.6	4.8	5.9
Mutton Price	142.3	219.0	440.7	582.5	9.3	12.0
Poultry Feed Price	125.7	201.7	380.5	499.1	7.9	8.8
Egg/Feed Price Ratio	0.99	0.80	0.72	0.66	-	-
Chicken /Feed Price Ratio	1.11	0.79	0.70	0.62	-	-
Chicken/Mutton Price Ratio	0.98	0.72	0.60	0.53	-	-

Further, the price of mutton which competes with poultry meat increased at 12 per cent, price of poultry meat increased at only 5.9 per cent. In other words, poultry meat has become relatively cheaper than mutton. This price trend is expected to increase the demand for poultry meat due to substitution effect. But the data on consumption, shown in the subsequent section, reveal that such substitution has not taken place. The increase in poultry production, despite the decline in their relative prices, must have been facilitated by technological changes, increasing returns to scale and rising export demand.

Consumer Preference Patterns for Poultry Products

Demand for livestock products depends not only on income and prices but also on the acceptance of non-vegetarian food. Once a household accepts non-vegetarian food, the levels of consumption are determined by income and prices. Data on the percentage of households reporting consumption of meat, fish or egg at the state and national levels during latest three rounds of NSS are presented in (Table 20). The proportion is higher in Andhra Pradesh than the national average and it is increasing in the rural areas. While only 58 per cent of the rural and urban households consumed these livestock products at all India level, 84 per cent of the rural households and 73 per cent of the urban households consumed such livestock products in Andhra Pradesh during 1999-2000. The proportion increased in rural areas from 77 per cent in 1987-88 to 84 per cent in 1999-2000.

Table 20. Percentage of Households Consuming Meat, Fish and Egg

Year	All India		Andhra Pradesh	
	Rural	Urban	Rural	Urban
1987-88	54.1	56.8	76.9	73.1
1993-94	56.4	57.0	82.6	76.1
1999-00	57.9	58.0	83.9	73.3

The consumption of egg is low in rural areas, which is not due to vegetarianism. While 83 per cent of the rural households accept non-vegetarian food, only 53 per cent consume egg. In the urban areas, 57 per cent of the households consume egg, though 73 per cent accept non-vegetarian food (Table 21). Between mutton and poultry meat, the consumer preference is clearly in favor of the former, though its price is twice that of the latter. While goat meat is consumed by 29 per cent of the rural and 39 per cent of the urban households, chicken is consumed by less than 20 per cent in both rural and urban areas. Given the fact that price of mutton is higher than that of poultry meat, the lower consumption indicates lower preference for poultry products than for mutton.

Table 21. Households Consuming Poultry Products : 1993-94

(Percentages)

Item	Rural		Urban	
	Andhra Pradesh	India	Andhra Pradesh	India
Egg	52.3	22.0	57.2	34.9
Poultry Meat	18.4	7.5	19.4	9.0
Mutton or Goat Meat	29.1	20.3	39.1	28.0
Fish	25.9	30.7	20.6	27.1

Levels of Consumption of Poultry Products

The nutritional norms suggest consumption of 180 eggs and 11 kgs of meat per capita per annum. As compared to this, the level of actual consumption is 17.3 and 25.6 eggs per capita per annum in rural and urban areas respectively (Table 22). However, the level of consumption is much higher than the national average. The level of consumption of total meat including fish is 4.0 kg. per capita per annum in rural areas and 3.7 kg. in urban areas, which is also lower than the recommended level. Poultry meat accounts for less than 25 per cent of total meat consumption in both rural and urban areas. Egg consumption has to rise ten times in rural areas and seven times in urban areas of Andhra Pradesh in order to satisfy the nutritional norm.

Table 22. Annual per Capita Consumption of Meat, Fish and Egg: 1993 – 1994

Item	Rural		Urban	
	Andhra Pradesh	India	Andhra Pradesh	India
Egg (No.)	17.28	7.68	25.56	17.76
Chicken (kg.)	0.60	0.24	0.60	1.08
Other Meat (kg.)	2.04	1.20	2.19	2.04
Fish (kg.)	1.32	2.16	0.96	2.40

Income and Price Elasticities

Growth of livestock sector depends partly on demand conditions and partly on supply conditions. Demand conditions are reflected in the income and price changes and responsiveness of demand for these changes. The income and price elasticities are estimated using the Linear Expenditure System for seven broad commodity groups (for details see Appendix). The estimates of expenditure and price elasticities for rural and urban areas are shown in Table 23. The results show some significant features. Firstly, expenditure (income) elasticities are higher than price elasticities indicating that income improvement generates relatively more demand than price reduction. Secondly, rural-urban differences in the elasticities are quite high and urban elasticities are far below the rural elasticities for all the food items. This result indicates that it is easier to generate demand in the rural areas than in the urban areas. Thirdly, though both price and income elasticities are lower in urban areas as compared to rural areas, the gap is higher for price elasticities than for income elasticities. For instance, price elasticity of milk products in urban areas in 0.35 while the corresponding value for rural areas is 1.05. Similarly, price elasticity of meat, fish and egg is 0.30 in urban areas while the corresponding elasticity for rural areas is 0.84. A comparison of income and price elasticities for various commodities reveals that livestock products have the highest elasticity with respect to income as well as price. Milk products have higher elasticity than meat products. For instance, income and price elasticities of milk products in rural areas are 1.20 and 1.05 respectively. The corresponding elasticities for meat products are 0.98 and 0.84. Thus, rural demand for the livestock products is highly sensitive to income and price changes. Urban demand is sensitive to income changes, but not to price changes. The price elasticity of demand for milk and meat products are 0.35 and 0.30 respectively while the corresponding income elasticities are 0.83 and 0.65. Thus, income growth in rural and urban areas and price reduction in rural areas increased the demand for livestock products.

Table 23. Income and Own Price Elasticities for Broad Commodity Groups

Commodity Group	Expenditure Elasticity		Price Elasticity*	
	Rural	Urban	Rural	Urban
Cereal	0.45	0.15	0.42	0.10
Pulses	0.77	0.45	0.67	0.18
Milk and milk products	1.20	0.83	1.05	0.35
Meat, fish and egg	0.98	0.65	0.84	0.30
Edible oil	0.74	0.41	0.65	0.18
Other Food	0.77	0.84	0.70	0.40
Non-Food	1.48	1.60	1.10	0.90

* Negative sign is omitted

Problems of Poultry Industry

A quick survey of a few poultry farmers in Nellore and East Godavari districts of Andhra Pradesh during May, 2002 revealed the problems the sector is facing. Some are on the demand side and some on the supply side. The problems on demand side are three-fold. Rural per capita consumption of eggs is very low due to poor marketing facilities. The commodity is highly delicate like glassware. Proper packing technology is not developed for moving small quantities. Only retail sellers participate in trade and they handle very small quantities. They keep high profit margin because of the low quantity handled by each seller. Further, rural retail prices are not sensitive to changes in egg prices. When egg prices fall, many vendors enter into the business and leave it when profit margin is reduced. Secondly, the commodity faces seasonality in demand while production is stable. Consumption is low in summer and during certain months of religious importance. This problem can be solved through the development of cold storage facilities in rural areas. It is suggested that the cold storage facilities available in the dairy units can be used for the storage of eggs in summer because the storage requirement for milk will be low in summer. Thirdly, the industry has to capture new export markets. Presently, the country is unable to enter the European markets because of the quality constraints imposed by these markets. There is a feeling that heavy vaccination of birds to prevent diseases and high use of pesticides in the cultivation of maize, the major feed ingredient, reduce the quality of egg. The high use of vaccine is partly due to disease proneness at the production premises caused by not maintaining adequate distance between units. It is suggested that the quality of maize can be improved by introducing contract farming between feed manufactures and maize farmers.

On the supply side, two major problems are identified. The viability of small poultry farmer has become a serious problem because of the economies of scale in production and seasonal fluctuations in input prices. Small producers are unable to purchase the feed in bulk. If the small farmer has to survive, there is need to establish an organization on the lines of NDDB to help small producers in rural marketing and input supply. Contract farming can also be encouraged between poultry units and processors.

5. SUMMARY AND CONCLUSIONS

Bovine population of Andhra Pradesh has been undergoing significant changes in size and composition since mid-sixties. The composition has been shifting from cattle to buffalo. Till mid-eighties the shift came through increase in female buffaloes and decline in female cattle, indicating that cow is not preferred for milk production and it is maintained only to produce bullocks. In the areas where mechanization is introduced, cow population declined at a faster rate. Since the mid-eighties, even the population of male cattle started to decline and the composition further tilted towards buffalo. The size of total bovine population also declined. Significant reduction in animal power with increase in tractors took place only during this period. Male buffalo has been declining continuously since mid-sixties as it is not preferred as draught animal.

Work animal density declined steeply in the mono-crop paddy areas. There is no significant decline in draught animal power in the areas where cropping pattern is diversified because certain operations cannot be performed by tractors. The density of bullocks per 100 hectares of net area sown is higher in North Coastal Andhra, North Telangana and South Telangana than in the other three zones. This high density cannot be attributed to the poor tillage capacity resulting from poor feeding. The quality of male animals maintained will depend on the type of soil and activities to be performed. With mechanisation of paddy cultivation, the need for very strong work animals is reduced. The indivisibility problem in maintaining work animals is resolved through tractor hire services. The correlations of work animal density with agro-climatic variables reveal that the positive association with paddy area as well as with the proportion of marginal and small farmers is reduced and the negative association with mechanisation is strengthened from 1987 onwards.

Milk production increased at a high rate of 7.67 per cent per annum between the mid-seventies and the mid-eighties, but the growth rate decelerated steeply in the later part of the eighties. However, the nineties witnessed revival with an annual growth rate rising to 5.69 per cent per annum. The demand for milk is likely to grow at about six per cent per annum during the first decade of this century. To meet this demand, production level has to be raised to 88 lakh tonnes by 2010 and 142 lakh tonnes by 2020. This growth in production has to come from breed improvement and better feeding. Crossbreeding programme has not succeeded because of the shift from cow to buffalo in all the areas. Breed improvement programme was successful in the canal irrigated areas of Krishna–Godavari zone comprising of four districts and Chittor district which is mostly dry. The dynamic changes in these districts reveal the importance of agro-climatic suitability for breed improvement. In Krishna-Godavari zone, there was a shift from cow to local buffalo in initial period and because of its suitability to the environment, local buffalo is graded up. Similarly, Chittor district experienced shift from cow to buffalo initially and buffalo is replaced by crossbred cow for further improvement in milk production as buffalo was found to be unsuitable for the environment. A significant decline in the work animal population is a common feature in both these areas. The experience indicates that the development of dairying requires replacement of work animals by tractors and adoption of cow in areas where buffalo is not suitable. It appears that cow is more suitable in the scanty rainfall and Telangana areas and parts of North Coastal Andhra.

The population of small ruminants remained stagnant till 1987, but grew at an annual rate of 1.95 per cent. Though the growth rate of the number of small ruminants is higher than that of human population, the high increase in per capita income coupled with the high income elasticity of demand since eighties led to steep increase in the demand for mutton. The population of goats which declined between 1983 and 1993, began to increase in the subsequent period. This could be partly due to bias against goats in anti-poverty programmes. In future, the population of goats will be increasing at a faster rate than sheep because of the higher demand for goat meat than sheep meat. The correlations between the density of small ruminants and agro-climatic factors indicate that this activity is confined to resource poor areas.

Andhra Pradesh specializes in poultry production, contributing as high as 20 per cent of the total eggs produced in the country. Per capita availability of eggs is 70 in Andhra Pradesh as against 30 at the national level. Egg production increased at a high rate of 21.6 per cent per annum during 1982-83 to 1986-87. The sector could achieve a high growth rate even under the adverse price conditions of higher growth of feed and mutton prices relative to the prices of egg and poultry meat. There is a lot of scope for improving egg consumption levels in the rural areas. While the consumption levels of chicken and other meat are same in both rural and urban areas, the rural areas lag far behind in egg consumption. This is due to poor availability of eggs in rural areas resulting from poor marketing infrastructure in rural areas. Development of cold storage and improvements in packing technology for moving eggs in small quantities go a long way in reducing the price of egg in rural areas. Livestock products have the highest income and price elasticities of demand among food products and they are higher in rural areas than in urban. Increase in incomes and reduction in prices of livestock products in rural areas will have a significant impact on growth in demand. The expansion of export market to European countries requires improvement in the quality of eggs. This can be achieved either through contract farming or development of cooperatives as in the case of milk production. These developments have the additional advantage of making the small producer viable.

References

Dandekar, V.M. (1969), "India's sacred cattle and cultural ecology", *Economic and Political Weekly*, Vol. 4, No. 39, September 27, pp.1559-66.

Dhas, A.C. (1989), "Changes in Draught Animal Population and Its Effect on the Composition of the Bovine Stock in Tamil Nadu", in Indian Society of Agricultural Economics (ed), *Livestock Economy of India*, Oxford and IBH, New Delhi.

Government of Andhra Pradesh (1999), *Andhra Pradesh: Vision 2020,* State Secretariat, Hyderabad.

Government of India (1976), *Report of the National Commission on Agriculture, Part VII, Animal Husbandry*, Ministry of Agriculture, New Delhi.

Mishra, S.N (1979), *Livestock Planning in India,* Vikas, New Delhi.

Mishra, S.N. and Sharma R.K.(1990), *Livestock Development in India*, Vikas, New Delhi.

Nair, K.N. and Dhas, A.C. (1989), "Cattle Breeding Technology and Draught Power Availability in Indian Agriculture", in Indian Society of Agricultural Economics (eds), *Livestock Economy of India*, Oxford and IBH, New Delhi.

Nadkarni, M.V. (1987), "Agricultural Development and Ecology-An Economist's View", *Indian Journal of Agricultural Economics*, Vol.42, No.3, July-September.

Raj, K.N. (1971), "India's sacred Cattle: Theories and Empirical Findings", *Economic and Political Weekly*, Vol.6, No.13.

Rao, Hanumantha, C.H. (1969), "India's surplus' cattle: some empirical results", *Economic and Political Weekly*, Review of Agriculture, December, pp.225-27.

Rao, Hanumantha, C.H. (1994), *Agriculture Growth, Rural Poverty and Environmental Degradation in India*, Delhi, Oxford University Press, pp.155-194.

Sharma, R.K. (1989), "Green Revolution and Draught Power (A Case study of a village in West Uttara Pradesh)", in Indian Society of Agricultural Economics (ed), *Livestock Economy of India*, Oxford and IBH, New Delhi.

Subrahmanyam, S. Rama Raju, V. and Nageswara Rao, R. (1996), "Inter-linkages Between Agriculture and Dairy Development", *Agricultural Situation in India*, April.

Vaidyanadhan, A. (1988), *Bovine Economy in India*, Oxford and IBH, New Delhi.

Appendix A

Linear Expenditure System: Data and Methodology Adopted

Price and income elasticities of demand are estimated for seven broad commodities using the linear expenditure system (LES). The commodity groups considered are: 1) cereals 2) pulses 3) milk and milk products, 4) edible oils, 5) meat, fish and egg, 6) other food, 7) non-food. The model assumes linear relationship between income and consumption of a commodity. This linearity assumption is valid within a narrow range of expenditure. Hence the model is estimated separately for four broad expenditure groups so that linearity is implied only within each group. The four expenditure groups are defined as follows. First, expenditure groups are classified into those below poverty line and those above the poverty line. In the second stage each of these two groups are again divided in to two categories. The poor are classified into very poor (households whose per capita expenditure falls below 0.75 times the poverty line) and moderately poor (poor households with per capita expenditure more than 0.75 times the poverty line). Households above the poverty line are classified into non-poor (per capita expenditure above the poverty line but less than 1.5 times the poverty line) and rich (households with per capita expenditure more than 1.5 times the poverty line). The consumption data relating to 18 NSS rounds beginning from 1970-71 to 1998-99 have been anchored to these groups and the model is estimated separately for these groups. Commodity prices have been constructed for this purpose separately for rural and urban areas using 1977-78 commodity weights derived from NSS 32nd round consumer expenditure survey data and Prices collected under Essential Commodities Act.

Since expenditure elasticity is used in projections, growth rate of per capita income is translated into growth rate of per capita expenditure by using the elasticity of consumption expenditure with respect to income. State domestic product at factor cost and consumer expenditure available from NSS data, both deflated by the state income deflator, are used. The elasticity of expenditure with respect to income is found to be 0.89. The income for the target year is projected from the trend equations estimated for the data from 1980-81 onwards.

Appendix B

Table: Classification of Districts into Agro-climatic Regions

Region	Districts included
North Coastal Andhra	Srikakulam, Vizianagarm, Visakhapatnam
Godavari-Krishna	East Godavari, West Godavari, Krishna, Guntur
Southern	Prakasam, Nellore, Chittor
Scanty Rainfall	Cuddapah, Anantapur, Kurnool
South Telangana	Ranga Reddy, Hyderabad, Medak, Mahaboobnagar, Nalgonda
North Telangana	Nizambad, Adilabad, Karimnagar, Warangal, Khammam

10

Structure and Growth of Industry

P. Venkatramaiah and
L.G. Burange

1. INTRODUCTION

Industrial sector plays a major role in the development process. It is well known that as the economy progresses, the share of industry in national product increases and that of agriculture comes down. At an advanced stage of development, the service sector dominates even the industrial sector. These changes in the relative importance of industry and service sectors are contributed by both demand and supply factors. On the demand side, income elasticity is the highest for services followed by industrial goods and then agricultural commodity. On the supply side, land being the basic resource, agriculture faces constraint even after considering its augmentation through quality improvements. Thus, industrialisation plays a crucial and dynamic role in widening and deepening the production base of the economy. Industrialisation has a vital role in enhancing the productivity of labour.

India adopted a development strategy based on central planning after independence. The industrial sector was highly controlled and was regulated through licensing mechanism. While the country achieved considerable progress in creating a sound and broad based industrial structure, its growth rate was modest. There has been a feeling since the eighties that the economy needs to be liberalised for achieving a high growth. A concrete shift in the policy towards liberalisation has been introduced in 1990-91. What is its effect on industry? Has it helped in accelerating industrial growth? This paper is an attempt to address these issues in the context of Andhra Pradesh. The industrial growth during the past four and half decades and the focus of the vision 2020 in respect of industrial sector are examined in section I. The growth and composition of factory sector in Andhra Pradesh is presented in section II. The performance of the factory sector in the pre and post liberalisation periods is examined in section III.

Share of Industries in State Income

Industrial sector comprises of four subsectors viz., mining and quarrying, manufacturing, electricity, gas and water supply and construction. The share of this sector increased slowly till 1991, but declined by 1995-96. From a low share of 12% in 1960-61, the state domestic product from industry increased to 14.8% by 1970-71, to 17.6% by 1980-81 and to 19.4% by 1990-91. It again came down to 18.5% by 1995-96 (Table 1). Manufacturing sector with a lion's share of 60% in industry also exhibited a similar trend. Thus, there is no improvement in the performance of industry as compared to other sectors in the nineties.

Table 1. Share of Industrial and Manufacturing Sectors in Net Domestic Product (1980-81 Price)

	Andhra Pradesh		India		Andhra Pradesh's Share in All India	
	Industry	Mfg	Industry	Mfg	Industry	Mfg
1960 – 61	12.0	7.3	19.45	13.47	4.29	3.74
1970 – 71	14.8	9.1	22.42	15.34	4.32	3.89
1980 – 81	17.6	11.2	24.34	16.95	4.81	4.39
1990 – 91	19.4	11.6	28.07	20.71	4.27	3.45
1995 – 96	18.5	10.7	28.77	21.61	3.62	3.58

Source: National Account Statistics and Directorate of Economics and Statistics, Andhra Pradesh.

The performance of the industrial sector at the national level is far superior to that of Andhra Pradesh. Its share at the national level was higher than at the state level. From 19.5% in 1960-61, its share rose to 28% in 1990-91. The poor performance of the state in industrial development in recent period can be seen from the fact that its share in all India declined from 4.8 per cent in 1980-81 to 3.6% in 1995-96. With a share of 7.8 per cent in India's population, this share of 3.6% in industrial income is very low.

The performance of the industrial sector in employment generation is very poor both at state and national levels. While the share of industry in state domestic product of Andhra Pradesh increased from 14.8 per cent in 1970-71 to 19.4% in 1990-91, the share in total workers remained stagnant around 11% (Table 2). At the national level the share of industry is only 12.7% in workers as against the high share of 28% in national income.

Table 2. Working Population in the Industrial Sector of Andhra Pradesh

Year	Percentage of total workers	Number of workers (in Lakhs)
1961	13.9	25.95
1971	11.1	19.99
1981	12.0	27.15
1991	11.3	32.14

Source: Census Publications.

Industry in Vision 2020

The vision 2020 envisages a growth rate of 10.3% per annum for gross state domestic product (GDSP) and a nine fold increase in per capita income over a period of 25 years (1995 to 2020). The share of industry stated to increase from 18% in 1995-96 to 21% in 2020-21. Though this target appears to be modest, it implied a 13 fold increase in 25 years and an annual growth rate of 11 per cent. It envisages an investment of Rs.11,65,000 over a period of 25 years. The capital output ratio works out to 6.85 and the sector is expected to absorb 8 million workers by 2020 from a low base of 3.5 million workers in 1995. The elasticity of employment with respect to value added in industry comes to 0.25.

All the three parameters viz., capital output ratio, employment elasticity and share in GSDP envisaged in the vision are eminently reasonable. But the required annual growth rates of income and as well as employment are unbelievably high when compared with the past performance. When the income from industrial sector increased three fold in 25 years, can it grow 13 times in the coming 25 years? Similarly, when it could absorb only 1.5 million workers in 25 years, can it be raised to 8 millions in the next 25 years? The answer can be in affirmative if the envisaged investment of Rs.11,65,000 crore materialises.

The vision document recognised that investment of such a high magnitude is not possible with internal savings, but believes that the state can be made an attractive destination of investment from foreign as well as domestic investors. Even if such funding is available, it would not enhance the levels of living by nine times as envisaged in the document because of the flight of income in the form of profits. Let us examine the likely extent of the flight of income due to dependence on external funds for investment. The total investment needed in all the sectors is put at Rs.30,00,000 crores, which represents 44% of GSDP till 2020. Even with improved saving rate, the state will have to depend for at least one third of the investment (Rs.10,00,000) on sources outside the state.

This outside investment generates an income of Rs.2,50,000 crores as the capital output ratio is assumed to be 4:1 but of this income, only wage component accrues to the population of the state and the non-wage income accrues to the outside owners of the capital. The wage component in the manufacturing income is only 28% in 1997-98. Even if we take it as 40% for the economy as a while, the non-wage component of the income generated with outside investment comes to Rs.1,50,000 crores and this amount is likely to flow out of the state. The incremental GSDP available for state's population would be Rs.6,00,000 crores rather than Rs.8,00,000 crores as envisaged in the vision 2020 document.

The government of Andhra Pradesh constituted cabinet sub-committees for operationlising the plan envisaged in the Andhra Pradesh Vision 2020 document. The sub-committee on employment envisaged an additional employment of 67.05 lakhs with an investment of Rs 78,994 crores in the industries and part of service sector by the year 2005. This implies an investment of Rs. 1.18 lakh per worker. But the Vision 2020 document expects an investment of Rs 15 lakhs per person. Small scale and tinny industries along with PMRY and CMEY are slated to create large employment with low investments. With globalization and consequent intense competition, units with such low investments can not survive and many of them would soon be sick. Thus, the employment targets based on this low investment for the year 2005 look to be unrealistic.

2. MANUFACTURING INDUSTRY IN ANDHRA PRADESH

The manufacturing sector in Andhra Pradesh generated an income of Rs 16,500 crores in 1997-98 accounting for 14.4% of the net state domestic product (in current prices). The manufacturing sector is usually divided into registered manufacturing consisting of the factory sector and unregistered manufacturing covering the remaining establishments. In 1960-61 the share of registered part was 39% which rose of 48% in 1970-71. Currently the share of the registered sector is over 60%. In what follows we focus attention on the registered manufacturing (factory) sector.

Share of Andhra Pradesh in the Nation's Factory Sector

The factory sector in Andhra Pradesh employed 9.75 lakh persons and generated an income of Rs 11,000 crores in 1997-98. The share of Andhra Pradesh in the All India factory sector has been rising consistently since 1980-81. But with a share of 8% in India's population the state accounted for only 4.5% of the value added and 5.2% of the output in the all India factory sector, But in terms of factory workers the share of the state was high at 8.7% in 1980-81. However, AP's share in value added, output as well as in employees went on consistently increasing over the decade of eighties and nineties. For instance, the shares in value added and output rose to 8.7% to 7% by 1997-98 (Table 3). Indicating that the factory sector of Andhra Pradesh showed a better performance than all India in terms of growth of output, value added and employment. But its performance in investment was poor. Net fixed capital has grown at 8.85% per annum in AP while the growth rate at the national level is 10.24% (Table 4).

Table 3. Share of Andhra Pradesh in All India Registered

Component	1980-81	1991-92	1997-98
Number of employees	8.73	10.99	11.18
Output	5.18	6.55	7.01
Value added	4.49	5.33	8.69
Emoluments	5.38	6.53	7.21
Net fixed capital	5.58	12.49	7.39

Table 4. Growth rate of Registered Manufacturing Sector in India and Andhra Pradesh

Description	India			Andhra Pradesh		
	1980-81 1997-98	1980-81 1991-92	1991-92 1997-98	1980-81 1997-98	1980-81 1991-92	1991-92 1997-98
Annual compound growth rate of						
i. Output	8.36	7.72	9.90	9.71	9.61	9.96
ii. Value added	7.68	6.66	10.14	9.59	6.54	17.18
Iii. Employment	1.63	0.60	4.15	3.05	2.31	4.82
Iv. Fixed capital	10.24	7.88	16.07	8.85	16.22	8.02
v. Wage rate	2.25	2.77	1.02	2.56	2.72	2.17*
Employment Elasticity						
i. Output	.212	.093*	.348	.313	.225	.355
Ii. Net fixed capital	.168	.057	.225	.156	.113	.264*
Elasticity of substitution between Lab and Cap	1.073	1.028	1.446	1.460	1.009	2.459

Andhra Pradesh is one of the major contributors in basic metals, non-metallic mineral products, beverages and tobacco, food products, textile products. But leather and leather products have an insignificant share in the total output (Table 5). The vision document identified textile and leather products for focus in the initial period in view of the large international market and high labour intensity. The state's share in the national output is only 1.3% in case of textile products and 0.8% in leather products. Considerable effort in building high class infrastructure is needed to augment production of these sectors.

Key Characteristics of AP's Factory Sector

Some key characteristics of the factory sector in Andhra Pradesh are presented in Table 6. The share in value added in the factory sector which decreased marginally during the eighties from 16% to 14% has increased significantly to 22% in 1997-98. The share of wages in value added witnessed a steep decline from 61% in 1980-81 to 28% in 97-98. The output and value added per employee more than trebled during the period. The net fixed capital per employee increased from Rs.16,000 to Rs.75,000 in 1981-82 prices. The return to net fixed capital which declined from 19% in 1980-81 to 12% in 91-92 rose sharply to 33% by 1997-98. While these rates do not give the correct picture of return to investment to be calculated on replacement values and not on capital values net of depreciation, these figures do indicate that return to capital has substantially increased in the state's factory sector. The average number of employees per factory which remained around 37 from 1980-81 to 1990-91 declined to 30 in 1997-98. Earlier it was observed that the share of the unregistered manufacturing was declining while the share of the registered sector has been increasing. The unregistered units may be moving into the registered category over a period of time. Thus the entire growth rate achieved by the factory sector should not be taken as fresh addition to the industry. A part of it is due to dynamic changes in the existing unregistered sector.

Table 5. Relative Share of Industry in the Registered Manufacturing Sector of Andhra Pradesh 1997-98

(Per cent)

Industry Group and Code Number	Output	Value added	Fixed capital	No. of employees
1	2	3	4	5
Food Products 20 –21	23.7	13.1	12.7	18.1
Beverage and Tobacco Products 22	5.2	6.4	1.2	38.1
Cotton textiles 23	8.4	3.7	4.5	6.7
Wool, Silk and Synthetic textiles 24	1.2	0.5	1.9	0.9
Jute, Hemp and Mesta textiles 25	0.3	0.5	0.1	0.8
Textile Products 26	0.5	0.3	0.4	1.0
Wood Products 27	0.2	0.3	0.1	0.3
Paper Products 28	2.3	2.8	3.8	2.8
Leather Products 29	0.1	0.1	0.1	0.2
Chemical Products 30	11.4	9.8	20.4	5.3
Rubber, Plastic, Petroleum and Coal Products 31	5.1	0.6	6.5	2.0
Non-metallic mineral Products 32	6.3	9.2	10.3	5.4
Metal and Alloy industries 33	22.6	36.3	29.9	4.5
Metal and Machinery Products 34	2.3	1.3	2.0	1.9
Machinery (Tools and Parts)35 – 36	7.8	11.2	3.6	5.4
Transport equipment 37	1.8	1.9	1.7	2.4
Other Manufacturing industries 38	0.3	0.1	0.8	0.7
Repair of capital goods #39	0.8	2.0	0.3	3.5
Manufacturing Mfg. (2-3)	100.00	100.00	100.00	100.0
AGRIND	41.7	27.5	11.6	69.0
N AGRIND	58.3	72.5	89.4	31.0
	Rs.50,34,80 1 crores	Rs.11,01,09 5 crores	Rs.22,00,719 crores	Rs.9,74,501 crores

Industry Composition

Food products basic metals and alloys manufacture of rubber, plastic and petroleum products and manufacture of machinery are the important industry groups in terms of their contribution to output, value added and net fixed capital. Though Andhra Pradesh is agriculturally advanced, non-agro-based industries which account for 58% of output of 73% of value added and 89% of net fixed capital (Table 5). This is not because the state is highly industrialized but because of the large scale public sector units which provided the foundation for industrialization of the state. The share of public sector factories in 1994-95 was 40% in output, 50% in value added and 95% in net fixed capital and 65% in emoluments, though the share was only 28% in employees*. The Hindustan Petroleum Corporation Visakhapatnam, Rashtriya Ispat Nigam Vizag and BHEL

Hyderabad, ECIL Hyderabad are very large units accounting for major chunk of the industrial output.

3. IMPACT OF LIBERALIZATION

The economic reforms of 1991 raised expectations about industrial growth in some quarters while there were apprehensions about its adverse impact in some. The devaluation of the rupee has enhanced the demand for exports there by boosting the Indian industry. The capital market reforms leading to the greater inflow of foreign exchange, the reduction in import duties leading to improved access to capital equipment, dismantling of controls leading to better capacity utilisation have all a positive impact on the Indian industry. At the same time the macro stabilisation measures of reducing the fiscal deficit, leading to reduction in government investment expenditure and the costlier imports have an adverse effect. The concessions to foreign capital (for eg, in tax treatment of capital gains) to accumulate foreign exchange drew protests from the Indian Industry that it would be adversely affected. What is the sum total effect of these factors on the Industry in Andhra Pradesh?

Table 6. Key characteristics of Factory Sector in Andhra Pradesh

Sl.No	Description	1980-81	1991-92	1997-98
1.	Number of factories (000)	16	22	32
2.	Number of employees (000)	594	795	975
3.	Output (in Crores)			
	a) Current prices	2,910	17,718	50,340
	b) 1981-82 prices	3,084	8,600	1,599
4.	Value added (in crores)			
	a) Current prices	462	2,513	1,101
	b) 1981-82 prices	545	1,179	3,247
5.	Net Fixed Capital (in crores)			
	a) Current prices	934	11,623	22,007
	b) 1981-82 prices	1,064	5,099	7,244
6.	Emoluments per employee			
	a) Current prices	4,739	15,288	31,540
	b) 1981-82 prices	5,851	6,981	8,617
7.	Net Capital per employee (current prices)	15,734	64,134	74,339
8.	Output per employee (in Rs.) in 1981-82 prices	51,946	1,08,150	1,64,091
9.	Value added per employee Rs. in current	9,173	14,831	33,314
10	Value added / Output (current)	.16	.14	.22
11.	Wages / Value added (current)	.61	.48	.28
12.	Capital /Value Added (current)	2.02	4.63	2.0
13.	Return to net capital	37	37	30
14.	Employees per factory	19%	12%	33%

Table 7. Relative share of industry in the Registered manufacturing sector of Andhra Pradesh 1997-98

(Per cent)

Industry Code Number	Output	Value added	Fixed capital	No. of employees	Emoluments
1	2	3	4	5	6
20 –21	11.5	12.5	13.1	13.3	11.5
22	17.6	18.4	6.8	62.1	37.5
23	9.5	7.7	5.2	7.6	4.6
24	2.1	1.1	2.8	2.6	2.0
25	3.9	4.2	2.8	3.7	3.0
26	1.3	1.0	1.9	2.6	2.1
27	4.5	9.2	1.7	3.5	4.3
28	6.2	8.7	7.1	8.1	8.7
29	0.8	0.2	1.2	1.4	1.3
30	4.9	4.7	6.8	6.6	5.1
31	3.7	0.9	6.0	5.6	3.8
32	12.7	18.2	10.7	11.8	10.9
33	12.2	20.2	10.8	6.6	9.1
34	6.1	4.7	7.3	6.5	4.5
35 – 36	4.6	6.8	3.5	5.9	6.5
37	1.8	2.2	2.5	4.2	3.1
38	1.5	0.6	5.4	4.3	4.7
#39	4.4	9.5	3.0	10.3	11.8
Mfg. (2-3)	7.0	8.7	7.4	11.2	7.2
DW2	8.7	8.7	7.0	15.8	8.8
DW3	6.2	8.7	7.5	6.8	6.4
APs	Rs 50,341 crores	Rs 11,011 crores	Rs 22,007 crores	Rs 9,74,501 crores	Rs 3,074 crores

Note: For a two-digit classification of the industries, see Appendix 1.

Data

To understand the impact of liberalization on the performance of the manufacturing sector of Andhra Pradesh, we examine the growth rates of output, value added, and employment of the factory sector. The summary results for factory sector of the Annual Survey of Industries provides the main data source. We examine the growth rates based on constant prices at the two digit industry level from 1980-81 to 1997-98. This period has been subdivided into pre-liberalization (1980-81 to 1991-92) and post-liberalization (1991-92 to 1997-98)

The index number of wholesale prices with base 1981-82 is used for deflating the current values of output. The fixed capital is deflated using a composite price index of building material, machinery (electrical and non-electrical), machine tools and transport equipment. The fixed capital considered in this study is net fixed capital, net of depreciation. The replacement value of capital would be more appropriate but those figures are not available. As such the observations based on fixed capital are of limited significance. Total emoluments to employees are deflated by the consumer price index for workers and the non-wage component of value added is deflated by the wholesale price index. The impact of liberalization on the manufacturing sector in the state is assessed by comparing the growth rates of output, value added, emoluments to employees, all in constant prices, between the pre and post liberalization periods. (Tables 8 to 10).

Table 8. Annual Compound Growth Rate of Value of Output and Net Value Added in the Registered Manufacturing Sector of Andhra Pradesh During 1980-81 to 1997-98. (@ constant prices, 1981-82=100)

(Per cent)

	Value of Output			Net Value Added		
Industry Code Number	1980–81 to 1997–98	1980–81 to 1991–92	1991–92 to 1997–98	1980–81 to 1997–98	1980–81 to 1991–92	1991–92 to 1997–98
1	2	3	4	2	3	4
20 –21	9.41	9.75	8.59	10.16	9.82	10.96
22	3.56	3.78	3.03*	8.52	9.96	5.18
23	9.62	9.02	11.06	5.59	3.75	10.11
24	22.39	23.78	19.14	20.43	22.04	16.12*
25	(-) 4.98	(-) 2.59	(-) 10.42	(-) 3.72	(-) 1.46*	(-) 8.87
26	17.41	14.37	24.97	19.52	13.03	36.48
27	0.75*	6.14	(-) 10.99	1.60*	4.71*	(-) 5.44*
28	5.57	6.45	3.50*	6.87	8.11	3.97
29	8.79	18.04	(-) 10.39	4.93*	17.35	(-) 19.67
30	11.99	8.89	19.74	14.17	9.86	25.10
31	13.07	19.15	(-) 0.18*	9.94	17.19	(-) 5.54*
32	11.26	12.95	7.35	11.43	7.77	20.62
33	15.29	14.24	17.84	17.55	9.03	37.19
34	12.62	12.15	13.75	13.13	12.86	13.78
35 – 36	5.42	6.60	2.68*	4.55	3.19*	7.86
37	5.91	1.16*	18.13	4.58	(-) 1.44*	20.39
38	15.13	15.75	13.67	6.77*	7.80*	4.41*
#39	13.33	-	-	8.54	-	-
Mfg. (2-3)	9.71	9.61	9.96	9.59	6.54	17.18
AGRIND	8.27	8.28	8.24	8.28	8.32	8.18
N AGRIND	10.91	10.81	11.16	10.31	5.54	22.81

- Statistically insignificant at 5% level of significance.

\# Data are available from 1989-90.

Output

The value output has grown at 9.7% per annum during the entire period 1980-81 to 97-98. The non-agricultural based industries (Div 3) grew at a higher rate (10.9%) as compared to agro based industries (8.3%). The synthetic textiles, textile products, basic metals, petroleum and chemicals have recorded high growth rate and the wood and wood products industry remained stagnant (Table 8).

Table 9. Annual Compound Growth Rate of Employment and Emoluments in the Registered Manufacturing Sector of Andhra Pradesh: 1980-81 to 1997-98.

(Per cent)

Industry Code Number	Employment (No. of Employees)			Emoluments (Per Employee Emoluments)		
	1980–81 to 1997–98	1980–81 to 1991–92	1991–92 to 1997–98	1980–81 to 1997–98	1980–81 to 1991–92	1991–92 to 1997–98
1	2	3	4	5	6	7
20–21	1.94	(-) 0.36*	7.63	3.97	5.34	0.80*
22	2.99	2.50	4.16	0.87*	1.47*	(-) 0.53*
23	2.16	0.82*	5.41	1.01	1.52	(-) 0.19*
24	6.41	4.16	11.97	2.39	1.33*	4.97
25	(-) 5.56	(-) 2.60*	(-) 12.24	1.62	1.39*	2.17*
26	15.18	9.13	30.95	4.71	5.87	2.00*
27	(-) 2.10	(-) 2.16*	(-) 1.94	2.43	4.30	(-) 1.89*
28	1.83	1.83	1.82*	3.07	3.18	2.81
29	6.05	12.81	(-) 8.43	2.89	3.32	1.88
30	2.80	(-) 0.55*	11.24	3.03	3.72	1.41
31	10.96	13.06	6.12	0.39*	0.45*	0.26*
32	4.17	4.47	3.47	1.44	0.46*	3.81*
33	7.73	10.39	1.65*	4.74	1.93*	11.72
34	6.94	10.17	(-) 0.35*	4.82	8.20	(-) 2.79*
35–36	1.46	2.27	(-) 0.44*	2.73	2.56	3.13
37	(-) 0.70*	(-) 4.63	9.30	1.17	0.66*	2.37*
38	5.12	3.71	8.55	2.36	2.29	2.52*
#39	8.17	-	-	1.58	-	-
Mfg. (2-3)	3.05	2.31	4.82	2.56	2.72	2.17*
AGRIND	2.40	1.38	4.85	1.74	2.27	0.51*
N AGRIND	4.69	4.70	4.65	2.25	1.70	3.55

• Statistically insignificant at 5% level of significance.
Data are available from 1989-90.

The growth rate in the post liberalization period (91-92 to 97-98) slightly accelerated to 9.96% from 9.61% in the pre-liberalization period (1980-81 to 91-92). It is the Non Agro industries (division 3) that contributed to the higher growth in the post liberalization period. The annual growth rate of chemical and chemical products, of which drugs and pharmaceuticals is an important component, has more than doubled from 8.89% to 19.74%. The transport equipment and parts (37) has also shown a phenomenal growth of 18.13% in the post liberalization period as compared to an insignificant growth of about 1% in the earlier period. On the other hand, the growth rate of agro industries (Div2) declined though marginally, in the post liberalization period. Among these industries, synthetic textiles and textile products, food, beverages and Cotton textiles have achieved higher growth rates in the post-liberalization period. But these gains were offset by the negative growth rates in jute textiles, food products and leather industry. The negative growth rate in leather industry is a cause for concern as it was identified as one of the growth engines in the Vision 2020 document.

Table 10. Annual Compound Growth Rate of Fixed Capital in the Registered Manufacturing Sector of Andhra Pradesh During 1980-81 to 1997-98. (at constant prices, 1981-82=100)

(Per cent)

Industry Code Number	1980 – 81 to 1997 – 98	1980 – 81 to 1991 – 92	1991 – 92 to 1997 – 98	Col. (4) – Col. (3)
1	2	3	4	5
20 –21	10.59	4.65	26.11	21.46
22	10.38	12.17	6.23	-5.94
23	9.98	6.34	19.13	12.79
24	30.34	31.05	28.66	-2.39
25	0.27*	2.50*	(-) 4.83*	-2.33
26	22.18	26.43	12.64	-13.79
27	(-) 8.47	(-) 11.83	0.02*	11.81
28	3.59	(-) 2.45 *	19.50	17.05
29	2.62	8.03	(-) 9.19	-1.16
30	10.67	0.77*	38.29	37.52
31	14.81	19.22	4.99	-14.23
32	14.78	22.58	(-) 1.83*	20.75
33	26.90	38.32	3.40*	-34.92
34	18.90	22.92	9.86*	-13.06
35 – 36	4.34	4.26	4.53	0.27
37	2.04	(-) 3.49*	16.49	13.00
38	24.26	31.25	9.12*	-22.13
#39	8.21	-	-	-
Mfg. (2-3)	13.72	16.22	8.02	8.20
AGRIND	8.85	3.77	21.94	18.17
N AGRIND	15.39	20.17	4.79*	-15.38

• Statistically insignificant at 5% level of significance.

Data are available from 1989-90.

Value added

Net value added increased at an annual rate of 9.6 per cent. There is accelaration in growth from 6.5% in the eighties to 17.2% in the nineties. While there is no change in the performance of agro-based industries between the two periods, the growth rate of non-agro-based industries quadruped from 5.4% to 22.8% per annum.

Petroleum products, Non metallic minerals, Basic metals and transport equipment are the major gainers (Table 8). The value added in textile product sector, which has been identified as one of the growth engines of industrial development in Vision 2020 document, grew at 36.5% in the nineties.

Employment

Employment in the factory sector of manufacturing grew at an annual rate of 3.05% over the period 1980-81 to 97-98. The growth rate of employment in Non Agro based industries is higher at 4.6% compared to 2.4% of Agro based industries. Textile products and Rubber, Plastic. Petroleum and Coal products showed high growth rates (Table 9). What is the impact of liberalization on employment? With economic growth there should be a structural transformation in the composition of domestic product in favour of industry and services. Also the surplus labour of agriculture should be absorbed in the other sectors. The vision 2020 document expects industrial sector to account for 43% of the 20 million new jobs in the state. Because of increasing competition with liberalization and globalization there is a need for the industry to improve its efficiency. Down sizing the labour force with voluntary retirement schemes is expected to enhance the efficiency. Thus there is a fear that the liberalized regime in the Indian context may lead to job less growth which would be highly detrimental. What does the data show ?

Employment in the registered manufacturing sector in Andhra Pradesh grew at a rate of 4.8% per annum in the post liberalization period as compared to a growth rate of 2.31% in the pre liberalization period. It is the agro-based industries which contributed to this rise. While the employment growth rate in the non Agro industries was more or less same (around 4.7%) in both the periods, the growth rate in employment in agro-based industries shot up to 4.85% in the post liberalization period from 1.38% in the eighties. Textile products, food products, wool, silk and synthetic fiber textiles contributed to this rise. Leather industry showed a negative growth rate in employment.

Employment Elasticity

Both the output and the employment grew at a higher rate in the nineties compared to eighties. Elasticity of employment with respect to output relates these two growth rates and indicates the labour absorptive capacity of the manufacturing sector. Contrary to popular perception, the data shows that the employment elasticity has increased in the post liberalization period as compared to pre liberalization period. This is largely because of agro-based industries, textile and leather products exhibited an employment elasticity of greater than ninety in the nineties. The chemical, rubber, plastic and petroleum products show improved employment elasticity while in metals and metal products the employment elasticity declined significantly. Considerly the factory sector as a whole, a 10% increase in output resector in a 3.5% increase in employment in the nineties as compared to 2.3% in the eighties (Table 11).

Table 11. Employment Elasticity in the Registered Manufacturing Sector of Andhra Pradesh During 1980-81 to 1997-98

Industry Code	Employment Elasticity with Respect to		Elasticity of substitution between labour and fixed capital
	Output	Fixed Capital	
20 –21	0.229	0.040*	1.356
22	0.550	0.270	0.084*
23	0.271	0.249	0.764
24	0.359	0.192	-
25	0.994	0.455	0.369
26	0.841	0.495	0.458*
27	0.439	0.208	0.941
28	0.448	0.220	1.207
29	0.713	0.682	-
30	0.309	0.272	1.753
31	0.667	0.135	(-) 0.028*
32	0.374	0.227	0.240*
33	0.498	0.283	-
34	0.734	0.355	0.424*
35 – 36	0.341	0.356	0.727
37	0.613	0.413	0.885*
38	0.358	0.211	-
39#	0.674	0.579	-
Mfg. (2-3)	0.313	0.156	1.460
AGRIND	0.316	0.216	0.374*
N AGRIND	0.430	0.269	1.663

• Statistically insignificant at 5% level of significance.

Data are available from 1989-90. Due to negative net value-added substitution elasticity for industries 24, 29, 33 and 38 is not estimated.

Growth of Wages and Employment

Employment in the organized manufacturing sector grew at a much higher rate than in the eighties both at the national and state level. How did the real wages grow during these two periods? Table 9 gives the annual compound growth rate of per employee emoluments in the factory sector of Andhra Pradesh. The growth of wages was lower in the nineties than in the eighties while the growth of employment showed opposite pattern. Similar is the case with agro-based industries. But the growth of wages in the non-agro industries is higher in the nineties as compared to eighties though growth rate of employment is lower in the nineties. Thus, there is a conflict between employment generation and wage improvements.

Naturally, in the liberalisation period, growth in employment takes place only at the cost of wage rate.

Growth Rates at the State and National Level

At the national level also the output, value added, net fixed capital and employment grew at a higher rate level in the post liberalization period as compared to the pre-liberalization. But the growth rates in Andhra Pradesh are higher than the national level in both the periods in all indicators except fixed capital. Both at the national and state levels the growth of wage rate was lower. Further, the growth rate of wages was lower in the nineties than in the eighties both at the state and national levels.

The employment elasticity with respect to output which was almost zero in the eighties has increased at the national level (Table 12). The elasticity of substitution which measures the ease with which labour and capital are substituted assumes a value greater than unity and increased

Table 12. Employment Elasticity with Respect to Output in the Registered Manufacturing Sector of Andhra Pradesh

Industry Code Number	Output			Fixed Capital		
	1980–81 to 1997–98	1980–81 to 1991–92	1991–92 to 1997–98	1980–81 to 1997–98	1980–81 to 1991–92	1991–92 to 1997–98
1	2	3	4	5	6	7
20–21	0.229	0.029*	0.490	0.040*	0.094*	0.218
22	0.550	0.609	0.130*	0.270	0.189*	0.223*
23	0.271	0.526	0.294	0.249	0.213	0.251
24	0.359	0.553	0.342	0.192	0.091*	0.113*
25	0.994	0.429*	1.012	0.455	0.778	0.228*
26	0.841	0.525	1.188	0.495	0.375	1.034
27	0.439	0.103*	0.454	0.208	0.127	0.301*
28	0.448	0.481	0.494	0.220	0.016*	0.139*
29	0.713	0.680	1.055	0.682	0.607	0.514*
30	0.309	0.073*	0.807	0.272	0.199*	0.306
31	0.667	0.548	0.946	0.135	0.142*	0.484
32	0.374	0.346	0.588	0.227	0.178	0.539
33	0.498	0.748	0.146*	0.283	0.266	0.205
34	0.734	0.839	0.210*	0.355	0.405	0.289
35–36	0.341	0.383	0.185*	0.356	0.535	0.103*
37	0.613	0.546	0.583	0.413	0.368	0.479
38	0.358	0.204	0.424	0.211	0.102	0.634
39#	0.674	-	-	0.579	-	-
Mfg. (2-3)	0.313	0.225	0.355	0.156	0.113	0.264*
AGRIND	0.316	0.235*	0.429	0.216	0.082*	0.168
NAGRIND	0.430	0.391	0.306	0.269	0.235	0.201*

* Statistically insignificant at 5% level of significance.
# Data are available from 1989-90.

during the post liberalisation period (Table 13). This indicates that increase in the wage rate relative to profit rate leads to a more than proportionate decrease in labour capital ratio there by decreasing the share of wages in value added. On the whole liberalisation had a positive impact on the growth parameters of the manufacturing sector both at the national and the state levels.

Table 13. Elasticity of Substitution between labour and Fixed Capital in the Registered Manufacturing Sector of Andhra Pradesh During 1980-81 to 1997-98

Industry Code Number	1980 – 81 to 1997 – 98	1980 – 81 to 1991 – 92	1991 – 92 to 1997 – 98
1	2	3	4
20 – 21	1.356	1.184	0.858*
22	0.084*	0.095*	2.342
23	0.764	0.733	(-) 3.746*
24	-	-	-
25	0.369	0.168*	1.074
26	0.458*	0.459*	(-) 0.032*
27	0.941	0.978	0.606*
28	1.207	2.054	(-) 0.233*
29	-	-	-
30	1.753	1.604	(-) 1.760*
31	(-) 0.028*	0.091*	(-) 5.411*
32	0.240*	(-) 0.062*	1.444*
33	-	-	-
34	0.424*	0.139*	(-) 0.837*
35 – 36	0.727	0.877*	1.021*
37	0.885*	(-) 0.654*	0.578
38	-	-	-
39#	-	-	-
Mfg. (2-3)	1.460	1.009	2.459
AGRIND	0.374*	0.322*	1.119*
N AGRIND	1.663	0.931*	2.523

• Statistically insignificant at 5% level of significance.
Data are available from 1989-90.

4. CONCLUSIONS

The share of the industrial sector in the state domestic product has increased from 12% in the Eighties to 19% in the Nineties. But in the nation's industrial income AP's share is around 4% while AP's population is nearly 8% of India's population. The increasing share of the industry in the domestic product is not accompanied by increase in the share of employment. During the last two decades, the factory component of the manufacturing industry in AP grew at a higher rate than that of the nation, in terms of output, value added and employment. By 1997-98 its share in value added in the nations factory sector increased to 8.5% from 4.5% in 80-81.

The registered manufacturing segment of the factory sector during the decades of Eighties and Nineties grew at a higher rate than the country's factory sector aided mainly by the public sector undertakings in Iron and Steel, Petroleum, Electrical Machinery and Electronics. The share of Public Sector Units is 50% in output and is 95% in net fixed capital.

The Vizag Steel Plant, Hindustan Petroleum Refinery at Visakhapatnam, BHEL and ECIL at Hyderabad are very large units accounting for a major chunk of output and capital investment. One would have expected that the backward and forward linkages provided by the large scale public sector units backed by the investable funds available from the surpluses of the agricultural sector would have resulted in rapid industrialization of Andhra Pradesh. Though in the eighties a few, new entrepreneurs (like Nagarjuna group) emerged from the landed aristocracy, much of the surpluses from the agricultural sector went into the tertiary sector like hotels and restaurants and film production.

Drugs and pharmaceuticals is one industry where AP has a dominant position in the country. Roughly one third of the country's bulk drugs is produced in and around Hyderabad. The public sector units, though now sick, did provide an impetus in terms of technocratic and skilled manpower for the growth of the drug industry in AP.

One may have to search for reasons as to why the state could not industrialize faster inspite of the advantages mentioned above?. Is it due lack of infrastructure? Or is it due to lack of Skilled manpower? Or is it due to lack of work ethics?. The vision document expects that the industrial sector would be multiplied by 13 times of the current size in real terms over the 25 year period. Can the state attract investment to realize such a phenomenal growth?.

In the general developmental process the service sector is gaining increasing prominence specially after the information technology revolution. Traditionally the declining share of agriculture was to be compensated by the industrial sector and subsequently by the service sector. But now it appears that service sector is getting prominence even before the industrial sector in sufficiently developed. Much emphasis is being placed on information technology both at the national level and at the state level. Because of the educated manpower available in the state and in the country with very favorable exchange rate mechanism, there is high external demand for IT service. As a result much emphasis is being laid on the IT sector.

As was seen the liberalisation process led to a higher growth in the manufacturing sector in the nineties compared to eighties. But after the initial pent up demand for manufactured articles is satiated, the industrial sector is facing a recession. The cheap imports consequent to trade liberalisation as per WTO norms also affect the demand for products of the domestic industry. In the stock market the shares of the companies producing manufactured articles are at very low levels. Manufacturing segment of the economy is now being called "old economy" as if it has no future as against the IT sector which is called the new economy.

The infrastructure that is being developed in the state is also largely focussed on IT sectors to the neglect to the industrial sector. It may be noted that the IT sector is growing because of export demand and there is very little domestic demand. In the long run this cannot be sustained unless domestic demand grows. The growth of domestic demand to a considerable extent depends on the increase in the production of the material sector of which industrial sector is an important component. The state may have to focus on selected localities by providing the necessary infrastructural facilities to promote industrial development.

Notes

* Rao V.H., N.K. Acharya and M.C. Swaminathan (eds.) (1998), *Andhra Pradesh at 50, A Data based Analysis,* Data News Features, Hyderabad (P. 323).

Appendix 1

Two-digit Industrial Classification

Industry Code	Description of Industry
20 –21	Mfg. Of food and food products.
22	Mfg. of beverages, tobacco and tobacco products.
23	Mfg. of cotton textiles.
24	Mfg. of wool, silk and synthetic fiber textiles
25	Mfg. of jute, hemp and mesta textiles.
26	Mfg. of textile products.
27	Mfg. of wood and wood products, furniture and fixtures.
28	Mfg. of paper and paper products.
29	Mfg. of leather and leather products.
30	Mfg. of chemical and chemical products.
31	Mfg. of rubber, plastic, petroleum and coal products.
32	Mfg. of Non-metallic mineral products.
33	Basic metal and alloys industries.
34	Mfg. of metal products and parts except machinery.
35 – 36	Mfg. of machinery, machine tools and parts.
37	Mfg. of transport equipment and parts.
38	Other manufacturing industries.
#39	Repair of capital goods.
Mfg. (2-3)	Manufacturing

11

Industry: Policy and Performance

Deepita Chakravarty

1. INTRODUCTION

The objective of this paper is to give an overview of the main aspects of the performance of industrial sector in Andhra Pradesh (A.P.) since the 1970s, with a specific focus on the role played by government policies both at the national as well as at the state level. In India, like many other developing countries, industrial development is a product of conscious government policy effort with public investment playing the crucial role. This is not to deny the role private investment played in industrializing the economy but to emphasize the predominance of industrial policy legislations in determining the private initiative. However, over the last 50 years Indian industrial policies have undergone major changes with the final turn around coming in the early 1990s.

Two important features emerge out of the extant literature concerning industrialization on the basis of the experiences of both developed and developing countries. First, it confirms that compared with the underdevelopment of the colonial past, the growth of industrial activity, as a whole has been impressive. Secondly, it also shows that industrial development within as well as between countries has been uneven over time and space. (Nayyar, 1994). This pattern of development has helped generate disparities between states regarding industrialization. The regional disparity in industrialization, is however, predominantly a developing country feature. The reasons behind this are diverse and often find their roots in the broader political processes. But the issue lies beyond the scope of this paper.

At the time of Independence, some states in India were already much ahead of the rest in terms of industrial development. An industrial atmosphere was already prevailing in those states. Thus the socio-economic conditions in those were not comparable with a post-war standard developing country situation. But Andhra Pradesh was not one of those states and was predominantly an agrarian economy with all developing country characteristics of the post war period. A nation-wide analysis of the impact of industrialization, as often done[1], thus is likely to hide the specificities of different states which may have important policy implications for development. Moreover, with the recent major change in the industrial policy regime, the importance of private investment has increased enormously. As a result, different states have to face direct competition from each other for attracting private investment both domestic and foreign. From this perspective, it has also become important to understand the nature and status of industrial development in a specific state in relation to the state's own policy incentives or disincentives.

According to the Indian Constitution, industry is predominantly a central subject. Consequently, in the relatively industrially underdeveloped states it is difficult to find a separate industrial policy at least at the early stages of development. In AP, the first-ever policy on industrial development was announced by the government only in the early 1990s (Rao *et al*, 1998). The nature of the state policies is essentially of incentive type. In this paper we try to relate the industrial performance of the state of AP with the broader policies at the one hand and the state incentives on the other.

The remainder of this paper is organized as follows. The next section deals with the constraints and availability of data with the major sources used for assessing the industrial policy performance of AP. This is followed by an overview of the implications of industrial policies for the industrial sector as a whole since the 1970s. Considering the extensive data set available and the importance of the registered manufacturing sector, we concentrate only on this sector in the fourth section. Finally some policy implications are suggested in the last section.

2. DATA

In order to capture the performance of the industrial sector in AP we have to look mainly at two crucial variables relating to this sector such as employment and output. Industrial sector constitutes of mining, manufacturing, electricity- gas and construction sectors. National Accounts Statistics (NAS) published by the Central Statistical Organization (CSO) provides time series data for net state domestic product (NSDP) in terms of broad industrial classifications at the single digit level. From this source it is easy to get the industrial output figures at the state level.

Unfortunately, it is not easy to capture the employment picture. The total employment figures are available in the Economic Tables of the Decennial Census. The main shortcoming of this data is the time lag. Moreover, at this juncture, it is available only up to 1991. So looking at this data set alone will not tell us any thing about the post 1990s. There is yet another important data source on the employment- unemployment situation provided once in five years by the National Sample Survey Organization (NSSO). Information for the latest year available from this data set is 1999-2000. While Census gives the absolute employment figures, NSSO gives the work participation rates. Moreover, the definitions used for the two sources are different. Thus, while these two sources are not strictly comparable, separately they provide important insights[2].

Considering the importance of manufacturing sector within the industrial sector in general and registered manufacturing in particular, we decide to narrow down our focus. Another important reason behind this decision is the availability of a rich data set for the registered manufacturing sector provided by the Annual Survey of Industries (ASI) published by the CSO. ASI provides a fairly detailed information regarding output, employment, capital formation, wages etc for the factory sector of manufacturing every year. Presently, the latest year available for the state of Andhra Pradesh is 1997-98. The state-wise wholesale price index in terms of two-digit level classification is not available. Thus for deflating the current values of output we have used the all India wholesale price index numbers for each industry groups with 1981-82 as base. We have deflated the fixed capital figures by a composite index of electrical and non-electrical machinery. ASI gives both the figures for employees and workers. In this paper we have considered the figures for workers to capture the employment picture. In order to calculate the trend growth rates we have fitted a semi-log equation.

3. INDUSTRIAL PERFORMANCE SINCE 1970

This section aims at giving a broad sketch of the industrial policy performance in AP since 1970 and tries to identify its role in the process of economic development. So far as the basic pattern of industrialization is concerned both developed (Kuznets, 1966) and developing (Pack, 1988; Weiss, 1988) countries share some common experiences. To begin with, compared to the growth rates of most developed countries during the 19th or early 20th century, the developing countries during the post war period recorded higher growth rates at the corresponding stage of development. Thus, the countries industrializing in the post war period could achieve a certain stage of industrial development within a relatively short span of time. This has been possible through extensive forms of government intervention[3] confirming the Gerschenkorn (1962) hypothesis regarding the pattern of industrialization among latecomers (Mookherjee, 1995)[4]. During the fifties and sixties the forms of government intervention especially showed major commonalities amongst most developing countries. These comprise import substitution, extensive public investment and emphasis on development of heavy industry. In this respect, Indian as well as AP's experience is not an exception.

Policies and the Industrial Sector

Growth of industries in the state of AP was propelled by the growth of public sector industry. During the years between 1960 and 1975 industrial estates came up in Hyderabad and some other districts of AP. This was followed by the building up of the power generating stations mainly to improve infrastructure for future industrial development. The essential feature of this public investment was heavy capital intensity in the large-scale industries (Rao *et al*, 1998). In the period 1960-61 to 1970-71, net state domestic product of AP industrial sector grew at 5.2 percent per annum. In this period the national average was 5.4 percent. The growth performance of the industrial sector of the state was not high by comparison with most other developing countries but it was slightly higher than growth rates achieved in the industrialized nations at the turn of the nineteenth century (see Pack, 1988).

Industrialization is supposed to change the relative importance of the manufacturing sector in the economy. Generally the share of manufacturing and services improve both in terms of output and employment at the cost of the agricultural sector. Cross-sectional experiences of countries at different stages of development confirm this trend. While the composition of output has altered notably in the state of AP during the period 1960-61 to 1999-2000, composition of employment reveals a different pattern. The relative shares of different sectors exhibit an almost constancy with a mild increase in the share of the services sector at the cost of agriculture (Table 1). The Indian experience is almost similar as well.

Table 1. Relative Share of Different Sectors in the Total Employment of AP (%)

Year	Agriculture	Industry	Services
1971	73.40	11.16	15.44
1981	72.02	11.94	16.04
1991	70.37	11.35	18.26

Source: Economic Tables, Population Census of AP .

This suggests a significant difference between the experiences of the structural transformation of the AP economy and the now-developed economies at comparable stages of development (Kuznets, 1966). The policy emphasis on heavy industry, import substitution and state-led investments in the industrial sector, probably resulted in high levels of capital intensity. While discussing the factory sector of manufacturing in the next section, we will take up this issue in more detail. As a consequence, the shift of output into industry has failed to match a corresponding shift in employment.

In the Population Census, information about industrial employment[5] is available mainly under two broad categories: household and non-household and rural and urban. Percentage of AP industrial employment has declined steadily both in the household sector and in the rural areas over the period 1971 to 1991. New industrial set ups are likely to come in urban areas due mainly to better infrastructural development and market. As a result, with industrial development it is expected to have a shift in the industrial employment towards the urban areas. The percentage of rural employment was 65 in 1971 and declined to 57 in 1991. It is worth mentioning here that this trend is more or less the same in all the major regions of AP with Hyderabad having no industrial activity in the rural areas. This has happened in spite of the Central and state government providing incentives for setting up industries especially in the backward areas. In fact, it has been well documented in the literature that industrial location decisions are usually determined more by infrastructural facilities and skilled labour than by such incentives.

While it is true that the definition of the backward areas and forms of incentives have changed substantially over this period, concentration of employment in terms of industries, however, has not changed much during this span of time. Regarding employment concentration, industrial categories of food products, textiles mainly handlooms and bidi making are the most important instances. Moreover, the prevalence of the industrial category of electrical and non-electrical machinery featured in 1991 population Census in the area around Hyderabad is significant. Within the machinery group, three digit classification shows the importance of the group 367, the software- based machinery, in the early 1990s itself. The active policy initiative of the state government to promote the software and hardware industries in the state in two consecutive industrial policies in the 1990s will probably lead to more activities in the industrial category of electrical and non-electrical machinery. We will come back to this issue in the context of the factory sector of manufacturing.

Because of the unavailability of the Census data for the year 2001, from the above analysis we cannot say anything about the post liberalization trends in employment. However, the quinquennial surveys on employment unemployment of the NSSO do provide some important information at the single digit classification level. NSSO provides information in terms of usual or current status of employment for rural and urban areas. For our analysis, we concentrate only on the usual status employment.

NSSO data show a similar pattern of structural change in terms of employment in the period 1983 to 1999-2000 (Table 2) as revealed from the Census data till the year 1991(Table 1) for the rural areas of AP. More importantly, this data set suggests a steady decline in the industrial activities in the rural areas. Services sector in the rural areas shows only a slight increase over the years. In the urban areas more than 50 percent of the activities are concentrated in the services sector and consistently increasing over the concerned period. However, industrial activities are relatively more important in the urban areas and show a steady but marginal increase during this period.

Table 2. Distribution of Employment by Sectors According to the Usual Status

Year	Rural persons				Urban persons				
	Agricul-ture	Industry	Manufa-cturing	Services	Year	Agricul-ture	Industry	Manufa-cturing	Services
1983	79.7	9.8	7.7	10.5	1983	14.3	29.6	22.42	56.1
1993-94	79.3	9.3	6.9	11.3	1993-94	16.4	30.0	19.1	53.7
1999-2000	78.8	8.7	5.6	12.5	1999-2000	9.5	32.2	19.4	58.2
	Rural female					Urban female			
1983	83.2	8.9	7.6	7.9	1983	27.5	29.9	24.56	42.6
1993-94	83.7	8.5	7.4	7.7	1993-94	30.8	29.7	22.7	39.2
1999-2000	84.3	7.5	6.0	8.2	1999-2000	16.8	33.5	22.2	49.6

Source: Report on Employment and Unemployment, NSSO for several years.

The relative importance of the services sector compared to industry, especially in the urban areas, in generating both output and employment might have its roots in the peculiar history of the beginning of the non-agricultural activities in the state. In the early seventies, with the advent of land reform, big farmers decided to diversify investment in non-agricultural activities. They started investing in film industry, hotels, bars, building construction, trading and in shares. The absence of the industrial entrepreneurial class and the necessary infrastructure probably thwarted the initiatives in investing resources to the development of industries unlike the states of Maharashtra, Tamil Nadu etc. (Rao *et al*, 1998, Naïdu, 1988). However, the growing importance of the services sector in generating employment even after a decade's conscious policy effort to boost industry in the state is a matter of serious concern. Services sector has produced more than 50 percent of the total net state domestic product in the year 1999-2000. The growth of the services sector is likely to be sustained only when the productive sectors, especially industry, of an economy grow at a sufficiently rapid rate to generate demand for the services.

The Small-scale Sector

Both in the theoretical literature (such as Brock and Evans, 1986) as well as in the policy questions small-scale industry plays a major role in the issues of development. In India, small-scale industry has been the recipient of numerous forms of government protection since the late 60s (Majumdar 1991, Bhavani, 1992). Moreover we find special mentions of incentives for the small-scale industrial activities in the state industrial policies since its emancipation. How is the small-scale industrial sector performing in AP? One of the difficulties in discussing small firms is defining what one means by small. For the purpose of analysis here we define small firms as the ones operating in the unregistered sector mainly, together with the sample sector of the ASI frame. The latter some times is referred to as modern small-scale sector (Gang, 1995). One more difficulty to handle the issues related to the small-scale industry is the problem of unavailability of data.

According to the Economic Census (a proximate source of information) number of enterprises, which employs at least one hired worker and not registered under the Factory's Act (1948) within the small-scale industry, has gone up from 88 thousand in 1980 to 1.3 lakhs in 1998. Table 3 brings out some salient features of the small-scale industrial activities[6] in AP in a comparative frame of the other three Southern states as well as the two industrially most developed states in India. Interestingly, while the size (in terms of employment) of the enterprises is generally of same magnitude (except in Gujarat), AP shows the lowest labour productivity among all states considered here. With the increasing importance of the small-scale manufacturing activities in terms of exports, this of course is a matter of concern. Low productivity is generally a result of obsolete technology and organizational inefficiency. The rising sickness of small-scale firms in AP (Rao et al, 1998) can be considered as an indirect evidence of inefficiency in both counts mentioned above. A study based on primary data suggests that non-availability of credit facilities and acute shortage of infrastructure, mainly power, leads to the use of inefficient technology in the small units (Singer et al, 2001). Moreover, limited-marketing avenues in some cases also plays an important role.

Table 3. Salient Features of the Unregistered Small-scale Sector of AP and a Few Other States

State	Number of Workers	Value added/ Worker(in Rs000)	Workers/ Factory	Percentage of Women Workers
Andhra Pradesh	2485210	12.05	2.00	37.22
Karnataka	1976698	17.80	2.25	39.11
Kerala	1201302	22.25	2.06	39.93
Tamil Nadu	3355725	18.42	2.16	43.71
Gujarat	1649244	27.40	2.64	15.49
Maharashtra	2869009	28.87	2.41	19.56

Source: Calculated from *Informal Sector in India*, 1999-2000, NSSO 55th Round.

From the policy perspective, small firms are held to be better at achieving intermediate development goals such as employment creation and particularly women's employment generation. In this context it is important to note that although the percentage of women's employment in the other Southern states is higher than AP, the state is much ahead of the two industrially perennially developed states in India. We will come back to this issue in the context of manufacturing sector once again.

The percentage compositions of crucial variables for the modern small firms sector as emerging from Table 4 indicate no clear direction of the relative performance of this sector visa vi the large ones. Incidentally Gang (1995) reports a similar finding for India as a whole. She also suggests that the relative share of small firms differs widely across industries. The scanty evidence that is available for the state of AP is not suggestive of some thing different. Possible determinants for the size of small-scale activities in an industry include industry's capital intensity, the degree of vertical integration in the industry, economies of scale in management etc. However, there is a clear indication that within the small firms relatively bigger ones have done well mainly at the cost of relatively smaller ones. Part of this might be due to dynamic transformation of the relatively smaller firms within the small firm group. It may be essential for the government to rethink about the incentive structure for the small-scale industrial sector on the basis of a detailed assessment of performance of disaggregated industrial classifications.

Table 4. Percentage Composition of Certain Important Variables by the Small Units within the Factory sector of AP (Size Class Distribution in terms of Employment)

Employment size class	Factories	Fixed Capital	Employment	Net value added
		1985-86		
Up to 49	74.9	6.7	25.0	10.9
50 to 99	17.9	4.0	19.3	7.8
100 and above	7.2	89.3	55.7	81.3
		1994-95		
Up to 49	68.03	4.03	18.63	7.13
50 to 99	24.70	3.08	27.95	7.54
100 and above	7.3	92.89	53.42	85.33
		1997-98		
Up to 49	65.86	4.41	16.80	8.02
50 to 99	25.86	3.31	26.46	11.01
100 and above	8.3	92.28	56.74	80.92

Source: Annual Survey of Industries Summary Results.

The Manufacturing Sector

In Andhra Pradesh industry generated 23.44 percent of net state domestic product in the year 1997-98. Within the domestic product generated by the industrial sector of AP, around 58 percent comes from the manufacturing alone. In India, the manufacturing sector can be divided broadly into registered and unregistered sectors. In terms of employment the unregistered sector plays a very important role, in fact more important than the registered sector. However, in terms of output the registered sector assumes more importance.

Table 5 shows the percentage distribution of employment and output in the registered and unregistered manufacturing in AP. The high percentage share of the registered sector in output and low percentage share in employment confirm our earlier statement in the case of AP. The percentage share of NSDP of the registered sector is not only much higher than the unregistered sector but is also increasing significantly over the years. However, the figures for 1999-2000 show a decrease in the percentage share of NSDP of the registered sector (around 60 per cent) when compared to 1991-92. It is important to note that AP shows a consistent increase in the share of registered sector employment during 1971 - 1991. A part of it is due to dynamic changes in the existing unregistered sector. Because of the unavailability of Census data mainly, we are not able to talk about the situation in the late 90s. However, the NSSO data provide some clue. Table 2 shows that while the share of manufacturing in the rural areas has declined consistently during the concerned years, in the urban areas there is a marginal increase in1999-2000 over 1993-94. The population dependent on the manufacturing activities in the urban areas is much more than the rural areas. Thus, according to NSSO data we probably can conclude that there is a marginal improvement in the total manufacturing employment in the late 90s compared to the early 90s.

Table 5. Percentage of Registered Manufacturing Employment[7] and Output

Year	Employment percentage	Output percentage
1971	20.88	42.46
1981	24.78	56.38
1991	27.17	66.87
2000	Not available	60.00

We are interested in looking at industrial performance from the perspective of development. Thus the structural changes become important in our analysis. From this point of view it becomes essential to look at the women's participation in the industrial activities such as manufacturing. According to the Population Census percentage of female employment has increased steadily from 21 in 1971 to 28 in 1991 in AP. Concentration of women's employment is the highest in the bidi making industry and notably, this concentration has increased over the concerned period. Thus while industrialization helped women to diversify the broad pattern of their work participation, it still is determined by the 'role models' for women set by the socio-economic consensus. Interestingly, while there were specific incentive measures for the small manufacturing undertakings headed by a person from the SC/ST community, there is no such incentive scheme for a woman entrepreneur.

4. REGISTERED MANUFACTURING SINCE THE 80s

In this section we discuss the major features of the industrial policy performance in the context of the registered manufacturing sector in AP with a special focus on the probable impact of the fundamental changes in the policy regime. For the analysis in this part the period chosen is 1980-81 to 1997-98. We consider 1980-81 to 1991-92 as pre liberalization and 1992-93 to 1997-98 as the post liberalization period. We have not discussed the rates of growth of different indicators in detail as it has already been done in the last chapter 'Structure and Growth of Industry' by Venkatramaiah and Burange in this volume. This paper is referred hereafter as 'last chapter'. However, it is worth mentioning here that the second period considered here is slightly different from the previous study. As this difference only leads to a difference in the numerical figures in precision and does not change the trend, we decide to follow the results of the previous study as and when required.

Percentage compositions

To begin with let us have a quick look at the relative position of AP in the total registered manufacturing in India along with the Southern states as well as the two industrially most developed states of Maharashtra and Gujarat (Table 6), in terms of gross value added. As the size of the different states varies considerably, there is a problem of standardization. However, leaving apart the problem of standardization, one can only look at the relative performance of a specific state in the decades of 80 and 90s.

Table 6. Share of Gross Value Added by some States of India (in per cent): Registered Manufacturing

State	1979-82	1995-98
Andhra Pradesh	5.0	6.9
Karnataka	5.0	5.5
Kerala	3.1	2.0
Tamil Nadu	9.9	9.7
Gujarat	9.4	11.8
Maharashtra	23.5	21.9

Source: Thomas (2002).

According to Table 6, AP's share in registered manufacturing of India is still much lower compared to the industrially developed states. However, the improvement in AP's share in the late 90s over the early 80s is considerable. This is more so in comparison with the other states except Gujarat. With this brief introduction to AP's performance in the context of the national economy, we move on to discuss various percentage compositions in the registered manufacturing of AP.

In economic analysis, we often classify industries either on the basis of the nature and source of input or on the basis of the nature of the final product. Our analysis is confined to the two-digit classification of industries of the ASI. The nature of this data set does not permit us to classify the industries in terms of its final product such as capital goods, consumer goods or intermediates. Thus we decide to confine our discussion within the ambience of the input-based classification such as agro-based, chemical-based and metal-based.

Figures (1), (2) and (3) depict the behaviour of the percentage composition of employment, output and net value added (NVA) respectively by the input-based classification. Percentage composition of output and net value added has been considered in nominal terms. From figures (1) and (2) it is clear that the agro-based industries significantly dominate both in terms of employment and output over the other two groups. This is, however, expected as AP is still in its early stages of industrial development. More important is the fact that there is almost no change in the trend in the later years even with the conscious government policy effort to industrialize the state since the 80s.

Let us now turn to the percentage composition of the net value added. Figure (3) shows that around 46 per cent of net value added were produced by the agro-based industries in 1980-81. After two consecutive years' decline, the share of agro-based industries showed an increasing trend throughout the 80s with little fluctuations. But from 1991-92 it started showing a declining trend. The percentage share of the metal-based industries was generally fluctuating but could keep its middle position till 1991-92. In the year 1991-92 it shows a steep decline. However, from the next year on, it started picking up but is still lower than the other two shares. The percentage share of the chemical-based industries was the lowest till 1991-92. The chemical-based industries experienced a steep increase in the year 1991-92 mainly at the cost of metal –based and to some extent agro-based industries. Another important feature is that from 1995-96 onwards the percentage shares have become significantly closer.

It is interesting to note the different behaviour of the percentage shares of the industrial classifications in terms of output and net value added. The concept of value added by an enterprise or an industry is very useful because, unlike the value of its total production or total output, the value added roughly measures the contribution made by the industry to the economy. The value of total output includes the value of purchased intermediate inputs which were not produced by the industry. It is likely that the input prices for the agro-based industries have increased relatively more than the other two categories and as a consequence the share of net value added started declining while the share of output has remained the same since 1991-92[8].

In its 1992 "New Industrial Policy Statement" the Government of AP has identified the agro-based industries as one of the most potential industrial activities in the state. The policy statement reiterates: "Government is endeavoring to boost up export efforts of agro-based and food processing industries in the state." It adds "Government of India has recently exempted certain food processing industries from Central Excise. The State Government welcomes and encourages foreign equity participation in food processed units on a large scale in consonance with the Central Government's policy" (New Industrial Policy Statement, 1992,

Figure 1

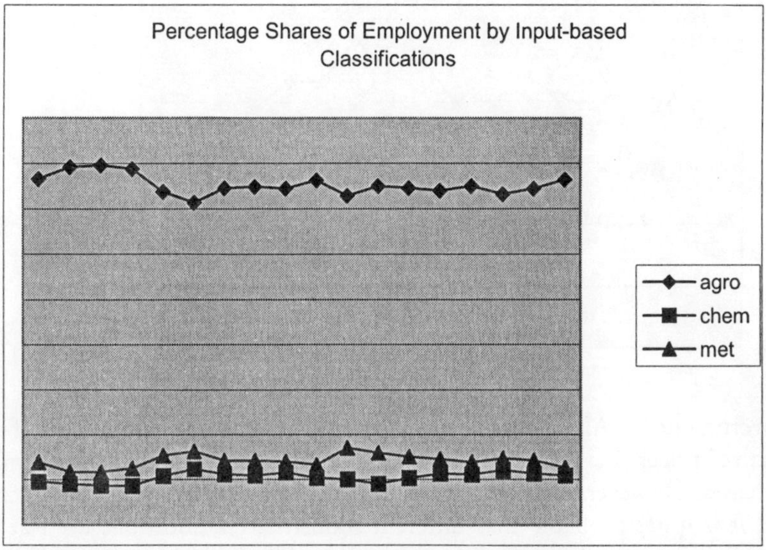

Figure 2

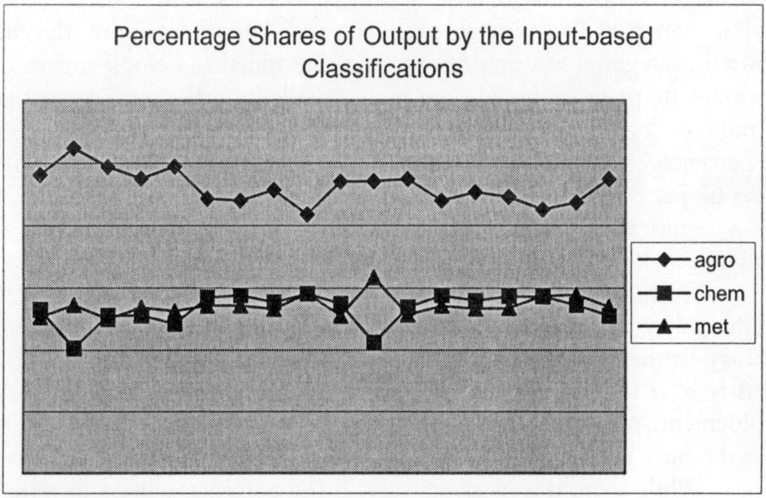

Figure 3

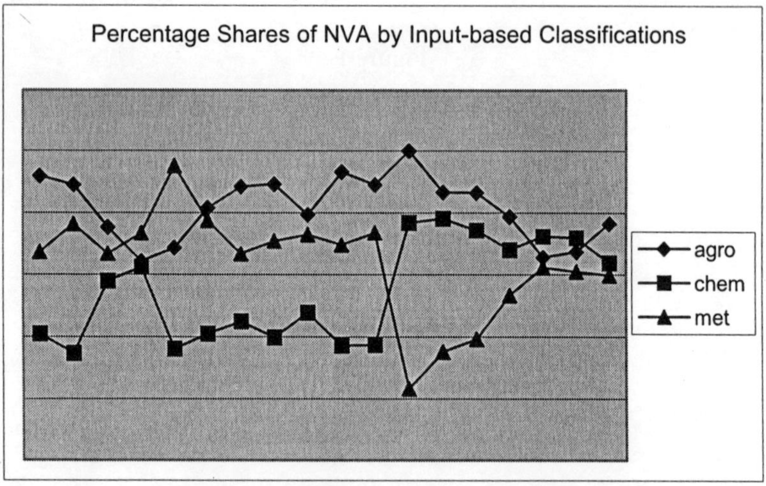

Government of AP. P.4). These incentive policies may not work if the relative prices of agricultural inputs compared to metal or chemical increases. However, 'agro-based industries' represent an aggregative picture and it is quite probable that different industrial classifications even at the two-digit level will show different trends. We will return to this issue shortly.

According to the summary results of the ASI in 1997-98 industrial classifications of food products, beverage and tobacco, cotton textiles, non-metallic mineral products and basic metal are the most important categories in terms of output, value added and employment. One important point to be noted here is that while all other percentage shares are more or less comparable among the above-mentioned industry groups, the percentage share of employment by the beverage and tobacco alone shows 62 per cent. Moreover, three-digit classification of ASI data indicates that a significant proportion of this employment is concentrated in the small bidi making factories of Nizamabad and Karimnagar.

We have already mentioned that the Government of AP has taken specific policy initiative to attract private investment in the food processing industry in the early 1990s. Let us have a look at the performance of this industry over the last two decades. Table 7 shows the percentage share of employment, net value added and output for the food products industry since the early 80s.

While there is a clear increase in the percentage share in terms of both output and nva there is a decline in the employment share in 1997-98 compared to 1980-81. However the growth rates have a different story to

Table 7. Percentage share of food products and machinery industry in some crucial variables

Year	Worker	Nva	Output
1980-81	5.98	21.48	15.28
1986-87	6.37	21.28	14.42
1991-92	5.98	19.61	11.36
1994-95	5.72	16.48	10.59
1997-98	4.23	19.20	9.67
Percentage share of food products in output, employment and nva			
1980-81	20.93	13.42	24.76
1986-87	14.89	13.97	23.60
1991-92	16.15	19.41	26.18
1994-95	16.61	15.11	25.54
1997-98	17.82	18.28	27.36

Source: ASI for various years.

tell. There is a marginal decline in the generally high rates of growth of output of this industry in the second period compared to the first (see the last chapter). On the contrary rate of growth of employment has increased significantly in the second period (Table 9). But this increase in the rate of growth of employment has to be considered in the context of no growth experienced in the earlier period (coefficient of time being insignificant) (Table 9). As a result the real increase may not be of much significance. Considering all these facts, it is difficult to judge the impact of the conscious policy effort to boost this industry in the 90s.

In the 'new industrial policy', 1992 of the AP State Government electronic and software-based industries have also been categorized as priority industry in the state. Together with the new agro-based and food processing industries, electronics and software industries have also achieved the thrust sector and sunrise industry status in the above mentioned policy document. Consequently, these industries have been offered the State incentives of investment subsidy, deferment of sales tax, concessions on power and water tariffs and subsidized allotment of developed industrial land and sheds. These policy incentives, however, were not applicable to the units within the municipal areas of Hyderabad and other big cities. But the concentration of software and hardware activities in and around Hyderabad in recent years shows that industrial location decisions are probably far more influenced by availability of power and other infrastructure and skilled labour than by such incentives as mentioned earlier. Moreover, the export –oriented nature of these IT companies which often come under the 100 percent export-oriented zone scheme do get an even more lucrative incentive package from the Central Government (Kundra, 2000)[9].

In this context it is worth looking at the contribution of this industry in the economic development of AP. Table 7 shows not only a low percentage of employment in the industrial classification for machinery but also declining during 1980-81 to 1997-98. Moreover, both the percentage shares of net value added and output declined over the years. However, software and hardware industries are only one component in the machinery category at the two-digit level. Let us have a look at the behaviour of some of the crucial variables in the IT industry in recent years.

Table 8. Some Crucial Variables Relating to the IT Industry
(Value figures are in Thousands and others are in Number)

	Factories	Employees	Workers	Nva	Output
1994-95	7	666	246	144662	442577
1995-96	6	258	166	31864	120370
1996-97	6	220	98	37455	121750
1997-98	7	312	115	17585	170239

Source: same as Table 7.

From Table 8 it is evident that there is a remarkable decline in the total net value added as well in the output of the registered IT industry in the 4-year period of 1994-95 to 1997-98 even in nominal terms. While number of factories remained around 6/7 over this period number of employees has declined to half and number of workers has declined more than half within a short spell of 4 years. These findings again lead us to feel unsure about the impact of incentive policy measures involving a loss of substantial amount. However, the considerable increase in the software exports from this state in the recent years (Rao *et al*, 1998) leaves a possibility of much of the activities taking place in unregistered sector. Moreover, our time period is constrained by the availability of data and it is quite likely that the picture has changed considerably in the recent years especially with the more focused incentive schemes for the IT industry.

Structural Ratios

We now turn to some of the important structural ratios of the registered manufacturing in AP. The time trends of the three important structural ratios viz, capital/labour, output/labour and capital/ output, for the AP registered manufacturing suggest a couple of facts. While both the ratios of capital labour and output labour show a significant positive trend during 1980-81 to 1997-98, capital output ratio shows an insignificant trend. However, on an average all the three ratios have increased in the second period compared to the first. Increase in the capital / output ratio in the second period is the result of a sharp decline in net value added in one year. A close look at the analytical relationship between the three crucial structural ratios can give some valuable insights into the implications of increase in the capital labour ratio that seems to have taken place in the concerned period in AP from the perspective of employment.

Algebraically, capital(c)/labour(L) = capital/output(O) X output/labour. Here, by output we consider net value added. Thus any change in the capital/labour ratio would imply some changes in either or both the ratios. Looking at the ratios in the pre and post liberalization periods for the disaggregated registered manufacturing we reclassify all the industrial categories into three different groups: capital/labour ratio increases with decline in capital/output ratio and increase in labour productivity; increases in all the three ratios and finally, capital/labour ratio decreases with decline in capital/output ratio and increase in labour productivity. We consider the rates of growth of employment for the different groups of industries as well (Table 9).

From Table 9, it is evident that in the first group of industries, the increase in productivity is a result of increase in capital per unit of labour. This increase in productivity has the potentiality of increasing the output to a great extent which, in turn, could also manage to lower the effect of increase in capital per unit of output in the second period in relation to the first. We can consider this as a case of technological change in the production process. What is the effect of this productivity growth on the rate of growth of employment? Among these industrial categories only food products beverage and tobacco and chemical products have shown an improvement in the rate of growth of employment in the second period over the first. Except chemicals the other two are labour intensive (industry) by nature. However, in all these cases the growth rate was either insignificant or negative in the first period. So, actually the improvement may not have a significant impact on the employment situation of registered manufacturing in the post liberalization period. Moreover, significant decline in the employment growth rates of the jute and machinery industry and insignificant growth rates for the rest of the industries in this group lead us to presume that the technological change is such that productivity gains take place at the cost of labour displacement.

But there is yet another possibility. Indian registered manufacturing, especially the public sector units, are known to be a case of 'feather bedding' or over-manning. It is possible that a number of people have retired or being retrenched through voluntary retirement scheme in the second period. This is possible in the cases where the rate of growth of employment is negative. This leads to an increase in the output as well as fixed capital per unit of labour without any change in the technological base.

Jute industry is a case in point. The behaviour of the structural ratios is suggestive of a technological change in this industry. But we note a negative rate of growth of output for this industry both before and after liberalization. The decline is, in fact, sharper after liberalization. We have noted an insignificant rate of growth of fixed capital in both the periods as well (see the last chapter). These results do not however indicate a case of technological modernization. Moreover, with the general decline in the demand for jute it is quite unlikely for the entrepreneurs to go for a significant change. Probably, the ratio between fixed capital and output has declined owing to selling off of the obsolete machinery without affecting the net value added. The other industrial category that shows a negative rate of growth of employment is the machinery industry. In this case while the rate of growth of output is insignificant in the second period, there is almost no change in the rate of growth of fixed capital. The capital/ output ratio has declined marginally.

The second group of industries is precisely those industries for which productivity growth could not lower the increase in capital per unit of output. But, here again the increase in the capital per unit of labour indicates a possibility of change in the technological base. According to Table 9 manufacturing activities which come under the category of others is the only member of this group. The insignificance of the rate of growth of employment for both the periods leads us to assume that the increase in productivity has not led to increase in employment.

The third group of industries shows a very interesting feature. While theoretically it is possible to have a combination of structural ratios considered under the third group, in reality it is quite unusual to achieve an increase in the labour productivity with decrease in capital/ labour ratio. Existence of significant unused capacity in the first period for the industries in this group can be a likely reason. Let us take up the industries one by one.

Decrease in capital per unit of labour for the industrial classification of 26 is in fact marginal (Table 9). It looks like a case of horizontal expansion leading to a significant increase in both output and employment (see the last chapter). The increasing share of ready-made garments, the most important component of textile products, in the total export of India since the mid eighties most probably played an important role here. The ready-made garment sector is supposed to be a labour intensive sector due to its typical nature of production and thus explains the phenomenal growth in employment in the second period. But the puzzle of labour productivity becoming almost tripled in the second period compared to the first without any increase in the capital per unit of labour still remains. The output per unit of labour might have increased partly because of the under-reporting of number of workers. Due to their labour intensive nature, the large units find it more profitable to go for subcontracting which necessarily lessens the labour cost. It happens to be so because quite a number of these subcontracting units are outside the purview of the factory sector as these subcontracting units often work in the households (Chatterjee *et al*, 1993). But if this is true, then the capital per unit of labour has to also decline with actual reporting of the number of workers. This may well lead to a situation where increase in productivity takes place with decrease in the capital labour ratio. However, the significant existence of the household sector activities in this sector may

Table 9. Rate of growth of employment in industries classified according to changes in structural ratios (% per annum)

Industry Groups	Rate of Growth of Employment	
	Period I 1980-81 to 1991-92	Period II 1992-93 to 1997-98
Group I		
C/L increases with		
C/O decreases		
O/L increases		
(20-21) Food Products	(-) 0 .6*	4.5
(22) Beverage and Tobacco	1.6*	3.7
(23) Cotton Textiles	0.4*	0.6*
(24) Other Textiles	2.9*	7.3*
(25) Jute	(-) 1.3*	(-) 5.4
(28) Paper Products	0.9*	0.4*
(31) Chemical Products	(-) 2.2	5.9
(32) Non Met. Min.	3.8	2.2
(33) Basic Met. Alloy	9	2.8*
(34) Metal Products	9.2	3*
(35-36) Machinery	1.5*	(-) 4
(37) Transport Equipment	(-) 3.7	6.4*
Group II		
C/L increases with		
C/O increases		
O/L increases		
(38) Others	1.9*	2.8*
Group III		
C/L decreases with		
C/O decreases		
O/L increases		
(26) Textile Products	7.6	30
(27) Wood Products	(-) 3.1	0.0*
(30) Rubber Products	13.3	6.3

Nots: (1)'*' represents statistical insignificance at 5% level.

(2) Industrial category of 29 has not been included because it shows an altogether contradictory behaviour of the structural ratios. It may have happened because of the aggregated nature of the data represented by the industry groups.

(3) Figures of this table are not strictly comparable with the employment growth rates given in the last chapter, because of two reasons. Fist, here we have considered number of workers while in the last chapter the authors have considered the figures for employees. Secondly, the second period in this chapter is slightly different from that of the previous one.

Source: calculated from various *ASIs*.

offer a probable solution. The nature of production in this sector may be such that the incremental capital labour ratio is quite low but it increases output per unit of labour significantly. Moreover, in the household sector it is possible to use single machinery more intensively than in the factory sector as the number as well as hours of work is not fixed. The same machine in the household sector can be used by several family members during different parts of the day.

It is clear that the decline in the rate of growth of employment in the manufacture of rubber and rubber products into half the times of the earlier period is a result of output remaining the same in real terms for both the periods (see the last chapter). The reason behind no growth in output of this industry in the second period probably is the drastic decline of the international price of rubber since the early 1990s. However, one needs more micro information about this industry to solve the main apparent contradiction of the behaviour of the structural ratios.

5. POLICY IMPLICATIONS

The inadequacies and gaps in the policy we have been discussing are meant to initiate some policy suggestions. During the last three decades AP economy is experiencing a slow but significant structural shift from agriculture to mainly services sector both in terms of employment and output. It is true that there is a slow increase in the share of output by the industry, but the low and unchanging share in employment turns out to be a serious matter of concern. However, NSSO data indicate a slight increase in the percentage of people engaged in industry in the late 1990s when compared with early 1990s. Our analysis shows while there is a probable positive impact of emphasis on export promotion on the textile product sector of the registered manufacturing of the state, some of the industries have performed unsatisfactorily in the post liberalization period. However, more intensive analysis is required to conclude that the failure of the industries to perform is a result of the opening up of the market in the post 1990s.

Since the early 1990s the state government has given a number of policy incentives to boost up the industrial performance of the state. While the rate of growth of output remained more or less the same, employment has, in fact, increased for the registered manufacturing in the second period[10]. However, Venkataramaiah *et al* (see the last chapter) claims that this growth of employment has taken place only at the cost of wage rate. This may have happened as a result of the increase in the contract and temporary employment in the organized manufacturing. Moreover, the percentage share of NSDP by the registered manufacturing has declined significantly in 1999-2000 compared to the early 1990s. The emphasis on the small-scale sector development in the state government's industrial policy may have encouraged the manufacturing activities of the non-factory sector more than that of the factory sector. However, compared to the Southern states as well as the industrially developed ones, unregistered industrial activity, a major part of small scale, in AP has not done well in the late 1990s. From the employment perspective, as long as the wage differential is not significant there is no harm if unregistered sector employment is increased. But in India the significant wage differential between these two sectors is an established fact. Thus it is important to ensure a decline in the wage differential between the two sectors. The registered segment of the manufacturing sector during the decades of the eighties and the nineties grew at a higher rate than the country's factory sector aided mainly by the public sector undertakings in Iron and Steel, Petroleum, Electrical Machinery and Electronics. The share of Public Sector Units is 50% in output and 95% in net fixed capital.

Among the public sector units, the large undertakings of Vizag Steel Plant, Hindustan Petroleum Refinery at Visakhapatnam, BHEL and ECIL at Hyderabad account for a major share of both output and capital investment. The backward and forward linkages generated by these large-scale public sector units were expected to be successful in attracting private investment from the surpluses of the agricultural sector. And this would have led to rapid industrialization in the state. While in the 1980s a few enterprenuerships have emerged from the agricultural surpluses, private investment still is being attracted by the services sector. Thus it is clear that to accelerate industrial growth increase in the private investment is essential.

Interestingly, rate of growth of fixed capital in the post-reform period has become half the rate of the pre-reform period. In order to compete both in the more open home market and the export market it is necessary to improve the quality of the product. This often calls for a modernization of technology. Technological modernization can be thwarted mainly for two reasons. First is the resistance from the workers. Theoretically, we cannot determine the nature of correlation between technological modernization and employment. It depends on the elasticity of substitution between capital and labour, factor shares and aggregate demand emanating due to the change in the relative price (Hall and Hefernan, 1985). Besides, labour militancy is much lower in AP compared to the industrially developed states such as Maharashtra, Tamil Nadu etc (CII, 2000, Chakravarty, 2001). Thus, probably labour militancy is not the reason.

Table 10. Investment Rankings of Selected States

States	Investment ranking	Value
AP	8	0.1
Gujarat	2	1.2
Maharashtra	3	1.0
Tamil Nadu	6	0.3

Source: CII (2000).

The second and more probable reason lies in the fact of unavailability of investible resources. According to the vision 2020 the amount of investment required for the envisaged remarkably high rates of growth is not possible only with internal savings. It needs to compete with other states in attracting foreign investment. Attractiveness of a state in terms of private investment depends on various economic and socio-political indicators. In the year 2000, Confederation of Indian Industries (CII) and Rajiv Gandhi Institute for contemporary studies carried out a detailed study on the relative performance of the different states in India. The exercise was done on the basis of various indicators of both economic and non-economic in nature. On the basis of this composite index, Andhra Pradesh stands 12th in the rank. They have also calculated the rankings in terms of the investment attractiveness of a state, which differ from the composite rankings. In order to understand the probability of Andhra Pradesh being the possible destination of private investment in industry, we compare the rankings of AP with the three most developed industrial states in India such as Marashtra, Gujarat and Tamil Nadu (Table 10). The low rank of AP in terms of investment attractiveness compared to the already industrially more developed states does make us feel a little unsure about the success of AP to attract significant private investment in the coming years.

However, it seems the situation of investment is improving considerably. The Economic Survey of AP 2001-2002 reports: " the state has received 410 new proposals for setting up of industrial units (large and medium) involving an investment of Rs.46524 crores with an employment potential of 56411 persons."(Government of AP, 2001-2002, p. 61). Regarding foreign direct investment (FDI), the above-mentioned source again claims: "AP has emerged as an attractive investment destination. Liberal policies of the state government and availability of good infrastructure have attracted giants in the sectors like information technology, agro-food processing and infrastructure based industries." According to the Economic Survey, 2001-2002 the state has received 533 FDI proposals up to October 2001. However, only 149 proposals among these were finally launched; it is worth probing into the reasons behind this.

A possible explanation can be the bureaucratic hazards. One of the main thrusts of the Indian industrial policy in the post 1990s is on reducing bureaucratic hazards in the process of setting up of a new industrial unit. If AP fails to assure this precondition no incentive package will work in the right direction and will lead to drainage on the state exchequer. This is all the more important in a state like AP where industrial climate is yet to develop properly. As a result, there is a natural tendency for the domestic investors within the state to invest in other sectors which apparently do not involve dealing with the government on one hand and do not need infrastructural support as much as the industry does, on the other.

The New Industrial Policy document of 2000- 05, however, shows the government's consciousness regarding this fact. A special thrust has been given to the 'Single Window' scheme to curb successfully the bureaucratic hazards involved in the registration procedure for an industrial activity. The following extract is a part of the policy document:

"Single Window registration for clearance will be made compulsory by law. Designated authorities will be created as: (A) District level authority headed by district collector for clearing cases up to Rs. one crore of investment. (B) State Investment Promotion Committee headed by Chief Secretary to clear cases up to Rs 25 crores of investment. (C) State Investment Promotion Board headed by the chief minister to clear cases beyond Rs. 25 crores of investment." (Incentives for Investment in Andhra Pradesh – 2000 – 2005, p: VI).

In the neighbouring states of Karnataka and Tamil Nadu a successful implementation of the 'single window' scheme played a very important role in attracting investment. It may be expected that a proper implementation of the above-mentioned policies would help AP to this end.

The Vision document 2020 has identified three types of industries as the engines for industrial growth in the coming years such as: knowledge-based, resource-based and labour intensive. The knowledge-based industries include IT, biotechnology and pharmaceuticals. While, a major part of these industries are service related activities, a considerable amount falls under manufacturing as well. Our analysis suggests a possibility of much of the manufacturing activities in the IT industry, taking place in the small-scale sector, especially in the unregistered sect. It may be essential to bring these activities more into the sphere of the large-scale in order to ensure sustained growth. It is true that India as well as AP has achieved a remarkably liberal regulatory environment for software exports. However, there are two serious problems which in future can thwart the growth of this industry and has to be addressed through policy measures: data communication link to the distant customer which is reported to be quite week and the availability of skilled IT professionals. The traditional importance of the pharmaceutical industry in AP in the country's bulk drug production and the rising percentage share of exports by this industry have been noted in the literature. However, studies indicate a low technological advancement in this industry except a few firms. With increased market competition in the recent years, it is essential for the firms to modernize. As a matter of fact production of drugs has stagnated over last three years in AP (Singer *et al*, 2001).

The resource-based industries are mainly the agro-based, especially the food processing industries. Our analysis indicates that in spite of having a strong agricultural base, the incentive policies for growth may not work properly if the input prices move in the wrong direction. Among the labour intensive industries, to begin with, the government has decided to focus on the manufacture of garments and leather goods industries. These industries not only generate substantial employment opportunities but also high potential of growth mainly through exports. The phenomenal growth both in terms of employment and output in the registered sector of textile product industry, as discussed above, reveals the advantageous position of the textile product industry compared to other labour intensive industries in the state. Moreover, Indian export performance in both these industries in the last five years is quite impressive.

The government has suggested industry-wide parks in the above-mentioned industrial categories. The firms in these parks will enjoy a number of lucrative incentive packages. Already a number of IT and garment making parks have been established in the state in the recent years (Government of AP, 2001-02). Let us have a quick look at the nature of incentives offered. Besides the whole lot of tax exemption and investment subsidies, the incentive package can be divided into two broad groups of policies related to easy access of power and exemption of policy constraints related to environment and labour (Government of AP, 2000). With assured power supply and more flexible labour market, it is expected to get cost efficient production which will help the firms to compete in the export market. The competing states for investment in IT like Tamil Nadu and Karnataka have already exempted the software industry from the pollution control act. Moreover, considering the nature of the product of this industry, negative externalities in terms of environment may not be of serious concern. Together with the exemption of labor laws the government has suggested a number of skill upgradation schemes for the workers specific to these parks. The skill upgradation schemes have several probable impact on the economy. To improve the quality of production skill improvement is one of the essential factors. As a result the increase in demand for skilled labour will increase the rate of wage on the one hand and increase in the scale of output will ensure more employment within a flexible labour regime. However, the implications of these policy exemptions are yet to be seen in reality.

To conclude, we would like to discuss two important factors related to the probable export performance of the above mentioned parks especially with reference to garment. First is the change in the international policy environment. The Uruguay Round Agreement on textile and clothing states a phase out programme, according to which during 1998 to 2005 international trade in textiles and clothing will be gradually incorporated into GATT/ WTO framework. At the beginning of each phase of incorporation, importing countries like EU, and US must integrate specified minimum portion of their textile and garment imports. This integration should be based on total trade volume in 1990 for the items listed in the annexure to the agreement given for progressive increase in quota growth rates for products remaining under a quota. However, the aim is to postpone the most sensitive products until the end of the 2005. As a result, the quotas for most import-intensive items in US and EU like shirts and women's outwear, in which India has an advantage, will not be removed until 2005. The permitted quotas for the developing countries like India, however, will be relatively more liberal (Ramaswamy *et al.*, 1998). Moreover, in the post Uruguay round tariff rates in the textile and clothing sector will be higher than that of all commodities. So, it is obvious that the sustenance of the attained level of garment exports by India is significantly vulnerable to the international trade policy changes and therefore it needs to develop a domestic market for readymade garments along with the production initiatives.

The second important issue, we would like to address is the question of quality of the products. As these parks are essentially export-oriented, not only the price but also the quality of the product is very important. Though an essentially micro issue by nature, in the vision document the question of 'quality control' has featured in the case of growth engines. It has been implicitly assumed in the document that development of skills through outside training with improved technology and an accreditation process will lead to a quality control regime. However, the concept of 'quality control' as against 'quality assurance' is highly influenced by the ideas of Taylor (1967). In this paradigm quality is maintained through a coercive hierarchical relationship. On the contrary the other paradigm of continuous quality assurance emphasizes the making of quality as the umbrella theme for an organization. Here, the effort of the management is to develop a common language of quality improvement through all operational and organizational levels (Cole, 1994). This is achieved by enhancing communication, understanding and acceptance of common objectives. The application of the second method has been found to be more useful in some export-oriented textile firms in Mumbai (Chakravarty, 2001). While it is not possible to formulate a macro policy regarding this issue, the issue can be considered in research agenda of the government relating the question of increase in efficiency of internal organization of firms, the actual growth engines.

Notes

1 Notable among them are Ahluwalia, 1991, Choudhuri, 2002.

2 However, researchers have combined the two sources and calculated the absolute figures.

3 There is yet another possibility that occurs from different states of technological improvement.

4 The industrial growth rates of centrally planned economies have tended to be even faster than of developing countries.

5 Here by industrial employment we mean employment in the manufacturing and electricity, gas, water supply group.

6 Here we have considered only manufacturing and construction activities within industry because data for informal mining and electricity gas sector is not available in the data source. Moreover, in the case of mining and electricity gas sector informal activities are almost irrelevant.

7 The percentage of registered sector in total manufacturing employment would have been a little higher if the number of 'total persons engaged' were considered rather than workers.

8 However, there is another possibility that input intensity of the agro-based industries may have increased over this period.

9 An example of this is an export-processing zone for 100 per cent software exports under a software technology park scheme in the early 90s in Hyderabad.

10 This is true in both the cases of employees and workers.

References

Ahluwalia, I. J (1991), *Productivity and Growth in Indian Manufacturing*, Oxford University Press, New Delhi.

Bhavani, T.A. (1992), "Small Industry Policy", (mimeo), Institute of Economic Growth, Delhi.

Brock, W. and D. Evans (1986), *The Economics of Small Business*, Holmes and Meier, New York.

Chakravarty, D (2001), *Technological Change, Organization of Work and Employment Contracts: Emergence of Decentralized Bargaining in the Indian Textiles*, Unpublished PhD Dissertation, Jawaharlal Nehru University, New Delhi.

Chatterjee, S and R. Mohan (1993), "India's Garment Exports", *Economic and Political Weekly*, Vol. 28, No.35.

Confederation of Indian Industries (CII) (2000), *How are the States Doing?*

Chaudhuri, S (2002), "Economic Reforms and Industrial Structure in India", *Economic and Political Weekly*, Vol.37, No.2.

Cole, Robert E. (1994), "Different Quality Paradigms and Their Implications for Organizational Learning" in Mashahiko Aoki (ed.) *The Japanese Firm*, Clarendon, Oxford University Press, New York.

Gang Ira N (1995), "Small Firms in India" in D Mookherjee (ed.) *Indian Industry: Policies and Performance*, Oxford University Press, New Delhi.

Gerschenkorn, A (1962), *Economic Backwardness in Historical Perspective*, Harvard University Press, Cambridge.

Government of India, *Annual Survey of Industries: Summary Results for the Factory Sector*, Central Statistical Organization, Ministry of Planning, Department of Statistics, New Delhi.

Government of India, *National Accounts Statistics*, Central Statistical Organization, Ministry of Planning, Dept. of Statistics, New Delhi.

Government of Andhra Pradesh (1992), *New Industrial Policy Statement*, Hyderabad.

Government of Andhra Pradesh (2000), *Incentives for Investments in Andhra Pradesh*, Hyderabad.

Government of Andhra Pradesh (2001-2002), *Economic Survey*, Hyderabad.

Hall, P.H. and S. A. Heffernan (1985), "More on the Employment Effects on Innovation", *Journal of Development Economics*, (Vol. 17).

Kundra, Ashok (2000), *The Performance of India's Export Zones*, Sage Publications, New Delhi.

Kuznets, S (1966), *Modern Economic Growth*, Yale University Press, New Haven, Connecticut.

Mookherjee, D (1995), "Introduction" in Dilip Mookherjee (ed.) *Indian Industry: Policies and Performance*, Oxford University Press, New Delhi.

National Sample Survey Organization, *Employment and Unemployment in India* for various years.

National Sample Survey Organization, *Informal Sector in India,* 1999-2000

Naidu, Muniratna K (1988), "Pattern of Industrialization in Andhra Pradesh and Inter-state Growth" in Muniratna K Naidu (ed.) *Industrialization and Regional Development in India,* Relience Publishing House, New Delhi.

Nayyar, D (1994), *Industrial Growth and Stagnation: The Debate in India,* Oxford University Press, New Delhi.

Pack, H (1988), "Industrialization and Trade", in H Chenery and T.N Srinivasan (eds.) *Handbook of Development Economics, Vol. I,* North Holland, Amsterdam.

Ramaswamy, K. V and Gary Gereffi (1998), "India's Apparel Sector in the Global Economy" *Economic and Political Weekly,* Vol.33, No.3.

Rao, V. H., N.K. Acharya and M.C Swaminathan (eds.) (1998), *Andhra Pradesh at 50,* A Data-based Analysis, Data News Features, Hyderabad.

Singer A, P. Dasgupta and S. Mahendra Dev (eds.) (2001), *Andhra Pradesh: Improving Business Environment for Sustained growth,* The World Bank.

Taylor, Fredrich (1967), *The Principles of Scientific Management,* W.W Norton, New York

Thomas J. J (2002), "A review of Indian Manufacturing" in Kirit S. Parikh, and R. Radhakrishna (eds.) *India Development Report, 2002,* Oxford, New Delhi.

Weiss, J (1988), *Industry in Developing Countries, Theory, Policy and Evidence,* Roultledge, London and New York.

12

Towards a Demographic Transition

K.S. James and
S. V. Subramanian

1. INTRODUCTION

There is no difference of opinion that Andhra pradesh is in the course of a rapid demographic transition in recent years although one would possibly debate on the underlying causes behind such transition. The accelerated pace of the transition began with a rapid decline in fertility in second half of the 1980s. With the state approaching towards a replacement level fertility, Andhra Pradesh would be undisputedly proving the possibility of high performing demographic indicators within the context of poor performing social and economic variables. The demographic debate particularly in the context of India now mostly hovers around the causes of rapid fertility transition with not only poor economic development but also social development. The theme of this paper is to look at such experience in Andhra Pradesh and to depict the pace as well as the conflicting arguments for such a transition.

However, fertility transition is only one aspect of overall demographic transition. The changes that occur in other demographic parameters, viz., mortality and migration are critical for any state. Firstly, these three demographic parameters determine the size and distribution of population in a particular geographical area for many years to come. Hence, for any concrete future planning trends in these variables are intensely monitored. Secondly, as population stabilisation is now broadly regarded as desirable particularly in the Indian context due to its impact on the economic development, the current trends and future movements in all the three events are particularly crucial. Thirdly, these parameters enter into the broad definition of economic development as crucial input variables and hence various governments eagerly seek improvement in the performance of these variables.

This paper, therefore, primarily tries to capture the progress of different demographic indicators in the state during the last quarter of the century and the socio-economic factors associated with the demographic phenomena. The purpose of this analysis is mainly to present the picture of demographic transition and its possible determinants in the state based on available information and studies.

This paper is based, for the most, on well –known existing data sets; Census, Sample Registration System and National Family Health Surveys Data. The data on census is available on a decennial basis. Sample Registration System gives annual series of data on demographic indicators like fertility and mortality for the last 25 years or more. There had been two rounds of National Family Health Survey in the state, 1992 and 1998. Both these Surveys give enormous amount of information on the demographic, health and social indicators.

2. GROWTH OF POPULATION

The decadal growth rate of population since the turn of the last century is presented in Figure 1. A negative growth of population between 1911-21 was due to the influenza epidemic throughout India, which is estimated to have killed nearly 5 percent of the population in the country (Visaria and Visaria, 1994). The decadal growth rate of population was below 15 per cent until 1961 and rose considerably thereafter. The growth rate between 1981-91 had been the highest ever recorded in the last century (24.2 per cent) and also was one of the highest among Indian states. However, the 2001 census results revealed a significant decline in the growth of population during the decade 1991-2001. While population of India grew at 1.93 per cent a year during the decade, the population of Andhra Pradesh grew at a much lower rate of 1.3 per cent a year. Thus the average annual rate of growth in the state declined from 2.17 per cent in 1981-91 to 1.30 per cent in 1991-2001, amounting to 40 per cent decline in the ten year period. This is largely due to high pace of demographic transition.

Figure 1: Population Growth in Andhra Pradesh, 1901-2001

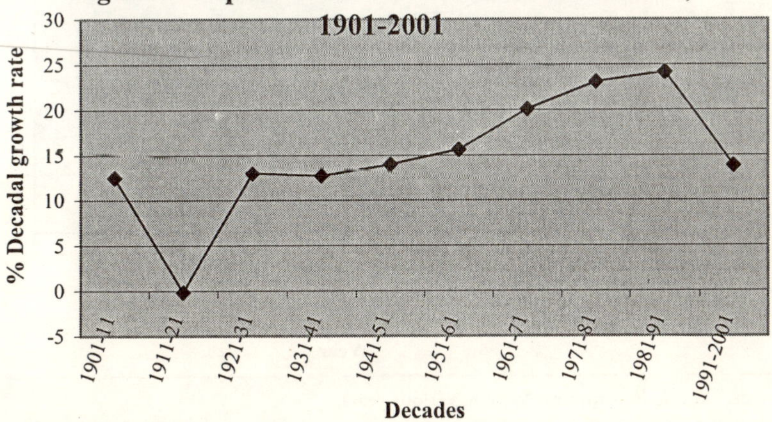

Source: Computed from Census figures.

The growth of population is the result of basic processes of births, deaths and migration. The current population growth rate is mainly the result of past demographic variables than its current performance. However, with mortality rate remaining low, the main cause of population growth, recently, is the changes in fertility. Inter-state migration can also alter the population scenario. Let us now look at these three parameters individually to understand the performance of the state in the demographic arena during the quarter of the century.

3. PACE OF FERTILITY TRANSITION

Since the introduction of Sample Registration Data in the second half of the 1960s, there is fairly large information on the levels of fertility in India. However, there is certain amount of skepticism on the quality of SRS estimates of fertility particularly in the initial years. The analysis, nevertheless, is carried out without making any adjustment. Figure 2 presents the trend in crude birth rate, crude death rate and natural growth rate (birth rate-death rate) in the state since the early 1970s. Interestingly, both birth rate and death rate nearly show a declining trend since the 1970s. However, the pace of decline in fertility has been slower in the first half of both 1970 and 1980. The mortality rate has been declining at a faster pace in the 1970s. As a result of this the rate of natural increase touched its highest level by the first half of the 1980s.

Figure 2: Birth Rate, Death Rate and Natural Increase, Andhra Pradesh1971-2000

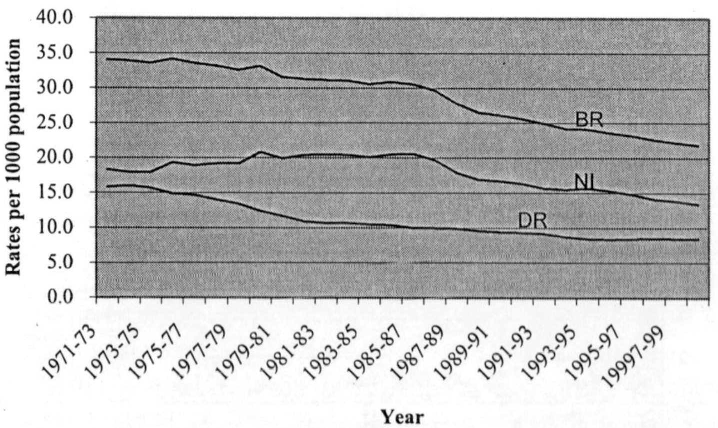

Source: Sample Registration System, various years.

A significant change in fertility rate is observable from the second half of the 1980s. Although mortality has been declining even during this period the pace of fertility decline outstripped the mortality decline resulting a significant decline in the natural increase of population.

A better measure to assess the magnitude of fertility decline would be total fertility rate. The TFR has fallen from nearly 4.6 children per woman in the early 1970s to 2.5 children by 1997, a decline to the tune of 2 children per woman during the 26-year period. The trend in TFR of the state since1971 is depicted in Figure 3.

Figure 3: Total Fertility Rate: Andhra Pradesh, 1971-97

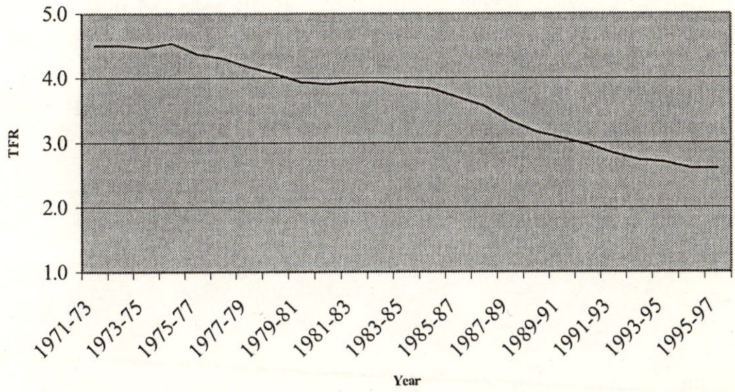

Source: Same as in Figure 2.

Of these two child decline per woman within a span of 26 years, more than 1 child decline is accounted during the last decade from 1987 to 97. It shows the rapidity in the pace of fertility decline since the mid 1980s. The estimate of fertility by National Family Health Survey is lower than the SRS estimate. The NFHS estimate of TFR is 2.25 during 1996-98 period with rural areas having slightly higher fertility (2.32) than urban areas (2.07).

The decline in fertility in the state was largely attained through the contraceptive use and particularly through female sterilisation. It is estimated that about 60 per cent of the married women are currently using contraceptive methods, mainly the female sterilization. The contraceptive prevalence rate recorded a phenomenal increase in the 1990s from 47 per cent in 1992-93 to 60 per cent in 1998-99. The NFHS-2 (1998-99) data showed that among all the states in India, the lowest median age of sterilization is in Andhra Pradesh (23.6 years).

Practically all the social and economic groups have experienced this decline in fertility in the state. Consequently, the wide difference in fertility usually observed between different social and economic classes is only marginally present in the case of Andhra Pradesh. Table 1 shows total fertility rate during NFHS-1 and NFHS-2 by various background characteristics of women.

At present the variation in total fertility rate across different social and economic groups is marginal. A comparison of NFHS-1 and 2 shows that there has been decline in fertility in all the groups except those with high school and above education and Christians. For these groups, however, the estimates of fertility in the NFHS-1 was quite low, even below replacement level. Considerable decline in fertility is observed among illiterate women and schedules tribe women within the 7 years period. Scheduled tribe fertility has declined to the tune of nearly one child. This is crucial in a state with levels of illiteracy as high as 64 per cent among

Table 1. Total Fertility Rate by Different Background Characteristics in Andhra Pradesh, 1989-91 & 1996-98

Characteristics	Total Fertility Rate		
	1989-91	1996-98	Difference
Residence			
Urban	2.35	2.07	0.28
Rural	2.67	2.32	0.35
Education			
Illiterate	2.97	2.35	0.62
Literate, < middle complete	2.23	2.22	0.01
Middle school complete	2.23	1.94	0.29
High school and above	1.84	2.20	-0.36
Religion			
Hindu	2.59	2.20	0.39
Muslims	2.89	2.53	0.36
Christian	1.71	2.53	-0.82
Caste/tribe			
Scheduled caste	2.61	2.51	0.10
Scheduled tribe	3.74	2.75	0.99
Other Backward Classes		2.26	
Other		2.00	
Standard of Living Index			
Low		2.29	
Medium		2.32	
High		1.99	
Total	2.59	2.25	0.34

Source: National Family Health Survey (1995) and (2000).

eligible women (according to the NFHS-2 report) and also as nearly 25 per cent belongs to Schedule caste and Schedule tribe population. Any significant decline in fertility for the state as a whole, therefore, depends substantially on the fertility reduction among these socially and economically backward sections of the society. Hence the fertility advancement of the state was primarily due to these sections of the society.

Andhra Pradesh is characterised by considerable regional heterogeneity which would also manifest in the levels of fertility. The estimates are available for 1981 and 1991 census periods and also an indirect estimate for 1994-2001 period using 2001 census results. Table 2 presents total fertility estimates for 1981, 1991 and 1994-2001. The

Table 2. Total Fertility Rate and Infant Mortality Rate in Various Districts of Andhra Pradesh, 1981-91

Districts	Total Fertility Rate				Infant Mortality Rate		
	1981 (1)	1991 (2)	1994-2001 (3)	Difference (4)= (3) - (1)	1981 (5)	1991 (6)	Difference 1991-81 (7)=(6)-(5)
Srikakulam	4.1	3.4	2.4	1.7	123	77	46
Vizianagaram	4.0	3.4	2.5	1.5	137	99	38
Visakhapatnam	4.0	3.4	2.2	1.8	97	73	24
East Godavari	3.8	3.4	2.1	1.7	77	54	23
West Godavari	3.9	3.0	2.0	1.9	84	65	19
Krishna	4.3	3.3	1.9	2.4	92	30	62
Guntur	4.1	3.2	1.9	2.2	80	38	42
Prakasam	4.6	3.5	2.3	2.3	89	46	43
Nellore	3.9	3.1	2.0	1.9	86	46	40
Chittoor	4.0	3.1	2.2	1.8	115	60	55
Cuddapah	4.5	3.4	2.3	2.2	105	44	61
Anantapur	4.9	3.9	2.4	2.5	121	70	51
Kurnool	5.0	4.3	3.0	2.0	96	68	28
Mahabubnagar	4.9	4.5	3.1	1.8	99	77	22
Rengareddy	4.8	3.9	2.6	2.2	82	56	26
Hyderabad	4.2	4.1	1.9	2.3	40	22	18
Medak	4.6	4.2	2.9	1.7	82	52	30
Nalgonda	4.5	4.32	2.6	1.9	90	58	32
Nizamabad	4.1	3.3	2.5	1.6	70	41	29
Adilabad	4.6	3.8	2.7	1.9	95	51	44
Karimnagar	4.1	3.4	2.2	1.9	81	35	46
Warangal	4.6	4.1	2.5	2.1	99	59	40
Khammam	4.7	3.7	2.3	2.4	87	47	40
Andhra Pradesh	4.3	3.4	2.3	2.0	91	55	36

Source: Column no. (3) is from Guilmoto and Rajan (2002) and the rest are from Census of India (1991).

variation in fertility ranges from 3.1 in Mahabubnagar to 1.9 in Krishna, Guntur and Hyderabad in 1994-2001. The districts in Coastal Andhra and Rayalaseema region have lower fertility levels. However, the decline in fertility was experienced in all regions between 1981 and 194-2001. Even in

Telangana region, the rate of decline was substantial. Curiously, the lowest decline was in Vizianagaram district of the state in the coastal Andhra region.

Determinants of Fertility

Conditions that create low fertility in any society are quite complex. Although different theories have been postulated to understand the fertility decline mechanism, the rapid nature of fertility decline now experienced in developing countries under extremely different circumstances make it difficult to predict how well these fit the theories. Traditional demographic transition theory primarily emphasised the role of economic or modernisation factors towards reduction in fertility. Similarly, the neoclassical demand theories too emphasised the role of economic forces primarily stressing two variables, viz., quantity-quality trade off and the allocation of mother's time (Schultz, 1981). However, as far as developing countries are concerned economic factors do not seem to explain the full course of fertility transition. First, the fertility decline has occurred in many countries and areas where the levels of economic development were comparatively poor. Second, the opportunities to ensure the quality of children are limited in the context of many developing countries. Third, the value of time is not particularly relevant when majority of women are illiterate and underemployed.

The other predominant argument was the emphasis on the role of social development (Caldwell, 1980). The experience of many parts of the developing world suggest that fertility decline can, in fact, take place with social development (Krishnan, 1976; Murthi et al., 1995). Two variables are being emphasised in the social development discourse, viz., female literacy level and health status. Improvement in the health status, however, is considered to be a necessary condition of fertility decline even by the demographic transition theorists. Hence the crux of social development argument was emphasising the role of female education. But experience from a few developing countries has clearly conveyed that neither high improvement in female education nor considerable reduction in infant mortality are necessary conditions for the onset of rapid decline in fertility.

As development indices became poor predictors of birth control use and fertility, there had been emphasis on diffusion theory of fertility in recent years (Retherford, 1985; Cleland and Wilson, 1987). Partly the diffusion framework results from the failure of other theories of fertility (Guilmoto and Rajan,1998). The major evidence on diffusion was gathered during the Princeton European Fertility Project. It showed that the fertility decline has occurred under a wide variety of social, economic and demographic conditions in Europe (Coale and Watkins, 1986). It had also established that the transition occurred primarily within the linguistic boundaries.

By contrast, there are other explanations of fertility decline, mainly of country specific context (Ratcliffe, 1978; Srinivasan et al., 1991; Martine, 1996; Pitt et al., 1999; James, 1999). The regional specific variables, however, are considerably varied and difficult to organise into any concrete theoretical framework. Probably, given the diversity in the nature of the population under study, factors determining fertility decline could be considerably different across groups. Many of these factors were thought to have originated in that particular geographical area either due to the policies of the government or by a group action. These studies point to an important fact that implementation of schemes that benefit the poor and its better governance had an important role to play even in familial decisions like number of children.

The important criteria would, therefore, be to understand how far these theories account for the rapid pace of fertility decline occurring in many developing countries recently and particularly in some states of India. Above all, how well the decline in fertility in Andhra Pradesh could fit the existing theories of fertility decline.

Role of Conventional Factors

Table 3 presents the various socio-economic indicators in Andhra Pradesh for the latest available years.

Table 3. Various Socio-Economic Indicators, Andhra Pradesh

Variables	Rates
Per Capita Income, 2000-2001 (1993-94 prices) (rupees)	9697
Percentage of female Literate, 2001	51.17
Infant Mortality Rate, 2000 (per 1000 live births)	65
Percentage of Workers in Primary Sector, 2001	62.3
Percentage of Urban Population, 2001	27.08

Most of the socio-economic variables in Andhra Pradesh depict deplorable levels of progress. The per capita income in the state is below national average. The female literacy level in the state is one of the lowest among the Indian states. The infant mortality rate is also fairly high. There is neither any significant structural change happening in the economy by way of shifting away from agriculture nor any considerable alteration in the rural-urban composition of the population.

It is, therefore, clear that both the modernisation and social development arguments fail to explain the fertility decline in Andhra Pradesh. This becomes even more evident by matching district level fertility with the socio-economic and health indicators of respective districts. Comparatively low levels of fertility is recorded in north coastal districts like Srikakulam and Vizianagaram where the female literacy levels are significantly low and infant mortality rate is as high as 77 and 99 per 1000 live births respectively. The regression analysis carried out at the district level based on several socio-economic and demographic indicators showed that none of these variables is significantly associated with fertility in Andhra Pradesh (Census of India, 1991).

As the economic and social theories fail to explain the fertility decline, probably, two broad explanations can be postulated for the decline in fertility in the state. First, the fertility decline in the state has occurred within the contours of diffusion hypothesis. Second, fertility decline occurs purely due to 'endogenous factors' that are being shaped at the state and do not really conform to the limits of a particular theory. The term 'endogenous' is used here to refer to those factors that are peculiar to the region under study. Can such variables explain a major part of the fertility decline in a region? No simple answer lies for these two questions. Both these explanations need careful examination.

Diffusion

The essence of diffusion dynamic is that the information or behaviour of one person can have spillover effects on the motivation of another which could be either positive or negative (Montgomery and Casterline, 1998). This spillover effect has both social and geographical dimension. Social diffusion can occur through different means, e.g. education, mass media, government IEC programmes and so on. It is yet to be established clearly which of these programmes is most important in fertility reduction. An important form of diffusion widely talked, of late, is geographical diffusion. The geographical diffusion is horizontal and this process is not yet clearly understood. When different geographical areas are linked by social networks, there could be spillover effects of one area to another.

The attempt to analyse Indian fertility decline through a diffusion process is quite new. There are now strong arguments that fertility decline has assumed a peculiar geographical pattern in the country (Guilmoto and Rajan, 1998). The decline has primarily emerged in the coastal districts of the state and now slowly spreading towards interior regions. At the same time it is highly difficult to quantify the diffusion and thus still remains at the theoretical level. It is rather easy to attribute diffusion when a change has already taken place. One of the major drawbacks of diffusion theory is that it only tries to give an answer when a change has already occurred. But it cannot convincingly predict why such phenomena do not continue to occur in other parts or at least why similar process is not taking place in other regions.

Probably an alternative view to diffusion process is looking at the role and specificity of a particular geographical region or state in fertility transition. Such attempt has been made to explain fertility decline across different countries and states in India. For instance, group based lending programme introduced in Bangladesh is estimated to have a significant impact on changing their reproductive behaviour too (Dev *et al*, 2001). Kerala's fertility decline was explained in terms of a social justice theory mainly in political and economic policies and development strategies identified through land reforms, increased wages of agricultural labourers peculiar only to the state (Ratcliffe, 1978). In the case of Tamil Nadu the role played by committed political leadership and social reformers in fertility decline is often emphasised (Srinivasan et al., 1991).

The State-specific Factors

It was pointed out that the rapid fertility decline began in Andhra Pradesh by the second half of 1980s and accelerated in the 1990s. The progress was phenomenal in the 1990s. Figure 4 presents number of sterilizations in the second half of the 1990s. The number recorded a consistent increase over this period. Hence, a careful analysis of the policy changes is called for particularly in the 1980s and more importantly in the 1990s.

Figure 4: Number of Sterilisations in Andhra Pradesh, 1995-96 to 2000-01

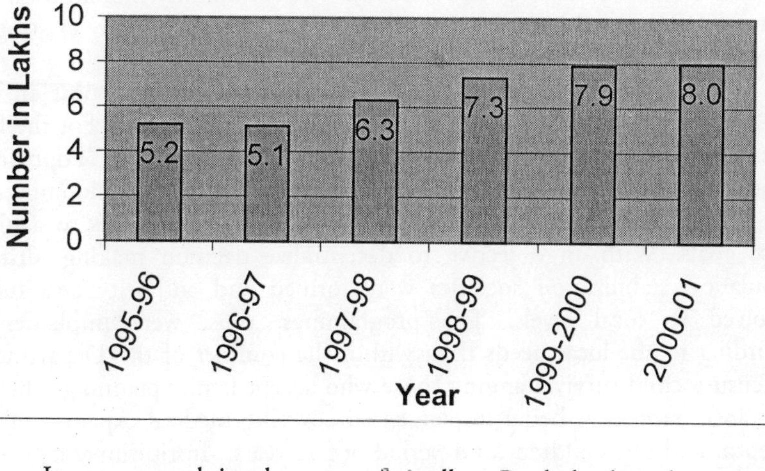

It was argued in the case of Andhra Pradesh that the policies followed and implemented since the early 1980s had not only profound impact on the economic life of the people but even paved the way for a social change. James (1999) brought out different measures followed in the state since early 1980s and its likely impact on the aspiration towards children as well. The implementation of vigorous public distribution system and large allocation and efficient administration of pro-poor schemes like ICDS was particularly mentioned. Ramachandurdu and Kamalamma (2002) argued that state adopted a two pronged strategy; poverty alleviation through people's participation and linked it to the adoption of small family norm which can be called as 'Welfare Induced Population Stabilisation'. Better governance is observed in many other government programmes in the state. For instance, an evaluation of group lending programme for women, DWACRA, has shown that it is quite successfully implemented in the state (Org-Marg Research Ltd., 2000).

It is likely that the better governance observed in the implementation of pro-poor programmes embraced even other sectors in the state, in particular, the effective delivery of family planning services. The family planning services are implemented through a network of Primary Health Centres (PHC) and sub-Centres at the lowest level. The number of Primary Health Centers had shot up considerably in the 1980s after a tardy growth in the 1970s. During the eighties the number of PHCs were increased from about 450 to 1100 due to introduction of Mandal administration in the state (Sawhney, 2000). The recruitment of doctors increased and they were trained for skill development. The family planning services, thus, become within easy reach of the majority of the acceptors. The implementation of the programme also was unique considering the prevailing situation in the district. It took advantage of programmes like self help groups, employment generation programme, literacy, community mobilisation and so on (Sawhney, 2000). The community mobilization has been very effective due to large number self-help groups already existing in the state.

The family planning programme received further boost in the 1990s through concrete policies and action (Chatterjee, 2001). For the first time in India, a state government in 1997 brought out a "Population Policy" to address core areas and specifying clearly demographic targets to be achieved in specified time and interventions and initiatives to achieve these goals. With an objective to decentralize decision making, district population stabilization societies were formed and authority and funds devolved to local levels. The programmes, thus, were implemented according to the local needs than within the confines of the Department. To ensure child survival among those who accept family planning a health insurance package is being implemented covering medical expenses of the acceptor and two children for a period of five years. Institutional deliveries were encouraged by paying Rs 300 for every woman delivering in a public health institution. Population control was a favoured topic in all grama sabhas during Janmabhoomi programme (Chatterjee, 2001).

Hence, the success of the state in controlling the population problem partly lies in the better provision and governance of both family planning related and welfare oriented programmes. The evidence available from other countries and other parts of India where the fertility decline has occurred with similar features also speaks about the importance of better governance in the success of any programme particularly the birth control.

The message simply, therefore, is that there are different routes to attain a given goal and economic development need not be a precedent for achieving a major social change.

Statistical Proof

Although it is possible to observe a link between state policies and fertility decline in the state, it is difficult to predict conclusively on such association given the lack of proper data linking these two events. A modest attempt, however, is made to link the fertility with the village level welfare programmes and family planning activities using data from the National Family Health Survey (NFHS-2). The details of the data used, statistical technique adopted and the coefficients are presented in Appendix 1.

The results reestablish the importance of several household level characteristics (demographic, social and cultural) in determining modern contraceptive use (Table 4 in Appendix 1). Two notable exceptions were exposure to mass media and work participation of women. While these results are fairly well known, where the present analysis makes a departure and improves is by estimating the 'village effects' and 'district effects' on women's fertility. Three village-level factors were included to assess whether individual contraceptive use is systematically related to some of village factors. The variable representing the diffusion process (distance to nearest town) was not significant. However, the first variable associated with government policy (beneficiaries in a village) showed a significant, but negative, relationship. This finding is contrary to the argument that development intervention increases the contraceptive use. This cannot be disproved, given that many villages typically tend to be benefited by the government on the basis of their being 'backward' – areas that typically show low levels of contraceptive use. But the interactive term with standard of living and SC/ST households also did not turn out to be significant. However, the second governance variable, family planning related group meeting at the village during the last one year showed a nearly significant positive relationship with the contraceptive use. This indicates that effective implementation of programme has a major effect on the contraceptive use in a village.

The model also clearly suggests that individual factors do not account for the total variation in contraceptive use. While a bulk of the variation continues to be at the individual level, nonetheless, significant differences between villages remain even after considering three village level variables. However, after considering household level and village level factors, no significant variation remains at the district level. Obviously there is a need to assess other village factors – which also makes a case for detailed village surveys that are purpose specific.

To conclude, the analysis demonstrated that village specific factors, which basically measure the government role in the family planning, have a significant impact on the contraceptive use in the state. This probably suggests that an able government through its policies and efficient administration can make inroads into those decisions that were earlier specifically considered as private. Andhra Pradesh, thus, shows a different path that can be followed to attain a reduction in fertility. Probably, the unexpected decline in fertility in other parts of the country and other developing countries also would have similar features which need to be examined clearly.

4. MORTALITY TRENDS

Mortality transition in India as a whole began far earlier than the fertility decline. With a progressive control of cholera and plague epidemics after 1921, the mortality rate dropped considerably in the country (Visaria and Visaria, 1994). This, as already stated, resulted in a widening gap between fertility and mortality decline leading to a rapid pace of population growth. The Figure 1 indicates a consistent decline in mortality throughout the last quarter of the century in Andhra Pradesh.

As a result of the mortality transition, remarkable progress has been achieved in attaining an increased life expectancy of the people. The life expectancy at birth which was around 49 in the early 1970s has increased to nearly 62 during 1992-96 period. The life expectancy was favourable to females even in the 1970s. The increase in life expectancy during this period was significant even in rural areas. (Table 5) As a result the magnitude of difference in life expectancy has reduced between rural and urban areas over the period.

Table 5. Life expectancy at birth by place of residence, Andhra Pradesh, 1970-75 to 1992-96

Period	Total	Rural	Urban
1970-75	48.8	47.3	57.2
1976-80	53.1	51.7	60.6
1981-85	58.4	57.1	63.8
1986-90	59.1	58.3	62.1
1991-95	61.8	60.7	65.1
1992-96	62.0	61.0	65.5

Source: Sample Registration System (1999).

Infant Mortality

An important measure to understand the mortality transition is considered to be the levels of infant mortality. All the more, infant mortality is also recognized as a sensitive measure to understand the health status of the population. Infant mortality is also often used as an excellent indicator to assess the overall socio-economic development of a particular geographical region. The reduction in the infant mortality rate has been one of the priority health goals of both national and state governments in India.

Figure 5: Neonatal, Postneonatal and IMR: Andhra Pradesh 1971-97

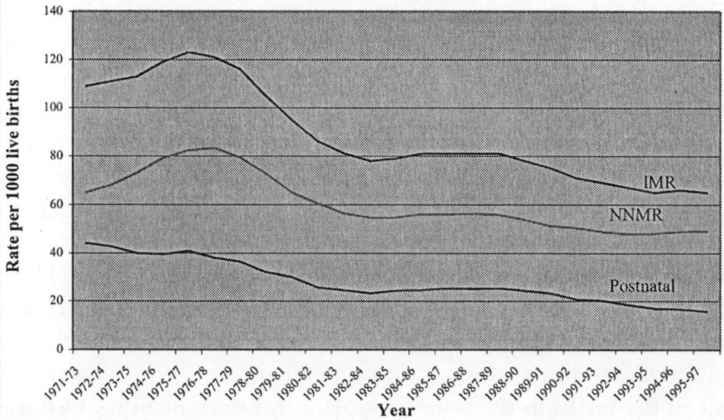

Source: Same as in Figure 1.

There had been some sharp decline in infant mortality in the state. Figure 5 depicts trends in infant mortality over the period 1971-97. From around mid 1970s, considerable decline is observed in IMR. This was nearly halted around mid 1980s and then picked up later. The over all decline in infant mortality has been around 2.8 per cent per annum during this entire period.

However, the present level of infant mortality (63 per 1000 live births in 1997) is relatively high compared to Kerala (12) which has the lowest infant mortality level in India. This relatively high infant mortality exists despite the fact that there has been a substantial decline in the fertility rate in the state particularly from the mid 1980s.

Infant mortality can be decomposed into two components; neonatal and postneonatal mortality primarily based on the cause of infant death. The infant deaths in the neonatal period (first 28 days) result from endogenous factors related to mother. The postneonatal mortality, (29 days to one year) on the contrary, occurs due to exogenous components viz., the larger environment.

The decline in postneonatal mortality has been quite consistent in the case of Andhra Pradesh over the last 25 years. It continues to decline and its present level (14.7) is quite lower than the all India average (25.1) in 1997. The reduction in post neonatal mortality is primarily due to great emphasis recently placed on controlling two major killers among children such as diarrhoea and acute respiratory infections. Further, vaccination of children had been taken up on a priority basis as a strategy to attain the National Health Policy goals. As a result, the percentage of children aged 12-23 months fully immunised constitutes nearly 59 per cent in Andhra Pradesh. Only around 5 per cent have not received any vaccination. These interventions primarily affected the mortality rate beyond one month of age.

Curiously, however, the decline in neonatal mortality has been sluggish particularly since the 1980s. At present the neonatal mortality constitutes nearly 77 per cent of the total infant mortality. The neonatal mortality in the state (48.4) is higher than at all India level (46.1), although the postneonatal mortality had been far lower than the national average. The state has recorded considerable decline in fertility since the late 1980s which has substantially cut down the high risk pregnancies. Also there has been considerable improvement in the adoption of prenatal care in the state. According to the latest data available from National Family Health Survey only 7.6 per cent of the women did not receive any prenatal care for the births three years preceding the survey in 1998. The number of institutional delivery has also gone up although it is still at a lower level. Nearly half of the births in the state took place in health institutions during the three years preceding the survey in 1998.

Probably, the high levels of neonatal mortality reflect on the poor socio-economic and health status of the mothers in the state. Although simple medical intervention could bring down the post neonatal mortality substantially, the same could not be replicated in the case of neonatal mortality with the incidence of illiteracy as high as 64 per cent among the eligible women. Another major reason could be the high incidence of under nutrition among women in the state. More than 37 per cent of the married women have a Body Mass Index (BMI) less than 18.5 per cent indicating high prevalence of nutritional deficiency according to NFHS-2. The prevalence of anemia is around 50 per cent.

National Family Health Survey also presents data on neonatal mortality by background characteristics of women in the state (Table 6). Although the relationship between educational level of the mother and postneonatal mortality is quite revealing, that of neonatal does not depict a clear direction. Even among women with high school or higher levels of education, the neonatal mortality is considerably higher. However, the relationship is more obvious in the case of the living standard index. The living standard index is calculated using household asset holding such as land, durable goods and household facilities like type of house, source of lightning, fuel for cooking, toilet facility etc. Women with low living standard have considerably higher neonatal mortality rate than other groups. It is not to deny the fact that the levels of neonatal mortality among the high living standard group is also far higher than that of post neonatal

Table 6. Neonatal, Postneonatal, Infant Mortality and Nutritional Status of Women by Different Background Characteristics in Andhra Pradesh, 1996-98

Characteristics	Neonatal	Postneonatal	IMR
Residence			
Urban	26.6	78.6	
Education			
Illiterate	54.3	28.0	82.4
Literate, < middle complete	32.9	20.2	53.0
High School Complete & above	40.5	8.4	48.9
Caste/tribe			
Scheduled caste	69.4	26.0	95.4
Scheduled tribe	57.7	45.9	103.6
Other Backward Classes	42.9	26.8	69.7
Other	35.7	11.4	47.1
Standard of Living Index			
Low	62.8	34.4	97.1
Medium	38.5	18.3	56.8
High	34.1	8.4	42.5
Total	47.5	23.4	70.8
33.1	13.3	46.4	
Rural	52.0		

Source: National Family Health Survey (2000).

mortality. It is therefore, difficult to predict what factors really determine neonatal mortality in the state which definitely needs further probing (James et al. 2000). However, on the whole, one would wonder whether overall living standard of the women where nutritional level becomes an important component, has a major role to play in the higher levels of neonatal mortality and thus the overall infant mortality.

It would also be quite interesting to look at the geographical distribution of infant mortality in the state (Table 2). Although higher level of fertility is recorded in Mahabubnagar in 1991, the infant mortality is highest in one of the low fertility district of Vizianagaram. As far as infant mortality is concerned the coastal districts do not seem to have any advantage over Telangana districts. Even in some of the developed districts like East and West Godavari the level of infant mortality is quite high. The decline in infant mortality is also taking place across all the districts.

To conclude, although the overall mortality level is low, the efforts of the state to attain a reasonable level of infant mortality decline along with fertility decline have not met with success. It is also observed that the major part of infant death is now occurring in neonatal stage which has direct link with mother's health. With the number of children substantially declining, the high levels of neonatal mortality now has to be addressed by emphasising the overall socio-economic and health status of the mother in general and nutritional status in particular.

5. MIGRATION

Information on migration is important not only as a possible factor in determining population growth at the state level but also to understand the development dynamics in each region within the state. Migration is considered to be a function of comparative underdevelopment of the place of origin. Understanding migration dynamics, therefore, provides useful insights into the development dynamics in a regional perspective.

It is now well established that inter-state and international in-migrants constitute only negligible proportion of total population in Andhra Pradesh (James, 2000). Table 7 presents the interstate net migrants mainly to understand as to whether the state attracts or releases people. Andhra Pradesh has recorded a net outflow of people to other states in India to the tune of nearly 0.2 million in the decade 1981-91. A net outflow is recorded even in earlier decades. The magnitude of net-outmigration is quite negligible indicating clearly that the population growth in the state is not determined by migration but due to natural growth resulting from the discrepancy between births and deaths.

Table 7. Inter-state net migration in Andhra Pradesh : 1961-91

Year	Net Migration (in 00's)
1961	-2846
1971	-3381
1981	-3205
1991	-2319

Note: 1961 and 1971 figures are based on place of birth data while 1981 and 1991 figures are based on place of last residence information and as such strictly not comparable.
Source: Computed from Decennial census, various years.

Inter-District Migration

As already stated, inter-district migration is considered to be a powerful means to understand the relative economic development of the different geographical regions. It is generally hypothesised that the movement of the people is uni-directional from underdeveloped to better-off regions. Hence an analysis of the migration streams across regions provides useful insights on the equitable regional development. For the present analysis, the districts in the state are divided into five regions1. Table 8 presents percentage of inter-regional in, out and net migration among males to total population in different regions of the state based on 1981 and 1991 census results. The data are based on 'place of birth' information. Hence, migrants are defined as those whose place of birth is different from the place of enumeration. A major disadvantage with the 'place of birth' data is the lack of time dimension. Therefore, those who migrated log ago are also included.

Table 8. Percentage of inter-regional in, out and net migrants among males to total male population in regions of Andhra Pradesh, 1981 and 1991

Regions	1981			1991			1991 Net-1981 Net*
	In	Out	Net	In	Out	Net	
North Coastal Andhra	2.73	3.53	-0.80	2.68	3.05	-0.38	0.31
South Coastal Andhra	2.08	3.68	-1.61	1.64	3.87	-2.23	-0.99
Rayalaseema	1.42	1.46	-0.04	1.15	1.56	-0.41	-0.42
South Telangana	3.86	2.42	1.44	4.58	1.10	3.48	2.76
North Telangana	3.67	1.82	1.86	2.68	1.89	0.79	-0.77

Note: (*1991 Net minus 1981 Net). For 1981 and 1991 the proportion is estimated using respective population figures from Census. But for calculating last column (1991 Net-1981 Net), mid year population between 1981-91 is used.

Source: Computed from Census of India, Migration Tables of Andhra Pradesh.

It is interesting to see that the net migration (in migration- out migration) is positive only in South and North Telangana regions both in 1981 and 1991. Although one would expect large-scale in-migration to South Coastal Andhra because of its advantage over other regions over development, the region records the highest level of net out migration. As the Hyderabad urban agglomeration is located in South Telangana, positive net migration into this region is not surprising. But North Telangana also recorded a positive net migration both in 1981 and 1991. It is strange that while one would expect more of out-migration from underdeveloped regions to developed pockets, nearly a reverse trend is portrayed in the case of Andhra Pradesh.

However, as already pointed out, the above analysis is based on lifetime migration, which includes even those migrated long ago. It necessitates a clear understanding of the economic and social scenario of these regions in the past. What is more interesting would be to find out the recent direction of inter-regional movements. If place of birth statistics are available for two consecutive census, this can be used to make an indirect assessment of intercensal net migration. The last column of Table 8 presents percentage of inter-district net migrants between 1981-912. The direction of movement observed while considering the lifetime migration is nearly absent during 1981-91 period. There are only two regions with net migration remaining positive between 198-91 indicating more of in migration. The highest percentage of net immigrants is recorded in South Telangana. This definitely is the influence of Hyderabad urban agglomeration. It indicates that although there had been movement of people in the past to other districts of Telangana region, currently the movements are restricted to two big urban centres of Hyderabad and Visakhapatnam.

It will also be interesting to see from which region the in-migrants to other region come from. This will show whether there is any concentration in the origin of in-migrants. If such concentration persists, it will have implication for the regional inequality. Table 9 presents the contribution of each region in the total in-migration in other regions.

Table 9. Percentage contribution of different regions towards in-migration in other regions among males in Andhra Pradesh, 1991

Regions	NCA	SCA	RLS	ST	NT
North Coastal Andhra (NCA)	0	91.77	3.56	3.14	1.53
Southern Coastal Andhra (SCA)	50.62	0	23.69	12.73	12.96
Rayalaseema (RLS)	10.05	70.94	0	15.82	3.18
South Telangana (ST)	4.70	54.18	12.91	0	27.58
North Telangana (NT)	4.78	53.61	3.96	37.66	0

Source: Same as in Table 8.

In most of the regions majority of in-migrants come from the neighbouring regions. For instance, bulk of in-migrants to North Coastal Andhra comes from South Coastal Andhra, probably due to the presence of Visakhapatnam urban agglomeration. There is hardly any movement from Rayalaseema and Telangana region to the North Coast. Conversely, Southern Coastal Andhra attracts nearly half of the migrants from North Coast and the other half come from other regions. In Rayalaseema, majority of the in-migrants are from the South Coastal Andhra. On the contrary, more than half of the Telangana migrants come from South Coastal Andhra. The migration from North Coastal Andhra and Rayalaseema to Telangana is negligible.

The above analysis of inter-regional migration, thus, brings out the several interesting points. First, the inter-regional migration shows a declining trend in the state over the last three decades. Second, although in the past there were large in-migration to Telangana regions (both to south and north Telangana), the current inter-district migration is mainly limited to big urban centres of Hyderabad and Visakhapatnam. Third, the inter-district migration pattern observed in the past is not in conformity with the existing migration theories or understanding of movement from underdeveloped to developed pockets. On the contrary, in the past, there had been migration from developed pockets of South Coastal Andhra to the poor Telangana region.

In a nutshell, migration definitely is not a major determinant of population growth in Andhra Pradesh. Overall the state recorded a net population outflow in a lesser magnitude. However, Andhra Pradesh had an interesting inter-district migration in the past from developed districts of coastal areas to poor Telangana region. This process also nearly halted in recent years. At present the only major migration stream in the state is the flow towards big cities especially to Hyderabad and Vishakhapatnam.

6. IMPLICATIONS OF DEMOGRAPHIC TRANSITION

With migration playing an insignificant role in the overall population dynamics of the state, the major challenges in the population front will be through the changes in fertility and mortality variables. Although higher levels of infant mortality confront a challenge, the overall mortality rate is not significantly high. Therefore, the declining fertility along with increasing life expectancy is going to be a major challenge as far as social and welfare policies are concerned. This is particularly important for a state eagerly looking forward to 2020 when the people are expected to lead a healthy and productive life.

The main macro demographic effect that comes through the demographic transition usually is reduction in population growth rate and resultant changes in the age structure of the population. These changes, however, are not sudden. The population growth does not respond to demographic changes in the short-term. Even after the fertility decline an increase in the number of births can still occur as the women who are already born in the past pass through the prime reproductive ages.

As a result of demographic transition, the first impact is often observed in age pyramid. The declining mortality rate would result in increased longevity of the people. Further, declining fertility would result in less number of people in the young ages. This would result in higher proportion of old age people. This is generally known as population ageing. The state machinery needs to be prepared to take care of old people and its associated socio-economic problems.

Secondly, there would also be shift in the size and proportion of labour force in the state which has major implication for the economic growth and standard of living of the people. However, it is difficult to predict what impact (negative or positive) the transition will have on the economy. Some studies attribute nearly one-third of East Asia's economic miracles between 1965-90 to the changes in the population dynamics especially rapid growth in labour force (Bloom and Williamson 1998). It would, therefore, be interesting to see the expected changes in both labour force and old age proportion in Andhra Pradesh in the coming decades.

The Vision 2020 has kept some ambitious target as far as many demographic indicators are concerned. The state is projected to attain a total fertility rate as low as 1.5, infant mortality rate of 10 per 1000 live births and life expectancy of 68.1 years for men and 70.6 years for women by 2020. The expected growth of population is 0.8 per cent. It is, however, difficult to predict how far the dream of total fertility rate coming to as low as 1.5 per women will materialise by 2020. Although the experience form the Western world does not rule out the possibility of achieving TFR even below 1.5, the related socio-cultural characteristics of those countries are extremely different from what is experienced generally in our country. The cultural change associated with such a low fertility such as large proportion of women remaining unmarried and without having any children is unlikely to be experienced in India within a span of 20 years.

Therefore a reasonable prediction to understand the relative size and structure of the population in the future would be the population projection carried out by Registrar General of India until the year 2016. This projection is based on the available trend and expected movement in the vital rates in the coming years. The expected changes in the age structure between 1991 and 2016 are provided in Table 10.

Table 10. Projected Population and growth of population in different age groups in Andhra Pradesh

Age Group	Population 1991 (in '000)	Percentage 1991	Population 2016 (in '000)	Percentage 2016	Growth Rate* 1991-2016
< 15	24176	36.35	20044	22.62	-1.25
15-59	37916	57.01	59309	66.92	2.98
60+	4416	6.64	9270	10.46	4.94
Total	66508	100.00	88623	100.00	1.91

Note: * Exponential growth rates are calculated.
Source: Registrar General of India (1996).

The registrar general's projection explicitly conveys two important challenges ahead and the real vision the state might have to set forth in the coming days. The first challenge is in the employment front and the second in ensuring old age security. However, the state has something to cheer about regarding the rapid decline in the young age population. Not only there is a reduction in the percentage of young age population but even the absolute number registers a sharp decline. This would give some leverage to the state in reallocating its resources spent on children's health and development.

At the employment front the working age population will be increasing at a faster rate in the next couple of decades. This is primarily due to the higher levels of fertility experienced in the past. Although the faster increase in working age population was found to be a blessing for the economic boom in the context of East Asian countries (Bloom and Williamson 1998), one is not sure how far this would be helpful for a state plagued already with high levels of unemployment and underemployment.

Employment creation, therefore, would be a real challenge as the size of the population in this age group considerably increases during the next 15 years.

The second major challenge will be the marked increase expected in the old age population which more than doubles during the 15 year period. The proportion of old age population will become more than 10 per cent of the total population by 2016. As the present old age security measures are scanty, how far the state would be able to allocate an increasing share of resources in this sector is going to be crucial.

7. CONCLUSION

The analysis of demographic transition in Andhra Pradesh, thus, brings out several interesting dimensions of the transition for the present and in the years to come. The achievement of state is commendable as far as fertility reduction is concerned. It is also interesting to see that the fertility reduction has embraced all sections of the society irrespective of economic, social or cultural differences. The state, thus, would achieve a replacement level of fertility in the very near future. However, this reduction does not conform to the classical theories, which thought fertility reduction necessitates considerable improvement either in economic or social development. This ultimately brings down the entire fertility reduction argument in the state to two major hypotheses. Whether the fertility reduction can be attributed to the diffusion process especially a geographical diffusion or whether it is the result of certain 'endogenous' policies and factors occurred within the state for the last couple of decades. It is however, difficult to predict the validity of both these arguments with precision using the existing data sets. However, a multi-level analysis was carried out by using the NFHS-2 data to assess the hypothesis viz., whether the government programmes (both welfare oriented and effective implementation of family planning) make a difference. The results confirmed that effective governance of family planning programme has an impact on the contraceptive use. However, the village-level factors representing diffusion process or government welfare programmes did not show the expected results mainly because of the inappropriate variable constructs.

The mortality transition in the state began earlier than the fertility transition. Although the overall mortality level is low the present level of infant mortality is comparatively high. A major part of infant mortality is now explained by neonatal mortality (28 days). Oddly, neonatal mortality has not recorded any marked decline even with dramatic decline in fertility level. The main causes of neonatal deaths are usually associated with mother specific factors. Given the poor social and health indicators of women in the state, major strides in infant mortality is unlikely to be achieved without addressing the overall socio-economic and health status of the women particularly the nutritional levels.

Inter-state or international migration plays an insignificant role in the population dynamics of the state. At present the internal migration is also limited to the big urban centres. A natural outcome of such migration would be growing big cities without adequate facilities to address it. The state, however, had a curious internal migration particularly in the earlier decades from comparatively developed pockets of coastal regions to poor Telangana districts. This would have been due to the availability of cheaper land in the poor regions.

Finally, the outcome of present demographic transition would be seriously felt in the coming years. There is going to be considerable increase in the working age population primarily due to the high fertility in the past. This would create severe pressure on employment by the year 2020. Also the old age population will be more than doubling between 1991-2016. At the same time, the younger population will be declining in numbers. This would result in a greying population and one wonders how far the social security measures will be geared up to face those challenges.

Notes

1 The districts comes under each region are North Coastal Adnhra=Srikakulam, Vizianagaram and Visakhapatnam, South Coastal Andhra= East Godavari, West Godavari, Krishna, Guntur, Prakasam and Nellore, Rayalaseema= Chittor, Cuddapah, Anantapur and Kurnool, South Telangana= Rangareddy, Hyderabad, Mahabubnagar, Medak and Nalgonda, and North Telangana= Nizamabad, Adilabad, Karimnagar, Warangal and Khammam.

2 These estimates will be slightly underestimates as no adjustment is made to account for mortality.

References

Bloom, David E. and J. G. Williamson (1998), “Demographic Transition and Economic Miracles in Emerging Asia”, *The World Bank Economic Review*, Vol.12, No.3.

Caldwell, J.C (1980), "Mass Education as a Determinant of the Timing of Fertility Decline", *Population and Development Review*, Vol.6, No.2.

Census of India (1991), *District level estimates of fertility and child mortality for 1991 and their inter relations with other variables*, Occasional Paper No.1 of 1997, New Delhi: Registrar General Of India.

Chatterjee, Rachel (2001), “Health Systems in Andhra Pradesh”, Indian Council for Research on International Economic Relations, New Delhi (Mimeo).

Cleland, J. and C. Wilson (1987), “Demand Theories of the Fertility Transition: An iconoclastic view, *Population Studies*, Vol 41, No.1.

Coale, A.J. and Susan Watkins (1986), *The Decline of Fertility in Europe*, Princeton: Princeton University Press.

Dev, Mahendra S., K.S. James and Binayak Sen (2001), "Causes of fertility decline in India and Bangladesh: An Investigation", Paper presented at the third annual conference of the South Asian Network of Economic Research Institutes, Indian Council for Research on International Economic Relations, New Delhi, August 28-31.

Duncan, C., K. Jones and G. Moon (1996), "Health related behaviour in context: a multilevel modeling approach", *Social Science and Medicine*, 42, No.6.

Goldstein, H. (1995), *Multilevel statistical models* 2nd edition, London: Arnold.

Guilmoto, Christophe Z. and S. Irudaya Rajan (1998), "Regional Heterogeneity and Fertility Behavior in India", Working Paper No 290, Centre for Development Studies, Trivandrum.

Guilmoto, Christophe Z. and S. Irudaya Rajan (2002), "District level estimates of fertility from India's 2001 census", *Economic and Political Weekly*, Vol 37, No. 7.

James, K.S. (1999), "Fertility Decline in Andhra Pradesh: A search for alternative hypotheses", *Economic and Political Weekly*, Vol. 34, No.8.

James, K.S. (2000), "Internal migration in Andhra Pradesh: A quantitative analysis", Working Paper No. 38, Centre for Economic and Social Studies, Hyderabad.

James, K.S., Iain Aitken and S.V. Subramanian (2000), "Neonatal Mortality in India: Emerging Paradoxes", Working Paper No.10.13, Harvard Center for Population and Development Studies, Cambridge, MA, November, 2000.

Janardhan Rao, B. (1987), *Land Alienation in Tribal Areas*, Kakatiya School of Public Administration, Warangal, India.

Krishnan, T.N. (1976), "Demographic Transition in Kerala: Facts and Factors" *Economic and Political Weekly* 11, No.31-33 (August).

Martine, George (1996), "Brazil's Fertility Decline, 1965-95: A fresh look at key factors", *Population and Development Review*, Vol 22, No.1.

Montgomery, Mark R. and John B. Casterline (1998), "Social Networks and the Diffusion of Fertility Control", Working Paper No. 119, Population Council, New York.

Murthi, Mamta, Anne-Catherine Guio and Jean Dreze (1995), "Mortality, Fertility and Gender Bias in India: A district level analysis", *Population and Development Review*, Vol. 21, No.4.

National Family Health Survey (1995), *Andhra Pradesh, National Family Health Survey India 1992-93*, Population Research Centre, Andhra University, Visakhapatnam and International Institute of Population Sciences, Bombay.

National Family Health Survey (2000), *Andhra Pradesh, National Family Health Survey India 1998-99*, Mumbai: International Institute of Population Sciences.

Org-Marg Research Ltd (2000), "Consultancy on strengthening of self help group in Andhra Pradesh- SWOT analysis of the groups surveyed in Andhra Pradesh", Sponsored by Department of Rural Development, Government of Andhra Pradesh, Hyderabad.

Pitt, Mark, M., Shahidur R. Khandker, Signe-Mary Mckernan and M. Abdul Latif (1999), "Credit programs for the poor and reproductive behaviour in low income countries: Are the reported casual relationships the result of heterogeneity bias", *Demography*, Vol 36, No.1.

Ramachandrudu, G and G. Kamalmma (2002), "Fertility Transition in Andhra Pradesh-The Welfare Induced Population Stabilization (WIPS) Model", Paper presented at the National Seminar on India' s Population Census-2001, Implications for human poverty, Department of Economics, Andhra University, Visakhapatnam, March 7-8.

Ratcliffe, John. (1978), "Social Justice and Demographic Transition: Lessons from Kerala state", *International Journal of Health Services*, Vol. 8, No.1.

Registrar General of India (1996), *Population Projections for India and States 1996-2016*, New Delhi: Registrar General.

Retherford, R.D. (1985), "A Theory of Marital Fertility Transition", *Population Studies*, Vol. 39, No.2.

Sample Registration System (1999), *Compendium of India's Fertility and Mortality Indicators, 1971-1997*, New Delhi: Registrar General of India.

Sawhney, Nilam (2000), "Family Planning Programmatic Implementation in Andhra Pradesh: A historical and contemporary perspective", Paper presented at the National Seminar on "Fertility Decline in Andhra Pradesh: A historical and contemporary perspective" on 13-15 March, 2000, Hyderabad: Indian Institute of Health and Family Welfare.

Schultz, T. Paul (1981), *Economics of Population*, Massachusetts: Addison-Wesley.

Srinivasan,K., P. C. Saxena, T.K.Roy and R.K.Varma (1991), "The Effect of Family Planning Components on Contraceptive Acceptance in Four Indian States", *International Family Planning Perspectives*, No.1.

Subramanian, SV, Jones K, Duncan C. (forthcoming), "Towards a multilevel geography of health". In Kawachi I, Berkman L (Eds.) *Neighborhoods and health*, New York: Oxford University Press.

Visaria, Pravin and Leela Visaria (1994), "Demographic Transition: Accelerating Fertility Decline in 1980s", *Economic and Political Weekly*, Vol. XXIX, No.51&52.

APPENDIX 1

Data Used For The Statistical Analysis

The data for the statistical analysis is from the household level survey carried out as part of the National Family Health Survey-2, 1998-99 in the state. The survey has obtained information on fertility and other background characteristics of 4032 ever-married in the age group 15-49 years. There is also a village survey as part of NFHS-2 providing information on various village services and programmes. As similar information is not available for the urban blocks, the analysis is restricted to rural areas of the state (3030 ever-married women).

Multi-level Analysis

The determinants to fertility are hypothesized to operate at several levels: individual-level (such as women's socio-economic status); village-level (programme implementation); district-level and so on. Conventional techniques fall short of recognizing the 'multi-level' structure of the issue under examination. However, in recent times multi-level modeling procedures have allowed us to address these concerns in a robust manner (Goldstein, 1995). Duncan, Jones and Moon (1996) and Subramanian, Jones and Duncan (forthcoming) provide a detailed introduction to the application of multi-level modeling techniques within health studies. Consequently, we adopt a multi-level modeling strategy to understand the variations in the fertility in Andhra Pradesh.

For the multilevel analysis, a three-level structure of women at level-1 nested within villages at level-2 and nested within district at level-3 is considered. By way of a summary, using multilevel techniques we essentially model, and provide estimate of:

- the overall relationship between individual, compositional factors and fertility ('fixed' parameters);
- the extent to which village-level factors relate to individual fertility and account for the between village-variation.
- the variation between villages and districts that cannot be accounted for by such factors ('random-intercept' parameters);

Notwithstanding the importance of the individual socio-economic factors, in terms of their direct impact on contraceptive use, it is also essential to account for these factors before any robust assessment can be made regarding the extent to which villages vary. For instance, a village could have high (low) levels of contraceptive use simply because it has a concentration of certain types of women who anyway are likely to report high (low) levels. In such cases, the variation between villages would simply be an artifact of its population composition. However, if differences between villages remain, then it suggests that over and above the individual factors, there are 'village-effects'. Consequently, we assess whether or not living in one village as compared to another has an impact on women's contraceptive use levels.

Variables Chosen for the Analysis

While the individual variables are expected to measure the impact of household level variables (socio-economic, cultural and demographic variables) on fertility, the village variables represent government programmes and diffusion process. Although district is also included as a third level, no variables are considered. Diffusion process is defined quite loosely here. Distance of a village from the nearest town is considered to represent diffusion process. This is based on the assumption that closeness to the town provides easy passage to the geographical diffusion. There are, nonetheless, many other ways geographical diffusion can take place. Hence this representation of diffusion process is rather weak and vague.

The effectiveness of the government policies and programmes is represented by two variables. First, the number of beneficiaries per household in each village in three employment generating programmes (IRDP,NREP and DWACRA). Even here the number of beneficiaries is not a direct measure of its efficiency. Further if the employment generating programmes were implemented selectively in poor districts or in poor villages, it will also affect our results. Hence, The programme variable is interacted with standard of living index and SC/ST families. This will capture if the programmes are implemented selectively for the poor or SC/ST villages. It is, however, thought that as more and more women come under the purview of a programme like DWACRA, it has an effect not only economically but as a social group as well. Second variable representing better governance is whether at least one group meeting on family planning programme was conducted in the village during the last one year. This variable is thought to represent the effective implementation of family planning programme which also partly represent better governance.

Results and Discussion

Table 4 presents the data definition, structure and the estimated coefficients from the model.

Table 4. Results of Multi-level Model for rural areas of Andhra Pradesh, 1998-99 (in logits)

Variables	Coefficient
Response	
Contraceptive use (1 = Yes; 0 = No)	
Fixed part	
Level-1: Women, *n =3030*	
Women-level predictors	
Constant	-10.834 (0.776)*
Age (in years)	0.509 (0.047)*
Age squared	-0.008 (0.001)*
Male children born	2.013 (0.112)*
Squared male children born	-0.251 (0.023)*
Female children born	1.368 (0.103)*
Squared female children born	-0.185 (0.020)*
Male children died	-0.798 (0.117)*
Female children died	-0.472 (0.120)*
Women's education (1=Yes; 0 = No)	0.474 (0.137)*
Husband's education (1 = Yes; 0 = No)	0.113 (0.117)
Muslim (1 = Yes; 0 = No)	-1.403 (0.293)*
Scheduled caste/tribe (1 = Yes; 0 = No)	-0.534 (0.154)*
Media exposure (1 = Yes; 0 = No)	0.098 (0.122)
Gainful employment (1 = Yes; 0 = No)	0.191 (0.129)
Standard of living index	0.056 (0.019)*
Level-2: Villages, *n = 98*	
Village-level predictors	
Distance to nearest town	-0.004 (0.005)
Number of beneficiaries per household	-2.886 (1.392)*
Group meeting on IEC activity in the village during the last year (1=yes; 0=No)	0.141 (0.074)*
Standard of living index*No.of beneficiaries	0.024 (0.190)
SC/ST* No.of beneficiaries	-1.996 (1.691)
Random part	
Level-3 Between district variation	0.136 (0.072)
Level-2: Between village variation	0.143 (0.063)*
Level-1: Extra-binomial variation	1.042

Note: Figures in the bracket indicate the standard error. Media exposure is the exposure to TV/Radio at least once a week or going to cinema at least once a month.

Standard of living index is calculated using asset holding and facilities at the household. For details of its estimation see National Family Health Survey (2000). Number of beneficiaries per household is calculated as the total number of beneficiaries in a village in three employment generating programme, IRDP, NREP and DWACRA divided by the total number of households in the village. IEC is the Information Education and Communication programme conducted in villages as part of the family planning programme.

* significant at 5 per cent level.

The demographic factors such as age, children born and died (males and females) are significantly related to contraceptive acceptance. Among the social factors, educational status of the woman showed a significant relationship but husband's educational level did not make a difference. Woman belonging to scheduled caste/tribe community and Muslim religion had lower contraceptive acceptance. As expected, standard of living (computed on the basis of total asset holding and selected household amenities) was positively related to contraceptive use. Strangely, neither exposure to media nor labor force participation of women outside household had any impact.

At the village level, the variable representing the diffusion process (distance to nearest town) was not significant. The variable associated with government policy (beneficiaries per household) showed a significant, but negative, relationship. The interactive term introduced also did not turn out to be significant. However, the other governance variable, group meeting at the village during the last one year showed a nearly significant positive relationship with the contraceptive use.

Random part results from model clearly suggest that significant differences between villages remain even after considering three village level variables. However, no significant variation remains at the district level.

13

Size and Nature of Healthcare System

K.V. Narayana

This paper deals with the size and nature of medical facilities in the public and private sectors and identifies the factors responsible for rapid growth of the private sector in recent decades. It also traces adverse impact of the private sector on the public hospitals and gives a brief sketch of major health sector reforms in the state.

1. PUBLIC AND PRIVATE MIX IN HEALTH CARE

There are no regular sources of information on the size of health care facilities (hospitals, beds, doctors etc.) in the private and voluntary sectors, as there is no law to enforce compulsory registration of health care institutions with any public or professional agency. The Health Information of India (published by the Director General of Health Services, the Government of India) does provide state-wise data on the number of hospitals and beds in different sectors but the occasional surveys conducted in some states show that it is a gross underestimation (Nandraj, 1994). For instance, according to the Health Information of India, there were only 266 hospitals and 11,103 hospital beds in the private sector in Andhra Pradesh (AP) in 1993. However, a survey of private hospitals by the Directorate of Health Services, Government of AP (GOAP) in 1992/1993 revealed that the actual number of private hospitals (3,151) and beds (46,550) was much more (Institute of Health Systems, 1996). The national surveys such as National Sample Survey (NSS) and the National Family Health Survey (NFHS) on utilisation of medical care and the local surveys on medical facilities also indicate the predominance of private sector and its rapid growth in the state.

Utilisation of Health Care Facilities

The 42nd (1986-1987) and 52nd (1995-96) rounds of NSS provide state-wise estimates on the private and public sources of inpatient as well as outpatient treatment (Central Statistical Organisation, 1986-87 and 1993-94). On average about 60 percent of inpatient care was provided by the public sector in the country in 1986-87 (Table 1). By 1995-96, the share of public sector was reduced to about 45 percent. However, the private sector was very predominant in AP even during 1980s. It accounted for about 70 percent of inpatient care in rural areas and 62 percent in urban areas, which was highest in the country. By mid 1990s, its share further increased to 77.5 percent in the rural areas, and a marginal increase in the urban areas. In the provision of outpatient care, the private sector was predominant in most of the states in 1990s as well as in 1980s. It accounted for about 70 percent of outpatient care in 1980s and 80 percent during 1990s (Table2). Similarly, the estimates of National Family Health Surveys on the type of medical attendance at the time of delivery show growing predominance of private medical facilities in A.P. (IIPS, 1992-93 and 1998-99). At the national level, the per cent of births taking place at the health institutions (public and private hospitals) had

Table 1. Percentage Distribution of Hospitalised (Inpatient) Cases by Type of Hospital

State	Rural				Urban			
	Private		Government		Private		Government	
	1986-87	1995-96	1986-87	1995-96	1986-87	1995-96	1986-87	1995-96
A.P.	70.09	77.5	29.91	22.5	62.02	63.8	37.98	36.2
Assam	9.98	26.2	90.02	73.8	17.67	34.8	82.33	65.2
Bihar	50.14	75.3	49.86	24.7	54.29	65.4	45.71	34.6
Gujarat	51.04	67.9	48.96	32.1	40.79	63.1	59.21	36.9
Haryana	49.04	69.5	50.96	30.5	44.69	62.7	55.31	37.3
Karnataka	41.98	54.2	58.02	45.8	51.10	70.2	48.90	29.8
Kerala	56.62	59.9	43.38	40.1	44.35	61.6	55.65	38.4
M.P.	20.77	46.7	79.23	53.3	23.02	44.0	76.98	56.0
Maharashtra	56.43	68.8	43.57	31.2	53.77	68.2	46.23	31.8
Orissa	11.94	9.4	88.06	90.6	18.52	19.0	81.48	81.0
Punjab	52.51	60.6	47.49	39.4	51.23	72.4	48.77	27.6
Rajasthan	19.99	35.1	80.01	64.9	14.38	26.9	85.62	73.1
Tamilnadu	43.85	58.9	56.15	41.1	41.96	64.3	58.04	35.7
U.P.	44.63	52.9	55.37	47.1	40.75	60.2	59.25	39.8
W. Bengal	8.38	18.0	91.62	82.0	26.10	27.9	73.90	72.1
All India	40.26	54.7	59.74	45.3	39.74	56.9	60.26	43.1

Source: 1. NSSO (1992).
2. NSSO (1998).

increased from about 26 percent in 1992-93 to 34 percent in 1998-99 (Table3). In A.P., it increased from about 34 to 54 percent during the same period. However, the private sector accounted for a high proportion of hospitalised births in AP. Its share increased rapidly from 58 percent in 1992-93 to 75 percent in 1998-99. Similar trend was manifested at all India level but it is less pronounced. The share of private sector increased from 43 to 52 percent.

In sum, the national surveys on utilisation of medical facilities indicate the rapid growth of private sector in the country during 1990s. The private sector seems to be rampant particularly in AP.

Table 2. Percentage Distribution Of Treatments (Outpatient) Over Source Of Treatment

State	Rural				Urban			
	Private		Government		Private		Government	
	1986-87	1995-96	1986-87	1995-96	1986-87	1995-96	1986-87	1995-96
A.P.	79.99	76.7	20.01	23.3	78.00	88.5	22.00	11.5
Assam	46.99	55.0	53.01	45.0	70.40	65.1	29.60	34.9
Bihar	83.13	94.9	16.87	5.1	82.00	80.9	18.00	19.1
Gujarat	67.50	81.6	32.5	18.4	81.44	81.8	18.56	18.2
Haryana	83.10	86.6	16.9	13.4	78.31	89.9	21.69	10.1
Karnataka	63.60	68.4	36.4	31.6	68.70	81.4	31.30	18.6
Kerala	65.48	70.1	34.52	29.9	63.68	69.5	36.32	30.5
M.P.	67.24	74.2	32.76	25.8	68.00	80.0	32.00	20.0
Maharashtra	73.68	88.1	26.32	11.9	74.98	89.9	25.02	10.1
Orissa	47.31	62.2	52.69	37.8	52.13	67.6	47.87	32.4
Punjab	87.23	93.0	12.77	7.0	89.08	92.8	10.92	7.2
Rajasthan	43.88	59.3	56.12	40.7	42.49	59.1	57.51	40.9
Tamilnadu	62.96	69.9	37.04	30.1	64.93	75.7	35.07	24.3
U.P.	-	95.8	-	4.2	83.80	89.7	16.20	10.3
W. Bengal	80.59	87.1	19.41	12.9	76.77	86.2	23.23	13.8
All India	74.42	81.8	25.58	18.2	72.85	82.6	27.15	17.4

Source : 1. NSSO (1992).
2. NSSO (1998).

Size of Public and Private Health Care Facilities

Occasional surveys of medical facilities also indicate the growing predominance of private medical care in AP. The GOAP survey of medical facilities had shown that the private hospitals accounted for 59 percent of total hospital beds in the state, leaving 35 percent in the public sector and 6 percent in the voluntary sector (Table 4). However, there were considerable regional variations in the relative strength of these sectors. The private sector was very developed in the Coastal districts which are more advanced in the socio-economic development. Within the Coastal region, the backward north coastal districts (Srikakulam, Vizianagaram and Vishakhapatnam) had a lower percent of private hospital beds. Similarly, the developed districts like Nizamabad, Nalgonda, Karimnagar and Khammam in Telangana region had a larger private sector while the public sector was still predominant in the backward districts like Adilabad and Mahbubnagar.

Table 3. Place of Delivery

A.P/India	Health Facility/Institution				Home	Others	Total
	Public	NGO/Trust	Private	Total			No. of Births
A.P							
1992-93	252	-	353	605	1207	28	1838
(%)	13.7		19.2	32.9	65.7	0.15	100
1998-99	141	25	396	562	557	10	1129
(%)	12.5	2.2	35.1	49.8	49.3	0.9	100
India							
1992-93	7208	-	5381	12589	36286	494	49369
(%)	14.6		10.9	25.5	73.5	1.0	100
1998-99	5284	227	5410	10921	21185	324	32393
(%)	16.2	0.7	16.7	33.6	65.4	1.0	100

Distribution of Institutional Deliveries

	Private Hospitals	Voluntary Hospitals	Public Hospitals	Total
A.P				
1992-93	353		252	605
(%)	58.3		41.7	100.0
1998-99	396	25	141	562
(%)	70.5	4.4	25.1	100.0
India				
1992-93	5381		7208	12589
(%)	42.7		57.3	100.0
1998-99	5410	227	5284	10921
(%)	49.5	2.1	48.4	100.0

Source: IIPS, National Family Health Surveys, 1992-93 and 1998-99.

The relative size of public and private sectors in some districts was affected by the presence of government medical colleges. The relative size of private sector was small in Kurnool district in Rayalaseema and Warangal district in Telengana due to presence of government teaching hospitals. But in the most developed districts like East Godavari, Krishna and Guntur in the Coastal Andhra, the private sector had become very predominant despite the presence of large teaching hospitals in the government sector. The growth of private medical care within the state is thus closely related to the overall development at district level.

Table 4. Hospital Beds in Public, Private and Voluntary Sectors

S.No.	District	Public		Private		Voluntary		Total	CMIE
		Beds	%	Beds	%	Beds	%	Beds	Index
Coastal Andhra		**10244**	**27.5**	**24193**	**65.0**	**2787**	**7.5**	**37224**	
1.	Srikakulam	552	50.1	510	46.3	40	3.6	1102	56
2.	Vizianagaram	321	79.5	83	20.5	0	0.0	404	65
3.	Visakhapatnam*	2418	57.8	1602	38.3	160	3.8	4180	92
4.	East Godavari*	1624	23.9	4765	70.1	404	5.9	6793	93
5.	West Godavari	638	12.9	4297	87.1	0	0.0	4935	115
6.	Krishna*	1463	26.7	3182	58.2	826	15.1	5471	119
7.	Guntur*	1764	25.6	4196	60.8	942	13.6	6902	114
8.	Prakasam	456	14.4	2601	82.4	100	3.2	3157	86
9.	Nellore	1008	23.6	2957	69.1	315	7.4	4280	96
Rayalaseema		**4389**	**51.6**	**3145**	**37.0**	**973**	**11.4**	**8507**	
10.	Chittoor*	1351	48.1	932	33.2	525	18.7	2808	84
11.	Cuddapah	573	31.4	939	51.5	313	17.2	1825	85
12.	Ananthapur	1085	69.4	479	30.6	0	0.0	1564	92
13.	Kurnool*	1380	59.7	795	34.4	135	5.8	2310	83
Telengana		**13307**	**40.0**	**19212**	**57.8**	**738**	**2.2**	**33257**	
14.	Mahbubnagar	736	41.0	968	54.0	90	5.0	1794	53
15.	Ranga Reddy	709	31.4	1505	66.7	42	1.9	2256	75
16.	Hyderabad*	6946	43.1	9153	56.9	0	0.0	16099	299
17.	Medak	578	47.1	649	52.9	0	0.0	1227	86
18.	Nizamabad	642	35.6	1119	62.1	40	2.2	1801	104
19.	Adilabad	688	59.4	446	38.5	25	2.2	1159	66
20.	Karimnagar	641	26.0	1617	65.5	210	8.5	2468	97
21.	Warangal*	1289	52.3	1077	43.7	97	3.9	2463	80
22.	Khammam	521	24.4	1501	70.4	110	5.2	2132	76
23.	Nalgonda	557	30.0	1177	63.3	124	6.7	1858	71
	Total	**27940**	**35.4**	**46550**	**58.9**	**4498**	**5.7**	**78988**	

Source: IHS (1996).

Note: * Districts with Govt Medical Colleges.

The per capita availability of beds in private sector also varied with overall development of districts (Table 5). In the public sector the per capita bed availability was more uniform across the districts. It was marginally high in the districts with the government teaching hospitals. However, the per capita availability of beds in the private sector tended to be higher in the developed districts. The number of hospital beds per 1000 population was around 1.0 in the developed south Coastal districts. In the backward north Coastal districts, Rayalaseema and in most of the Telengana districts it was about 0.5 bed per thousand population in the private sector.

Table 5. District wise Availability of Beds per 1000 Population

Districts		Private	Public	Voluntary	Total
Coastal Andhra					
1.	Srikakulam	0.22	0.24	0.02	0.48
2.	Vizianagaram	0.04	0.15		0.19
3.	Visakhapatnam	0.49	0.74	0.05	1.28
4.	East Godavari	1.05	0.36	0.09	1.5
5.	West Godavari	1.25	0.18		1.43
6.	Krishna	0.86	0.4	0.22	1.48
7.	Guntur	1.02	0.43	0.23	1.68
8.	Prakasam	0.94	0.17	0.04	1.15
9.	Nellore	1.24	0.42	0.13	1.79
Rayalaseema					
10.	Chittoor	0.29	0.42	0.16	0.87
11.	Cuddapah	0.41	0.25	0.14	0.8
12.	Ananthapur	0.15	0.34		0.49
13.	Kurnool	0.36	0.63	0.06	1.05
Telengana					
14.	Mahbubnagar	0.32	0.24	0.03	0.59
15.	Ranga Reddy	0.59	0.28	0.02	0.89
16.	Hyderabad	2.91	2.21		5.12
17.	medak	0.29	0.25		0.54
18.	Nizamabad	0.56	0.32	0.02	0.9
19.	Adilabad	0.22	0.34	0.01	0.57
20.	Karimnagar	0.53	0.21	0.07	0.81
21.	Warangal	0.38	0.46	0.03	0.87
22.	Khammam	0.69	0.24	0.05	0.98
23.	Nalgonda	0.41	0.2	0.04	0.65
	Total	0.71	0.43	0.07	1.21

Source: IHS(1996).

Medical facilities in the private, public as well as voluntary sectors were located mainly in the urban areas. About 80 per cent of total hospital beds in the state were located in the urban areas. When compared to the private sector (78 per cent), the urban concentration was actually more in the public(86 per cent) and voluntary sectors(93 per cent) (Table 6). As a result, the presence of private sector was much stronger in rural areas (72 per cent) when compared to urban areas (56 per cent), although in both the areas the facilities were more in private sector (Table 7).

Table 6. Rural-Urban Distribution of Hospital Beds (In Per Cent)

S.No.	District	Private		Public		Voluntary		Total	
		Rural	Urban	Rural	Urban	Rural	Urban	Rural	Urban
Coastal Andhra		**26.9**	**73.1**	**14.8**	**85.2**	**7.3**	**92.7**	**22.1**	**77.9**
1.	Srikakulam	1.2	98.8	19.6	80.4	0.0	100.0	10.3	89.7
2.	Vizianagaram	0.0	100.0	24.9	75.1	0.0	0.0	19.8	80.2
3.	Visakhapatnam	2.9	97.1	6.0	94.0	0.0	100.0	4.6	95.4
4.	East Godavari	28.4	71.6	6.6	93.4	5.9	94.1	21.9	78.1
5.	West Godavari	37.7	62.3	97.5	2.5	0.0	0.0	45.5	54.5
6.	Krishna	33.5	66.5	9.6	90.4	3.0	97.0	22.5	77.5
7.	Guntur	25.5	74.5	5.2	94.8	11.7	88.3	18.4	81.6
8.	Prakasam	25.8	74.2	15.1	84.9	0.0	100.0	23.5	76.5
9.	Nellore	23.1	76.9	15.5	84.5	14.3	85.7	20.6	79.4
Rayalaseema		**35.7**	**64.3**	**10.2**	**89.8**	**6.5**	**93.5**	**19.2**	**80.8**
10.	Chittoor	17.7	82.3	8.9	91.1	3.8	96.2	10.9	89.1
11.	Cuddapah	3.9	96.1	7.0	93.0	13.7	86.3	6.6	93.4
12.	Ananthapur	26.3	73.7	11.7	88.3			16.2	83.8
13.	Kurnool	100.0	0.0	11.7	88.3	0.0	100.0	41.4	58.6
Telengana		**16.0**	**84.0**	**14.5**	**85.5**	**7.9**	**92.1**	**15.2**	**84.8**
14.	Mahbubnagar	70.9	29.1	26.6	73.4	0.0	100.0	49.2	50.8
15.	Ranga Reddy	16.9	83.1	86.2	13.8	0.0	100.0	38.4	61.6
16.	Hyderabad	0.0	100.0	0.0	100.0	0.0	0.0	0.0	100.0
17.	medak	31.4	68.6	25.1	74.9	0.0	0.0	28.4	71.6
18.	Nizamabad	41.6	58.4	20.2	79.8	0.0	100.0	33.1	66.9
19.	Adilabad	0.0	100.0	26.7	73.3	0.0	100.0	15.9	84.1
20.	Karimnagar	25.7	74.3	33.5	66.5	0.0	100.0	25.6	74.4
21.	Warangal	58.1	41.9	13.8	86.2	0.0	100.0	32.6	67.4
22.	Khammam	8.2	91.8	37.0	63.0	0.0	100.0	14.8	85.2
23.	Nalgonda	25.8	74.2	14.4	85.6	46.8	53.2	23.8	76.2
	Total	21.7	78.3	13.8	86.2	7.2	92.8	17.9	82.1

Source: IHS(1996).

A survey undertaken by the Centre for Economic and Social Studies confirmed these trends in the size of private sector and identified characteristics of medical care at different stages of development (Narayana, 1998). It was a comparative study of public and private hospitals in Eluru, Cuddapah and Mahbubnagar towns that are head quarters of West Godavari, Cuddapah and Mahbubnagar districts respectively. Excluding Hyderabad, West Godavari was ranked second on the index of infrastructure development by the Centre for Monitoring Indian Economy (CMIE, 1992). In contrast, Mahbubnagar was the least developed district with the lowest rank on the CMIE index. Cuddapah was at a medium level with its rank of 15 among the 23 districts in the State. An earlier study on ranking of districts on the basis of overall development also gave similar ranks to these districts (Iyengar and Sudarshan, 1982). A sample of three towns located in three regions (Coastal Andhra, Rayalaseema and

Telengana), which are at widely different levels of development, was purposively selected to observe the emerging pattern in the medical care in the process of development.

Table 7. District wise Rural-Urban Distribution of Hospital Beds

S.No.	District	Rural			Urban		
		Private	Public	Voluntary	Private	Public	Voluntary
Coastal Andhra							
1.	Srikakulam	5.3	94.7		51.0	44.9	4.0
2.	Vizianagaram	0.0	100.0		25.6	74.4	0.0
3.	Visakhapatnam	24.4	75.6		39.0	57.0	4.0
4.	East Godavari	91.2	7.2	1.6	64.3	28.6	7.2
5.	West Godavari	72.3	27.7		99.4	0.6	0.0
6.	Krishna	86.6	11.4	2.0	49.9	31.2	18.9
7.	Guntur	84.1	7.2	8.6	55.5	29.7	14.8
8.	Prakasam	90.7	9.3		79.8	16.0	4.1
9.	Nellore	77.2	17.7	5.1	67.0	25.1	7.9
Rayalaseema							
10.	Chittoor	54.1	39.3	6.6	30.6	49.2	20.2
11.	Cuddapah	30.8	33.3	35.8	52.9	31.3	15.8
12.	Ananthapur	49.8	50.2		26.9	73.1	
13.	Kurnool	83.2	16.8			90.0	
Telengana							
14.	Mahbubnagar	77.8	22.2		30.9	59.2	9.9
15.	Ranga Reddy	29.4	70.6		89.9	7.1	3.0
16.	Hyderabad				56.9	43.1	
17.	medak	58.5	41.5		50.7	49.3	
18.	Nizamabad	78.2	21.8		54.2	42.5	3.3
19.	Adilabad	0.0	100.0		45.7	51.7	2.6
20.	Karimnagar	65.9	34.1		65.4	23.2	11.4
21.	Warangal	77.9	22.1		27.2	67.0	5.8
22.	Khammam	38.9	61.1		75.9	18.1	6.1
23.	Nalgonda	68.8	18.1	13.1	61.7	33.7	4.7
	Total	71.7	26.1	2.2	55.9	37.5	6.5

Source: HIS (1996).

In terms of number of doctors the size of private sector was larger than the public sector in all the towns (Table 8). About 75 per cent of doctors in Eluru and Cuddapah, and a little more than half (57 per cent) of them in Mahbubnagar were in the private sector. In addition, the private sector includes the private practice of doctors in the government service. About 85 per cent of government doctors in all the towns have private practice, mostly clinic based. For instance, the government doctors accounted for about 32 per cent of private clinics and 25 percent of outpatients in Eluru. The proportion of government doctors in the private sector was higher in the less developed towns. In the less developed Mahbubnagar town, the share of government doctors was about 45 percent of private clinics and outpatients (Table 9). In terms of hospital beds, the government sector was still predominant in Mahbubnagar (55 per cent) but its share was reduced to 45 per cent in Cuddapah and 40 per cent in Eluru (Table 8). Thus there was a gradual shift

Table 8. Public and Private Mix in Medical Care

	Eluru			Cuddapah			Mahbubnagar		
	Govt	Private	Total	Govt	Private	Total	Govt	Private	Total
MBBS	21	73	94	17	54	71	16	18	34
MS	9	17	26	6	17	23	5	7	12
MD	5	25	30	5	12	17	6	6	12
BDS	1	5	6	2	5	7	1	5	6
MDS	0	3	3	0	3	3	0	0	0
Total Doctors	36	123	159	30	91	121	28	35	63
Nurses									
a).Trained	73	85	158	82	105	187	52	20	72
b).Un Trained	0	146	146	0	77	77	0	43	43
Male Assistants	28	116	144	9	82	91	5	69	74
Ayas & Sweepers	25	57	82	6	62	68	26	35	61
Other Employees	91	69	160	133	39	172	83	30	113
Lab Technicians	5	45	55	3	64	67	2	26	28
X-Ray Technicians	3	29	34	3	14	17	3	10	13
Beds (No.)	340	509	849	352	434	786	215	165	380
Inpatients (per day)	230	236	466	210	207	417	89	72	161
Out Patients (per day)	1020	2001	3021	795	1927	2722	891	1190	2081

In Percent

	Eluru			Cuddapah			Mahbubnagar		
	Govt	Private	Total	Govt	Private	Total	Govt	Private	Total
MBBS	22.3	77.7	100.0	23.9	76.1	100.0	47.1	52.9	100.0
MS	34.6	65.4	100.0	26.1	73.9	100.0	41.7	58.3	100.0
MD	16.7	83.3	100.0	29.4	70.6	100.0	50.0	50.0	100.0
BDS	16.7	83.3	100.0	28.6	71.4	100.0	16.7	83.3	100.0
MDS	0.0	100.0	100.0	0.0	100.0	100.0	0.0	0.0	0.0
Total Doctors	22.6	77.4	100.0	24.8	75.2	100.0	44.4	55.6	100.0
Nurses									
a). Trained	46.2	53.8	100.0	43.9	56.1	100.0	72.2	27.8	100.0
b). Un Trained		100.0	100.0		100.0	100.0		100.0	100.0
Male Assistants	19.4	80.6	100.0	9.9	90.1	100.0	6.8	93.2	100.0
Ayas&Sweepers	30.5	69.5	100.0	8.8	91.2	100.0	42.6	57.4	100.0
Other Employees	56.9	43.1	100.0	77.3	22.7	100.0	73.5	26.5	100.0
Lab Technicians	9.1	81.8	100.0	4.5	95.5	100.0	7.1	92.9	100.0
X-Ray Technicians	8.8	85.3	100.0	17.6	82.4	100.0	23.1	76.9	100.0
Beds (No.)	40.0	60.0	100.0	44.8	55.2	100.0	56.6	43.4	100.0
Inpatients	49.4	50.6	100.0	50.4	49.6	100.0	55.3	44.7	100.0
Out Patients	38.3	61.7	100.0	31.7	68.3	100.0	46.7	53.3	100.0

in the medical infrastructure towards the private sector with increasing levels of development.

In all the towns, the diagnostic facilities were largely concentrated in the private sector. More than 80 per cent of the laboratory and x-ray technicians were in the private sector (Table 8). A relatively higher proportion of diagnostic facilities when compared to their share in the number of hospital beds and inpatients imply excess capacity and scope for unnecessary testing in the private sector.

Table 9. Number of Clinics Owned by the Govt and Pvt Doctors

	Eluru			Cuddapah			Mahbubnagar		
	Govt Doctors	Private Doctors	Total	Govt Doc-tors	Private Doctors	Total	Govt Doc-tors	Private Doctors	Total
Doctors									
1.MBBS	14	31	45	12	27	39	11	14	5
2.MS	5	3	8	5	7	12	4	2	6
3.MD	2	8	10	5	5	10	5	4	9
4.BDS	2	5	7	2	5	7	1	4	5
5.MDS	0	3	3	0	3	3	0	0	0
Total	23	50	73	24	47	71	21	24	45
Outpatients (Per Day)	295	882	1177	335	795	1130	385	490	875

In Percent

	Eluru			Cuddapah			Mahbubnagar		
	Govt Doctors	Private Doctors	Total	Govt Doc-tors	Private Doctors	Total	Govt Doc-tors	Private Doctors	Total
I. Doctors									
1.MBBS	31.1	68.9	100	30.8	69.2	100	44.0	56.0	100
2.MS	62.5	37.5	100	41.7	58.3	100	66.7	33.3	100
3.MD	20.0	80.0	100	50.0	50.0	100	55.6	44.4	100
4.BDS	28.6	71.4	100	28.6	71.4	100	20.0	80.0	100
5.MDS		100.0	100		100.0	100			
Total	31.5	68.5	100	33.8	66.2	100	46.7	53.3	100
Outpatients (Per Day)	25.1	74.9	100	29.6	70.4	100	44.0	56.0	100

A majority (55 per cent) of trained nurses/paramedicals in Eluru as well as Cuddapah were in the private sector. In the less developed Mahbubnagar, only about 28 per cent of them were in the private sector. However, when compared to its share in number of doctors and beds, the private sector had a low per cent of trained nurses in all the towns. The private hospitals depend more on untrained paramedical personnel, which is not a positive indicator for the quality of care in the private hospitals. Excepting the "Other Employees" consisting of clerical staff, a majority of other menial staff (Male Assistants, Ayas etc.) are in the private sector.

Table 10. Size wise Distribution of Private Hospitals (In Percent)

	Eluru		Cuddapah		Mahbubnagar	
	Hospitals	Beds	Hospitals	Beds	Hospitals	Beds
Bed Size						
<=10	55.9	25.9	48.3	26.7	50.0	18.8
11-20	26.5	29.1	37.9	42.2	30.0	29.7
21-30	8.8	15.5	10.3	19.6	10.0	15.2
Sub Total	**91.2**	**70.5**	**96.6**	**88.5**	**90.0**	**63.6**
31-40	2.9	7.9				
41-50	2.9	9.8	3.4	11.5		
51-60	2.9	11.8			10.0	36.4
Total	100.0	100.0	100.0	100.0	100.0	100.0

No Preference for Private Sector

However, it may be noted that the utilization pattern of public and private hospitals, as indicated by the NSSs and the NFHSs, does not imply any specific preference for private hospitals in AP. The proportion of people going to public and private hospitals broadly corresponds to their bed strength in the state. The private hospitals accounted for about 72 per cent of beds in the rural areas and 56 per cent in the urban areas in 1993(Table 7). The NSS (42nd round) had also shown that the private hospitals accounted for 69 per cent of inpatient care in the rural areas and 58 per cent in the urban areas. Similarly, the NFHS (1992-93) revealed that 58.5 per cent of total births in the hospitals have taken place in the private sector. It is almost equal to the share of the private sector (59 per cent) in the hospital beds in Andhra Pradesh. It is therefore erroneous to cite the NSSs and NFHSs as an indication of people's preference for private sector. It is lack of facilities and poor quality of services in the public sector that may be driving even the poor to the private sector. It doest not imply their preference for and ability to pay for the services in the private sector.

Nature of Private Sector

Although the private sector accounted for a higher per cent of medical facilities in the state, the size of private hospitals was relatively small. In all the towns, the average bed strength of hospitals was about 15 only (Table 12). And, about 90 per cent of the hospitals had bed strength less than 30 (Table 10). Together, the hospitals with less than 30 beds accounted for more than two-thirds of hospital beds in the private sector. The GoAP survey also showed this pattern at the state level. About 66 per cent of beds were located in hospitals with the bed strength of 30 or less (Institute of Health Systems, 1996). In addition, a majority of the private hospitals treat all types of cases and a few were confined to a single speciality. Among various specialisations, the obstetrics in combination with other specialisations was the single largest specialisation in the private sector.

Apart from having a higher number of doctors in the private sector, a majority (about 60 per cent) of the private doctors had hospital-based practice in Eluru (Table 11). In Cuddapah also nearly a half (47.8 per cent) of the doctors were hospital based. In contrast, the private sector in Mahbubnagar was mainly clinic based. Only 31 percent of the private doctors had hospital-based practice. In other words, there was a gradual shift from clinic to hospital-based practice with increase in levels of development.

In all the towns, the doctors with postgraduate degrees tended to have hospital-based practice but the trend was more conspicuous at higher levels of development. On average about 40 per cent of doctors were postgraduates in all the towns but the per cent of postgraduate doctors with hospital-based practice was very high in Eluru (75.6) when compared to Cuddapah (58.6) and Mahbubnagar (53.8). Hence in Eluru, the most developed town, the private sector is predominantly hospital based and specialists oriented.

The differences in the composition of private medical sector were also reflected in the average number of outpatients treated at hospitals and clinics. The private sector accounted for a high per cent of outpatients in all the towns but the proportion of outpatients treated at hospitals in Eluru and Cuddapah (41 per cent) was higher when compared to and Mahbubnagar (26.5 per cent). Thus, there was a gradual shift in the outpatient care from clinics to hospitals with the increase in the levels of development. The higher share of hospitals in the outpatient care within the private sector in AP was reported in the NSS 42nd survey also.

About 90 per cent of the hospitals in these towns were family owned and headed by a single doctor or doctor-couples. However, the per cent of hospitals jointly headed by the doctor-couples was increasing with increasing levels of development (Narayana, 1998). In Eluru, 41 per cent of hospitals were headed by the doctor-couples as against 31 per cent in Cuddapah and 10 per cent in Mahbubnagar. Perhaps it indicates that the private hospitals are turning into family enterprises in the small towns in the developed regions.

Corporatisation of Medical Care

The growing capital intensity in medical technology, requiring huge capital investments, has been encouraging corporatisation of medical care. The private nursing homes owned by the individual doctor-entrepreneurs are not in

Table 11. Nature of Private Sector

	Eluru				Cuddapah				Mahbubnagar			
	Hospitals	Clinics	D.C's	Total	Hospitals	Clinics	D.C's	Total	Hospitals	Clinics	D.C's	Total
MBBS	42	31	0	73	27	27	0	54	4	14	0	18
MS	14	3	0	17	8	7	0	15	5	2	0	7
MD	17	8	0	25	7	5	0	12	2	4	0	6
BDS	0	5	0	5	1	5	0	6	0	4	0	4
MDS	0	3	0	3	0	3	0	3	0	0	0	0
Total	73	50	0	123	43	47	0	90	11	24	0	35
Nurses												
Trained	73	12	0	85	105	0	0	105	19	1	0	20
Un Trained	77	69	0	146	18	59	0	77	14	29	0	43
Male Assistants	53	63	0	116	22	49	11	82	30	39	0	69
Ayas&Sweepers	52	5	0	57	58	4	0	62	19	16	0	35
Other Employees	39	14	16	69	28	11	0	39	5	20	5	30
Lab Technicians	5	0	40	45	30	8	26	64	3	0	23	26
X-Ray Technicians	3	0	26	29	8	1	5	14	2	0	8	10
Beds(No.)	509	0	0	509	434	0	0	434	165	0	0	165
Out Patients (Per Day)	824	1177	0	2001	797	1130	0	1927	315	875	0	1190

In Percent

	Eluru				Cuddapah				Mahbubnagar			
	Hospitals	Clinics	D.C's	Total	Hospitals	Clinics	D.C's	Total	Hospitals	Clinics	D.C's	Total
MBBS	57.5	42.5		100	50.0	50.0		100	22.2	77.8		100
MS	82.4	17.6		100	53.3	46.7		100	71.4	28.6		100
MD	68.0	32.0		100	58.3	41.7		100	33.3	66.7		100
BDS		100		100	16.7	83.3		100		100		100
MDS		100		100		100		100				
Total Doctors	59.3	40.7		100	47.8	52.2		100	31.4	68.6		100
Nurses												
Trained	85.9	14.1		100	100.0			100	95.0	5.0		100
Un Trained	52.7	47.3		100	23.4	76.6		100	32.6	67.4		100
Male Assistants	45.7	54.3		100	26.8	59.8	13.4	100	43.5	56.5		100
Ayas&Sweepers	91.2	8.8		100	93.5	6.5		100	54.3	45.7		100
Other Employees	56.5	20.3	23.2	100	71.8	28.2		100	16.7	66.7	16.7	100
Lab Technicians	11.1		88.9	100	46.9	12.5	40.6	100	11.5		88.5	100
X-Ray Technicians	10.3		89.7	100	57.1	7.1	35.7	100	20.0		80.0	100
Beds(No.)	100			100	100			100	100			100
Out Patients	41.2	58.8		100	41.4	58.6		100	26.5	73.5		100

a position to generate necessary investments. It required a large-scale mobilization of resources from financial institutions, public etc., and the corporate hospitals are mobilising resources through promoters' share capital, borrowing from financial institutions and the share market. The state also played a very active role in the corporatisation of medical care by extending financial and other benefits.

The corporate phenomenon in medical care in Andhra Pradesh began with the establishment of a multi-specialty diagnostic centre (Medinova) with outpatient consultancy by a local pharmaceutical company in 1985. In the hospital sector, the corporate phenomenon began with the establishment of Apollo Hospital in the state capital in 1989 by the Non-Resident Indian (NRI) doctors from USA. The state government encouraged the corporatisation of medical care by providing government land while the central government offered tax concessions on import of medical equipment. The existing corporate hospitals are opened by the doctors (either NRI or local) and local business families. All of them are promoted by the local dominant agricultural castes (Kamma, Raju, Reddy and Velama) and most of them are family controlled and managed by their family members who are doctors by profession.

There is no study yet on the exact size and nature of the corporate sector. There are about 6 big corporate hospitals in Hyderabad. In recent years, the corporate phenomenon is spreading fast through acquisition of medium level private hospitals by the corporate hospitals. For instance, the Apollo hospital has acquired four private hospitals located in different parts of Hyderabad. Similarly, the CDR hospital has established a number of emergency medical centres in different localities in Hyderabad. It is basically intended to widen the catchment area to ensure steady flow of patients for its main super speciality hospital for high tech treatment. The corporate hospitals are spreading their network also by giving franchise to small diagnostic centres, speciality clinics and pharmaceutical stores. Similarly, the Medinova diagnostic centre has established its branches in a large number of towns in the state. The corporate hospitals have also come up in agriculturally prosperous towns like Vijayawada and in the port city of Visakhapatnam. They too have their own referral centres in the neighbouring towns. In addition, a good number of specialists from Hyderabad visit clinics and hospitals in the towns every weekend and refer complicated cases to the super speciality hospitals with which they are associated in the city.

There is also a trend towards trans-nationalisation of corporate hospitals. For instance, the Apollo hospital has a tie-up with a Singaporean Health Group in a joint-venture company to undertake management of hospitals in the south and Southeast Asia. While the Parkway Health Group of Singapore takes the responsibility to secure the contracts for hospital management, the Apollo would supply doctors, nurses, engineers etc. to manage hospitals that would be under their contract. The basic objective is to take advantage of India's medical manpower that is far less expensive when compared to US and Europe. Recently, the Apollo group has established a hospital in Colombo, capital of Srilanka.

2. ORIGINS AND GROWTH OF PRIVATE SECTOR

Although the origin of private sector in AP can be traced even to pre-independence days in the state, the real spurt in the growth of private hospitals occurred mainly in the 1980's and the 1990's. About 75 to 90 per cent of existing hospitals in Eluru, Cuddapah and Mahbubnagar were established during the last two decades (Table-12). The growth of private diagnostic centers is an even more recent phenomenon; most of them were established only during 1990s.

The government has been responsible for encouraging the growth of private sector indirectly by neglecting the quality and quantity of services in the government hospitals and directly by providing subsidies, tax concession etc. to the private hospitals. During 1980s there was a marked shift in the government policy in the health sector. In the Health Policy Document (1982), the state had given up its proclaimed objective to meet the health care targets on its own (Ministry of Health and Family Welfare, 1981). Instead, it started emphasizing the role of private sector and non-government organisations in achieving the objectives in the health sector. The main factors responsible for the rapid growth of private hospitals in the state are analysed below.

Stagnation in Expansion of the Public Hospitals

Expansion of facilities in the public sector did not keep pace with the increase in population. It resulted in excess load on the public health care system and decline in its quality. The shortfall in the quantity as well quality of services had provided tremendous opportunities for the growth of private sector.

The availability of hospital beds in the public sector had declined from 6.2 beds per 10,000 population in 1961 to 4.8 beds during 1970s and 1980s and 5.1 beds in 1990s (GoAP, Annual Series). The inadequacy of facilities in the public sector was further worsened by the lopsided distribution of medical facilities and public expenditure between the primary, secondary and tertiary hospitals. Keeping in view the inpatient load at different levels, the Planning Commission (the seventh five-year Plan) suggested 70 per cent of hospital beds at the secondary level and 15 per cent each at the primary and the tertiary hospitals (Government of India, Planning Commission, 1985). However, the secondary level hospitals have only 30 per cent of total beds.

Table 12. Establishment of Private Medical Facilities

Period	Hospitals and Beds						Diagnostic Centers		
	Eluru		Cuddapah		Mahbubnagar		Eluru	Cuddapah	Mbnagar
	Hospitals	Beds	Hospitals	Beds	Hospitals	Beds			
1950s			1	4					
1960s	4	65	1	50				1	
1970s	3	72	5	86	1	25		1	2
Sub Total	7	137	7	136	1	25		2	2
1980s	12	215	7	103	6	101	7	8	2
1990s	15	157	15	191	3	39	17	41	11
Total	34	509	29	434	10	165	24	51	15

In Percent

Period	Hospitals and Beds						Diagnostic Centers		
	Eluru		Cuddapah		Mahbubnagar		Eluru	Cuddapah	Mbnagar
	Hospitals	Beds	Hospitals	Beds	Hospitals	Beds			
1950s			3.4	0.9					
1960s	11.8	12.8	3.4	11.5					
1970s	8.8	14.1	17.2	19.8	10.0	15.2		2.0	13.3
Sub Total	20.6	26.9	24.1	31.3	10.0	15.2		2.0	13.3
1980s	35.3	42.2	24.1	23.7	60.0	61.2	29.2	15.7	13.3
1990s	44.1	30.8	51.7	44.0	30.0	23.6	70.8	80.4	73.3
Total	100.0	100.0	100.0	100.0	100.0	100.0	100.0	100.0	100.0

Source: K.V.Narayana (1998).

The government has been responsible for encouraging the growth of private sector indirectly by neglecting the quality and quantity of services in the government hospitals and directly by providing subsidies, tax concession etc. to the private hospitals. During 1980s there was a marked shift in the government policy in the health sector. In the Health Policy Document (1982), the state had given up its proclaimed objective to meet the health care targets on its own. Instead, it started emphasizing the role of private sector and non-government organisations in achieving the objectives in the health sector. The main factors responsible for the rapid growth of private hospitals in the state are analysed below.

The problem of overcrowding was further worsened by the failure of referral mechanism in the public health care system. Due to uncertainty in the availability of staff and medicines at the Primary Health Centres (PHCs), the patients go directly to the first referral (district and area/sub-divisional hospitals) and teaching hospitals even for the minor health problems. It is the overcrowding of the hospitals in the urban centres which had created vast demand for the private hospitals/ nursing homes from the urban middle classes.

Decrease in Allocations to Health Sector

The overall decline in the share of the health sector in the government budget, particularly after the initiation of Structural Adjustment Programme (SAP), has further worsened the scarcity of resources in the health sector.

The share of the health sector in the state budget was highest (6.5 per cent) in the 5th FY Plan. Thereafter it declined continuously and fell to 5.2 per cent in the 8th FY Plan(Table 13). The

Table 13. Share of Social and Economic Services in Public Expenditure (In Percent)

Year	Health Services	Social Services	Economic Services	Total Expenditure
5th FY Plan (1974-79)	6.5	34.2	42.9	100
1979-80	5.9	35.6	42.7	100
6th FY Plan (1980-85)	6.2	40.1	37.9	100
7th FY Plan (1985-90)	5.8	38.0	38.4	100
1990-91	5.6	36.2	37.5	100
1991-92	5.6	35.2	37.3	100
8th Plan (1992-97)	5.2	34.3	37.5	100
1997-98	5.4	35.5	33.3	100
1998-99	5.7	39.2	29.7	100
1999-00	5.8	37.7	28.0	100
2000-01	5.0	32.2	33.8	100

Source: Govt of AP, Budget Estimates, Detailed Demands of Grants.

share of the health sector declined even in the 6th and 7th FY Plans in which the aggregate share of social services increased. In fact, the share of social services was more than the share of economic services in the 7th FY Plan. The allocation to health sector remained low in the 1990s also.

At constant (1993-94) prices, the per capita public expenditure on health care was about Rs.58 during the Fifth five-year Plan (Table-14). It increased by about 45 percent in the next two five-year plans and reached Rs.85 per capita during the seventh five-year Plan (1985-1990). However, the 1990s witnessed a sudden fall in the per capita public expenditure on health care and other services. It declined from Rs.85 in the 7th plan to Rs.73 in the 8th plan. When compared to the economic services, the social services experienced a steep fall in public expenditure. Within the social services, the decline was more in the case of health care. It clearly indicates adverse impact of the SAP on the provision of health and other social services.

Moreover, there was a continuous increase in the share of salaries in the hospital budgets from about 52 per cent in 1974 to 80 per cent in 1995 which left very meagre resources for the supply of materials and maintenance of the infrastructure (Table-15). The decline in allocations to

Table-14. Per Capita Net SDP and Public Expenditure in AP at 1993-94 Prices

(In Rs.)

Year	Health Services	Social Services	Economic Services	Total Expenditure	SDP
5th FY Plan (1974-79)	58	304	381	888	5306
1979-80	66	402	481	1128	5508
6th FY Plan (1980-85)	75	480	454	1197	5999
7th FY Plan (1985-90)	85	558	565	1470	6526
1990-91	75	488	506	1350	7050
1991-92	72	463	492	1318	7164
8th Plan (1992-97)	73	487	533	1420	7695
1997-98	79	515	483	1451	7964
1998-99	88	607	453	1550	8790
1999-00	93	605	451	1610	8980
2000-01	97	627	658	1945	9386

Source: 1. Govt of AP, Budget Estimates, Detailed Demands of Grants.
2. Bureau of Economics and Statistics (AP), Estimates of SDP.

Table 15. Public Expenditure on Secondary Hospitals (In Percent)

Plan/year	Salaries	Materials &Supplies	Others	Total
Vth Plan(1974-78)	51.7	32.5	15.8	100.0
(1979-80)	54.1	30.9	14.9	100.0
VIth Plan(1980-84)	59.2	27.8	13.0	100.0
VIIth Plan(1985-89)*	61.4	30.2	8.4	100.0
1990-91*	67.8	17.8	14.3	100.0
1991-92	68.3	18.6	13.1	100.0
1992-93	73.1	18.2	8.7	100.0
1993-94	74.4	15.1	10.5	100.0
1994-95	78.4	11.7	10.0	100.0
1995-96	75.5	11.3	13.2	100.0

* Excluding Grants to APVVP.

the medical supplies and maintenance has contributed to faster degeneration in the quality of treatment in the public hospitals.

Prior to the Structural Adjustment Programme (SAP), there was increase in the ratio of public expenditure on the health sector in the State Domestic Product (SDP), in spite of decrease in allocations to health in the state budget, because of overall increase in the size of state budget. The share of health sector in SDP increased from 1.09 per cent in the 5th plan to 1.29 per cent in the 7th plan (Table 16). During the 6th and 7th FY Plans the share of Social Services was actually higher than the share of Economic Services. However, with the beginning of SAP in 1990s there was a sudden decline in the share of social sectors including health. The proportion of public expenditure on the health sector to the SDP declined from 1.29 per cent in the 7th FY Plan to 0.94 in the 8th FY Plan. Thus, after the beginning of SAP, there was decline in the allocations to health services despite all the talk of safety net.

Table 16. Share of Public Expenditure in SDP (In Percent)

Year	Health Services	Social Services	Economic Services	Total Expenditure
5th FY Plan (1974-79)	1.09	5.7	7.2	16.8
1979-80	1.20	7.3	8.7	20.5
6th FY Plan (1980-85)	1.25	8.1	7.6	20.2
7th FY Plan (1985-90)	1.29	8.5	8.5	22.3
1990-91	1.06	6.9	7.2	19.1
1991-92	1.00	6.5	6.9	18.4
8th Plan (1992-97)	0.94	6.3	6.9	18.4
1997-98	0.99	6.5	6.1	18.2
1998-99	1.00	6.9	5.2	17.6
1999-00	1.04	6.7	5.0	17.9
2000-01	1.03	6.7	7.0	20.7

Source: 1.Govt of AP, Budget Estimates, Detailed Demands of Grants.
2. Bureau of Economics and Statistics (AP), Estimates of SDP.

Encouragement to Private Sector

The growth of private hospitals and diagnostic centres was encouraged directly by the Central and State governments by offering tax exemptions, land at concession rates etc. in return for provision of free treatment for the poor: free treatment to at least 40 percent of outpatients and 10 percent of inpatients. Apart from availing the tax concessions, some hospitals received special benefits like allotment of government land at an insignificant part of market price. For instance, in 1989 a corporate hospital in Hyderabad was given 30 acres of government land in a posh locality at a throw away price on the condition of reserving additional 15 percent of beds for the poor.

In 1995, the A P Legislative Assembly had appointed a House Committee to find out whether or not the corporate hospitals, private nursing homes and other medical centres honoured the conditions (i.e., free treatment to the poor) imposed for granting tax concessions, exemptions and other benefits (Andhra Pradesh Legislative Assembly, 1996). The committee was also to examine the efforts made by the concerned authorities in seeking the compliance of these conditions and to make suitable recommendations to regulate the private medical establishments in future.

The Committee found that "most of the Corporate Hospitals who have availed the benefit of customs duty exemption were not treating the poor patients free of cost". The State Government was equally lax about implementing the conditions on the private hospitals. "The Committee observed that there was no check as to whether the Apollo Hospital was adhering to the condition of 15 percent of the beds to be reserved to the poor for free treatment. All these years, there was no check and no one was made responsible. The committee was at a loss to understand on the failure of the State Government in implementing the conditions." It appears that neither the private hospitals nor the government were serious about the provision of free service to the poor. It was only a ploy to dole out these benefits to the private sector.

Apart from subsidies, the private corporate hospitals receive huge amounts of public funds in the form of reimbursements from the public sector undertakings, the state and the central governments (eg.CGHS) for treating their employees. Another major source of revenue is the inflated and fraudulent claims from the public insurance companies under various medical insurance schemes.

Lack of Regulation

The lack of government or any other regulation on the minimum standards in terms of staff, facilities etc. and on the pricing of services in the private hospitals has contributed to the rapid expansion of private sector in medical care. Having no controls on its size, quality and pricing, the medical care became a very attractive outlet for private investment.

Before the era of reform that began in 1991, the public sector dominance and pervasive controls over the private sector were the key elements in the development strategy of India. Yet, the private medical care remained beyond the purview of any regulation for more than 4 decades during which the private sector achieved "Commanding Heights" of medical care industry in the country.

Realising that the State Government has no control over the private hospitals, the House Committee recommended a comprehensive legislation on nursing homes, diagnostic centres etc. To curb the practice of unnecessary investigations and prescription of drugs in the private sector, the Committee recommended preparation of "Clinical Manuals" in consultation with the Medical Council of India and other professional bodies. The Committee also suggested a law prescribing minimum standards in terms of buildings, equipment, medical staff etc. for private hospitals and a mechanism to enforce those standards. The legislation was also intended to ensure that all private hospitals maintain inpatient and outpatient registers and case sheets which should be given to the patient at the time of discharge.

Recently, the state legislative assembly passed a bill to regulate the private sector in medical care but not yet operationalised it. It appears that the government does not have either the will or ability to regulate the private practice in medical care.

Role of Public Sector

Like in other areas of economy, the establishment of public sector laid foundation for the growth of private sector in medical care. The establishment of public hospitals generally preceded the growth of private medical care and in many towns its origin can be traced to the private practice of government doctors. While most of the government doctors have private clinics, some of them are also involved in establishment of private hospitals and diagnostic centres. A good number of private hospitals in small towns still belong the doctors who were or are in the government service.

In addition, the public investment in free medical education has created a vast network of medical professionals who provided basis for the expansion of the private sector.

Impact of Urbanization

Rapid urbanization, expansion of middle class with higher purchasing power and growing health awareness have together provided necessary conditions for the rise of private sector in medical care. Urbanisation, accompanied by the increase in size of middle classes, created market for the medical care.

3. IMPACT OF PRIVATE SECTOR ON PUBLIC HOSPITALS

The state's patronage to the private sector is sometimes justified on the ground that it would ease out pressure on the government hospitals. But in reality, the private hospitals are replacing rather than complementing the public hospitals by weaning away the resources from the government hospitals. The adverse impact of privatization on public hospitals is identified in the following subsections.

Lack of Patronage to Public Hospitals

With the large-scale expansion of private health care in 1980s and 1990s, the rich and middle classes no longer go to the government hospitals. The public hospitals are used mostly by the poor at present (Mahaptra et al, 2002: P.43 and GoAP, 2001). While the rich have deserted the government hospitals in favour of the corporate hospitals, the middle classes rely on the small private hospitals. As a consequence, the public hospitals are facing unfair competition in mobilising resources since the state (politicians and bureaucrats) is more interested in extending facilities to the private, mainly corporate, hospitals.

Apart from depravation of resources, the day-to-day maintenance of public hospitals is also neglected. Whenever public services (hospitals, schools etc) are used exclusively by the poor, the quality of services tend to degenerate due to lack of resources and effective supervision

Since public hospitals are used exclusively by the poor, there is little scope for generating additional resources through user charges. The growth of private corporate hospitals was found to have adverse impact on the demand for paid wards in the government hospitals, particularly the teaching hospitals. The bed occupancy in the paying wards was only about 35 per cent in the Osmania Hospital (Prasad, 1995). In the past, there used to be waiting lists for paying wards in the same hospitals.

Luring away Specialists from Public Hospitals

A study of public and corporate hospitals found that the popularity and use of corporate hospitals depend mainly on the reputation of individual doctors (Prasad, 1995). The patients still choose the doctors, not the hospitals. As a result, there is severe competition between the corporate hospitals to attract the reputed specialists by offering higher remuneration, better service conditions etc. In the process, many reputed specialists are lured away from the government teaching hospitals and the shortage of specialists has further adverse impact on the image of government hospitals.

While the big corporate hospitals offer attractive service conditions for the senior specialists, the junior doctors, nurses and other staff have low salaries, long working hours and no job security. The junior doctors prefer government service on account of job security, better working conditions, diversified experience i.e. greater exposure to a variety of cases. Once they gain enough experience in the government hospitals, the corporate hospitals lure them away with better salaries and service conditions. The government sector has thus become a cheap source of well-trained specialists for the corporate hospitals.

Transfer of Critical Cases from Private to Public Hospitals

Public hospitals are used by the private hospitals for dumping unwanted cases. The private hospitals transfer serious/terminal cases to the government hospitals to avoid medico-legal problems and to maintain the image of being efficient. Even the super-specialty corporate hospitals transfer terminal cases, AIDS patients etc. to the government hospitals. The problem has become widespread after the extension of Consumer Protection Act to the medical care in recent years. As a consequence, the public hospitals face the problem of adverse case mix, apart from overcrowding.

Growing Capital Intensity, Cost Escalation and Supplier Induced Demand

With privatization and corporatisation, the medical care became very capital intensive and added to escalation of cost inflation in the medical sector. Because of growing competition in the private sector, there is excess investment in diagnostic and other equipment to attract patients. The government policy of tax exemptions on import of medical equipment and easy loans from public financial institutions has further encouraged the capital intensity and excess supply in the private sector. This in turn led to unnecessary tests and treatment to recover huge investments on the equipment. It was found that between the public and private hospitals, the latter have a higher proportion of Caesarian deliveries. In Eluru, Cuddapah and Mahbubnagar towns, the incidence of the Caesarian operations in the private hospitals was about 16 per cent higher than that in the public hospitals (Narayana, 1998). The problem of supplier-induced demand has become so rampant that the state unit of Indian Medical Council publicly warned the private hospitals against the unnecessary tests and surgeries.

4. REFORMS IN PUBLIC HEALTH SECTOR

With the avowed objective to improve the financial viability and quality of care in the public hospitals the State Government initiated a series of reforms, mainly at the secondary and primary levels. To begin with the reforms were introduced on its own but later on the reforms were initiated and guided mainly by the World Bank. The following sections describe reforms in the public hospitals at the secondary and primary levels.

The Andhra Pradesh Vaidya Vidhana Parishad

The scarcity of funds and declining standards in the government hospitals led to the creation of the Andhra Pradesh Vaidya Vidhana Parishad (APVVP), an autonomous Commission for the management of secondary level hospitals in 1986. The objective was to grant financial and administrative autonomy to the secondary hospitals. Autonomy to the hospitals was aimed at reducing the financial burden on the government through more efficient use of existing resources and mobilising additional resources. It is also expected to improve the quality of care and patient satisfaction in the public hospitals.

As a part of financial autonomy, the APVVP is empowered to receive funds and donations from general public and financial institutions. Apart from receiving grants-in-aid from the state government, it is empowered to take loans from domestic and foreign financial institutions and collect user charges for diagnostic and treatment services. It can even construct and maintain commercial complexes in the hospital premises, and organise lotteries to achieve financial self-sufficiency.

To provide administrative autonomy, the Commission is empowered to make its own rules and regulations in running the secondary hospitals. However, all the new rules and regulations are to be placed before the State Legislative Assembly for its ratification and in case of any dispute between the Government and Commissionerate, the former would prevail. In practice, such clauses nullified the very objective of autonomy and reduced the APVVP to one among many other government agencies.

In spite of limited autonomy, the APVVP seems to have achieved considerable improvement in the functioning of public hospitals at the secondary level (Chawla, no date). Creation of a single apex agency is credited with elimination of bureaucratic delays in getting sanctions from the State Secretariat. It is also supposed to have improved the medical supplies and maintenance of diagnostic equipment and other infrastructure facilities.

However, the APVVP failed in achieving two of its basic objectives: recruitment of independent staff on contract basis and financial independence. One of the objectives of APVVP was to introduce flexible manpower policy based on contract system. The APVVP has legal authority to recruit its staff, independent of the Department of Health, Medical and Family Welfare (DHMFW), but in practice it faced many hurdles. The APVVP tried to recruit staff on contract basis but could not sustain due to internal resistance. The doctors complained about the feeling of insecurity, discrepancy in the service conditions between the existing and newly recruited staff etc. Finally, the newly recruited doctors were absorbed by the DHMFW and the APVVP does not have any doctors on its own.

A major objective in establishing the APVVP was to introduce user charges. However, the matter was so sensitive politically that the first commissioner of APVVP was sacked within three months by the government for announcing the introduction of user charges which created furore in the State Legislative Assembly. Other financial proposals also did not materialise. As a result, the revenue receipts remained an insignificant part of its expenditure that is financed mostly from the block grants from the state government. The financial self-sufficiency of the APVVP is very doubtful because there is very limited scope for raising revenues through user charges.

Andhra Pradesh First Referral Health Systems Project (1995-2002)

With the aid from World Bank, the Andhra Pradesh First Referral Health System (APFRHS) Project was launched to introduce reforms at the secondary level hospitals that are under the management of APVVP (World Bank, 1994). Apart from renovating and upgrading the secondary level hospitals through huge investments (US $159 million/Rs.6.08 billion, 90 percent of which is funded by the IDA) in civil works, medical equipment, additional staff and medical supplies, the project aims at introducing major changes in the health policy and institutional structures.

The major policy changes proposed in the health policy include the introduction of user charges at secondary hospitals, contracting out supportive services and shift in allocations from the tertiary to secondary level hospitals. To strengthen the policy development capacity it proposed a Strategic Planning Cell in the Health Department to organise workshops and seminars, and commission studies on key issues like implementation of cost recovery mechanisms in public hospitals, and cost effectiveness of public health intervention.

Under the institutional development, the basic of objective of the World Bank Project is to secure complete autonomy to the APVVP in introducing user charges, contracting out supportive services, recruitment of staff on contract basis etc. As a part of the project, the APVVP is revising all employment regulations and seeking the government approval to implement them. The project envisages that the state government would revise all cadre regulations and transfer all staff to APVVP.

The APFRHS project stipulates introduction of user charges to recover at least the non-salary component of incremental recurrent costs. It is estimated that the expansion of beds and improvements in the quality of care would result in additional recurrent costs of Rs.300 million per annum. It is aimed at recovering Rs.45 to Rs.55 million per annum or 15-18 percent of incremental recurrent costs. It is also proposed to decide the extent and level of user charges on the basis of cost effectiveness of medical interventions: to impose user charges on the services which are low in cost-effectiveness and subsidise the ones high in cost-effective procedures.

The project approach represents two major shifts in the health policy. Firstly, the shift in emphasis from the incidence of disease to economic burden of disease in setting health sector priorities. The cost-effectiveness of health interventions was assessed in terms of gains in the Disability Adjusted Life Years (DALYs). In other words, the economic value of people is taken into consideration in the provision of health services. Any emphasis on investment aspects of health care would go against the interests of the poor and socially disadvantaged groups, whose productivity levels tend to be low due to lack of adequate access to education, nutrition, health care etc. In other words the DALY based health policy would perpetuate the vicious circle of poverty. One of the basic objectives of free medical care is to reduce distributional inequalities through creation of human capital among the poorer sections of population.

Second, the project lays emphasis on greater role for market forces in the health care provision. The ultimate objective of World Bank-sponsored health sector reforms in the third world countries is to increase the role of market forces in the health care provision by introducing user charges and contracting out of services in the public hospitals and by encouraging the growth of private sector. It is assumed that by providing an efficient public health care system at the secondary level, the World Bank aided project "would encourage a greater participation of the private sector in health care through improved functioning of referral mechanisms" (World Bank, 1994). The project proposes incentives, financial schemes and training to private providers in order to encourage them in case-finding, referral treatment etc. Apart from extending patronage to the private sector, the project introduces market mechanism in the public sector. Introduction of paid wards and user charges in the general wards in the APVVP hospitals is one of the preconditions in the project. It also encourages contracting out of supportive services to the private sector with the assumption of increasing efficiency and reducing costs. Even in deciding the range and level of services in the APVVP hospitals, the "availability and accessibility of alternate sources of equivalent services" is to be taken into account. In other words, the project is safeguarding the interests of the private hospitals by not creating similar facilities in the public hospitals.

The APFRHS Project represents the first reform-based lending of World Bank to the health sector in the country and a major policy initiative in the health sector. It appears that the main reason for selecting A.P. is the existence of an autonomous organisation, APVVP, to manage secondary level hospitals in the state. In spite of severe restriction on its autonomy in the day to day functioning, the very existence of a corporate entity is seen as an opportunity to implement its agenda of reforms in the state and extend it subsequently to other states. "While APVVP functions in effect like a Directorate within the Department of Health, Medical and Family Welfare, the use of a corporate vehicle provides significant potential for non-governmental participation in the health sector. The flexible organisational structure of APVVP has not been adequately utilized in the past. The proposed project would make it possible to fully use the organisational flexibility assigned to APVVP through investments in first referral facilities" (World Bank 1994: p.71). It is with this intention that the APVVP is given central role in implementing the project and intends to secure complete autonomy for APVVP from the state government.

Primary Health Care Project 1998-2002 AD

The GoAP has initiated reforms at the level of primary health care also as a part of the World Bank sponsored A.P. Economic Restructuring Project (APERP) which encompass reforms in primary education, nutrition, irrigation, communications and the state administration (GoAP, 1998). The total estimated cost of the primary care project is $76.5 million of which $62.2 million would be financed by the World Bank. About 70 per cent of the project cost is meant for the civil works and 30 per cent for the capacity and institution building (22 per cent) and community participation (8 per cent). The basic objective of project is to integrate the primary health care with the first referral hospitals, which are already subjected to major reforms under APFRHS project. The reforms at the primary care are expected to add value to investment at the secondary level by strengthening the referral system and reducing the patient-load at the secondary hospitals.

The primary health care project has 3 components. First, strengthening the institutional capacity at the state, district and PHC. Second, upgrading the primary health care facilities by constructing/renovating the PHC buildings. Third, enhancing community participation through IEC and other innovative schemes including health care delivery through the private sector. The proclaimed objectives of project are improving the quality and effectiveness of health services at the primary care level and improving its accessibility to under-served population.

At present there are about 1335 PHCs in the state. The project aims at upgrading 500 existing PHCs to provide enhanced service package consisting of prenatal and delivery care, family planning services, management of sick children etc., which require the presence of doctor. The project aims at running the remaining PHCs with the help of paramedical personnel. About 100 upgraded PHCs would work round the clock to improve access to outpatient care and maternity services.

Indirectly, the project aims at enhancing the space for the growth of private sector. It criticises the existing population norms in locating PHCs and proposes to take into account the availability of private services. The project discourages the up-gradation of PHCs where there are private facilities and wants to gradually reduce the availability of doctors at PHCs in places where there are private doctors.

5. CONCLUSION

Andhra Pradesh in one of the few states where the private sector in medical care has outgrown the size of public sector through direct and indirect state patronage. The financial incentives to the private sector and overcrowding at the public hospitals have created conditions for the rapid growth of private hospitals in the state. Further, absence any control on the quality as well as pricing has made the medical care a very attractive source of investment for the private capital. The private sector consists mainly of small hospitals owned by the individual doctors/doctor-couples but the corporate phenomenon is gradually spreading in the state. In achieving the predominant position, the private sector, mainly the corporate segment, has exploited all the financial and other incentives offered by the state but did not honour the precondition of providing free medical care to the poor. Because of growing criticism against the misuse of incentives by the corporate hospitals, tax exemptions on the imported medical equipment were withdrawn recently. However, the corporate hospitals still siphon of huge amounts of public resources through inflated bills for the treatment of employees in the government and public sector undertakings, medical insurance claims from public sector insurance companies and through income tax concessions by registering themselves as trusts and research centers. The past experience shows that the poor did not benefit from the huge amounts of public resources doled out to the private hospitals. The state should withdraw all financial incentives, including the reimbursement facility, to the private providers. Any attempts at partnership with the private sector are bound to be detrimental to the public sector. The private sector in medical care forms a very strong bureaucratic and political lobby and would manipulate the state and further weaken the public health care system by draining out the resources. Immediate attention of the government should be on enforcing the provision of free care to the poor by the private hospitals, which utilized the financial incentives, land grants etc. Otherwise, the public policy towards the private sector should confine to the regulation of quality and pricing of medical care. The professional bodies like Indian Medical Association and Indian Medical Council have been acting more like trade unions of doctors and did not safeguard the interests of public. And, given the experience with 'the license raj', the direct state regulation might not improve the situation. Instead, the state should create independent regulatory institutions with representation to all stakeholders like consumer societies, NGOs, government officials, private medical establishments etc. to ensure basic standards in the quality and pricing of medical care. The state legislature has recently enacted a law to create regulatory framework for private medical establishments but the operational guidelines are not yet finalized.

Due to lack of adequate resources, there was stagnation in the size and degeneration in the quality of care at the public hospitals. With the initiation of the SAP in 1990s, there was further decline in per capita public expenditure on health services. The growth of private sector has also weakened the position of public hospitals in resource mobilisation because the state patronage is shifted to the corporate hospitals, which are increasingly used by the policy makers. However, it may be noted that the high proportion of outpatient and inpatient treatment in the private sector in the state does not anyway indicate the underutilization of public hospitals. In fact, there is overcrowding and more than full capacity utilization of public hospitals, particularly the maternity and children's wards. There is still widespread unmet demand for medical care among the poor and the government should expand facilities in the public sector to meet this demand. The recent investments in the secondary level hospitals had perceptible improvement in the quality of care and attracting more and more patients particularly from the poorer sections of population. However, the improvements in the secondary hospitals may not be sustainable unless the government is willing to bear the additional expenditure from its general revenues. Financing of even a part of additional recurring expenditure through user charges, which is visualized in the reforms project, may not be achieved. Since a great majority of the patients in the government hospitals are desperately poor and not in a position to bear even the minimal indirect expenditure on travel, medicines etc., the feasibility of user charges is very doubtful. The APVVP studies reported that only 7 percent of the patients were pink ration cardholders people above poverty line and the remaining were either white ration card holders (about 75 percent) or have no ration card, most of whom are likely from the poorer sections of population. The possibility of bringing back the well-to-do patients to the public hospitals through improved quality is also unlikely. The paid wards in the secondary level hospitals, which are created as a part of the World Bank project, are mostly unoccupied.

At present the public sector investment in the medical care is very meager. It accounts for about 1 percent of SDP and its share in the total health expenditure incurred together by the state and households in the state was less than 25 percent ((Central Statistical Organisation, 1986-87 and 1993-94). In the OECD countries the state accounts for about 90 of total health expenditure. The basic need is to increase the allocations to the health sector in the state budget. In addition, instead of paying huge sums of money to the corporate hospitals, the government should restrict the reimbursement facility to the government hospitals and invest these resources to improve the facilities in the public hospitals. It would augment the resources in the government hospitals and the presence of senior bureaucrats and politicians would create pressures to improve the quality of care in these hospitals. It might attract the well-to-do sections of population and provide scope for user charges and cross subsidization in the future.

Apart from additional resources, there is need for professional management and accountability to improve the quality of care in the public hospitals. A major weakness in public health care system is poor performance of the primary health centers, mainly due to staff absenteeism. Apart from providing adequate incentives to motivate the staff to stay in rural areas, community participation should be encouraged to bring accountability of staff and to improve the maintenance. As a part of health sector reforms, the state government has created the Hospital Advisory Committees (HACs) to bring community control over the public hospitals but they seem to be not effective. Recently, there is a proposal to transfer the subject of health to the PRIs but the health department is opposing it. Either way, the state should encourage the community participation to improve the functioning public health care system.

Since the reforms in the health sector are only a part of drastic reforms in other major sectors undertaken as a part of APERP, the overall impact on the health conditions of people and their access to medical care depend more on the changes proposed outside the health sector. For instance, while exempting the white ration card holders (i.e. people below poverty line) from the user charges in the government hospitals, the project insists on reducing the number of white cards to half in the state. The net effect would be to reduce the percent of population eligible for free treatment. The basic thrust of APERP is to enhance the role of private sector in core areas like power, irrigation, communications, higher education etc. and to reduce the government subsidies.

Similarly, the World Bank advocates staff recruitment on contract basis and contracting out of certain services, particularly the supportive services like laundry, dietary services, sanitation etc to the private agencies. Contracting out to private sector is considered more efficient than the directly hired labour because of slow recruitment process and rigid labour laws. Contracting out of services to the private sector is prone to many serious problems in the long run. It creates nexus between private contractors and hospital authorities and leads to siphoning off of public resources. The contract system creates inhuman labour conditions by shifting employment from formal to informal sector. It is not a long-term solution to create a healthy society. To avoid labour problems, it is more sensible to introduce a flexible entry and exit system in the labour market rather than encouraging the expansion of informal sector in the economy.

The health sector reforms, guided by the World Bank, are aimed at limiting the role of the state mainly to the provision of primary care and to encourage the private sector in the provision of tertiary care (GoAP, 1999). In the provision of primary health care, the Vision 2020 document lays emphasis on what it considers two "innovative approaches" i.e. Community Health Workers programme and mobile health centres. Actually, both these schemes were introduced quite sometime ago in the country but are defunct now in most of the states. At the secondary care level, the basic objective is to secure complete autonomy to the APVVP in introducing user charges, subcontracting of services, staff recruitment on contract basis etc. The ultimate objective of complete autonomy, financial and administrative, would imply privatization of public hospitals. Financial self-sufficiency, for instance, requires large-scale mobilization of additional resources through user charges that would drive out the poor from the public hospitals.

The government hospitals have their limitations in terms of overcrowding, lack of cleanliness etc. which are basically due to lack of adequate resources and absence of professional management and accountability, but the private hospitals have built in limitations in the crucial aspects of medical care. Medical care has unique economic characteristics which deviate from the basic prerequisites of market model of economy. Consumer ignorance and scope for supplier-induced demand in the medical care lead to overcharging, excess medication/testing, unnecessary treatment etc. As a system, the private hospitals are highly prone to unethical and harmful practices. Given the complexity of medical care, it may be more difficult for the state to regulate private sector than providing the medical care directly.

References

Andhra Pradesh Legislative Assembly (1996), *Report of House Committee on Corporate Hospitals*, Andhra Pradesh Legislature Secretariat, Hyderabad.

Central Statistical Organisation (1986-87 and 1993-94), *National Sample Surveys*, Department of Statistics, Ministry of Planning, Government of India, New Delhi.

Central Statistical Organisation (1995-96), *NSS 50th Round*, Department of Statistics, Ministry of Planning, Government of India, New Delhi.

CMIE (1992), *Profile of States*, Centre for Monitoring Indian Economy, Bombay.

Chawla, Mukesh and Alex George (nd), "Hospital Autonomy: The Experience of APVVP Hospitals", IHS Working Paper XVI, Institute of Health Systems, Hyderabad.

GoAP (2001), "Beneficiary Assessment Study (PHCs)", AP Economic Restructuring Project, APERP Cell, Hyderabad.

GoAP (1999), *Vision 2020*, Government of Andhra Pradesh, Hyderabad.

GoAP (1998), *Project Implementation Plan for the Primary Health Care Component of AP Economic Rehabilitation Project,* Department of Health, Medical & Family Welfare, Government of Andhra Pradesh, Hyderabad.

GoAP (Annual Series), *Statistical Abstract of Andhra Pradesh* (Annual Publications), Directorate of Economics and Statistics, Government of Andhra Pradesh, Hyderabad.

Government of India, Planning Commission (1985), *Seventh Five-Year Plan*, New Delhi.

Institute of Health Systems (1996), *Andhra Pradesh Health Institutions Database (APHID), Technical Note, Working Paper No. XI (1-27),* IHS, Hyderabad.

IIPS (1992-93 and 1998-99), *National Family And Health Surveys*, International Institute for Population Studies, Bombay.

Iyengar, N.S. and P. Sudarshan (1982), "Method of Classifying Regions from Multivariate Data", *Economic and Political Weekly*, Vol. 17, No.51.

Mahapatra, P., P. Sridhar and K.T. Rajshree (2002*), Structure and Dynamics of Private Health Sector*, Institute of Health Systems, Hyderabad, p.43,

Ministry of Health and Family Welfare, Government of India (1981), *Health Policy Statement*, New Delhi.

Nandraj, S. (1994), "Beyond the Law and the Lord: Quality of the Private Health Care", *Economic and Political Weekly*, Vol.29, No.27.

Narayana, K.V. (1998), *Public and Private Mix in the Medical Care in AP, Report*, Centre for Economic and Social Studies, Hyderabad.

NSSO (1992), *Sarvekshana*, National Sample Survey Organisation, Vol. 15, No.4, April-June,Issue No.51.

NSSO (1998), *Morbidity and Treatment of Ailments*, National Sample Survey Organisation, Fifty-second Round.

Prasad, Sheela (1995), *Urban Health Care,* Delta Publishing House, Delhi.

World Bank (1994), *Andhra Pradesh First Referral Health Project*, Report No.13402-IN.

14

Primary Education: Causes and Constraints

V. Ratna Reddy and
R. Nageswara Rao

1. INTRODUCTION

Education is one of the most important social indicators, which are directly linked with economic development. Level of literacy or education is directly associated with gross domestic product, indirectly with poverty, population growth, health and crime rate. Despite its importance education continues to be a neglected area at the policy level. After fifty years of planning, enormous funding and promises total literacy remains to be a distant dream. The deadline for achieving total literacy keeps postponing year after year. Apart from overall low levels of literacy at the national level, disparities across regions, genders, social groups, etc., are of serious concern. Education is recognised as a basic input for empowerment to individual and overall development of the society. Expenditure on education and its intra sectoral allocation, in general, appears to be the main factor influencing the literacy levels (Sharif and Ghosh, 2000). At the national level the expenditure on education in relation to Gross Domestic Product (GDP) continues to be much below the desired 6 percent level. The share of elementary education in the total expenditure on education continues to be below 50 percent as against the required 65-70 percent to achieve universal literacy. At the same time expenditure on education *per se* is influenced by non-economic factors rather than economic factors (Tilak, 1995). For, some of the moderately developed states like Andhra Pradesh seem to be doing badly as far as education is concerned.

Andhra Pradesh ranks 22nd among 28 states (2001 census) in terms of adult literacy while it ranks 11th in terms of per capita state domestic product in descending order. That is, Andhra Pradesh is in the middle category in the case of per capita SDP while it is in the bottom category in the case of literacy. This indicates that the relation between economic development and education development (literacy) is not automatic. However, education development is a necessary condition for economic development and poverty alleviation.

This paper makes an attempt to examine various aspects of education in the state of Andhra Pradesh at a disaggregate level with a view to pinpoint the causes for its poor performance in primary education. Some of the important issues that need attention in this regard include: a) trends in the status of primary education and public expenditure on primary education in a regional context, b) factors (demographic, socio-economic, etc.) influencing literacy levels in a regional context, and c) constraints (economic, institutional and policy) on achieving total literacy in the state. The intention here is to examine the problem of schooling (primary) at the district level and also between rural and urban situations. It may be noted that primary education and literacy represent different levels or degrees of learning. However, the differences between these two seem to be narrowing. For, during 1991 census all children below the age of 7 years have been treated as illiterate even though some school going children might have picked up reading and writing. This is departure from the previous practice when children below the age of 5 years only were treated as illiterate (Govt. of India, Census-1991, Andhra Pradesh, Series-2, p. 5). Similarly, as per NSS 42nd round (Sarvekshna, Vol, XVI, No. 4, April-June, 1993) one will be considered as 'literate' if he/she can read and write a simple message in any language, which is possible only through some primary education. For the purpose of our study, we consider primary education (up to class V in Andhra Pradesh) as necessary for attaining appropriate literacy. Though the paper mainly relies on secondary sources of data, it also draws from some of the recent micro and macro studies conducted in the state and elsewhere.

2. TRENDS IN LITERACY RATES

Literacy rate in Andhra Pradesh has been much below the all India level during the last four decades (Table 1). The gap between the two has narrowed down during the last decade (2001). The gap is more in the case of male literacy than that of female literacy. The estimates of literacy rates from different sources, especially National Council for Applied Economic Research (NCAER), during the 1990s have also shown some improvement in the state's performance. Female literacy has recorded a significant improvement in the state when compared to all India level. This could be attributed to the literacy campaign focused on women (*akshara sankranti*) in the state during the year 2000.

The literacy rates of Scheduled tribe and Scheduled caste population at all India are relatively high indicating a social gap in rural Andhra Pradesh. The female literacy rates of these groups are still only around 10 percent. In rural Andhra Pradesh, there are 731 households for every thousand households without a female literate and 465 households without any literate in the family. At the all India (rural) level these figures are 633 and 331 households respectively. As a result the effective literacy rate will be much below that of all India level. For, an illiterate in a household with at least one literate (proximate illiteracy) will be much better off than an illiterate in a household without any literate person (isolated illiteracy) due to the externality affect of literacy (Basu, Foster and Subramaniam, 2000). The externality (positive) affect will be stronger in the households in which at least one female member is literate. The female literacy in the state is low even in urban areas as compared to all India. This may be because the Zamindars of the Telugu speaking areas have not encouraged universal education in the Coastal as well as Telangana regions. Further, the missionaries who were working in the education field had concentrated only in the rich Godavari and Krishna delta region. Therefore, educational development in Andhra Pradesh did not take off during the early years. It was only after the state's formation in 1956 that a systematic attempt was made for universaliasation of primary education in all the districts of the state, though delta region had always had the benefit of early Christian missionary work.

Table 1. Trends in Literacy Rates in India and in Andhra Pradesh (Percentages)

Year	ALL INDIA			ANDHRA PRADESH		
(Source)	Persons	Male	Female	Persons	Male	Female
1971 (census)	34	46	22	25	33	16
1981 (census)	44	57	30	36	48	25
1991 (census)	52	64	39	44	55	33
1994 (NCAER)	54	66	40	50	61	39
1997 (NSSO)	62	73	50	54	64	43
2001 (census)	65	76	54	61	71	51

As per 2001 census Coastal Andhra region attained 62.5 per cent while Rayalaseema and Telangana regions have attained 60.7 and 58 per cent literacy levels. Between 1971 and 2001, along with the increase in the literacy rates, the regional disparities have come down substantially (Table 2).

Rural-Urban Disparities

Three fourths of the urban and more than half of the rural people have attained literacy by the year 2001 in Andhra Pradesh. The increase in literacy rate is higher in 1991-01 compared to earlier decades in all the regions except coastal Andhra, in both rural and urban literacy rates. Inter district variations are steadily decreasing over the period both in rural and urban areas. Interestingly by 1991 all the regions attained equal status in urban literacy rates but by 2001 Rayalaseema has fallen behind marginally.

We have calculated the disparity indices by taking the ratio of urban to rural literacy rates multiplied by hundred. The index ranges from '0' to '100'. Disparities tend to decline along with the ratio and vice versa. Rural-urban disparities in Andhra Pradesh are higher when compared to all India though the gap is narrowing over the period (Table 3). The rural-urban disparity is the highest in the Telangana region in all the four periods. Rayalaseema region has performed well in reducing the rural-urban disparities over the period.

Table 2. Trends in Literacy Rates across the Regions of the State

Region	Category	1971		1981		1991		2001	
		Mean	C. V	Mean	C. V	Mean	C. V	Mean	C. V
Coastal	Male	35.5	13.5	48.3	13.1	55.0	8.4	70.9	6.0
Andhra	Female	19.5	34.8	27.8	32.5	35.0	24.5	54.1	17.2
	Total	27.61	20.9	37.63	19.9	45.07	14.4	62.5	10.6
Rayala-	Male	35.2	2.6	51.0	2.8	58.7	7.3	72.9	6.6
seema	Female	13.1	6.0	21.8	7.0	30.6	13.4	48.1	12.5
	Total	24.39	2.9	36.76	3.3	45.01	9.1	60.7	8.8
Telangana	Male	27.4	29.5	43.9	28.8	52.1	19.6	69.0	9.5
	Female	10.7	66.3	20.5	67.1	28.5	45.2	47.0	22.7
	Total	19.14	39.8	32.18	41.7	40.47	28.5	58.0	14.8
Andhra	Male	33.18	22.8	46.7	20.6	55.1	14.5	70.9	8.0
Pradesh	Female	15.8	51.4	24.9	47.6	32.7	33.9	51.2	20.1
	Total	24.57	30.9	36.43	29.6	44.09	21.1	61.1	12.7

Note: C. V= Coefficient of Variation in percentages.
Source: Population Census.

Table 3. Rural-Urban Disparity Index across Regions of the State

Region	1971	1981	1991	2001
Coastal Andhra	50.4	49.5	41.2	23.3
Rayalaseema	55.4	49.4	38.7	21.8
Telangana	67.3	63.4	54.4	35.0
Andhra Pradesh	58.2	54.8	46.2	27.6
All India	60.1	46.4	38.9	---

Gender and Social Disparities

Telangana region is lagging behind in terms of both male and female literacy rates for the last four decades (Table.2). Over the period inter district variations in female literacy have declined faster than that of male literacy rates (Table 2). The decline was prominent during 1990s, which may be due to the realisation of the importance of female literacy. The gender disparity in the state has been shrinking steadily from 55 percent to 28 percent, though the gap is still substantial (Table 4). Among the regions, disparities have declined faster in Rayalaseema and Telangana

Table 4. Gender Disparity Index across Regions of the State.

Region	1971	1981	1991	2001
Coastal Andhra	45.1	42.4	36.4	23.7
Rayalaseema	62.8	57.3	47.9	34.0
Telangana	60.9	53.3	45.3	31.9
Andhra Pradesh	54.7	47.8	42.3	27.8
All India	52.2	46.8	38.7	29.0

when compared to Coastal Andhra and hence the narrowing of the inter-regional variations. Similarly social disparities are also shrinking though quite high at the present level (Table 5).

Table 5. Social Disparity Index

Region	1971		1981		1991	
	SC	ST	SC	ST	SC	ST
Coastal Andhra	50.8	76.9	36.0	68.3	26.9	60.5
Rayalaseema	66.7	74.7	57.7	69.0	39.1	52.1
Telangana	69.4	71.2	53.4	74.4	43.4	64.7
Andhra Pradesh	60.8	74.5	47.2	71.1	46.2	60.8
All India	63.5	72.5	58.6	68.3	50.0	60.7

To sum up, the performance of Andhra Pradesh in literacy does not reflect its position in economic development. As per the 2001 census it occupies the 28th position among the 35 states and union territories in the country (Census 2001). In fact its position has marginally deteriorated between 1981 and 1991 (moved from 25th to 26th position) while it maintained its position in 2001 census. Moreover, its growth in literacy rate was slightly better than Bihar, Uttar Pradesh and Rajasthan but lower than Madhya Pradesh and Arunachal Pradesh among the low literacy rate states. It compares poorly with the all India averages in all respects except in the case of ST literacy rates. These figures do not augur well for a state that boasts of an Information Technology hub. The inter census period (91-01) has improved the literacy rates in all the regions in comparison with 81-91 census period. Telegana region reflects the highest disparities in the case of rural-urban and social disparities while Rayalaseema reflects highest gender disparities.

3. ACCESS TO EDUCATION

The poor performance in attaining higher literacy rates could be viewed from the supply as well as demand sides. The supply side aspects include availability of schools in the vicinity, infrastructure, quality of education, etc. On the demand side the problems are high opportunity costs, high costs of education, low returns from education, etc. Since primary education is made a fundamental right the stress is often on the supply side factors though demand factors also play an important role. Moreover, the demand side factors are directly linked with economic development provided a threshold level of development has been achieved with reasonable equity across regions and socio-economic groups. The ranking of states by literacy rates and economic development clearly indicates that development does not guarantee literacy automatically, which is true even across countries (UNDP, 1990). This emphasises the role of supply side aspects in improving the literacy levels. This is more so in the case of backward and rural areas due to the iniquitous distribution of gains between less-endowed and well-endowed regions and between rural and urban areas. Here we focus our analysis on the supply as well as demand side aspects.

Physical access to school is an important dimension in terms of both supply and demand factors. Access is often defined as availability of school to all the school going children within a distance of 1 kilometer. Of late location of the school is also considered important in defining access. For, it is observed that children from lower social groups are not comfortable going to school located in the higher social group region and vice versa (Aruna, 1999, PROBE, 1999). In this section we deal with the aspects of access at disaggregate level in the state. Besides, an attempt is made to look into the schemes implemented by Central and State Governments to counter the access problem.

At all India level every two out of three villages have less than 500 population and a quarter of the rural population lives in these small villages (1991). Only a sixth of the total villages were in the category of above 2000 population housing less than 50 percent of the people. Therefore, majority of the people live in villages with unfavourable conditions for the supply of basic amenities including education. In this regard Andhra Pradesh is placed in a favourable position. For, 70 percent of the rural population in the state lives in 32 percent of the large size (above 2000) villages. Only 10.5 percent of the population lives in villages of less than 1000 population (Census, 1981 & 1991; NCERT, 1997). Compared to the all India situation, a large proportion of the state's rural population has the advantage of easy access (supply side). Though the distribution of habitations by their size explains the social disparities it does not really explain the overall poor performance of the state in literacy rates.

The All India Educational Surveys have attempted to examine the problem of remoteness in terms of access to primary and upper primary schools. In Andhra Pradesh, the percentage of habitations having a primary school has increased (Table 6). This is clearly reflected in the coverage of scheduled tribe population by primary schools (Table 7a). However, only 82 percent of the tribal population is being covered by primary schools within 3 km of the habitations as against above 97 percent in the case of scheduled castes and all categories of population. The situation is similar even in the case of upper primary schools. The sixth All India Educational Survey estimated that about 93 percent of population in 70 percent of habitations was covered by primary schools. One kilometre from the centre of the habitation to school is considered as convenient distance for children by walk. The proportion of population having access to a school within walking distance is 98 percent in 89 percent of the habitations (Tables 7a and 7b).

Table 6. Expansion of Primary and Upper Primary Schools in Andhra Pradesh

Survey No	Primary School			Upper Primary School	
	% Of habitations	% Of Population Served	% Of Habitations	% Of Population Served	With in 3 kms
I (1957)	44.8 (48.1)	81.1 (60.0)	2.2 (3.1)	– (–)	– (–)
II (1965)	60.8 (38.0)	90.7 (71.5)	6.1 (7.1)	25.7 (–)	55.4 (–)
III (1973)	61.1 (44.3)	87.5 (76.1)	9.3 (8.7)	31.3 (28.9)	64.6 (72.0)
IV (1978)	64.0 (46.8)	91.8 (78.5)	10.3 (10.7)	36.0 (33.5)	71.2 (78.8)
V (1986)	72.1 (51.2)	92.7 (80.4)	15.5 (13.1)	42.4 (36.9)	97.3 (84.0)
VI (1993)	69.7 (49.8)	92.5 (77.8)	13.5 (–)	43.0 (37.1)	79.4 (85.0)

Notes: Figures in brackets pertain to all India.
Source: All India Education Survey 1997 (NCERT).

Table7a. Availability of Primary Schools in Andhra Pradesh by Social Groups (1993)

Category	Primary Schools in		Primary school with in 1 km	
	% Of Habitations	% Of Population Covered	% Of Habitations	% Of Population Covered
Scheduled Tribe	46.7 (45.9)	69.8 (71.4)	67.5 (76.3)	82.0 (88.6)
Scheduled Caste	50.0 (37.0)	82.1 (64.3)	93.2 (82.3)	97.2 (91.3)
All	69.7 (49.8)	92.5 (77.8)	88.6 (83.3)	97.6 (93.8)

Note: Figures in brackets pertain to all India.
Source: All India Education Survey 1997 (NCERT).

Table 7b. Access to Primary Schools by Regions and Social Groups

Region	Scheduled Castes		Scheduled Tribes	
	% Of Habitations	% Of Population	% Of Habitations	% Of Population
1. Coastal Andhra	91.2 (83-96)	91.4 (83-96)	91.3 (85-95)	80.8 (58-94)
2. Rayalaseema	72.3 (58-93)	62.7 (42-97)	81.7 (66-100)	65.2 (37-97)
3. Telangana	88.6 (78-98)	89.6 (80-98)	75.8 (59-93)	68.9 (52-87)
Andhra Pradesh	84.2 (58-98)	82.1 (42-98)	80.2 (59-100)	69.8 (37-97)

Note: Figures in brackets indicate range across the districts.
Sources: All India Education Survey 1997.

Density of Primary Schools

The Primary school density in terms of number of schools per 1000 Sq. Kms and per 1 lakh children (6-11 years), average area (catchment) per school and children (6-11) per school, student teacher ratio and share of private schools reflect the quantitative and qualitative aspects pertaining to access to schooling. The Rayalaseema region has highest school density followed by Coastal Andhra (Table 8). The average area per school gives some idea regarding the efficient coverage in terms of distance. It is interesting to note that although Coastal Andhra schools are crowded (assuming enrolment is directly linked to the number of school going children), it has better density of schools. On the contrary, in

Rayalaseema and Telangana regions schools are not only sparsely located but also crowded.

Table 8. School Density and Catchment Area Across the Regions (1999-2000)

Region	School Density		Catchment area			Total Sch-ools
	Per 1000 sq km	Per lakh Children (6-11)	Area in Sq. km	Children	Share of Private School	
Coastal Andhra	298 (167-519)	608 (413-858)	3.6 (1.9-6.0)	178 (117-242)	8.8 (1.3-25)	25287
Rayalaseema	187 (108-292)	689 (405-889)	6.1 (3.4-9.3)	161 (113-247)	4.5 (2.8-7.9)	12317
Telangana	155 (138-1626)	437 (70-846)	6.0 (0.6-8.2)	228 (121-1551)	2.8 (0.7-43.9)	17794
Andhra Pradesh	213 (108-1626)	523 (70-889)	5.0 (0.6-9.3)	191 (113-1551)	5.9 (0.7-43.9)	55398

Source: Department of Education, Government of Andhra Pradesh.

There are about 5.9 percent of private schools but the concentration of these schools is high in delta districts of Coastal Andhra. Krishna District has the highest proportion of private schools (25.6 per cent). Availability of teachers and infrastructure facilities in the schools reflects the quality of education. Student teacher ratios have gone up between 1981 and 1999-2000 reflecting the declining quality of education at the primary level (Table 9). However, the trend has reversed between 1991 and 1999-00, which may be due to the special emphasis on primary education during the 1990s. In comparison with all India Andhra Pradesh has a better student-teacher ratio in all the periods. Though Telangana region has the most unfavourable ratio the regional disparities have narrowed down substantially over the last two decades (Table 9).

Table 9. Trends in Student-Teacher Ratios at the Primary Level

Region / year	1981	1991	2001	Percentage Change	
				1981-91	1991-01
1. Coastal Andhra	37.5	56.3	44.0	50.1	-21.8
2. Rayalaseema	33.4	49.7	46.6	48.8	-6.2
3. Telangana	23.0	48.5	50.6	110.9	4.3
Andhra Pradesh	27.5	51.9	46.5	88.7	-10.4
All India	54.0	59.4	58.8*	10.0	---

Note: * pertains to the year 1998-99.

Source: Census and Department of Education, Government of Andhra Pradesh.

As far as infrastructure facilities are concerned, seventy five percent of the primary schools have *pucca* buildings but nearly half of the schools have single rooms and about 40 percent of the schools have single teacher. The provision of drinking water, toilets, blackboards, etc., in the schools is below the minimum requirements. Only 30 percent of the schools have drinking water, 14 percent of the schools have urinal facilities. Moreover, only 8 percent of the schools have separate toilets for girls.

In order to bridge the access gap and improve the literacy levels, non-formal education centres (NFECs) have been promoted to bring the non-enrolled and dropout children to formal education. In 1996-97 there were 31245 NFECs in the state enrolling about 6.38 lakh children. However, this accounts for only 23.9 percent of the out of school children reflecting the huge demand-supply gap. Of the total NFECs 25400 are state run centres and the remaining are run by Non-Governmental Organisations (NGOs). Between 1992-93 and 1996-97 there was no increase in the number of state run centres while the number of NGO run centres have recorded a growth of 92 percent (GOI, 1998). The average allocation of funds for the state run centres was about Rs. 16 crores (between 1992-97) at the rate of Rs. 6280 per centre. Despite the expenditure, the performance of the NFECs is not encouraging. Even in the case of NFECs the performance of the state is poor compared to that of all India level. Only 22.8 percent of the students in the state completed the course as against 30.8 percent at the all India level in the year 1996. Of this only 13.5 of the total students (5.4 percent of the girl students) have entered the formal system in the state as against 28.7 (12.4 percent of the girls) at the all India level. These figures also indicate that non-formal system of education is no substitute for the formal system. In terms of infrastructure facilities in the NFECs also the state is placed badly, which may explain the poor performance. More importantly, above 80 percent of the teachers in these schools are having below secondary or secondary education qualification (GOI, 1998).

Enrolment vis-à-vis Dropouts

Enrolment is a necessary condition for obtaining literacy in a formal system but not sufficient to attain literacy. Higher enrolment leads to higher literacy rates provided dropouts do not increase at the same rate. As per the estimates of the education department enrolment ratio in the state was as high as 90 percent in 2000 compared to 73 percent in 1991-92 (Table 10). Coastal Andhra region seems to have reached saturation in enrolment ratios and Rayalaseema has the highest enrolment ratios in both the periods, while Telangana moved from third position to second position.

Interestingly, dropout ratios are also high in the state, which may be due to the fictitious enrolment. There are wide variations in dropout ratios across the districts (7-63) (Table 11). Telangana recorded the highest dropout ratios followed by Coastal Andhra and Rayalaseema regions. Rayalaseema with highest enrolment ratio recorded the lowest dropout ratio. Similarly, girls have recorded higher dropout ratios too. Over the years enrolment ratios have increased while dropout ratios have declined indicating a positive impact on effective enrolment and literacy. Overall the

Table 10. Enrolment Ratios in Primary Schools (5-9 age group)

Region	1992			2000		
	Boys	Girls	Total	Boys	Girls	Total
1.Coastal Andhra	86.4	78.3	82.6	82.0	81.2	81.6
	(75-96)	(68-91)	(73-94)	(70-101)	(71-97)	(71-99)
2. Rayalaseema	99.2	70.4	84.9	97.5	94.8	96.1
	(88-122)	(64-79)	(76-96)	(81-116)	(80-106)	(81-111)
3. Telangana	81.0	53.9	68.1	92.6	87.0	89.8
	(68-102)	(45-76)	(59-79)	(67-103)	(72-98)	(69-101)
Andhra Pradesh	86.2	58.9	72.7	87.7	84.8	86.3
	(68-122)	(45-91)	(59-96)	(67-116)	(71-106)	(69-111)

Note: Figures in brackets indicate the range across the districts.
Source: Department of Education, Government of Andhra Pradesh.

enrolment ratio has increased by 19 percent whereas the dropout ratio has declined by 31 percent. Telangana has recorded the highest increase in enrolment ratio and the lowest dropout ratio. Coastal Andhra recorded no improvement in the enrolment ratio and recorded 41 percent decline in dropout ratio. In fact, both Coastal Andhra and Rayalaseema recorded a decline in boys' enrolment ratios. On the contrary, girls have gained substantially in terms of enrolment (positive and high) but lost in terms of dropout ratios (negative and high).

Table 11. Dropout Ratios in primary Schools

Region	1992			2000		
	Boys	Girls	Total	Boys	Girls	Total
1.Coastal Andhra	44.4	53.7	48.9	33.1	36.2	34.6
	(23-61)	(44-64)	(42-63)	(27-44)	(30.49)	(29-46)
2. Rayalaseema	39.6	51.6	45.0	27.2	33.8	30.4
	(21-47)	(43-57)	(31-51)	(18-35)	(23-41)	(20-38)
3. Telangana	55.3	61.7	57.0	46.2	47.2	46.7
	(25-72)	(27-75)	(26-73)	(8-62)	(6-64)	(7-63)
Andhra Pradesh	48.5	56.4	52.6	39.4	41.2	40.3
	(21-72)	(27-75)	(26-73)	(8-62)	(6-64)	(7-63)

Note: Figures in brackets indicate the range across the districts.
Source: Department of Education, Government of Andhra Pradesh.

One of the recent field studies in the three regions of Andhra Pradesh vindicates the high enrolment ratios though the variations across the regions are not the same (Rao, 2002). On the contrary, dropout ratios are quite low (between 10 and 15 percent) in all the three regions. However, there are differences between developed and backward regions within each region. While the differences across regions are marginal in the case of enrolment they are substantial in the case of dropouts. This is true even in the case of developed and backward regions within the regions. Backward regions record the highest dropout ratios. This indicates that the problem is of retention rather than enrolment.

4. EXPENDITURE ON EDUCATION

Public spending on education is critical for improving the literacy levels. Though economic variables like per capita gross domestic product, etc., do not explain the variations in the literacy rates, public expenditure on education seems to have a strong bearing on the performance of literacy. However, it is not necessary that public expenditure on education be directly linked with per capita incomes, as the former is usually influenced by non-economic factors like political will, etc. Moreover, the performance of primary education is directly influenced by the inter-sectoral allocation of funds within the education sector i.e., allocation towards primary, secondary, technical and higher education sectors. In this section an attempt is made to examine the financial allocations to education in the state in comparison with the country as a whole. The idea is whether the poor performance of the state in literacy rates can be explained in terms of expenditure on it. However, lack of data on public expenditure at the district or regional level limits our analysis to the aggregates of Country and the state. The regional and district level analysis of public expenditure and financial resources is recognised as an important variable in understanding the status of education only recently (after the 1990 conference in Jomtien, South Africa and the revised National policy on education in1992).

Inadequate allocation of funds to elementary education is due to inadequate recognition of the importance of elementary education by our planners and policy makers (Tilak, 1999). International agencies view this as a problem of under investment (Varghees, 1998). The central government has increased its role in support of primary education since 1986, mainly by supporting interventions to improve learning achievement. It has adopted both uniform and specially tailored interventions (World Bank, 1997). At the all India level expenditure on education accounts for 3.1 percent of the gross domestic product. Investment in education at all India level needs to be more than doubled from the present level of 3.1 per cent of the GDP and a greater allocation to primary education is necessary if every child in India is to be got into school in the next five years (Sharif and Ghosh, 2000). These studies indicated the decline in allocation of funds to education due to structural adjustment following economic reforms and the lack of political will towards achieving universal education. The sources of funds for education include central and state government budget allocations, aid from International Agencies, mobilisation of funds from local Non-governmental Organisations (NGOs) and village level education committees. The funds from the last two agencies are marginal. It is suggested that the collection of education cess from the people is necessary to augment the financial resources for funding elementary education.

The total expenditure on education at all India as a proportion of gross national product (GNP) accounts for 3.8 percent during 1995-96. The share of education in GNP has recorded an increase between 1980-81 and 1995-96 though there was a decline between 1990-91 and 1995-96. The growth rates indicate a clear decelerating trend and decline even in absolute terms. In Andhra Pradesh the situation is one of stagnation. Though there is an increase in the public expenditure on education between 1980-81 and 1995-96, in terms of its ratio to the NSDP it remained more or less around 3.0 percent (Table 12). Unlike in the case of all India, Andhra Pradesh has recorded faster deceleration in the share of education during 1985-86 through 1995-96. This reflects the low priority accorded to education in the state.

However, budget allocations are better indicators of the priority given to education. Andhra Pradesh is providing a lesser share of its budgetary allocations to education compared to the national budget. Allocation is low even when compared to southern states. Allocations have declined both at the aggregate and state levels though the gap between the state and the central allocations (all states) is narrowing over the period (Table 12). While the share of education in Andhra Pradesh's budget has come down from 19.1 percent in 1980-81 to 16.6 percent in 1995-96, in the case of all states it has come down from 25.5 percent to 19.6 percent during the same period. This might aggravate the situation further given the fact that allocations in Andhra Pradesh had experienced sharper declining trend (-2.4) during the period 1990-91 and 1995-96. In the absence of any political or popular support education sector becomes the first victim. One cannot attribute this to the reform process alone, as there are other pressures on the state finances such as populist programmes.

The share of elementary education in the total budget as well as in the education budget is the ultimate indicator of literacy performance in the state. As in the case of education, elementary education gets a lower share in the State budget when compared to the central budget allocations. Similarly, the share of elementary education in the education budget in Andhra Pradesh is not only on the lower side but also declined after 1985-86. The share of primary education in the state has declined from 44.1 percent to 41.7 percent, while in the case of all states level it has increased from 48 percent to 49.6 percent. This is mainly due to the high priority given to higher education in the state. As it is, the allocations for elementary education are much below the requirements (above 60 percent) both at the national and state levels. The decline in the allocation in the state is of serious nature. If this trend continues, the state will be pushed to the lowest rungs of the literacy ladder. These trends are sharply reflected in the quality of education (per student expenditure). Per student expenditure in the state is declining since 1985-86 (Table 12). In this regard, the gap between all India and the state is widening fast, as per student expenditure at the all

Table 12. Public Expenditures on Education and its Allocation.

(at constant prices 1980- 81=100)

Public Expenditure on Education and its shares	Andhra Pradesh				All States			
	80-81	85-86	90-91	95-96	80-81	85-86	90-91	95-96
Total Expenditure (Rs. in millions)	2291	3521 (10.7)*	3925 (2.3)+	3987 (0.3)@	29306	43785 (9.9)*	64605 (9.5)+	75474 (3.4)@
As Percentage of GNP	2.9	4.0 (7.6)*	3.3 (-3.4)+	3.0 (-2.2)@	3.0	3.6 (4.4)*	4.1 (2.6)+	3.8 (-1.4)@
As percentage of budget	19.3	18.4 (-0.9)*	18.8 (0.4)+	16.6 (-2.4)@	25.5	20.5 (-4.0)*	21.1 (0.6)+	19.6 (-1.4)@
Share of primary education in the budget	8.5	8.5	8.4	6.9	12.2	10.1	10.5	9.8
Share of primary education in education	44.1	46.1	44.9	41.7	48.0	49.5	50.0	49.6
Expenditure per Student (total) (in Rs)	316	376	357	330	291	344	440	426
Expenditure per student (primary) (in Rs)	189	232	225	222	185	230	311	305

Note: Figures in brackets are growth rates, *= between 1980-81 and 1985-86; +=between 1985-86 and 1990-91; @=between 1990-91 and 1995-96.
Source: Sharif and Ghosh (2000).

India level has recorded substantial increase. These trends are similar for the total student population as well as elementary student population.

There seems to be some improvement in the allocations towards education in the late 1990s in terms of its ratio to GSDP and per student expenditure (Table 14). But, there is no improvement in the case of primary education. In fact, the allocations towards primary education in 2000-01 and 2001-02 are lower than that of 1995-96. More importantly, a lion's share (above 80 percent) of the expenditure is spent on salaries leaving little for improving the quality of education. This is despite the introduction of District Primary Education Programme (DPEP) during 1994-95. The expenditure on DPEP mainly goes towards infrastructure. This could be the reason why there was some dip in the per pupil expenditure in the late nineties (Table 13). Per pupil expenditure of DPEP ranges from less than Rs. 200 in Kurnool to above Rs. 600 hundred in Nizamabad district. These variations exist in the case of per classroom expenditure also. However, there is no significant relationship between per pupil expenditure and level of literacy across districts, though one expects a negative relationship i.e., more expenditure per unit in the low literate districts in order to reduce inequalities (DFID, 2001). Similarly, tribal districts like Adilabad, Srikakulam and Visakhapatnam do not attract higher per unit expenditure even under DPEP. This indicates that expenditure flows do not match the existing disparities. This is reflected in the perpetuation of social and gender disparities in literacy levels in the state. Dropout rates continue to be a nagging problem while enrolment

Table 13. Recent Trends in Expenditure on Education in Andhra Pradesh

Particulars	95-96	96-97	97-98	98-99	99-00	00-01	01-02
Expenditure on education as % of GSDP	2.4	2.6	2.7	2.9	3.1	3.3	3.2
Real expenditure/ student (Rs.)	219	258	269	316	345	398	405
Share of primary education (%)	55	54	53	57	57	51	53
Share of salaries in primary education	93	88	94	85	93	90	84

Source: DFID, 2001.

rates have improved. This problem is more among the SC, ST communities and females. Therefore, retention at primary level and improving the enrolment at the upper primary level are the main concerns as far as ST community is concerned.

5. DETERMINANTS OF LITERACY

Thus, the above analysis explains the poor performance of the state in literacy to some extent. However, the analysis was mainly supply-sided, though demand as well as supply factors influence the literacy levels. In this section an attempt is made to explain the variations in literacy levels across the districts of the state in order to identify the factors influencing the literacy levels based on the secondary data. Besides, we have also examined the reasons for dropout and non-enrolment of children based on the household level data in the three regions of the state. This is based on the perceptions of 3000 households spread over 12 villages in three districts belonging to Coastal Andhra, Rayalaseema and Telangana regions.

Using the secondary data we have estimated the regression equations across the districts for different literacy segments such as rural, urban, male, female, SC&ST, etc. A number of explanatory variables, both from demand and supply side, were used in the analysis. The specification and other details of the selected variable are presented in the appendix.

At the theoretical level the expected relationships between literacy and various independent variables are rather unclear, as the literature is a bit controversial due to the location specificity of the results (for an exhaustive review see Bhatty, 1998). The controversy is mainly on the issues of supply and demand side aspects of literacy. Some argue that the poor performance on the literacy front is mainly due to the low priority accorded to primary education at the policy level in terms of financial allocations. These views are supported by some micro level studies where impact of access and quality of primary education was found to have a strong bearing on literacy, enrolment and dropout ratios. More clinching argument is that poor economic status forces the households to keep their children away from the schools. The opportunity cost of time (children's) is not only positive but also important for the household's survival. In other words, the ability of the poor households to send their children to school is very low not only because they loose children's income but without grown-up children at home they will not be able to fully devote themselves to wage employment. Apart from income, the ability of the household to send their children to school is dependent on the composition of the family. If the family consists of older people who are not fit for physical labour but can take care of less demanding household chores like looking after siblings, then the family does not require the school going children at home. This could be the reason why half the poor are able to send their children to school. In a study of 93 schools in Karnataka it was observed that access to primary education and its quality, retention and dropout rates are related to the prevailing caste, class and gender divides in the region (Kaul, 2001). Besides, the costs (direct) of schooling are substantial in comparison with their low-income levels (Krishnaji, 1997). Costs will be much higher when indirect costs are also taken into account. The total costs explain the low parental motivation. Lack of relevance and quality of the curriculum results in poor returns from education and hence benefits are not conspicuous or dramatic. This dimension needs to be taken into account when talking about parental motivation.

Synthesizing the wide spectrum of views, the PROBE (Public Report on Basic Education, 1999) report, after an extensive field study in four states, has categorized some of the conventional views as myths. The four important myths listed are: i) "parents are not interested", ii) "child labour is the main obstacle", iii) "elementary education is free" and iv) "schools are available". The first two myths are largely misrepresented. They are taken on the face value of the statements, as they do not go into the underlying relationships. As mentioned above, parent's interest or motivation is closely linked with their dependence on children in household activities. This in turn is determined by the household's economic status and structure. In the absence of an intensive probe it is difficult to understand the underlying factors. Opposite responses are elicited when questions are posed differently e.g., why are you not sending your children to school? / Are you not interested in your children's education? Similarly, child labour is taken as labour market participation. Children may not be directly participating in the labour market or earning wages, but they facilitate greater work participation at the household level by taking care of household chores like fetching water, fuel wood, herding cattle, looking after infants, etc. In fact, unpaid household work is the most common form of child work (Bashir, 1994 as quoted in Bhatty, 1998). It is estimated in the four PROBE states (Uttar Pradesh, Madhya Pradesh, Rajasthan and Bihar) that 20 percent of the boys and 22 percent of the girls have worked for more than 8 hours on the preceding day of the survey while only 5 percent of the boys and 1 percent of the girls performed wage labour (PROBE, 1999, p.16). Therefore, it is not correct to say for these states that child labour is an obstacle to literacy on the basis of children's participation in the labour market.

It is now widely accepted that elementary education is not free. The direct costs of primary education are estimated to be in the range of Rs. 20 to Rs. 85 (PROBE, 1999, Krishnaji, 1996, Majumdar, 1996 as quoted in Bhatty, 1998). These costs are substantial especially to low income categories. More importantly, opportunity cost of child time is also a major deterrent. Though physical access (availability of primary school with in one kilometre of the habitation) is not a serious problem, socio-cultural constraints aggravate the problem. Access needs to be defined in a socio-cultural context rather than simple physical access. This would explain the low literacy rates among the socially disadvantaged sections, but not a serious constraint on the overall literacy performance. In what follows we explore some of these issues in the context of Andhra Pradesh.

The explanatory power of the specifications is quite high (above 90 percent in some cases). Specifications turned out strong in the case of rural and female segments, which are lagging behind in terms of literacy levels (see appendix table 1). The estimates are theoretically consistent and robust between the periods 1981 and 1991. Broadly our results corroborate with Krishnaji's (1996) study of 1981 census data. Though our findings are not new, some of the variables we have employed are different and hence add to the explanation. Our results for both the periods strongly support the demand side aspects of literacy performance in the state. Access and gender aspects have also turned out important. As far as access is concerned the variable proportion of habitations with primary school (% HWS), turned out significant during 1980-81 but not in 1990-91. Same is the result with the quality variable, student-teacher ratio (S-T ratio). Gender variable, proportion of female teachers (%FTECH), turned out significant only in 1991. In 1981 it did not turn out significant.

Indicators of prosperity at the district level such as percentage of gross irrigated area (% GIA) and value of yield per hectare (YIELD) have a positive impact on literacy. While % GIA turned out significant in 1981, YIELD turned out significant in 1991. In other words, literacy rates are high among the prosperous regions due to the demand for education. Interestingly percentage of private schools (% PS) has a major bearing on the literacy performance at the district level. Its influence has substantially improved by 1991. Advent of private schools reflects the demand drive for literacy. Besides, their increasing influence also reflects the declining quality of public schools. We hasten to add that this should not be taken as a case for privatisation of primary education. This trend (growth in private schools at the primary level) would aggravate inter and intra regional disparities in the absence of improvement in the public systems. Proportion of female teachers to the total teachers (% FTECH) has a strong and positive impact on literacy in most categories in 1991. Some of the micro studies clearly indicate that female teachers represent better teacher attendance and better quality of education (Bhatty, 1998).

Determinants of Enrolment

Given the wide variations across the districts in the enrolment ratios at the primary level an attempt is made here to identify the factors that explain the variations. At the theoretical level economic prosperity is expected to have a positive impact on enrolment rates. Therefore, we have incorporated all the demand factors, discussed above, as independent variables. Besides, adult literacy rates, SC/ST literacy rates, access factors such as schools per one lakh population are included. Proportion of children in the age group 0-5 years is also included in the analysis, as this variable is found to have a significant negative impact on enrolment at the state level (Reddy, 1995). The estimates were obtained for the year 1991.

The linear regression exercises revealed that none of the demand factors turned out significant. Even work participation rates do not have any impact on the enrolment ratios. Adult literacy rates and access to schools (number of schools/1 lakh population) turned out significant (see appendix Table 2). Both of them have a positive impact on the enrolment ratios of male and female. Access to schooling has a strong influence on enrolment. Increasing the density of schools, especially in remote areas, is a better alternative than merely fixing the targets for enrolment. Fixing targets for enrolment under various literacy programmes and *Janmabhoomi* programme in the absence of requisite facilities is resulting in fictitious enrolment. This, in turn, causes the high dropout ratios. This clearly brings out the point that policies to improve literacy ought to integrate demand and supply aspects. While supply factors ensure higher enrolment, demand factors help improving the retention rates.

The importance of demand factors on dropouts and non-enrolment is conspicuous in our analysis of household level data[1]. Reasons expressed by households are grouped under demand and supply factors. Supply related problems are captured under school problems and others (includes gender and social discrimination), while all other reasons reflect the demand side problems. Poverty and economic activity are the most important reasons for dropout / non-enrolment among male as well as female children, though male children dropout rates are more dependent on these reasons (Table 14). Here economic activities include wage labour as well as unpaid labour such as work on own farm, supporting the parents in their activities. While poverty appears to have greater influence in the backward regions, economic activity seems to play a greater role in the developed regions. This may be due to the pull factors consequent to

Table 14. Reasons for Dropout and Non-Enrolment (% of Households)

Category	Poverty	Eco. Activity	Dom. activity	No. Interest	School problems	Others
Male						
Developed	37	41	04	14	02	02
Backward	41	24	07	18	07	03
Overall	39	35	05	15	04	03
Female						
Developed	23	31	16	22	05	03
Backward	23	10	15	31	00	21
Overall	23	21	16	25	03	12

Source: Field Survey of 300 households in three districts of Guntur, Anantapur and Medak.

greater labour demand, especially during the peak seasons, in the developed regions. Domestic activity and lack of interest among parents are important deterrents, especially in the case of females. On the other hand, school problems seem to be secondary as far as dropout / non-enrolment of children is concerned, in backward as well as developed regions.

The cost of education further accentuates demand problems. The costs of education at the primary level seem to be much higher when all the costs such as uniform, transport costs, pocket money, etc., are included. The costs range from about Rs. 400 to about Rs. 800 per annum in the case of government schools (Table 15). The gender differences are marginal as

Table 15. Expenditure per Student at Primary Level by Type of School (in Rs./year)

Region		Expenditure per student by School Type (Rs./year)			
		Government		Private	
		Boys	Girls	Boys	Girls
Coastal Andhra	Developed	840 (1.1)	833 (1.0)	2065 (51.6)	2068 (41.9)
	Backward	497 (1.1)	429 (1.1)	1335 (50.1)	1001 (41.2)
Rayalaseema	Developed	516 (0.9)	550 (0.9)	1984 (58.9)	1547 (53.7)
	Backward	532 (1.3)	536 (1.6)	2795 (35.8)	—
Telangana	Developed	398 (4.8)	376 (2.2)	1060 (39.0)	2150 (27.9)
	Backward	451 (2.0)	442 (2.2)	1467 (25.3)	—

Note: Figures in brackets indicate proportion of expenditure on school fee.
Source: Rao (2002).

far as costs are concerned. The costs are about four times higher in the case of private schools. More than a third of this expenditure goes towards uniform followed by notebooks, pocket money, etc (Rao, 2002). On the other hand, direct costs of school fee and textbooks account for less than 3-4 percent of the total costs in the public schools while it is above 40 percent in the case of private schools.

Analysis of factors influencing literacy rates and effective enrolment rates brings out interesting aspects. While demand factors rule the extent of literacy and dropout rates, access or supply factors or quality factors influence enrolment rates. This indicates the need for an integrated approach of demand and supply factors in order to bring the children to school and retain them. Bringing the children to school, keeping them in school and make them literate goes beyond access factors. This demands, apart from demand factors, intensive institutional arrangements such as social mobilization of the community on child labour and education (Dev, 2001). Such attempts are very successful at the micro level as demonstrated by the MV foundation. Its replicability at the macro level needs to be explored. This calls for addressing the problem through evolution of proper institutional arrangements rather than focusing on demand (poverty) and supply (simple access) factors.

6. POLICY INITIATIVES AND IMPLICATIONS

The performance of Andhra Pradesh in attaining literacy has been dismal. Despite its better economic status in comparison with number of other states, its position in terms of literacy levels is sliding. It compares poorly with all India averages in almost all the indicators such as rural-urban disparities, gender disparities, etc. It is doing better only in terms of ST literacy rates. The poor performance of the state is somewhat puzzling if we look at the other indicators. For, the state is doing better in access indicators like school density, size distribution of habitations, student-teacher ratios, etc. However, in terms of expenditure, the state's budgetary allocations to education are lower in comparison with all states taken together. The declining allocations to primary education may further aggravate the situation. On a comparative scale the state may slide further if the increasing trend at the aggregate level (all states) in terms of the two indicators, viz., the share of primary education and per pupil expenditure at the primary level, is any indication.

The Vision 2020 document rightly identifies the problems ailing the education system in the state. The document identified low literacy of parents, poverty, lack of access to school and poor infrastructure facilities as the main causes of low literacy rates. These are in tune with our findings. Though it emphasizes increasing access to schooling by building more schools, employing more teachers, etc, the declining allocations go against this objective. Moreover, any increase in allocation is due to the salary component. Expenditure is further diluted due to the allocations towards non-formal system, which is neither effective nor sustainable. The impact of these non-formal modes is moderate at the best. The emphasis ought to be on formal education in order to achieve genuine literacy.

The three major important programs initiated in tune with the new education policy (1986) are Operation Black Board (OBB), Andhra Pradesh Primary Education Project (APPEP) and District Primary Education Project (DPEP). The OBB programme, supported by the Government of India, focuses on the supportive infrastructure such as construction of school buildings, providing teaching aids, play grounds and creation of additional teacher posts. The APPE project was assisted by the Overseas Development Authority (ODA) with the objectives of improving the quality of schooling, construction of additional classrooms and teacher training centres. This program was merged with the DPEP after 1995. DPEP in Andhra Pradesh was launched initially in five backward districts in 1996 and later extended to 14 districts with an objective of involving local community and NGOs in designing, implementation and participation in the education programmes through education committees. This programme has many incentive schemes such as mid day meal / supply of dry ration to enhance enrolment, regular attendance of the students and to reduce dropout and also to maintain the nutritional status of the students. The Andhra Pradesh government has also designed schemes such as "*Mabadi*" (our school) "*Chaduvkundam*" (Back to school) and "*akshara sankranti*" to improve access to children, women and of disadvantaged communities in tiny habitations. The '*vidya* volunteer' scheme was started to support single teacher schools. Educational technology institutions at the district level were established to improve the teachers' training quality.

The recent programmes seem to have undue focus on enrolment resulting in high dropouts. The dry ration programme has encouraged fictitious enrolment (Dev, 2001). Even the District Primary Education Programme (DPEP) initiated in 1993 did not appear to be effective in the state. Instead the stress needs to be on meeting the social needs of rural population, which inhibits access to education, such as elder children participating in economic activities, looking after younger siblings or attending domestic chores, etc. Equal importance should be given to retention of the enrolled children, especially among the scheduled tribes and scheduled caste children. This calls for a balanced approach to tackle supply as well as demand problems pertaining to primary education.

The schemes designed to solve these problems such as residential schools, anganwadi centres, pre-primary schools, supply of dry ration, textbooks, uniform, etc., are more supply sided in nature. The state government has also adopted the 'bridge school' concept of M. V. foundation in the name of 'back to school' programme. However, in order to make the schemes effective, intensive institutional arrangements are required. Some of the innovative approaches are followed by NGOs such as M. V. foundation (Dev, 2001). These institutional arrangements could be replicated with suitable modifications.

From the demand side, generation of productive employment and minimum wages go a long way in reducing the household's dependence on children. In other words, rural economy has to be liberated from the vicious circle of agricultural involution, that is, low employment, low wages and high participation rates. Only through creation of productive employment with a decent (minimum) wage rate could one reduce the work participation rates. As rightly argued in the recent Human Development Report (UNDP, 2000): good health, education and jobs cannot be attained by legislation. Economy should be strong enough to provide them. For that people should be productively (economically) engaged. The role of state is to provide conducive environment for such activities. Specific policies are required to address the problems of the disadvantaged groups such as gender and social disparities. Employment of more female teachers appears to be an effective instrument in improving the female literacy and enrolment. This would take care of the cultural taboos surrounding female education to some extent. Sociocultural aspects ought to be taken into account while planning more schools for SC and ST populations. Even designing of the curriculum for these groups needs special attention.

Notes

1 The analysis is based on the data collected from all the households (3000) in 12 villages spread over the 3 regions of Andhra Pradesh. For the sake of simplicity these villages are grouped as developed and backward.

References

Aruna, R. (1999), "Learn Thoroughly: Primary Schooling in Tamilnadu, *Economic and Political Weekly*, Vol. 34 No.18.

Basu, Kaushik., James E. Foster and S. Subramaniam, (2000), "Isolated and Proximate Illiteracy: And Why These Concepts Matter in Measuring Literacy and Designing Education Programmes", *Economic and Political Weekly*, Vol. 35, Nos. 1 and 2.

Bhatty, Kiran (1998), "Educational Deprivation in India: A Survey of Field Investigations, *Economic and Political Weekly*, Vol. 33, Nos.27-28,

Chakrabarty, G. (1999), "SCs and STs in Rural Andhra Pradesh" *Journal of Rural Development*, Vol. 18, No. 2.

Chalam, K.S. (1998), "Education" in V.Hanumatha Rao et.al (ed), *Andhra Pradesh at 50: A data based analysis.* (Hyderabad: Data News features).

Dev, Mahendra (2001), "Social Mobilization for Getting Children out of Work and into School: Impact of MV Foundation Activities", Evaluation Report of the UNDP/NORAD supported MV Foundation Project, March.

DFID, (2001), *Andhra Pradesh- Impact and Expenditure Review for School Education*, DFID, Hyderabad.

GoAP (1992), "Eighth Five year plan (1992-97)" Planning Department, Government of Andhra Pradesh, Hyderabad.

GoAP (1999), *Selected Statistics for the Years: 1995-96, 1996-97, 1997-98 and 1998-99*, Commissioner and Director of School Education, Government of Andhra Pradesh, Hyderabad.

GoAP (2000), Vision 2020, Government of Andhra Pradesh, Hyderabad.

GoI (1993), *Education for all: Indian Scene,* Ministry of Human Resource Development, Government of India, New Delhi.

GoI (1998), *Evaluation Study of Impact of Non-formal Education*, Planning Commission, Government of India, New Delhi.

Kaul, Rekha (2001), " Accessing Primary Education-Going Beyond the Classroom", *Economic and Political Weekly*, Vol. XXXVI, No. 2, 13-19 January.

Klein, L. R. (1962), *An Introduction to Econometrics*, Printice Hall Inc., New Jersy.

Krishnaji, N. (1998), "Poverty, Gender and Schooling: A Study of Mahaboobnagar and Adilabad districts,

PROBE (1999), *Public Report on Basic Education in India*, Oxford University Press, New Delhi.

Rao, Nageswara, R. (2002), Determinants of Demand for Primary Education in Rural Andhra Pradesh, Project Report, Centre for Economic and Social Studies, Hyderabad.

Reddy, V. N. (1995), "Gross Enrolment, Dropout and Non – enrolment Ratios in India", *Journal of Educational Planning and Administration*, Vol. 9, No. 5, July.

Saldanha, Denzil (1999), "Residual Literacy and Uneven Development- Parts I, II and III", *Economic and Political weekly*, Vol. XXIV, Nos. 27, 28 and 29.

Sarvekshana (1996), Vol. XIX, No. 4, 67th issue April-June.

Shariff, A. and P. K. Gosh (2000), "Indian Education scene and Public expenditure Gap," *Economic and Political Weekly*, April 15, P.1396-1406.

Tilak, J.B.G. (1995),"Student Loans as the Answer to Lack of Resources for Higher Education", *Economic and Political Weekly*, Vol. 34, No. 1 and 2, January 2-8.

Tilak, J.B.G. (1999), "Exploding some Economic Myths of Elementary Study" *The Hindu*, October 5th.

UNDP (2000), Human Development Report, Oxford University Press.

Varghese, N.V. (1998), "Primary Education: Priorities for Public intervention" *Labour and Development*, Vol. 3, No. 1&2.

APPENDIX

Lit_i = F (Access, Quality, Gender, Demand and Social factors) + U_i ------- I

Where,

Lit_i = Percentage of literate population in the 'i^{th}' segment of the population. i = total female literacy, total literacy (male + female), rural female literacy, rural total literacy, urban female literacy, urban total literacy and SC and ST literacy.

Access factors include school density per 1000 KM (SD/1000km) and per one lakh population (SD/ 1lakh) and percentage of habitations with a school (% HWS). All these factors are expected to have a positive impact on literacy levels.

Quality factors include student-teacher ratio (S-T ratio), proportion of private schools in total schools (% PS), urbanization defined as percentage of urban population (% URB), road length per 100 square kilometres (ROAD). These factors are expected to have a positive impact on literacy rates.

Gender factors include percentage of female and male teachers (% FTECH and % MTECH), female work participation rates (FWPR) and adult female and male literacy rates (Lit.ADLF and Lit.ADLM).

Demand factors include the development indicators or proxies of economic prosperity. Factors considered are percentage of population living below poverty line (% BPL), relative development index (RDI), farm size (FSIZE), percentage of gross irrigated area (% GIA), yield per hectare (YIELD), work participation rates of total population, SC and ST population (TWPR, SC/ST WPR), percentage of workers depending on agriculture (% AGLAB). Of these factors % BPL, WPRs and % AGLAB are expected to have a negative impact and the remaining factors are expected to have positive impact on literacy rates.

Social factors include proportion of scheduled caste population (% SC) and proportion of scheduled tribe population (% ST). These two factors are expected to have a negative impact on literacy rates, as these sections are having the lowest literacy levels.

Linear regressions were estimated across the 22 districts of the state. Hyderabad district was not included due to its cosmopolitan and urban nature. Analysis was carried out for the 1981 and 1991 census periods to examine the changes, if any, between the periods and also to test the robustness of the results. Analysis was focused on the priority areas of literacy such as rural literacy, female literacy and SC/ST literacy. Number of permutations and combinations of the selected (listed above) independent variables were estimated to arrive at the best specifications in terms of explanatory power and significance of the variables. In order to eliminate less important variables and avoid multi-colinearity problems we have used the correlation matrices. For checking multi-colinearity problem we have adopted the statistical criteria: if the simple correlation coefficient of two independent variables is greater than the value of multiple 'R', then one of the two correlated variables has to be dropped (Klein, 1962, p.64 and 101). However, as long as the multi-colinearity between the two variables is not too severe to vitiate the results by affecting the signs of the coefficients, no great caution need be exercised in this regard. Based on the correlation matrices we have selected the variables for incorporating in the final specifications. The coefficients of the selected equations are presented in appendix Table 1.

Appendix Table 1. Gist of the Linear Regression Estimates

Dependent Variable	1981	1991
Total female Literacy	TWPR (-); % GIA (+); % PS (+); % HWS (+); S-T ratio (+)	% PS (+); TWPR (+); % FTECH (+); YIELD (+)
Total literacy (male+female)	TWPR (-); % PS (+); % HWS	FTECH (+); TWPR (-); % PS (+); YIELD (+)
Rural female literacy	% GIA (+); TWPR (-); % HWS (+); S-T ratio (+); % PS (+)	YIELD (+); % PS (+); % FTECH (+)
Rural total literacy	% GIA (+); TWPR (-); % HWS (+); S-T ratio (+)	FTECH (+); YIELD (+); % PS (+)*
Urban female literacy	TWPR (-)	No variable is significant
Urban total literacy	TWPR (-)	No variable is significant
SC/ST total literacy	TWPR (-); % PS (+); S-T ratio (+); % BPL (-)@	% PS (+); YIELD (+); SC/ST WPR (-); FWPR (-)

Note: All the variables are significant at less than 10 percent level indicated with their respective signs in the brackets. @ Significant at 11 percent level; * significant at 12 percent level.

Appendix Table 2. Linear Regression Estimates of Effective Enrolment Ratios

Independent Variable	Dependent Variable	
	Female enrolment ratio	Male enrolment ratio
1.Adult male literacy	----	0.5920888* (0.1113)
2.Adult female literacy	0.7308674* (0.0697)	----
3.Number of Schools/1 lakh population	0.1125391* (0.0216)	0.1283589* (0.0260)
R Square	0.88	0.77
Adjusted R Square	0.87	0.75
Number of Observations	22	22

Note: Figures in brackets are standard errors. * Significant at less than 1 percent level.

PART - IV

EMPLOYMENT, POVERTY AND REGIONAL DISPARITIES

15

Employment and Unemployment

S. Mahendra Dev and
Vijay Mahajan

1. INTRODUCTION

Expanding productive employment is central to sustained poverty reduction as labour is the main asset for majority of the poor. The Vision 2020 document says " by 2020, every individual of Andhra Pradesh will be able to lead a comfortable life, filled with opportunities to learn and develop skills". Regarding employment, around 18-20 million new jobs will have to be created by 2020. The document says that presently around 70 per cent of the workers are dependent on agriculture. By the year 2020, only 35-40% of the workers is expected to be dependent on agriculture. However, the experience of the last decade shows that employment opportunities created is inadequate inspite of rapid growth. The general perception in the country is that although GDP growth has accelerated, it has not been accompanied by a commensurate increase in employment leading to a worsening in the employment situation in the post-reform period. These considerations have led to a demand for greater attention to the employment objective[1]. There is also a concern on youth and educated unemployment as increase in it will lead to waste of human resources and social tensions.

In this paper, we present an assessment of the nature of the employment problem in Andhra Pradesh based on the recent trends in employment and unemployment. The paper also offers some policy suggestions for employment promotion in the state. The study is organised as follows. Section 2 examines the employment situation by presenting the trends in employment and unemployment in recent years while Section 3 analyses about the quality of employment. Section 4 deals with strategic options at macro level by presenting projections of employment upto the year 2020. Section 5 discusses policies needed for promotion of employment. Last Section provides concluding observations.

2. EMPLOYMENT SITUATION AND TRENDS

In this section, we examine employment situation and trends in employment and unemployment based on National Sample Survey (NSS) data.

As shown below, employment in A.P. is largely unorganised, rural and non-industrial nature. Labour market in A.P. has some unique characters[2]. Women in A.P. have the highest participation rates in rural areas. It also records the highest proportion of agricultural labour households in the country next only to Tamil Nadu. Among these labour households, casual labour forms large majority and has been growing over period.

Work Participation Rates

Worker-population ratios provide an idea about the participation of population in economic activity[3]. Table 1 provides the worker population ratios for the period 1983 to 1999-2000. The participation rates in rural A.P. increased in 1993-94 before declining significantly in 1999-2000. The decline occurred for both rural and urban areas. The worker-population rates for rural A.P. are much higher than for rural India. Even in urban A.P., the participation rates are higher than that for all India.

Table 2 presents participation rates for males and females for the 1990s. It shows a decline of rates for both males and females in 1999-00 as compared to 1993-94. The female work participation rates in rural A.P. are the highest in the country[4].

Table 1. Work Participation Rates : A.P. and All India

Year	Andhra Pradesh		All India	
	Rural	Urban	Rural	Urban
1983	53.5	34.8	44.5	34.0
1987-88	53.3	35.8	43.4	33.7
1993-94	57.6	37.6	44.4	34.7
1999-2000	54.2	34.8	41.7	33.7

Source: NSS Rounds on Employment and Unemployment (38th, 43rd, 50th and 55th Rounds).

Table 2. Work Participation Rates for Males and Females: A.P. and All India

Year	Andhra Pradesh		All India	
	Rural	Urban	Rural	Urban
Male				
1993-94	63.1	54.4	55.3	52.0
1999-2000	60.5	51.1	53.1	51.8
Female				
1993-94	52.1	19.9	32.8	15.4
1999-2000	47.8	17.8	29.8	13.9

Source: NSS Rounds on Employment and Unemployment (50th and 55th Rounds).

Incidence of Child Labour in A.P is the highest in the Country: There seems to be some correlation between the women's work participation rate and the child labour. A.P. has the highest incidence of child labour and high women's participation rates. In rural areas, around

25.1 per cent of children work in the age group of 10-14 in A.P. while the corresponding number for Kerala is only 0.7 per cent in 1999-00 (Table 3) . Even in urban areas, A.P. has the second highest incidence of child labour in the country.

Table 3. Percentages of Child Labour among Children across States: 1999-00

States	Rural		Urban	
	5-9 age group	10-14 age group	5-9 age group	10-14 age group
Andhra Pradesh	2.7	25.1	0.7	7.1
Assam	0.4	4.6	0.3	7.8
Bihar	0.2	5.0	0.1	3.4
Gujarat	0.7	11.5	0.0	3.6
Haryana	0.1	2.6	0.0	2.4
Karnataka	1.1	15.2	0.1	5.9
Kerala	0.0	0.7	0.0	0.5
Madhya Pradesh	0.3	10.6	0.2	2.5
Maharashtra	0.8	8.5	0.0	2.3
Orissa	0.4	9.0	0.0	1.7
Punjab	0.5	5.5	1.8	3.5
Rajasthan	2.5	16.7	0.4	5.1
Tamil Nadu	0.4	8.6	0.1	4.7
Uttar Pradesh	0.2	6.4	0.3	5.5
West Bengal	0.4	8.8	0.2	6.2
All India	0.7	9.3	0.3	4.3

Source: NSS 55th Round , Report No. 458.

Employment Growth

Have economic reforms reduced employment growth? Table 4shows that employment growth declined drastically in the 1990s as compared to the decade of 1983 to 1993-94. In rural A.P., it declined from 2.40 per cent per annum during 1983 to 1993-94 to 0.29 per cent during 1993-94 to 1999-2000. The corresponding numbers for urban areas were 4.28 per cent and 0.01 respectively. Similar decline can be noticed for all India. Special Group on Employment (GOI, 2002) estimates employment growth based on current daily status. According to this report, rural employment growth in all India declined from 2.40 during the period 1983/94 to 0.67 during the period 1994/2000. During the same periods, urban employment growth in all India declined from 3.59 per cent to 2.32 per cent. In the case of A.P., the employment growth (rural+urban) during 1993-94 to 1999-00 was only 0.35 per cent per annum.

What are the reasons for the decline in employment growth in the 1990s? One of the reasons could be decline in participation rates of younger age groups. A decline in the participation rates of younger age groups is expected as younger people try to gain access to education and stay in school for a longer period. Rising income levels also reduce the pressure to enter the labour market(GOI, 2001). However, it may be noted that participation rates declined for all age groups although the decline was shaper for younger age groups. Another explanation given is that labour force growth itself has declined. In other words, many are joining the category of 'not in the labour force'. It is not, however, clear why labour force participation has declined. It is possible that economic opportunities have not increased in the post-reform period inspite of higher growth.

Table 4. Employment Growth (per cent per annum): Usual status (principal and subsidiary), A.P. and All India

Period	Rural		Urban	
	A.P.	All India	A.P.	All India
1983 to 93-94	2.40	1.73	4.28	3.34
1993-94 to 1999-2000	0.29	0.67	0.01	1.34

Source: Computed by the author based on NSS and Census data. For absolute numbers, Census figures are used.

Proliferation of Marginal and Small Farmers

Due to demographic pressures, the number and shares of marginal and small farmers have been increasing. The distribution of land holdings show that the share of marginal and small farmers in area and no. holdings increased significantly over time(Table 5). The data for 1995-96 show that around 81 per cent of the land holdings belong to marginal and small farmers with area share of 42.7 per cent. There are 80.70 lakh small and marginal farmers in the state and they are mostly underemployed. The size of land holding of these farmers is uneconomical and majority of them also work as agricultural labourers to sustain their livelihood. In A.P. the share of agricultural labour has been increasing while the share of cultivators has been declining. The share of agricultural labourers has increased from 37 per cent in 1981 to 41 per cent in 1991. The cultivators seem to have become agricultural labourers over time. Also 60 per cent of the female workers in A.P. are agricultural labourers in 1991.

Employment in A.P. is largely unorganised

It is known that most of the social security laws in the country are applicable only to organized workers who are less than 10 per cent of the total workforce. In Andhra Pradesh, 20.5 lakh workers are in the organized sector in 1998. There are approximately 387.5 lakh total workers in the state in the same year. In other words, organised workers form only around 5.5 per cent while unorganized workers constitute 94.5 per cent of the total in A.P. The vast majority of the workforce including agricultural labour, construction labour and labour in traditional leather tanning, handloom, fishing, forestry, salt making, household industry etc. as also village artisans, urban informal workers coming under the general categories of unorganised sector are wholly out of any reckoning in the various statutory laws in the country. These workers are unprotected by legislation and most of them tend to be poor. The Economic Census conducted in the years 1990 and 1999 revealed that the employment in the unorganized sector increased from 67.34 lakhs to 72.46 lakhs respectively recording a growth rate of 0.80 per cent per annum.

Table 5. Distribution of Operational Holdings and Area by Size Classes: 1970-71 and 1995-96

Size	No.of Holdings (mil.)		Area (million ha.)		No.of holdings (%)		Area (%)	
	1970-71	1995-96	1970-71	1995-96	1970-71	1995-96	1970-71	1995-96
Marginal	2.49	6.30	1.09	2.90	46.0	59.4	8.0	20.2
Small	1.06	2.26	1.53	3.23	19.6	21.3	11.3	22.5
Semimed	0.94	1.40	2.61	3.74	17.4	13.2	19.2	26.0
Medium	0.69	0.56	4.79	3.23	12.7	5.3	35.2	22.5
Large	0.24	0.08	3.57	1.27	4.3	0.8	26.3	8.9
Total	5.42	10.60	13.59	14.37	100.0	100.0	100.0	100.0

Note: Marginal (below 1 hect.); Small (1.0 to 2.0 hect.); Semi-medium (20. To 4.0 hect.); Medium (4.0 to 10.0 hect.); Large (above 10.0 hect.).
Source: GoAP (2000).

Employment in the Organised Sector: Public and Private Sector

Much of the concern about the lack of employment reflects a strong preference for employment in the organised sector. The jobs in organised sector generally provide much higher levels of wages than in the unorganised sector and also provide much greater job security and other benefits. The available information summarized in Table 6 shows that it increased from 12.36 lakhs in 1975-76 to 20.72 lakhs in 1999-2000. The table also shows deceleration in growth of employment in organised sector over time. In the later part of 1990s, the growth rate was around 1.6 per cent per annum. In fact, since 1996-97, increase in organised employment

Table 6. Employment in Organised Sector

Years	Employment (In lakhs)	Period	Compound growth rate
1975-76	12.36	1975-76 to 1980-81	3.2
1980-81	14.46	1980-81 to 1985-86	2.2
1985-86	16.11	1985-86 to 1990-91	1.8
1990.91	17.63	1990-91 to 1995-96	1.9
1995-96	19.42	1995-96 to 1999-2000	1.6
1996-97	20.42		
1997-98	20.51		
1998-99	20.59		
1999-2000	20.72		

Source: Various issues of *Economic Survey*, GoAP.

in A.P. has been marginal. One of the main reasons for the lower growth in organised employment is the slowdown in public sector employment in the 1990s. Public sector accounts for 70 to 80 per cent of the organised employment in the state. The growth rate in public sector employment in the 70s and 80s was quite high. In the 1990s, however, growth of public sector employment was around 1 per cent only (Table 6a). On the other hand, private sector employment has been growing at the rate of 4.8 per cent per annum in the 1990s. But, growth in private sector has not been able to compensate the loss in the public sector.

Table 6 a. Public and Private Employment in Organised Sector: 1990-91 to 1999-2000

Year	Public Sector (In Lakhs)	Private Sector (In Lakhs)	Period	Growth rate in Public sector(%) per annum	Growth rate in private sector(%) per annum
1990-91	13.68	3.72	1991 to 1996	1.16	5.79
1991-92	14.04	3.83	1996 to 2000	0.92	3.56
1992-93	14.27	4.16	1991 to 2000	1.05	4.79
1995-96	14.49	4.93			
1996-97	15.07	5.35			
1997-98	15.03	5.43			
1998-99	15.09	5.50			
1999-2000	15.03	5.67			

Source: same as Table 6.

Changes in Sectoral Distribution of Workers and Rural Non-farm Employment

Here we examine diversification in terms of shifts across broad sectors in rural areas for the period 1983 to 1999-00. Diversification of rural livelihoods is important for several reasons. At the economy level, the demographic pressures on land have been increasing significantly in the state. With its share of around 30 per cent in GDP, Agriculture has to bear the burden of 65 per cent of workers. Therefore, labour productivity has been low in agriculture. Urban areas have their own problems of demographic pressures. As a result, rural non-farm sector becomes an escape route for agricultural workers. In order to increase wages in agriculture and to shift the workers to more productive areas, rural diversification is advocated.

While examining the trends we may have to disregard the numbers in 1987-88 because it was a drought year. The percent of workers in primary sector in rural A.P was lower than that of all-India rural in 1983 (Table 7). However, by 1999-2000, the share of primary sector in A.P. was higher than all India. This is because, the diversification has been much slower in A.P. as compared to all India.

The percent of workers in secondary sector in rural A.P was 9.8 per cent in 1983 and 8.6 per cent in 1999-2000; that in all-India it increased from 9 per cent to11.4 percent during the same period. In 1983, the tertiary sector's share in A.P. was higher than that for all India. By 1999-2000, the share of tertiary sector in A.P. and all India are similar.

Table 7. Broad Sectoral Distribution of Workers in Rural A.P. and India

Year	Rural A.P.			Rural all India		
	Primary	Second.	Tertiary	Primary	Second.	Tertiary
1983	79.7	9.8	11.9	81.5	9.0	9.4
1987-88	76.7	11.2	12.1	78.3	11.3	10.3
1993-94	79.0	9.5	11.5	78.2	10.2	11.5
1999-00	78.8	8.6	12.6	76.1	11.3	125

Source: NSS Rounds.

Table 8 shows that the percentage of rural non-farm employment in AP increased significantly from 17.6 % in 1977-78 to 22.8 % in 1983, and thereafter it tended to stagnate or show a decline. This is true for both males and females. In other words, jobs in the rural non-agricultural sector in rural areas were created very slowly. Since rural labor absorption in the non-farm sector is crucial for poverty reduction, the Andhra Pradesh experience in the 1990s with regard to non-farm employment creation is disturbing.

Table 8. Percentage of Non-farm Employment in rural Andhra Pradesh and Rural All India

Year	Males		Females		Total	
	AP	All India	AP	All India	AP	All India
1977-78	19.7	19.3	14.6	11.8	17.6	16.6
1983	25.6	22.4	18.7	12.2	22.8	18.4
1987-88	25.9	25.7	17.9	15.3	22.4	21.6
1993-94	24.4	26.0	16.3	13.9	20.7	21.7
1999-2000	25.6	28.7	15.7	14.6	21.2	23.8

Source: NSS data on Employment and Unemployment.

Trends at One-digit Level

NSS provides data at different levels of disaggregation based on National Industrial classification (NIC). Table 9 provides the trends in rural employment in A.P. at one digit level. In comparisons over time, we ignore 1987-88 as it is a drought year. As mentioned above the increase in rural non-farm employment has been slow in A.P. Whatever the increase is mainly concentrated in construction, trade and, services.

Table 10 provides recent changes for males and females. For males, marginal increases were noticed in non-farm employment such as construction, trade and transport. Manufacturing sector's share has not increased over time. In the case of females, the raise was mainly in services.

Table 9. Percentage Distribution of Workers by Industry at One Digit Level : Rural A.P.

Sector	1983	1987-88	1993-94	1999-2000
Agriculture & Allied	79.7	76.7	79.0	78.8
Mining and Quarrying	0.7	0.9	0.8	0.8
Manufacturing	7.7	8.0	6.9	5.6
Electricity, Water etc.	0.1	0.1	negl.	negl.
Construction	1.3	2.2	1.8	2.2
Trade, Hotel & Restaurant	4.0	4.7	4.5	4.6
Transport etc.	2.3	1.1	1.0	1.7
Real Estate business activities etc.	0.2	0.4	0.2	0.2
Services	5.4	5.8	5.7	6.2
Total	100.0	100.0	100.0	100.0

Source: NSS Rounds.

In the case of rural males in all India, sectors like construction, trade, hotels and restaurants , transport, storage, communications showed faster growth than those for A.P. In the case of females for all India, the shares of manufacturing and services increased over time. The share of manufacturing in all India increased from 5.9% in 1977-78 to 7.6% in 1999-2000. The diversification in A.P. has been much slower than that for all India.

Unemployment

Unemployment rate is the ratio of unemployed to labour force. Similar to work participation rates, NSS provides unemployment rates by usual status, current weekly status and current daily status.

Usual Status: The unemployment rates are relatively high in urban areas than rural areas in A.P as well as all India (Table 11). Unemployment rates among males are higher than females in rural areas (except in 1987-88) while female unemployment is almost similar to that for males in urban areas of A.P.

If we ignore 1987-88, there was no sign of increase in unemployment for rural and urban areas of A.P. In 1999-2000, significant increase occurred for urban males. The rates in rural and urban areas of A.P are less than that for All-India for both males and females.

Current Daily Status: As can be seen from Table 11, the unemployment rates according to CDS are higher than those of usual status. The rate declined upto 1993-94 but there was significant increase in 1999-2000 in rural A.P and India. In urban areas there was only a marginal increase in unemployment rates. Increase in rural unemployment in A.P. is a matter of concern.

Table 10. Distribution of Workers by Industry at One Digit Level : Males and Females (%)

Sector	Rural Males		Rural Females	
	1993-94	1999-2000	1993-94	1999-2000
Agriculture & Allied	75.6	74.4	83.7	84.3
Mining and Quarrying	0.9	0.9	0.5	0.7
Manufacturing	6.5	5.3	7.4	6.0
Electricity, Water etc.	0.1	0.1	0.0	0.0
Construction	2.6	3.4	0.6	0.8
Trade, Hotel & Restaurant	5.4	5.8	3.4	3.0
Transport etc.	1.9	3.0	0.0	0.1
Real Estate business activities etc.	0.4	0.4	0.1	0.0
Services (public adm.. Comm. etc)	6.7	6.7	4.2	5.1
Total	100.0	100.0	100.0	100.0

Source: NSS Rounds.

Underemployment

Underemployment is commonly defined as the underutilisation of labour time of the workers. Some of the workers classified as usually employed do not have work throughout the year due to seasonality in work or otherwise and their labour time is not fully utilised – they are therefore underemployed.

Table 11. Usual status and current daily status unemployment rates in A.P and India

Year	M	F	M	F	M	F	M	F
	Usual Status				Daily Status			
	A.P.		India		A.P.		India	
				Rural				
1983	1.4	0.9	2.1	1.4	7.9	10.5	7.5	9.0
1987-88	2.5	4.5	2.8	3.5	4.9	9.4	4.6	6.7
1993-94	1.0	0.5	2.0	1.3	5.9	7.0	5.6	5.6
1999-'00	1.2	0.7	2.1	1.5	8.8	8.7	7.2	7.0
				Urban				
1983	5.4	5.1	5.9	6.9	9.4	12.1	9.2	11.0
1987-88	6.4	9.0	6.1	8.5	10.1	13.2	8.8	12.0
1993-94	3.5	4.3	5.4	8.3	7.5	9.5	6.7	10.4
1999-'00	4.3	4.4	4.8	7.1	7.7	9.7	7.3	9.4

Note: Usual Status refers to Principal status. M-male, F-female.
Source: Different rounds of NSS data.

The unemployed person days for rural males in A.P. has increased from 5.0% in 1993-94 to 6.7 % in 1999-00 (Table 12). Similarly it increased for rural females. The unemployed person days are higher for A.P. than all India. For the females, the percentage of employed increased significantly while that of 'not in the labour force' declined during the period 1993-94 and 1999-2000.

Table 12. Underemployment: Per 1000 distribution of person-days of usually employed (principal and subsidiary) by their current daily status in Rural A.P.

Current daily status	Males		Females	
	1993-94	1999-2000	1993-94	1999-2000
Employed	898	881	722	739
Unemployed	50	67	53	59
Not in labour force	53	51	226	202
Total	1000	1000	1000	1000

Source: NSS Rounds.

Unemployment Rates for Educated

The problem of long term unemployment (usual status) seems to be more with educated and the youth. As shown, in Table 13, educated unemployment is higher than normal unemployment rate particularly for females. Although unemployment rate for urban female educated has declined, it is still high at 15 per cent. The unemployment for educated females in rural A.P. increased from 7.9% to 15.0% in the 1990s. Youth unemployment is also higher as compared to overall unemployment in A.P[5].

Table 13. Unemployment Rate Among Educated: Usual Status, 1993-94 (%)

Category	Andhra Pradesh		All India	
	1993-94	1999-00	1993-94	1999-00
Rural Males	7.6	7.2	8.8	6.8
Rural Females	7.9	15.0	24.9	20.4
Urban Males	7.4	6.1	6.9	6.6
Urban Females	24.9	14.5	20.6	16.3

Source: NSS 50th Round.

The proportion of Educated is high Among the total Unemployed: Earlier, illiterate persons used to dominate the unemployed population. In recent years, the proportion of educated among unemployed is quite high as shown in Table 14. Even in rural areas, around 76 per cent of the male unemployed are educated. These proportions are high for the urban males and females.

Table 14. Proportion of Educated Among Unemployed: 1993-94 (%)

Category	Andhra Pradesh	All India
Rural Males	75.8	61.4
Rural Females	22.5	59.1
Urban Males	73.8	59.5
Urban Females	94.1	73.2

Source: NSS 50th Round.

The above numbers indicate that there is a need to increase jobs for educated employed and also to raise the job quality of those who are presently employed.

3. QUALITY OF EMPLOYMENT

Focusing on employment and unemployment fails to capture an aspect of the employment problem, which is extremely important, and this relates to what may be called the quality of employment. Income or wages is one of the variables reflecting quality. Many people are employed but they get low wages and income. That is why there is so much gap between unemployment (based on time criterion) and poverty and we have many numbers of 'working poor'. In this section, we examine changes in variables representing quality of employment such as casualisation, labour productivity, real wages and, poverty by sectors.

Casualisation of Labour

The proportion of self-employment has been declining over time (Table 15). One of the reasons is the decline in farmers cultivating their own land owing to fragmentation of holdings. There has been sharp increase in casual labour. Andhra Pradesh has the second highest percentage of casual labour in the country in rural areas. The percentage of casual labourers was 48.3 while the corresponding percentage of casual labour is only 37.4 per cent for all India in 1999-00. As shown in Table 16, the percentage of casual labour increased for both males and females.

Employment and Education

Education is important for workers in order to get qualitative employment. Literacy alone is at best only one indicator. Literacy definition covers anyone who can write their name and this means many people may be classified as literate although they may not understand simple written instructions. Unless we have these abilities for workers, the efficiency of the labour force in many occupations is likely to remain low. Table 17 provides the educational standards of the workers in Andhra Pradesh and All India. It shows that in A.P. 88 per cent of the rural workers are either illiterate or have been educated only up to primary level. In other words, less than 15 per cent of the workers have education of middle school or above. Similarly in urban areas of A.P., 63 per cent are either illiterate or have education up to primary school. Education of workers in A.P. is much lower than that for all India.

Labour Productivity

Gross state domestic product (GSDP)at constant prices per NSS worker–provides one meaningful absolute measure of employment quality.

Table 15. Distribution of Usually Employed by Category of Employment

Year	Rural A.P.			Rural All India		
	Self Employed	Regular Employed	Casual Labourers	Self Employed	Regular Employed	Casual Labourers
1983	47.3	8.9	43.9	61.0	7.3	31.3
1987-88	49.1	6.8	44.2	59.4	7.7	32.9
1993-94	47.5	5.2	47.3	58.0	6.4	35.6
1999-00	45.8	5.9	48.3	55.8	6.8	37.4

Source: NSS Rounds.

Table 16. Percentage of Casual Labour in Rural Areas for Males and Females

Year	A.P.		All India	
	Males	Females	Males	Females
1977-78	32.4	50.8	26.6	35.1
1983	34.3	50.4	29.2	35.3
1987-88	38.1	49.7	31.4	35.5
1993-94	42.8	52.8	33.8	38.7
1999-00	44.0	53.8	36.2	39.6

Source: NSS Rounds.

Table 17. Percentage Composition of Workers of Age 15 years and above by Level of Education: Andhra Pradesh and All India: 1999-00

Level of Education	Andhra Pradesh		All India	
	Rural	Urban	Rural	Urban
Not Literate	59.7	30.7	51.3	21.5
Literate up to Primary	27.9	32.0	23.3	21.1
Middle Level and Above	12.4	37.3	25.4	57.4
Total	100.0	100.0	100.0	100.0

Note: Computed from NSS 55th Round (1999-00) data.

Bhalla (2000, 2001) provides estimates of labour productivity by sectors for states during 1983 to 1999-2000. All India estimates are given upto 1993-94. Sector wise labour productivity since 1983 are provided in Table 18. Labour productivity in agriculture declined between 1983 and 1993-94 before increasing significantly in 1999-2000. In construction it declined in 1999-2000. On the other hand, manufacturing sector recorded significant increase continuously since 1983 – the highest increase was noticed in 1999-2000. In general, late 1990s witnessed a significant growth in major sectors of A.P. economy.

A comparison with All India upto 1993-94 shows that the levels of labour productivity in A.P. in all the sub-sectors were lower in A.P. as compared to all India (Table 18). Sundaram (2001) provides growth rates of labour productivity for sub-sectors of all India during the period 1993-94 to 1999-2000. These estimates show that agriculture and manufacturing showed 3.36 per cent and 6.13 per cent per annum respectively. As compared to these, A.P. recorded growth rates of 4.38 per cent and 12.86 per cent respectively in agriculture and manufacturing. On the other hand, the growth rates in construction and transport were lower in A.P. as compared to all India.

Table 18. Labour Productivity (GSDP per UPSS worker) in different sectors (Rs. In constant 1980-81 prices)) in A.P. and All India

Year	Agriculture	Construction	Services	Manufacturing	Transport	Trade
A. P. (GSDP per person)						
1983	2261.85	8446.73	6862.32	4471.86	7986.78	7521.94
1987-88	2109.76	6462.13	7718.27	4938.16	9464.31	7805.19
1993-94	2183.45	9602.92	8852.11	5498.23	10685.26	8494.62
1999-2000	2706.00	6597.00	N.A.	9460.00	11296.00	N.A.
Average of 16 states GSDP per person						
1983	2491.65	9450.89	9196.60	7529.89	8761.21	8210.72
1987-88	2532.92	8160.88	10714.26	8453.60	10005.86	8359.71
1993-94	2870.87	9139.12	12326.58	10800.23	11468.26	9678.27

Source: Bhalla (2000), Bhalla (2001).

Real Wages

Trend in real wages is an important indicator of changes in livelihoods. Table 19 indicates that real wages increased in the 1980s, but growth rate was low in the 1990s for both men and women. The trend rate

Table 19. Nominal and Real Wages of Field Labor in Agriculture

Year	Nominal Wages		Real Wages (80-81=100)	
	Males	Females	Males	Females
1981	5.9	4.4	5.9	4.4
1983	8.0	6.0	6.6	4.9
1985	10.4	7.7	7.8	5.8
1987	12.0	8.9	8.4	6.2
1989	14.6	10.6	8.1	5.9
1991	19.6	14.2	9.0	6.5
1993	25.1	17.8	9.0	6.4
1995	31.1	22.2	9.3	6.6
1997	37.9	28.5	9.7	7.3
1999	43.5	32.2	9.8	7.2
Trerd Growth Rates (%)				
1981-90	11.64	9.84	5.74	4.76
1990-99	10.70	1023	1.53	1.94

Note: Real wages are obtained by deflating the money wages with Consumer price index for agricultural labourers.

of growth for males declined from 5.74 % in the 1980s to 1.53 % in the 1990s. Similarly for women, the trend rate of growth in real wages has declined from 4.76 % in the 1980s to 1.94 % in the 1990s. Growing rural wages in real terms was one of the key determinants of poverty reduction in India in the 1980s. The trend in Andhra Pradesh is therefore worrying. It is also not clear why the increase in real wages are not commensurate with that of labour productivity.

Table 20 shows real wages for agriculture and non-agriculture. The non-agricultural wage levels are higher than those for agriculture. It indicates that diversification to non-agriculture may be due to pull factor rather than push factor. Real wages in both agriculture and non-agriculture seem to have increased over time. However, as shown above the rate of growth has been slower in the 1990s as compared to 70s and 80s.

Table 20. Real Agricultural and Non-Agricultural Wage Earnings among Wage worker in Rural Labour Households at 1960-61 prices: A.P. and All India (in Rs.)

Year	Adult Males		Adult Females	
	Agricultural	Non-Agricultural	Agricultural	Non-Agricultural
Andhra Pradesh				
1964-65	0.9	1.0	0.4	0.7
1974-75	0.8	1.0	0.6	0.6
1977-78	1.2	1.6	0.8	0.9
1983	1.1	1.4	0.8	0.8
1987-88	1.6	1.9	1.1	1.3
1993-94	2.0	2.6	1.4	1.5
All India				
1964-65	1.0	1.3	0.6	0.8
1974-75	0.9	1.1	0.6	0.6
1977-78	1.2	1.9	0.8	0.9
1983	1.0	1.5	0.7	0.8
1987-88	1.4	1.7	1.1	1.2
1993-94	1.9	2.8	1.3	1.5

Source: Unni (1999).

Rural Poverty by Sectors: Is Diversification to non-agriculture due to push or pull factors?

Poverty ratios in different sectors provide a less direct but equally valuable indicator of the relative productivity of work in different sectors of the economy. The head count poverty ratios by sectors are available for rural areas. Table 27 provides these estimates for rural A.P. estimated by Bhalla (2000). The numbers show that in the rural areas, three poorest segments are: agricultural labourers, construction workers, and persons in households mainly engaged in manufacturing, in that order, followed by other services, then households mainly engaged in cultivation, trade, and finally, far below all others, rural health and education services. It may be noted that rural workers in manufacturing and construction are poorer than cultivators. The numbers show that for agricultural labourers, shift to any other sector seems to be a better option and one can say that it reflects a pull factor. On the other hand, if cultivators shift to manufacturing or construction or transport, they would be worse off and it may reflect a push factor in rural areas. However, most of the poor (nearly 90%) are concentrated in agriculture.

Table 21. Rural Head Count Poverty Ratios for Persons in Households Engaged in Specified Sectors: 1987-88 and 1993-94 : A.P.

Reference Year	Cultivators	Agricultural labourers	Construction	Manufacturing	Trade	Transport	Health & Education	Other Services
1987/88	12.53	32.58	25.98	16.83	13.13	13.13	2.55	16.4
1993/94	9.67	23.30	18.71	12.97	8.90	8.90	0.83	9.89

Source: Bhalla (2000).

4. STRATEGIC OPTIONS

Challenge

The above facts on macro scenario shows that the immediate challenge is to diversify the activities which include shifting the workers to non-agriculture sector to improve the livelihoods of poor workers. It may be noted that agricultural growth would not be sufficient to absorb the growing labour force. As shown above, In India as well as in A.P., unemployment rates are not high. The rates are around 7 to 8 per cent in both all India and A.P. This is because unemployment rates are based on time criterion. Poor people are too poor to be unemployed for a long time. We have the concept of "working poor". In other words many people are working at low wages, low working conditions in agriculture and informal sector. Therefore, the challenge is to shift these workers to high productivity sectors and also create new jobs in the non-agriculture sector. Thus, the real nature of the unemployment problem is not that people are not 'employed' in some activity but that large number of those classified as employed are engaged in low quality employment, which does not provide adequate income to keep a family above the poverty line. Besides, the employment opportunities available in the market too often do not come up to expectations of the new and increasingly educated entrants to the labour force. The employment strategy we need therefore is not a strategy, which ensures an adequate growth in the volume of employment but one, which ensures a sufficient growth in high quality of employment opportunities.

Around 95 per cent of the A.P. workers arc in thc unorganised sector. Therefore policies have to take into account the unorganised sector.

Projections and Strategic Options [6]

In order to have macro strategies, we need to know the likely scenario of employment, investments needed in future. Therefore, we have made projections for the workers and investments in the five-year period and 20 year period. Also, five scenarios of projections were made in order to know the impact of investments in different sectors on poverty and inequality. The procedure followed for projections are the following:

- Using employment data of Census 1981 and 1991 for 10 NIC (National Industrial Classification) categories (one digit level) and State Domestic Product (SDP) data, we computed the Compound annual growth rate (CAGR) of output per worker.
- Based on this, we projected employment and output in each category for 2005 & 2020.
- The employment and output along with the Incremental Capital Output Ratio (ICOR) was used to estimate the investments needed and the CAGR of SDP for 2005 and 2020.

The following assumptions were made regarding ICOR:

- In general, productivity enhancement has been assumed to be coincidental with increase in ICOR.
- Accordingly, ICORs have been increased where they were low.
- However, ICORs have been reduced where efficiency gains are likely to set in due to private ownership, competition etc.

The projections show that employment would increase from 36 million in 1999-2000 to 57 million in 2020 i.e. by 21 millions. If we add 3 million backlog of unemployed in 2000, labour force increase by 2020 would be 24 million. The Cabinet Sub-Committee on Employment Generation and Manpower Planning provides different figures regarding the projection of workers in A.P. According to the Committee, the workforce in A.P. would increase from 47.1 million in 1999-2000 to 56.2 million without intervention (61.5 million with intervention) in the year 2020. The differences between Committee's and our projections could be due to some assumptions regarding shifts in workforce.

Employment Strategies: Five Options

Next question is to examine the strategic options, which would give an idea of the likely impact on employment, poverty and inequality. The following are the five options used in the study.

- Status Quo: No change from 1981-91 trends.
- Agricultural and allied sectors productivity has been enhanced, as also employment in allied sectors: Here we are not increasing the employment of agriculture because we need reduction in the workers in agriculture.
- Agriculture, allied and services sectors productivity has been enhanced, as also employment in the latter two sectors. Here also we are assuming that there is no increase in agricultural employment.
- Services sectors productivity and employment has been significantly enhanced.

- Manufacturing Sector productivity and employment significantly enhanced.

Findings

Our estimates of the key indicators of different strategic options for employment generation in A.P. reveal the following

- The agri+allied+services option seems to be the most desirable from the point of view of increasing employment, while reducing poverty and income disparity significantly
- The services led option is even better but needs more investment and does not reduce income disparity as much
- The manufacturing led option increases incomes, but with higher disparity, and requires high investment

5. CONSTRAINTS, POLICIES AND RECOMMENDATIONS

In section 2, we have discussed that public sector can not generate jobs and the future employment has to be created in organised and unorganised private sector. Government should act as a facilitator to increase private sector investment, which in turn increases employment. In this section, we will discuss about constraints for private sector participation and suggest recommendations for promotion of employment in different sectors of A.P.

Market Failure and Other Constraints

Market failure and other constraints prevent active private sector participation in promising subsectors. This in turn has a negative impact on employment. The direct control of and access to natural resources such as land, water and forests, as well on infrastructure such as power and roads, by the Government has restricted action by private sector and civil society institutions. Some examples of market failure and other constraints are given below.

Labour Market Failure

A large amount of seasonal unemployment in Rayalaseema and Telangana areas co-exists with shortage of agricultural labour in the coastal region and in urban manual activities. The "shortage" of labour has led many construction contractors to go in for mechanical equipment for digging, earthwork, road laying, and so on. The problem is even more severe when one moves up slightly the skill ladder, such as for carpenters, masons, plumbers and electricians. Unemployment for the powerloom and handloom weavers, for example in Sircilla co-exists with a shortage of garment workers at the new Apparel Park of Gundla Pochampally, just 150

Table 22. Key Indicators of Different Strategic Options for Employment Generation in AP

Key Indicators	Base Data	Same as 1981-1991		Agri+Allied		Agri+Allied+ Services		Services		Manufacturing	
	2000	2005	2020	2005	2020	2005	2020	2005	2020	2005	2020
Ag lab % (Poverty ratio)	44	44	42	44	40	42	25	42	15	43	26
Aglab per worker output	5675	6083	7492	6265	9761	6420	10756	6420	10756	6265	9761
Avg per worker output	14528	16705	26362	16856	28013	18123	48050	18356	55434	17817	51943
Aglab/Avg Output as %	39	36	28	37	35	35	22	35	19	35	19
Investment reqd Rs Cr pa		18025	11739	16988	11940	22377	29418	26267	39794	24541	42555
CAGR of SDP		5.28	5.53	5.47	5.89	7.01	9.24	7.29	10.19	6.65	9.93

kms away. Promoters there complain that not enough persons are available even to undertake skill training.

There is an absence of mechanisms for moving workers out of subsectors where demand is declining, such as handloom and powerloom, into those subsectors where demand is increasing, such as apparel and construction. This failure in the labour market can partly be explained by the lack of information, inadequate rural-urban transportation linkages (although considerably eased by the recent introduction and popularity of seven seater tempos) and inadequate difference in wage rates to compensate for the risk of migration.

Credit Market Failure

There is a huge unmet demand for credit. As per the State focus Paper of NABARD, the total potential demand for rural credit is Rs 11,899 crores in 20001-02 whereas the expected supply is Rs 9650 crores, leaving a gap of Rs 2248 crores. At the same time, there is no constraint of funds , as is obvious from the Credit deposit ratio of the state at 68 percent in March 1999[7]. There is a huge network of banks, even in rural areas, with 2322 rural and 467 semi-urban branches. There are even targets and priority sector lending obligations.

Table 23. Five Options: Key Results by 2020

Option	Poverty (agri-labour as % of total)	Income disparity*	Growth CAGR %
No change	42	28	5.53
Emphasis toAgri + Allied	40	35	5.89
Emphasis to Aagri+Allied+ Services	25	22	9.24
Emphasis to Services	15	19	10.19
Emphasis to Manufacturing	26	19	9.93

* Income disparity is the ratio of agricultural labour productivity and total productivity.

Yet, the availability of credit, both for fixed asset purchases and for working capital, has been a problem area both in terms of access and transaction costs. Due to the inadequacy of loan amount, time delay and excessive paper work in getting a loan from formal institutions, a majority of the producers rely on informal channels, such as traders for working capital. The SHG movement in the state testifies the extent to which the poor face credit constraints and the extent to which they are willing to invest their time in having access to flexible and friendly credit sources.

Apart from credit market failure, the newer rural subsectors fail to attract private investment as the private sector seeks opportunities with an assured return considerably higher than the bank interest rates. If the return is higher but perceived risk is also higher, then private sector hesitates from investing. Thus an attempt needs to be made to reduce risk perception through information sharing and appropriate regulatory frameworks. For example, investments in the forestry sector will not come as long as restrictions on felling and transport of timber are not rationalised.

Commodity/Product Market Failure

Lack of information about new market opportunities has restricted the participation of the private sector or constrained micro-entrepreneurs to continue catering to declining market segments. For example, in groundnut, while there is a competitive squeeze in the edible oil market due to cheap palm oil imports, the market for whole nuts for confectionery and other purposes is growing. Yet very few units have responded to this, while oil mills are closing down. This is due to lack of information on new market segments.

Generally the role of middlemen in marketing is criticized as they siphon off a major share of the value added. However, the positive role of "middlemen" has to be recognised in marketing products which are produced by the unorganised sector. It includes their role in identifying the market demand pattern, transportation and taking risk of the product damage and price changes in between transporting it from the producer to market. In several cases, members of SHGs find it difficult to market their products. They could actually benefit by dealing with competitive middlemen. Indeed, where they can, many SHGs have themselves become "middlewomen", marketing products on behalf of Hindustan Levers and Philips.

Infrastructure Constraints

Lack of power in rural areas seems to be an important constraint for agriculture as well as some of the rural non-farm subsectors, such as powerloom. Even handloom weavers want power so that they can weave late in the night using electric light. Power is in general available for 8 to 9 hours in rural areas. The farmers are willing to pay more provided they get assured supply and voltage, but APTRANSCO cannot assure that so it is unwilling to supply more power to rural areas since it loses over Rs 2 for every unit it supplies! Water problem is also acute in some areas. Road network is important to improve the business environment in rural areas. There has been some improvement in rural roads. There has been significant improvement in telecommunications but in some areas network is poor.

The lack of training and infrastructure was lamented by all concerned. Yet we found that the provision for up to 20 percent expenditure on infrastructure and 10 percent on training of borrowers (all as a grant) under SGSY was not being used by most DRDAs. The MDOs were not even aware of these. The main reason for this "market failure" is the long chain of decision making from the GoI to RDC to the DRDA to the MDO, resulting in unrealistic norms and non-implementation.

Policy Suggestions and Recommendations

The Government has to act as a facilitator and create favourable conditions for private sector participation and identify and prioritize key sectors with employment potential and ensure successful implementation. The Government appointed A.P. Employment Generation Mission and issued a strategy paper on employment. The strategies are, however, biased towards higher educated population. We recommend the following strategies for increasing employment for unskilled workers and educated workers.

- Twin Sub-strategies
- Focus on Selected Growth Engines and Clusters
- Selected Growth Engines for the un/semi-skilled masses
- Selected Growth Engines for the Educated Unemployed
- Strategy for Self Employment
- Employment Programmes
- Labour market flexibility
- Public-private partnership

Twin Sub-strategies:

Given the problem of unemployment for educated and unemployment and underemployment for the masses, there is a need to have twin strategies for improving the livelihoods. The first sub-strategy should aim at rural and urban masses who are illiterate/semi-literate, unskilled, semi-literate/skilled. About 10 lakhs persons per year are being added to the workforce due to population growth, land pressure etc. The second sub-strategy is to address the approximately 31 lakhs educated unemployed, registered in employment exchanges. The policy goal should be to improve economic growth in rural areas with emphasis on employment for the poor, and shift workers from agriculture to non-agriculture activities, particularly services in rural areas. To achieve this goal, it is necessary to focus on selected growth engines and clusters: In order to have a focussed intervention, the Vision 2020 had suggested 18 "growth engines" for vertical (e.g. leaf to cloth) subsectoral interventions. However, our analysis shows that these may not be adequate to generate near full employment and that the number of growth engines may have to be increased to between 30 to 40 for that purpose. Further, nearly 200 poorest mandals can be selected for focus. The Government can then identify which of the above growth engines can be promoted in each mandal.

Selected Growth Engines for the un/semi-skilled masses
Primary activities: (a) Agro-processing and agro-services (spraying, tractor operation, repairs); (b) vegetable growing, trading and processing; (c) Horticulture and floriculture; (d) sericulture and silk handlooms; (e) Forest produce processing

Secondary Activities: (a) Handlooms and handicrafts; (b) apparel parks - tailors, cutters; (c) leather tanning and goods; (d) stoneware and ceramics; (e) cement and construction materials

Tertiary Activities: (a) construction - workers, masons, barbers, carpenters, painters etc. (b) paramedicals and paravets; (c) transport of goods and passenger (d) housekeeping services; (e) Child care and pediatric services.

Selected Growth Engines for the Educated Unemployed
The selected growth engines are:

Agricultural services - extension, input supply, repairs, produce marketing; Utility retailing - electricity, water, sanitary and telecom services; IT and IT enabled services - data entry, medical transcription and financial back-office services, CAD/CAM, low-end programming; Apparel/fashion design; construction - draftsmen, site supervisors; Tourism - catering, hotel management, guides; Educational services- English teaching; Health care services - including administrative and support jobs in hospitals and clinics; Business services - accounts, sales etc.; Financial services - capacity building of SHGs, housing and consumer loan retailing, insurance retailing etc.

Strategy for Self Employment

- Training of educated unemployed to become self-employed service professionals in travel, transport, tourism, education, health, financial and IT enabled services
- Self employment in petty trading, hotels, transport, repairs, miscellaneous services
- Retraining of self employed in response to changing market demand

Employment Programmes

For helping the poor, the government has many wage and self employment programmes Swarna Jayanti Swarojgar Yojana (SGSY), Development of Women and Children in Rural Areas (DWCRA), Employment Assurance Scheme (EAS) etc. They generally act as providers of supplementary employment. The effectiveness of these programmes can be improved by involving panchayati raj institutions, NGOs and CBOs. There is also a need to link these programmes to sectoral activities[8].

Labour market flexibility

It is possible that labour market reforms attract private investment including foreign direct investment. The entrepreneurs may prefer contract labour to permanent labour. However, productivity enhancing measures like technology and infrastructure are more important for raising output than labour market reforms.

Public-private Partnership

There is a need to have public and private partnership to improve the livelihoods. Government can only be a facilitator for enhancing private investment. There are some private industry initiatives with Government acting as facilitator e.g. Apparel Park at Gundlapochampally, Philips - sale of energy efficient fluorescent lamps in rural areas, linkage of SHGs with Hindustan Lever Limited for retailing of consumer products, and linkage of SHGs to supply items to Food World outlets. The partnership of BASIX with APDDCF (Andhra Pradesh Dairy Development Co-operative Federation) in revitalising milk chilling plants is another example. Private Training Institutions (Engineering, IT, polytechnics) have come up in response to market demand while the government has confined itself to ensuring standards. In general, as the GoAP faces fiscal constraints and the need for investments goes up manifold, it may be necessary to think of establishing new infrastructure on the "build, own, operate" model.

Sectoral Strategies

Agriculture

Experience from all over India, and indeed from other developing countries, shows that the greatest stimulant for the growth of the non-agricultural economy in rural areas is dynamic agricultural growth9. The linkages between agriculture and non-agriculture are well known. Unfortunately, the growth rate of agricultural and allied activities has been less than 2 per cent in AP in the 1990s. Enhancing agricultural productivity requires as a first step, soil and water conservation measures, using the watershed management approach in undulating and dryland areas, and tank rehabilitation in all areas. Water users associations formed under canal areas should be activated also in the tankfed areas and in small lift irrigation fed areas.

Only after these steps are taken should farmers be encouraged to use improved varieties of seeds, fertilisers including a judicious mix of organic manure, and integrated pest management techniques. As several field level studies show, there is no point in pushing the old style HYV-chemical fertiliser-pesticide package to farmers in poorer areas without first addressing soil and water conservation10. Programs like the Andhra Pradesh Rural Livelihoods Programme (APRLP) of DFID and the District Poverty Initiative Project of the World Bank should be used for this. Three issues that need policy attention with respect to irrigation water are:

- Control over indiscriminate use of ground water in dryland areas, to grow paddy, for example.
- Ensuring higher quality and more number of hours of power to irrigation pumpsets but at the same time enforcing metering and steadily increasing the tariff charged to farmers.
- A mechanism to extend benefit of irrigation to landless labourers, through a combination of land allotment and extending common borewells/lift irrigation schemes

After agriculture, the next important livelihood is animal husbandry, particularly dairy. The already considerable network and infrastructure of the APDDCF and the Animal Husbandry department needs to be revitalised, as has been done in certain milk chilling plants in Mahaboobnagar district[11]. The delicensing of milk processing up to 10,000 litres has created opportunities for private plants to come to smaller places. This should be encouraged by offering incentives to "pioneer" dairy plants in backward mandals. Animal husbandry support activities which can be encouraged is breed upgradation and veterinary services, as is being done by the APDDCF and BAIF through Livestock Breeders Associations and the "Gopal Mitra" scheme of private para-veterinarians. Among animals other than cattle, sheep rearing is one potential activity, particularly as forest cover is beginning to be restored in the state and there is increasing possibility of pastures. The Deccani variety needs to be upgraded for wool and wool carding and spinning units can then come in various dryland mandals. In the tank/canal irrigated areas particularly, north coastal districts and "agency" areas, fishery is an important possibility. The experience of fishery development in Kolleru lake can be replicated elsewhere in the state.

Diversifying beyond agriculture and allied activities

The structural transformation of the rural economy of AP will not happen merely by targeting agriculture and other primary sectors: animal husbandry, fishery. Non-farm sectors, particularly forestry, mining, and quarrying, processing, manufacturing, construction, utilities, trade, warehousing, transport, services - health, education, business, financial and other services also require progressive policies for their promotion. The scope for forest based livelihoods is large, whether it is bamboo work or tamarind processing or medicinal plants. As the JFM schemes successfully increase the usufructs, time has come to build NTFP based livelihood strategies. The experience of Girijan Development Corporation and NGOs such as Outreach can be used as a basis for this. In the rural tourism there is a lot of scope for promoting this composite services subsector in numerous locations across the state.

Credit

It as emerged as a constraint across all the sectors of A.P. economy. Though a large network of banks exists in the state, and nearly Rs 8,000 crores is disbursed as credit every year to rural AP, the supply is well below demand. The following steps can be taken:

- To ensure timeliness of bank credit, which is particularly crucial for crop loans, the Kisan Credit Card scheme should be universalised in the state.
- Strict monitoring of the CD ratios of banks at the sub-district level to ensure that in backward locations.
- Building on the successful experience of bank-SHG linkage model, ensuring high coverage in poorer 200 mandals. Programs like DPIP should be used for this.
- To encourage a large number of microfinance institutions to come up to provide rural finance on a commercial basis.
- To provide term loans and start up finance for establishing small to medium sized units for commercialized primary activities (cash crops, horticulture, forestry, medicinal plants, dairy, fishery) and agro-processing in backward mandals.

Infrastructure and marketing

Power, water, roads, communications should be improved to improve the business environment. There is also a need to develop counseling and enterprise escort services. There is a need to have more market facilities as market is considered one of the important constraints in rural areas. Marketing channels for the mass e.g. Rythu Bazars, DWCRA Bazars and ten percent of SHGs to serve as market agents for other SHGs, have to be increased. Infrastructure development can be done without using the limited resources of the GoAP,

- By relying on the "build, own, operate" model for infrastructure development.
- By using NABARD's Rural Infrastructure Development Fund loans
- By making full use of the allocations under SGSY for infrastructure development
- By reviving, with limited investments, existing infrastructure such as defunct lift irrigation schemes and milk chilling plants

- ➢ The network of Training and Technology Development Centres in each district which can improve some of the technologies in rural areas.

By establishing Rythu and DWCRA bazars for marketing of rural products.

Finally, major effort to promote literacy and more importantly to bring about improvement in skill levels of those in working age group consistent with their level of education should therefore have high priority. One weakness of government supplied and directed education and training has been a divorce of the supply of skills from the demands of the market for skills.

6. CONCLUSIONS

This paper examines employment situation in Andhra Pradesh by providing a profile of trends in employment and unemployment including quality of employment. The paper also discusses about constraints and provides policy suggestions and recommendations for promoting productive employment.

The nature of employment problem in A.P. can be summarized as follows.

- Employment in A.P. is largely unorganised, rural and non-industrial. The work participation rates declined significantly in both rural and urban areas in the 1990s. The incidence of child labour is the highest in the country.
- The employment growth recorded a drastic decline during 1993-94 to 1999-2000 as compared to those for the period 1983-84 to 1993-94. Probably the expectations of increasing employment opportunities due to economic reforms has not materialized at the aggregate level.
- There has been a proliferation of small and marginal farmers over time. The share of cultivators in the total declined while those of agricultural labourers increased.
- Only around 6 per cent of the total work force is in the organised sector in A.P. The growth of employment in the organised sector has declined over time. In the post-reform period, the growth of public sector employment declined drastically while that of private sector employment increased. However, the growth of private sector employment has not been able to compensate for the loss of jobs in the public sector.

- The share of non-farm employment in rural areas has been stagnant in 1983. The diversification of employment has been slower in A.P. as compared to all India in the 1990s.
- There is no sign of increase in the usual status unemployment rates. However, the daily status unemployment recorded significant increase in the 1990s. It is a matter of concern for the state. The problem of unemployment is more with the educated and youth.
- Casualization has been increasing over time. Rural A.P. has the second highest percentage of casual labourers in the country.
- Labour productivity showed high growth in agriculture and manufacturing in the 1990s. Inspite of this, the growth of real wages in rural areas declined significantly in the 1990s.
- Around 91 per cent of the rural workers in A.P. are either illiterate or have been educated only upto primary level.

Our macro projections show that focus on agriculture & allied and services option seems to be the most desirable from the point of view of increasing employment, while reducing poverty and income disparity significantly.

We have discussed about the constraints for private sector participation. Market failure in labour, credit, product are some of the constraints. Low infrastructure is another important constraint.

The study recommends that given the problem of unemployment and underemployment for the masses and unemployment for educated, there is a need to have twin strategies for improving the livelihoods. The first sub-strategy should aim at rural and urban masses who are illiterate/semi-literate, unskilled, semi-literate/skilled. The second sub-strategy has to address the educated unemployed. The policy goal should be to improve economic growth in rural areas with emphasis on employment for the poor, and shift workers from agriculture to non-agriculture activities, particularly services in rural areas. To achieve this goal, it is necessary to focus on selected growth engines and clusters: In order to have a focussed intervention, the Vision 2020 had suggested 18 "growth engines" for vertical (e.g. leaf to cloth) subsectoral interventions. However, our analysis shows that these may not be adequate to generate near full employment and that the number of growth engines may have to be increased to between 30 to 40 for that purpose.

In conclusion, we can say that the task of generating employment is an urgent one and needs a range of concerted actions from the government, donors, banks, and the private sector and from civil society institutions.

Notes

1 For details see GOI (2001).
2 See Parthasarathy (1995).
3 In order to capture the complexities of the employment situation in a predominantly agrarian and unorganised economy like India, the estimates of employment and unemployment by NSSO are derived on three concepts, Usual Status (US); Current Weekly Status (CWS) and Current Daily Status (CDS). The three concepts are based on three different reference periods for ascertaining the activity status of a person. Under the Usual Status concept the reference period is one year and the activity status of a person as employed, unemployed or out of labour force is determined on the basis of activity pursued by him for the major part of the year. On the CWS criterion, a person is considered as employed or unemployed if he has worked or has not worked though was available for work, respectively, even for one hour during the week. Under the CDS approach, the unit of classification is half day. Under this approach the person days are distributed by activity category during an average week. A deficiency of the present time criterion based estimates of employment is that one gets to know little about how well employed (income etc.) are the persons who are seen as employed. They also do not provide the multiple activities by persons/households.
4 In 1999-2000, Himachal Pradesh has the next highest women's participation rate (47.1%) in rural areas.
5 Usual status estimates show that youth unemployment in urban areas of A.P. was 9.3 per cent while the overall unemployment in urban areas was 1.5 per cent in 1999-00.
6 This sub-section is based on Mahendra Dev and Mahajan (2000).
7 Lower credit-deposit ratio indicates not necessarily 'surplus' but utilization of funds elsewhere. In general, credit-deposit ratio for rural areas in the country is lower than for urban areas indicating that rural areas are net savers whereas urban areas are net investors.
8 More on this see chapter on poverty.
9 See Ravallion (2000).
10 On field level experiences, see Mahajan and Mahendra Dev (2001).
11 For details of this experiment, see Mahajan and Mahendra Dev (2001).

References

Bhalla, S. (2000), "Behind Poverty: The Qualitative deterioration of Employment Prospects for Rural Indians", Working paper number 7, Institute for Human Development, Delhi.

Bhalla, S. (2001), "Assessing Quality of Employment Growth using National Sample Survey data", paper presented at NSSO Golden Jubilee Seminar, Pune, April 6-7, 2001.

GoAP (1999): *Vision 2020, Swarna Andhra Pradesh*, State Secretariat.

GoAP (2000): *Economic Survey, 1999-2000*, Finance and Planning Department.

GOI (2001), *Report of the Prime Minister's Task Force on Employment Opportunities*, Planning Commission, Government of India.

Mahajan, Vijay and S.Mahendra Dev (2001) "Enhancing Livelihood Security for the Rural Poor in Andhra Pradesh" paper written for Employment Mission of GOAP and DFID.

Mahendra Dev, S and Vijay Mahajan (2000), "Challenge for Generating Pro-poor Employment in A.P.: An Options Paper", paper written for Employment Mission of GOAP and DFID.

NSSO (1983), "Sarvekshana, Issue no.18, Vol.6. No.3-4, Jan-April 1983, Survey results of second quinquennial survey on employment and unemployment (1977-78)" National Sample Survey Organisation, Department of Statistics, Ministry of Planning, Government of India.

NSSO (1988), "Sarvekshana, Issue no.35, Vol11, no.4, April 1988, Survey results of the third quinquennial (1983) survey on employment and unemployment".

NSSO (1990), "Sarvekshana, Issue no.44, vol XIV, No.1, July-September 1990, Some selected important results of the third quinquennial survey on employment and unemployment for 9 major status, NSS 38th round" .

NSSO (1990), "Sarvekshana, Special number, September 1990, Results of the fourth quinquennial survey on employment and unemployment (All-India)".

NSSO (1993), " Sarvekshana, Vol.16, no.3, January-March 1993, Survey results of fourth quinquennial survey on employment and unemployment for 9 major status (1987-88)".

NSSO (1997), " Sarvekshana, Issue no.68, Vol. 20, No.1, July-September 1997, Survey results of fifties quinquennial survey on employment and unemployment (1993-94)".

NSSO (2000), "Employment-Unemployment in India 1999-2000, Key Results ".

Parthasarathy, G. (1995) " Trends and Dimensions in Employment and Unemployment in Andhra Pradesh", in S. Sudhakar Reddy and K. Lakshminarayana (eds.), *"Review of Employment Trends and Programmes in Andhra Pradesh : Potential Impact of Liberalization"*, Booklinks Corporation, Hyderabad.

Ravallion, M. (2000), "What is needed for a more pro-poor growth process in India?" *Economic and Political Weekly*, Vol.35, No.13.

Sundaram, K. (2001), "Employment and Unemployment Situation in the Nineties: Some results from NSS 55th Round Survey", *Economic and Political Weekly*, March 17.

16

Trends and Determinants of Poverty

S. Sudhakar Reddy, S. Galab and P. Padmanabha Rao

1. INTRODUCTION

The major thrust of planning in India has always been reduction in the incidence of poverty. There are differences in the incidence of poverty and composition of the poor among the Indian states. The incidence of poverty and the factors underlying its persistence differ significantly from state to state. While there was a significant reduction in poverty in the country, the decline in the incidence of poverty in rural Andhra Pradesh, according to official estimates, was very steep between 1973-74 and 1999-00 and the poverty level was much lower than the national average. However, the incidence of urban poverty in the state of Andhra Pradesh was more or less similar to the national level. It was rural poverty which showed drastic decline compared to the national poverty. Hence, it is necessary to examine the source of this puzzle to have a realistic estimate of rural poverty in A.P for which different estimates of the incidence of poverty were provided by a number of researchers for the period 1973-74 to 1999-00. There are differences in the magnitude of poverty due to the adoption of different poverty lines.

The objectives of this paper are: i) to examine the trends in rural and urban poverty; ii) to analyse the determinants of rural poverty; iii) to explain the role of the poverty alleviation programmes in eradicating poverty. The estimates of poverty in A.P are based on secondary data and the analysis is based on the existing literature. Wherever possible, an attempt has been made to analyse interrelationships between various factors using secondary data. These relationships provide guidelines for state interventions in improving the quality of life. This paper is organised as follows: the incidence of rural and urban poverty at the state level, human poverty index and the determinants of rural poverty are presented in the second section; the third section deals with the poverty alleviation programmes; and summary and conclusion are provided in the last section.

2. RURAL POVERTY IN ANDHRA PRADESH

In the literature relating to poverty, different estimates of rural poverty in A.P are available from 1973-74 to 1999-00 for both rural and urban areas. Six quinquennial surveys-two each in the last three decades - have been carried out. Their respective rounds and survey periods are: i) 27th round from November 1973 to October 1974; ii) 32nd round from July 1977 to June 1978; iii) 38th round from January to December 1983; iv) 43rd round from July 1987 to June 1988; v) 50th round from July 1993 to June 1994; and vi) 55th round from July 1999 to June 2000 (Table 1). The Expert Group (1993) and the Planning Commission (2001) have estimated the incidence of poverty for the period from 1973-74 to 1999-00 (Table 2). The poverty line for rural A.P was found to be the lowest of all the Indian states whereas the poverty line for urban A.P was higher than the urban India.

Table 1. Estimates of Poverty of Andhra Pradesh From 1973 -74 To 1999-00

Areas	Name of the researcher	Incidence of poverty					
		1973-74	1977-78	1983-84	1987-88	1993-94	1999-00
Rural	Expert Group & Planning Commission	48.41	38.11	26.53	20.92	15.92	11.05
	Datt	56.84	47.84	37.99	34.02	28.93	
	Deaton and Dreze				35.00	29.20	26.20
	Datt et al					28.90	23.80
Urban	Expert Group & Planning Commission	52.56	46.46	40.13	44.63	41.51	26.63
	Datt	51.02	43.53	35.63	39.98	30.82	
	Deaton and Dreze				23.40	17.80	10.80
Rural + Urban	Expert Group & Planning Commission	49.25	39.96	29.88	27.20	23.08	15.77

Source: i) Expert Group (1993); ii) Datt (1997); iii) Deaton and Dreze (2002); iv) Datt, Kozel and Ravallion (2002) and v) Planning Commission (2001 and 2002).

The urban poverty line was found to be Rs.457.40 for A.P against Rs.454.11 for all India. When urban prices are higher in A.P as compared to all India, rural prices cannot be lower by 20 per cent. Moreover, the urban poverty lines for three rounds starting from 1987-88 onwards are around 74 per cent higher than the corresponding rural poverty lines. As a result, the incidence of poverty in urban Andhra Pradesh is higher than the rural A.P. The Planning Commission used a low poverty line of Rs.262.94 per capita per month for A.P and a high poverty line of Rs.374.79 per capita per month for Kerala and Rs.327.56 per capita per month for all India for the year 1999-2000. The poverty lines for the other three Southern States indicate a smaller deviation from all India poverty line (Table 2).

Is the poverty line of rural A.P estimated by the Expert Group Method a realistic one? When the poverty lines of A.P and all India are considered, the poverty lines of A.P are found to be about 80 per cent of the all India poverty line. Are the prices really lower by 20 per cent in A.P? As price adjustment has been a controversial issue in Indian literature and policy discussions, some illustrations may be helpful. The incidence of poverty in rural India is computed by using the Consumer Price Indices for Agricultural Labourers (CPIAL). The Expert Group (1993) has used the CPIAL to estimate the consumer price index for middle rural population (CPIMR) in order to derive poverty lines. The CPIAL for food is available but the CPIAL index for non-food is not available. The CPIAL was derived from the general index and the weighing diagram. Having obtained food and non-food CPIALs for each state, a combined index is estimated

Table 2. State Specific Poverty lines for South Indian States and all India from 1973-74 to 1999-00

Areas	Year	Tamil Nadu	Karnataka	Kerala	Andhra Pradesh	All India
	1973-74	45.09	47.24	51.68	41.71	49.63
		(90.9)	(95.2)	(104.1)	(84.0)	
	1977-78	56.62	51.95	58.88	50.88	56.84
		(99.6)	(91.4)	(103.6)	(89.5)	
Rural	1983	96.15	83.31	99.35	72.66	89.45
		(107.5)	(93.1)	(111.1)	(81.2)	
	1987-88	118.23	104.46	130.61	91.94	115.43
		(102.4)	(90.5)	(113.2)	(79.6)	
	1993-94	196.53	186.63	234.84	163.01	205.84
		(95.5)	(90.7)	(114.1)	(79.2)	
	1999-00	307.64	309.59	374.79	262.94	327.56
		(93.9)	(94.5)	(114.4)	(80.3)	
	1973-74	54.34	57.87	62.08	55.11	56.96
		(95.4)	(101.6)	(109.0)	(96.7)	
Urban	1977-78	71.18	71.25	71.82	71.56	72.50
		(98.2)	(98.3)	(99.0)	(98.7)	
	1983	123.73	121.23	127.84	111.84	117.64
		(105.2)	(103.0)	(108.7)	(95.0)	
	1987-88	174.82	171.23	175.11	159.50	165.58
		(105.6)	(103.4)	(105.7)	(96.3)	
	1993-94	313.36	303.23	298.91	289.94	286.72
		(109.3)	(105.8)	(104.2)	(101.1)	
	1999-00	475.60	511.44	477.06	457.40	454.11
		(104.7)	(112.6)	(105.0)	(100.7)	

Note: Figures in brackets indicate the ratios of state specific poverty lines to all India poverty lines.

Source: i). Expert Group (1993); ii). Malhotra (1997); iii) Planning Commission (2001 and 2002).

making use of the consumption pattern of the people around the poverty line in rural areas at the national level for 1973-74. The base year price index for CPIMR was much lower for AP as compared to all India in 1973-74. As a result of the lower CPIMR, the poverty lines in AP in the base year were lower than all India. The price index of CPIAL for AP at 1960-61 prices is lower by 15 per cent in all the years (Table 3). The price of firewood has been held constant in the official CPIAL series since 1960-61 (Datt, 1997). According to Deaton and Dreze (2002), CPIALs are based on fixed and frequently outdated commodity weights. These could be the major reasons for the lower levels of poverty in A.P.

Table 3. Consumer Price Indices Of Agricultural Labour At 1960-61 Prices

Year	CPIAL – AP	CPIAL All India	Ratio between AP and all India prices %
1973-74	242	283	85.51
1977-78	297	323	91.95
1983	426	502	85.03
1987-88	537	650	82.61
1993-94	999	1215	85.22
1999-00	1539	1802	85.40

Source: i). Expert Group (1993), ii). Malhotra (1997), iii). Planning Commission (2001 and 2002).

The poverty estimates reveal that the incidence of poverty has continued to decline more decisively since the 1970s. The incidence of poverty in A.P showed a dramatic decline in all the years for which the estimates are available. The proportion of poor in the rural areas declined from 48.41 per cent in 1973-74 to 15.92 percent in 1993-94 and further declined to 11.05 percent in 1999-00 (Table 1). Though the sample survey of 55th NSS round pertaining to 1999-00 indicates a steep decline in the incidence, the results are not dependable because of the simultaneous use of two reference periods namely, week and month, in the same questionnaire. The 55th round (1999-00) is not directly comparable to the 50th round (1993-94) due to changes in questionnaire design. The NSS introduced an experimental questionnaire with different recall periods for different classes of goods. The experimental questionnaire of the 30-day recall and seven day recall periods for food, paan, tobacco and intoxicants were used for the same households in two adjacent columns on the same page of single questionnaire. In addition, 365-day recall period questionnaire was used for the less frequently purchased items, namely, clothing, footwear, durables and health expenditure (institutional) instead of the traditional 30-day recall period questionnaire. Some critics have alleged that the two sets of questionnaires may have confused both respondents and enumerators such that even the 30-day recall estimates for 1999-00 are not comparable with those of the earlier large sample studies. But when month and week are introduced in the same questionnaire, the estimates based on the month reference period appear to have been distorted and the incidence came down to a very low level and became close to the estimates based on 'week' reference period. The 'head count ratios' estimated from the 55th round with a 7-day reference period for food, paan, tobacco and intoxicants had been found to be uniformly lower than those based on a 30-day reference period. The consumer expenditure data of the 55th round on a 30 day recall basis yields poverty ratios of 11.05 per cent in rural areas, 26.63 per cent in urban areas and 15.77 per cent for the state as a whole for the year 1999-00. The corresponding figures from the 7-day recall period are 9.15 per cent in rural areas, 24.48 percent in urban areas and 13.79 percent for A.P as a whole. In terms of absolute numbers of rural poor, there was a decline of 29.08 lakh persons between 1973-74 and 1977-78; 35.67 lakh persons between 1977-78 and 1983; 18.57 lakh persons between 1983 and 1987-88; 16.89 lakh persons between 1987-88 and 1993-94; and 21.36 lakh persons between 1993-94 and 1999-00 (Table 4).

Table 4. Number of people below the poverty line

(in lakhs)

Year	Andhra Pradesh			All India		
	Rural	Urban	Combined	Rural	Urban	Combined
1973-74	178.21	49.31	227.52	2612.90	603.12	3216.03
	(78.33)	(21.67)	(100.0)	(81.25)	(18.75)	(100.0)
1977-78	149.13	57.64	200.77	2642.46	677.40	3319.86
	(74.28)	(25.72)	(100.0)	(79.60)	(20.40)	(100.0)
1983	113.46	56.07	169.53	2517.15	752.93	3270.08
	(69.93)	(33.07)	(100.0)	(76.98)	(23.02)	(100.0)
1987-88	94.89	72.88	167.77	2293.96	833.52	3127.48
	(56.56)	(43.44)	(100.0)	(73.35)	(26.65)	(100.0)
1993-94	79.49	80.64	160.13	2440.29	794.17	3234.46
	(49.64)	(50.36)	(100.0)	(75.45)	(24.55)	(100.0)
1999-00	58.13	60.88	119.01	1932.43	670.07	2602.50
	(48.84)	(51.16)	(100.0)	(74.25)	(25.75)	(100.0)

Note: Figures in brackets are percentages to combined figures.
Source: Expert Group (1993); Planning Commission (2001 and 2002).

Deaton and Dreze (2002) recalculated the poverty lines and poverty estimates by using new prices. They estimate the distribution of total consumption as if there had been no change in survey design under two key assumptions of 7 day recall (7/30/365 day recalls) and 30 day (30/30/365 day recalls) recall for food. Firstly, the reported expenditures on the intermediate goods, for which the recall period is unchanged, are unaffected by the changes elsewhere in the questionnaire. Secondly, the relation between intermediate-goods expenditure and total expenditure is much the same in 1999-00 as in 1993-94. Applying this method, Deaton and Dreze found a fall in poverty in 1999-00, though not as great as implied by the 55h round. The results of Deaton and Dreze suggest that the fall in the incidence of rural poverty between the 50th and 55th rounds obtained by the Planning Commission (2001) is attributable to the change in survey design. They presented two estimates of poverty for 1993-94 viz., 29.20 per cent and 33.47 per cent. The incidence of poverty was 35 percent in 1987-88, 29.20 percent in 1993-94 and 26.20 per cent in 1999-00. The incidence of rural poverty in A.P estimated by Deaton and Dreze was higher by 15.15 percentage points compared to the official estimate for the year 1999-00. A comparison of the incidence of poverty has been made from the estimates provided by different studies (Table 1).

Datt (1997) has estimated the levels of rural poverty for A.P and All India using the poverty lines of Rs.49 for the rural and Rs.57 for the urban areas for 1973-74 at all India prices. For rural areas corrected CPIAL series were used by making upward adjustments to the nominal price of firewood as it has been kept constant at 1960-61 prices in the official CPIAL series for urban areas. The Consumer Price Indices for Industrial Workers (CPIIW) with 1960-61 prices was used. Datt has provided poverty estimates in terms of three poverty indicators, viz., the Head Count Ratio (HCR), the Poverty Gap Index (PG) and the Squared Poverty Gap Index (SPG). The estimates of rural poverty declined fairly steadily from 64 per cent in 1972-73 to 34 percent in 1986-87 (Table 5). The rate of decline of poverty slowed in the late 1980s despite the public distribution system, through which rice was supplied at Rs.2 per kg, and poverty alleviation programmes. A.P reduced the depth and severity of poverty even faster than the overall poverty rate. The Poverty Gap Index and the Squared Poverty Gap Index have declined from 17 to 6; 7 to 2 percent respectively over the last two decades in A.P (Table 5), which is faster compared to

Table 5. Estimates of Poverty, Poverty Gap Index and Squared Poverty Gap Index for Andhra Pradesh: 1973 - 74 to 1993 – 94

Year	Andhra Pradesh					
	Incidence of Poverty		Poverty Gap Index		Squared Poverty Gap Index	
	Rural	Urban	Rural	Urban	Rural	Urban
1973-74	56.84	51.02	17.029	13.763	6.921	4.968
1977-78	47.84	43.53	13.606	12.196	5.477	4.879
1983	37.99	35.63	9.555	9.376	3.291	3.537
1986-87	33.96	38.63	8.775	10.998	3.545	4.209
1987-88	34.02	39.98	7.538	10.113	2.270	3.380
1989-90	31.85	31.96	6.844	8.037	2.046	2.738
1990-91	36.90	27.91	7.843	7.398	2.351	2.759
1992	41.85	33.05	9.422	8.776	3.148	3.141
1993-94	28.93	30.82	5.819	6.842	1.801	2.032

Source: Datt (1997).

all-India. There has been a continuous decline in the incidence of poverty in rural A.P. All the measures of poverty indicate that A.P has performed extremely well compared to all India.

Datt, Kozel and Ravallion (2002) used a model-based approach for projecting poverty in India after 1993-94. Using the poverty lines of the Planning Commission (1979) viz., Rs.49 for rural and Rs.57 for urban areas at 1973-74 prices, they have constructed a consistent set of price indices across states and survey periods using monthly data on consumer price indices from the labour Bureau over the whole 35 year period. Theirprimary deflators were the Consumer Price Indices for Industrial Workers (CPIIW) for the urban sector and the adjusted all India Consumer Price Indices for Agricultural Labourers (CPIAL) for the rural sector. The adjustment carried out to the CPIAL was for the price of firewood that has been held constant in the official CPIAL series since 1960-61. The nominal state level distributions were further normalised into inter-state cost of living differentials estimated separately for urban and rural areas, anchored to the consumption pattern of households in the neighbourhood of the poverty line. Datt et al, in their projections up to 1999-00, suggest that the incidence of poverty has been falling in A.P. The rural poverty reduction implied by their results is 0.9 percentage points per year for the period since 1993-94. In other words, the incidence of poverty has declined from 29.5 per cent in 1993-94 to 24.1 per cent in 1999-00.

Urban Poverty

The urban poverty line was around 15 percent higher than the rural poverty line in 1973-74. Subsequently, urban poverty lines for AP are around 73 to 78 percent higher than the corresponding rural poverty lines for 1987-88, 1993-94 and 1999-00 (Table 6). The rate of decline in urban poverty has been slower in AP up to 1993-94 but declined much faster between 1993-94 and 1999-00. According to the Expert Group and the

Table 6. Rural and Urban Poverty Lines in Andhra Pradesh

Year	Rural poverty lines	Urban poverty lines	Percentage difference between rural and urban poverty lines
1973-74	41.71	55.11	32.13
1977-78	50.88	71.56	40.64
1983	72.66	111.84	53.92
1987-88	91.94	159.50	73.48
1993-94	163.01	289.94	77.87
1999-00	262.94	457.40	73.96

Source: Expert Group (1993), Planning Commission (2001 and 2002).

Planning Commission, the urban poverty ratio in A.P declined from 52.56 per cent in 1973-74 to 26.63 per cent in 1999-00 (Table 1). There was a decline of 6.1 percentage points between 1973-74 and 1977-78; a decline of 6.33 percentage points between 1977-78 and 1983; an increase of 4.5 percentage points between 1983 and 1987-88; a decline of 3.12 percentage points between 1987-88 and 1993-94 and a decline of 14.88 percentage points between 1993-94 and 1999-2000. The estimates show an increase in the number of urban poor in A.P for the period between 1973-74 and 1993-94 and marginal decline in the nineties between 1993-94 and 1999-00. There was an increase of 31.33 lakh persons between 1973-74 and 1993-94 and a decline of 19.76 lakh persons between 1993-94 and 1999-00 (Table 4).

The incidence of urban poverty was estimated by Datt (1997) from 1973-74 to 1993-94. It fluctuated around 50 percent in the fifties and the sixties (Table 6), and started declining since 1977-78. In the two decades starting from 1973-74 to 1993-94 the incidence of urban poverty declined by 20 percentage points. But the decline was the highest during 1973-74-1983. The pace of decline slowed down during 1983-1993-94. A comparison of the performance of A.P with all-India reveals that A.P has done extremely well in terms of decline in the incidence of poverty. Similar trends could be seen from the Poverty Gap Index and the Squared Poverty Gap Index (Table 5).

Deaton and Dreze (2002) recalculated the urban poverty line for the 55th NSS round for the year 1999-00. According to them, with this recalculated urban poverty line (Rs. 344.76), the incidence of urban poverty for 43rd round (1987-88) was 23.40 per cent; 17.80 per cent in 1993-94 and 10.80 per cent in 1999-2000. The incidence of urban poverty in A.P estimated by Deaton and Dreze was lower than the official estimate by 15.83 percentage points for the year 1999-00. The decline in the incidence of urban poverty between 1987-88 and 1993-94 was 5.60 percentage points and between 1993-94 and 1999-00 was 7.0 percentage points (Table 1).

Human Poverty Index

The United Nations Development Programme (UNDP) has devised a Human Poverty Index (HPI) in 1997 report to redefine poverty, since it felt that the income measure of poverty was inadequate. While the reports draw attention to human deprivation to complement income measures of poverty, their focus is on the percentage of poor who lack basic capabilities as well as access to minimal facilities. The Human Poverty Index (HPI) includes three indicators: a) Vulnerability to death at a relatively early age as quantified in the percentage of people expected to die before the age of 40 years; b) Deprivation in respect of reading and communication measured by the percentage of adults who are illiterate (adult illiteracy); and c) Deprivation in overall economic provisioning which is a combined index of three variables; i) Percentage of people without access to safe drinking water; ii) Percentage of people without access to health services; and iii) Percentage of children under five who are moderately and severely underweight. The values of the human poverty index for the South Indian states are presented in Table 7. The highest deprivation among the South Indian states is observed to be in A.P i.e. 40.78 percent which is higher than all India, while it is lowest in Kerala (23.19 per cent) (Prabhu, 1999).

Table 7. Human poverty index for south Indian states, 1991-93

(per cent)

States	Health	Knowledge	Provisioning	Human poverty index
Andhra Pradesh	14.88	49.51	42.88	40.78
Karnataka	15.68	39.14	41.12	35.42
Kerala	5.14	8.47	33.22	23.19
Tamil Nadu	13.45	30.69	32.98	28.19
India	17.99	42.69	48.70	40.49

Note: The Human Poverty Index has been computed using the methodology of the UNDP.
Source: Prabhu (1999).

Determinants of Rural Poverty

An attempt is made to examine the relationship between poverty and economic growth. Much of the recent literature emphasizes an inverse relationship between poverty and economic growth. In the context of rural areas, the focus is on the poverty-alleviating role of agricultural growth. This effect varies, however, depending on the nature of the agricultural growth process. If, for example, growth takes place in a setting of extreme inequality in endowments, its benefits are not likely to 'trickle down' to large segments of the poor. Relevant evidence is therefore reviewed here to illustrate the conditions under which impoverishment occurs. Ahluwalia (1978) observed an inverse association between the incidence of rural poverty and agricultural performance. A faster rate of economic growth (GDP), especially when it is biased towards agriculture, under favourable institutional framework, will have a considerable impact on the incomes of the poor (Rao, 1994). Dharm Narain showed that changes in the incidence of poverty are positively related to changes in the consumer price index, while the growth of output per head has a negative impact on poverty (Desai, 1986). Ahluwalia (1986) questioned the role of prices basing his arguments on statistical grounds: Since poverty calculations themselves are based on price adjustments, the use of prices again on the right hand side of regression equation would amount to an incorrect specification. However, Amartya Sen explains that it is not an incorrect specification (Desai, 1986), and, in general, the effect of inflation on poverty is not denied. Ravallion and Datt (1998) constructed a simultaneous equation model to include wages, prices and agricultural productivity as explanatory variables and each of these variables influenced poverty. A negative relationship exists between poverty and agricultural growth. If there is rapid agricultural growth, which is labour using and hence wage enhancing, there is reduction in poverty (Acharya and Papanek, 1995). If agricultural growth is related to the increasing use of labour, demand for labour would push up agricultural wages, increasing the incomes of casual labourers and thus reduce poverty.

In order to find out the annual change in the incidence of poverty, a trend equation is used for pre-green revolution and post-green revolution periods separately. The results show a declining trend in the incidence of poverty in both the periods. But the first period experienced a very slow rate of decline at 0.4 percentage points per annum, which is not statistically significant. On the other hand, the second period i.e., the post-green revolution period experienced a high rate of decline in poverty at 1.3 percentage points, a statistically significant rate of decline (Table 8).

Table 8. Results of Regression with Incidence of Poverty as Dependent Variable

Period	Constant	Independent Variables			R^2
		Wage Rate	Agricultural Output	Time	
1957-58 to 1999-00	69.0507	-	-	-0.9958 (-11.282)	0.852
1957-58 to 1969-70	64.4287	-	-	-0.3905 (-1.712)	0.227
1970-71 to 1999-00	76.4688	-	-	-1.2605 (-5.909)	0.795
1957-58 to 1999-00	145.154	-22.6042 (-3.651)	-15.9453 (-3.266)	-	0.928
1957-58 to 1969-70	166.706	-7.9809 (-0.530)	-21.4225 (-2.616)	-	0.480
1970-71 to 1999-00	131.840	-25.5373 (-2.644)	-13.0736 (1.339)	-	0.871

Note: Figures in parentheses are t values.

Any decline in rural poverty is discernible only when the real wages increase. Datt and Ravallion (1998) found a strong interlink age between real wage rates and rural poverty. In fact, the authors found a more significant relationship of the real wage with the poverty gap and squared poverty gap measures of poverty than with the head count ratios. The implication is that the real wages have a strong effect not only on poverty but also on the distribution of income below the poverty line. Hence, a better understanding of recent trends in agricultural wages are important for greater clarity about the nature of rural poverty and possible means of removing it. The rise in the money wages will not be of much significance if the prices of commodities purchased by the poor also rise at a high rate (Desai, 1986). The trends in real wages and Consumer Price Indices for Agricultural Labourers are estimated for the periods under consideration (Table 9). The results clearly indicate a steep rise in the Consumer Price Indices for Agricultural Labourers in the nineties at an annual rate of 9 per cent. Such a high rate was not observed in the earlier three decades. Even during the sixties when the agricultural sector experienced slow growth, the increase in prices was only 7.4 per cent per annum. In the eighties, the growth rate of Consumer Price Indices for Agricultural Labourers was only 5.6 per cent per annum. The real wages of rural male labourers increased at 1.2 per cent in the nineties as compared to 5.6 per cent in the eighties. A similar trend is also observed for wage rates of rural female labourers. The only feature in the nineties was a slightly higher growth rate of female wages (1.6 per cent) as compared to male wage rate (1.2 per cent). Thus, the above evidence indicates that poverty might not have declined significantly during the economic reform period.

Table 9. Growth Rates of Consumer Price Indices and Real Wages

(percentages)

Dependent Variable (in logs)	1960s	1970s	1980s	1990s
Consumer Price Indices of Agricultural Labour	7.40	6.41*	5.67*	9.03*
Males Real Wage	-0.76	2.49	5.60*	1.23*
Female Real Wage	-0.27	2.99	4.83*	1.64*

Note: Computed from logarithmic trend regression equations estimated for each decade.
* Significant at one per cent level.

Another pertinent question is the relative importance of agricultural growth and growth of wages in reducing poverty. Agricultural growth can have an indirect effect on poverty reduction in so far as the trickle down operates through wage increase and increase in employment. On the other hand, growth rate of real wages, impelled partly from forces other than agricultural growth, is expected to have direct impact on poverty alleviation. In order to understand the relative importance of these forces, the incidence of poverty is regressed on real wage rate and agricultural output index (Subrahmanyam and Sudhakar Reddy, 2001). These are found to be statistically significant for all the periods. The results show that in the post green revolution periods (1970s and 1980s) increase in real wages played a more important role than the growth of agricultural output. On the other hand, the effect of real wages was low in the pre green revolution period. For instance, a 10 per cent increase in the agricultural output reduced poverty by 1.3 percentage points, whereas the same growth in the real wage rates resulted in the reduction of poverty by 2.6 percentage points in the post green revolution period. In the pre-green revolution period, a 10 per cent increase in agricultural output facilitated a decline in poverty by 2.1 percentage points whereas a 10 per cent increase in real wage rate could reduce poverty by only 0.8 percentage points (Table 8). It is possible that the gains from agricultural growth were shared more widely in the pre-green revolution period. Also, poverty in the post-green revolution period was concentrated more among the wage labour.

An increase in real wage rates of labourers engaged in the farm sector was mainly attributed to the rise in the demand for labour in the non-farm sector mostly in construction and service sector. Since the wages in the non-farm sector have been consistently higher than the wages in the farm sector, it is inferred that a part of the significant decline in rural poverty was due to opening up of employment opportunities in the non-farm sector. In other words, real wage rates in the farm sector are directly related to the availability of non-farm employment leading to a decline in the incidence of rural poverty.

3. PUBLIC INTERVENTIONS FOR POVERTY ALLEVIATION

Poverty alleviation programmes have been designed from time to time to enlarge the income earning opportunities for the poor. In the fifties and sixties, measures like land reforms, credit reforms, introduction of Panchayati Raj and others were implemented to improve the income earning power of the poor. In the seventies, special programmes were launched to strengthen the income earning power of the small and marginal farmers, scheduled castes and tribes. In the eighties, the endowment of assets to the poor for self-employment under the IRDP, the special programmes for wage employment, programmes for women like DWCRA were designed to empower the poor (Rao, 1995). Human development is given priority so as to enable the vast majority of people to benefit from growth. Our failure to invest sufficiently in our biggest and most valuable asset i.e. our human resources is one of the primary reasons for the persistence of large-scale poverty. Investment in human resources, in their health, education and nutrition would tend to reduce rural poverty. Education and health services in A.P face three fundamental problems viz., a) lack of easy access for the needy, b) high costs and c) poor quality. The problem of poverty is tackled through infrastructural development like roads, well-designed irrigation systems, flood control, electrification etc., sustained over a period of time. The impact of various poverty alleviation programmes on poverty is analyzed in the following sections.

Land Reforms

The relationship between rural poverty and access to land is complex. Many factors are involved, including differences in land quality, the availability of complementary inputs, access to credit and markets and opportunities for off-farm employment. When the land quality is poor and access to inputs and markets is limited, access to land – even large quantities – may not significantly reduce the risk of poverty. Nevertheless, to the extent that land is a major source of income in rural areas and its distribution has important linkages with the non-farm sector, land reforms are crucial to poverty alleviation. Land reforms comprise a wide range of measures, including land redistribution, regulation of tenancy contracts and land titling, with varying degrees of targeting on the poorer population segments. While some aspects of land reforms have received attention in the recent literature, there has been a waning of interest in the redistribution of land as a key component of reform. This is in a large measure attributable to the dismal record of land redistribution in many developing countries. In the few countries that undertook land redistribution, it met with strong resistance and the pace consequently slowed down. Moreover, the benefits to the poorest groups were quite limited. Nevertheless, it is argued below that land redistribution plays a major role in poverty alleviation (Lipton, 1991). The distribution of ownership holdings of land, given in Table 10 at four points of time from the early 1960s to early 1990s, shows that the number of small and marginal holdings (up to 2 ha) has increased from about 78 per cent to about 94 per cent, while the large holdings (>10 ha) have decreased from about 2.26 per cent to less than half per cent, medium holdings from about 8.6 per cent to 5.5 per cent and semi-medium from about 10.6 per cent to about 3.5 per cent. It is similarly seen that the area under small and marginal holdings has risen from about 18 per cent to about 51 per cent while area under medium and large holdings fallen from about 65 per cent to about 32 per cent. In absolute terms, thus, there is a move towards smaller holdings because of the demographic pressure leading to land fragmentation, which is compounded by the limited occupational diversification.

Ownership holdings may not reflect access to land since many smaller holdings are too small to be operationally viable. Some small land pieces may be merged with others through lease systems to form a single operational holding. Data in Table 11 show that at the all-India, as well as at the level of A.P, the operational holdings are proportionately more in thesemi-medium and medium sized categories, and fewer in the smaller sized groups. Naturally, the total number of operational holdings is less compared to ownership holdings. It is no coincidence that around 40 to 50 per cent of the agricultural workers are engaged as casual agricultural labourers.

Distribution of Surplus Land

The earliest of public interventions for poverty alleviation was provision of access to land through land reforms. Abolition of intermediaries did not change the ownership structure of landholdings directly. But, it had two indirect effects: first, growth through its percolation effect on poverty; second, it freed rural labour from the grip of the Zamindar and his control over common property resources (Parthasarathy, 1995). Under the land ceiling legislation, against an estimated surplus of 20 lakh acres by 1992, about 8 lakh acres were found

Table 10. Percentage Distribution of Households and Area Owned Over five Broad Holding Size Categories in Andhra Pradesh and All India

Region	Year	Marginal (less than 1 ha.)		Small (1-2 ha.)		Semi-medium (2-4 ha.)		Medium (4-10 ha.)		Large (10 ha. & above)	
		House hold	Area Owned	House hold	Area Owned	House hold	Area Owned	House hold	Area Owned	House hold	Area Owned
AP	1961-62	66.32	8.15	11.46	9.69	10.60	16.97	8.61	31.29	3.01	33.90
	1971-72	65.30	9.92	13.65	13.16	11.22	21.22	7.57	30.15	2.26	25.58
	1981-82	67.49	11.26	14.03	15.29	10.01	20.70	6.69	29.83	1.78	22.92
	1991-92	73.74	21.30	20.34	39.91	3.50	15.53	5.46	30.74	0.43	8.06
India	1961-62	60.06	7.59	15.16	12.40	12.86	20.54	9.07	31.23	2.85	28.24
	1971-72	62.62	9.76	15.49	14.68	11.94	21.92	7.83	30.75	2.12	22.91
	1981-82	66.64	12.22	14.70	16.49	10.78	23.38	6.45	29.83	1.42	18.07
	1991-92	69.38	16.93	21.75	33.97	5.06	17.63	2.84	17.64	0.95	13.83

Source: NSS 17th (1961-62), 26th (1971-72), 38th (1981-82), and 48th (1991-92) rounds.

Table 11. Changes in Percentage Distribution of Operational Holdings and Area Operated by size Categories of Operational Holdings in Andhra Pradesh and india

Region	Year	Marginal		Small		Semi-medium		Medium		Large	
		Number	Area	Number	Area	Number	Area	Number	Area	Number	Area
AP	1961-62	41.90	6.76	18.59	9.31	19.10	17.83	14.80	30.60	5.61	35.50
	1971-72	47.29	9.28	19.14	11.74	18.23	21.91	11.87	31.32	3.47	25.75
	1981-82	48.64	10.25	22.13	15.37	15.51	21.08	10.80	30.20	2.92	23.10
	1991-92	59.27	17.54	21.38	23.34	13.16	26.23	5.38	23.49	0.81	9.40
India	1961-62	39.07	6.86	22.62	12.33	19.8	20.70	13.99	31.17	4.52	28.94
	1971-72	45.77	9.21	22.38	14.80	17.66	22.52	11.11	30.49	3.08	22.98
	1981-82	56.00	11.50	19.32	16.59	14.23	23.55	8.56	30.15	1.89	18.21
	1991-92	62.79	15.60	17.79	18.70	11.99	24.13	6.10	26.37	1.33	15.20

Source: NSS 17th (1961-62), 26th (1971-72), 38th (1981-82), and 48th (1991-92) rounds.

surplus and around 5.11 lakh acres were distributed, although much of this was dry land of inferior quality. A.P holds the third position in the country with respect to the extent of land distributed (Sankaran, 1996). A study conducted recently in Nalgonda district to assess the impact of distribution of surplus land reveals that the land distributed per household for agriculture, mining, and free putta categories is 1.83 acres, 2.82 acres and 3.00 acres respectively. Twenty-five percent of the beneficiaries have sold the agricultural land to meet their expenses and to clear debts and due to their inability to cultivate the land because of lack of finances and experience. Lack of access to inputs, viz., credit and technology constrains the beneficiaries from deriving the potential benefits from the lands distributed. But the indirect impact of land reforms contributes to a shift from rentier to entrepreneurial agriculture, to growth and thereby to a reduction in poverty through percolation effects in the deltas of Coastal Andhra (Parthasarathy, 1995).

The distribution of land at the disposal of the Government, commonly known as Banjar land, constitutes an important component of the land reforms programme in A.P. It has been estimated that by the end of 1992, about 37.29 lakh acres have been assigned to the landless poor, catering to about 19.13 lakh beneficiaries. Of this, 11.24 lakh acres were allotted to members of Scheduled Castes and 6.06 lakh acres to Scheduled Tribes. In this regard, distribution of land to the landless poor in AP is perhaps, the highest in the country. While the surplus land alone would constitute only 1.5 per cent of operated area, taken along with the Government land, the land allotted to the poor would constitute about 12.5 per cent of the operated area, and this cannot be considered insignificant (Sankaran, 1996).

Tenancy Reforms

The gains from tenancy legislation were considerable for the tenants in the Telangana area, though the impact was very little in the Andhra area (Sankaran, 1996). Recent trends in the districts of A.P suggest a rise in tenancy due to a number of factors: increasing shift of large and middle class owners into more lucrative non-agricultural occupations, along with a shift from rural to urban locations; entry of the entrepreneurial agriculturist class into trading ventures in rural areas and partial leasing out by resident land owners; growing shortage of labour especially during peak seasons, resulting in increased leasing out by large landowners (Parthasarathy, 1995).

Depriving tribals of their land, which in turn may have resulted in the growing Naxalite movement, should be considered an important issue for public policy. Tribal deprivation takes two major forms: alienation of land, and declining access to forests, a source of livelihood (Subba Reddy, 1988 and 1989). Access to common property resources (CPRs) viz., village forests, developed under watershed development projects in the dry land areas of A.P, for collecting fodder has enhanced the capacity of landless agricultural labour, marginal and small farmers to rear animals and induced them to take up dairy activity. Thus, access to CPRs also constitutes a strategy for poverty reduction (Sharma, 1997).

Asset Development

Integrated Rural Development Programme (IRDP)

The concurrent evaluation (Fifth Round) of IRDP during 1995-96 in A.P has revealed that the programme has covered 12 per cent of rural households (Table 12). The coverage of the Scheduled Castes and Scheduled Tribes is higher than their share in the population but is lower than the target of 50 per cent of total coverage. The coverage is marginally less than proportion in the population of women headed households and manual labour households. The selection by the Grama Sabha was to the extent of 60 per cent of beneficiaries' - this percentage has declined from 92 in the fourth round of evaluation. The percentage of old beneficiaries whose current non-IRDP income is higher than the old poverty norm (Rs.6400) is 66 and those whose non-IRDP income is higher than the revised poverty norm (Rs.11000) is 25 - an indication of the non-poor covered under the programme. The assistance provided has ranged between Rs. 3000 and Rs. 10000 - higher proportion of SCs, STs and manual labour beneficiaries have received smaller investment assistance than others. More than half of the schemes financed are in the primary sector, more than a third in the tertiary sector and less than a tenth in the secondary sector. The IRDP is contributing to diversification of rural occupations/employment, with self-employment in non-agriculture being the principal gainer. Three fifths of the assets of old beneficiaries are in productive use, most of the rest having been sold or transferred and in respect of new beneficiaries 91 per cent are in productive use. The average net income from IRDP asset is Rs.1898 per annum and is equivalent to less than two months of prevailing wage earnings for the male agricultural field labour in the State. A rupee of investment in IRDP assets yielded an income of Rs.0.55. There has been a sizeable reduction in the proportion of the poor among old beneficiaries - from 75 per cent to 56.6 per cent; and the very poor from 34 per cent to 16 per cent. Some of the beneficiaries (3 per cent) continue as bonded labour (Venkatramaiah, *et al*, 1997). An overwhelming majority of the respondents expressed satisfaction with the IRDP. Studies done on regional variation revealed that the more developed regions and those families near the poverty line showed a better performance when compared to others (Subba Rao, 1985; Rao and Rangaswamy, 1988).

The entry of non-poor into the programme is around 26 percent across the selected districts viz., Anantapur, Nalgonda, and Vizianagaram.

Table 12. Total Allocation, Utilisation and total families covered under IRDP from 1994-95 to 1998-99 in Andhra Pradesh and All India

(Rs. in lakh)

Items	Regions	Total Allocation				
		1994-95	1995-96	1996-97	1997-98	1998-99
Total Allocation	Andhra Pradesh	8,344.00 (135.27)	8,336.41 (103.45)	8,336.41 (65.85)	8,612.23 (102.68)	7,734.30 (83.21)
Utilisation (Rs. in lakhs)	All India	1,09,822.00 (92.90)	1,09,721.16 (98.16)	1,09,721.16 (43.72)	1,13,351.23 (92.12)	1,45,627.78 (52.87)
Total Families	Andhra Pradesh	1,59,908	1,22,863	75,341	1,27,776	86,238
Covered	All India	22,14,390	20,50,678	7,91,063	16,03,775	11,32,044

Note: Figures in brackets are percentage utilization.
Source: 1. *Basic Rural Statistics,* 1996, Ministry of Rural Areas and Employment, Government of India.
2. *Rural Development Statistics,* 1998, NIRD, Hyderabad and,
3. *Annual Reports,* Ministry of Rural Areas and Employment, Government of India.

The expenditure incurred in obtaining the assets under the programme accounted for 7 percent of the subsidy provided to the poor. The average net income from IRDP assets is Rs.1273 per annum. While 77 percent of the beneficiaries retained the assets, 71 percent of poor beneficiaries crossed the poverty line. The employment gain to the beneficiary households came to around 120 man-days in the selected districts. The income gains are more pronounced in the developed districts and among the relatively better off among the poor. The income mobility matrix also indicated that the crossing of poverty line is more pronounced among the near poor rather than among the poorest. The banks are found to be indifferent in providing credit to the poorest of the poor, as they are unsure about the repayment from the poorest. As a result, the poorest of the poor are not covered under the programmes. The absence of institutional building to enhance social capital among the poor for undertaking collective actions with regard to market intermediation may be one of the main reasons for this (Dev and Rao, 2002).

Development of Women and Children in Rural Areas

Development of Women and Children in Rural Areas (DWCRA), as one of the sub-schemes of IRDP, was initiated in 1982-83 and was extended to all the districts gradually. DWCRA targets poor rural women for income generating activities through credit and organizational support. Lack of adequate staff and proper coordination between the staff located at different levels of administrative hierarchy is constraining the performance of the programme. The size and composition of the group and institutional arrangement for maintaining the group activity and the support mechanism provided by the programme implementation authority are the determinants of the success of the programme. Heterogeneous groups could also perform better as against the popular belief that only the homogeneous groups perform well, provided appropriate support from the implementing authority is ensured. The programme has benefited the members of the groups in terms of diversifying their activities from their traditional economic activities and increasing their income levels which ultimately resulted in increased intake of nutritious food (Kanchanya, 1998). On the other hand, there are some DWCRA groups in the drought-prone and the backward district like Anantapur which are not undertaking any economic activity either individually or collectively but utilizing the financial assistance as an interest free loan among themselves (Galab et. al, 1997). It has generally been found that this programme had done relatively better in A.P. The performance of DWCRA had established that group approach centering on women produced better results than individual oriented schemes of IRDP leading to a big increase in the number of such groups.

In a study conducted in three districts of A.P viz., Adilabad, Kurnool, and Visakhapatnam, it was concluded that DWCRA groups are homogeneous and cohesive (i.e., based on income, caste and neighbourhood). 22% of the members belong to SCs, 11% to STs, 67% to BCs and the remaining 4% to others. The average age of members is 35 (i.e., high percentage of women in the fertility group). For 60% of the groups, saving is the main purpose of group formation. Majority (94%) of groups showed no defaulters in the last three months. There is high regularity in saving. There is a high rotation of group corpus (80% internal loans). An active participation in pulse polio immunization (30%) and Janmabhoomi (80%) was observed. There was a gradual shift from consumption loans (40%) to production loans (60%). In fact, 61% would have gone to moneylenders had there been no Women's Self Help Groups. Whereas 7.5% of the women are illiterate, book keeping and maintaining records is poor. A majority of the leaders and the members are aware of DWCRA Bazaars. There is a need to strengthen marketing facilities for the products of DWCRA groups (Dev and Rao, 2002).

Self Help Group Approach

Providing the poor with access to financial services will help to increase their incomes and productivity. Hence, micro credit and cooperative programmes have been developed to fill this gap. Many of these programmes provide credit using social mechanisms such as group based lending to reach the poor and other clients including women, who lack access to formal financial institutions. Women's Self-help group approach is a success story and has formed a central element in the State's social mobilization and community empowerment strategy for poverty reduction. The key findings of the latest evaluation, on the basis of a SWOT-analysis performed in 7 districts (East Godavari, Kurnool, Mahabubnagar, Nalgonda, Nellore, Prakasam, and Ranga Reddy) are very encouraging. Future security is becoming a more important purpose for the women to be active within the group. Dependency on moneylenders and landlords seems to be declining and particularly, there is a gradual shift from consumption loans to productive loans. The women self help groups now number 3.57 lakh covering 49 lakh women. They have established a corpus fund (own savings, government grants and bank loans) of Rs.750 crores. In the last 2 years, 96000 groups have accessed Rs.156 crores from banks.

Joint Forest Management

A.P has taken steps to demonstrate that a convergence of conservation and development objectives can be achieved through Joint Forest Management (JFM). At present JFM is implemented in a total of 6575 villages covering an area of 16.32 lakh hectares. About 5.28 lakh hectares of degraded forests have been treated through JFM. Around 13 lakh people, including 6 lakh women are participating in the activity of bringing back greenery to the forests. SC/ST beneficiaries account for nearly 5.5 lakh out of these 13-lakh beneficiaries. Pursuing one of the most proactive JFM programmes in India, A.P has committed 100% of minor forest produce to the forest user groups. Widespread implementation of JFM is leading to an increased flow (both value and volume) of minor forest products to communities and an increase in environmental benefits resulting from improved forest condition particularly with respect to soil and water regimes. Formation of JFM Committees in A.P has successfully targeted remote and under-served communities, in particular tribal populations.

Deepam Scheme (LP Gas Scheme)

The cooking fuel crisis of the rural poor has particularly affected women and children by adding many hours in search of fuel with rapidly diminishing yields; by harming the schooling prospects of the poor female children as they become engaged in either fuel gathering or sharing the house work and by exposing women to dangerous amounts of smoke inhalation from cooking with twigs and plant debris on open stoves. In this backdrop, providing LPG stoves becomes a necessary component of the programme to alleviate poverty. Deepam Scheme was launched on 9-7-1999 for distribution of 10 lakh L.P. Gas Connections to women among families below poverty line in rural areas. The objectives of the scheme are i) to provide relief to women from drudgery of cooking with firewood and ii) to improve the health status of the rural women.

Area Development Programmes

Two major programmes of area development are Drought Prone Area Programme (DPAP) and Desert Development Programme (DDP). The Rural Manpower Programme of 1978 was redesigned as DPAP and

DDP for mitigating the severity of scarcity conditions by organizing labour intensive and production oriented works through augmenting land and water resources. Watershed approaches have come to be the primary strategy under these programmes. A.P has done fairly well in the earlier years. In general, over the years, the utilization of resources had seen a steady decline indicating that the delivery mechanism did not get strengthened in correspondence with the increase in resource flow. Since the introduction of watershed approach, land and water conservation and augmentation measures through DPAP, DDP and also EAS received substantial resources.

Area development on watershed basis is an important programme for employment generation and poverty reduction. A 10-year (1998-2007) action plan aimed at treating 10 million hectares using participatory processes has been initiated. So far about 3 million hectares have been treated. The Government of A.P has recently embarked on a programme in five districts with the financial support from Department for International Development (DFID). This programme aims to address some of the shortcomings of the existing watershed programmes and to provide support for strengthening participatory processes and providing sustained capacity building for the community-based organizations involved in watershed management. Watersheds programmes can be successful in harmonizing the use of water, soil, forest and pasture resources, particularly in the rain-fed areas to raise agricultural productivity. Consequently, they offer an opportunity to increase growth and reduce poverty in a sustainable way.

Janmabhoomi

The Janmabhoomi programme is unique as a people centered development process launched in 1997. The Janmabhoomi process has created a positive impact because it provides an opportunity for direct interaction between government officials and people. The following are the five core areas of Janmabhoomi viz., i) Community Works; ii) Primary Education iii) Primary Health and Family Welfare; iv) Environmental Conservation and v) Responsive Governance.

Rural Employment Programmes (Rural Public Works)

Rural Public Works (RPW) are now an integral part of a poverty-alleviation strategy – especially in densely populated agrarian economies because of their self-targeting nature and beneficial impact on labour market in terms of increase in wages The rural public works undertaken under rural employment programmes like the National Rural Employment Programme (NREP); the Rural Landless Employment Guarantee Programme (RLEGP); the Jawahar Rozgar Yojana (JRY) and presently Jawahar Gram Samridhi Yojana (JGSY) and Employment Assurance Scheme (EAS) have resulted in the creation of community assets as well as assets to the down-trodden sections besides providing wage employment to the poor. The benefits derived by the poor from the wage employment programmes are higher than those derived from the self-employment programmes (Sudhakar Reddy, *et al*, 1997). However, these programmes have not contributed to a rise in wages (Galab, *et al*, 1997). The JRY programme could cover 15 per cent of the unemployed and this should be considered significant (Table 13). This programme has contributed to generating interest among elected representatives. It has provided greater flexibility to village Panchayats in the choice of projects. However, the programme needed improvements in two vital respects: it is not adequately related to agricultural development, and its location and timing need improvement (Rao, 1996).

Table 13. Total Allocation, Utilisation and mandays generated under JRY from 1994-95 to 1998-99

(Rs. in lakh)

Items	Region	Total Allocation				
		1994-95	1995-96	1996-97	1997-98	1998-99
Total Allocation Utilisation (Rs. In lakh)	Andhra Pradesh	27099.96 (86.57)	34118.65 (82.16)	17372.39 (23.99)	10410.49 (53.92)	14629.93 (71.66)
	All India	349872.39 (82.34)	434869.77 (76.66)	223679.48 (51.87)	249921.18 (78.09)	259702.47 (55.97)
Total Mandays Generated (lakh mandays)	Andhra Pradesh	946.90 (67.51)	675.74 (94.95)	373.67 (18.69)	336.97 (65.08)	254.01 (41.34)
	All India	7997.37 (93.20)	8042.80 (98.92)	4288.58 (44.44)	3864.90 (94.40)	3966.57 (47.97)

Note: Figures in brackets are percentage utilization out of total allocation.
Source: i). *Basic Rural Statistics*, 1996, Ministry of Rural Areas and Employment, Government of India. ii). *Annual Reports*, Ministry of Rural Areas and Employment, Government of India, 1996-97, 1997-98 & 1998-99.

Under JRY, employment generated per person on an average per year is around 40 days across the sample villages of selected districts. The employment created is not adequate enough to influence the wage rates in labour market. The socio-economic backgrounds of the participants indicate that the poorer sections of the society are depending on JRY works. The villagers of sample villages have expressed that the wage employment programmes should be implemented in lean seasons in the backward and drought prone areas (Dev and Rao, 2002)

Food Security

Some sections of the poor like the old, the infirm and the handicapped are not likely to benefit from the direct anti-poverty interventions. Neither land reforms nor Rural Public Works (RPW) will help them to augment their incomes. Special interventions designed to raise their income levels are therefore necessary. There is now sufficient empirical evidence which points to the greater vulnerability of the poor to abrupt price changes of food items (Radhakrishna *et al*, 1997). Unanticipated fluctuations in agricultural output may, for example, cause a spurt in food prices with serious consequences for the 'entitlements' of agricultural labourers. The effects are more severe for rural labourers and casual labour in urban areas for two reasons: i) food accounts for a large share of their household budget and ii) liquidity constraints prevent the storage of food. In this context, there is a strong justification for food subsidies. However, the design and implementation of food subsidies raise many contentious issues. Such subsidies take a number of forms like general food subsidies, food rations, food stamps, and the choice of an appropriate form is often very difficult. Their effects vary, depending on whether a partial equilibrium or a multimarket analysis is carried out. If the food subsidies account for a large share of public expenditure, the macro effects may well be significant. These may, for example, neutralize the favourable nutrition effects through higher inflation (Radhakrishna *et al*, 1997).

Public Distribution System

The Public Distribution System (PDS) has been a part of the larger food policy, which has all along aimed at providing inexpensive food to rural and urban dwellers. PDS also distributed a wide basket of goods including food grains, sugar, edible oil, cheap cloth etc. The Government of A.P introduced the subsidized rice scheme in the early 1980s to improve the consumption levels of the weaker sections of the society. Since August 1996, a poor household is entitled to 5 kg of rice per person per month subject to a ceiling of 20 kg at Rs.3.50 per kg. Besides rice, they are entitled to sugar and kerosene.

A micro-level study reveals that most of the people had access to food from this scheme in the developed villages, but a large percentage of beneficiaries are non-poor. In the backward villages, a large percentage of poor are excluded while a sizeable percentage of the non-poor is included (Indrakant, 1996).

The impact of all consumer subsidies on poverty was better in A.P during 1986-87. Subsidies reduced poverty by 4.64 percentage points in rural areas and 3.24 percentage points in urban areas. About 2.53 million persons (2.09 million in rural and 0.44 million in urban areas) may have moved out of poverty in 1986-88 due to income transfers from PDS. It has been estimated that the per capita monthly gain in income for the poor due to PDS in 1986-87 was nearly Rs.5.67 in rural areas and nearly Rs.8 in urban areas; and consequently, there was reduction in poverty by 5 percentage points and 3 percentage points in rural and urban areas of the State (Radhakrishna *et al*, 1997).

Human Capital

Human capital measured in terms of health status and education are considered critical measures of non-monetary dimensions of welfare as well as important inputs into an individual's earning ability (Sen, 1981). The poor are disadvantaged in terms of human capital measures and that improving their human capital will not only redress these inequalities but may also help reduce economic poverty.

Education

The relationship between human capital and poverty is a complex one in as much as each influences the other (Behrman, 1990). Lack of human capital among the poor takes a variety of forms – illiteracy, lack of income-augmenting skills, morbidity resulting in loss of physical stamina etc. This tends to perpetuate their poverty. On the other hand, given limited facilities for acquiring human capital in rural areas, acutely poor households fail to invest in human capital. Once caught in this vicious circle, poverty reinforces itself. Empirical evidence suggests that access to basic education has the most dramatic effect on poor children's chance to escape from poverty. It plays a catalytic role for poor women, weaker sections, and people living in rural areas. Basic education is expected to lead to increased earning potential, improved labour mobility, and better health for both adults and their children. In spite of considerable success in increasing education coverage over the last decades, A.P has one of the lowest literacy rates in the country. Expenditures on education in A.P are low compared to all India averages. A.P does not compare favourably with its neighboring states in its spending on education. Moreover, the composition of spending on education is also not optimal. Compared with its neighboring states in Southern India, A.P has lower school enrollment and attendance rates and also the state faces a considerable problem of school dropouts. The gross enrollment ratio in primary schools was 85.2 in 1998-99,and 47.07 in upper primary schools during the same period. As regards the dropouts in class I-V, it was more than 43 per cent among general categories, 51.5 per cent among Scheduled Castes and 71.7 per cent and Scheduled Tribes in 1998-99. The social attainment indicators of A.P along with Kerala and all India are presented in Table 14.

Health

The availability of medical services is believed to reduce the risk of poverty among agricultural labour households. This seems plausible since the loss of employment on account of sickness and a consequent termination of contract may entail a more substantial loss of income for agricultural labourers. Since health is a merit good and it calls for government intervention, individuals left to them may under provide health care. It is of course debatable whether all types of health care ought to be

Table 14. Select Social Attainment and Deprivation Indicators for Andhra Pradesh, Kerala and all India

Item	Unit	Year	Andhra Pradesh	Kerala	All India
Attainment Indicators					
1. Literacy					
Persons	Per cent	2001	61.11	90.92	65.38
Females		2001	51.17	87.86	54.16
2. Life expectancy at birth					
Males	Years	1993-97	61.20	70.40	60.40
Females	Years	1993-97	63.50	75.90	61.80
Deprivation Indicators					
3. Total illiteracy rate	Per cent	2001	38.89	9.08	34.62
4. Female Illiteracy rate	Per cent	2001	48.83	12.14	45.84
5. Non-enrollment rate	Per cent	1994	31.30	8.90	38.10
6. Drop-out rate (class I-V)	Per cent	1999-00	40.28	(-)1.22	36.27
7. Infant mortality rate (MR)	Per 1,000 live births	1998-99	66.00	16.00	72.00
8. Non-institutional births	Per cent	1998-99	50.20	9.70	66.40
9. Morbidity – diseases					
a) Reflecting poor living conditions	Per lakh population	1992	2782.51	2468.87	1530.90
b) Preventable by immunization	Per lakh population	1992	15.78	47.80	21.55
10. Maternal mortality	Per lakh live births	1987-96	283.00	a	479.00
11. Death rates	Per 1,000	1998	8.20	6.40	9.00
12. Under nourished children (0-4 Yrs)					
a) Weight for age	% below –2sd	1998-99	37.70	26.90	46.00
b) Weight for age	% below –3sd	1998-99	10.30	4.70	18.00
c) Height for age	% below –2sd	1998-99	38.60	21.90	45.50
d) Height for age	% below –3sd	1998-99	14.20	7.30	23.00

Note : 'a 'indicates that maternal mortality is so low that estimating its level from sex differentials in adult mortality for the reproductive ages is not possible.

Source: 1. Census of India, (2001), 2. International Institute for Population Sciences, (2000), 3. Statistical Abstract of India, (2001), 4. Bhat *et al* (1995), 5. Bhat (2002), 6. Duraiswamy, (2000).

the exclusive concern of the government. The case for government intervention is nevertheless strengthened by some recent findings suggesting that economic growth by itself will not improve significantly the health and nutrition status of the poor. For example, among the poor and allegedly malnourished individuals in rural southern India, the responsiveness of nutrient intakes to income changes was found to be very low and almost close to zero (Behrman and Deolalikar, 1987). The improvements in health and nutrition do indeed have a positive effect on labour productivity and income of the poor (Behrman, 1990). Table 14 presents important deprivation indicators wherein Kerala and all India indicators are also given.

Nutrition Programme

Under nutrition results in lower productivity. In a sample of rural households in southern India, weight-for-height – a medium-term indicator of an individual's nutrition status – significantly raised on-farm labour productivity as well as the wage rate earned in casual agricultural labour families (Deolalikar, 1988). Integrated Child Development Scheme (ICDS) is a nutritional and health programme targeted towards children and women. The ICDS project covered 150 blocks during 1998-99, 185 blocks during 1999-2000 and 220 blocks during 2000-2001. The total beneficiaries covered in ICDS are as follows: i) 27 lakh children (under six years); ii) 7 lakh adolescent girls and iii) 6.35 lakh expectant and nursing mothers during 1999-2000. This programme is found to be beneficial to the poor.

Rural Infrastructural Development

In the context of the need for stepping up agricultural growth rate to 4.5 per cent in the Ninth Five-Year Plan, emphasis was considered necessary for developing rural infrastructure in sectors like irrigation, roads, bridges, etc., as an essential requirement for better productivity of capital and labour. Such an emphasis would help check the migration of rural population to urban areas. High rates of growth in agriculture and allied activities generate a lot of employment opportunities in the rural areas. Non-availability of work from time to time would be a major cause of low incomes and high incidence of poverty. Poverty alleviation would naturally require creating work for the agricultural labourers who are also casual labourers. Firstly, the development of good physical infrastructure is very important for rapid and balanced economic growth. Most of our villages are still poorly connected or not connected at all by proper roads. Markets do not develop in areas where there are no roads. Another form of physical infrastructure needed for economic development is power. Rapid increase in electrification not only contributes to growth in agricultural productivity by encouraging private investment in irrigation, but it also contributes to reduction in rural poverty through the generation of non-agricultural employment. Thirdly, the development of other rural infrastructure like well designed irrigation systems and watersheds and other irrigation facilities are most important, as a high proportion of rural people derives their livelihood from agriculture. Irrigation has increased dramatically but with considerable regional variation.

4. SUMMARY AND CONCLUSION

The incidence of poverty in A.P shows a distinct pattern and is unique in showing a statistically significant declining trend. According to official estimates, the proportion of poor in the rural areas declined from 48.41 per cent in 1973-74 to 15.92 per cent in 1993-94 and to 11.05 per cent in 1999-00. Deaton and Dreze recalculated the poverty lines and poverty estimates by using new prices. The incidence of rural poverty was 35 percent in 1987-88, 29.2 percent in 1993-94 and 26.2 per cent in 1999-00. According to the Expert Group, the urban poverty ratio declined from 52.56 per cent in 1973-74 to 26.63 percent in 1999-00. On the other hand, estimates of urban poverty show an increase in the number of urban poor in A.P for the period between 1973-74 and 1993-94 and a decline between 1993-94 and 1999-00.

On the basis of official estimates, annual decline in the incidence of poverty was 0.39 percentage points in the first period from 1957-58 to 1969-70 and 1.26 percentage points in the second period from 1970-71 to 1999-00. The decline in the first period was not statistically significant. The impact of agricultural growth on rural poverty was significant in the first period but the impact of the wage rate was not significant. In the second period, the impact of wage rate was significant but the impact of agricultural growth was not significant. When the entire period is considered, both the wage rate and agricultural growth made significant contributions in reducing poverty.

Agricultural wages provide important information on poverty. Firstly, real wages are highly correlated with head count ratios. In other words, wherever incidence of poverty is higher, wages tend to be lower and vice versa. Secondly, the real wages act as rough indicators of poverty. A better understanding of recent trends in agricultural wages are important for greater clarity about the nature of rural poverty and possible means of removing it. The real wage rates of agricultural labourers have grown at 1.45 per cent per annum for males and 1.42 for females. In the eighties, the real wage rates increased substantially in A.P at 5.60 per cent per annum for males and 4.83 for females. In the nineties, there was a declining/stagnating trend in the real wage rates at a growth state of 1.23 per cent per annum for males and 1.64 for females. The increase in real wage rates despite the declining trend in agricultural growth indicates that the expansion of non-farm employment might have contributed for the rise in the agricultural wages during nineties. An increase in real wage rates of labourers engaged in the farm sector is mainly attributed to the rise in the demand for labour in the non-farm sector mostly in construction and service sector. Since the wages in the non-farm sector have been consistently higher than the wages in the farm sector, it is inferred that a part of the decline in rural poverty is due to opening up of employment opportunities in the non-farm sector.

It is argued that agricultural growth by itself may not make a dent in rural poverty. Even if the growth process is such that the poor participate in it, some segments, for instance the old and infirm, are likely to be left out. In fact, there is often a large hard core of the chronically poor who fail to benefit from agricultural growth. Hence, direct anti-poverty interventions such as food subsjdies and rural public works are necessary. The development of human capital through education and health has been neglected in poverty alleviation strategy. However, in order to make the poor self-reliant, it is necessary to include the provision of human capital. Besides the inadequacy of public expenditure in this area, the allocation has been lopsided, for instance, primary education has been relatively neglected. There is a growing awareness that the promotion of self-employment opportunities is likely to benefit only a limited segment of the rural poor and, therefore, rural public works can play a significant role in poverty alleviation. An important feature of RPW is that they are self-targeting and only the needy are likely to come for manual labour.

Food subsidies must continue for some specific groups of the poor such as the old, infirm and pregnant and lactating women. Since testing of means at frequent intervals is prohibitively expensive, it is imperative to identify other targeting indicators, viz., location. Also, the use of simple registration procedures would reduce transaction costs for the poor and enhance their access to subsidized food. Greater emphasis on the provision of human capital is necessary to enable the poor to break out of the vicious circle of poverty. However, allocations of public expenditure within the education and health sectors have been both insufficient and inequitable. Shifts in favour of programmes for primary education as well as for primary health care and control of communicable disease are necessary. Selectively imposed user fees for services for which there is private willingness to pay like hospital care and on certain groups like middle- and upper-income urban consumers would yield revenues both to expand primary education and primary health care facilities in rural areas and to improve their quality. At the same time, it is important to continue subsidies on health care, food and education for the poor. Women's education and health are important in their own right and warrant imaginative, wide-ranging interventions. For example, the expansion of female education requires not just a lowering of the opportunity cost or attending a school but also concerted efforts to overcome parental resistance.

Some broad areas of policy intervention are suggested: the provision of transport services, electricity, education and health care facilities and credit; access to arable land and extension services; the creation of non-farm employment activities in rural areas in order to open new avenues of employment for rural labourers and to add to their bargaining power; and the provision of safety nets (food subsidies) for mitigating acute and chronic deprivation – especially for those unable to participate in the growth process.

Reference

Acharya, S. and G.F. Papanek. (1995), "Explaining Agricultural wage Trends in India", *Development Policy Review,* Vol. 13, No.1, March.

Ahluwalia, M. S. (1986), "Rural Poverty, Agricultural Production and Prices" in J.W. Mellor and G.M Desai (eds.) *Agricultural Change and Rural Poverty,* Oxford University Press, New Delhi.

Behrman, J. R and Anil, B. Deolalikar. (1987), "Will Developing Country Nutrition Improve with Income? A Case Study for Rural South India", *Journal of Political Economy,* Vol.95, No.3.

Behrman, J. R. (1990), *The Action of Human Resources and Poverty on One Another. What we have yet to learn,* LSMS Working Paper No.74, The World Bank, Washington DC.

Bhat, P.N.M; K. Navaneethan and S. Irudaya Rajan. (1995), " Maternal Mortality in India: Estimates from a Regression Model", *Studies in Family Planning,* Vol. 26, No.4.

Bhat, P. N. M. (2002), "Maternal Mortality in India : An Update" *Studies in Family Planning*, Vol. 33, No.3.

Census of India, (2001), *Provisional Population Totals,* Government of India, New Delhi.

Datt, Gaurav. (1997), *Poverty in India and Indian States: An Update,* International Food Policy Research Institute, Washington, D.C.

Datt, Gaurav and Martin Ravallion. (1998), "Why have some Indian states done better than others at reducing rural poverty"?, *Economica,* Vol 65, No. 257.

Datt, Gaurav, Valerie Kozel and Martin Ravallion. (2003), "A Model Based Assessment of India's Progress in Reducing Poverty in the 1990s", *Economic and Political Weekly,* Vol. 38, No. 4, January 25-31.

Desai, G.M. (1986), "Trends in Rural Poverty in India: An Interpretation of Dharm Narain", in J.W. Mellor and G.M. Desai (eds.), *Agricultural Change and Rural Poverty,* Oxford University Press, New Delhi.

Deaton, Angus and Jean Dreze. (2002), "Poverty and Inequality in India: A Re-Examination", *Economic and Political Weekly,* Vol. 37, No.36, September 7-13.

Deaton, Angus. (2003), "Prices and Poverty Rates in India, 1987-2000", *Economic and Political Weekly,* Vol. 38, No. 4, January 25-31.

Deolalikar, Anil. B. (1988), "Nutrition and Labour Productivity in Agriculture: Wage Equation and Farm Production Estimates for Rural India", *Review of Economics and Statistics,* Vol. 70.

Dev, S.M. (1988), "Regional Disparities in Agricultural Labour Productivity and Rural Poverty in India" *Indian Ecnomic Review,* Vol. 22, No.2.

Dev, S.M. and S. Galab. (1999), "Eradication of Poverty and Generation of Productive Employment in South India" Paper Prepared for the IASSI Regional Seminar on India on Threshold of the New Millennium: The

Unfinished Agenda and the New Challenges, organized at the Institute for Social and Economic Change', Bangalore, 15-16 December 1999.

Dev, S. M. (2000), "Draft Report of the Rural Poverty Reduction Task Force: Andhra Pradesh,"(mimeo) Centre for Economic and Social Studies, Hyderabad.

Dev, S.M. and P. Padmanabha Rao. (2002), "Poverty Alleviation Programmes in Andhra Pradesh – An Assessment", (mimeo) Centre for Economic and Social Studies, Hyderabad.

Duraiswamy, P. (2000), "Changes in Returns to Education in India 1983-94: By Gender, Age Cohort and Location" (NCAER data), Center's Discussion Paper No. 815, Economic Growth Center, Yale University.

Galab. S, M. Gopinath Reddy, K.S. Reddy, G.K. Mitra and M. Krishnaiah (1997), "District Poverty Initiatives Project: Anantapur", Centre for Economic and Social Studies, Hyderabad.

Galab, S. (1999), "Some Micro-Level Arrangements of Social Security in Andhra Pradesh", *The Indian Journal of Labour Economics,* Vol. 42. No. 3, July-September.

Government of India. (1979), *Task Force on Projections of Minimum Needs and Effective Consumption Demand,* Perspective Planning Division, Planning Commission, Government of India.

Government of India. (1993), *Report of the Expert Group on Estimation of Proportion and Number of Poor,* Perspective Planning Division, Planning Commission, Government of India, New Delhi.

Government of India. (2001), *Number and Percentage of Population Below Poverty Line by States 1999-2000,* Perspective Planning Division, Planning Commission, Government of India.

Indrakant, S. (1986), *Effects of Price and Income on Household Expenditure Pattern on A.P: Some Policy Implications,* Ph.D Thesis, Department of Economics, Osmania University, Hyderabad.

International Institute for Population Sciences. (2000), *National Family Health Survey, India: 1998-99,* IIPS- Bombay.

Kakwani, N and K. Subba Rao. (1990), "Rural Poverty and its Alleviation in India", *Economic and Political Weekly,* Vol. 35, No.13, March 31.

Kanchanya, K. (1998), *Women and Development: A case study of DWACRA Programme in West Godavari District.* Unpublished M. Phil thesis, Centre for Economic and Social Studies, Hyderabad.

Lipton, M. (1991), "Land reform as Commenced Business: The Evidence Against Stopping", (mimeo), Cornell University, USA.

Malthotra, R. (1997), "Incidence of poverty in India: Towards a Consensus on Estimating the Poor", *The Indian Journal of Labour Economics,* Vol. 40, No.1.

Parthasarathy, G. (1995), "Public Intervention and Rural Poverty: Case of Non-Sustainable Reduction in Andhra Pradesh", *Economic and Political Weekly.* Vol. 30, Nos. 41&42, October 14-21.

Parthasarathy, G and C. Durgaparameswari. (1998), "Andhra Pradesh", in V.M. Rao (ed) *The Poor in a Hostile Society: Glimpses of Changing Poverty Scenario in India,* Vikas, New Delhi.

Prabhu, K. Seeta. (1998), "Economic Growth, Income Poverty and Human Development: A Study of Andhra Pradesh", (mimeo), Department of Economics, University of Bombay, Mumbai.

Prabhu, K. Seeta. (1999), "Dimensions and Measures of Human Poverty", in Raja J. Chellaiah and Sudarshan (eds.), *Income Poverty and Beyond : Human Development in India,* Social Science Press, New Delhi.

Radhakrishna, R, K. Subba Rao, S. Indrakant and C. Ravi. (1997), *India's Public Distribution System: A National and International Perspective,* World Bank Discussion Paper No.380, The World Bank, Washington D.C.

Rao, C.H.H and P. Rangaswamy. (1988), "Efficiency of Investment in IRDP: A Study of Uttar Pradesh", *Economic and Political Weekly,* Vol. 23, No.26, June 25.

Rao, C.H.H. (1992), "Integrating Poverty Alleviation Programmes with Development Strategies – Indian Experience", *Economic and Political Weekly,* Vol. 27, No.48, November 28.

Rao, C.H.H. (1994), *Agricultural Growth, Rural Poverty and Environmental Degradation in India,* Oxford University Press, New Delhi.

Rao, C.H.H. (1995), "Attack on Poverty and Deprivation: Role of Structural Change and Structural Adjustment", *The Indian Journal of Labour Economics,* Vol. 38, No. 1, January – March.

Rao, C.H.H, and Linnemann, Hans. (eds.) (1996), *Economic Reforms and Poverty Alleviation in India,* Sage, New Delhi.

Rao, C.H.H, and R. Radhakrishna. (1999), "National Food Security: Policy Perspective for India" in Peter, G.H. and Braun, J.V. (eds.), *Food Security Diversification and Resource Management: Refocusing of Agriculture,* International Association of Agricultural Economics, Ashgate.

Ravallion, Martin and Datt, Gaurav. (1998), " Farm Productivity in India", *Journal of Development Studies,* Vol. 34, No.4.

Sankaran, S.R. (1996), "Organisational and Administrative Inputs for Poverty Alleviation Programmes" in V.M. Rao (ed.), *The Poor in a Hostile Society: Glimpses of Changing Scenario in India,* Vikas publishing House: New Delhi.

Sen, A. (1981), "Public action and the quality of life in developing countries", *Oxford Bulletin of Economics and Statistics,* Vol. 43.

Sharma, V.P. (1997), *Impact of Watershed Development Programme on Dry-Land Agriculture,* Unpublished Ph.D thesis, Centre for Economic and Social Studies, Hyderabad.

Statistical Abstract of India. (2001), Central Statistical Organization, Ministry of Statistics and Programme Implementation, Government of India, New Delhi.

Subba Reddy, N. (1988), "Depriving Tribals of Land: Andhra Move to Amend Land Transfer Laws", *Economic and Political Weekly,* Vol.23, No. 29, July 16.

Subba Reddy, N. (1989), "Sword of Damocles over Tribal People of Andhra Pradesh", *Economic and Political Weekly,* Vol. 24, No. 26. July1.

Subba Rao, K. (1985), "Regional Variations in impact of Anti-Poverty Programmes: A Review of Evidence", *Economic and Political Weekly,* Vol. 29, No. 43.

Subrahmanyam, S and S. Sudhakar Reddy. (2001), "Economic Reforms, Agricultural Growth and Rural Poverty in Andhra Pradesh", (mimeo), Centre for Economic and Social Studies, Hyderabad.

Sudhakar Reddy, S. (1991), "Poverty and Agricultural Growth in Rural Andhra Pradesh: Inter-district Analysis", Centre for Economic and Social Studies, Hyderabad.

Sudhakar Reddy, S, K.S. Reddy, P.Padmanabha Rao and G. Santhana Babu. (1997), "District Poverty Initiatives Project: Adilabad", (mimeo), Centre for Economic and Social Studies, Hyderabad.

Venkatramaiah, P, S.Galab, M. Gopinath Reddy and M.C. Swaminathan (1997), "Concurrent Evaluation of Integrated Rural Development Programme Report for Andhra Pradesh (5th Round: July, 1995 – June, 1996)" (mimeo), Centre for Economic and Social Studies, Hyderabad, Andhra Pradesh.

World Bank. (1997), *India: Achievements and Challenges in Reducing Poverty*, A World Bank Country Study, The World Bank, Washington.

17

Women and Self Help Groups: Poverty Alleviation and Empowerment

S. Galab and
N. Chandrasekhara Rao

1. INTRODUCTION

Accelerating economic growth and creating an environment for ensuring 'spread effect of growth' have been emphasised, especially during 90s, for poverty alleviation. This macro-strategy contributes to the emergence of production indivisibilities (Rao, 1994). Poor should be able to respond to these stimuli for poverty alleviation (Vyas and Bhargava 1995). But, the poor can internalise the production indivisibilities in groups only. Moreover, the participation of the poor in the planning and implementation of anti-poverty programmes is required to reduce the chain of intermediaries between the government and the actual beneficiaries and to improve their bargaining power (Rao, 1994). Further, the institutions – joint-family system, patron-client relationships and traditional occupation-based institutions, that provide social security to the poor are breaking down at the grass-roots level. Thus, there is an institutional vacuum at the grass-roots level to safeguard the interests of the poor (Galab, 1999). In this context, there is substantial evidence that organising women around thrift and credit services is one of the most effective methods, not only for alleviating poverty but also for empowering women (World Bank, 1995, 2000/2001). Thus, the macro and micro concerns are giving rise to the demand for women-based collectives centred around thrift and credit services. Then, the issue is how the Government of Andhra Pradesh has responded in this regard.

The Government of Andhra Pradesh has provided larger space for women self help groups in its strategy for poverty alleviation and women empowerment. The promotion of women groups under Development of Women and Children in Rural Areas (DWCRA) programme and adoption of the model of South Asia Poverty Alleviation Programme (SAPAP) with suitable improvements to develop and implement Andhra Pradesh District Poverty Initiatives Project (APDPIP) and the Andhra Pradesh Rural Poverty Reduction Project (APRPRP) stand as a testimony to this. Therefore, the contribution of these groups, spread in the length and breadth of the state, to poverty alleviation and women empowerment needs critical examination. But, the APDPIP and the APRPRP spread in the most backward mandals of the State are not amenable for assessment as they are still under implementation. However, the assessment of South Asia Poverty Alleviation Programme, the basic model of APDPIP and APRPRP, can help to predict the probable impact of APDPIP and APRPRP. On the other hand, the model promoted by Cooperative Development Foundation (CDF), which is purely a micro-finance model, helps to assess the contribution of DWCRA beyond micro-finance induced impacts. The assessment of these three models helps to identify the strengths and weaknesses of DWCRA groups and thereby helps to improve the DWCRA programme. In this backdrop, this paper addresses itself to the following issues:

i. What are the characteristics of the three women-based group models of poverty alleviation and women empowerment that are being implemented in Andhra Pradesh? And, how do they differ among themselves in their approach?
ii. How are the poor women organised into groups? And, how these groups are functioning?
iii. What is the contribution of these models to poverty alleviation and women empowerment?
iv. What are the improvements, if any, to be made in case of DWCRA groups for their better functioning and impact on poverty and women's empowerment?

This paper is based on the review of some of the relevant studies. The studies reviewed are excellent source to understand the process of change, though they do not provide precise estimates of impact assessment parameters. Formation, functioning, and impact are the broad issues examined in the studies. The impact assessment covered two aspects, viz., poverty alleviation and women empowerment. Regarding women empowerment, three dimensions are considered (Ranjani et al, 2002). They are 'power to', 'power with' and 'power within'. The 'power to' dimension of empowerment indicates the power of women to control their lives. This includes power to survive, control over their labour and access to family labour, access to and control over resources, freedom to move and interact, access to leadership positions, control over reproduction and control over body. The 'power with' indicates the collective power of women members to negotiate their gender, caste, class and other interests vis-à-vis institutions of the market, the State, and the community. This includes collective interventions in the institution of family, community, market organization, the State including statutory local bodies. The third dimension 'power within' indicates the strategic gender awareness. An indicator of the 'power within' at the individual level is the ability of women to challenge gender related attitudes and social norms in their own personal lives. Another indicator of the power, women gaining at a deeper level, is the perception of others on women's confidence, assertiveness, and independence. This framework of empowerment is utilized to assess the empowerment in all the studies.

2. BASIC CHARACTERISTICS OF THE SELECT MODELS

Model of the Cooperative Development Foundation (CDF)

Among the three selected models, the CDF model is the simplest model. Women Thrift Cooperatives (WTC) is the basic entity promoted under CDF model. Any adult woman, irrespective of her economic status, can become member of the WTCs. Members save Rs. 20 per month and earn a monthly interest of one per cent. Monthly interest of 2 per cent is charged on the loan. The loanable funds are generated from member's savings only. Credit is linked to savings. A maximum of three times of savings of a member is provided as credit. The WTCs help the members, who like to utilise their accumulated thrift during their economically active life span as a social security during their economically inactive life span, on the one hand and on the other they also help members to obtain thrift-linked credit for the economic empowerment. Thus, the WTC is an intervention in village credit market to provide safer place for thrift accumulation and thrift linked-credit at the prevailing market interest rates at lower transaction costs with social collateral without any external funds. The WTC is organised into small groups with group leaders to monitor loan repayment, savings collection and disbursement of loan. Two guarantors are required for sanctioning loans. These two mechanisms are adopted to mobilise savings, loan disbursement and loan repayment. Loan insurance fund (LIF) scheme is introduced to safeguard against the risk of bad debts due to the death of any member. The repayment schedule is not specific to the economic status of the members. The Women Thrift Cooperatives are federated into Association of Women Thrift Cooperatives (AWTC) to facilitate better functioning of WTCs, perform higher order functions and inter-flow of loanable funds among WTCs. The CDF model is based on the premise that lack of access and higher interest rates perpetuate poverty. As noted earlier, both the poor and the non-poor are the members of the WTCs. Thus, the CDF model is a model of untargeted micro-finance institution (MFI) (Biswas and Mahajan, 1997). This suggests the need to examine whether poor are discriminated in favour of non-poor in CDF groups.

Model of Development of Women and Children in Rural Areas (DWCRA)

The Development of Women and Children in Rural Areas (DWCRA) programme was started in 1982-83 in the State with UNICEF cooperation to provide opportunities of self- employment on a sustained basis for the rural poor women. Women living in neighbourhood with similar socio-economic background form groups. The size of the groups ranges from 10-15 members. The SHGs of DWCRA are federated into Mahila Banks under Andhra Pradesh Mutually Aided Cooperative Societies Act, 1995 for the better functioning of SHGs and to provide more access to credit for the poor. The women in groups take up economic activities suited to their skills and local resources. Training in leadership, attitudinal changes, skill for income generation is the mandate of the DWCRA model. A lump sum grant of Rs.25, 000/- is provided to the group for undertaking economic activities. This is a common fund, which is recouped and revolved periodically. The IRDP subsidy and bank loans over and above the grant can be accessed. In addition to these funds, groups mobilise monthly savings for inter-lending to meet the consumption needs of the members. This programme also aims to improve women's access to basic services (health, education, chid care, nutrition, water and sanitation) and other rural development programmes of the government. The organizing of women around thrift and credit services should result in the enhancement of their bargaining power and the power to resist exploitation. DWCRA 'Bazaars' and linkage with corporate sector are the initiatives undertaken by the government to capture non-local markets for the DWCRA group products (GOAP, 1999).

Model of South Asia Poverty Alleviation Programme (SAPAP)

The South Asia Poverty Alleviation Programme (SAPAP) assisted by United Nations Development Programme (UNDP) was a response to Dhaka declaration of the SAARC Summit held in 1993 on eradication of poverty by 2002 in all SAARC countries. In India, SAPAP Pilot project was initiated in 1995 in Andhra Pradesh. The programme was implemented in the three poverty striken- drought prone-districts, viz., Anantapur, Kurnool and Mahaboobnagar. Thus, SAPAP was concentrated in 20 of the poorer mandals. This programme is based on two premises, viz., an elite, who appropriated public resources for their private and sectional gain has captured the South Asian State and this State is deemed to be misgoverned and unaccountable. The misgoverned system has adversely affected the poor as follows:

- The poor, as individuals, are paying unacceptable transaction costs of a socio-political and financial nature for accessing resources from the State;

- The poor, as individuals, are incapable of augmenting their own production capacities through enhanced savings and skill formation; and
- The gains made by the poor are insecure because of the random risks emanating through ill-health, old age, environmental factors, and social and political oppression (UNDP, 2000)

In the above backdrop, the SAPAP has contemplated the process of social mobilisation as an institutional mechanism to mobilise the poor into self help groups (SHGs) for their collective empowerment at the grass-roots level. The collective body facilitates the poor to interact with the government machinery for better accessing of public resources and services and also acts as a pressure group to keep the State more accountable to the institutional power of the socially mobilised poor. Thus, the empowerment model of SAPAP includes three components, viz., social mobilisation, capital formation and capacity building of the poor which help to remove the obstacles that perpetuate poverty and enable them to overcome their vulnerable conditions (UNDP, 1998). The SAPAP was implemented in collaboration with local NGOs and the State government. The programme was initially implemented through 18 Partner Voluntary Organisations (PVOs) or NGOs and was served by a project office backed by 22 Coordinators and 121 Community Volunteers. The programme has covered 66,000 households, who constitute 34 percent of the total households of the project area and 64 percent of the total target group households. As high as 5201 self help groups (SHGs) have emerged. These groups have been federated into 380 village organisations (VOs)at the village level. The Mandal Mahila Samakhya (MMS), the apex body of VOs at the mandal level, plays a crucial supporting role in sustaining the VOs (UNDP, 2000).

Comparative Perspective of the Select Models

These models are rooted in three premises, viz., lack of access to credit at favourable terms and conditions for poor is resulting in perpetuation of poverty; social capital contributes to poverty alleviation; and women's empowerment reduces general and gender poverty. Women Self help Groups (SHGs) are promoted as basic entities under all the models. The SHGs are federated to tackle higher order functions and improve the functioning of SHGs. The SHGs of DWCRA are federated into Mahila Banks. The SHGs of SAPAP are federated into Village Organizations (VOs) and in turn the VOs are federated into Mandal Mahila Samakhyas (MMSs). The SHGs of CDF are called Women Thrift Cooperatives (WTCs) and these are federated into Association of Women Thrift Cooperatives (AWTCs). The poor are eligible to become members in the SHGs of DWCRA and SAPAP models, whereas all the adults of village, irrespective of their economic status, are eligible to become members of Women Thrift Cooperatives of CDF model. This is the reason why the size of the WTCs of CDF runs into hundreds at the village level, while it varies between 12-15 across other models, on an average. The CDF model depends only on internal funds, while the other models depend on internal as well as external funds to generate loanable funds. The CDF model contemplates no linkages of WTCs/AWTCs with any other organizations. The DWCRA model contemplates linkages of SHGs/ Mahila Banks with the Line Departments (LDs) of the Government, the formal financial institutions and Corporate Sector. The SAPAP model contemplates linkages with the State including (Line Departments, local governance bodies), civil society and the market. The DWCRA and SAPAP models have child centred intervention strategy also. The DWCRA model lies between CDF model and SAPAP model. It is a micro-finance plus model. Besides micro-finance operations, this model links the DWCRA groups to the services and programmes provided by the State and also to Corporate Sector. This programme is being implemented by the State through out the length and the breadth of the State of Andhra Pradesh. Economic and social empowerment of poor women is the bottom line of the DWCRA model. The SAPAP model is assisted by UNDP. It is also a micro-finance plus model. But it contemplates economic, social and political empowerment of poor women. Thus, they represent NGO model (CDF), Government model (DWCRA) and an international model (SAPAP), which has been implemented in SAARC countries. Among the NGO models, the CDF has the distinction of being non-targeting micro-finance model, whereas the models of other NGOs are being targeted micro-finance plus. So, it may be difficult to find only micro-finance centred model among the NGOs except that of CDF.

The rate of coverage of people -the number of people covered per year, on an average- is the highest under DWCRA model (1,25,508) followed by the SAPAP (11,251) and the CDF (4560). These variations across the models can be attributed to four factors, viz., the area of operation; the age of the models; the nature of the models; and the nature of the implementing agency. The DWCRA is being implemented in the entire state, while the other two models are confined to a few mandals of the two/three districts of the state-the CDF model is in two districts (Warangal and Karimnagar) and the SAPAP model was in three districts (Anantapur, Kurnool and Mahaboobnagar). The DWCRA is 20 years old, while the CDF and the SAPAP are 12 years and 5 years old respectively. The CDF model is being implemented in and around the Mulkanoor Cooperative (a well-functioning diversified cooperative) area to take advantage of the acceptability of the cooperatives by the people-both the poor as well as the non-poor. The Mutually Aided Cooperative Societies Act, 1995 (MACS Act, 1995) of Andhra Pradesh has given impetus to the growth of the cooperatives of CDF. This is evident from the fact that the growth of the WTCs is phenomenal after 1995 only (CDF, 2001). The MACS Act, 1995 ensures freedom from bureaucratic pressures as well as excessive reliance on easily available external funds, that had often proved to be a source of weakness for the cooperative movement (Ghosh, 1998). The Government of Andhra Pradesh has promoted DWCRA model to contain the negative effects of the economic reforms, pursued rigorously since 1995, on poor and harness the collective strength of women demonstrated through the anti-liquor movement of women in early 90s. This is evident from the fact that the growth of DWCRA groups (as well as other self help groups) is significant only after 1995 (GOAP, 1999). The SAPAP model was implemented in collaboration with the local NGOs and the State intensively as it was an experimental model. It is striking to note that the State has focussed more on marginalised sections of the society. The size of the savings and loan per member, on an average, is larger under SAPAP (even DWCRA) compared to CDF because the saving contributions are related to the local wage rates and the funds are accessed through multiple sources other than own savings (Table 1). Thus, the unmet credit needs may be more pronounced among the CDF groups.

3. FORMATION, FUNCTIONING AND IMPACT OF THE MODELS

The detailed analysis of the formation, functioning and impact of the models on poverty and women empowerment is in order.

CDF Model: Formation and Functioning of Groups

The WTCs are untargeted micro-finance institutions (MFIs), since any woman irrespective of her socio-economic status can become a member of WTC. The caste composition of 37 WTCs promoted by CDF in Warangal and Karimnagar reveals that BCs, OCs, SCs and STs constitute 61, 13, 12 and 2 percent of the total participant members respectively. The landholding pattern of member households shows that landless, marginal and small farmers, and other farmers (including medium and large) constitute 55, 41 and 4 percent respectively (CDF, 1999). The relatively low amounts of both share capital per member (Rs 10 or 20) as well as monthly-required thrift (typically Rs. 20) allow women from across the income spectrum of the village to participate. This has led to coverage of ninety percent of village women across all social strata in most of the villages (Ghosh, 1998). On the other hand, there are few members who do not appear to be in great financial need but who are members for the sake of companionship and the sense of solidarity with other women (Ray and Vasundhara, 1996). This indicates that women from all socio-economic spectrums, except the very privileged participate in groups.

Table 1. Macro Dimensions of the Models

Sl. No	Description of the Dimension	Cooperative Development Foundation (CDF) Model	Development of Women and Children in Rural Areas (DWCRA) Model	South Asia Poverty Alleviation Programme (SAPAP) Model
1	Project Area	Warangal and Karimnagar Districts	Entire state	Anantapur, Kurnool and Mahaboobnagar Districts
2	SHGs/ WTCs formed (in number)	200	1,90,083 out of 4,27,927 SHGs	5201
3	VOs/MMSs/Mahila Banks/AWTCs (in numbers)	27 (AWTCs)	NA	308 (VOs)
4	Members (in Numbers)	45,605	25,10,075	56,256
5	Members per SHGs /WTCs (in number)	228	13	15
6	Caste composition of members (in percentages)			
	Scheduled Castes	12	34	28
	Scheduled Tribes	2	10	7
	Backward Castes	61	40	50
	Other Castes	13	16	15
7	SHGs/WTCs per habitation (in number)	1	2	4
8	Entry of non-poor (in percentage)	NA	16.65	28.00
9	Savings (Rs.in crores)	4.71	316.00	8.18
10	Savings per member (in Rs.)	1034	1260	1092
11	Total corpus (Rs. In crores)	6.48	589	NA
12	Loans per member (in number) (during the current year)	0.68	NA	NA
13	Loan amount (Rs. in crores) (during the current year)	7.00	NA	77.7
14	Average loan size (in Rs.) (during the current year)	2248	NA	2763*
15	Grade 'A' SHGs/WTCs (in percentages)	NA	18.9	47.6

Source: GoAP (1999); GoAP (2002); UNDP (1998); UNDP (2000) ; CDF (1999); CDF (2001); CESS (2001).

Note: 1. NA indicates not available.

2. The figures for CDF and SAPAP relate to the year 2000 and the same for DWCRA relate to September, 2002.

3. * Indicates estimated figures.

4. In case of CDF, the caste distribution of the members is not equal to 100 as the caste affiliation of some of the members is not known.

The proportion of leadership from SCs and STs was slightly higher than their proportion in membership, where as in case of the BCs, this was slightly lower. However, this was relatively higher from OCs than their proportion in membership. The landless were underrepresented in relation to their proportion in membership, whereas the other categories were over represented in relation to their proportion in membership. This could be due to the pressure of daily work on the landless, and likely loss of wages for days spent in committee meetings. Most WTCs are now discussing the payment of sitting fee for directors, equal at least to the daily agricultural wage in their area (CDF, 1999). Majority of the members attend meetings on a regular basis. Most women actively engage in decision-making process during the meetings. They take the responsibility to ensure that others repay loans regularly and occasionally make the thrift contribution on behalf of other members who may be away ((Ray and Vasundhara, 1996).

The resistance from the husbands and mothers-in-law for the women to actively participate in WTCs has been gradually coming down. The dependency of WTCs on CDF staff also has been declining slowly ((Ray and Vasundhara 1996; Ghosh 1998). The WTCs and AWTCs are able to meet the transaction costs through the interest amount earned on the credit operations (Biswas and Mahajan, 1997). The credit provided by the WTCs is enabling the women to utilise the existing skills they possess. However, this is restricting the fuller utilisation of credit potential, as new opportunities are not expanding in the villages. Moreover, due to lack of effective forward linkages, some of the women are not able to generate adequate surpluses from the existing economic activities to make repayments of loans. As a result of this, women are afraid of obtaining loan from the WTCs. All these factors result in the reduction of utilisation of funds and loan repayments overtime. This may threaten the sustainability of Women Thrift Cooperative System in years to come, if these trends are not countered.

Impact of the WTCs

As noted earlier, the WTCs should provide access to credit at reasonable interest rates and enable the women to undertake economic activities, besides meeting pressing needs. This ultimately should result in reduction in poverty (income poverty). These are the intended impacts of the WTCs. However, there may also be unintended consequences of the WTCs. As the intervention impacts of WTCs do not confine to the credit transactions and thereby economic empowerment, it may also stretch to social and political domains of empowerment since they are interrelated. Further, the externalities of WTCs may also contribute to the changes in credit market at village level.

Impact on Poverty

Some of the women reported that they didn't know earlier where to get loan. Some others have reported that they used to knock on several doors and beg for loan before joining the Women Thrift Cooperatives. Others told that they did not have access to loans without pledging or pawning articles of value or alternatively they had to pledge their produce to merchants at lower than market rates. Some others mentioned that they used to borrow at higher rates of interest and face lot of problems previously. Some have revealed that they have to desperately depend on their husbands for getting money before joining the WTCs. They have also reported that their ability to repay the loan was low since loan has to be repaid in lump sum and at a time. But all of them reported that they are able to obtain loan that can be repaid in easier instalments without collateral in timely manner whenever necessary at a reasonable interest rate from the WTCs. Women also noted that as a result of their participation in the WTCs, their creditworthiness with other financial institutions and other money providers had improved, thus giving them access to more funds ((Ray and Vasundhara, 1996). The relatively low amount of both share capital per member (Rs.10 or 20) as well as monthly-required thrift (typically Rs. 20) allows women from across spectrum of the village to participate and accumulate their savings. Poor women, and sometimes others, often have nowhere to keep their money safely. At home, their husbands may take it away at any time. There are no reliable and suitable organizations to mobilise small savings to retain local surpluses within the region (Ghosh, 1998). Local reliable self-managed WTCs filled this gap. Some women reported that their ability to save was a sign of security. Others noted the improvement of their financial situation and having `money at hand' as their reasons for feeling secure. The proportion of borrowers from each caste is in line with their proportion of membership. The proportion of borrowers from landless is less than the proportion of their membership. Similarly, the proportion of loans received by this category, too, was lower than the membership percentage. Further the size of the loan received is also low compared to other category of members (CDF, 1999). This indicates the lower credit absorption capacity of this category of members. The cooperatives' interest rate of 24 percent per annum has forced other lenders to lower their rates. Women reported that the interest rate outside the WTCs dropped from 36 percent to 30 percent per annum ((Ray and Vasundhara, 1996). This indicates the impact of women's thrift cooperatives on the village credit market. Further, this also reveals that the cost of credit also has come down for the members as well as non-members of WTCs. Similar observations are made in case of CDF sponsored women cooperatives in Cuddapah district (Parthasarathy and Kalyani, 1995).

The pattern of utilisation of loans taken from WTCs provides indications for assessing the income improvements of the member households of WTCs. It is interesting to note that 50 percent of the loans have been utilised for immediate generation of income and the rest 50 percent of the loans have been utilised for creation of productive assets. Agriculture (including irrigation), animal husbandry and small business constitute 23, 13 and 11 percent of the loans respectively. Human capital formation (health, education and consumption) acquisition of assets (physical assets including irrigation) constitutes 23 and 12 percent, respectively (CDF, 1999). These observations are similar to those observed in case of WTCs sponsored by the CDF in Cuddapah district (Parthasarathy and Kalyani, 1995). Women's involvement in economic activities has increased substantially, as they have accessed loans. Women have been able to start new business and expand old ones. The business, both old and new, consist of small grocery stores, tea/ coffee and 'paan' shops, spice grinding units, vegetable vendors, home-based cut piece cloth business and tailoring, bangle selling and desilting crane. The access to credit at lower interest rates and patterns of utilisation of credit indicate that there should be improvement in the incomes of the households. The husbands of members of WTCs also reported that their wives are adding additional income to the households' income ((Ray and Vasundhara, 1996). These observations have support from WTCs in Cuddapah also (Parthasarathy and Kalyani 1995). All these indicate the possibilities for reduction in income poverty of the member households of WTCs.

Impact on Women's Empowerment

Women have reported that they have started non-traditional tasks and enterprises vis-à-vis the activities they were already doing. The tasks and enterprises noted earlier provide substantial evidence to this. These women reported that their access to and control over savings have improved. Another key asset for women is jewellery. Though jewellery is a non-productive asset, women perceive it as their own to a greater extent. Besides livestock and shops, women members reported acquisition of other physical assets. They have also reported that they have become more mobile as a result of their WTC activities. Most of the members agreed that mobility outside the village has increased with travelling between villages for WTC meetings. Some women have reported that they have travelled for the first time outside of their district to attend group activities. Women have reported that the members consider the unity and solidarity among the women in the WTCs to be one of the most important benefits of membership. Women of different castes and classes met for a common purpose in the WTC. Women noted that the absence of caste segregation in the WTCs was an important change in their villages. The solidarity in the cooperatives has given scope to share their problems and seek help. The cooperatives have become a shelter for the widows and single women who face particular pressures in the society. Caste and class based norms are slowly broken in the cooperatives. Thus, freedom to interact and make friends outside the four walls of the family has been improved. The WTCs have expanded avenue for women to assume leadership positions. Most women reported that they are able to spend money on their own needs like health care, clothing and jewellery. Some of the women reported that they are consulted by their husbands in regard to what crop to grow. This indicated that the role of women in decision-making in the family has improved. There are collective interventions in the institution of family. Arbitration in a divorce case by one WTC is a case in point. However, there are collective interventions vis-à-vis the State and statutory local bodies. The leaders of WTC were consulted about the installation of sanitary latrines in one of the villages; politicians have started coming to the WTCs to find out how their members vote. Four women members contested in elections from women reserved constituencies in the local government Mandal elections. Many of the husbands reported that their wives are more independent than before joining the WTCs (Ray and Vasundhara, 1996; Ghosh, 1998).

DWCRA Model: Formation and Functioning of Groups

Women from all caste groups are covered under the programme (ORG- MARG 2000). However, the composition of coverage is varying across the districts (ORG-MARG, 2000; Raju and Ali, 1996; ICM, 1996; Jayalakshmi, 1997; Narayanaswamy and Jagannathan, 1999; YFA, 1996; Kanchanya, 1998; Mahendra Dev and Rao, 2002). This may be due to variations in the caste composition of poor across the districts. However, backward castes, scheduled castes, and scheduled tribes put together constitute significant proportion of the beneficiaries covered. Further the participation of widows, who constitute the poorest of the poor, is nine percent (ORG-MARG, 2000; Raju and Ali, 1996). The composition of the members according to pre-DWCRA income status of their households reveals that the coverage of the poorest of the poor is low on the one hand and on the other the coverage of non-poor is considerable. (GOAP, 1999; Raju and Ali, 1996). The reasons for this include: the poor are not sure of their savings capability and hence do not join the groups; many a time the initial mobilisers may exclude the poorest due to their bias and underestimation of the capacities of the poor to save, avail loans and repay them; and sometimes, the poor are indifferent to such programmes and thus never join the groups (APMAS, 2002). The mean age of members in DWCRA groups is 35 years (ORG-MARG, 2000). The groups are formed on the basis of the income, caste and neighbourhood. Hence these groups are more homogeneous (ORG-MARG, 2000).

About 39 percent of groups do not hold meetings. 23 percent of the groups are not practicing bookkeeping. There are mainly two reasons for this: gross illiteracy of members; and equal distribution of external grants and funds where groups don't see the need for book maintenance. Regularity on savings is observed and defaulters are found to be only eight percent of the members in the last three months (ORG-MARG, 2000). 78 percent of SHGs save regularly. It was found that savings per month equal the average daily wage. Savings were collected by a door-to-door practice and not during meetings. There is no penalty for not saving in time. It was observed that some groups discontinue savings, once the revolving fund is availed by the group. Few groups lack the motivation to save due to the absence of external linkages, in spite of functioning for a period of two years or more. Interest on savings is not a common feature in any of the districts. Additional savings apart from the mandatory savings are absent. Only two percent of the groups carry out voluntary savings (APMAS, 2002). Equal distribution of funds dominates the pattern of lending. This has been due to four factors: fear of repayment in case of need-based loans; the members feel that every member has an equal share in the loan amount; unwillingness to pay interest on internal loans (from savings) by the members; banking system and the DRDA staff together encourage equal distribution as a pattern of lending to inculcate cohesiveness among the group members. Internal lending activities have not developed fully in the districts.

Idle funds as a percent of total funds available, (member's savings, grants, interest amount, other inflows) is 33 percent. However, 78 percent of internal funds are in rotation (ORG-MARG, 2000). Selection of leaders is democratic in 87 percent of the groups. In the SHGs, there was imposed leadership and it was due to the lack of initiative among the members to become leader. Leadership rotation was absent in 94 per cent of the SHGs. (APMAS, 2002; ORG-MARG, 2000). Thus, development of leadership among other members is lacking. Groups are over dependent on the leader. The leader manages all activities regarding accounts, loans and attendance. Member's involvement in mobilisation of savings is only four percent (ORG-MARG, 2000). In the absence of the group leader, meetings are not held up to six months or more (APMAS, 2002). 84 percent of leaders and 93 per cent of members are not part of other institutions including local bodies. This indicates the poor growth of leadership in the groups (ORG-MARG, 2000). The grading of DWCRA groups according to their functioning by the Government of Andhra Pradesh has revealed that 18,63,19 per cent of the groups are found to be A,B and C categories respectively. Similarly, Andhra Pradesh Mahila Abivrudhi Samithi has confirmed this grading, by and large (APMAS, 2000). Thus, only 18 percent of the groups are functioning very well.

Impact on Poverty

The dependency on moneylenders among members is declining due to the access to credit from SHGs of DWCRA programme. As high as 61 per cent of members reported that they would have gone to moneylenders had there been no SHGs. Of course, this percentage varies across districts- 90 percent in East Godavari and 69 percent in Mahaboobnagar (ORG-MARG, 2000). The access to credit has enabled the women to undertake economic activities. Around eight per cent of the members of SHGs reported that they might not have started the economic activity, had there been no SHGs. The incidence of such members varies across the districts (ORG-MARG, 2000). The economic activities undertaken by the members of SHGs fall under three categories, viz., agriculture, animal husbandry, and industry, service and business (ISB) sectors (YFA, 1996; Kanchanya, 1998; Raju and Ali, 1996; ICM, 1996; Jayalakshmi, 1997; Narayanaswamy and Jaganathan, 1999). The activities are dominantly production oriented rather than service. They are largely continuous activities rather than seasonal. The ownership of DWCRA sponsored enterprises (activities) is equally divided into individual and family ownership. This reveals that the enterprise is actually owned, assisted and managed by other members of the family also, though the financial assistance is provided to the women members of the family. Majority of the women of SHGs reported that the assistance provided under DWCRA is not adequate to meet the initial requirements in case of some activities (Raju and Ali, 1996).

A large proportion of women, who are mostly from artisan families engaged in traditional occupations become members of the groups to further strengthen and expand their ongoing economic activities. These women are continuing with their earlier (pre-DWCRA) occupations. As a matter of fact, the DWCRA groups that formed with common interest in expanding/strengthening their existing traditional activities have been significantly successful (BASIX, 1999). However, a smaller proportion of them have taken up new occupations rather than remaining in traditional activities (Raju and Ali, 1996). These women are not able to manage these activities due to lack of previous experience. Moreover overcrowding in some of the activities like vegetable vending and fruit vending has forced some of the women to close down their activity (Raju and Ali, 1996; Kanchanya, 1998; ICM, 1996; Jayalakshmi, 1997; Narayanaswamy and Jagannathan, 1999). Thus, most of the enterprises (activities), which are facilitated through DWCRA groups helped to utilise the existing skills by using the credit assistance provided. The attempts of the Government to impart new skills and upgrade existing skills have not reached many areas of the State. As a result, many of the women groups are not able to derive the benefits from the government facilitated DWCRA 'Bazaars' as marketing outlet. It has been reported that some of the unemployed and wage employed have become self-employed. Interestingly, four per cent of the members who were housewives earlier became self-employed. The diversification of occupation to non-agriculture activities has enhanced the quality of income of the households since the dependency on risk- based agriculture has come down to some extent.

The additional income accrued to the beneficiary women from the economic activities undertaken due to DWCRA programmes varied between Rs 10-30 per day on an average. This has contributed to considerable improvement in the incomes of the poorest of the poor and enables the near poor to cross the poverty line. It is reported that considerable proportion of beneficiary adult female family members has full employment under the DWCRA scheme. At the same time, some of the male family members have also derived employment under the DWCRA scheme. A part of the income gained was spent, by some of the women member households, on nutritious food for family especially children (YFA, 1996; Kanchanya, 1998). Considerable proportion of the sampled beneficiaries has taken up kitchen garden activities near their homesteads. This has brought changes in the quality of consumption that might have led to the enhancement of the nutritional status of children, pregnant and lactating mothers among the DWCRA families (YFA, 1996). Similarly, part of the income gained also spent on the health care of the family (Kanchanya, 1998). It is not out of place to mention that the state has achieved impressive reduction in the growth rate of population from 2.42 during 1981 to 1991 to 1.39 per cent during 1991 to 2001 (Economic Survey, 2001). In fact, the dramatic decline in decadal growth rate of population has also been attributed to the phenomenal growth of SHGs in the state (James, 2002). Most of the eligible among DWCRA members in sampled groups have undergone family planning. Most of the pregnant women, similarly, had tetanus coverage. Majority of the children of the beneficiaries are going to school as the women had become aware of the need for basic education. Thus, women are able to improve their access to health care and educational institutions to some extent. However, the groups in the interior villages and Scheduled Tribes have not been benefited to the extent of the exterior villages and other caste beneficiary households (YFA, 1996; Kanchanya, 1998).

Impact on Women's Empowerment

The women members of SHGs seem to have embarked on the non-traditional tasks like marketing and non-traditional enterprises. The women have improved control over their labour to this extent. Women's access to and control over their savings, credit and income have improved. Women have improved freedom to move and interact with the officials and other women after joining the SHGs of DWCRA. The DWCRA groups themselves have expanded avenues for women to assume leadership position. The adoption of family planning and contraceptive methods by the women members of SHGs indicate the improvement of the control of women over their reproductive choice. On the whole, it is clear that women are able to improve control over their labour, resources (saving, credit and income), freedom to move and interact, leadership, and reproductive choices, to some extent. Thus, there is improvement to some extent with regard to 'power to' dimension of empowerment. But, there is no improvement in the 'power with' dimension of empowerment. This is evident from the absence of the collective initiatives of women members to negotiate their gender, caste, class and other interests vis-à-vis institutions of the market, the State, the community and family. The women are able to handle some of the issues relating to their lives independently. This indicates that 'power within' dimension of empowerment is impacted due to participation in SHGs to some extent.

SAPAP Model: Formation and Functioning of SAPAP Groups

The poor from Scheduled Castes, Scheduled Tribes, Backward Castes and Other Castes have participated in the programme. Women constitute 90 per cent of the total participants in the programme. Men groups were also formed, but they are less in member. Women groups were dominantly promoted. Homogeneous as well as heterogeneous groups of women with respect to caste dimension of the women are formed. Female-headed households constitute 17 per cent of the members. 72 per cent of members were very poor or poor at the time of group formation. Self Help Groups (SHGs) of poor women are promoted at the cutting edge level, habitation and below. The principles underlying the group formation were physical proximity, homogeneity and affinity. The number of members in a SHG is found to be 15, on an average, in the villages covered under the programme. There are 4 SHGs on an average per each habitation in the project area. Community Coordinators, Community Volunteers and Village Specialists (Para- professionals) were trained. This process makes it possible for members of the SHGs to access specialised knowledge from within the community. All the SHGs in a village are federated into Village Organization (VO) and these VOs are again federated into Mandal Mahila Samakhya (MMS) at mandal level. There is no proper follow-up of the periodical rotation of leadership of SHGs, as no one is willing to take responsibility. Constantly, the increased dependence on the existing leader may create the possibility for exploitation. All the members are not participating in group discussions. Micro planning for proposing productive economic activities has to be strengthened among the members (Outreach, 2001). 47.6 per cent of the SHGs are graded as 'A' category based on the functioning of the groups (UNDP, 1998).

These SHGs, VOs and MMSs have to interact with the State, market and civil society to achieve the objectives of alleviating poverty and empowering women, besides making the State accountable and transparent to poor and transforming the civil society to become more pro-poor and markets (labour, financial and commodity markets) to become more perfect. The economic, caste and gender homogeneity of the SHG, VOs and MMSs lends itself to collective action. Moreover, because of exclusive character of the SHGs, there is less scope for the groups to be captured by better-educated and more affluent leaders. The interest amount generated from their credit transactions is enabling the SHGs, VOs and MMSs to meet the running cost (UNDP, 2000). However, the institutions can become unsustainable unless adequate attention is focused on livelihood related issues (Mahendra Dev et al, 2002). The SAPAP programme has been replicated with suitable modification in the most backward mandals of Andhra Pradesh in the form of Andhra Pradesh District Poverty Initiatives Project (APDPIP) and Andhra Pradesh Rural Poverty Reduction Project (APRPRP). This shows the replicable potentiality of SAPAP for poverty reduction.

Impact on Poverty

The financial status has improved due to improvement in access to formal credit institutions, apart from improvement in their savings status. Dependency on money -lenders had declined (Outreach, 2001; Ranjani et al, 2002; and Mahendra Dev et al, 2002). The presence of money -lenders and the interest rate charged by those who are in place have declined (Ranjani et al, 2002). The single most important benefit of the project is that the members are relieved from the clutches of money- lenders whom they had to approach earlier even for small consumption loan of Rs. 100. The negotiations of SHGs to obtain loans from bank, the initiatives of MMS to obtain loan from government (DRDA, SC Corporation, UNDP) and NGOs (BASIX and Friends of Women World Banking) for on lending to SHGs and establishing women's own bank together contributed for enhancing the financial status of the household. Each person availed on an average 2 loans. The very poor members, who joined groups have not been able to access as much number and quantum of loans as the poor, moderately better off farmers. (Ranjani et al, 2002). The credit accessed was reported to be inadequate (Outreach, 2001).

The possession of livestock rather than land has increased considerably among the households. A very thin scaling up of extent of land owned is recorded after the participation in groups (Outreach, 2001; Ranjani et al, 2002; and Mahendra Dev et al, 2002). However, the households who had pledged land in the past but started redeeming the same are on increase (Ranjani et al, 2000). The physical capital base has increased only due to increase in consumer durables holding status in Anantapur district (Mahendra Dev et al, 2002). Possession of diesel or electric motors has not improved (Outreach, 2001). But, there is evidence that the purchase of equipment and setting up of shops is dominant among the households (Ranjani et al, 2002).

Occupational diversification has taken place among the members. This is evident from the increase in the number of sources of livelihoods of women members and their husbands and larger proportion of member households shifting from agriculture to service and trade. The strengthening of skill base of members in a limited way through providing training on tailoring, embroidery, knitting and word processing has helped women to diversify their occupations to some extent. The credit enabled the poor to make more effective use of skills they already possessed rather than skill development induced demand for credit. Women have undertaken micro-enterprises relating to petty business activities. The initiatives made, though in limited way, to reduce the transaction, production, marketing and storage costs by promoting appropriate collective arrangements like bulk purchase of inputs, vehicles and establishing milk and agricultural market societies have improved the livelihoods. But there are large variations across the groups in this regard. There was a slight improvement in the quality of employment i.e., shift from casual /bonded employment to self-employment. Dependency on migration as a livelihood strategy has declined. Demand for higher wages and equal wages, releasing women members or members of her family from bondage, and also establishing "Ammavadis" (Baby care centres) to facilitate poor women with young children to work without pulling their elder daughters out of school have improved the labour market conditions in favour of poor.

The levels of income of households have increased in all the categories of participants of the SHGs. However, the increase was higher among relatively better off among the poor. As high as 47 percent of sample households were found to be above the poverty line (Outreach, 2001). The wealth-ranking exercise carried out with 83 SHGs suggests that poverty declined among 69 percent of the members and the proportion of the very poor reduced from 48 percent to 18 percent - 75 percent of them had become poor and the rest become moderately poor. The reduction in poverty was less pronounced among Dalits and women-headed households compared to non-Dalits and male-headed households. However, some of the women reported that there is a decline in their living conditions due to the failure of the economic activities undertaken by them after joining the groups. Further, they have also reported that the distress events they have experienced, in the absence of insurance coverage, also hurt them badly. The gender poverty measured in terms of gender bias with respect to norms of eating, male preference in distribution of food and access to clothing has not declined significantly. Interestingly, gender poverty is lower among the Dalits compared to other communities despite relatively higher levels of poverty among the Dalits (Ranjani et al, 2002). Food security has improved after the participation in groups. On the other hand, there is evidence that there had been no significant change in food security status among the households in Anantapur district (Mahendra Dev et al, 2002). Cutting down consumption as a coping strategy when households faced with food shortage has come down. However, women and girl children mostly bear the brunt of food shortage. Acute malnutrition among children, infant and child mortality/premature adult death have declined. The school enrolment and regularity in attending school by children have improved. Gender disparities were much lower among the member households with respect to nutrition, child/adult premature death and ability of women to sign. Gender differences in children's education and infant mortality have declined moderately. Young children using government child-care services have increased. Drainage facilities, toilet facilities and access to pucca houses, electricity and gas have improved. The improvements in the access to productive assets, improved livelihoods and control over all aspects of life of women have contributed to the decline of disparities (Ranjani et al, 2002).

Impact on Women's Empowerment

The women of SHGs have improved their control over their lives. More specifically, women have improved access and/or control over power to survive, their labour/family labour, resources, freedom to move and interact, leadership positions, reproduction, and body. Thus there is all round improvement with regard to control over their lives. However, there are variations with regard to improvement in access and/or control over the different aspects of this dimension of improvement. Highest achievements are made with respect to their mobility, breaking of gender division of productive labour, access to their own savings, access to friendship outside their family and access to leadership positions in gram panchayat; moderate achievements are made with respect to reproductive rights and body rights (freedom from violence); and lower achievements are made with respect to extent of access of women to husband's labour (productive and reproductive), rights of women to land and house, their ability to control male alcohol consumption and their ability to influence setting of wages. Women have intervened collectively in several institutions, viz., family, community, markets (labour, commodity and financial), and State including local self-government institutions. Within the family, higher collective achievement has been with respect to girl child education followed by release of bonded labour. At the community level, women groups at various levels are changing attitudes on girl child education and caste-based discrimination. The interventions in labour and commodity markets have to be strengthened, though the interventions in financial market are impressive. Linkages with government departments are stronger with those departments that deal with women's reproductive tasks or women managed productive activities and weaker with those activities which are controlled by men. This has resulted in accessing the government services and resources (Mahendra Dev *et al,* 2002). However, the women groups have to begin to play their role in making gram panchayats function more transparently. The women members' husbands feel that their wives are more independent. Lesser degree of son preference shown by women members and breaking of caste norms within the group indicate that women in their own lives also pursue gender specific concerns. Thus, a considerable and balanced impact in all three levels of empowerment – power to (individual), power with (collective) and power within (consciousness) was achieved (for details see Ranjani *et al,* 2002).

4. CONCLUSIONS AND POLICY IMPLICATIONS

Participation in SHGs has improved the access of women to credit. This has helped women in reducing their dependence on moneylenders. The interest rates in informal credit sector have declined. This has to be confirmed with further evidence as the interest rates are generally declining overtime due to the penetration of formal banking system in the village economies. The access to credit has helped women to meet their consumption as well as production needs. The women have invested the credit obtained from SHGs in new economic activities and/or strengthening the old activities. They have contributed to the occupational diversification at the household level. The non-agricultural activities undertaken by the women helped the households to obtain income from low risk activities. Thus, the quality of income of the households has gone up. The quality of employment, indicated by shift from wage to self-employment, of women as well as their families (when the other family members also participated in the activity undertaken by the women) is enhanced. All these indicate that the incomes of the poor have increased and as a result the intensity of poverty (poverty gap) among the poor has come down. The women acquired some non-land assets; health, nutrition and education status of children has improved. This indicates that the inter-generational transmission of poverty has reduced. The women have met their basic needs to some extent. The reduction of gender inequalities is also recorded to some extent. However, failure of the economic activities undertaken coupled with the effect of distress events brought a decline in the living conditions of some of the poor women.

These are the changes observed across the models considered for the analysis. Then, the issue in question is whether these changes are varying across models and/or across different socio-economic groups among of the poor? And whether the process of reduction in poverty as well as reduction in intergenerational transmission of poverty is sustainable? The evidence available reveals that some of the aforementioned changes vary across models. However, there are also some similar changes across the models. A considerable proportion of the poorest of the poor are not included at all in the process of poverty alleviation under the DWCRA and SAPAP models. On the other hand, there are indications that non-poor have entered the DWCRA and SAPAP groups. Entry of non-poor itself might have hindered the entry of the poorest of the poor. The poorest of the poor, who are in the groups have absorbed relatively lower volume of credit among the poor covered under SAPAP and CDF. This is due to low asset base including skills. The profile of economic activities undertaken by the members under SAPAP, DWCRA and CDF also support this. The activities undertaken with low level of credit and existing skills, given the demand, may not generate adequate surplus to repay the loans. As a matter of fact, a few among them opted out of these activities as the existing demand is inadequate. This has led to decline in the living conditions in case of SAPAP group members. But, the poor who could withstand competition have improved their incomes. Some of the members, mostly the poorest of poor from SAPAP groups are repaying the loans taken from groups by resorting to reduction in consumption and/or borrowing from informal credit sources. These are the two escape routes available to comply with peer monitoring for repayment of loans. These processes make the poorest of the poor much worse than before. This indicates that the poorest of the poor should stay out of these groups at least to maintain their earlier welfare levels. Does this mean that the micro-credit alone cannot address the problems of poverty of the poorest of the poor? This problem can be tackled to some extent by adopting repayment schedule suitable to the poorest of the poor. The improvement in skill base, given the other assets base, can also be a solution to tackle the problems of the poorest. Proper livelihood planning, bulk purchases of inputs and collective marketing of outputs help the poorest of the poor to organize their economic activity effectively. Thus interventions in commodity markets help the poorest of the poor. Then, how about the aged and migrant agricultural labours that constitute larger share of the poorest? The welfare programmes for the aged and wage employment and land rights including usufruct rights on common property resources to arrest migration coupled with micro-credit for migrant agriculture labour may be the solution. Thus micro-credit has to augment other programmes to address the concerns of the poorest of the poor.

Further, some of the poor are not taking loan from the SHGs with the apprehension that they may not be able to repay the loan, given the peer monitoring for the repayment of loans. This is ultimately resulting in lower utilisation of loanable funds in case of DWCRA and CDF. This in turn may threaten the very sustainability of SHGs of DWCRA and CDF. Thus low levels of self- employment opportunities available in the local economies are constraining the poor to avail credit from SHGs. Thus, there may not be a change in the income of some of the poor who are in SHGs.

The attempts to reduce the transaction costs of production and marketing by resorting to collective purchase of inputs (bulk purchases), collective storage of output to sell the product at right time and marketing collectively has definitely improved the income levels of the poor. This is evident from the initiatives of the poor under SAPAP. However, this is confined to a very few groups. Thus, there is a need to replicate these initiatives under all the models. At the same time, there was resistance from the upper caste landlords and employers to such type of initiatives by the poor. Does this mean that the benefits of social capital are constrained in the context of existing class relations? Or does this mean that the micro-process of poverty generation that emanate from the existing class relations cannot be arrested with the strength of social capital? However, a detailed and systematic examination is required in this regard.

The other issue is whether widening the skill base of the poor can improve incomes of the poor. The skill base of women has not been broadened at all either through imparting new skills or upgrading existing skills to take up new activities or refining the quality of old product under CDF. But, this was done in a limited way in case of SAPAP and DWCRA, given the spread of DWCRA across the State of Andhra Pradesh. The recent initiatives of the Government of Andhra Pradesh in the form of DWCRA Bazaars and linking SHGs with the corporate sector to capture the non-local markets besides local markets is an indication that the local markets are not adequate to absorb the products emanated as a result of widening the skill base of the poor. However, the poor who are in this process have gained considerably. But the SCs and women headed households have not improved considerably compared to non- SCs and male-headed households under SAPAP.

The raise in incomes, to whatever extent it may be, coupled with the conscious efforts to enable the poor to access public services has facilitated the poor women to improve their own health status and children's health and educational status under all the models. However, the interior villages and the tribals have not benefited to the extent others had benefited from the efforts of the State. This is evident in case of DWCRA groups. The women could also meet their basic needs in terms of water tap and LPG gas connections and sanitation facilities under all the models. Then, the issue is whether the process of reduction in poverty as well as reduction in intergenerational transmission of poverty can be sustained. The enhancement in the asset-base of the poor provides evidence to the fact that the reduction in poverty as well as reduction in intergenerational transmission of poverty can be sustained at least in case of some of the poor, may be better off among the poor, under all the models. Thus, it is evident that the poverty reduction is varying across different socio-economic classes given the low level of self-employment opportunities in the local economies. Similarly, the reduction in gender inequalities is highly pronounced in case of SAPAP model.

There is improvement in the empowerment of women. Then, the issue is whether the improvement in empowerment of women is varying across models and/or across different socio-economic classes. The women could establish their access and/or control over their labour (to some extent), access to resources (credit, savings and income), mobility and interaction, leadership positions, reproduction choices (to some extent) under all the models. There is no evidence to conclude that the women have improved their control over their body (free from domestic violence and violence in work place and public) in case of DWCRA and CDF models. However, the women under SAPAP model have achieved access and control over all the aspects of individual dimension of women empowerment significantly compared to the other two models. But, the access and control over land-based assets and control over body has not been achieved much by women even under SAPAP model. This indicates that the existing property relations (with respect to non-movable properties) and the deep-rooted patriarchal value system may be hindering this process. The involvement of men in this process of handling the problems relating to women may facilitate decline in gender inequalities.

The DWCRA and CDF models did not facilitate power for women to intervene as a group into family, community, State including local governance institutions and market to address strategic and livelihood concerns. However, the women of SAPAP have achieved improvement in regard to strategic and livelihood concerns through interacting with the civil society, State and market to some extent. The women have become more confident, assertive and independent under all the models. But, the practice of strategic gender concerns in the personal lives is only pronounced among the women who are in the SHGs of SAPAP. This is completely absent in case of DWCRA and CDF. Thus, there is considerable and balanced impact in all three levels of empowerment – power to (individual), power with (collective) and power within (consciousness) under SAPAP model compared to DWCRA and CDF models. This is due to the fact that comprehensive processes of change with regard to strategic and general concerns of gender are institutionalised under SHGs of SAPAP. Thus, the issues relating to strategic and general concerns of gender cannot be addressed effectively unless the processes in this direction are institutionalised under the models. In this context, lessons have to be drawn from SAPAP model to improvise the DWCRA model. The achievements in empowerment varied across different social groups since the issues of women empowerment are interlocked with caste, religion and headship of the households and age of the women. The women headed households, the aged women (those who are above 45 years) and Dalits, on the whole, have benefited more in the process of empowerment. However, the women from other communities have made impressive beginning in the process of women empowerment.

Then the issue is whether this process of empowerment of women is sustainable. The fundamental pre-requisite is that women should participate intensively in this process. The intensive participation involves some costs to be born by them in the form of wage losses and transportation costs. Hence, the leaders and the members of the groups should be compensated. The leaders are compensated under SAPAP very aptly. The members can be compensated through organising Mahila Banks on the lines of Midtur Grameena Mahila Bank in Kurnool under SAPAP, where women have their share capital and bonus claim. Along with this, women should be provided facilities to meet their basic needs, so that they can be relieved from drudgery and find time to participate in group activities. There are efforts by women to reduce time in fetching water and collecting fuel wood by resorting to water tap and LPG gas connections. The time released by reducing drudgery can be utilised not only to participate in the process initiated by the SHGs but also to undertake main economic activities. Thus, initiatives of the Government of Andhra Pradesh to provide LPG gas connections to poor women through "Deepam" programme is highly justified. Thus, the government has to take all the initiatives to meet the women-specific needs. On the whole the SAPAP model is found to be superior over DWCRA and CDF given the mandate of poverty alleviation and women empowerment. However, the model has to address adequately the issues relating to coverage of the poorest of the poor like specially abled persons, migrant agriculture labour; broadening the skill base, infrastructure bottlenecks, vulnerability, women-specific basic needs, and linkages with the State, market and civil society. In view of these concerns, the SAPAP with suitable modifications is replicated as Andhra Pradesh District Poverty Initiatives Project (APDPIP) and Andhra Pradesh Rural Poverty Reduction Project (APRPRP) by the State of Andhra Pradesh in the most backward mandals of all the districts of the State. These projects cover the former SAPAP groups and also DWCRA groups in these mandals. This may help the Government of Andhra Pradesh to realise the goals contemplated in vision 2020 in respect of poverty alleviation and women empowerment. However, the government should focus attention on developing the rural economy by activating agriculture and non-agriculture sectors and removing infrastructural inadequacies to widen the self-employment choices for the SHG members. Otherwise, the potential benefits of APDPIP and APRPRP cannot be realised on a sustainable basis.

Refereces

APMAS (2002), "Evaluation of Self Help Groups in Adilabad, Cuddapah, and Visakapatnam Districts," Draft report prepared for the Government of

Andhra Pradesh, Mahila Abhivruddhi Society, Andhra Pradesh, Hyderabad.

BASIX, CARE – AP and Vikasdharshini (1999), "Women's Savings and Credit Movement in Andhra Pradesh and A Proposal for a New Institution APMAT", Report prepared for DFID (UK) India Office and Commissionarate of Rural Development, Bhartiya Samuruddhi Investments Consultancy, Government of A.P, July.

Biswas, Arun and Vijay Mahajan (1997), "Sustainable Banking with the Poor: A Case Study on Women Thrift Cooperative System in Warangal and Karimnagar Districts of Andhra Pradesh", July.

CESS (2001), "Report on Baseline Survey for Andhra Pradesh District Poverty Initiatives Project," Report prepared for the Society for Elimination of Rural Poverty, (mimeo) Centre for Economic and Social Studies, Hyderabad, November.

CDF (1999), *Member Participation in New Generation Thrift Cooperatives Around Warangal Town in A.P: 1997*, Cooperative Development Foundation, Hyderabad. (2001), Annual Report, Cooperative Development Foundation, Hyderabad.

Ghosh, Jayati (1998), *Cooperatives under the Andhra Pradesh Mutually Aided Cooperatives Societies Act, 1995*. Centre for Economic Studies and Planning, Jawaharlal Nehru University, New Delhi, December.

Galab, S. (1999), "Some Micro-Level Arrangements of Social Security in Andhra Pradesh", *The Indian Journal of Labour Economics*, Vol. 42, No. 3, July-September.

GOAP (1999), *DWCRA and Women's Empowerment: A Success Story of Self Help Movement in A.P*, Panchayat Raj and Rural Development Department, Government of Andhra Pradesh, Hyderabad.

— (2002), Achievements under Women Action Plan 2002-2003, Rural Development Department, Government of Andhra Pradesh, Hyderabad.

— (2002), *Economic Survey 2001-2002*, Department of Planning, Government of A.P, Hyderabad.

ICM (1996), "Evaluation of Rural Development Programmes in Nizamabad District of A.P", Institute of Cooperative Management, Hyderabad.

Jayalakshmi, R. (1997), "Evaluation of Rural Development Programmes in Adilabad District", Report submitted to the Government of Andhra Pradesh, Institute of Cooperative Management, Hyderabad.

James, K.S. (2003), "Towards a Demographic Transition of A.P", *Economic and Political Weekly*, Vol 38, Nos. 12 and 13, March 22-28/29-April 4.

Kanchanya, K. (1998), *Women and Development: A Case Study of DWCRA Programme in West Godavari District of A.P*, Unpublished M.Phil dissertation submitted to Dr. B.R. Ambedkar Open University, at Centre for Economic and Social Studies, Hyderabad.

Mahendra Dev, S. and P. Padmanabha Rao (2002), "Poverty Alleviation Programmes in A.P: An Assessment," Report submitted to the Planning Commission, Government of India, (mimeo) Centre for Economic and Social Studies, Hyderabad.

Mahendra Dev, S, S. Galab, M. Gopinath Reddy, K.S. Reddy, C. Ravi, K.S. Babu and G.K. Mitra (2002), "Baseline Survey Report in Sustainable

Livelihood Framework", Report prepared for the Society for Elimination of Rural Poverty, (mimeo), Centre for Economic and Social Studies, Hyderabad.

Narayanaswamy, R. and P. Jagannathan (1999), "Evaluation Study of IRDP, TRYSEM, Tool Kits and DWCRA Schemes in Adilabad District", Report submitted to the Government of Andhra Pradesh. Institute of Cooperative Management, Hyderabad.

Outreach (2001), "South Asia Poverty Alleviation Programme: Policy Lessons Emerging in Andhra Pradesh in India". Report submitted to the UNDP (India), Outreach, Hyderabad.

ORG-MARG (2000), "Consultancy on Strengthening of Self Help Groups in Andhra Pradesh: SWOT Analysis of the Groups Surveyed in A.P", Report submitted to the Department of Rural Development, Government of A.P, Hyderabad.

Parthasarathy, G. and R. Kalyani (1995), *Economic Impact of Women's Thrift and Credit Societies*, Institute of Development and Planning Studies, Visakapatnam, Andhra Pradesh.

Raju, B.Y and Ali A Firadausi (1996), "Evaluation of DWCRA in Cuddapah District," Report submitted to Government of Andhra Pradesh. Administrative Staff College of India, Hyderabad.

— (1996), "Evaluation of DWCRA in Adilabad District," Report submitted to the Government of Andhra Pradesh, Administrative Staff College of India, Hyderabad.

Ranjani, K. M, K. Raju and Amitha Kamath (2002), "Towards Women's Empowerment and Poverty Reduction: Lessons from the Participatory Impact Assessment of South Asian Poverty Alleviation Programme in Andhra Pradesh, India". Report of the Study Commissioned by United Nations Development Programme.

Rao, C.H.H (1994), *Agricultural Growth, Rural Poverty and Environmental Degradation in India*, Oxford University Press, New Delhi.

Ray, Nandita and D.P. Vasundhara (1996), "Like My Mother's House: Women's Thrift and Credit Cooperatives in South India", in M. Carr, M Chen and R. Jhabvala (ed) *Speaking Out-Women's Economic Empowerment in South Asia*, Vistaar Publications, New Delhi.

UNDP (1998), *South Asia Poverty Alleviation Programme: Progress Report, 1996-1998*, UNDP,RAS/96/600 India , Hyderabad.

— (2000), *South Asia Poverty Alleviation Programmes, Regional Progress Report*, Hyderabad.

Vysas, V. S. and Pradeep Bhargava (1995), "Public Intervention for Poverty Alleviation: An Overview", *Economic and Political weekly*, Vol. 30, Nos. 41 and 42, October 14-21.

World Bank (1995), *World Bank Participation Handbook*, IBRD Social Policy and Resettlement Division, Washington DC.

— (2000/2001), *World Development Report 2000/2001: Attacking poverty*, Oxford University Press, New York.

Youth for Action (1996), "Evaluation Report on DWCRA in Mahaboobnagar District of Andhra Pradesh," Report of a study submitted to UNICEF, Hyderabad.

18

Food Security and Public Distribution System

C. Ravi and
S. Indrakant

1. INTRODUCTION

Access to adequate food is an important element of welfare of people. The development agenda at the National and at State level include food security in one form or the other. Although national food security is necessary, what is important is to provide food security for each and every household and within it to every member of the family. Achieving food security has thus three dimensions. "It is necessary to ensure a safe and nutritionally adequate food supply both at the national level and at the household level. It is necessary to have a reasonable degree of stability in the supply of food, both from one year to the other and during the year. And most critical, is the need to ensure that each household has physical, social and economic access to enough food to meet its needs" (Nawani, 1994). At the household level the resources available and the prices it faces together determine the level of its food security. There are a wide range of employment and income generating programs, which aim to raise the purchasing power of the poor. The national food policy aims to stabilize year-to-year fluctuations in availability of foodgrains, giving support prices to the producers, building buffer stocks and consumption subsidies to the needy.

This Paper addresses the food security issues in Andhra Pradesh. The foodgrain production in the state, which was slightly less than 60 lakh tones during the mid fifties, increased to 140 lakh tonnes by the turn of last century. The production of rice, which is a staple food in the states, more than trebled during the same period from 33 lakh tones to 110 lakh tonnes. The state is considered as foodgrain surplus and food secure at macro level. Thanks to the low 'official' calorie-based poverty line, Andhra Pradesh is credited with remarkable success in poverty reduction during the seventies and eighties and is 11 percent in rural and 27 percent in urban areas in 1999-2000. However, the Poverty estimates in general and of 1999-2000 in particular is embroiled in different controversies. Alternative estimates of Deaton and Dreze (2002) indicated a higher rural poverty at 23 percent and considerably low levels of urban poverty at 11 percent. That would mean that about one-fifth of the state's population still suffers from chronic food insecurity with consumption levels below the poverty line. There is a widespread prevalence of malnutrition among the children, especially in rural areas. About one-third of rural children below the age of 5 year suffer from moderate undernourishment and another one-tenth are severely undernourished. In urban area almost one-third suffer from undernourishment either in severe or moderate form. Nearly one-half of the women suffer from anaemic conditions.

The reorientation of priorities, policies and programs in the wake of recent reform process initiated in the state do have an impact on the household food security. This Paper addresses some of the food security concerns emerging in the recent periods. Specifically we ask, what are the consumption levels across different sections of population and what do they imply in terms of nutrition security? How surplus is the state with respect foodgrains? What is the nature of state intervention and how effective is it in ensuring food security? What are the problems and prospects of ensuring food security for all by the year 2020- the year much dreamed about in the state?

2. FOOD SECURITY: A NATIONAL PERSPECTIVE

Thanks to the green revolution, India achieved self-sufficiency and eliminated the transient food insecurity to a large extent. With surplus foodgrain production, there was no further need to depend on the volatile external markets. The transition of the food economy from scarcity to surplus has been tremendous. The surplus food situation at the national level led to complacency (Rao, 1995). The achievements on the production front did not result in matching success in ensuring food and nutrition security at household level. Despite favourable movements in prices and real incomes, the cereal consumption declined across all the states for all income groups with a few exceptions. There has also been a substantial diversification of consumption of the poor in favour of non-cereal food from cereal and to non-food from food. A substantial amount of these shifts in consumption patterns has been attributed to changing tastes and preferences (Radhakrishna and Ravi, 1992). There seems to be divergence in the need based and want or demand based consumption basket of poor. All this resulted in stagnation in energy intake level of poor (Ravi, 2000). One view is that the reduced level of physical labour and drudgery among the rural masses due to improvements in rural infrastructure and mechanization is to some extent responsible for the diversifying food basket although it is less energy efficient and to that extent this phenomenon can be associated with improvements in the welfare of rural consumers (Rao, 2000). The long-term consequences of such trends are yet to be explored. Evidence from regional (state level) studies also reveals similar changing preference patterns in consumption (Meenakshi, 2000, Murthy, 1997). In the post-reform period of nineties, the slow down in the growth of real expenditures in rural areas and inequitous urban growth coupled with increasing relative price of cereals have accentuated the decline in foodgrain consumption substantially (Ravi, 2000). The consequences of these trends on the food economy were adverse.

Food economy in India is managed through an elaborate system of procurement and distribution. The Government of India procures, stocks and distributes foodgrains through Food Corporation of India (FCI). In terms of the budget involved and the coverage of its operations, the procurement and Public Distribution System (PDS) in India is one of the most important policy initiatives during the post-independence era. In addition, the FCI maintains a certain level of buffer stocks to augment the supplies during the periods of shortages. The central government announces minimum support prices at which the FCI procures foodgrains from producers. This policy served well during the past three decades. Price collapses during the bumper crop years have been averted and productivity levels have increased (Radhakrishna and Rao, 1994). Over time, especially in the nineties, the support price increased at a rate higher than the wholesale prices and became increasingly remunerative for producers (GOI, 2002). As a result procurement levels of foodgrains rose sharply to 39.3 million tonnes in 2000-2001 with a total stock reaching 58.1 million tonnes.

With a network of more than 4.62 lakhs Fair Price Shops (FPS), the public distribution system in India is one of the largest in the world. As making foodgrains available to the consumers is the primary responsibility of the states, the PDS depends heavily on the initiatives of state governments and their political commitment. A few states like Andhra Pradesh, Karnataka and Tamil Nadu have further contributed additional subsidies from their own exchequer to raise the total subsidy and issued foodgrains at significantly lower prices. As a result, there are large inter-state variations in the functioning of this system (Ahluwalia, 1993, Dev and Suryanarayana.1991 and Parikh, 1994). Andhra Pradesh is the earliest state to give additional subsidy to reduce the issue price considerably and build an extensive network of ration shops.

3. FOOD SECURITY IN ANDHRA PRADESH

The consumption data of 6 rounds of quinquennial Consumer expenditure Surveys of National Sample Survey Organisation (NSSO) between 1972-73 and 1999-2000 have been analysed to examine the food trends. The unit prices implicit in the value-quantity consumption data, CPIAL, CPIIW and Wholesale price of the state form the basis for computations in real terms. In order to examine the relative movements in the cereal price over a long and continuous period (1970-71 to 1999-2000), cereal price indices were constructed for rural and urban consumers using the wholesale price series of the state and weighting diagram from 1972-73 consumption data. Consumption estimates were made separately for rural and urban and for three broad income groups viz. poorest 30%, middle 40% and top 30%. The parameter estimates of LES taken from Subrahmanyam et al (2000) are used to estimate the demand projections and analyse the impact of PDS on consumption levels of poor.

Cereal Consumption

Consumption data from 6 rounds of quinquennial Consumer Expenditure Survey data of NSSO, from 1972-73 through 1999-2000 indicate that the per capita monthly consumption of cereals is declining across all the income groups in rural and urban areas of Andhra Pradesh (Tables 1 and 2). It declined from 15.25 kgs to 12.66 kgs in rural areas and from 12.67 kgs to 10.94 kgs in urban areas during the period 1972-73 to 1999-2000. During this period the rural cereal consumption declined at 0.79 percent per annum, while it declined at the rate of 0.32 percent per annum in urban areas. The rate of decline increases as one moves from the lower income group to the higher. What is interesting is that the declining cereal trend is visible even among the rural poor though it is almost stagnant for the urban poor. The net decline during this period is about 2.5 kgs in rural areas and about 1 kg in urban areas. Cereals is a cheap source of energy among all the food items. Its decline in the food basket of the poor will have serious nutritional implications, unless the decline is compensated by increase in non-cereal food.

Rice is a staple food in Andhra Pradesh (about 97 percent of the rural and 94 percent of urban households have reported rice consumption during 1999-00). The trends in rice consumption are mixed. In the case of the poorest 30 percent in rural areas, the rice consumption increased at 2 percent p.a. from 5.2 kg to 9.7 kgs, while for their counterparts in the urban areas it fluctuated around 9 kgs. For the middle-income group, rice consumption increased at 1 percent p.a. and for the rich group, the decline began in the nineties. The average rural per capita consumption of rice increased from 9 kg to 12 kg with a growth rate of 0.75 percent p.a.. In urban areas the rice consumption for the middle 40 percent and the rich 30 percent population declined at 0.2 and 0.86 percent p.a. respectively. For the poorest 30 percent of the urban there is an increase in rice consumption from about 8 kgs to 9.7 kgs in this period. The overall urban trend shows declining rice consumption at 0.2 percent. Other cereals (Coarse cereals) and wheat form the remaining components of cereals in AP. The consumption of wheat is negligible (less than a half kilo in rural and around a kilo in urban areas during 1999-2000). The trends in the other cereal and rice consumption together indicate dramatic shifts from other cereals in favor of rice in case of bottom and middle classes of rural areas and the bottom class of urban areas. For the rich 30% of rural and urban, these trends indicate that the consumption shifts seem to be away from rice also. During 1972-73 the consumption of other cereals in rural areas was as high

Table 1. Percapita Monthly Consumption of Cereals in Rural Andhra Pradesh

Class	CEREALS (Kg/person/month)						Growth Rate (1972/73-1999/00)
	1972-73	1977-78	1983	1987-88	1993-94	1999-00	
Bottom 30%	11.25	12.73	10.53	12.51	11.25	10.89	
		(2.50)	(-3.72)	(-3.51)	(-1.75)	(-0.54)	-0.19
Middle 40%	15.20	15.85	15.39	14.25	13.24	12.81	
		(0.84)	(-0.58)	(-1.52)	(-1.22)	(-0.54)	-0.76
Top 30%	19.31	18.97	20.19	16.32	15.33	14.21	
		(-0.35)	(1.25)	(-4.17)	(-1.04)	(-1.25)	-1.23
All	15.25	15.85	15.37	14.35	13.27	12.66	
		(0.77)	(-0.61)	(-1.36)	(-1.30)	(-0.79)	-0.79
	RICE (Kg/person/month)						
Class	1972-73	1977-78	1983.00	1987-88	1993-94	1999-00	
Bottom 30%	5.23	6.79	8.41	8.54	9.07	9.75	
		(5.35)	(4.37)	(0.31)	(1.01)	(1.20)	2.02
Middle 40%	8.98	10.96	11.79	11.55	11.71	12.04	
		(4.07)	(1.47)	(-0.41)	(0.23)	(0.47)	0.83
Top 30%	12.66	14.80	15.17	14.03	13.88	13.30	
		(3.17)	(0.50)	(-1.55)	(-0.18)	(-0.71)	-0.03
All	8.96	10.86	11.79	11.39	11.57	11.73	
		(3.92)	(1.66)	(-0.69)	(0.26)	(0.23)	0.75
	OTHER CEREALS (Kg/person/month)						
Class	1972-73	1977-78	1983.00	1987-88	1993-94	1999-00	
Bottom 30%	5.96	5.91	2.10	3.93	2.13	1.06	
		(-0.17)	(-18.69)	(13.35)	(-9.70)	(-11.03)	-5.67
Middle 40%	6.12	4.82	3.53	2.61	1.39	0.60	
		(-4.66)	(-6.04)	(-5.86)	(-9.97)	(-13.11)	-8.05
Top 30%	6.44	3.92	4.74	1.98	1.05	0.49	
		(-9.45)	(-3.87)	(-16.02)	(-10.03)	(-12.07)	-9.12
All	6.17	4.88	3.46	2.82	1.51	0.70	
		(-4.58)	(-6.65)	(-4.01)	(_9.89)	(-11.99)	-7.49

Note: Figures in the parenthesis are annual growth rates. The growth rate between 1972/73 to 1999/00 is estimated using semi-log trend line.
Source: NSSO reports.

Table 2. Percapita Monthly Consumption of Cereals in Urban Andhra Pradesh

Class	1972-73	1977-78	1983	1987-88	1993-94	1999-00	Growth Rate (1972/73-1999/00)
CEREALS (Kg/person/month)							
Bottom 30%	10.88	11.00	10.66	10.54	10.43	10.41	
		(0.24)	(-1.00)	(-0.04)	(-0.26)	(0.21)	0.05
Middle 40%	12.99	13.62	11.92	11.63	11.56	11.14	
		(0.93)	(2.63)	(-0.16)	(0.04)	(-0.65)	-0.36
Top 30%	14.05	14.00	13.48	13.32	11.94	11.21	
		(-0.09)	(-0.75)	(-0.49)	(-1.6)	(1.04)	-0.57
All	12.67	12.95	11.95	11.81	11.34	10.94	
		(0.42)	(-1.60)	(-0.42)	(-0.58)	(-0.53)	-0.32
RICE (Kg/person/month)							
Class	1972-73	1977-78	1983	1987-88	1993-94	1999-00	
Bottom 30%	8.30	8.89	8.95	9.15	9.51	9.74	
		(1.40)	(0.13)	(0.44)	(0.65)	(0.39)	0.51
Middle 40%	10.71	11.51	10.66	10.45	10.52	10.18	
		(1.43)	(-1.51)	(-0.39)	(0.11)	(-0.53)	-0.23
Top 30%	11.83	11.77	11.60	11.45	10.26	9.72	
		(-0.11)	(-0.29)	(-0.26)	(-1.82)	(-0.89)	-0.75
All	10.32	10.80	10.43	10.36	10.14	9.91	
		(0.91)	(-0.69)	(-0.13)	(-0.36)	(-0.36)	-0.20
OTHER CEREALS (Kg/person/month)							
Class	1972-73	1977-78	1983	1987-88	1993-94	1999-00	
Bottom 30%	2.20	1.77	1.33	1.11	0.63	0.37	
		(-4.26)	(-5.51)	(-3.50)	(-9.08)	(-8.47)	0.51
Middle 40%	1.50	1.33	0.58	0.51	0.38	0.28	
		(-2.51)	(-15.23)	(-2.38)	(-4.76)	(-5.24)	-0.23
Top 30%	0.94	0.78	0.53	0.37	0.33	0.05	
		(-3.77)	(-7.34)	(-6.79)	(-2.24)	(-26.63)	-0.75
All	1.54	1.29	0.73	0.65	0.44	0.24	
		(-3.44)	(-10.83)	(-2.25)	(-6.38)	(-9.73)	-0.20

Note: Figures in the parenthesis are annual growth rates. The growth rate between 1972/73 to 1999/00 is estimated using semi-log trend line.
Source: NSSO reports.

as 6.2 kg but it declined to less than a kilo by 1999-2000. High rate of decline in other cereal consumption is visible across all the three income groups. In urban areas, the level of other cereals consumption is much lower than that of rural areas and is almost disappearing from the food basket. The average urban consumption of other cereals declined from 1.54 kg in 1972-73 to as low as 0.24 kg in 1999-00. For all the income groups its consumption is below half a kilo in 1999-2000. Though coarse cereal is nutritionally equivalent to rice, it is cheaper compared to rice. Therefore, the energy content per rupee spent on cereals will decline with shifting consumption from coarse cereal to rice.

Food Consumption

An analysis of budget shares (at 1972-73 prices) indicates a striking decline in the food share among all the income groups of rural and urban areas (Tables 3 and 4). Even among the poorest 30 percent the share of food in their budget has shrunk from about 80 percent to 67 percent in rural areas and from three fourths to two thirds in urban areas. Within

Table 3. Budget Shares of Broad Commodity Groups in Rural Andhra Pradesh (in percentage)

Class	1972-73	1977-78	1983	1987-88	1993-94	1999-00
CEREALS						
Bottom 30%	59.27	49.46	37.25	44.44	36.41	31.11
Middle 40%	52.34	40.38	36.56	34.44	29.85	26.59
Top 30%	37.40	25.06	24.67	19.63	17.79	17.80
All	46.14	34.06	30.56	28.48	24.90	23.44
NON-CEREAL FOOD						
Bottom 30%	22.47	27.67	36.21	27.18	35.77	34.95
Middle 40%	26.94	31.61	31.04	32.35	38.03	37.94
Top 30%	29.13	30.77	26.80	31.11	32.34	37.37
All	27.29	30.50	29.73	30.77	34.69	37.03
FOOD						
Bottom 30%	81.74	77.13	73.46	71.62	72.18	66.06
Middle 40%	79.29	71.99	67.59	66.79	67.88	64.54
Top 30%	66.52	55.83	51.47	50.74	50.13	55.17
All	73.44	64.56	60.30	59.26	59.59	60.48
NON-FOOD						
Bottom 30%	18.3	22.9	26.5	28.4	27.8	33.9
Middle 40%	20.7	28.0	32.4	33.2	32.1	35.5
Top 30%	33.5	44.2	48.5	49.3	49.9	44.8
All	26.6	35.4	39.7	40.7	40.4	39.5

Note: The budget shares are derived from group-wise expenditures expressed at 1972-73 prices.
Source: NSSO reports.

food, while the share of cereals is declining, that of non-cereals is increasing among all income groups except for the middle and rich classes in urban areas. What is interesting is that the decline in the cereals share is not commensurate with the increase in the share of non-cereal food. For the average rural budget, the share of cereals declined at 2.25 percent p.a. while that of non-cereals increased at half this rate. In urban areas the average shares of both these items is declining.

Table 4. Budget Shares of Broad Commodity Groups in Urban Andhra Pradesh (in percentage)

Class	1972-73	1977-78	1983	1987-88	1993-94	1999-00
CEREALS						
Bottom 30%	43.86	38.12	40.07	45.49	40.11	33.90
Middle 40%	36.12	29.73	28.88	31.44	29.32	23.29
Top 30%	24.94	16.56	18.48	17.01	15.96	12.71
All	32.07	23.98	25.16	25.23	23.87	19.40
NON-CEREAL FOOD						
Bottom 30%	30.08	37.42	31.06	23.85	28.65	28.33
Middle 40%	35.44	38.64	34.81	29.11	32.47	30.34
Top 30%	37.69	32.54	28.87	27.56	28.93	26.70
All	35.61	35.22	31.21	27.54	29.96	28.02
FOOD						
Bottom 30%	73.9	75.5	71.1	69.3	68.8	62.2
Middle 40%	71.6	68.4	63.7	60.5	61.8	53.6
Top 30%	62.6	49.1	47.4	44.6	44.9	39.4
All	67.7	59.2	56.4	52.8	53.8	47.4
NON-FOOD						
Bottom 30%	26.06	24.46	28.88	30.66	31.24	37.78
Middle 40%	28.44	31.63	36.31	39.45	38.21	46.37
Top 30%	37.38	50.90	52.65	55.43	55.12	60.59
All	32.32	40.80	43.63	47.23	46.17	52.58

Note: The budget shares are derived from group-wise expenditures expressed at 1972-73 prices.
Source: NSSO reports/Sarvakshena.

Cost of Calories and Calorie Intake Levels

The implications of these trends for the cost of energy and energy intake levels are adverse. The Calorie-rupee ratio (the ratio of calorie intake to real food expenditure) is declining for all the income groups (Tables 5 and 6). It is of great concern that it is declining faster among the poor compared to that of the richer groups. Given these trends, any price rise in food items will further erode the calorie content of the food expenditure for the poor. For the rural poor, the calorie-rupee ratio is declining at 1.8 percent p.a., while for the richest group it is declining at 1.6 percent p.a. Corresponding rates of decline in urban area are 1.3 and 1.0 respectively. Though the difference is marginal, the higher rate of decline is a cause of concern as the calorie intake levels of the poor is much lower compared to that of the rich. It is clear that the consumption shifts among the poor is more adverse in terms of their implications on energy intake levels. In 1999-2000, the calorie intake level of the poorest was 1400 K.cal compared to 2614 for the rich in rural areas. Similarly, the urban rich consume almost 80 percent higher calories than the poor whose intake level is about 1400 K.cal. For the poorest 30 percent of the rural, the per capita per day calorie intake declined at 0.7 percent p.a., while for the rich the rate of decline is 1.02. Corresponding rates of decline in the urban areas are 0.6 and 0.5.percent p.a. The average intake levels of both the bottom and the middle-income groups in rural as well as urban areas are below the respective minimum norms.

Table 5. Calorie-Rupee Ratio and Total Percapita Calorie Intake Levels in Rural Andhra Pradesh

CALORIES PER RUPEE SPENT ON FOOD (K.cal/Rupee)					
Class	1977-78	1983	1987-88	1993-94	1999-00
Bottom 30%	79.78	73.07	66.76	58.09	54.39
		(-1.74)	(-1.79)	(-2.29)	(-1.09)
Middle 40%	91.39	67.71	59.25	59.09	50.73
		(-5.82)	(-2.64)	(-0.05)	(-2.51)
Top 30%	82.49	58.77	52.50	50.83	48.22
		(-6.56)	(•2.57)	(-0.54))	(-0.88)
All	89.35	65.37	57.39	56.41	51.80
		(-6.06)	(-2.57)	(-0.29)	(-1.41)
TOTAL CALORIES (K. Cal/ day)					
Bottom 30%	1764	1690	1499	1443	1400
		(-0.85)	(-2.37)	(-0.63)	(-0.50)
Middle 40%	2536	2306	2032	1968	1841
		(-1.88)	(-2.50)	(-0.53)	(1.10)
Top 30%	3557	3118	2776	2692	2614
		(2.60)	(-2.29)	(-0.51)	(-0.49)
All	2611	2365	2095	2028	1980
		(-1.96)	(-2.39)	(-0.55)	(-0.39)

Figures in the parenthesis are annual growth rates.

Source: NSSO reports. For 1987-88 the estimates are made using commodity-wise consumption data and calorie – rupee ratios.

Table 6. Calorie Rupee Ratio and Total Percapita Calorie Intake Levels in Urban Andhra Pradesh

CALORIES PER RUPEE EXPENDITURE ON FOOD (K.cal/Rupee)					
Class	1977-78	1983	1987-88	1993-94	1999-00
Bottom 30	71.94	63.91	66.18	62.61	58.47
		(-2.34)	(0.70)	(-0.91)	(-1.13)
Middle 40	64.88	57.58	59.70	57.43	52.56
		(-2.36)	(0.72)	(-0.64)	(-1.47)
Top 30	53.55	49.75	50.00	50.34	45.67
		(-1.46)	(0.10)	(0.11)	(-1.61)
All	61.21	55.37	56.25	55.26	50.96
		(-1.99)	(0.32)	(-0.30)	(-1.34)
TOTAL CALORIE INTAKE (K. Cal/ day)					
Bottom 30	1691	1512	1342	1406	1423
		(-2.21)	(-2.36)	(0.78)	(0.21)
Middle 40	2317	2091	1836	1938	1863
		(-2.03)	(-2.60)	(0.90)	(-0.65)
Top 30	2989	2738	2746	2695	2530
		(-1.74)	(0.06)	(-0.31)	(-1.04)
All	2331	2111	1961	2006	1942
		(-1.96)	(-1.46)	(0.38)	(-0.53)

Note: Figures in the parenthesis are annual growth rates.
Source: NSSO reports. For 1987-88 the estimates are made using commodity-wise consumption data and calorie – rupee ratios.

Prices and Income

What are the factors responsible for these shifts in the consumption patterns? Can changes in real income and prices alone explain these shifts? Table 7 presents the real expenditures of the three income groups for the years considered along with the growth rates. In rural areas, with the exception of 1999-2000, the growth rate is positive for all the years. Even in this year the negative growth is due to the decline in the top income group. In urban areas also, the real expenditures have positive growth rates. For the entire period, the trend growth rate indicates a faster rural growth compared to that of urban. However, in the nineties the reverse is true-higher growth in urban and lower in rural areas. Another interesting observation regarding the growth pattern is that in urban areas the growth inequality is rising, while in rural areas higher growth can be seen among the bottom classes. It may be mentioned here that there is controversy regarding the comparability of 1999-2000 survey with the earlier one because of 'defective questionnaire design'. The survey results are supposed to have overstated the consumption. If correction is made for the 'design', as was done by Deaton and Dreze (2002) the growth rate for 1999-00 may indicate sharper deceleration in rural areas. Accordingly, the consumption patterns may indicate sharper shifts with 'corrected data'. The estimates of Deaton indicate a real growth of about 0.5 and 2.87 percent p.a. in the per capita expenditures of rural and urban areas of the state between 1993-94 and 1999-2000, as against our estimates of –0.04 and 3.12. The differences in the price indices used could be the reason for the lower rural growth estimated by us.

Table 7. Total Expenditures at 1972-73 Prices and Growth Rates

TOTAL EXPENDITURES (Rs/person/month)						
RURAL						
Class	1972-73	1977-78	1983	1987-88	1993-94	1999-00
Bottom 30%	21.14	27.85	31.71	33.12	34.59	38.39
Middle 40%	35.00	46.17	51.04	52.13	53.70	57.31
Top 30%	64.82	93.59	103.09	107.14	108.45	99.33
All	39.79	54.90	60.85	62.93	64.39	64.24
URBAN						
Bottom 30%	31.58	33.07	36.55	34.67	37.05	42.95
Middle 40%	49.72	54.74	61.17	57.56	60.24	70.94
Top 30%	89.87	116.43	121.15	131.94	126.18	146.41
All	56.32	66.75	71.78	73.01	73.06	85.18

GROWTH RATES (percent per annum)						
RURAL						
	1977-78	1983	1987-88	1993-94	1999-00	1972/73-1999/00
Bottom 30%	5.67	2.63	0.87	0.73	1.75	1.86
Middle 40%	5.70	2.03	0.42	0.49	1.09	1.49
Top 30%	7.62	1.95	0.77	0.20	-1.45	1.30
All	6.65	2.08	0.67	0.38	-0.04	1.46
URBAN						
Bottom 30%	0.93	2.02	-1.05	1.33	3.00	0.94
Middle 40%	1.94	2.25	-1.21	0.92	3.32	1.03
Top 30%	5.32	0.80	1.72	-0.89	3.02	1.41
All	3.46	1.46	0.34	0.02	3.12	1.20

Note: The inter round growth rates are annualized. The annual growth rate between 1972/73 -1999/00 is estimated using semi-log trend line.
Source: NSSO reports.

With positive expenditure elasticities and growth in real expenditures, the consumption patterns should have indicated rising food consumption, unless there are adverse movements in relative prices. From available wholesale price in the state, cereals price indices have been estimated separately for rural and urban sectors (Table 8). The relative price

Table 8. Trends in Cereal Prices

Year	Cereal Index		General Index		Relative Price Index of Cereal	
	Rural	Urban	CPIAL	CPIIW	Rural	Urban
1970-71	100.00	100.00	100.00	100.00	1.000	1.00
1971-72	113.98	113.18	107.91	106.67	1.056	1.06
1972-73	135.67	134.86	125.42	120.00	1.082	1.12
1973-74	164.62	161.68	158.19	142.78	1.041	1.13
1974-75	174.74	173.60	184.75	158.33	0.946	1.10
1975-76	138.65	140.11	151.41	155.00	0.916	0.90
1976-77	150.68	154.06	167.80	167.22	0.898	0.92
1977-78	139.97	145.34	155.93	173.89	0.898	0.84
1978-79	141.15	146.73	163.28	185.00	0.864	0.79
1979-80	158.23	164.60	183.62	204.44	0.862	0.81
1980-81	197.86	200.72	220.90	232.78	0.896	0.86
1981-82	210.23	217.38	232.20	252.78	0.905	0.86
1982-83	223.04	231.72	238.98	272.22	0.933	0.85
1983-84	233.28	238.78	252.54	301.11	0.924	0.79
1984-85	233.17	239.82	260.45	319.44	0.895	0.75
1985-86	251.27	258.15	268.36	344.44	0.936	0.75
1986-87	264.15	273.68	284.18	374.44	0.930	0.73
1987-88	321.43	333.76	331.07	418.33	0.971	0.80
1988-89	341.16	345.73	350.85	451.67	0.972	0.77
1989-90	332.72	345.94	349.72	488.89	0.951	0.71
1990-91	411.68	422.07	415.82	556.11	0.990	0.76
1991-92	521.48	527.06	543.50	622.78	0.959	0.85
1992-93	494.74	513.29	530.51	667.78	0.933	0.77
1993-94	574.29	598.00	564.41	727.22	1.018	0.82
1994-95	621.95	629.90	638.98	815.00	0.973	0.77
1995-96	687.15	696.85	697.18	890.56	0.986	0.78
1996-97	732.46	755.50	746.33	942.22	0.981	0.80
1997-98	811.67	853.23	820.34	1046.11	0.989	0.82
Annualised growth rates						
1970s	3.20	3.83	6.62	7.20	-2.51	-3.81
1980s	6.27	6.34	7.11	7.71	-0.79	-1.92
1990s	8.95	9.16	9.14	8.15	-0.27	0.27

Note: 1. The price indices for cereal are computed using the wholesale prices of cereals and weighting diagram based on NSSO consumption data of 1972-73.

CPIAL-Consumer Price Index for Agricultural Labour.

CPIIW-Consumer Price Index for Industrial Workers.

Source: Wholesale Prices are taken from various issues of Andhra Pradesh Statistical Abstracts.

indices in rural areas show a declining trend over the past three decades. However the rate of decline is coming down gradually in each of the last two decades. The rate of decline, which was 2.5 percent p.a. during the seventies slipped to 0.8 percent p.a. in eighties and further down to 0.3 in the nineties. In urban sector the relative price index declined in the seventies and eighties, but increased in the nineties. The rate of decline in urban areas came down from 3.8 percent p.a. during the seventies to 1.9 during the eighties. In the nineties, the cereal relative price index started rising at 0.3 percent p.a. Though these trends do not indicate anything adverse as of now, the trend if continues may have adverse impact on the poor who derive substantial portion of their energy intake from cereals consumption. The shift in the consumption patterns in spite of favourable price and income movements is attributed to the changes in tastes and preferences. Given the existing patterns of consumption, ensuring adequate food security for the poor is possible by raising their purchasing power and by subsidizing their consumption. With the decline of other cereals, the prominence of rice in foodgrains consumption is increasing. The consumption prospects therefore would depend much on what is happening in the rice sector. The state is said to be surplus with respect to rice.

4. FOODGRAIN PRODUCTION TRENDS

During the last four decades Andhra Pradesh achieved a significant growth in foodgrain production, in general, and cereal production in particular. The foodgrain production of the state almost doubled (Table 9). The quinquennial average production increased steadily from 72 lakh tonnes in 1960-65 to 130 lakh tonnes in 1995-2000. The growth rate of foodgrain production, which was negative during the 60s, increased substantially to 3.16 percent p.a. in the seventies, mostly because of the improvements in the yield rates (3.0 percent p.a.). During the eighties in spite of its declining area (at 1.84 percent p.a.), foodgrain production registered a growth rate of 1 percent p.a., because of sustained yield improvements (at 2.9 percent p.a.). With a slowdown in the yield improvement and declining areas, the growth rate of foodgrain production dropped to 1.6 percent during the nineties. Cereals account for almost three-fourths of the foodgrain area and for more than 90 percent of its production. The growth pattern of cereal production is almost similar to that of foodgrains. The decline in the area under foodgrains during the last two decades is due to the decline in the area under cereals. The production of rice, which is the staple food in the state trebled in the last four decades. The acceleration of rice production began in the seventies during which period it increased at 4.12 percent p.a. This was the period when area under rice expanded from 33 lakh hectares in the sixties to 37 lakh hectares. The productivity levels improved from 1.3 tonnes per hectare in the

Table 9. Area, Yield and Production of Foodgrains

Year	RICE			CEREALS			FOODGRAIN		
	Area (Lakh He.)	Yield (Kg./He)	Prodn (Lakh Tonnes)	Area (Lakh He.)	Yield (Kg./He)	Prodn (Lakh Tonnes)	Area (Lakh He.)	Yield (Kg./He)	Prodn (Lakh Tonnes)
1960-65	32.74	1334.60	43.61	81.50	849.25	69.23	95.23	758.93	72.30
1965-70	32.30	1291.37	41.78	78.29	809.42	63.44	92.35	715.38	66.12
1970-75	32.84	1524.20	50.08	77.66	957.16	74.45	91.62	853.48	78.32
1975-80	37.14	1651.04	61.45	80.70	1093.99	88.49	94.49	972.20	92.07
1980-85	37.45	2040.09	76.50	73.70	1397.23	103.08	88.05	1226.95	108.15
1985-90	37.08	2241.31	83.74	63.62	1625.85	103.66	78.35	1403.41	110.22
1990-95	37.52	2485.57	93.07	55.82	2017.50	112.29	71.88	1664.62	119.43
1995-00	39.26	2575.00	101.45	54.37	2237.73	122.04	70.47	1832.94	129.54
2000-01	42.43	2936.13	124.58	57.72	2594.25	149.74	76.75	2088.34	160.28
Growth Rates									
1961-70	0.34	-0.35	-0.01	-0.49	-0.36	-0.85	-0.26	-0.62	-0.87
1971-80	1.89	2.23	4.12	0.73	3.12	3.86	0.61	3.00	3.61
1981-90	0.54	1.94	2.48	-2.38	3.23	0.85	-1.84	2.91	1.07
1991-00	0.55	1.13	1.68	-0.75	2.39	1.64	-0.59	2.16	1.57

Note: The decadal growth rates are based on semi-log trend lines.
Source: Various issues of Andhra Pradesh Statistical Abstracts.

sixties to 1.6 tonnes per hectare. The production levels reached 60 lakh tonnes from around 40 lakh tonnes in the sixties. Eighties and nineties saw a deceleration in the growth rate of rice production. The area expansion nearly stopped and the growth rates in productivity levels declined. As a result the production growth rate dropped to 2.5 percent p.a. in the eighties and further down to 1.7 percent p.a. in the nineties. The rate of growth of area under rice remained at about 0.5percent p.a. during nineties and that of productivity dropped to just over 1 percent. The year 2000-01 was very good in terms of foodgrain production. The production of foodgrain reached an all time high of 160 lakh tonnes of which rice was 124 lakh tonnes.

However, the achievements in per capita terms are not as impressive as they are in aggregate terms (Table 10). The average per capita production of foodgrains fluctuated between 200- 170 kgs during the four decades. After achieving an impressive growth of 1.6 percent p.a. in per capita production in the seventies there was a sudden decline in production and fluctuated around 180 kgs. The trends in rice look slightly better. The growth rate of rice production in the seventies was 2 percent. Thereafter it dropped to a low of 0.3 in the eighties and nineties.

Table 10. Per capita Production of Rice, Cereals and Foodgrains in Andhra Pradesh (Quinquennial Averages)

(Kilograms)

Year	Rice	Cereals	Foodgrains
1960-65	118.87	188.72	197.09
1965-70	103.57	157.27	163.91
1970-75	112.74	167.60	176.29
1975-80	124.86	179.80	187.08
1980-85	139.90	188.52	197.79
1985-90	137.41	170.10	180.86
1990-95	138.35	166.93	177.53
1995-00	145.49	174.96	186.05
2000-01	166.66	200.32	214.42
	Growth Rates		
1960s	-1.91	-2.75	-2.77
1970s	2.07	1.81	1.56
1980s	0.32	-1.32	-1.10
1990s	0.33	0.30	0.22

Note: The decadal growth rates are based on semi-log trend lines.
Source: Various issues of Andhra Pradesh Statistical Abstracts.

Demand – Supply Balances of Rice

Since there are no estimates of the total exports to other states and private stocks in the state, it is difficult to estimate the net availability of rice at state level. As a result a complete food balance sheet cannot be prepared. Therefore an attempt is made to estimate surpluses of production over and above household consumption and net procurement (total FCI procurement less distribution under PDS and other welfare schemes). The surpluses thus estimated should consist of exports to other states, requirement of seed and private stocks. The aggregate household consumption for the 5 NSSO survey years indicate that, the state rice production is lower than the household consumption and net procurement for all the years except for 1983 (Table 11). The order of deficit ranges from 27 lakh tonnes in 1999-98 to about 7 lakh tonnes in 1972-73. Over time the deficits seem to be rising. These deficits would increase if we account for changes in private stocks, feed and seed requirements and exports to other states. A similar observation is made by the High Level Committee headed by Abhijit Sen (GOI, 2002) for the year 1999-2000, which found that except West Bengal, Haryana, Punjab, Madhya Pradesh and Uttar Pradesh all other states are deficit in rice. This counter intuitive picture is puzzling. The state of Andhra Pradesh is known to be a rice surplus state and exports rice to other states. In the absence of any rationale for this anomaly, the only explanation could be underestimation of production or overestimation of consumption or both.

Table 11. Balance Sheet for Rice in Andhra Pradesh

(in Lakh Tonnes)

Years	Aggregate Household Consumption (NSS)			Net Procurement	Gross Out put	Deficit	
	Rural	Urban	Total			Actual	Adjusted
1972-73	38.63	11.06	49.69	0.00	42.56	-7.13	NA
1977-78	50.60	13.95	64.55	0.00	56.05	-8.50	NA
1983.00	60.02	16.79	76.81	5.90	87.91	5.20	18.38
1987-88	62.61	19.46	82.07	5.40	70.87	-16.60	NA
1993-94	69.69	22.50	92.19	18.20	95.62	-14.77	6.27
1999-00	76.27	23.89	100.16	35.90	106.38	-29.68	NA

Note: Net Procurement = Procurement by FCI – Distribution through PDS.

Deficit = Aggregate household consumption +Net Procurement – Gross output.

The estimates of per capita consumption of foodgrains from NSS data at national level have been lower than those derived in the National Accounts Statistics. Though the issue is still unresolved, the analysis of the NSS/NAS data does not indicate any overestimation of consumption (Sundaram and Tendulkar, 2002). Another possibility could be the underestimation of production, which is not totally unfounded and has been nagging the Indian Statistical system since long.

Agricultural statistics in Andhra Pradesh, as in most parts of the country draws heavily on 'land records' for area estimates. Aggregation of the village-wise abstracts prepared based on land records give land use and cropping pattern in the state. Over time, the land record system all over India, specifically in the state, deteriorated due to various reasons. The abolition of traditional patwari system in the early eighties further distorted the quality of agricultural statistics in Andhra Pradesh. The Government of India launched a scheme called Improvement of Crop Statistics (ICS) to identify and rectify the lacunae in area and yield statistics. One of the components of the scheme is to compare the areas recorded in the land records with actual areas on a sample basis. From the sample data the crop areas are estimated and compared with the aggregated (from land records) area statistics. The results reveal large variations between the recorded areas and the actual areas in case of major crops like paddy, wheat, jowar, etc. Invariably, the recorded areas are lower than the actuals. The extent of under estimation varies between 13 percent to as high as 30 percent during 1993-94 to 1997-98 (GOI, 1999). In Andhra Pradesh the extent of underestimation of area under rice crop was around 10 percent during the eighties (CESS, 1987). This is a matter of serious concern with severe implications for food policy and food security. However, this has somehow escaped the attention of the government at the state and centre and no effort is made to strengthen the land record system. However, the present sampling scheme of ICS is not adequate to give a 'factor' for correcting the area statistics.

In the absence of any alternative, we adopted the available 'correction factors' from ICS to re-estimate the production and adjust the balance sheet. The under estimation ratios of 15 and 22 are adopted for the years 1983 and 1993-94, for which they are available. The adjusted estimates show a rise of surplus from +5.20 to +18 lakh tonnes in 1983 and –15 to +6 lakh tonnes in 1993-94. But there are still seed and exports to account for. There seems to be an indication that the status of Andhra Pradesh as 'surplus' is under cloud. The strains on the rice balance sheet could partly be responsible for the rising rice price, especially during the recent times. Inflation rates in rice price (wholesale) were 4, 6 and 9 percent during the seventies and eighties and nineties respectively. Notwithstanding the digression into defective agricultural statistics, there appears to be no room for complacency.

5. PUBLIC DISTRIBUTION

The Government of Andhra Pradesh introduced the subsidized rice scheme in early 80s to improve the consumption levels of the weaker sections of the society. Eligible households were given green coloured ration cards and the other households were issued yellow cards. A household with a green card was entitled to 5 Kgs of rice per person per month subject to a ceiling of 25 Kgs. at Rs.2 per kg. In 1991 the ration cards changed colours-from green to white and from yellow to pink. The ration price for the white cardholders was increased to Rs. 3.50. per kg. and the ceiling was reduced to 20 kg. per card. On political and economic grounds the ration price and the scale of ration have been altered couple of times. Presently, the ration price of rice is Rs. 5.25 per kg and the quantity distributed per head is 4 kgs per month subject to a ceiling of 20 kgs. per card. The subsidised rice scheme is covering nearly 70% of the population while only about 20% of the population is estimated to be poor. Thus, a large number of non-poor households also enjoy the benefit of the subsidized rice scheme. At the same time micro-level studies reveal that large number of poor households do not have ration cards.

Procurement and Distribution

Right up to 1980-81, the procurement of rice in the state was generally low (Table 12). In 1981-82, the procurement crossed one million tonne mark. In the following years i.e., 1982-83 on account of introduction of subsidised rice scheme and procurement by the A.P State

Civil Supplies Corporation (APSCSC) the procurement of rice crossed the mark of 2 million tonnes. From 1982-83 to 1989-90 the state civil supplies corporation purchased about one million tonne of rice from rice millers at a negotiated price (which happened to be higher than the procurement price

Table 12. Trends in Procurement and Distribution in Andhra Pradesh

Year	Procurement (Lakh Tonnes)	Production (Lakh Tonnes)	Distribution (Lakh Tonnes)	Proc as % of prod	Net Procurement as % to Production	Percapita Quantity Distributed (Kg/annum)
1980-81	7.0	70.1	NA	10.0	NA	NA
1981-82	11.0	78.7	NA	14.0	NA	NA
1982-83	20.0	76.7	13.7	26.1	6.3	25.0
1983-84	24.2	87.9	18.3	27.5	5.9	32.6
1984-85	27.4	69.1	18.9	39.7	8.5	32.9
1985-86	24.8	76.1	21.5	32.6	3.3	36.6
1986-87	23.0	65.9	22.1	34.9	0.9	36.8
1987-88	24.1	70.8	18.7	34.0	5.4	30.5
1988-89	27.8	106.2	20.0	26.2	7.8	31.9
1989-90	35.9	99.6	21.2	36.0	14.7	33.2
1990-91	33.2	96.5	24.2	34.4	9.0	37.1
1991-92	22.6	92.5	22.4	24.4	0.2	33.7
1992-93	33.0	87.9	18.2	37.5	14.8	27.0
1993-94	39.7	96.0	21.5	41.4	18.2	31.5
1994-95	40.2	92.7	22.6	43.4	17.6	32.6
1995-96	36.7	90.1	25.2	40.7	11.5	31.1
1996-97	45.0	106.8	23.6	42.1	21.4	33.1
1997-98	38.5	85.1	22.8	45.2	15.7	31.7
1998-99	50.7	106.6	22.8	47.6	27.9	31.3
1999-2000	55.2	106.4	22.1	51.9	33.1	29.9

Source: Annual Reports of APSCSC.

of Food Corporation of India) as quantity received from FCI (about one million tonne) for distribution was insufficient to implement the subsidised rice scheme. However, this practice was given up in 1989-90 as the FCI started releasing sufficient quantity of rice. There has been a upward trend in procurement of rice during 90's. In 1998-99, procurement of rice has crossed 5 million tonnes and in 1999-2000 it touched a record level of 5.52 million tonnes. The procurement as a percentage of production has increased gradually from a low level of 14 per cent in 1981-82 to nearly 52 percent in 1999-2000. The high procurement levels during the recent years could be due to the high support prices, which might have induced recycling of some of the distributed rice, especially under the welfare schemes outside regular PDS, back to the FCI godowns – a fear expressed by GOI (2002).

The quantity of rice distributed through PDS generally varied in the range of 2 to 2.5 million tonnes. Generally, 50-60 percent of rice procured in the state is distributed within the state. The annual per capita quantity distributed through the PDS generally varied in the range of 30 to 37 kgs. During the last five years the quantity of rice distributed through the PDS has not changed much, while the population of state has been steadily increasing. Therefore, the per capita quantity distributed has been declining indicating a decline in the extent of food security provided by PDS in the State.

Subsidies

The Subsidised rice scheme involves the provision of subsidy by both the State and Central Government. The Central subsidy per tonne increased from Rs.1275 in 1990-91 to Rs.5771 in 2001-02 (Table 13). This increase was partly due to regular enhancement in procurement price and partly due to rise in administrative cost of FCI. During the same period, the State subsidy per tonne increased from Rs.1512 to Rs.4138. The introduction of Targeted Public Distribution System (TPDS) in 1997 provided some relief to the state government. Under the scheme, a quantity

Table 13. Central and State Subsidy on Rice Distributed in Andhra Pradesh (Rs./Tonne)

Year	Central	State	Total
1990 - 91	1275	1512	2787
1991 - 92	1315	1568	2883
1992 - 93	1429	1894	3323
1993 - 94	1647	1900	3547
1994 - 95	940	3415	4355
1995 - 96	1495	4463	5958
1996 - 97	2482	3351	5833
1997 - 98	3104	2885	5989
1998- 99	3473	3416	6889
1999-00	3344	4803	8147
2000-01	4390	4026	8416
2001-02	5771	4138	9909

Source: 1) *Economic Survey*, Ministry of Finance.
2) AP Budget Papers.

of 10 kgs of rice per month per family living below the poverty line was released by the Central Government at half of the Central Issue Price (CIP).

Consequently the state government is able to obtain 30% of requirement of rice at a reduced rate. In other words, the introduction of TPDS has merely amounted to a partial transfer of state burden to the Centre. The state subsidy increased to Rs. 4138 by 2001-02 as the Central Issue Price was enhanced from Rs. 7.50 per Kg to Rs. 9.05 per Kg. in 1999 and from Rs. 9.05 to Rs. 11.80 per Kg. in 2000. But to clear the accumulated stock the CIP for BPL rice was reduced by 25 paise per kg and that of APL rice by 50 paise per kg in August 2000.

There are some critical studies on the extent and usefulness of subsidy provided by the State Government. For instance, Olsen (1989) has examined the cost involved in the subsidised rice scheme. She points out that in 1987-88 the subsidy on rice scheme was more than the entire State expenditure on public health. It matched with entire cost of elementary education in the State. Subba Rao (1987) found that in 1985-86 the cost to the State for providing Re.1.00 worth of subsidy was Re.1.00.

Utilisation of PDS: Some Evidence form 1999-2000 data

National Sample Survey Organisation (NSSO) in its 55th round in 1999-2000 collected information on purchases of rice, wheat, sugar and kerosene made in fair price shops. These data have been analysed to examine the utilization of PDS.

The all India picture of PDS utilization is dominated by a few better performing states (Table 14). Andhra Pradesh is one of them. According to the 1999-2000 data, the PDS is accessible (Percentage of households purchases in Fair Price Shops) to about 30 percent of Indian rural households for rice and only 17 percent for wheat. The corresponding figures for states show large variations – from 75 percent for Kerala to 17 percent in West Bengal (barring other Wheat eating States) in case of rice and 34 percent in Gujarat to 0.21 percent in Punjab (barring Rice eating states) in case of wheat. In AP, PDS is accessible to 63 percent of rural and 29 percent of urban households for rice. In terms of access, the state of Andhra Pradesh ranks 4th and 6th in rural and urban areas respectively. Dependence on PDS (percentage purchase of rice and wheat from PDS to total purchases) also shows similar pattern. At all India level about 12 and 10 percent of total rice and wheat purchases were from PDS supplies in rural and urban areas respectively. Himachal Pradesh, Jammu and Kashmir, Karnataka and Tamil Nadu have dependency ratio of more than 30 percent in the rural areas. Andhra Pradesh, Gujarat and Maharashtra have about 20 percent dependency on PDS in rural areas. The rest of the states have the ratio below 20 percent and show large variations. Andhra Pradesh ranks 6th in terms of dependency in both rural and urban areas. Do these inter state variations anything to do with poverty? The correlation coefficient of the dependency ratio with the poverty ratio (alternative estimates of Deaton and Dreze (2002) estimates) is -0.24 and – 0.37 in rural and urban areas. It

Table 14. Statewise Indicators of Utilisation of PDS

State/ Group	Poverty Ratio	MPCE (Rs.)	Percentage of Household Accessing PDS		Dependency on PDS (Rice+ Wheat)	Income Gain		MPCE (Rs.)	Poverty Ratio	Percentage of Household Accessing PDS		Dependency on PDS (Rice+ Wheat)	Income Gain	
			Rice	Wheat		Rs. 0.00	% to MPCE			Rice	Wheat		Rs. 0.00	% to MPCE
	RURAL							URBAN						
Andhra Pradesh	26.20	454.02	62.93	1.84	21.47	17.74	3.91	773.22	10.80	29.34	15.86	14.50	15.15	1.96
Assam	35.50	425.58	37.22	1.74	8.55	7.83	1.84	803.17	11.80	22.28	1.25	5.77	6.52	0.81
Bihar	41.10	383.85	5.40	8.98	1.85	3.52	0.92	600.24	24.70	2.30	4.66	0.99	2.98	0.50
Gujarat	20.00	551.21	43.98	34.32	20.06	11.27	2.04	892.18	6.40	17.54	12.78	7.85	7.59	0.85
Haryana	5.70	715.11	0.72	2.16	0.90	5.08	0.71	910.14	6.40	0.35	1.34	0.41	4.05	0.45
Himachal Pradesh	9.80	681.14	34.90	20.08	35.04	7.06	1.04	1245.30	1.20	17.23	10.98	15.53	5.97	0.48
J&K	6.10	676.58	36.55	21.44	39.28	9.70	1.43	965.49	1.30	42.89	26.13	46.90	21.35	2.21
Karnataka	30.70	499.28	68.24	61.96	29.16	13.49	2.70	912.57	10.80	40.19	37.49	16.10	12.80	1.40
Kerala	10.00	764.98	68.52	37.08	49.67	23.67	3.09	926.39	9.60	59.99	39.88	47.62	23.42	2.53
Madhya Pradesh	31.30	401.36	16.10	10.90	5.20	3.77	0.94	690.58	13.90	6.81	3.45	1.98	2.91	0.42
Maharashtra	31.90	497.15	44.26	43.43	19.74	7.67	1.54	971.84	12.00	15.17	14.75	7.17	9.03	0.93
Orissa	43.00	373.50	51.38	4.98	14.00	11.06	2.96	617.84	15.60	29.76	17.72	10.15	9.59	1.55
Punjab	2.40	741.12	0.24	0.21	0.21	4.68	0.63	893.79	3.40	0.14	0.10	0.04	5.25	0.58
Rajasthan	17.30	548.74	0.61	5.46	3.62	3.74	0.68	796.31	10.80	0.28	2.41	1.61	3.37	0.42
Tamil Nadu	24.30	513.61	75.21	15.09	35.86	31.67	6.17	972.04	11.30	52.59	30.32	27.56	33.70	3.47
Uttar Pradesh	21.50	466.57	8.07	7.34	4.07	3.71	0.79	687.99	17.30	3.29	2.93	1.93	4.82	0.70
West Bengal	21.90	454.30	17.49	16.06	3.17	7.65	1.68	863.82	11.30	6.87	18.36	4.98	9.27	1.07
All India	26.30	485.69	32.38	16.59	12.41	9.48	1.95	853.78	12.00	20.28	15.12	10.35	9.87	1.16

Source: Estimated from NSSO 1999-2000 consumer expenditure data.

Access indicates the percentage of households reporting purchases from PDS.

seems the consumer support of PDS as reflected in the dependency is weak in the poorer states compared to the relatively richer states. The distortion gets sharper if we exclude foodgrain rich states like Punjab and Haryana from analysis. Another indicator of performance of PDS is income gain to the consumer through PDS supplies.

Fig. Dependence on PDS and Poverty

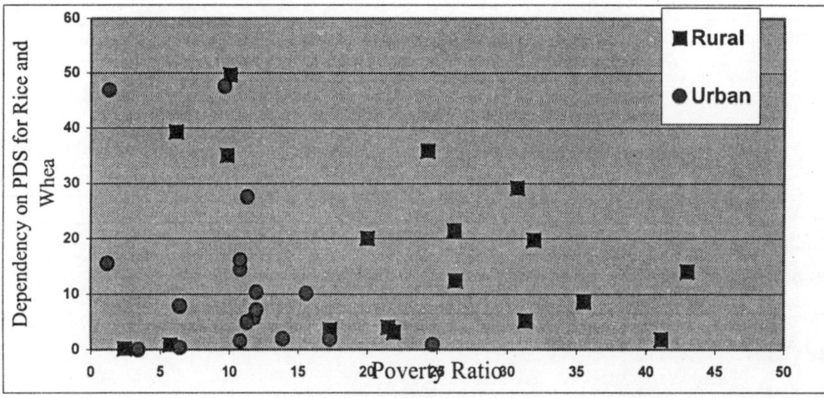

Income gain for the consumer is the difference between the value of the quantity of goods purchased in PDS when evaluated at market prices and the actual value of PDS purchases. The NSSO data gives the purchases made in PDS and open market in both quantity and value terms. Prices implicit in these data are used to derive the income gain. The income gains vary with quantities purchased in PDS, open market prices and PDS price. Though the central issue price is the same for all states, the income gains can be higher for some states even if the market prices are the same on account of lower PDS prices due to additional state subsidies. The income gains through PDS form about 2 percent of the total monthly per capita expenditure in rural areas and 1.2 percent in urban areas. The Highest income gain is in rural Tamil Nadu (6.17%), followed by Andhra Pradesh rural (3.91%). In Kerala, where the dependency on PDS is as high as 50%, the income gain is about 3%. Income transfers through PDS do not show any relation to poverty. The correlation coefficient of average income gain and poverty ratio is almost zero in both rural and urban areas. It is evident that except for a few states the performance of PDS is poor. Andhra Pradesh is one of the better performing states.

Leakages in PDS

Due to the policy of delivery of foodgrains at the doorsteps of FPS the leakages in Andhra Pradesh at the first level i.e., at FCI godown level is minimal in the existing PDS Network. The system of delivering the foodgrains at the doorstep of the fair price shop appears to be working reasonably well in most parts of the State. In States like Uttar Pradesh and Bihar, the FPS dealers have to lift their allotment from FCI godowns and transport it to their shops at their own expense. Consequently, leakages at this level are high and many times the foodgrains do not reach the villages.

Table 15. Utilization of PDS in Southern States

State/Group	RURAL					URBAN				
	MPCE (Rs.)	Percentage of Household Accessing PDS (Rice)	Dependency on PDS (Rice+ Wheat)	Income Gain		MPCE (Rs.)	Percentage of Household Accessing PDS (Rice)	Dependency on PDS (Rice+ Wheat)	Income Gain	
				Rs. 0.00	% to MPCE				Rs. 0.00	% to MPCE
	RURAL					URBAN				
Andhra Pradesh										
Poor	264.26	77.13	28.54	17.35	6.57	301.58	49.18	21.98	16.1	5.34
Nonpoor	521.38	57.86	19.47	17.62	3.38	830.33	13.63	13.69	14.74	1.78
All Classes	454.02	62.93	21.47	17.74	3.91	773.22	29.34	14.5	15.15	1.96
Karnataka										
Poor	294.11	78.45	42.05	10.18	3.46	325.66	58.89	26.17	8.86	2.72
Nonpoor	590.17	63.8	25.64	14.3	2.42	983.63	30.53	15.32	13.01	1.32
All Classes	499.28	68.24	29.16	13.49	2.70	912.57	40.19	16.1	12.8	1.4
Kerala										
Poor	320.68	85.79	73.26	18.88	5.89	331.75	82.8	73.46	22.02	6.64
Nonpoor	814.35	66.63	47.62	24.05	2.95	989.54	46.03	45.65	23.41	2.37
All Classes	764.98	68.52	49.67	23.67	3.09	926.39	59.99	47.62	23.42	2.53
Tamil Nadu										
Poor	260.98	87.91	45.07	25.37	9.72	323.02	71.87	43.01	32.56	10.08
Nonpoor	594.71	71.11	33.55	33.02	5.55	1054.7	38.74	25.88	33.03	3.13
All Classes	513.61	75.21	35.86	31.67	6.17	972.04	52.59	27.56	33.7	3.47

Source: Estimated from NSSO 1999-2000 consumer expenditure data.
Access indicates the percentage of households reporting purchases from PDS.
Income gains indicate the total income accruing from purchases of rice, wheat, sugar and kerosene.

The leakages at the second stage i.e., village or town level in Andhra Pradesh is likely to be substantial. The income of FPS dealers is very low. The dealers gross margin per month varied in the range of Rs.700-1165 (Indrakant 1996). The FPS dealers tend to increase income through bogus cards, through diversion of quantities not taken by cardholders etc. Venugopal (1992) found that in 1986 the number of ration cards in circulation (139 lakhs) exceeded the estimated number of households (121 lakhs) by about 15% or by 8 lakhs.

To check the diversion of PDS supplies to the open market by the FPS dealer and to improve the targeting of the Public Distribution System, the state government in recent years has introduced coupon system. Under this scheme, the officials of the Civil Supplies Department distribute coupons to the cardholders. The Cardholder is supplied with ration at Fair Price Shop against these coupons. The FPS dealer has to hand over these coupons to the Civil Supplies Department to get fresh supply. This procedure enables the Civil Supplies Authorities to know the actual off take by the cardholders. On this basis, the quota for the next month to the FPS dealer is released. This system, it is hoped, is likely to weed out some of the bogus cards. The system first implemented for kerosene was found successful by reducing the off-take by 15-20 percent. Therefore, the coupon system was extended for the distribution of rice throughout the state. The cardholder has to collect the coupons sufficient for two years in person. The cardholder besides ration card has to take the trouble to preserve the coupons. This may be difficult for the poor and illiterate persons. There are reports that many FPS dealers are expressing their reluctance to continue the job on account of coupon system. The introduction of coupons system weeded out about 8 percent of white cards.

The leakages at the third level i.e., household level is not likely to be much because the price of rice in the fair price shop is much lower than the open-market price of coarse cereals.

Targeting of PDS

According to 1999-2000 NSS data, more than three-fourths of poor in the state had access for PDS rice (Table 15). Not all of them may be beneficiaries of the subsidized rice scheme. On the other hand, out of the 58 percent of non-poor, who are accessing PDS, some may be beneficiaries of the subsidized rice scheme. The estimates indicate that almost 23 percent of rural poor and 50 percent of urban poor are altogether excluded from the PDS - subsidized or otherwise. An idea about the extent of exclusion of poor persons and inclusion of non-poor persons in PDS (subsidized rice scheme) can be obtained from a recent field study (Indrakant, 2000). The study covered two backward villages viz. Nettampadu and Singtham, two developed villages viz., Narsayapalem and Machavaram, and a moderately developed village i.e., Jaggasagar spread in the districts of Mahaboobnagar, Medak, Karimnagar and Guntur.

In the backward villages nearly half of the poor (i.e., monthly per capita expenditure below Rs.182) did not posses white card. On the other hand, in the two developed villages almost all the poor households had the white card. It is interesting to note that a large percentage of non-poor households in the developed villages manage to obtain a white card.

Cornia and Stewart (1993) have classified the errors of targeting into two types viz. 'E' error i.e., inclusion of non poor in the scheme and 'F' error i.e., exclusion of poor from the scheme. The extent of these two types of errors in targeting in the five selected villages indicated that in the two developed villages almost all the poor households are covered by the scheme. However, a large percentage (70-80 per cent) of beneficiaries of the scheme belong to non-poor category. In irrigated area, households having less than 2 acres have been issued white cards. There are many non-poor households having less than 2 acres of land. Venugopal has estimated that in 1983 there were about 30-45 lakh ineligible white cardholders in the state. In backward villages, both types of errors in targeting are large. A large percentage of poor households are excluded from the scheme while a sizeable percentage of beneficiaries of the scheme belong to the non-poor category. In developed villages, the scheme has provided access to food to most of the poor. However, a large percentage of beneficiaries are non-poor households. The impact of the targeting inefficiency on the cost of the subsidized rice scheme is considerable. With the present level of targeting, the cost of transferring a rupee to poor through PDS is Rs. 6.46. If the benefits are confined only to the poor, the cost would come down to Rs. 1.59 only.

Impact of PDS

In participatory assessments it is found that poor rate PDS and other programmes like Antyodaya, Annapurna and FFW very highly (ITAD, 2002). This is because poor, in general and the poorest of the poor in particular are not food secure and depend on these safety nets to a large extent for survival. Attempts have been made to provide macro level estimates of gains to the poor from the scheme. The macro simulation exercises of Radhakrishna and Indrakant (1987) provide some insights of welfare implications of different policy interventions. Estimates shows the net gain after allowing for changes in the open market prices brought about by reduction of supplies due to procurement as well as the farm income feedback effects on demand. Ignoring the secondary effects the per capita per month income gain due to PDS in 1999-2000 is estimated to be Rs. 17 for both poor and non-poor in rural areas of the state (Table 15). However, in terms of percentage to MPCE the gains work out to be 6.6 and 3.4 percent for poor and non-poor respectively. In urban areas the income gain for the poor is Rs. 16 (5.3 percent of MPCE) as against Rs. 15 (1.8 percent of MPCE) for the non-poor. In an earlier study, Radhakrishna et al (1997) have estimated the per capita monthly income gain to the poor due to PDS in 1986-87. These estimates indicate that for the poor, the percentage of income gains to MPCE was 6.8 percent in rural areas and nearly 7.6 percent in urban areas. In other words between 1986-87 and 1999-2000 the welfare gain to poor due to PDS remained more or less the same in rural areas while it actually declined in urban areas.

The impact of food subsidies on food consumption is estimated using the income elasticities of Subrahmanyam et al (2000). As a result of income gains the consumption of non-cereal food increased by 7.52 percent for the rural poor and by 3.6 percent for urban poor. Similarly, the total food consumption increased by 6.5 percent and 4.6 percent for the poor of rural and urban areas respectively. In case of non-food, the increase in consumption is 6.9 percent for the rural poor and 4.6 percent for urban poor. Thus, the diversification of food basket of the poor due to PDS seems to be considerable.

As a result of the income gains to the poor, there was 6-percentage point and 4-percentage point reduction in poverty in rural and urban areas of the State. With better targeting much better results could have been achieved. A more rational policy to provide food security would be to issue larger quantities of foodgrains through PDS at a price higher than existing ones instead of issuing a small quantity of foodgrains at a highly subsidised price.

6. PROBLEMS AND PROSPECTS

Based on results of Linear Expenditure System of Subrahmanyam et al (2000), demand for rice has been estimated for 2020 under various assumptions. Since the model does not incorporate the changes in tastes, the resultant growth rates were moderated (Table 16). These estimates indicate that additional 30 to 40 lakh tonnes of rice will be demanded by 2020. Will the state be able to meet the demand of this scale?

Given the stagnant net area, the possibility of increasing the production seems to depend on the improvement in the productivity levels. Increasing irrigated areas, resource use efficiency and deregulating trade are some of the strategies outlined in the *Vision 2020* to boost rice production in the state. The prospects do not look bright considering the present declining trends in the investments. The impact of abnormal increases in MSP is already felt at national level in terms of mounting stocks and rising costs. The policy alternatives seem to be based on rationalizing MSP and moving towards greater role for the market. The need for direct intervention in providing food security to the poor is greater in this context.

The coverage of PDS is large coupled with targeting errors. The extent of benefits from PDS in terms of PDS quantity in total cereal consumption, income gain to the beneficiary households and consequent declining poverty is modest when compared to the huge amount of subsidy incurred on the subsidised rice scheme. A more rational policy to provide food security would be to issue larger quantities of food grains through PDS at a price higher than the existing one instead of issuing a small quantity of food grains at highly subsidised price. The present rice scheme in AP can be modified to make it cost effective so that the poor can be protected without

Table 16. Projections of Household Demand for Rice in Andhra Pradesh

Scenario	ATE Growth	2000	2005	2010	2020
		Aggregate Household Demand (Lakh tonnes)			
I	3.00	100.16	109.64	119.52	129.79
II	4.00	100.16	111.50	123.52	136.21
III	4.50	100.16	112.44	125.57	139.53
IV	5.00	100.16	113.39	127.65	142.93
		Annual Growth Rate			
I	3.00	-	1.82	1.74	1.66
II	4.00	-	2.17	2.07	1.97
III	4.50	-	2.34	2.23	2.13
IV	5.00	-	2.51	2.40	2.29

Note: The scenario I-IV present projected demand under the assumption of different growth rate for Aggregate Total Expenditure (ATE). All the projections are made at 1999-2000 relative prices.

straining investments in other sectors of human development, which are as essential as the food security. The demand for cereals is declining because of changes in tastes and insufficient growth of the income of the poor households. To improve the food security of the people in general and the poor in particular it is essential to see that farmers get remunerative price and the income of the poor is increased. Therefore, the prospect of future food security to a great extent depends upon the success of government policies in increasing the income of the poor and to provide necessary infrastructure facilities etc. to the domestic farmers to make them competitive in the context of globalisation of trade.

References

Ahluwalia, Deepak (1993), "Public Distribution of Food in India" *Food Policy,* February.

Centre for Economic and Social Studies (1987), *Statistical System for Multilevel Planning- Findings of Committee of Experts to Report Improvements to Andhra Pradesh Statistical System,* Centre for Economics and Social Studies, Hyderabad.

Cornia, G. A. and Franc Stewart (1993), "Two Errors of Targeting", *Journal of International Development,* Vol.5, No.5.

Deaton, Angus and Dreze (2002), "Poverty and Inequality in India. A Re-Examination" *Economic and Political Weekly,* September 7, 2002.

Dev, S. Mahendra and M. H. Suryanarayana (1992), "Is PDS Urban Biased and Pro-rich? An Evaluation", *Economic and Political Weekly,* Vol.26, No.41.

Government of India (1999), *Status Report on Estimation of Area and Production,* National Sample Survey Organisation, Government of India, New Delhi.

Government of India (2002), *Report on Long Term Grain Policy,* Ministry of Consumer Affairs and Public Distribution, Government of India, New Delhi (available at http.//fcamin.nic.in/hlc_mrep.htm).

Indrakant, S. (1996), *Food Security and Public Distribution System in Andhra Pradesh - A Case Study,* Centre for Economic and Social Studies, Hyderabad, (mimeo),.

Indrakant, S. (2000), "Food Security and Public Support . A Study of Andhra Pradesh in N. Krishnaji and T.N. Krishan (eds), *Public Support for food Security- The Public Distribution System in India,* Sage Publications, New Delhi.

ITAD(2002), *Livelihood Assessment Report*, ITAD, West Sussex, U.K.

Meenakshi, J. V. (2000), "Food Consumption Trends in India. A Regional Analysis, in N. Krishnaji and T. N. Krishnana (ed), *Public Support for Food Security*, Sage, New Delhi.

Murthy, K. N. (1997), "Trends in Consumption and Estimates of Income and Price Elasticities of Demand for Major Crops in the Semi-Arid Tropics of India- A compendium", International Crops Research Institute for Semi-Arid Tropics, (mimeo), Hyderabad.

Nawani (1994), "Indian Experience on household food and nutrition security" Presented at Regional Expert Consultation, August 8-11, 1994, FAD-UN Bangkok,(Available at www.fao.org/DOCREP/x0172e/),.

Olsen, Wendy K. (1989), "Eat Now Pay Later "Impact of Rice Subsidy Scheme", *Economic and Political Weekly* Vol. 24 No.28.

Parikh K.S. (1994), "Who Gets How Much from PDS . How Effectively Does it reach the Poor", *Sarvekshana,* Vol. 17 No.3.

Radhakrishna, R and K. Hanumanta Rao (1994), *Food Security, Public Distribution and Price Policy,* Centre for Development Studies, Thiruvananthapuram. Mimeo.

Radhakrishna, R and S. Indrakant (1987), "Effects of Rice Market Intervention in India. The Case of Andhra Pradesh" in *Evaluating Rice Market Intervention Policies. Some Asian Examples,* Asian Development Bank, Manila.

Radhakrishna, R. and C. Ravi (1992), "Effects of Growth Relative Price and Preference on Food and Nutrition", *Indian Economic Review,* Vol, XXVII.

Radhakrishna, R., K. Subba Rao, S. Indrakant and C. Ravi (1997), *India"s Public Distribution System - A National and International Perspectives,* World Bank Discussion Paper No.380, Washington, D. C.

Rao, C.H. (2000), "Declining Demand for Foodgrains in Rural India. Causes and Implications" *Economic and Political Weekly,* January 22.

Rao, V. M. (1995), "Beyond 'Surpluses': Food Security in Changing Context", *Economic and Political weekly,* Vol 30, No.4 January 28.

Ravi, C. (2000), *Complete Demand Systems, Welfare and Nutrition. An Analysis of Indian Consumption Data,* Ph.D thesis , Centre for Economic and Social Studies, Hyderabad.

Subba Rao, K. (1987), *Interventions to Fill Nutrition Gaps at the Household Level. A Review of India"s Experience,* Institute of Economic Growth, New Delhi.

Subrahmanyam, S, S. Indrakant and C. Ravi (2000), *Consumption Patterns and Demand in Andhra Pradesh*, Research and Monitoring Wing for Essential Commodities in Andhra Pradesh, Andhra Pradesh State Civil Supplies Corporation, Hyderabad, (mimeo),

Sundaram, K and S. Tendulkar (2002), "Recent Debates on Database for Measurement of Poverty in India" Presented at Government of India/World Bank Poverty Workshop, New Delhi, January 2002. (Available at http://www.worldbank.org/indiapovertyworkshop).

Venugopal, K.R. (1992), *Deliverance from Hunger . The Public Distribution System in India*, Sage Publication, New Delhi.

19

Regional Disparities: Causes and Remedies

S. Subrahmanyam

1. INTRODUCTION

There is hardly any country, developed or developing, which does not face the problem of regional disparities in development as certain regions enter the process of development earlier than others either due to historical reasons or differences in natural resources or cultural-institutional factors. If the differences persist over time, political discontent is bound to emerge sooner or later. Regional problems become complex when income differences overlap with differences in race, religion, language or culture of the people living in different regions. Interventions to correct regional imbalances are justified not only socially, but also on economic grounds because development of backward areas can contribute to the utilization of unexploited resources.

Many development theories showed that regional disparities are inherent in the process of development. Myrdal (1957), in his theory of cumulative causation, argues that market forces create regional inequalities and this tendency is more dominant in poor countries. He explains this tendency in terms of spread and backwash effects. Regional inequalities widen when backwash effects become stronger than the spread effects. He suggests that backwash effects have to be controlled through policy interventions. The analysis of long period data showed that income inequalities across Indian states increased mildly till mid eighties and rapidly afterwards (Subrahmanyam and Rajagopala Rao, 2000; Govida Rao et.al, 1999).

Regional disparities within a State need not increase because corrective steps can be easily implemented at the State level as compared to the national level because all regions in a State are under one administrative control. This paper focuses on trends in regional disparities in Andhra Pradesh since its formation. The state was formed on 1st November 1956 by merging the nine districts of Telangana belonging to the erstwhile Hyderabad state with the Andhra State formed in 1953 by combining Coastal Andhra comprising of seven districts and Rayalaseema comprising of four districts. Later on three new districts were formed: Vizianagaram was carved out of Srikakulam and Visakhapatnam districts, Prakasam was formed by combining parts of Guntur, Nellore and Kurnool districts and

Ranga Reddy was formed by taking out the rural parts of Hyderabad district.

The first step in regional analysis is the delineation of regions. Regions are generally demarcated on the principle of relative homogeneity. When the analysis covers a long period, regions which were homogeneous in the initial period may develop intra-regional variations over time. In such a case, it is proper to consider smaller regions which remained relatively homogeneous throughout the period. Andhra Pradesh is usually divided into three regions viz., Coastal Andhra, Rayalaseema and Telangana. But in the recent period, northern part of Telangana attained rapid agricultural growth. Similarly, the northern part of Coastal Andhra experienced slow growth in agriculture. In view of these variations in performance within the regions, there is a need to consider the three northern districts in Coastal Andhra as a separate region for analysis. Similarly, the five districts in the northern part of Telangana, which receive higher rainfall than the other districts in Telangana and also experienced higher growth in agriculture, have to be considered as a separate region. In South Telangana, Hyderabad district is completely urban and shows different characteristics of development. It is appropriate to classify Hyderabad as a separate region. The State is thus classified into six regions. Hyderabad district consisted of the present Ranga Reddy and Hyderabad districts in the earlier period. When comparisons are made with the earlier period (before 1980), both Ranga Reedy and Hyderabad are considered together (see Appendix A for districts included in each region).

The analysis focuses on trends in regional disparities in agriculture, industry and social sectors. In social sectors, education, health, poverty and status of women are considered. The main focus of the paper is on four aspects. First, what is the extent of regional disparity in different aspects of socio-economic development? Second, have they declined over time? Third, what are the factors responsible for the disparities? Fourth, what interventions are needed in different regions? The issue of increase in regional disparities after liberalization is also examined within the data constraints.

2. GENERAL FEATURES

With a population of 775 lakh and an area of 2.75 lakh KM^2, Andhra Pradesh is the fifth largest State in India. The six regions in the State show distinct demographic features. North Coastal Andhra has the highest density of population which is due to historical reasons rather than high population growth after the formation of the State. The growth rate of population in the region is lower than the State average.

South Coastal Andhra is also densely populated, which can be attributed to its high agricultural development. But population growth rate in the region is the lowest among the regions in the State. Urbanization is also low in the region. Rayalaseema has the lowest population density of 200 persons per KM^2. All the four districts in the region have the same extent of urbanization. North Telangana has a high growth rate of population. Density of population is also low in the region. South Telangana has low density of population, but higher than that of North Telangana due to its proximity to Hyderabad. Urbanization is very low in all the districts in the region except Ranga Reddy which has the highest proportion of urban population among the districts other than Hyderabad.

3. LEVEL AND GROWTH OF PER CAPITA INCOME

Despite many limitations, per capita income is considered as an important indicator of development. The Directorate of Economics and Statistics, Hyderabad, estimates gross district domestic product using the methodology adopted in State income estimation. Though the process was initiated in 1960-61, there was break from 1979-80 to 1992-93. The estimates for the earlier period are available at 1970-71 prices and the estimates for the latter period are available at 1993-94 prices. The data for the earlier period is also converted to 1993-94 prices using the State income deflator. In order to avoid the problem of fluctuations, five year averages of income are computed for three periods viz., 1960-65, 1974-79 and 1995-2000. Per capita income of a region is calculated as weighted average of per capita district incomes.

In Andhra Pradesh, per capita state domestic product increased at a slow rate till mid seventies. The increase was only 12.8 per cent in 15 years. On the other hand, per capita income grew at about 4 per cent per annum in the latter period. Let us examine the position of the six regions in relation to State average during 1995-2000. Hyderabad district occupies top position with 22.3 per cent higher per capita income than the State average. Among the remaining five regions, South Coastal Andhra occupies the top position with 5.8 per cent higher per capita income and North Telangana occupies the lowest position with 8.8 per cent lower income than the State average (Table 1). The other three regions have slightly higher income than North Telangana. South Telangana occupies the middle position and North Coastal Andhra and Rayalaseema occupy second and fourth positions respectively. While per capita incomes vary marginally across regions, the differences across districts are quite high because of the concentration of industries in selected locations. Medak district in South Telangana recorded the highest per capita income in the State which is due to its closeness to Hyderabad. Most of the industrial development surrounding Hyderabad is taking place in areas belonging to Medak district. Mahabubnagar district in the same region recorded the lowest per capita income among the 23 districts in the State. Similar variations are found in North Coastal Andhra region. Visakhaptnam occupies second position in industrial development after Hyderabad and hence its per capita income is found to be the second highest in the State. Srikakulam district in this region is second lowest in per capita income. The high per capita income at regional level may not necessarily indicate high per capita income in rural areas. The situation in the rural areas can be captured better through the analysis of the agricultural sector.

Table 1. Index of Per Capita Gross Domestic Products at 1993-94 Prices (State = 100)

Region	1960-65	1974-79	1995-2000
Coastal Andhra	109.1	103.6	103.7
Telangana (excl. Hyd & RR districts)	85.0	87.5	92.9
Telangana	90.4	97.2	99.6
Rayalaseema	96.3	96.9	92.1
North Coastal Andhra	89.8	79.2	98.0
South Coastal Andhra	116.6	112.6	105.8
North Telangana	85.2	92.1	91.2
South Telangana (excl. Hyd. districts)	84.7	80.7	95.4
Hyderabad & Ranga Reddy	117.8	140.6	122.3
State	100.0	100.0	100.0
	(3758)	(4239)	(9859)
Coefficient of Variation (%)	17.9	22.8	20.4

Note: 1. Figures in brackets are absolute values in rupees. Coefficient of variation is calculated considering district as unit.
2. For districts in each region, see Appendix A.

Let us now consider the situation in the early sixties. Disparities in per capita income were quite high and the ranking of the regions was also different. Though Hyderabad (including Ranga Reddy) occupied the top position even in this period, its per capita income was only 17.8 per cent higher than the State average. South Coastal Andhra, which occupied top position among the other five regions, recorded 16.6 per cent higher income and was close to Hyderabad. Rayalaseema occupied the second highest position and maintained a wide gap from the other three regions. South Telangana occupied the bottom position and North Telangana was very close to it. The main factor for these changes in ranks between these two periods is rapid industrialization of Visakhapatnam and areas surrounding Hyderabad. Rayalaseema was pushed from second to fourth and North Telangana was pushed to the bottom from fifth position.

The position by the mid-seventies was different. Hyderabad recorded very high growth and reached an all time high position of 40.6 per cent higher per capita income than the State average. Rayalaseema maintained its relative position. North Coastal Andhra experienced steep deterioration in its relative position and was pushed to the bottom since industrialization in Visakhapatnam picked up only later. Similarly, industrialization in Medak district also came later and hence the growth of

South Telangana was slower than that of North Telangana. The gaps between the per capita incomes of regions and the State average reveals that disparities widened between 1960-61 and 1978-79. In the subsequent period, North Coastal Andhra and South Telangana, the two lagging regions in mid-seventies picked up industrialization and reduced their gap with the State average. On the other hand, Hyderabad and South Coastal Andhra could not achieve the high growth rate recorded by the above two regions and hence their relative positions deteriorated. Thus, there is decline in the regional disparities between 1974-79 and 1995-2000. The increase in regional inequalities in the earlier period and reduction in the later period is also found across districts. The unweighted coefficient of variation in per capita income across districts increased from 17.9 per cent in sixties to 22.8 per cent by the end of seventies and then declined to 20.4 per cent by the end of nineties (Table 1).

Fig.1. Index of Per Capita GDP (State=100)

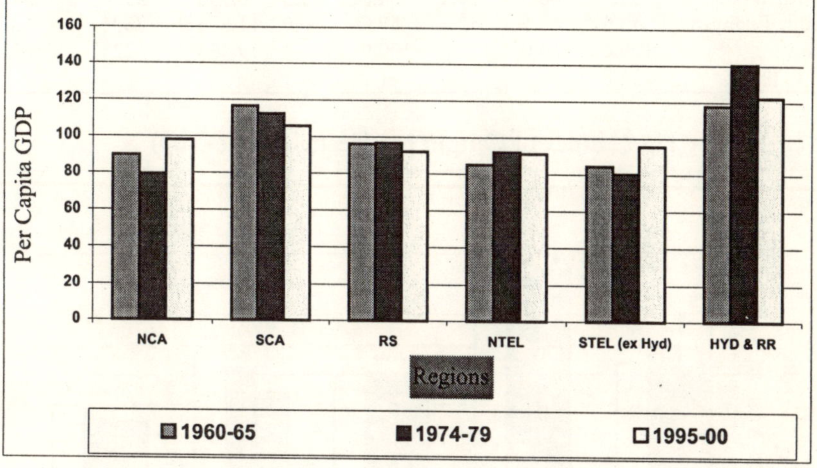

4. AGRICULTURAL DEVELOPMENT

While industrialisation generates employment and income in the urban areas, the well-being of the rural populace is largely determined by agricultural development because of the low share of industry in total employment as well as income. Since land is scarce, performance of agriculture has to be evaluated in terms of land productivity. To suppress the effect of year-to-year fluctuations in output, triennium average of the value of crop output is worked out for different years. The value of output per hectare of major 18 crops is estimated and it is blown up for the entire cropped area proportionately (Table 2). Since Hyderabad district is completely urban and has no agricultural land, there are only five regions for analysis.

Table 2. Value of Crop Output per Hectare of Net Area Sown at Current Prices

Region	Index of Output Per Hectare					Value of Output (Rs.) (1996-99)		
	1955-58	1969-72	1979-82	1989-92	1996-99	Per Hectare	Per Capita Rural	Index of Per Capita (%)
Coastal Andhra	184.8	142.7	140.3	133.7	134.4	26,163	4655	110.2
Telangana	49.0	58.6	61.8	71.5	77.9	15,171	3338	79.0
Rayalaseema	58.7	81.0	73.4	81.3	70.9	13,799	4199	99.4
North Coastal Andhra	148.7	121.0	94.9	99.2	87.5	17,036	2910	68.9
South Coastal Andhra	194.0	149.7	154.1	144.6	149.1	29,019	5239	124.0
North Telangana	54.9	68.3	71.1	84.7	95.3	18,555	3910	92.5
South Telangana	43.5	49.5	52.7	58.6	60.0	11,678	2693	63.7
State	100.0	100.0	100.0	100.0	100.0	19,466	4225	100.0
C. V. (%)	54.8	55.3	54.8	41.2	44.3	-	-	-

Fig 2. Index of Output per Hectare (State=100)

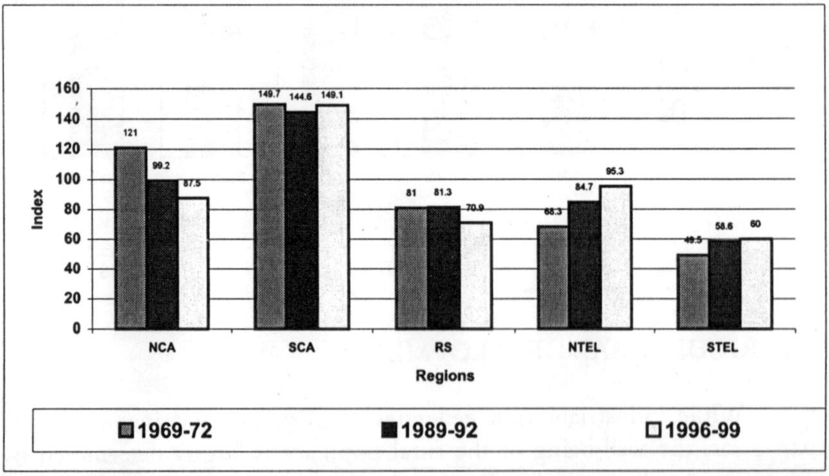

While South Coastal Andhra and North Telangana occupy the first and second positions, Rayalaseema and South Telangana are in the fourth and fifth positions in agricultural development. The results indicate that aggregation of the districts into three regions hides the backwardness of North Coastal Andhra and South Telangana regions in agricultural development.

Let us now examine the trends in regional disparities. During the triennium ending 1998-99, the gap between the top and bottom districts was 89.1 percentage points. As against this, in the initial period (1955-58), the same regions occupied the top and bottom positions with a wider gap than at present. While South Costal Andhra recorded 94 per cent higher productivity than the State average, South Telangana was 56.5 per cent below the State average, creating a gap of 146.5 percentage points. The data for other years also indicate decline in inter-regional disparities in agricultural productivity. However, the changes in the nineties indicate increase in the inequalities. This is clearly observed in the trends in the coefficient of variation, which declined significantly in the eighties and increased in the subsequent period, supporting the widespread view that inter-regional inequalities are widening in the liberalisation period. This phenomenon could be explained in terms of changes in public investment in agriculture, especially irrigation.

While the decline in regional disparities is a positive achievement, the performance of North Coastal Andhra is very poor requiring special attention. The region experienced deterioration in its relative position from 48.7 per cent above the State average to 12.5 per cent below the State average during the four decades. On the other hand, North Telangana showed commendable improvement by reducing its gap from the State average to 4.7 per cent from 45.1 per cent.

While land productivity indicates agricultural development, agricultural output per head of rural population indicates welfare levels. The ranking of regions on these two may not be the same because pressure of population on land may vary. While South Coastal Andhra and South Telangana occupy top and bottom positions even on this basis, Rayalaseema rose to second position from fourth and North Coastal Andhra is pushed to fourth position from second. North Telangana is placed at the middle. Thus, North Coastal Andhra suffers from not only slow growth of land productivity, but also heavy pressure on land. On the other hand, Rayalaseema has low pressure on land and hence per capita output is high despite low productivity of land. South Coastal Andhra also has high pressure on land as indicated by the fact that its superiority in land productivity is significantly reduced when per capita output is considered. A comparison of land productivity and per capita output in relative terms at district level shows that the problem of low per capita output in the three districts of North Coastal Andhra cannot be solved by mere improvement in productivity to the State average level since the gap in per capita output is much higher than the gap in per hectare output. There is a need to reduce the pressure of population on land through the development of non-farm sector. The problem of low per capita output in Cuddapah, Ranga Reddy, Mahabubnagar, Medak, Nalgonda and Adilabad can be tackled by improvement in agricultural productivity. Among the 23 districts in the

State, Adilabad, Ranga Reddy and Mahabubnagar deserve special attention as land productivity in these districts is less than one half of the State average.

Besides land productivity, expansion of area and growth in cropping intensity also influence growth of agricultural output. To understand the overall performance of the crop sector, growth rates of crop output at constant prices are computed from the logarithmic trend equations (Table 3). The growth rate of output for the period 1955-56 to 1998-99 is found to be 2.5 per cent for the State. North Costal Andhra and Rayalaseema recorded very low growth rates of 1.7 per cent and 1.9 per cent per annum respectively. Even the least developed South Telangana could attain the State average growth rate of 2.5 per cent. North Telangana, which improved its position in land productivity from fourth to second during the four decades, could reach that position because of its highest growth rate at 3.1 per cent per annum. The growth rates recorded in sub-periods indicate that Rayalaseema and North Coastal Andhra showed poor performance throughout the period. Only during the period of seventies and eighties, they could attain positive and statistically significant growth. It is significant to note that all the regions except North Telangana showed poor growth performance in the nineties. Even North Telangana showed high fluctuations in the nineties as a result of which the growth rate turned out to be statistically insignificant.

Table 3. Growth Rates of Crop Output in Different Periods

Region	1955-69	1970-89	1990-99	1955-99
Coastal Andhra	1.65*	3.01*	0.57	2.49*
Telangana	2.85*	3.03*	2.13	2.87*
Rayalaseema	-0.38	1.40**	0.78	1.88*
North Coastal Andhra	0.25	1.63***	-1.19	1.72*
South Coastal Andhra	2.00*	3.31*	0.92***	2.67*
North Telangana	3.45*	3.45*	3.07	3.12*
South Telangana	2.06*	2.43*	0.66	2.52*
State	1.52*	2.70*	1.16	2.47*

Note: *, ** and *** indicate significance at 1 per cent, 5 per cent and 10 per cent respectively.

Regional Variations in Crop Yields

Regional disparities in per hectare output can be traced to low yield performance of certain crops grown in the area. North Coastal Andhra has a very low yield of rice and sugarcane. The yield of rice is 1.7 tonnes per hectare as against 2.6 tonnes at the State level (Table 4). As rice is grown mostly under irrigated conditions in Andhra Pradesh, the low yield appears to be due to uncertainty of tank irrigation, the major source in this region. Because of the complementary relation between irrigation and fertiliser use, irrigation uncertainty may be leading to low fertiliser use. Yield of sugarcane is only 53 tonnes per hectare as against 74 tonnes at the State level. In this region, sugarcane is cultivated partly under irrigated conditions and partly under rain-fed conditions. The yield of sugarcane grown under dry conditions is very low due to low fertiliser use.

Table 4. Yields (quintals per hectare) of Selected Crops: 1996-99

Crop	N.CA	S.CA	R.Seema	S.Tel	N.Tel	STATE
Rice	17.18	28.52	24.91	24.34	26.62	26.06
Jowar	5.22	8.74	9.43	6.04	6.72	6.95
Pulses	4.01	5.81	5.76	3.04	3.69	4.61
Groundnut	11.33	16.56	8.35	7.51	11.46	8.95
Cotton(lint)	2.56	3.26	2.06	1.97	2.41	2.51
Sugarcane (Gur)	53.17	82.00	93.30	70.84	80.45	74.26
Tobacco	15.18	11.47	8.77	7.94	13.78	11.32
Chillies	19.52	27.30	13.19	14.89	21.22	21.49

Note: N.CA – North Coastal Andhra, S.CA – South Coastal Andhra, R.Seema – Rayalaseema, S.Tel – South Telangana, N.Tel – North Telangana.

The performance of South Telangana is poor in almost all the crops grown in the region. The region has low irrigation ratio (27.6 per cent) and receives low rainfall. In such an agro-climatic situation, moisture stress appears to be the major factor contributing for the low yield. Rayalaseema is the region with the lowest irrigation ratio (23.3 per cent) among the five regions in Andhra Pradesh. It also has the lowest precipitation. Groundnut is the major crop in the region and it is grown under rain-fed conditions. The yield of groundnut in Rayalaseema is one-half of the yield in South Coastal Andhra. In the absence of some protective irrigation, it is difficult to improve the yield of groundnut in the region.

North Telangana, the second best in crop output per hectare, is showing poor performance in cotton, which is expanding in the region in recent times. Yield of cotton lint is 74 per cent of the yield in South Coastal Andhra. This lower productivity is not attributable to low irrigation as the share of irrigated cotton is higher (39 per cent) than in South Coastal Andhra (24 per cent). Soil conditions appear to be the major factor for low yield of cotton in North Telangana region.

Growth of Irrigated Area

Water being the main source of agricultural development, regional disparities arise mainly due to differences in irrigation development. Irrigation improves yields of existing crops and also facilitates shift to high valued crops. Andhra Pradesh achieved significant growth in irrigation during the last four decades (Table 5).

The major feature of agricultural development in the State is the positive association between rainfall and irrigation ratio. North Telangana, North Coastal Andhra and South Coastal Andhra have high rainfall and also high irrigation ratio. North Telangana has the highest performance with a growth rate of 2.3 per cent per annum, followed by South Telangana with a growth rate of 1.5 per cent per annum. However, growth rate of

Table 5. Trends in Irrigated Area

Region	Percentage of Irrigated Area in Net Area Sown		Growth Rate of Irrigated Area		Rain fall Normal (mm)
			Gross @	Canal (Net)**	
	1955-58	1996-99	1955-99	1955-99	
Coastal Andhra	47.0	58.0	0.93*	0.34	1024
Telangana	15.8	36.0	1.96*	1.78	939
Rayalaseema	12.6	23.3	0.71*	1.20	689
North Coastal Andhra	50.1	44.8	0.24	0.68	1111
South Coastal Andhra	46.2	62.6	1.09*	0.29	981
North Telangana	19.6	44.2	2.29*	1.37	1036
South Telangana	12.7	27.6	1.49*	2.65	817
State	24.8	40.7	1.19*	0..57	942

@ Derived from exponential trend equations. * significant at less than 1%

** Calculated from triennial averages of 1955-56 to 1957-58 and 1996-97 to 1998-99.

canal irrigated area is higher in South Telangana region as compared to North Telangana because of its low base. Though South Coastal Andhra recorded a lower growth rate (1.1 per cent) than the two Telangana regions, its initial level was very high. Despite significant improvement in irrigation ratio at the State level, certain districts show very poor improvement. Adilabad has the lowest irrigation ratio of 12.4 per cent and Anantapur is the second lowest with a ratio of 14.2 per cent. While the former has high precipitation, the latter has the lowest. Despite this disadvantage, Anantapur district could achieve higher land productivity than Adilabad. Adilabad being predominantly tribal, the backwardness in respect of agricultural practices may be an important factor for low productivity of land.

Changes in Source of Irrigation

Source of irrigation influences sustainability of agricultural growth. Canal irrigation is highly dependable and sustainable and facilitates groundwater recharge. Conjunctive use of canal and tube-well leads to high growth of the agricultural sector. Tank is a less assured source than canal, but it also has a lot of potential to support ground water recharge. Wells and tube-wells require high groundwater potential and regular recharge which is possible only when surface irrigation exists or high rainfall is received.

In the initial period (1960-61), South Telangana was predominantly under tank irrigation and Rayalaseema had both tanks and wells. All the irrigation expansion in these regions came through wells and simultaneously area under tanks declined. The share of wells in net irrigated area increased from about 25 per cent to more than 70 per cent. Rainfall being low, such intensive development of well irrigation is leading to drying up of wells (Table 6).

Table 6. Percentage Distribution of Net Irrigated Area by Source

Region	Canal		Tank		Well	
	1960-61	1999-2000	1960-61	1999-2000	1960-61	1999-2000
Coastal Andhra	61.3	56.0	33.9	22.7	4.8	21.3
Telangana	19.1	17.7	62.6	18.6	18.3	63.7
Rayalaseema	22.7	20.2	49.8	9.4	27.5	70.4
North Coastal Andhra	32.7	38.0	63.0	52.2	4.3	9.8
South Coastal Andhra	69.8	60.4	25.3	15.5	4.9	24.1
North Telangana	23.6	18.3	63.5	24.0	12.9	57.7
South Telangana	12.8	16.8	61.0	9.4	26.2	73.8
State	45.8	37.3	42.9	19.4	11.3	43.3

Irrigation expansion was all time high at 8.4 lakh hectares in the eighties. Surface irrigation accounted for 38 per cent and groundwater 62 per cent. During the nineties, irrigated area expanded by only 0.8 lakh hectares. But area under groundwater increased by 6.0 lakh hectares and area under canals and tanks declined by 5.5 lakh hectares. This trend of abnormal increase in ground water exploitation and simultaneous decline in surface irrigated area is not conducive for sustainable agricultural development.

Because of the rapid ground water exploitation, there is a significant decline in the inter-district inequality during both eighties and nineties. In fact, the decline is much sharper in the nineties because of the expansion of ground water in areas of low irrigation. However, this is a high cost and uncertain source. The requirement of power increases with the increase in the depth of water. Significant decline in area under canal irrigation took place in districts like Nellore, Nalgonda and Nizamabad. This aspect requires thorough examination and identify remedial measures. In the case of tanks, almost all the districts suffered heavy decline in area under tanks. This pattern of irrigation expansion, though reduced regional inequality, is not conducive for sustainable development.

Agricultural growth in the coming years depends heavily on the expansion of irrigation, especially canal irrigation, since tank irrigation is unsustainable and well irrigation is not only unsustainable, but also costly. According to the information provided by the Department of Irrigation, Government of Andhra Pradesh, the State could utilize 52.95 per cent of the ultimate potential. Rayalaseema and Telangana have high unexploited potential for canal irrigation (Table 7). Since area under tanks declined steeply in the last two decades, even restoration of the lost area leads to a significant improvement in irrigation in the drought prone areas.

Table 7. Ultimate Irrigation Potential and Potential Created: 2000

Region	Ultimate Potential (Lakh Hectares)			Potential Created As Per cent of Ultimate Potential			Possible Expansion (Lakh Hectares)		
	Canal*	Tank	Total	Canal	Tank	Total	Canal	Tank	Total
Coastal Andhra	22.79	25.10	47.89	87.30	20.32	52.18	2.90	20.00	22.90
Telangana	11.92	24.90	36.82	73.40	57.19	62.44	3.17	10.66	13.83
Rayalaseema	8.59	10.20	18.79	42.26	31.37	36.35	4.97	7.00	11.97
State	43.3	60.20	103.5	74.50	37.44	52.95	11.03	37.66	48.69

Note: * Aggregate of Major and Medium Projects.
Source: Department Irrigation, Government of Andhra Pradesh, Hyderabad.

Under-utilisation of Land

Land is left fallow when crop cultivation is not remunerative. Andhra Pradesh has a larger proportion of fallow land than all India and it is increasing over time (Reddy, 1991). The proportion of fallow land in cultivable land (net area sown plus fallow) increased from 20.9 per cent at the beginning of seventies to 29.3 per cent in 1999-2000 (Table 8). It is

Table 8. Changes in Cultivated and Fallow Land

Region	Triennium Average Ending					
	Net Area Sown (Lakh ha)		Fallow Land (Lakh ha)		Fallow in Cultivable Land (%)	
	1972-73	1999-2000	1972-73	1999-2000	1972-73	1999-2000
Coastal Andhra	37.47	38.04	7.49	7.52	16.65	16.50
Telangana	47.65	40.42	16.26	26.78	25.45	39.85
Rayalaseema	28.49	26.63	6.21	9.30	17.89	25.88
North Coastal Andhra	9.21	9.75	1.39	1.21	13.08	11.03
South Coastal Andhra	28.25	28.29	6.10	6.31	17.76	18.23
South Telangana	25.27	19.89	8.06	15.46	24.18	43.73
North Telangana	22.38	20.53	8.20	11.32	26.82	35.54
State	113.60	105.09	29.96	43.59	20.87	29.32

Note: Cultivable land is defined as net area sown plus fallow land.

concentrated in the two Telangana regions. The low productivity of the dry land in relation to the wage rates could be one of the factors for increase in fallow land (Subrahmanyam, 2002). Ranga Reddy, Nalgonda, Nizamabad and Karimnagar have very high (about 40 per cent) extent of fallow land. Except seven districts in Coastal area, Khammam and Anantapur, all the remaining districts in the State have more than 20 per cent of the cultivable land under fallow. Identification of the reasons for leaving land fallow and development of these lands could be an important source of rural development in the near future.

5. DEVELOPMENT OF MANUFACTURING SECTOR

The Vision 2020 of Andhra Pradesh has a target of 11 per cent growth for the industrial sector and also to provide 43 per cent of the new jobs in this sector (GOAP, 1999). But the present level of development is very low. Manufacturing sector contributed only 12.3 per cent to net State domestic product of Andhra Pradesh during 1997-00 as compared to more than 20 per cent at the national level (Table 9). The growth rate of manufacturing workers was lower than that of total workers between 1981 and 1991, which led to decline in their share from 10.1 per cent to 8.8 per cent. Except South Telangana and North Telangana, all the remaining four regions experienced this decline. Rayalaseema and South Coastal Andhra experienced decline in absolute number of manufacturing workers also. Information for 1990s is available only for the registered manufacturing. The annual compound growth rate of registered manufacturing was only 1.5 per cent per annum between 1979-81 and 1997-99. South Telangana and North Telangana could achieve very high growth rate of 4.8 per cent and 3.4 per cent respectively. Rayalaseema also showed good performance during the period with a growth rate of 2.2 per cent. South Coastal Andhra has experienced decline in manufacturing employment and North Coastal Andhra attained a low growth of 0.9 per cent. Due to the decline of workers, the share of South Coastal Andhra declined steeply from 30.9 per cent during 1979-81 to 20.4 per cent during 1997-99. Another significant feature of industrialization in the State is the shift of industries from Hyderabad to neighbouring areas of Ranga Reddy, Medak and Nalgonda districts in order to avail of the concessions under backward area development. This is reflected in the fact that employment in Hyderabad declined at 5.7 per cent per annum, while it increased at a high rate of 4.8

Table 9. Share of Manufacturing Workers in Total Workers

Region	Total Manufacturing		Growth Rate	Registered Manufacturing		Growth Rate
	1981	1991	1981-91	1979-81	1997-99	1979-99
Coastal Andhra	9.63	7.43	-0.52	39.65	28.1	-0.4
Telangana (excl Hyd)	11.54	13.46	2.68	40.0	61.2	4.0
Telangana	11.49	11.27	2.44	54.2	64.9	2.6
Rayalaseema	8.33	6.76	-0.03	6.3	7.0	2.2
North Coastal Andhra	9.12	7.61	0.37	8.6	7.7	0.9
South Coastal Andhra	9.82	7.36	-0.84	30.9	20.4	-0.8
North Telangana	11.62	11.72	2.44	25.0	34.7	3.4
South Telangana (excl. Hyd)	9.26	9.4	3.04	15.0	26.5	4.8
Hyderabad	23.52	19.06	0.93	14.3	3.7	-5.7
State	10.11	8.83	0.93	100.0	100.0	1.5

per cent in South Telangana. Thus, regional disparities in manufacturing growth widened and North Telangana and Rayalaseema showed higher growth than the State average. The growth of South Telangana is also high, but its spread to areas beyond the vicinity or neighbouring areas of Hyderabad is not clear. The low manufacturing employment in Mahabubnagar district in South Telangana is an indication that industrialization in South Telangana is confined to surrounding areas of Hyderabad.

The nature of industrialization in different regions is reflected in capital–labour ratio and size of the unit. But data on capital stock cannot be used without proper adjustments because the value represents historical depreciated values, not representing any particular year. Hence, gross value added per worker is used as an indicator of capital intensity. Workers per factory is taken as the indicator for size of the unit. These values are expressed in relative terms, taking the value for the State as 100 (Table 10).

Table 10. Index of Value Added Per Worker and Workers Per Factory

Region	Value added per worker (Rs)		Workers per factory	
	1979-81	1997-99	1979-81	1997-99
Coastal Andhra	79.9	113.9	109.7	75.8
Telangana (incl Hyd)	114.9	89.8	99.5	131.6
Telangana (excl Hyd)	77.3	87.2	82.9	133.4
Rayalaseema	98.4	139.5	65.9	51.4
North Coastal Andhra	150.4	128.1	135.4	118.5
South Coastal Andhra	60.2	108.5	104.2	66.7
North Telangana	33.9	24.5	68.6	146.2
South Telangana	149.7	169.3	127.1	119.7
Hyderabad	220.0	131.2	227.6	107.2
State	100 (9,600)	100 (1,05,387)	100 (73.4)	100 (56.2)

Note: Figures in brackets are absolute values in Rupees.

At the State level, value added per worker is Rs. 1.5 lakh and employment per unit 56 persons during 1997-99. Value added per worker (capital intensity) differs widely across regions. North Telangana shows a distinct pattern with a very low value added per worker. It is only 25 per cent of the State average. On the other hand, South Telangana has the highest value added per worker (69 per cent higher than the State average). Thus, these two regions exhibit quite opposite patterns of industrialization. Rayalaseema, North Coastal Andhra and Hyderabad also exhibit higher capital intensity than the State average. Capital intensity increased in Rayalaseema, South Coastal Andhra and South Telangana, but declined in the other three regions. The steep decline in the capital intensity in Hyderabad indicates that capital intensive industries are moving away from

Hyderabad. Size of the unit is the highest in North Telangana. Rayalaseema and South Coastal Andhra have lower unit size than the State average.

Another approach to understand changes in the pattern of industrialization is to examine the growth of modern industries. The general practice is to treat all industries with NIC code 2 as traditional and those with code 3 as modern. Industries in code 2 broadly consist of agro-based, forest-based and leather-based industries. On the other hand, NIC code 3 consists of chemical-based, mineral-based, metal-based and machinery and equipment. The share of employment in modern industries in the factory sector is worked out for 1985-86 and 1998-99 (Table 11).

Table 11. Changes in the Share of Modern Sector in Manufacturing

Region	Percentage of workers in modern registered manufacturing*	
	1985-86	1998-99
Coastal Andhra	22.9	34.2
Telangana (incl Hyd)	27.1	25.4
Telangana (excl Hyd)	29.3	24.7
Rayalaseema	28.0	36.2
North Coastal Andhra	44.5	62.1
South Coastal Andhra	16.1	20.7
North Telangana	3.3	2.8
South Telangana	69.7	52.4
Hyderabad	19.6	38.0
State	25.8	28.6

Note: Industries with NIC code 3.

The share of modern industry is only 28.6 per cent in 1998-99 at the State level and the improvement during the last 13 years is negligible. North Telangana is conspicuous by its very low share of 2.8 per cent in modern industries. On the other hand, North Coastal Andhra and South Telangana have a majority of workers (62.1 and 52.4 per cent respectively) in modern industries. Hyderabad and Rayalaseema also have more than average level of modernization. However, it is significant that Hyderabad has significantly lower share of modern industry than South Telangana. South Coastal Andhra is also less modernized than the State average. It is clearly observed that the agriculturally developed regions have not gone for industrialization which is needed for further development of the region. They have to diversify and strengthen industrially. A significant aspect in regional industrialization is decline in the share of modern sector in South Telangana and simultaneous increase in Hyderabad region. While traditional industries are located in the neighbouring three districts, modern industries are being located in Hyderabad.

6. RURAL POVERTY

The Expert Group constituted by the Planning Commission estimated poverty line for all-India for the year 1973-74 using the norm of 2400 calories per capita for rural areas and 2100 calories for urban areas and then derived state specific poverty lines using differences in prices between the State and all-India (GOI, 1993). The poverty line for rural Andhra Pradesh was found to be the lowest among all the Indian States and Union Territories. The Consumer Price Index for Agricultural Labourers for the year 1973-74 on the basis of which State specific poverty lines are derived appears to be defective (Mahendra Dev and Ravi, 2003). As the poverty lines for other years are derived by updating the line for 1973-74 for price changes, the absolute difference in the poverty line between Andhra Pradesh and other States is magnified. As a large proportion of population will be concentrated around the poverty line expenditure, incidence of poverty is highly sensitive to the poverty line. The State Sample data of the 55th round of the National Sample Survey shows that the incidence of rural poverty as only 12 per cent in 1993-94 in Andhra Pradesh. However, this underestimation may not affect inter-regional comparisons as the same poverty line is used for all the regions. As we are interested only in relative position of each region and trends, the incidence of rural poverty in each region is expressed as a ratio of State average (Table 12).

Table 12. Indices of Head Count Rural Poverty

(State=100)

Region	1977-78	1983	1987-88	1993-94	Annual Decline
North Coastal Andhra	121	143	100	167	2.7
South Coastal Andhra	75	63	55	75	1.9
Rayalaseema	104	131	123	117	2.5
South Telangana	102	94	132	133	2.3
North Telangana	121	114	123	67	3.4
State	100	100	100	100	2.5

Source: Calculated by using the data available in Mitra, G.K. (2002).

7. LITERACY AND PRIMARY EDUCATION

Andhra Pradesh is one of the educationally backward states with a literacy rate of 61.1 per cent as compared to 65.4 per cent at the national level. The backwardness of the State in literacy is due to extremely poor performance of certain areas and certain social classes (Subrahmanyam, 2003).

Hyderabad, being completely urban, attained the highest literacy rate (79 per cent). Among the remaining five, South Telangana, North Telangana and North Coastal Andhra are the most backward with a literacy rate of 56 per cent (Table 13). Rayalaseema occupied the middle position with 60.5 per cent and South Coastal Andhra is at the top with 66 per cent literacy.

Table 13. Level and Improvement in Literacy during Nineties

District	1991	2001	Increase	Very Low(<44) Literacy Mandals (No.)
Coastal Andhra	46.2	63.6	17.4	37
Telangana (Excl Hyd)	37.1	55.9	18.9	108
Telangana	41.3	58.8	17.5	108
Rayalaseema	45.0	60.5	15.6	19
North Coastal Andhra	39.6	56.4	16.8	25
South Coastal Andhra	48.6	66.2	17.6	12
South Telangana	37.1	55.9	18.8	68
North Telangana	37.1	56.0	18.9	40
Hyderabad	71.5	79.0	7.5	-
Andhra Pradesh	44.1	61.1	17.0	164
Coefficient of variation (%)	21.6	12.9	-	-

Two issues become important for policy interventions in literacy improvement. Have regional disparities in literacy declined? Second, which are the low literacy districts in the State? It has to be noted that the country achieved very high improvement in literacy in the nineties because of the National Literacy Campaign supported by the National Literacy Mission established in 1988. What was achieved in two decades in the earlier period could be attained in one decade. And more significantly, the more backward the State, the higher is the literacy improvement. Andhra Pradesh improved its literacy level by 17 percentage points during the decade. Two of the three low literacy regions (North Telangana and South Telangana) achieved more than average improvement while the other (North Coastal Andhra) achieved less than average improvement. Rayalaseema which has a literacy rate close to the State average showed poor performance. The high literacy Coastal Andhra achieved more than average improvement in the nineties. These changes do not give a clear indication of decline in regional inequalities. In order to get a firm evidence on trends in regional disparities, decadal improvement in literacy is regressed on initial (1991) literacy rate using the cross-section data of districts. The estimated equation is as follows:

$$\Delta LIMP_i = 25.64 - 0.195\ LIT_i \qquad R^2 = 0.393$$
$$t\ value = -3.687$$

where ΔLIMP stands for literacy improvement between 1991 and 2002 and LIT stands for literacy rate in 1991.

The slope coefficient is negative and statistically significant, indicating that initially low literacy districts could achieve a higher improvement during the decade as compared to the districts with initially higher level of literacy.

Vizianagaram in North Coastal Andhra, Kurnool in Rayalaseema, Mahabubnagar and Medak in South Telangana and Nizamabad and Adilabad in North Telangana have very low literacy rates of less than 53 per cent in 2001. In the entire state of Andhra Pradesh, 164 Mandals (15 per cent of the total) have very low literacy rate of less than 44 per cent, which is the State average in 1991. These Mandals are concentrated in three contiguous areas. Vizianagaram and Visakhapatnam districts constitute one area with a concentration of 23 very low literacy Mandals, Kurnool and Mahabubnagar districts constitute another area with a concentration of 59 very low literacy Mandals and Medak, Nizamabad and Adilabad constitute the third location with 42 very low literacy Mandals. Mahabubnagar shows extremely poor performance with 44 Mandals falling in the very low literacy category and even the remaining 20 Mandals belong to low literacy category. The reasons for low literacy rates in these Mandals have to be identified and suitable programmes have to be implemented.

Primary education suffers from high drop out rate. Drop out rates worked out from the school data on the basis of adjusted cohort method, according to which the difference between enrolment before five years and completion of primary stage this year is defined as drop out, are available at district level. These rates include stagnation and hence give a higher estimate of drop out rate. On the other hand, they exclude direct admissions in higher classes leading to downward bias in the estimate of drop out rate. The estimate represents wastage rather than drop out.

Drop out rate at primary stage is 37.1 per cent for the State level. The rate is very high at 65.8 per cent among Scheduled Tribes and 44 per cent among Scheduled Castes (Table 14). Gender difference in primary education exists only among Scheduled Tribes and to some extent among scheduled Castes. But among other communities, drop out rate is higher among boys than girls as revealed from the fact that the dropout rate for all communities does not differ between boys and girls while it varies in the case of Scheduled Castes and Scheduled Tribes. Inter-district variations in drop out rates are lower among Scheduled Castes and Scheduled Tribes as compared to others.

Regional disparities in drop out rate are quite high. Very high drop out rates of 51.0 per cent and 48.4 per cent are recorded in South Telangana and North Telangana respectively. These are the regions with low literacy rate also. But North Coastal Andhra with the same low literacy level has very low drop out rate of 26.1 per cent, which is lower than the drop out rate recorded by the region with the highest literacy rate (South Coastal Andhra). Among the districts in the State, Adilabad and Mahabubnagar have very high drop out rate of about 62.5 per cent. The other districts with high drop out rates are Medak, Nizamabad, Warangal, Khammam, Ranga Reddy and Nalgonda. It is striking that Nellore recorded high drop out rate of 43.8 per cent, though it is a part of highly

Table 14. Drop Out Rates at Primary Education Stage: 2000-01

Region	All Boys	All Girls	S. C. Boys	S. C. Girls	S. T. Boys	S. T. Girls	All Total	S. C. Total	S. T. Total
Coastal Andhra	29.4	28.2	33.0	36.8	51.3	57.7	30.3	34.9	54.3
Telangana (excl Hyd)	49.8	49.3	54.9	56.5	70.3	77.8	49.6	55.6	73.1
Telangana	45.8	44.8	53.2	53.2	65.9	71.8	45.3	56.6	68.1
Rayalaseema	22.6	25.5	29.2	35.3	35.4	44.6	24.0	32.1	39.7
North Coastal Andhra	24.9	27.3	25.5	28.5	45.6	56.8	26.1	27.0	50.9
South Coastal Andhra	31.7	28.7	36.8	40.9	54.1	58.1	32.4	38.8	56.0
North Telangana	48.7	47.9	53.3	54.8	69.5	76.3	48.4	54.0	72.0
South Telangana (excl Hyd)	51.1	50.9	57.0	58.5	71.3	79.7	51.0	57.6	74.4
Hyderabad	10.2	4.4	37.2	23.7	26.7	17.9	7.3	65.2	23.0
State	37.2	37.1	42.8	45.3	63.2	69.0	37.1	44.0	65.8
C. V. (%)	40.7	45.8	32.0	30.8	30.0	28.7	40.3	31.1	28.6

Note: Dropout rate is calculated as simple average of district-wise drop out rates in the region.
Source: Selected Educational Statistics, Commissioner of School Education, Hyderabad.

developed region. The levels of drop out across regions indicate that the reasons are complex and deserve special attention. Generally, child labour is treated as an important factor for primary drop out. But the work participation rate among out of school children in the primary school age are found to be only at 4.8 per cent, indicating that 95.2 per cent of the children not attending school are not working. They are entering labour market only after 11 years of age. This indicates that primary education is not properly organized to stop the children, especially first generation learners, from dropping out of school (Subrahmanyam and Jagan Mohan Reddy, 2002).

8. STATUS OF WOMEN AND CHILDREN

Status of women is examined with the help of sex ratio and work participation rates. Child mortality rate is used as the indicator for status of children (Tables 15&16). Sex ratio in Andhra Pradesh is 978 in 2001. It is the highest in North Coastal Andhra at 1001 and the lowest in Hyderabad. These two regions have extreme values due to migration, the former has out migration and the latter has in-migration. Migration, being sex-specific, influences sex ratios both the sending and receiving regions. The high sex ratio in North Coastal Andhra may also be due to high proportion of tribal population. South Telangana also has low sex ratio because migrants into Hyderabad stay outside the city, which comes under Ranga Reddy or Medak districts. North Telangana has high sex ratio (900) and South Coastal Andhra stands next to it (981). On the other hand, Rayalaseema has low sex ratio, despite no in-migration into the region. Thus, the two agriculturally developed regions have high sex ratio without much impact from migration.

Sex ratio increased at the State level by six points between 1991 and 2001. All the regions, except South Coastal Andhra and South Telangana, showed significant rise. Very strikingly, the improvement is very high (12 points) in Hyderabad region and low in the adjacent South Telangana region. It appears that all recent migration is into Ranga Reddy and Medak areas in the vicinity of Hyderabad. Rayalaseema and North Telangana have high improvement in sex ratio.

Though improvement in sex ratio indicates improvement in the status of woman, sex ratio in the 0-6 age group declined significantly (11 points) at the State level. It is striking that all the regions experienced this decline. However, the decline is steep in South Telangana, North Telangana, North Coastal Andhra and Hyderabad. Migration is not expected to have any influence on this decline. Decline in sex ratio clearly shows deterioration in the status of woman. Sex ratio improvement is due to higher resistance of women for diseases. In each region, certain districts are showing abnormal decline in juvenile sex ratio. Vizianagaram, East Godavari, Guntur, Cuddapah, Mahabubnagar, Medak, Nalgonda, Adilabad and Warangal experienced steep decline in juvenile sex ratio.

Table 15. Sex Ratio, Juvenile Sex Ratio and Child Mortality Rate

Region	Sex Ratio		Juvenile Sex Ratio		Child Mortality Rate
	1991	2001	1991	2001	1991
Coastal Andhra	984	986	977	969	74
Telangana (excl Hyd)	971	977	980	965	66
Telangana	967	973	978	963	62
Rayalaseema	955	970	963	955	72
North Coastal Andhra	993	1001	988	976	100
South Coastal Andhra	981	981	973	966	61
North Telangana	980	990	980	966	61
South Telangana (excl Hyd)	962	963	979	963	72
Hyderabad	933	945	963	951	25
State	972	978	975	964	68
C. V. (%)	2.2	2.0	1.4	1.0	-

Work participation rate of females is 43.2 in rural areas and 12.6 in urban areas. North Telangana and South Telangana have high participation rates and South Coastal Andhra has the lowest. As expected, higher per capita income is associated with lower work participation rates among females. The increase in participation rates of females in the State, despite the rise in per capita income, needs further investigation.

Child mortality is the lowest in Hyderabad at 25 per thousand live births. Among the remaining five regions, the incidence is the highest in North Coastal Andhra at 100. South Telangana and Rayalaseema have the same incidence of 72 and South Coastal Andhra and North Telangana have the lowest incidence at 61. There is positive association between incidence of rural poverty and child mortality. The agriculturally prosperous districts have the lowest incidence of child mortality.

Table 16. Work Participation Rate among Females

Region	Rural		Urban	
	1991	2001	1991	2001
Coastal Andhra	39.0	39.8	12.6	13.2
Telangana (excl Hyd)	46.8	47.7	13.4	13.6
Telangana	46.8	47.7	11.0	11.7
Rayalaseema	41.7	44.5	12.9	15.2
North Coastal Andhra	44.9	43.7	10.8	11.2
South Coastal Andhra	37.0	38.4	13.3	14.0
North Telangana	47.5	48.2	14.1	14.4
South Telangana (excl Hyd)	45.9	47.2	12.6	12.6
Hyderabad	-	-	7.4	8.8
State	42.5	43.2	11.9	12.6
C. V. (%)	14.4	15.6	26.0	21.3

9. HUMAN DEVELOPMENT INDEX

The Human Development Report of the United Nations Development Programme (UNDP) uses Human Development Index (HDI) as a summary measure of human development in a country. The index measures the average achievements in a country in three dimensions namely, a long and healthy life as measured by life expectancy at birth, knowledge as measured by the adult literacy rate (with two-thirds weight) and the combined primary, secondary and tertiary gross enrollment ratio (with one-third weight) and a decent standard of living as measured by Gross Domestic District Product (GDPP) per capita. A dimension index is generated for each of these three indicators using minimum and maximum values (goal posts) and then HDI is then calculated as a simple average of the three dimension indices:

$$\text{Dimension index} = \frac{\text{actual value} - \text{minimum value}}{\text{maximum value} - \text{minimum value}}$$

Using the methodology adopted by the UNDP, HDI is computed for each of the 23 districts in the State and also for the six regions. However, variables used in the calculation of the index are slightly different. As data on expectation of life at birth is not available at district level, Child (0-4 age group) mortality rate (CMR) is used in its place. Since low child

Table 17. Human Development Index: 2001

District	Education Index	Health Index	Standard of Living Index	HDI	Rank
Srikakulam	0.559	0.668	0.174	0.467	20
Vizianagaram	0.518	0.556	0.226	0.433	21
Visakhapatnam	0.595	0.761	0.813	0.723	4
North Coastal Andhra	0.564	0.662	0.466	0.564	F
East Godavari	0.655	0.795	0.534	0.662	11
West Godavari	0.740	0.810	0.563	0.704	6
Krishna	0.699	0.922	0.619	0.747	3
Guntur	0.628	0.917	0.586	0.710	5
Prakasam	0.579	0.839	0.373	0.597	14
Nellore	0.659	0.849	0.540	0.683	7
South Coastal Andhra	0.662	0.855	0.543	0.687	B
Chittoor	0.675	0.883	0.474	0.677	9
Cuddapah	0.64	0.893	0.368	0.634	12
Anantapur	0.567	0.717	0.400	0.560	17
Kurnool	0.544	0.707	0.378	0.543	18
Rayalaseema	0.605	0.800	0.408	0.604	D
Mahbubnagar	0.455	0.683	0.156	0.431	22
Rangareddy	0.663	0.888	0.763	0.771	1
Medak	0.532	0.834	0.874	0.747	2
Nalgonda	0.578	0.795	0.496	0.623	13
South Telangana(Excl Hyd)	0.559	0.800	0.441	0.600	E
Nizamabad	0.533	0.863	0.311	0.569	15
Adilabad	0.535	0.854	0.297	0.562	16
Karimnagar	0.560	0.946	0.534	0.680	8
Warangal	0.584	0.771	0.246	0.534	19
Khammam	0.577	0.829	0.586	0.664	10
North Telangana	0.560	0.853	0.419	0.611	C
Hyderabad	0.790	1.029	0.656	0.825	A
Coefficient of Variation (%)	12.9	12.8	41.4	16.9	-

Note: 1. Literacy data relates to 2001, gross domestic district products (GDDP) to triennium ending 1999-2000 and CMR for 1991.
2. A, B, C, D, E and F represent ranking of the regions in descending order of development.

mortality rate indicates better health, the dimension index for long and healthy life is derived by subtracting dimension index of CMR from unity. Literacy rate alone is used in calculating the dimension index of knowledge as enrollment data available from school records gives a misleading picture of educational performance. The HDI index for each region is derived from the dimension indices calculated for the region. The goalposts for literacy are taken as 100 for maximum and zero for minimum. The goalposts for

CMR are taken as 205 and 31, the extreme values of child mortality rates observed across districts in India. The goalposts for standard of living are taken as Rs. 15,000 and Rs. 5000, which represent 1.5 times and one half of the average value of per capita gross district product for the period under consideration (Table 17).

While the coefficient of variation is 13 per cent for both education and health, it is as high as 41 per cent for standard of living. Hyderabad district, the sixth region in the State, occupies the top position. This high position is due to its top position in education and health among the districts in the State. Though the index of standard of living is higher than the indices for other regions, it is below the values for Medak, Visakhapatnam and Ranga Reddy districts. Among the other five regions, South Coastal Andhra is at the top and North Coastal Andhra is at the bottom. Srikakualam and Vizianagaram show very poor performance in North Coastal Andhra, occupying 21st and 22nd positions among the districts. All the districts in South Coastal Andhra show good performance in health and education. But Prakasam district lags far behind the other districts as well as the State average in standard of living.

North Telangana occupies the second position among the five regions. But the performance in standard of living is highly divergent across the five districts in the region. Rayalaseema and South Telangana occupy the third and fourth positions with negligible difference in the index. However, there is a difference between these two regions in the pattern of development. While Rayalaseema is more developed than South Telangana in education, the latter has higher per capita income. But development of South Telangana is highly lop-sided. Mahabubnagar in the region occupies the lowest position in all the three indicators and Medak shows very poor performance in education. On the other hand, Medak occupies the top position in per capita income.

9. CONCLUSIONS AND POLICY IMPLICATIONS

Balanced regional development is going to become the major issue in future because of the sharp increase in inter-State inequality in the era of liberalization. The experience at sub-State level may also be the same. But policy interventions can be easily implemented at sub-State level because all regions are under a single administrative control.

The ranking of the regions on the basis of per capita gross domestic regional product shows that Hyderabad (including Ranga Reddy) occupies top position during 1995-2000. Among the other five regions, South Coastal Andhra is at the top and North Telangana at the bottom. South Telangana occupies the middle position with North Coastal Andhra above it and Rayalaseema below. The changes in the relative positions are interesting. Hyderabad improved its relative position till mid-seventies and then started losing with the development of areas close to Hyderabad, which fall under South Telangana. South Coastal Andhra has been losing its position continuously because of the slow growth of agriculture as well as industry. With high industrial development in Medak since 1980s, South Telangana improved to the third rank from the bottom. Similarly, North Coastal Andhra improved from bottom to second position after seventies with rapid industrial development in Visakhapatnam. In this process, Rayalaseema slipped gradually from second to fourth and North Telangana slipped from fourth to fifth. Inequality in per capita income declined significantly with a higher growth of low income regions than high income regions. There is an increase in the inequality among the districts in the nineties.

Regional disparities in land productivity declined in the last four decades, but increased between 1980s and 1990s. This reversal in the trend can be attributed to lack of public investment in irrigation and the consequent stagnation in irrigated area. Irrigation expansion was all time high in the eighties and surface irrigation contributed about 40 per cent for this expansion. On the other hand, the nineties witnessed steep decline in surface irrigated area. While this change helped in reducing regional disparities, it is not conducive for sustainability. The neglect of surface irrigation is reflected in low yields in tank irrigated areas. Rice and sugarcane in North Coastal Andhra, almost all the crops grown in South Telangana and groundnut in Rayalaseema showed low yields as compared to other regions. Because of lack of irrigation, dry areas in low rainfall areas are left fallow and this has led to increase in the extent of fallow land.

The State is highly backward in manufacturing sector. The growth rate of manufacturing workers is lower than the growth of total workers. Further, regional disparities in manufacturing sector are widening. North Telangana has high growth of workers, but has the lowest capital intensity. On the other hand, South Telangana has the highest capital intensity. Most of the manufacturing activity in the State is traditional. Modern industry accounts for only about 28.6 per cent without much change in the nineties. However, modern sector is concentrated in certain regions. North Coastal Andhra has the highest concentration of modern sector with a share of 62 per cent in total workers followed by South Telangana. Modern sector is almost absent in North Telangana. Both the agriculturally prosperous regions have not gone beyond agro-based industrial development.

Incidence of Rural poverty based on Head Count declined in all the regions. Both the agriculturally prosperous regions have lower incidence of rural poverty than the incidence at the State level. North Coastal Andhra has the highest incidence followed by South Telangana. There is a clear increase in regional disparities in the incidence of poverty measured by the Head Count ratio. Regional disparities in literacy rates declined in the nineties because of the rapid improvement in literacy rate in the two low literacy regions viz., South Telangana and North Telangana. Rayalaseema showed poor performance. South Telangana and North Telangana have high drop out rates of more than 50 per cent. Caste differences in drop out rates are more significant than gender differences. The rate is as high as 66 per cent among Scheduled Tribes.

What are the remedial measures for achieving balanced regional development? Given the slow growth of the manufacturing sector, the solution in the immediate future lies in the development of agriculture. Irrigation should play a major role in the development process. Public investment in surface irrigation, especially canal irrigation, should be increased. Priority should go to presently backward regions and low rainfall regions. In the absence of surface irrigation expansion, sustainability of the present well irrigation in low rainfall areas is doubtful. Since North Telangana receives high rainfall, renovation of tanks is needed for conservation of water. The region also has heavy pressure on land. Though productivity improvement solves the problem of poverty to some extent, reduction of pressure on land is needed. This is possible through the development of non-farm sector in the region. The situation in Rayalaseema can improve only by exploiting the irrigation potential available in the region. Too much exploitation of ground water is already creating problems. Expansion of surface irrigation wherever possible and implementation of watershed programmes is the only way for the development of the area. Since water is scarce in the region, incentives should be provided to use water saving technology and crop systems. South Telangana requires partly implementation of new irrigation schemes and partly renovation of existing irrigation sources. South Coastal Andhra should focus on productivity improvement and rural diversification to reduce pressure on land. On the other hand, North Telangana, South Telangana and Rayalaseema should focus on utilisation of fallow land. In respect of social sector, the focus has to be on the backward Mandals to bring them on par with the district level first. The most backward districts in respect of important agricultural and social variables have to be identified and programmes should be implemented with close monitoring of progress.

References

Govida Rao, M. R. T. Shand, K P Kalirajan (1999), "Convergence of Incomes Across Indian States: A Divergent View", *Economic and Political Weekly*, Vol. 34, No. 13, March 28,

GOAP (1999), *Andhra Pradesh – Vision 2020*, Government of Andhra Pradesh, Hyderabad

GOI (1993), *Report of the Expert Group on Estimation of Proportion and Number of Poor*, Perspective Planning Division, Government of India, New Delhi, July.

Krishna Rao, Y. V. and S. Subrahmanyam (eds.) (2002), *Development of Andhra Pradesh: 1956 – 2001: A Study of Regional Disparities*, N. R. R. Research Centre, Hyderabad.

Mahendra Dev, S. and C. Ravi (2003), "Macro-economic Performance and Policies", *Economic and Political Weekly*, Vol. 38, Nos. 12&13, March.

Mitra, G. K. (2002), "Regional Disparities in Rural Poverty and Levels of Living", in Krishna Rao, Y. V. and S. Subrahmanyam (eds), *op. cit.*

Myrdal, G. (1957), *Economic Theory and Under Developed Regions*, University of Stockholm, Vora & Co. Publishers, Bombay.

Reddy, R. V. (1991), "Under-utilisation of Land in Andhra Pradesh: Extent and Determinants", *Indian Journal of Agricultural Economics*, Vol. 46, No. 4.

Subrahmanyam, S. and N. Rajagopala Rao (2000), "Liberalization and Income Convergence Across Indian States", *Working Paper* No. 36, January, Centre for Economic and Social Studies, Hyderabad.

Subrahmanyam, S. (2003), "Literacy and School Education in Andhra Pradesh", Paper presented at the Second Development Convention held at Institute for Social and Economic Change, Bangalore, 19-21 February.

Subrahmanyam, S. and G. Jagan Mohan Reddy (2002), "Literacy and School Education in Andhra Pradesh", in Krishna Rao, Y. V. and S. Subrahmanyam (eds.) *op. cit.*

Appendix A. Classification of Andhra Pradesh into Five Regions and Districts Falling Under the Regions

Region	Districts
North Coastal Andhra	Srikakulam, Vizianagaram, Vishakhapatnam
South Coastal Andhra	East Godavari, West Godavari, Krishna, Guntur, Prakasam, Nellore
Rayalaseema	Chittor, Cuddapah, Anantapur, Kurnool
South Telangana	Rangareddy, Mahabubnagar, Medak, Nalgonda
North Telangana	Nizamabad, Adilabad, Karimnagar, Warangal, Khammam
Hyderabad	Hyderabad
Coastal Andhra	North Coastal Andhra, South Coastal Andhra
Telangana	North Telangana, South Telangana

Appendix B. Select Indicators of Development

District	Sex Ratio 2001	Sex Ratio Increase In 90's	Density Per KM² 2001	Urbanization (%) 2001	CMR 1991	Crop Output TE 1998-99 Per hec. % to Total	Crop Output TE 1998-99 Rural per capita % to Total	Fallow Land* (%) 2000-01	% of N I A Triennium nding 1980-81	% of N I A Triennium nding 1990-91	% of N I A Triennium nding 2000-01
Srikakulam	976	-11	433	11.0	99	81.0	58.1	11.0	52.5	56.9	58.0
Vizayanagaram	981	-15	343	18.4	122	82.5	76.1	5.7	40.5	43.2	42.9
Visakhapatnam	973	-12	340	40.0	80	86.2	67.5	7.1	37.1	39.0	34.9
East Godavari	978	-16	451	23.3	73	146.8	88.0	12.5	65.5	62.6	64.7
West Godavari	977	-7	490	20.0	70	196.7	146.2	7.0	77.2	96.4	79.7
Krishna	959	-5	483	32.4	47	179.2	157.5	9.9	65.9	72.8	66.8
Guntur	956	-14	387	28.0	48	162.6	164.7	5.3	52.5	59.0	57.3
Prakasham	966	-4	173	15.3	64	95.0	103.2	26.2	24.1	31.6	34.7
Nellore	955	19	203	23.0	62	135.7	110.7	31.0	67.5	80.4	79.6
Chittoor	959	-10	247	22.0	55	119.4	103.5	32.3	30.8	32.1	38.9
Cuddapah	952	-16	168	23.3	53	62.2	63.6	24.6	28.9	30.8	36.4
Anantapuram	963	1	190	25.3	89	59.3	111.5	17.2	12.9	16.1	14.0
Kurnool	944	-11	199	23.0	91	58.7	113.0	22.3	12.4	16.5	19.9
Mahabubnagar	957	-24	190	11.0	96	48.3	59.3	32.4	14.2	17.9	20.8
Rangareddy	969	-3	468	53.3	54	45.7	43.3	38.7	14.3	20.6	25.5
Medak	964	-17	274	14.4	65	75.5	73.8	30.5	22.5	29.4	30.8
Nalgonda	962	-19	227	13.3	73	96.7	94.0	45.4	28.4	34.8	42.1
Nizamabad	966	-14	294	18.0	59	155.3	102.0	42.1	46.8	57.0	65.5
Adilabad	964	-22	154	26.5	61	40.7	62.7	32.0	7.0	9.6	14.6
Karimnagar	977	-3	294	19.5	42	160.3	114.0	39.5	32.7	59.0	67.7
Warangal	955	-22	252	19.2	78	124.4	109.5	25.8	27.5	54.2	57.8
Khammam	968	-12	160	19.8	66	101.9	117.8	17.7	20.3	38.6	43.4
Hyderabad	951	-12	16988	100.0	25	-	-	-	-	-	-
Andhra Pradesh	964	-11	275	27.1	68	100.0 (4580)	100.0 (915)	25.1	32.1	39.4	41.0

contd...

Appendix B. Select Indicators of Development (Contd.)

District	Drop Out Rates			Tank Area			Canal Area		
	All Castes	SCs	STs	1980-81	1990-91	2000-01	1980-81	1990-91	2000-01
	Total	Total	Total	'000' Hectares			'000' Hectares		
Srikakulam	22.5	26.9	50.7	100.15	76.9	80.1	74.1	102.1	91.9
Vizayanagaram	21.3	20.6	49.1	100.8	97.1	83.2	22.1	31.8	39.3
Visakhapatnam	34.5	33.5	53.0	42.3	46.6	35.8	47.8	52.8	46.5
East Godavari	30.6	36.4	60.5	42.9	42.5	34.5	207.4	202.1	180.6
West Godavari	29.0	36.6	44.7	49.5	48.0	34.5	216.7	212.4	188.7
Krishna	26.2	32.6	49.8	44.7	38.7	34.4	270.4	277.4	232.7
Guntur	33.0	40.2	56.0	3.0	5.9	5.8	292.7	316.9	304.5
Prakasham	32.1	39.1	55.0	22.2	36.6	30.9	78.7	89.6	72.3
Nellore	43.5	48.0	69.8	83.9	100.4	62.3	69.4	84.7	68.0
Chittoor	26.9	35.8	54.6	28.9	45.0	25.0	5.6	1.4	0.9
Cuddapah	21.9	31.1	41.6	10.0	18.0	8.1	23.0	21.3	20.6
Anantapuram	29.0	36.9	33.5	12.8	5.1	6.1	31.2	35.7	30.4
Kurnool	18.2	24.7	29.2	9.1	14.9	16.3	84.4	88.8	72.6
Mahabubnagar	62.2	67.1	83.1	47.2	42.8	18.9	24.1	20.1	17.5
Rangareddy	43.8	54.0	73.3	7.8	11.9	6.6	2.9	2.5	2.3
Medak	58.2	65.2	76.3	47.2	50.7	18.6	7.5	5.6	3.0
Nalgonda	40.0	44.3	64.8	15.2	23.0	15.2	94.7	95.0	72.0
Nizamabad	50.1	59.2	75.6	32.4	36.9	22.4	80.0	64.1	38.4
Adilabad	62.7	61.3	83.8	20.4	23.0	22.0	16.6	18.9	18.9
Karimnagar	34.1	46.9	64.2	39.6	55.3	34.7	21.6	72.4	79.2
Warangal	48.1	53.5	73.0	79.0	95.3	78.1	0.8	3.5	2.7
Khammam	46.8	49.2	63.6	60.6	53.4	53.00	20.9	69.7	66.3
Hyderabad	7.3	65.2	23.0	-	-	-	-	-	-
Andhra Pradesh	37.1	44.0	65.8	899.9	967.8	726.8	1692.7	1868.9	1649.4

Note: * Relates to Net Area Sown + Fallow Land. C M R: Child Mortality Rate.
Figures in brackets are absolute values at 1980-81 prices.

PART - V

ENVIRONMENT

20

Environment and Sustainable Development: Status and Strategies

V. Ratna Reddy and
Bhagirath Behera

1. INTRODUCTION

Integrating environmental concerns with developmental issues has become *sine qua non* of policy planning. There is widespread agreement that development is critically linked with the state of environment and vice versa. Environmental degradation, in most of the developing countries, is becoming a major constraint on future growth and development. The real costs of environmental degradation are increasingly felt in terms of health costs, declining productivities of natural resources like land, water, grass lands, etc. The impacts are widespread and conspicuous in land hunger agrarian economies like India. Though the impacts, in terms of loss of production, are not discernible at the macro level, the problem is of very serious concern at the regional level. In fact, it is observed that environmental degradation is reaching irreversible levels (desertification) in some regions of India, especially in arid and semi-arid tracts. On the other hand, the replacement costs (in terms of enhanced input use, abatement and conservation costs), are mounting and would make a dent in the national income if these costs were taken into account. Unless effective measures are adopted to arrest the degradation, achieving sustainable development would remain a distant dream. For, sustainable development requires keeping the natural capital (K_n) constant in the long run. More importantly, the environmental degradation would thwart the goals of food self-sufficiency and food security in the medium run apart from vitiating the inter-generational equity (inter and intra regional).

This paper is an attempt to look at the status of environment from a regional perspective. Here, we intend to examine the trends (across the years for which data are available) and patterns of natural resource degradation across the regions of Andhra Pradesh in order to understand their likely impact on different sectors of the economy. Specific objectives of the study include: a) to provide a comprehensive view on the status of environment in terms of important natural resources at the state and sub-regional levels, b) estimating the costs of environmental degradation to the extent possible, and c) establish linkages between degradation and development and suggest strategies for sustainable development. The study relies mostly on the available secondary sources at the state and district level apart from using the case studies from the existing literature. The scope of the study is constrained by the availability of the data. At the outset it may be noted that environmental data generation in the state is still at an infant stage. An attempt is made here to compile the data from all the available sources in order to make it as comprehensive as possible. Given the data constraints the main focus of the study is on the following resources: land, water, forests, livestock, fisheries, minerals, industrial pollution (air and water) and urban environment (solid waste, vehicular pollution, etc.).

2. LAND AND WATER

As far as sustainability is concerned, land and water resources are inter linked. Poor management of one resource could lead to the degradation of both the resources. For instance, improper water management can lead to salinity, alkalinity and desertification of soils. Similarly, intensive land use practices (high fertiliser and pesticide use) will lead to contamination of ground as well as surface water bodies. Therefore, an integrated approach is needed for the sustainable management of land and water resources.

Land Resources

There have been marginal changes in land utilization in Andhra Pradesh between 1960-61 and 1998-99 (Table. 1). Area under irrigation and cropping intensity continued to increase in the state during 1980s and 90s. Area under current fallows in the state is higher (9 percent) when compared to all India (4 percent). This indicates that the extent of land under-utilisation is more in Andhra Pradesh. Area under current fallows reflects the year-to-year fluctuations in cropped area due to rainfall. Area under forests is higher in the state when compared to all India while area under common pool resources is more or less at the same level. Common pool resources include cultivable waste, pastures and grazing lands and other fallow lands.

Qualitative aspects are equally, if not more, important as far as natural resources are concerned. For, it is now common knowledge that common pool resources (CPRs) are declining, quantitatively as well as qualitatively. Household's dependence on these resources is also declining. Similarly, degradation of croplands is being noticed in the recent years. Land degradation takes place largely in the form of soil erosion due to water. Water related erosion is in the form of direct and indirect erosion. Direct erosion is due to floods and surface run off while indirect erosion is due to excess or inappropriate use of water resulting in salinity and alkalinity. Another water related degradation is from industrial pollution.

Table 1. Changes in Land Utilization in Andhra Pradesh
(in Million Hectares)

(Three-year averages)

Classification	1960-61	1970-71	1980-81	1990-91	2000-01
ANDHRA PRADESH					
1. Geographical Area	27.42	27.44	27.44	27.44	27.44
2. Forests	5.97 (22)	6.34 (23)	6.18 (22.5)	6.27 (23)	6.20 (23)
3. Not available for cultivation	4.11 (15)	4.35 (16)	4.50 (16)	4.44 (16)	4.62 (17)
4. Misc. Tree Crops & Groves	0.29 (neg)	0.29 (neg)	0.27 (neg)	0.26 (neg)	0.27 (neg)
5. Common pool resources	3.52 (13)	3.04 (11)	3.19 (12)	3.01 (11)	2.82 (10)
6. Current Fallows	2.23 (08)	2.07 (7.5)	2.27 (08)	2.60 (09)	2.31 (08)
7. Net Area Sown	10.74 (39)	11.36 (41)	11.03 (40)	10.84 (39)	11.22 (41)
8. Cropping Intensity (%)	110	112	115	120	123
ALL INDIA					
1. Geographical Area	328.73	328.73	328.73	328.73	328.73
2. Forests	54.69 (17)	66.38 (20)	67.34 (20)	67.99 (21)	68.83 (21)
3. Not available for cultivation	50.52 (15)	45.22 (14)	39.70 (12)	40.92 (12)	42.39 (13)
4. Misc. Tree Crops & Groves	4.52 (01)	4.45 (01)	3.56 (01)	3.71 (01)	3.49 (01)
5. Common pool resources	32.68 (10)	37.72 (11)	38.12 (12)	36.14 (11)	35.16 (11)
6. Current Fallows	11.26 (03)	12.90 (04)	14.15 (04)	14.13 (04)	13.81 (04)
7. Net Area Sown	134.94 (41)	139.29 (42)	141.35 (43)	142.09 (43)	142.21 (43)
8. Cropping Intensity (%)	115	118	123	131	132

Note: Figures in brackets are respective percentages to geographical area. All India figures in last column pertain to 1995-96.

Source: Economic Survey 2001-02, Government of AP. Agricultural Statistics at a glance, 1996 and CMIE, 1999.

Industrial effluents pollute surface (rivers, tanks, etc) as well as subsurface (groundwater) water bodies. The use of these polluted water sources is resulting in severe damage to crop lands with significant decline in yield rates. Though the magnitude (in terms of area affected) of this problem is on a lower scale, its economic impact could be substantial, if not equivalent to other water related degradation. Agrochemical degradation is also looming large, as the impacts are getting conspicuous year after year. Punjab and Haryana (the prime green revolution belt) are experiencing declining wheat yields due to soil degradation, which is a consequence of excess and improper fertiliser and pesticide use. Wind erosion is another major problem though it is limited to only three states. On the other hand, CPRs, especially grazing and pasturelands, are degraded due to improper use and management practices owing to their public good nature. Most of these problems, except perhaps wind erosion, are manmade and are likely to aggravate along with the development activities.

At the aggregate level there appears to be no warning signal of an impending environmental problem relating to soil degradation. However, as mentioned earlier the problems are micro specific and hence may not be reflected at the macro level. Moreover, degradation may not reflect in yield rates but in increased input use, which will result in declining profit margins of the farmers. In Andhra Pradesh, while the crop yields have less than doubled during the last two decades, consumption of fertilizers has gone up by more than three times. Therefore, it is necessary to examine the actual extent of land degradation in the state.

As far as actual degradation is concerned about 32 lakh hectares of land in the state is degraded in one form or other while about 36 lakh hectares come under wasteland, as per the National Remote Sensing Agency estimates in 1988-89 (Table 2). Wastelands are not necessarily degraded lands, but are not used for cultivation purposes presently. The extent of wastelands indicates the potential for extensive cultivation in the state. Degraded lands are part of wastelands that need protective measures in order to keep the land quality intact. From the sustainability point of view degraded lands are of prime importance. The main reasons for degradation in the state are water and wind erosion (land with or without scrubs). The extent of degradation in the sate accounts for 10 percent of the geographical area and 19 percent of the cultivable area. Across the districts, extent of degradation ranges from about 3 percent in west Godavari district to about 50 percent in Visakhapatnam district. There appears to be no relationship between the extent of degradation and level of development of the district. For, some of the backward and poverty ridden districts such as Medak and Adilabad are showing lower levels of degradation compared to a developed district like east Godavari[1]. In fact, all the development indicators such as irrigation, fertiliser use, availability of credit, output per hectare are positively related with the extent of degradation though not significant. This indicates that development does not guarantee sustainability. However, on the whole, incidence of degradation seems to be more in less irrigated districts / regions like Rayalaseema and Telangana.

Given the extent of degradation we have estimated the costs of degradation using the treatment costs of degraded lands. It may be noted that these figures pertain to 1988-89 level of degradation and costs. Treatment costs across agroclimatic regions range from Rs. 600 to Rs. 1500 per hectare i.e. on an average Rs. 732 for the country as whole. At the average level the costs of degradation work out to be about Rs. 2328 lakhs (Table 2). This amounts to 1.2 percent of the state gross domestic product, 3.63 percent of states gross domestic product from agriculture and 0.85 percent of the asset value of land. These are annualised costs, which means that state's GDP will be higher by 1.2 percent if there is no land degradation.

Hitherto agriculture in less endowed (dry land) regions has been the victim of the defective policies. This neglect is mainly due to the concentration of public resources in the well- endowed regions for meeting the country's food requirements through irrigation development and promotion of green revolution technologies. While the policy bias has paid off in terms of meeting the country's food demands in the short run, it is

Table 2. Extent of Land Degradation in Andhra Pradesh

District	Extent of Degradation (ha)	% of Degraded land	% of waste land	Replacement Costs of Degradation (Rs.)#
Srikakulam	49876	13.24	13.72	36509232
Vizianagaram	65640	17.95	58.21	48048480
Visakhapatnam	195491	49.97	16.78	143099412
East godavari	84454	14.96	16.38	61820328
West godavari	14777	2.65	2.75	10816764
Krishna	55387	8.72	9.35	40543284
Guntur	137817	17.46	24.01	100882044
Prakasam	231840	23.88	27.35	169706880
Nellore	293455	43.01	47.20	214809060
Chittoor	266910	36.11	36.45	195378120
Ananthapur	289644	20.96	23.27	212019408
Cudapah	297540	48.07	57.79	217799280
Kurnool	94476	7.61	14.08	69156432
Karimnagar	95058	12.14	14.15	69582456
Mahaboobnagar	213323	28.86	30.51	156152436
Medak	64539	4.48	7.01	47242548
Nalgonda	187952	16.31	18.21	137580864
Nizamabad	61698	12.22	15.60	45162936
Ranga reddy	95229	17.00	19.70	69707628
Warangal	107180	13.35	14.39	78455760
Adilabad	98500	11.83	12.54	72102000
Khammam	179642	28.55	28.87	131497944
Andhra Pradesh	3180428	18.98	21.69	2328073296

For a detailed methodology on Replacement costs see Reddy (2000).
Source: NRSA (1995).

proving to be unsustainable, economically as well as environmentally, in the long run. State can ill-afford to continue this bias, lest it will not only aggravate the existing regional inequalities but also threaten the food security. For, development of dry regions, in terms of enhancing crop yields, holds the key for future food security. Besides, these regions are increasingly being confronted with environmental problems such as wind and soil erosion. In fact, it is feared that degradation is reaching irreversible levels in some specific locations. Andhra Pradesh is one of the first states to address this problem on a massive scale, which we will discuss later.

Water Resources

Water is among the most ill managed resources resulting in severe scarcity, both for drinking and irrigation, as well as environmental problems such as water logging in endowed regions and desertification in fragile regions. Andhra Pradesh is experiencing three types of environmental problems as far as water resources are concerned. Firstly, large and medium irrigation projects are facing the problem of under-utilisation of the created capacities in the recent years. This is mainly attributed to the mismanagement of the distribution systems resulting in siltation, water logging, poor drainage, etc. Consequently water availability is increasingly shrinking for the tail end and middle reaches of the distributory systems. The gap between capacity created and actual utilization increased from 23.5 percent in 1950-51, to 46.2 per cent in 1991-92 and to 56.4 percent in 1995-96 for major and medium irrigation projects (Reddy, 1998). Minor irrigation received low priority during the post independence period though it is less expensive. Development of well irrigation was totally left to private sector resulting in inter and intra regional disparities in resource distribution and development. Instead groundwater should be treated as common pool resource and institutional arrangement ought to be made to ensure equitable distribution of this scarce resource.

Secondly, the age-old water harvesting and storage systems such as tanks and ponds are becoming the things of past due to the absence of any maintenance by the State or civil society. Traditionally local people through institutional arrangements managed these systems. These traditional systems of resource management have degenerated over time due to the State interventions and due to the socio, political and economic dynamics at the village level. As a result irrigation under these water bodies too experienced a growing gap between capacities, often created much before independence, and the net area irrigated. In fact, by 1998-99, the net area irrigated by tanks was just 8.10 lakh hectares, much less than the 10 lakh hectares potential inherited under tanks in 1950-51. Loss of capacity of the tanks is not only the loss of tank irrigation but also loss of groundwater recharge in the tank dominant regions, which are relatively dry and drought-prone and dependent on wells (Reddy, 1998). Thirdly, the decline in groundwater tables in some of the regions has become alarming in the recent years resulting in the widespread desertification. Well irrigation recorded a phenomenal rise during the last three decades, i.e., moved from third position to first position in terms of area irrigated by a single source. This coupled with the declining area under tanks is a recipe for disaster, creating enormous ecological and social problems.

The most strident consequence of the above three environmental problems is with regard to drinking water. Scarcity of surface water coupled with the degeneration of traditional water harvesting systems are resulting in serious water shortages i.e., declining per capita water availability and unhygienic water, especially in rural areas. It is often observed, especially in dry regions, that rural households spend substantial amounts of time in fetching water and even spend money on buying water. Compared at the all India level, Andhra Pradesh is doing better in terms of coverage of households by tap water. But it seems to be the worst hit as far as the actual availability of drinking water is concerned. For, 8 percent of the state's population has to manage with inadequate water in both rural and urban areas as against 3 percent at the all India level (Table 3). Besides, the increased use of agro-chemicals and urbanisation are rendering groundwater and surface water bodies like tanks unusable for drinking as well as irrigation purposes. The problems of industrial pollution are acutely felt in the villages surrounding the industrial townships (see the separate section in this regard). This has further reduced the quantity of usable water.

Table 3. Access to Safe Drinking Water

State / Country	% of HH with access to tap water		% of HH reporting inadequate water		% of HH managing with inadequate water	
	Rural	Urban	Rural	Urban	Rural	Urban
Andhra Pradesh	26.2	75.6	22.1	30.1	08	08
All India	18.7	70.1	13.0	14.9	3.1	2.6

Source: NSS 54th Round, January – June 1998, NSSO, GOI, July 1999.

Initiatives in Land Management[2]

Andhra Pradesh has adopted the watershed development programmes by strictly adhering to the new watershed guidelines since 1995-96[3]. Coverage of these programmes since inception (1995-96) till 2001-02 is presented in Table 4. As per the guidelines implementation of the watershed has to be completed in four years covering 500 hectares of area to be treated with an amount of Rs. 20 lakhs per watershed (Rs.4000 per hectare)[4]. Anantapur district receives Rs. 22.5 lakhs per watershed (Rs. 4500 per hectare) due to its severe agro-climatic conditions. The average area under watershed is about 500 hectares in line with the guidelines. However, there is a gap in terms of amount sanctioned and utilised by the watershed committees.

Twenty two districts are covered under this programme till 2001-02. In terms of distribution across districts, coverage is more in dry districts. Though there are variations across districts, the utilisation ratio is about 70 percent, which varies from 34 percent in West Godavari district to 102 percent in Ranga Reddy district. Till 2001-02 the proposed number of watersheds in the state were 7809 covering about 47 percent of the unirrigated area (Table 5). Though the coverage is impressive, it would have been better if some of the low irrigated districts like Ananthapur were given greater priority.

On the whole, the state government's approach to dry land agriculture is laudable. For, the numbers in terms of watersheds and area covered are impressive. Even the impact in terms of groundwater recharge, cropping pattern changes etc., seem to be impressive as compared to the

Table 4. Watershed Development Programme in Andhra Pradesh across Districts (1995-96 to 2001-02)

District	No. of Water-sheds	Area (ha)	Area per Watershed	Money Sanctioned (Rs '000')	Money spent (Rs '000')	% Utili-sation
1. Srikakulam	313	149313	477	893.19	570.86	64.0
2. Vizianagaram	138	61663	446	341.92	316.14	92.5
3. Visakhapatnam	97	55957	577	397.14	263.55	66.4
4. East Godavari	137	63102	461	416.13	329.36	79.1
5. W. Godavari	22	10606	482	80.19	27.60	34.4
6. Krishan	269	123901	461	308.77	161.71	52.4
7. Guntur	43	19806	461	267.05	122.50	45.9
8. Prakasam	597	289251	485	1362.96	1328.28	97.4
9. Nellore	277	127586	461	593.34	433.69	73.1
10. Chittoor	628	321185	511	1326.65	1295.21	97.6
11. Cuddupah	372	167828	451	843.09	747.79	88.7
12. Anantapur	838	371381	443	2889.17	1678.50	58.1
13. Kurnool	792	365917	462	2297.20	1353.56	58.9
14. Mahaboobnagar	864	371208	430	1972.00	1093.61	55.5
15. Ranga Reddy	411	194907	474	664.21	680.38	102.4
16. Medak	350	167126	478	963.60	517.51	53.7
17. Nizamabad	215	100844	469	139.24	115.16	82.7
18. Adilabad	504	265096	526	960.72	651.71	67.8
19. Karimnagar	90	44130	490	549.21	527.74	96.1
20. Warangal	131	60339	461	404.14	298.89	74.0
21. Khammam	210	61444	293	903.28	640.46	70.9
22. Nalgonda	669	314047	469	947.00	601.89	63.5
Andhra Pradesh	7809	3633860	465	19519.20	13756.10	70.5

Source: Status Report on Watersheds., October 2002, Commissioner of Rural development, Government of AP.

earlier programmes (Rao, 2000). It was observed in some of the best-implemented watersheds that the impact is clear in terms of improvements in livelihoods despite three below normal rainfall years. The externalities are conspicuous in the case of new watersheds when compared to the older ones (Reddy, et.al., 2001). In general, impact is visible in terms of availability of *insi tu* moisture and water for longer periods in the vicinity of check dams. In fact, some of the enterprising farmers are making use of it by planting horticultural crops in the, hitherto, degraded lands. While, there is no second opinion regarding the economic impact of watershed technology, as long as implemented properly, it is too early to capture this in a tangible way. Recent field studies clearly established that economic impact is visible in the places wherever Project Implementing Agency (PIA) is good (Reddy, et.al., 2001 and Reddy, 2000). Further, there are differences between the good PIAs (Such as RDT in Ananthapur, CEO-WCUSS in Kurnool, DDS in Medak and VIP in Mahaboobnagar) as far as economic impact is concerned. These differences may be explained in terms of modus operandi adopted by each PIA in implementing the watershed apart from the differences in the local endowments (Reddy, et. al, 2001).

Table 5. Coverage of Rain-fed Agriculture by the Watershed Programmes

District	GCA(ha)	GIA(ha)	% Irrigated	Unirrigated area(ha)	% Unirrigated area covered by WS prog.
1.Srikakulam	419907	200956	47.8	218951	68.2
2.Vizayanagaram	436235	158032	36.2	278203	22.1
.Visakhapatnam	441886	157848	35.7	284038	19.7
4.East Godavari	764914	468547	61.2	296367	21.3
5.West Godavari	696925	607265	87.1	89660	11.8
6.Krishna	714923	448875	62.1	266048	46.6
7.Guntur	864464	378837	43.8	485627	4.1
8.Prakasam	662078	223265	33.7	438813	65.5
9.Nellore	327421	252578	77.1	74843	***
10.Chittoor	481819	210709	43.7	271110	***
11.Cuddapah	456342	171453	37.5	284889	58.9
12.Anantapur	1102856	175276	15.8	929780	39.9
13.Kurnool	991843	220915	22.2	770928	47.5
14.Mahaboobnagar	976662	234605	23.5	762057	48.7
15.Ranga Reddy	325499	99474	30.5	226025	86.2
16.Medak	560565	198468	35.4	362097	46.2
17.Nizamabad	399234	297325	74.4	101909	98.9
18.Adilabad	558776	97768	17.5	461008	57.5
19.Karimnagar	572132	419761	73.3	152371	29.0
20.Warangal	640913	375381	58.5	265532	22.7
21.Khammam	471380	208860	44.3	262520	23.4
22.Nalgonda	658359	309819	47.0	348540	90.0
Andhra Pradesh	13545263	5916147	43.6	7629116	47.6

Note: *** figures are not consistent with the unirrigated area in these two districts, so avoid giving the figures.

Source: Season and Crop Report, 2001-2002, Directorate of Economics and Statistics, Hyderabad.

In the watersheds managed by long standing NGOs (PIA) groundwater improvement, availability of water and fodder for livestock, greenery, etc., are conspicuous. This, in general, has resulted in an overall positive environmental impact. From the field studies it is clear that bore-wells are proliferating rapidly, particularly on middle and wealthier farmers' lands. Many landowners are sinking bore-wells adjacent to the new check dams and tanks to take advantage of whatever increased water harvesting has occurred. Since most of the DPAP harvesting structures have only existed for the last few years the trend in water tables is as yet uncertain.

But, there is no sign at present of any attempts to harmonise the level of extraction with the level of recharge. On the whole, a more intensive approach rather than an extensive one would have been better as far as the impact is concerned. If uncorrected the programme, like many others, will fail to create any productive assets despite its grand objectives. It would be wise to use the available funds more intensively covering limited number of watersheds and area rather than spreading them thinly. In the former case implementation and monitoring will be much more effective (Reddy, 2000).

3. FORESTS, PASTURES AND BIO-DIVERSITY

Forest resources are among the most crucial links in the ecosystem. Apart from providing direct use values, forests provide numerous environmental benefits such as watershed protection, nutrient cycling, pollution control, micro-climatic regulation, carbon sequestration, etc. Degradation of these precious resources affects the economy and environment locally as well as globally. In fact, forest degradation could become a major constraint on future growth and development in most of the developing countries like India. The real costs of such degradation are increasingly felt in terms of declining productivities of inter linked natural resources such as land, water, grass lands, etc. Depletion of forest resources can be viewed from two angles, i.e., quantitative and qualitative. Hitherto quantitative aspects in terms of forest cover were given priority over qualitative aspects by researchers as well as policy makers. Recent years have shown an improvement in the area under forests, though contradictions still exist among different data sets. In Andhra Pradesh forest depletion is taking place quantitatively as well as qualitatively. Area under forest cover declined, though marginally, during the eighties and nineties when compared to 1970s (Table 1). Besides, the official statistics often over-estimate the area under forests and other common pool resources and under-estimate the net sown area as the official data does not reflect illegal encroachments.

As per the official estimates about 29 thousand hectares of forest area has been encroached and legalised till 1994. The main causes for the loss of forests include agriculture, irrigation projects, encroachments, etc., (Table 6). Between 1983-84 and 1991-92 about 30, 000 hectares of forests were lost due to developmental activities. Conversion of forestlands to agricultural uses was the major source of loss followed by mining (Singareni coal mines). Area lost due to encroachments remained constant because only the legalised encroachments are recorded here, while the illegal encroachments far exceeds the legalised encroachments. Area lost due to rehabilitation activities between the periods is negligible, though it accounts for the second largest component of the forest area lost.

Table 6. Loss of Forests in Andhra Pradesh (in hectares)

Purpose	Up to 1983-84	% to total area lost	Up to 1991-92	% to total area lost
1. Rehabilitation	66759	32.18	66767	28.30
2. Agriculture	87289	42.07	104902	44.47
3. Non-agriculture	18816	09.07	19154	08.12
4. Singareni colories	5461	02.63	15907	06.72
5. Encroachments	29160	14.05	29160	12.36
6. Total	207485	100.00	235889	100.00

Source: Facts and Figures 1999, Forest Department, Government of Andhra Pradesh.

The qualitative decline is reflected in the area under degraded forests. The estimates of the extent of forest area degraded are given by the National Remote Sensing Agency (NRSA) for the year 1988-89. As per these estimates about 38 percent of the forest area in the sate is degraded as against 24 percent at the all India level (Table 7). The situation is precarious in some districts where over 90 percent of their forest areas are degraded (Guntur, Medak and Nalgonda). The only factor that seems to be associated with degradation of forests is the area under forests. Incidence of forest degradation is lower in the districts with higher forest coverage, though there is no set pattern in this regard (Table 7). The declining quality of forests is reflected in the revenue generated from forests in the state. The contribution of forests to the net domestic product has come down from Rs. 94 lakhs in 1980-81 to Rs. 85 lakhs in 1996-97. Similarly, 8.53 percent of the pasture and grazing lands in the state are degraded reflecting the declining quality of common pool resources. Interestingly, incidence of pasture and grazing land degradation is limited to four districts only. Prakasam district accounts for about 90 percent of the total pasture degradation in the state.

The vision document envisages massive afforestation of wastelands, other public and private lands. The state has 84 lakh hectares of wastelands. An estimated 17-lakh hectare of degraded forestlands will be developed over the next ten years through promoting appropriate institutional arrangements. The state government has initiated the Joint Forest Management Programme in 1992 as a strategy for rehabilitation of degraded forestlands through the formation of Vana Samarakshana Samithis (VSS) in the vicinity of forest areas. Such committees were entitled to 100 per cent right over forest produce such as NTFPs, grasses and dry fuel-wood besides a 50 per cent share from the final harvest in lieu of forest protection. This arrangement was modified in 1996 allowing the village communities a 100 per cent share of the usufructs instead of the earlier 50 per cent. So far about 6600 (VSS) have been formed covering 16.7 lakh hectares of forests, i.e., 25 percent of the forest area. So far about 5.75 lakh hectares of forest area has been treated. JFM has benefited an estimated 13 lakh people of which 47 percent are women. Till 1998-99 about Rs. 35 crores have been spent on JFM. Some of the initial evaluation reports

Table 7. Extent of Forest Degradation in Andhra Pradesh

District	Total Forest Area (ha)		Degraded Forest area (ha)	% of degraded forest to total Forest Area
1. Srikakulam	67568	(14.98)	39997	59.20
2. Vizianagaram	93092	(30.25)	71319	76.61
3. Visakhapatna	405012	(32.87)	132417	32.69
4. East Godavari	295762	(21.18)	51571	17.44
5. West Godavari	87945	(18.08)	22831	25.96
6. Krishna	58650	(16.41)	42563	72.57
7. Guntur	150205	(07.70)	136847	91.11
8. Prakasam	443352	(06.03)	85335	19.25
9. Nellore	244763	(07.51)	174606	71.34
10. Chittoor	449845	(20.85)	301197	66.96
11. Cuddupah	505737	(12.37)	141852	28.05
12. Kurnool	302022	(09.70)	89337	29.58
13. Anantapur	164078	(41.51)	129765	79.09
14. Mahaboobnagar	293801	(17.72)	68933	23.46
15. Ranga Reddy	72245	(12.05)	63071	87.30
16. Medak	70521	(28.85)	66179	93.84
17 Nizamabad	168665	(42.43)	78097	46.30
18 Adilabad	696637	(29.87)	178837	25.67
19 Karimnagar	229954	(47.97)	87465	38.04
20 Khammam	785539	(13.78)	145461	18.52
21 Nalgonda	83188	(07.54)	79689	95.79
22 Warangal	368743	(10.41)	108316	29.37
Andhra Pradesh	6037324	(20.46)	2295685	38.02
All India	65710815	(19.99)	16274270	24.77

Note: Figures in brackets are percent of forest cover to the geographical area.
Source: NRSA (1995).

provide a positive picture of the programme (Sethi and Singh, 1999), though more intensive studies are needed to understand the implementation and impact of the programme in the long run. For, most of these studies are impressionistic in the absence of any usage of scientific methodology or systematic analysis. According to the FAO study there is a 270 per cent increase in natural regeneration of red sanders, average tribal income has increased from Rs. 3570 in 1994 to Rs. 5600 by the year 2000, the practice of shifting cultivation has come down by 81 per cent and urban migration has come down by 70 per cent due to the JFM project (as quoted in Gopal and Upadhyay, 2001).

On the other hand, it was pointed out that the afforestation programmes in Andhra Pradesh often ignore tribal customary rights over *podu* (shifting cultivation) lands. Although forest department does not evict *podu* cultivators, includes old *podu* lands within the scope of JFM, which creates risk of losing their food security (OXFAM, 1998 as quoted in Saxena, 1999). It was observed that the current approach to participatory forestry is suicidal for the poor, as the department is focusing on high-income areas such as timber, etc. Where as low value products constituting sources of livelihoods for the poor have low priority. The rich farmers tend to monopolise the usufruct rights by bidding for fodder and fuelwood from the forest department thus denying the rights of small and marginal farmers. Similarly forest protection has led to improvement of fodder for big ruminants while the owners of free grazing small ruminants have not gained much (Gopal and Upadhyay, 2001). Besides, at the institutional level, it was pointed out that forest department's control has extended from forests to people with the advent of JFM, transparency is inadequate, community involvement is stifled due to lack of long-term assurance and legislation on VSS entitlements, etc. Hence there is need to democratise the functioning of the department and holding it accountable (Gopal and Upadhyay, 2001). Of late there are proposals to involve industry and corporate sector to take up afforestation through VSS. Though afforestation is being carried out in the industrial premises, involvement of industry in afforestation is marginal.

Bio-diversity

Bio-diversity is the totality of genes, species, and ecosystem. It is not just the total stock of living things that matter, but it is the range of different living things. In ecology, biodiversity plays a significant role of enriching soil, maintaining water and climate cycle and recycling and conservation of waste material into nutrients. Hence, ecological diversity is of great significance to human society, as it provides food, medicine and raw material for industry and household purposes from various living resources.

Andhra Pradesh has relatively richer biodiversity because of its strategic location in the central region of the Indian subcontinent. The topography of the state varies from the hilly range of Eastern Ghats to the Bay of Bengal, which support variety of flora and fauna. There are several rare and endemic flora found in Andhra Pradesh. So far around 1800 medicinal plants were documented in Andhra Pradesh. Nallamalais, one of the 13 Centres of Plant Diversity sites across the world, is located in Andhra Pradesh. It alone has 615 varieties of plant species; most of them are endemic. There are at least 16 flora species reported to be rare and threatened in Andhra Pradesh.

Similarly, in case of fauna, there are varieties of fauna species existing along with flora species especially in the forest areas of the state. The data about the identification of various fauna species is weak in the state, still it is estimated around 43 endemic and rare fauna including the Jerdons Courser and the Golden Gecko species. Tigers are considered to be the top carnivores from the ecological point of view. Andhra Pradesh has a tiger population, which is under severe stress, as the tiger population in the state has gone down by 37 percent between 1989 and 1997 despite the tiger project. Tiger project was initiated at the all India level to ensure the maintenance of viable tiger population and to preserve the habitats of biological importance. Warangal district has recorded more than 50 percent decline in the tiger population within 8 years due to illegal poaching.

Andhra Pradesh has got about 532 sq.km of mangrove forest area mostly in the regions of the Godavari and Krishna rivers. There are around 13 flora species found in the mangrove forest. The mangrove forest of Andhra Pradesh also attracts varieties of fauna as well, as it provides food and shelter to birds, mammals, fishes, insects and other species. However, due to constant pressure from the anthropogenic activities, the mangrove forests are disappearing and deteriorating. In addition the state has 2.33 lakh hectares of wetlands[5] of which 1.32 lakh hectares are natural and the rest are man-made. Krishna, West Gadavari and Adilabad districts account for 87 percent of the natural wetlands while 90 percent of the man-made wetlands are located in Kurnool and Nalgonda districts.

4. LIVESTOCK AND FISHERIES

Livestock is an integral part of the rural economy. Livestock is complementary, economically as well as ecologically, to the agricultural sector. Ecologically it provides the much needed manure to crop production. Though its economic contribution accounts for about 8 percent of the nation's gross domestic product, its contribution will be much higher if ecological considerations are taken into account. For, livestock contributes organic manure, which is required to neutralise the adverse affects of chemical fertilisers. It also contributes drought power that is ecologically more sustainable compared to tractor. However, livestock's contribution to agriculture is on the decline due to the subsidised chemical fertilizer and promotion of tractorisation.

The share of Andhra Pradesh in the country's livestock is on the decline during the last two decades. It has come down from 8.52 percent in 1976-77 to 6.99 percent in 1992-93. Livestock concentration (livestock/cultivable area) in Andhra Pradesh has declined between 1982 and 1993 while it has been rising at the all India level (Table 8). The state has experienced further decline in the concentration between 1993 and 1999. But its share in the country's milk production has gone up from 5.32 percent in 1971-72 to 6.62 percent in 1993-94. This indicates a qualitative change in the milch cattle. Also, the composition of livestock is moving in favour of small ruminants (sheep and goat), which have gone up from 36 percent in 1976-77 to 41 percent in 1998-99. Andhra Pradesh is the seventh largest milk producing state in the country. The dairy sector has grown by 17 percent during the period 1993-98. Milk production alone contributed 11 percent of the agricultural economy in 1995 (current prices), which is second only to rice. The dairy sector is poised for a big leap in the coming years. The Vision 2020 document targets for an increase in the share of milk production to 12-15 percent in the state gross domestic product by the year 2020. This would necessitate a qualitative and quantitative shift towards milch cattle. New initiatives in collaboration with private agencies like JK trust are underway. This would increase the availability of milk and milk products and the availability of organic manure.

The concentration of small ruminants (number/hectare of geographical area) in the state is lower compared to the all India level till 1992-93 but the data for 1998-99 indicates that there is a significant increase during the last five years (Table 8). It is often argued that small ruminants are one of the causes of pastureland degradation. But, the recent micro evidence suggests that the shift towards small ruminants is a result of degraded commons, as they can survive in such environments (Reddy, 1999). Households in degraded environments shift towards small ruminants. Across the regions of the state, only Telangana recorded an increase in the concentration of small ruminants between 82-83 and 92-93. This trend needs to be altered in order to realise the goals of Vision 2020. The declining concentration of livestock also indicates lower ratios of organic to inorganic input (fertiliser) use and higher dependence on tractors for cultivation purposes. Both these practices are expected to have an adverse impact on the environment.

Fisheries

Andhra Pradesh has a long and productive coastline of 974 km. As a result fisheries has evolved as a major economic activity. Despite its long coast line the share of marine fish in the total fish production of the state is lower than that of inland fish. Inland fisheries are well developed in the state and are mostly exported to other states like West Bengal. The state has 723 sq. km of area under aquaculture including an area of 400 sq. km of fresh water fish culture (APPCB, 2000). Besides, shrimp farming has come up on a large scale in some of the coastal districts like Nellore, Prakasam, Krishna and East Godavari, though its economic and ecological sustainability is of serious concern.

Statistics collected from the most developed fishing area (Visakhapatnam) in the state indicate the unsustainable nature of fishing activities. Despite the increase in the fishing fleet from 59 in 1981 to 180 in 1991 the catch has declined from 1649 tonnes to 1565 tonnes during the same period (APPCB, 2000). In terms of per fleet, the productivity has become one third (2.9 tonnes in 1991) of what it was in 1981 (8.7 tonnes). This indicates overexploitation of fish in this particular region, which would ultimately make the activity unviable.

Table 8. Livestock Concentration in the State
(Livestock per hectare of Cultivable area).

Region	1976-77	1982-83	1986-87	1992-93	1998-99+
1. Coastal Andhra	1.49	1.69	1.69	1.53	1.31
2. Rayalaseema	1.17	1.44	1.44	1.21	1.08
1. Telangana	1.38	1.53	1.54	1.48	1.15
2. Andhra Pradesh	1.36 (1.4)	1.56 (1.6)	1.56 (1.7)	1.43 (1.8)	1.30
3. % of sheep &Goat	36 (32)	36 (34)	35 (35)	37 (35)	41
6. Sheep & Goat / ha*	0.42 (3.7)	0.47 (3.4)	0.43 (4.8)	0.44 (5.2)	0.54

Note: Figures in brackets pertain to all India. * Sheep and goat concentration is measured in terms of geographical area.
Source: Quinquinannial livestock census, Government of India (for various years) till 1992-93. +Figure for the year 1998-99 are obtained from the Statistical Abstract of Andhra Pradesh, 1999, Government of AP. All India figures are not available for 1998-99.

The recent surge in aquaculture activity is creating serious environmental problems. More than 72 thousand hectares of land is under aquaculture of which more than 40 percent is in Krishna district itself (APPCB, 2000). Lack of proper environmental management practices and policies have caused severe stress on the surrounding environment. In the absence of any regulation the activity is spreading beyond the coastal regulation zone. As a result seawater is being pumped in to the hinterland leading to soil salinity and groundwater contamination. Besides, in order to keep the optimum salinity level in the ponds (about 25000 mg / l) huge quantities of fresh water has to be mixed with seawater. This would not only aggravate the fresh water scarcity in the regions but also result in land subsidence due to rapid depletion of groundwater table. Disposal (in the form of sludge) of unconsumed feed, shrimp excreta, chemicals and antibiotics would contaminate water bodies in the vicinity. Collection of natural tiger shrimp larvae for seed purposes would adversely affect the bio-diversity. For, every kilogram of larvae collected about 10 kilograms of other fish and shrimp are killed (APPCB, 2000). Though there is some kind of lull in this activity during the recent years (due to the spread of some viral disease) any further expansion of this activity has to be treated with caution given its environmental consequences. The proposals made in the vision document for expanding fisheries activity in the state need to take these environmental concerns into account. The document targets for 10 lakh tonnes of fish production by the year 2010 as against the present 4.1 lakh tonnes.

5. MINES AND MINERALS

Mining is the most demanding activity as far as environment is concerned. It leads to direct and indirect environmental impacts. Directly it results in the loss of soil, flora and fauna due to large scale clearing of mining fields. Often mining and environment come into direct conflict, especially when mineral reserves are found underneath forest areas. Indirectly, environment is degraded due to the development of infrastructure related to mining and establishment of processing industries like cement, etc. Andhra Pradesh stands second in mineral resources and fifth in mineral production contributing about Rs 8000 million to the national economy and Rs. 4500 million to the state exchequer.

The Vision 2020 document visualises the likely environmental impact of the large-scale mining activity in the state and plans to tackle it through policy instruments that guarantee restoration of mined lands. The instruments could be in the line of 'performance bonds' used in the western Australia. Similarly, taking care of displaced local people and tribals due to mining is another major concern. Privatisation of mining in the absence of other policy instruments to protect the environment and local people will be a disaster. Orissa is a living example in this regard. Though praised for its lead in privatising mining activity, it is one of the worst affected by the mining related pollution. As planned the state has started off by proposing the legislation regarding tribal lands for bauxite mining, which has generated some controversy. Such controversies will be on the rise if proper measures are not taken to compensate and rehabilitate the people. The state will be exploiting coal on a large scale in the coming decade. Coal, perhaps, is the least environment friendly resource and needs utmost care in its exploitation as well as processing and end-use. This calls for proper implementation of the policy instruments suggested in the Vision 2020 document. Similarly, appropriate policy instruments ought to be introduced to check the degradation at the already commissioned mining sites. As mentioned earlier Singareni coalmines is second important cause of forest loss in the state.

6. INDUSTRIAL POLLUTION

There is one to one correspondence between industrial growth and environmental degradation. Experience suggests that industrial growth results in adverse environmental problems, as the industrial policies do not take environmental aspects into account. Although environmental measures are envisaged there are no effective policy instruments to guarantee compliance. For instance, the Andhra Pradesh Pollution Control Board has identified 60 grossly polluting industries, but only 19 industries complied with the direction issued by the board (APPCB, 2000). Most of the defaulters fall in the category needing a common effluent treatment plant (CETP). Some of the most polluting industries include mining (especially coal), drugs and pharmaceuticals, fertilisers, pesticides, textiles, paper, sugar, thermal power, etc.

During the last two decades the most polluting industries have shown the highest investments, as also returns (APPCB, 2000). Though the environmental impact of these industries is on the decline on most of the major rivers in the state (Table 9), some of the minor river basins like Musi are among the worst polluted in the country (Down to earth, August, 1999). Six industrial estates (Patanceru, Bolaram, Kazipally, Pashamylaram, Bonthapally and Gaddapotharam) were established between 1975 and 1985 within 30 km radius of Hyderabad in the two sub-basins of Musi River. Environmental aspects were not taken in to account while establishing these industries. As a result surface and groundwater as well as the soil in these two sub-basins got polluted making them redundant for use. A detailed study of Patancheru industrial estate brings out vividly the environmental consequences of unplanned industrial development.

Table 9. Trends in River Pollution in the State (selected locations)

River / Location / Period	DO	BOD	COD	EC	TA	Sulph-ate	Chlo-ride
1. Godavari (Manchiriala)							
1980-87	NT	NT	UT	DT	UT	DT	UT
1993-95	NT	NT	DT	DT	NT	--	NT
1. Godavari (Polavaram)							
1980-87	NT	UT	NT	DT	DT	DT	DT
1993-95	UT	DT	DT	UT	DT	--	UT
2. Krishna (Gadwal bridge)							
1980-87	DT	NT	NT	DT	UT	NT	UT
1993-95	DT	UT	NT	--	--	--	--
3. Krishna (Vijayawada)							
1980-87	NT	UT	UT	--	--	--	--
1993-95	NT	DT	DT	--	--	--	--
4. Pennar (Nellore)							
1980-87	NT	NT	UT	NT	NT	NT	UT
1993-95	UT	NT	UT	--	--	--	--

Note: DO= Disolved Oxigen; BOD= Biochemical Oxigen Demand; COD= Chemical Oxigen Demand; EC= Electro Conductivity; TA= Total Alkalinity.
NT= No Trend; DT= Downward Trend; UT= Upward Trend.
Source: Water Quality Statistics of India (1979-87), Water Quality- Status and Statistics (1993-94) and 1995, CPCB, Delhi.

Patancheru is one of the most environmentally degraded industrial areas in Andhra Pradesh as well as in India. This region is among the most unplanned industrial estates, where there is no specific plan for establishing industrial units. Industrial units were established in a haphazard and scattered manner. The industrial belt is housing around 80 units of which about half are chemical units, including life-saving drugs. Major chemical and bulk manufacturing units are located here. These units generate significant quantities of hazardous wastes, which are not controlled or treated effectively. As a result these hazardous wastes lead to contamination of soils, surface and groundwater.

A study conducted to assess the magnitude of damages and costs of industrial pollution to agriculture, health and livestock brought out the severity of the problem in the Patancheru Mandal (Behera and Reddy, 2002). It was found that irrigation systems are the worst affected due to industrial pollution. At least 15 irrigation tanks in Patancheru Mandal were found to be either totally or partially polluted resulting in heavy losses to agricultural production, health and livestock. Tests of water samples from different sources such as bore-wells and tanks indicated that all the parameters are in excess of normal range. The impact of pollution has been estimated for different activities i.e., agriculture, livestock and human health. It is estimated that the average annual loss to a household was about Rs. 36,000 including agriculture (Rs.23156), human health (Rs.9379) and livestock (Rs.3550) due to the industrial pollution. Apart from the economic impact, pollution has led to severe social stress among the village people. The village has become both socially and economically isolated from the other parts of region. The major social impact is that their relatives from other villages stopped visiting and nobody was coming forward to marry their daughters to the villagers due to the fear of pollution. Their products like milk, rice remain unsold or they have to sell at a very cheap rate in the market.

As mentioned earlier, lack of pollution controls and compliance on the part of industry is the root cause of this mess. There are three common effluent treatment plants (CETP) in the state and all of them are located in these six industrial estates near Hyderabad. More importantly, not only their capacities are inadequate but also their treatment is substandard. The APPCB recognises this fact but not in a position to do anything about it. In fact, the treated water released by these plants turns out to be more dangerous than the untreated groundwater in the region (Behera and Reddy, 2002). The study village, Gandigudem, seem to have fallen victim to the effluent let out by the CETP located in the Bollarum industrial Belt. Initially the village was affected due to direct discharge of industrial effluents into the village land by the factories of the Bollarum industrial belt. After lot of protest by the villagers the CETP was established at the entrance of the village to treat effluents from 13 units with a capacity of 0.25 mld. The water from this CETP was tested and found that all the parameters are much higher than the standards. In most of the cases the values are higher for CETP when compared to bore well and tank water (Table 10). Therefore, it is clear that the standard of treatment is not up to the mark. In fact, the treated water is being injected into the ground through ditches and wells, which is contaminating the groundwater sources. A portion of treated water is being discharged into the village land, which is directly seeping into the agricultural field. Therefore, establishing a CETP at the entrance of the village does not serve any purpose of protecting the water and land resources.

The expected spurt in the industrialisation in the coming years is bound to aggravate the problems related to environment. The thrust sectors of coal mining and pharmaceuticals are among the worst polluters and hence extra caution is needed. Strengthening the institutional structure is a precondition for proper implementation of the existing pollution controls and ensuring compliance. Equal priority should be given to clear the present mess. The sufferings of the people continue unabated despite numerous protests and the appointment of a judicial committee (four years old) to look in to the problems in the Patancheru region. Nothing much is expected from these enquiries unless there is a change in the attitude of the state, implementing agencies and the industry.

Table 10. Levels of Pollution in Different Sources of Water.

Parameters	Sample I	Sample II	Sample III	Sample IV
PH	6.6 (7.0-8.5)	7.6	6.8	7.4
EC mho	7210 (750)	6000	4870	17780
TDS mg/l	4326 (500)	3002	2922	10668
Chloride mg/l	504 (200)	420	594	1392
Sulphates mg/l	220 (200)	250	359	732
Phosphates mg/l	0.025	0.020	0.25	3.0
COD mg/l	38 (3)	50	217	651
BOD mg/l	14 (3)	20	76	251
Calcium mg/l	315 (75.0)	500	261	553
Magnesium mg/l	151 (30.0)	180	129	388
Total hardness mg/l	1541 (100)	1269	1199	2998
Alkalinity mg/l	460 (75)	480	380	1000
Arsenic mg/l	0.2 (0.05)	0.1	0.75	2.0

Note: Tested at the Central Laboratory, Andhra Pradesh Pollution Control Board, Hyderabad.
TDS = Total Dissolved Solids, EC = Electrical Conductive, COD = Chemical Oxygen Demand, BOD = Biological Oxygen Demand. Figures in brackets indicate Normal range of parameters.
Sample I = bore- well –I; Sample II = bore-well- II; Sample III = tank water; Sample IV = CETP water.
Source: Behera and Reddy, 2002.

7. URBAN ENVIRONMENT

Unplanned urbanisation leads to serious environmental problems, which are more strident due to their link with health and microenvironment. The increased incidence of health problems such as cancer, heart deseases, stress, etc., in recent years is directly attributed to deteriorating urban environment. The major environmental problems related to unplanned urbanisation include scarcity of potable water and sanitation facilities, air pollution, poor management of solid waste, congestion, climatic change, etc.

Andhra Pradesh is one of the fast urbanising states in the country with a growth rate of urban population at 4.50 percent per annum. According to 1991 census there were 213 towns in the state. The level of urbanisation in the state as indicated by the proportion of urban population was 26.89 percent, which is expected to cross 35 percent by the year 2011. Across the regions Telangana has the highest level of urbanisation (30.18 percent), which is due to the presence of Hyderabad, the capital city. Telangana region has 39 percent of state's urban area housing 44 percent of state's urban population, while coastal Andhra region has 41 percent of urban area housing 41 percent of its population and Rayalaseema has 19 percent of urban area but only 15 percent of state's urban population lives there. Therefore, urban congestion is more in Telangana and Coastal regions. However, most of the environmental problems are concentrated in a few major city regions namely, Hyderabad, Vizag and Tirupati. These regions account for 70 per cent of hazardous waste generating units and 90 per cent of the waste generated per month (APPCB, 2000). Due to the unplanned urbanisation slums seem to be growing at a faster rate than the urbanisation. Between 1962 and 1994 the number of slums have gone up by 8 times (from 106 to 811) and the slum population by 13 times (1 lakh to 13 lakhs) (APPCB, 2000). Slums face severe water and sanitation problems, as they fall under unapproved settlements. Increasing population density lured by employment opportunities in the major cities is at the root of the problem. The decentralised planning for locating industries in the hinterland and rural industrialisation programmes are non-starters. Unless serious efforts are made in this direction, it is difficult to address the problems of urban congestion effectively.

Water Supply and Sewerage

The present position of water supply in almost all the municipalities in the state is below the national standard. The water shortage is as high as 75-100 percent in 9 municipalities, between 50-75 percent in 24 municipalities, between 25-50 percent in 26 municipalities and below 25 percent in 32 municipalities. Only in 12 municipalities there is no deficit at the moment but the distribution systems need immediate upgradation (PHED, Hyderabad). Overall, the shortage is about 36 percent at the state level and Rayalaseema is the worst affected with 43 percent of deficit (Table 11). The tentative capital investment based on per unit cost to cover the entire urban population expected by 2001 is estimated at Rs. 1292 crores. There exist wide disparities within and across the regions. In per capita terms the shortages (demand-supply gap) vary between 1.7 percent in Anantapur district to 83.15 percent in Prakasam district. The situation is likely to aggravate as none of these towns have any supply support for future demands, which will continue to increase with population. The important reasons for this state of affairs are financial constraints and the absence of demand management policies. Under the existing price policies water supply agencies are not in a position to generate their own funds for enhancing the existing water supply and distribution systems. In the absence of policies to promote conservation, water is being used inefficiently and wasted. This has resulted in unequal distribution of water across various sections of the population.

Table 11. Supply-Demand Gap in Urban Residential Water Supplies in Andhra Pradesh (in Million Gallons)

Region	Demand per day	Supply per day	Shortage (in %)
1.Coastal Andhra	79.77	52.56	34 (43)
2.Rayalaseema	46.20	26.45	43 (53)
3.Telangana	56.69	38.05	33 (42)
Andhra Pradesh	182.66	117.06	36 (47)

Source: Rath (1999). Figures in brackets are the figures for the year 2000 as given in Prasad and Rao (2000). These figures are for 111 municipalities in the state.

The situation is disturbing if we look at the treatment of sewerage water. Most of the towns do not have proper underground sewerage systems, let alone, collection systems. Even in a city like Hyderabad only 40 percent of the areas are covered with underground sewerage system. As a result most of the sewerage is left into open drains causing groundwater pollution. And the existing sewerage facilities are too few to meet the demand. Except Tirupati, no other municipality has adequate treatment facilities[6] (Table 12). This could be mainly due to the fact that in most of the places there are no facilities even to collect the sewerage for treatment, as they have open drainage systems. Most of the towns, except Hyderabad,

Table 12. Sewerage Treatment Facilities in Andhra Pradesh

Municipality	Present water supply (MLD)	Expected Sewage (MLD)	% of Sewage Treated
1. Hyderabad	670	536	25
2. Visakhapatnam	62.7	50.16	60
3. Vijayawada	140.9	112.72	24
4. Guntur	75	60	42
5. Nellore	52.7	42.16	06
6. Eluru	16.4	12.91	42
7. Tirupati	14.6	11.68	100
8. Tenali	10.7	8.56	53

Source. APPCB (2000).

Secunderabad, Vizag, Vijayawada and Tirupati do not have sewerage facilities. Even in Hyderabad, often sewer water gets into drinking water distribution systems causing widespread health problems such as gastro-enteritis. This problem assumes serious proportions during the monsoon months.

Solid Waste Management

Another important environmental problem is that of solid waste disposal and the hazardous waste disposal. About 83000 tonnes of hazardous waste is being generated in the state by 479 units. Hyderabad region accounts for 66 percent of this waste followed by Tirupati and Vizag (Table 13). Growth of chemical industry in the state is one of the main reasons for the generation of hazardous waste. Presently there are no facilities to treat the huge amounts of hazardous waste. The industries generating this waste are authorised to store it in their premises. But, mostly the waste finds its way to open dumping grounds, including those in the residential areas. In order to tackle this problem the state pollution control board is proposing to establish three units of TSDFs (Treatment, Storage and Disposal Facilities) in three regions of the state.

Table 13. Municipal Solid Waste and Hazardous waste Generated in Major Regions

Region	Municipal Solid waste (MT/Day)		Hazardous Waste (MT/month)	
Hyderabad	1566	(55.27)	4466	(66.04)
Vizag	300	(10.58)	663	(09.80)
Tirupati	85	(03.00)	969	(14.33)
Rest of the State	882	(31.15)	665	(09.83)
Total	2833	(100)	6763	(100)

Source: APPCB (2000).

Besides, 2833 metric tonnes of municipal solid waste is generated per day in the state. Again Hyderabad accounts for 55.27 percent of this waste. Eighty percent of this waste is lifted on a regular basis. But, only 40 percent of the waste is sent for compost or manure pits (APPCB, 2000). According to the latest NSS estimates, only 14.5 percent of the garbage is lifted bylocal authorities and the rest by households themselves, either by some arrangement or on their own (Table 14). The situation at the all India level is no different. Of the garbage generated only 1.1 percent is taken to biogas plants or manure pits and the rest is dumped in the community or household dumping spots. This unhygienic disposal of waste is resulting in surface as well as groundwater pollution besides odour and unpleasant microenvironment.

Air and Noise Pollution

Man-made air pollution is the main cause of concern. The important air pollutants include Sulphur dioxides (SO_2), Nitrogen (NO_x), Particulate Matter (SPM), HydroCarbons (HCs), Carbon Monoxide (CO), Lead (P_b), etc. Though the air pollution levels in most of the cities is within the permissible levels, cities like Hyderabad, Visakhapatnam, Vijayawada and Tirupati are showing dangerous trends in the levels of C_o and SPM (APPCB, 2000). While power sector contributes 70 percent of the SO_2 pollution, vehicular pollution contributes most in the case of the remaining pollutants. Details on pollution levels are available only for Hyderabad city.

Table 14. Municipal Solid Waste Management (% of Households)

Item	Andhra Pradesh	All India
I. Removal of Garbage by		
a) Municipality	14.50	13.70
b) Private arrangement	08.10	11.90
c) Household Members	75.30	71.20
II. Site of Garbage Dumping		
a) Bio gas /manure pit	01.10	01.40
b) Community Dumping Spot	55.90	47.42
c) Households Dumping Spot	29.80	29.60

Source: NSS, Round (1999).

According to the PCB as on March 31 2002 the city had 12.04 lakh vehicles on road with 1.25 lakh vehicles added every year. These vehicles emit an estimated 1,123 tonnes of pollution load every day which has jumped from 475 tonnes per day in 1995. It was estimated that the citizens of Hyderabad breathe 691 tonnes of pollutants every day. Hyderabad has the highest concentration of vehicles per kilometre of road length, i.e.; traffic density is 220 vehicles compared to 90 in Delhi, 70 in Channai and 45 in Mumbai. The biggest pollutants are the two wheelers. Between 1991 and 1999 the number of two wheelers rose from 357,000 to 678,000 and is now 720,000. By the end of 1999 there were 140, 000 cars, 49, 000 auto rickshaws, 38, 475 goods vehicles, 4, 000 taxis and 2, 322 Andhra Pradesh State Road Transport Corporation (APSRTC) buses. Among the vehicles two wheelers contribute 56 percent of the total pollution, trucks contribute 19 percent and four wheelers contribute 14 percent. And petrol vehicles contribute 77 percent of the pollution while diesel vehicles contribute 23 percent. Government has prepared some harsh measures to check the vehicular pollution in December 1999, which is yet to see the light as far as implementation is concerned. Some of the important measures include phasing out the 15 year old vehicles and two stroke engine vehicles (Venkateswarlu, 2000). Phasing out of 15 year old vehicles would help reduce the pollution load by 470 tonnes per day. Public places and parks, which are the lungs of the urban environment, are shrinking in the recent years. Most of the newly developed colonies do not provide space for these facilities flouting the norms. This is a potentially dangerous trend.

Noise pollution can cause severe health hazards both physical and mental, which can lead to long-term consequences on communication, working efficiency and comfort. The main sources of noise pollution are heavy traffic and commercial places of the city. The levels of noise pollution have been assessed in different parts of the city and found to be 15 to 20 decibels (db) above the standards. There are marginal variations in the level of noise pollution across locations in the city. In the commercial places the noise pollution varies from 64.8 to 78.9 db, whereas in case of residential places it varies from 61.5 to 83.8db. In case of industrial areas, the noise pollution varies from 59.2 to 67.2 db[7]. Though the noise pollution levels in the city are nearly equal to that of other major metros, stringent action should be taken in order to control the noise pollution in specific locations. Another source of noise pollution is that of movie theatres. In the name of dts (digital track sound) the theatre managements blast the volume. Though frequent movie goers might have got used (if not gone deaf) to the intolerable sound levels, it is very unpleasant and disturbing for a normal person.

8. STRATEGIES FOR SUSTAINABLE DEVELOPMENT

The status of environment in Andhra Pradesh does not indicate that sustainable development path is being pursued. However, recent policy pronouncements amply demonstrate the fact that environmental concerns are indeed among the policy priorities. In fact, the Vision 2020 document provides a blueprint for environmental management (apart from other things). However, the past experience in this regard casts doubts on the seriousness in implementing these policies. Our analyses of the present status of environment in the state identifies the following priority areas: land and water management, mining, industrial pollution and urban environment.

Judicious management of land and water resources is recognised (at the policy level) as a crucial ingredient for sustainable agricultural development. It is estimated that the cost of soil degradation alone is about 1.2 percent of its GDP. That is, by checking degradation of soil the growth in GDP can be increased by 1.2 percent. Since land and water resources are inter-linked it is necessary to follow an integrated approach. Land and water management are crucial for food security at the household level. Provision of irrigation can check land degradation to a large extent and hence dry land agriculture should be given priority.

The state's experiments with watershed development programme to promote dry-land agriculture and the irrigation development programme are the most innovative in the country. The success of these programmes will be a trendsetter for the future development policy. Here, perhaps, for the first time participatory approach is being implemented from above. Impact of watershed development under the new guidelines, in general, has an overall positive environmental impact. Unfortunately, more importance is given to the spread of the programmes than to their intensity or quality in terms of institutional preparedness. As a result, the long run sustainability of these programmes is at stake.

As far as water resources management is concerned an integrated approach is missing. The most important component of water resources (groundwater) is left out of the policy purview. The problem of groundwater is as serious, if not more, as that of tank and canal waters. The rate at which groundwater tables are depleting is alarming. The *de facto* privatisation of groundwater coupled with the populist programmes such as subsidised power supply is the main culprit. Continuation of these practices could result in economic deprivation and ecological disaster. For the sake of populism economic considerations of resource management (pricing, etc.,) are bypassed. While restructuring the irrigation management in the state there is hardly any attempt to rationalise the canal water pricing, despite the fact that various committees have suggested cost based pricing. As long as political aspects overrun the economic aspects of policies, however innovative they may look, sustainable management and development of resources cannot be ensured.

An appropriate strategy should integrate institutional approaches with market principles. Unless beneficiaries have a stake in the developmental activities, it is unlikely tha.-sustainability is ensured. Despite the fact that beneficiary contribution is imbibed in some of the recent programmes like watershed development, somehow it is undermined at the implementation level. Similarly cost based pricing in the canal commands has a long way to go. Unless the beneficiaries of canal irrigation are made to share their benefits the state does not have any ethical / moral right to expect the contribution from the poor dry land farmers. Since institutional innovation has already taken place as far as canal irrigation is concerned, now it is time to implement the cost and voumetric pricing. At the same time institutional development and strengthening the social capital needs to be taken more seriously, as these aspects are critical in the process of sustainable development. At the policy level there is an immediate need to de-link water rights from land rights, especially in the case of groundwater. In the absence of such de-linking it is near impossible to talk about equity and sustainability.

Mining is another sector, which is expected to take a big leap during the next two decades. The impact of mining on environment would be widespread and manifold. Mining could lead to irreversible damages if follow up action is not taken after the mining activity is completed. There are a number of ways to reduce the damage. They include, collection of environmental cess, issuing of safety bonds or deposits, which can be used for the purpose of reclamation, etc. The vision document proposes to issue the safety bonds for the future mining activity. This would escalate the initial costs of production and may deter competition. In such an event imposition of environmental tax (on value basis) would facilitate the distribution of the burden. The amount from this cess could be deposited in a separate account for usage (specific purpose) at a later stage. The proposed privatisation of mining would also cause social problems like displacement of local populations (tribals). Any conflict would adversely affect the developmental efforts. The recent tribal land legislation is a case in point. To avoid such conflicts policies ought to be made transparent and involve the local people in the process of policy making itself. The state should follow the strategy of conflict resolution through appropriate institutional arrangements rather than postponing the process. Though the vision document mentions about such arrangements (western Australian model), they are not taken seriously at the policy making level.

Industrial pollution is a clear case of policy failure. Both policy makers and implementing agencies are aware of the mess and appropriate measures are in place (paper) to tackle the market failure situations. But, nothing concrete is being done about it. Only in a few cases the intervention of judiciary has brought some relief. Compliance is the major problem at the industry level. The main reasons for this include weak institutions (implementing agencies), lack of cost effective technologies, political interference, nexus between industry, bureaucracy and politicians, absence of awareness and weak bargaining power of the victims. The problem could be solved only through awareness building and promoting environment friendly technologies through proper incentive / disincentive structures. In the short-run, planning the location of the industries will solve the problem to a large extent.

Unplanned urbanisation is at the root of the environmental problems. There cannot be better example than the recent floods in Hyderabad. Unplanned growth coupled with illegal occupation is resulting in serious stress on drinking water and sanitation facilities. Slum populations are the worst victims. Urban planning is a necessary condition for improving the situation. Illegal occupations need to be dealt with strictly. Rekindling the rural industrialisation process would go a long way in addressing the problem of urban congestion. During the 1990s the objective of rural industrialisation has been relegated to back seat. Unless industries are shifted to hinterlands and rural areas it is difficult to bring the rural-urban balance and reduce the rural-urban migration.

Demand management of urban amenities such as drinking water should be given top priority. Efficient provision of services fostered with progressive pricing of services would result in efficient use of services. Solid waste management is another area of importance. Appropriate institutional arrangements need to be worked out to collect, recycle and dispose the waste. Some of the colonies already have arrangements (privately) to collect the household waste by payment (Rs. 15 - 20 / month / HH). Such arrangements need to be strengthened and made more professional. Division of garbage (organic, inorganic, glass, etc.) should be encouraged for easy and efficient recycling.

Awareness and involvement of the civil society is a precondition for checking environmental degradation. Environmental protests and movements would have a discerning impact in this regard. Environmental protests or movements may not, on their own, solve the problems but they are instrumental in bringing awareness among policy makers and the civil society. This would put pressure on the polity to have a full-fledged environmental policy rather than having an adhoc approach. Although there is no dearth of policies the crux of the problem lies with implementation. Compliance to rules and regulations can be achieved only through strengthening the hands of the implementing agencies and tightening the environmental legislation.

Notes

1 We have also estimated the regression equations to examine the relationship between the extent of degradation and other socio-economic variables across the districts. None of the variables turned out significant.

2 Initiatives on water management are discussed separately in the chapter on irrigation (this volume).

3. Prior to this the National Watershed Development Project for Rainfed Areas (NWDPRA) has been introduced in 1990-91. Till 1996-97, under this programme, 94 watersheds covering 1.76 lakh hectares were treated with an expenditure of Rs. 5116 lakhs.

4 These rates are now revised to Rs. 30 lakhs per watershed (Rs. 6000 per hectare).

5 A general term applied to open water habitats and seasonally or permanently water logged land areas, including lakes, rivers and estuarine and fresh water marshes.

6 The expected sewerage is estimated under the assumption that 80 percent of the water supplied will come out as sewer.

7 Noise levels above 90db are hazardous to health.

References

APPCB (2000), *State of Environment in Andhra Pradesh*, Andhra Pradesh Pollution Control Board, Hyderabad.

Behera, Bhagirath and V. Ratna Reddy (2002), "Accountability and Environment: Impact of Industrial Pollution on Rural Communities", *Economic and Political Weekly*, Vol. 36, No. 3, 19 January.

CMIE (1999), *Agriculture*, Centre for Monitoring Indian Economy, Mumbai.

CPCB (1988), *Water Quality Statistics of India (1979-87)*, Central Pollution Control Board, New Delhi.

CPCB (1995), *Water Quality- Status and Statistics (1993-94, 95)*, Central Pollution Control Board, New Delhi.

Echeverrt-Gent, John (1992), "Public Participation and Poverty Alleviation: The Experience of Reform Communists in India's West Bengal", *World Development*.

GoAP (1999), *Economic Survey* (1999-2000), Government of Andhra Pradesh, Hyderabad.

GoAP (1999), *Facts and Figures* (1999), Department of Forest, Government of Andhra Pradesh, Hyderabad.

GoAP (1999), *Vision 2020*, Government of Andhra Pradesh, Hyderabad.

GoAP (various years) *Statistical Abstract of Andhra Pradesh*, Government of Andhra Pradesh, Hyderabad.

GoI (1993), *HandBook on Fisheries Statistics*, Ministry of Agriculture, Government of India, New Delhi.

GoI (various issues) *Quinquinannial Livestock Census*, Government of India, New Delhi,

NRSA (1995), *Report on Area Statistics of Land Use / Land Cover generated Using Remote Sensing Techniques*, National Remote Sensing Agency, Department of Space, Govt. of India, Balanagar, Hyderabad.

NRSA (2000), *Wasteland Atlas of India*, National Remote Sensing Agency, Department of Space, Government of India, Balanagar, Hyderabad.

NSSO (1999), *Drinking Water, Sanitation and Hygiene in India*, National Sample Survey, 54th Round, Government of India, New Delhi.

PHED (1997-98), *Augmentation of Urban Water Supply in A.P*, Public Health and Engineering Department, Hyderabad.

Prasad, D. Ravindra and K. Rajeswara Rao (2000), *Handbook of Municipal Statistics: Andhra Pradesh*, RCUES, Osmania University, Hyderabad.

Rao, C.H. Hanumantha (2000), "Watershed Development in India: Recent Experience and Emerging Issues", *Loveraj Kumar Memorial Lecture Delivered at SPWD*, New Delhi.

Rath, S. (1999), *Status of Urban Water Supply in Andhra Pradesh*, M.Phil dissertation submitted to University of Hyderabad, Hyderabad.

Reddy, D. Narasimha (1998), "Irrigation Crisis in Indian Agriculture: A Case Study of Andhra Pradesh", Paper Presented at Policy Dialogue on a National Emergency: The Crisis of Agriculture and Food Security, Research Foundation for Science, Technology and Ecology, New Delhi, 3rd August.

Reddy, V. Ratna (1996), "Liberalisation and the Poor: A Case of Rajasthan", Paper presented at the International Seminar on Liberalisation and the Poor: Impact, Opportunities and Barriers, IDPAD- ICSSR- CESS, Hyderabad, 7- 9 February.

Reddy, V. Ratna (1999), "Quenching the Thirst: Cost of Water in Fragile Environments", *Development and Change*, Vol. 30, No. 1, January.

Reddy, V. Ratna (2000), "Watershed Development in AP", *Deccan Chronicle*, 23 June, Hyderabad.

Saxena, N. C. (1999), "Participatory Issues in Joint Forest Management in India" Proceedings of the Seminar on Joint Forest Management and Sustainable Development, IMAGE, Chennai, 23-24 September.

Sethi, Pia and T. P. Singh (1999), "Institutional Issues and Productivity of Joint Forest Management", Proceedings of the Seminar on Joint Forest Management and Sustainable Development, IMAGE, Chennai, 23-24 September.

Springate, O., V. Ratna Reddy, M. Gopinath Reddy, S. Galab and Anjan Datta (2001), "Watershed Development in Andhra Pradesh: Policy Design, Implementation and Impact", (mimeo), Center for Economic and Social studies, Hyderabad.

Venkatswaralu, K. (2000), "All for a Whiff of Fresh Air", *The Hindu Survey of Environment*, The Hindu, Chennai.

21

Urbanisation and Urban Services

C. Ramachandraiah

1. INTRODUCTION

It has been argued that the spatial organisation of the big urban centers in Third World countries has often been articulated in accordance with the exploitative requirements of the colonial powers. Most of the cities of the Third World today grew as 'enclaves' integrated more closely with the economy of the colonial powers than with their national economies. The large urban centers have retained extreme parasitism over the regional economy and the process of underdevelopment in the vast rural hinterlands has accentuated over the years. The migration of people from rural areas was, therefore, not mainly due to the vertical mobility of workforce from the primary to the secondary and tertiary sectors in urban centers but was in the nature of out-migration from rural to urban areas, which did not have the capacity to sustain them (Chattopadhyay and Raza, 1975). In the Indian context the rural-urban migration stream, which is an instrumental factor in the urbanisation process, is highly disparate and polarised. It consists of one large stream of illiterate poor in search of livelihood, and another of the rich, educated and elite in search of better opportunities. The poor are pushed out of villages while the rich are pulled into the cities (Prakasa Rao, 1983).

In the present paper, an attempt has been made to analyse the trends of urbanisation and urban services like urban water supply, solid waste, households without sanitation facilities, and road length in the municipal towns of Andhra Pradesh. In the second section, a detailed analysis of urbanisation trends in the state in terms of composition of population in different size classes, levels of urbanisation and urban growth rate at district level from 1971 to 2001 has been attempted. In the third section, urban water supply levels have been analysed in terms of per capita litres per day (LPCD). Apart from water supply, the availability of house service connections (HSCs) and public stand posts (PSPs) as a ratio of population has also been analysed. The fourth section deals with the other urban services for which the information is available for 1997. The concept of rainwater harvesting is briefly discussed in fifth section. The concluding remarks are presented in the last section.

2. PATTERN OF URBANISATION

Macro Level Scenario-All India

The level of urbanisation in the state has been a little less than that of the national average since 1901 except in 1951 and 1991. The level of urbanisation in India has increased at a slower pace from about 11 per cent in 1901 to only about 28 per cent in 2001 despite relatively high growth of urban population in several decades. This is mainly due to high growth of total population as well. The magnitude of urban population and its concentration in big cities has contributed to the decline in the quality of urban life in India. More than one-third of the total urban population of 285 million in 2001 was concentrated in 35 'million plus' cities (Table 1). The small and medium towns (with below 50,000 population) accounted for only about 22 per cent of the urban population. During 1981 and 2001, the share of urban population has declined in all the categories of towns except 'million plus' cities. The 'top-heavy' nature of urbanisation seems to be getting accentuated over time which may not be a healthy trend in a vast agricultural country like India. At a comparable level of urbanisation (30 per cent in 2000) the structure of urbanisation in China seems to have expanded at the bottom and shrunk at the top. The proportion of urban population in cities with over one million population has come down from 8.4 to 5.8 per cent whereas that of cities of less than 2 lakh people has increased from 50.6 to 60.2 per cent during 1982 to 1993 (Chen and Parish, 1996). This is in total contrast to the scenario in many developing countries where a few large cities account for overwhelmingly high proportion of urban population.

Table 1. Distribution of Urban Population by Size Class of Urban Centres in India: 1971-01

Year	Total urban centres	Million Plus Cities		Cities with pop. of One lakh to One Million		50,000 to 1,00,000		Less than 50,000	
		Number	Per cent	Number	Per cent	Number	Per cent	Number	Per cent
1971	2476	9	25.5	139	31.7	173	10.9	2155	31.9
1981	3245	12	26.4	204	34.0	270	11.6	2759	28.0
1991	3697	23	32.5	277	32.4	345	10.9	3052	24.2
2001	4368	35	37.9	358	30.7	401	9.67	3574	21.7

Note: Percentage refers to share in the total urban population.
Source: Bose (1994) and Planning Commission (1983) as cited in Tewari (1997) upto 1991. For 2001, based on census data.

As per the Census definition in India, there should be a minimum population of 5000 for a settlement to be classified as 'urban'. There were, however, 13376 villages in India (1991) which had more than 5000 population and some of them had a population of more than 15000. While the number of urban centres has gone up by only about 2000, the number of these villages has increased by more than 9000 during 1961-91.[1] The predominantly rural character (i.e. primary sector) of these settlements, lack of diversification of economy towards non-farm activities, and their inability to acquire urban characteristics have resulted in this situation. Development of these places would go a long way in the promotion of urbanisation and growth of small and medium towns in large number that would provide urban support to rural economy. About 18 per cent of India's rural population would be added to urban population if the villages with population of 5000 and above were developed in this way. Ever since the reform process began in China in 1978, about 50000 small towns have been added by developing Town and Village Enterprises (TVEs) aimed at promoting economic development in rural areas and discourage migration to big cities (Wang and Hu, 1999).

Urban Scenario of Andhra Pradesh

In tune with the national trend, the urban population of the state is also getting concentrated in big cities. The share of class I cities has gone up from 42.7 to 75.3 per cent and their number from 13 to 39 during 1971-01 (Table 2). Though the number of towns in classes II has also increased, there is a decline in their share. The number of towns in classes IV and V has been declining since 1971. These are the towns that are closer to rural areas. This trend indicates that while the existing towns are getting

Table 2. Distribution of Urban Population by Size Class in Andhra Pradesh: 1971-01

Year	Total urban centres	Million-plus cities		Cities with pop. of one lakh to one million		50,000 to 1,00,000		Less than 50,000	
		Number	Per cent	Number	Per cent	Number	Per cent	Number	Per cent
1971	207 (224)	1	21.4	12	27.0	17	13.4	177	38.3
1981	234 (252)	1	20.5	20	32.7	30	16.2	184	30.2
1991	213 (264)	2	29.9	30	36.9	34	12.6	147	20.5
2001	173 (210)	2	33.5	37	41.8	43	13.9	91*	10.7

Note: 1. Percentage refers to share in the total urban population.
2. Figures in parentheses refers to the number of urban centres when the individual towns under urban agglomerations are treated separately.

* Declassification of many towns in this category is one of the reasons for such a steep decline in the number of towns.

Source: Based on census data.

promoted into higher classes, not many new ones are added to the list of towns in the lower categories. This may further suggest that the necessary diversification of economic activities towards non-agricultural activities is not taking place in big villages in the state. Hyderabad Urban Agglomeration (HUA) alone accounts for one-fourth, and, together with Visakhapatnam and Vijayawada, about 35 per cent, of urban population in the state. Though the level of urbanisation is low, it is the magnitude of urban population, about 20.5 million in 2001, which is posing problems in the provision of basic amenities in urban areas in the state.

The level of urbanisation at district level suggests that Hyderabad is hundred percent urban which largely coincides with the municipal corporation area (Table 3). In recent years, Hyderabad has emerged as an important software centre in India and has attracted considerable attention in the media both nationally and abroad. The next highly urbanised district, Rangareddy, surrounds Hyderabad. The ten municipalities, which are part of Hyderabad urban agglomeration, are located in this district. If these ten municipalities were excluded from the urban population of Rangareddy district, the level of urbanisation would be very low in this district as against the figure of 53.3 as per 2001 census. Similarly, the literacy rate would be only 47.1 per cent in Rangareddy (as against 66.3 per cent). In the districts of Mahabubnagar, Medak and Nalgonda that are neighbouring HUA the level of urbanisation is very low. The only other two districts that have urban levels of above 30 per cent are Visakhapatnam (40.0) and Krishna (32.4) because of the location of two big cities of Visakhapatnam and Vijayawada respectively. The coastal districts of Srikakulam and Prakasam have low levels of urbanisation. The level of urbanisation has remained more or less stagnant at around 27.08 per cent in 2001, compared to 26.8 per cent in 1991. It has declined in several districts during nineties, which have also witnessed very low urban growth rate during 1991-01. In Krishna and Kurnool districts there has been a decline in the level of urbanisation (by 3 percentage points).

The urban growth rate has come down sharply in nineties in the state. In several districts the growth rates are much below the state average of 15.11 per cent, with seven of them recording as low as 2 to 5 per cent. There is a fall in the urban population of Srikakulam district by 4.1 per cent. Of the 23 districts in the state, the urban growth rates are higher than the state average in only 8 districts (5 in Telangana, 2 in Rayalaseema and 1 in Coastal Andhra). The scenario changes slightly with the adjustments made in the data as given in the last column of Table 3. Rangareddy district experienced highest growth rate of 56.32 per cent though this is a decline from that of 209.2 per cent in eighties. While the high urban growth in Rangareddy district may be attributed to the growth of employment opportunities in and around Hyderabad and the consequent rural-urban migration, persistent backwardness might have induced higher urban growth in the other Telangana districts of Adilabad and Nalgonda in the

Table 3. Levels of Urbanisation and Urban Growth Rates at District Level in Andhra Pradesh: 1971-01

Sl. No	Name of the District	Per cent of Urban to Total Population				Decadal Urban Growth Rate			
		1971	1981	1991	2001	1971-81	1981-91	1991-01	1991-01*
1	Srikakulam	9.2	11.1	12.5	11.0	32.7	35.7	-4.1	8.3 (4-0)
2	Vizianagaram	13.9	16.0	17.2	18.4	31.7	25.9	13.8	13.4 (1-4)
3	Visakhapatnam	25.4	31.6	39.8	39.9	52.9	61.7	16.0	22.3 (8-2)
4	East Godavari	19.2	22.2	23.9	23.3	38.5	31.8	5.0	8.0 (3-0)
5	West Godavari	17.7	20.8	20.8	19.7	41.6	22.8	1.9	10.5 (2-0)
6	Krishna	27.3	32.7	35.8	32.4	46.1	33.5	3.2	14.4 (12-0)
7	Guntur	25.0	27.6	28.9	28.0	33.1	25.5	3.7	6.4 (4-0)
8	Prakasam	11.1	14.2	16.5	15.3	64.1	29.7	3.1	25.4 (4-2)
9	Nellore	15.6	20.8	23.8	22.7	64.4	36.0	6.2	24.5 (4-0)
10	Chittoor	13.6	16.8	19.8	21.7	50.2	39.6	25.6	37.4 (2-4)
11	Cuddapah	14.2	19.4	24.0	23.3	67.3	45.1	10.5	32.1 (5-2)
12	Ananthapur	17.8	20.3	23.5	25.3	41.1	40.8	23.0	23.0 (2-1)
13	Kurnool	20.3	24.5	25.9	22.6	46.5	30.1	3.4	7.7 (4-2)
14	Mahabubnagar	9.0	10.9	11.1	10.6	54.1	27.8	8.8	23.3 (4-0)
15	Rangareddy	–	24.0	47.1	53.3	141.6	209.2	56.3	57.0 (1-3)
16	Hyderabad	65.9	100.0	100.0	100.0	33.2	37.4	19.2	17.2
17	Medak	8.5	11.8	14.5	14.5	73.2	51.5	17.4	27.7 (2-3)
18	Nizamabad	15.9	19.3	20.3	18.0	54.7	27.9	2.4	2.3 (3-0)
19	Adilabad	15.9	19.3	23.1	26.5	54.5	51.8	36.4	38.7 (2-6)
20	Karimnagar	10.7	15.7	20.6	19.5	82.0	62.2	8.8	18.8 (5-2)
21	Warangal	13.4	17.3	19.4	19.2	58.1	37.7	13.7	13.6 (3-0)
22	Khammam	13.6	16.8	20.9	19.8	57.5	50.4	13.7	14.4 (3-2)
23	Nalgonda	6.7	11.4	11.9	13.3	113.0	30.3	26.9	41.0 (1-2)
	Andhra Pradesh	19.3	23.3	26.8	27.1	48.3	42.6 36.2*	15.1	20.5 (79-35)
	All-India	19.9	23.7	25.7	27.8	46.1	36.5	31.1	–

Note: 1. * Growth rates after the population of declassified towns, with more than 30 per cent male workforce in agriculture, are excluded from 1991 population.

2. Figures in parentheses in the last column indicate the number of declassified towns and new towns added in 2001 in each district. For instance, (3-2) indicates 3 declassified towns and 2 new towns.

Source: Census records for different years.

nineties. This hypothesis, however, needs to be examined with more empirical analysis.

An important aspect related to urbanisation in nineties in the state is the declassification of as many as 79 towns whereas 35 new census towns were added to the list in 2001 (Table 4). As a result, the urban area (i.e., geographical area under towns/cities) has come down from 5074.08 sq.km in 1991 to 4480.02 sq.km in 2001. As a proportion of the state's geographical area it has accordingly come down from 1.84 to 1.63 per cent during this period. The population of the declassified towns accounts for about 8 per cent of the total urban population of 1991 whereas that of new towns constitute only 2 per cent of the urban population of 2001. The fact that about half of the declassified towns are in Class III category, and many of them have been towns in the last couples of decades or so, indicates that the criteria for identifying urban centres might have not been applied properly at different census periods.

Table 4. Declassified and New Towns of 2001

Size class	Declassified towns		New towns	
	Number	Population (1991)	Number	Population (2001)
Class III (20,000 - 49,999)	35 (22)	923,658 (586,580)	4	103589
Class IV (10,000 - 19,999)	27 (17)	396,273 (232,873)	15	204289
Class V (5,000 - 9,999)	14 (6)	117,813 (51,423)	15	100302
Class VI (Below 5,000)	3 (1)	8,525 (3889)	1	2701
Total	79 (46)	14,46,269 (874,765)	35	410881

Note: Figures in parentheses indicate the distribution of the 46 declassified towns and their population by size class.
Source: Based on Census of India 2001, Andhra Pradesh, Paper 2 of 2001.

An analysis of the male workforce in these 79 towns for 1991 reveals that in 46 towns more than 30 per cent of the male workforce was engaged in agricultural activities, which means that they should not have been considered as 'urban' in 1991 itself had this criterion been applied more rigorously (Nagarpalika Network, 2002). The population of the 46 towns adds up to 8.75 lakhs and constitute 4.89 per cent of the urban population in 1991. The revised urban population in 1991 for A.P. would be 17.01 million instead of 17.89 million as per Census. The revised urban decadal growth during 1991-01 would be 20.5 per cent instead of the low Census figure of 15.1 per cent. The percentage of urban to total population would be 25.6 instead of 26.8. When the 46 towns are excluded from 1991 population the urban growth rate during 1981-91 works out to 36.2 per cent instead of 42.6 per cent, a decline of 6 percentage points. Even with the revised figures, the adjusted decadal growth rate in the state would still show a significant decline from 36.2 in eighties to 20.5 per cent during nineties. At the regional level, the 46 towns are concentrated more in Coastal Andhra (26) than in Telangana (12) and Rayalaseema (8). With the adjusted figures the growth rates at regional level show similar trend as the unadjusted figures but with more variation for Coastal Andhra and Rayalaseema (Table 5). Similarly at district level one finds a different scenario with the adjusted figures (last column of Table 3). In those districts where the growth rates (as per census figures) were negative (Srikakulam) or very low (Krishna, Prakasam, Nellore, Kurnool, Mahabubnagar, Karimnagar, Warangal and Khammam), the growth rates worked out appear more plausible. Certainly, declassification of towns has significantly affected their growth rates. Even after adjustment of the data, the districts of East Godavari, West Godavari, Guntur and Kurnool are showing below 10 per cent urban growth rates. Some of the backward districts have experienced higher urban growth rates compared to others. An in-depth analysis needs to be done before coming to definite conclusions regarding the reasons for the steep decline in urban growth in the state.

Table 5. Urban Growth Rates in Andhra Pradesh (Region-wise): 1991-01

Regions	Population ('000)		Growth rate	
	1991	2001	1991-01 (census)	1991-01 (adjusted)
Coastal Andhra	7304	7754	6.2	14.1 (42-8)
Rayalaseema	2703	3123	15.5	23.5 (13-9)
Telangana	7805	9626	23.3	25.2 (24-18)
Telangana (excluding Hyderabad/Rangareddy districts)	3518	5339	51.8	21.4 (23-15)
Andhra Pradesh	17813	20504	15.1	20.5 (79-35)

Note: Same as in Table 3 for the growth rates and figures in parentheses in the last column.
Source: Based on census records.

The slowing of urban growth at all-India level has been attributed to, among other things, near saturation in the growth of employment in unorganized sector, reduction in the gap between real wages of casual workers in urban and rural areas, and frequent invocation of legal systems for eviction etc., which have dampened rural-urban migration during nineties. Reduction in public expenditure on urban development and social sectors, and lack of access to basic amenities are also estimated to have adversely affected the pace of urbanisation in nineties (Kundu, 2001). The urban rural growth differential (URGD), which was at a high of 2.39 for 1971-81, has become a very low of 0.10 in nineties (Table 6). There is very less difference between urban and rural population growth rates in Andhra

Pradesh. With the adjusted figures also, there is a steep fall in URGD in nineties.

Table 6. Urban Rural Growth Differential (URGD) in Andhra Pradesh

Decade	Annual compound growth rate (Per cent)		URGD
	Rural	Urban	
1961-71	1.67	2.92	1.25
1971-81	1.57	3.96	2.39
1981-91	1.69	3.59	1.90
1991-01	1.27	1.37	0.10
		(1.88)	(0.61)

Note: The adjusted figures are given in the parentheses.
Source: Census of India, 2001, Andhra Pradesh, Paper 2 of 2001 (Rural Urban Distribution).

Based on the demographic figures of 1961 for the towns with a population of 30,000 and above, four urban regions were identified in the state (Alam, 1968) viz., (1) Hyderabad urban region comprising all the districts of Telangana; (2) Vijayawada-Guntur urban region comprising the four delta districts; (3) Visakhapatnam urban region with Srikakulam and Visakhapatnam districts; and 4) Kurnool-Nellore urban region comprising the four districts of Rayalaseema and Nellore district. In the light of the developments and patterns that have emerged in the last four decades, it may be inferred that the urban scenario of A.P has a mixed pattern, and has not emerged on the predicted lines as above.

The primacy of Hyderabad has been reinforced to a large extent over the years and seems to be casting a shadow-effect on the growth of other towns in Telangana region. This city is about eight times bigger than the next city, Warangal, in the region. It appears as a huge urban island amidst a vast underdeveloped area. As the city is attracting global capital and is emerging as an important software centre in India, there are indications that the dichotomy with its immediate hinterland may get accentuated. As Raza (1991) had observed, such a scenario appears common in India where many big cities and project centres of heavy industry are characterised by 'sharp gradients of their areas of influence giving them an enclave character...so that one sometimes moves from the world of the most advanced metallurgy to the realm of shifting cultivation, traversing four millennia in fifteen miles'.

The Vijayawada-Guntur urban region appears to have emerged distinctly but the delta districts of East and West Godavari seem to be not able to catch up with the region in this regard. Like Hyderabad in Telangana, Visakhapatnam has emerged as a metropolitan city leaving the two backward districts of Srikakulam and Vizianagaram[2] far behind. There is no evidence of the emergence of Kurnool-Nellore urban region centered around any one or more urban centres. Rayalaseema presents a more balanced urban settlement pattern. The presence of three big cities viz., Hyderabad in the north, Bangalore in the west, and Chennai in the south may be one of the important factors for the emergence of this pattern in Rayalaseema.

3. URBAN WATER SUPPLY

The data on water supply have been collected from a recently published source (Ravindra Prasad and Rajeswar Rao, 2000) for 105 municipalities out of a total of 107 municipalities in the state. The population of these 105 municipalities account for about 52 per cent of the state's total urban population.[3] The rest of urban population is spread over the six municipal corporations and a number of other small towns, which are excluded in this study. The sub-regions within Andhra Pradesh. viz., Coastal Andhra, Telangana and Rayalaseema, are mentioned in the analysis as R1, R2 and R3 respectively for convenience. The municipal towns have been grouped into the three regions and three population size classes of Class I, Class II and Class III, which are referred to as C1, C2, and C3 respectively (Table 7)[4]. Within each region, inter-class differences in water supply have been analysed. The data on slum population was available only for 63 municipalities, which had a population of 50,000 and above. Based on the of norms of 140 litres per capita per day (LPCD) in Class I and 100 LPCD in Class II and Class III towns, shortage in water supply has been estimated as a per cent of the demand. An attempt has also been made to analyse the ratio of public stand posts (PSPs) and house service connections (HSCs) and their availability to the slum and non-slum population.

The 105 municipalities are estimated to be supplying about 705 million litres of water daily (MLD) as against the total demand of about 1328 MLD in 2000. There is thus a shortage of 47 per cent if the water were to be supplied as per the prescribed norms. The deficit is more than 75 per cent in 10 municipalities, 50-75 per cent in 33, 25-50 per cent in 39, and less than 25 per cent in 18 towns. As per the Public Health Engineering Department, which is the agency responsible for undertaking water supply works in municipalities, groundwater is the major source of supply in 57 towns whereas 45 towns depend on rivers and canals (PHED, 1995). In terms of the size of towns, the shortage is higher in Class I towns (51 per cent) followed by Class III (41 per cent) and 36 per cent in Class II towns. Higher shortage in bigger towns may be attributed to higher per capita norms in these towns. At regional level, Telangana (R2) has higher shortage (53 per cent) compared to others. Several towns in this region are located in highly backward districts wherein in low level of development may be adversely affecting the provision of urban water supply as well.

Table 7. Water Supply in Municipal Towns of Andhra Pradesh: 2000

Class and Region	Number of Munici-palities	Per capita water supply (LPCD)	Per cent shortage in water supply	Per cent o slum population (2001)	PSPs as per cent of HSCs	Number per 250 population	
						PSPs (slum)	HSCs (non-slum)
1	2	3	4	5	6	7	8
C1 Total (Class I)	38	69	51	36.1 (36)	8	2.4	16.1
C2 Total (Class II)	46	64	36	46.4 (27)	11	2.3	18.3
C3 Total (Class III)	21	59	41	N.A	14	N.A	N.A
R1 Total (Coastal Andhra)	47	70	43	39.3 (23)	11	2.8	18.3
R2 Total (Telangana)	42	59	53	38.0 (25)	7	1.6	15.6
R3 Total (Rayalaseema)	16	75	42	39.2 (15)	12	3.0	16.0
All municipalities	105	66	47	38.7 (63)	9	2.4	16.6

Note: 1. Per cent of slum population is given by considering only those towns for which data was available.

2. Figures in parentheses in column 5 represent number of towns for which data was available for slum population.

3. Figures in columns 7 and 8 are for slum and non-slum population respectively.

Source: Based on data obtained from Ravindra Prasad and Rajeswar Rao (2000) and Census of India, Paper 2 of 2001, for Andhra Pradesh.

The municipal towns in Andhra Pradesh are providing only about 66 LPCD of water on average. Most of the towns are not able to supply even minimum prescribed standards of water supply as suggested by the National Commission on Urbanisation (1988)[5]. The water supply figures vary significantly in terms of regions and size class of towns. In general the level of per capita supply is higher in bigger size towns (C1) and it declines from Class I to Class III (from 69 to 59 LPCD), which suggests that the larger towns are able to manage resources to provide higher level of services. The towns in Rayalaseema (R3) are able to provide higher level of water supply (75 LPCD) compared to Coastal Andhra region (70) and Telangana (59) regions. There is less difference between R1 and R3 in this regard. The level of supply is much less in Telengana in which there are also a large number of municipalities. There are 16 municipalities in Class I in this region (R2) in which shortage in supply is the highest (57 per cent) compared to any other group of towns in the state. In this group, the per capita supply is also low (60 LPCD) compared to similar size towns in the other two regions. In these 16 towns, shortages are above 50 per cent in 11 towns. Within these 11 towns, 8 are located around Hyderabad city. Water supply to Hyderabad and the surrounding municipalities is provided by the Hyderabad Metropolitan Water Supply and Sewerage Board (HMWSSB), which is not able to meet the growing demand for water. In Telangana region (R2) the per capita supply in Class II (C2) towns is also much less compared to the other two regions.

The foregoing analysis based on aggregate levels of supply does not reveal intra-town variations. The experience in India reveals that those households with house service connections (HSCs) get higher levels of supply whereas the poor are served by public stand posts (PSPs) through which per capita availability is low. Proportion of population living in slum areas and the availability of PSPs provides an indication of the access of poor to this facility. In the 63 towns, for which data on slum population is available, about 39 per cent of the people are living in slum areas (Table 8)[6]. There is not much difference between the three regions in this aspect. However, in terms of size, Class II towns have higher percentage of slum population (46.4 per cent). With such a high proportion of population in slums, the aggregate supply of 66 LPCD of water does not reflect intra-town variations and water availability to the poor. The norms suggested by the NCU (1988) were 'subject to overhaul of the distribution systems in such a way that even the poorest colony is ensured at least 70 litres of supply per head per day on a regular basis.'

As a proportion of HSCs, PSPs constitute only 9 per cent in the 63 towns. This figure goes up from bigger to small towns, which indicates that relatively higher proportion of people are dependent on PSPs in small towns. At regional level, the situation in Telangana (R2) is more depressing with only 7 PSPs per hundred HSCs. The density of these taps separately for slum and non-slum population indicates that there are only 2.4 PSPs for 250 slum population, which means that there is only one public tap for 100 population in slums. While there is no difference between Class I and Class II in this regard, it may be noticed that in the towns of Telangana (C1-R2 and C2-R2), dependence of poor on public taps is much higher than in the other two regions. This situation makes poor people spend more time in collecting water and that too in less than adequate quantities as discussed earlier. The number of HSCs for non-slum population (16.6) also does not appear high. In this regard also the situation in Telangana (R2) is lower compared to the other regions. These low level of figures indicate that more than one family may be dependent on HSCs. It may be noted in this context that, as per the National Sample Survey Organisation (54th Round) for 1998, for those urban households who depend mainly on tap water the source is located within the dwelling for about 46 per cent only. For about 25 per cent, the source is located outside the dwelling unit but within the premises. For the remaining 29 per cent of the urban households, the tap lies outside the premises within a distance of up to 0.2 km (NSSO, 1999).

During the one decade of economic liberalization in nineties, the access to safe water in urban areas has declined in India. As per the NSSO (1999), only about 70 per cent of urban households had access to piped (tap) water supply in India in 1998 and this proportion has come down from 72.1 per cent in 1988 (44th Round). Along with this decline, the proportion of households going outside their house premises to fetch water has also gone up during 1993-98, which indicates "declining quality of social consumption in terms of availability of piped water" and the increased efforts in fetching it (Ratna Reddy, 2001). As per this survey, proportion of urban households reporting insufficiency of drinking water is high in Andhra Pradesh (30.1) as against the national average of 14.9 per cent. The corresponding figures in the southern states are 17.5 in Karnataka, 15.4 in Kerala and 12.9 in Tamil Nadu.

During the International Drinking Water Supply and Sanitation Decade (1981-91) the objective in India was to cover 100 per cent of urban population by water supply and 80 per cent by sanitation by 1991. During the mid-decade review in 1985, however, the objectives were lowered in the name of resource constraints to 90 per cent and 50 per cent respectively. By 1991, water supply coverage was estimated to be about 84 per cent, i.e., an increase of only 10 percentage points over 1981. The Eighth Five Year Plan (1992-97) has set a target of achieving 100 per cent coverage of population by safe drinking water by the turn of the century. The Ninth Five Year Plan (1997-2002) document admits that "in terms of estimated 1997 population, the coverage of urban population is unlikely to increase from the level attained in the Seventh Plan," which means that the coverage may be about 84 per cent (Planning Commission, 1997). Like in earlier proclamations, the document declares that "the government is committed to provide drinking water to every settlement in the country within five years." In the last fifty years since independence, setting new targets and extending deadlines for providing drinking water and sanitation facilities has become a routine practice in India's successive Five Year Plans. It was never given the urgency and priority that it deserved.

It was estimated that 21 per cent of all communicable diseases in India are related to water. About 1.5 million children under five years are dying and about 200 million person-days are lost each year in India due to these diseases (citing from other sources in Parikh *et al*, 1999). In view of the growing importance of urban centres in economic growth, it is imperative that quality of life is improved in the urban centres by increasing the levels of water supply. Urban local bodies in Andhra Pradesh have been making serious efforts in recent years to meet the growing demand for water. They are borrowing mainly from the Housing and Urban Development Corporation (HUDCO), New Delhi for undertaking capital works. Loans for water supply accounted for about 72 per cent of the total borrowings by municipalities in the state in 1996-97 (Ramachandraiah, 1999). Unless the distribution systems are overhauled, as recommended by the NCU (1988), minimum levels of supply cannot be ensured to all citizens. As the volume of water supplied is increased, it is those households who already have HSCs that may become the major beneficiaries.

4. URBAN INFRASTRUCTURE

Certain variables relating to density, health (garbage collection and households with toilets), and transport (road length) have been analysed for 105 municipalities[7] by grouping them into size Classes of I, II and III, and also into three regions. As the size of towns increases the overcrowding in them is also going up. There is nearly fifty per cent decline in density from Class I to Class II and from the latter to Class III (Table 8). With rising densities, the pressure on civic infrastructure will also increase. It is interesting to note that the towns in R3 have a higher density probably because more municipalities are in Class I category in this region. The density is low in Telangana (R2) which may also be due to several municipalities being in small and medium category. Though it is generally known that bigger cities will have higher densities, the situation calls for suitable strategies to see that the overcrowding does not increase beyond manageable limits.

Municipal Garbage

The existing literature on urban environment reveals that the per capita garbage generated increases as the level of development of towns increases (World Resources Institute, 1997). In Andhra Pradesh, about 0.50 kilograms (kg) of garbage is generated per person daily i.e., about 180 kilograms (kg) per person per year in the municipalities. This level of garbage generation is higher than that of Hyderabad (138 kg) and Visakhapatnam (144 kg), which are the two metropolitan cities in the state (CPCB, 1997). Though there is not much variation in the size classes, it is surprising that the per capita garbage generated is higher (209 kg) in Class III followed by 180 kg in Class I and 166 kg in Class II towns. The data for this component in small towns may require closer scrutiny. At regional level, per capita generated is high in R1 (198 kg/year) followed by 173 kg in R2 and 155 kg in R3. There are only three towns, Ongole (Class I), Markapur and Bhainsa (Class III) that are generating more than one kg per capita daily (i.e. 360 kg/year). The data for these three towns may also need a scrutiny. The towns generating less than 0.30 kg (i.e. 108kg/year) are more in Rayalaseema (Guntakal, Adoni, Proddatur, Dharmavaram) and Telangana (Qutubullapur, Mahabubnagar, Kothagudem, Adilabad, Nirmal, Mandamarri, Sangareddy, Jangaon) regions. There are only three towns in this category in the entire Coastal Andhra (Ichapuram, Jaggayyapet, Macharla) region. The distribution of these towns over many of the backward districts indicates that low level of garbage may be due to backwardness and low levels of consumption in these towns.

A qualitative change that has occurred in the nature of garbage in recent years is the increase of non-biodegradable waste with the growth of 'use & throw' culture of consumerism. As the experience from around the

Table 8. Infrastructural Facilities in Municipalities of Andhra Pradesh: 1997

Size Class and Region	No. of municipalities	Population ('000)	Area (Sq. Km.)	Density (persons/ sq.km)	Per capita garbage generated daily (kgs)	Per cent of garbage lifted daily	Per cent of households without individual toiltes	Road length per thousand population (kms)	Road length per sq.km of area (kms)
1	2	3	4	5	6	7	8	9	10
Class I	28	6313	745	8477	0.50(180)	89	23	1.03	8.75
Class II	38	3343	829	4030	0.46(166)	87	29	0.86	3.47
Class III	39	1829	784	2333	0.58(209)	85	36	0.92	2.15
R1 (11,14,23)	48	5014	954	5254	0.55(198)	91	25	0.99	5.18
R2 (7,18,14)	39	4159	990	4203	0.48(173)	82	30	1.02	4.27
R3 (10,6,2)	18	2311	414	5584	0.43(155)	91	26	0.82	4.59
Andhra Pradesh	105	11484	2358	4871	0.50(180)	88	27	0.96	4.70

Note: 1. R1 - Coastal Andhra; R2 - Telangana; R3 - Rayalaseema.
2. The figures in parentheses after R1, R2, R3 in column 1 indicate number of towns in Class I, II and III categories in that order in each region.
3. The figures in parentheses under per capita garbage generated relate to kilogram per year.
Source: Based on the data obtained from the Directorate of Municipal Administration, Government of Andhra Pradesh.

world indicates, share of this type of garbage would increase with increasing urbanisation and change of lifestyles. Municipalities that are already struggling with poor finances do not have the capacity to create recycling and incineration facilities. Even for normal garbage, the ill-maintained landfill sites cause groundwater contamination. Dumping of garbage in open spaces provides a breeding ground for disease vectors such as flies, mosquitoes, rats and other pests. It is necessary that municipalities are equipped to handle this problem in sustainable ways like compost making, conversion of garbage into pellets, sanitary land fills, incineration and power generation etc., to create a better urban environment.

The efforts of state government in improving the physical cleanliness in towns seems to be yielding positive results, which is indicated by the high level of garbage clearance (88 per cent) in the municipalities. With the decline in the size class there is also a decrease in the per cent of garbage clearance from 89 in Class I to 87 in Class II and to 85 in Class III towns though the variation is less. From this it is also possible to infer that bigger size towns have the necessary financial capacity to undertake such exercises as compared to small towns. Among the regions, the towns of

Telangana are falling behind the rest in the state. The number of towns that are able to manage hundred per cent clearance of garbage is more in Coastal Andhra region.

Sanitation Facilities

Availability of sanitation facilities is one of the very important aspects of health. About 27 per cent of households did not have individual toilets in municipalities of the state. The NSSO (1999) figures for 1998 also reveal that 30.8 per cent of urban households do not have access to sanitation (latrine) facilities in the state as against the national average of 25.5 per cent. This indicates that about 13.6 lakh poor households in urban areas in the state depend either on community toilets or use open spaces for sanitation purposes. The scenario seems to be no better in the other southern states with the exception of Kerala. The percent of households without sanitation (latrine) facilities in 1998 was 32.5 in Tamil Nadu, 30.0 in Karnataka and only 5.0 in Kerala.

The ill-maintained community toilets and filth-ridden open spaces in the vicinity of their living areas are the major sources of infectious diseases to poor people whose immunity levels are the low due to malnutrition and other related problems. In terms of size class of towns, it may be noticed that the small towns have a higher share i.e., one-third of households without individual toilets: Class III has 36 per cent while it is less in Class II (29 per cent) and in Class I (23 per cent). While such number may be high in big towns, proportionately it is the small and medium towns that are facing serious problems of sanitation and public health. This may also indicate relatively higher levels of poverty in small towns. The NCU (1988) had observed that the coverage of sanitation facilities is biased against the poor in India.

At regional level in the state, prevalence of this problem is high in Telangana since most of the municipalities in this region are in the small and medium category. There are a number of towns, many of them in small and medium and a few in Class I, in which the lack of sanitation facilities appear to be a gigantic problem. It is astonishing to note that in two Class III towns (Bhainsa and Bhongir in Telangana) about 80 per cent of households do not have individual toilets. This figure is also high in three Class I towns, Adoni (67) in R3, and Khammam (67) and Qutubullapur (52) in R2. It is interesting to note that Mahabubnagar, which is located in one of the most backward districts, has only 11 per cent of households in this category compared to more than one-third in Guntur (37) and Warangal (35) cities. These two cities have a population of over 5 lakhs each and have been made municipal corporations in nineties after the Constitution (74th) Amendment Act, 1992. In several other towns like Gudur, Amadalavalasa, Bobbili, Parvathipuram, Samalkot, Pedana, Macherla (all in R1), Nirmal, Mandamarri, Sangareddy, Suryapet,

Yellandu, Vikarabad, Zaheerabad (all in R2), and Rayadurg (R3), the number of households without individual toilets is in the range of 50-70 per cent. In several other towns also it is in the range of 40-50 per cent. Lack of adequate housing to large sections of urban poor may be the most important reason for the absence of individual toilets. Small and medium towns seem to be facing a bigger problem in this regard.

The Low Cost Sanitation Programme (LCSP) has been going on since 1982-83 in many municipalities in Andhra Pradesh with the main objective of conversion of dry latrines as sanitary latrines. Scavenging Elimination Programme, Vimukthi Programme and Integrated Low Cost Sanitation Programme (ILCS) (stage I) etc., have been implemented for this purpose. From 1993-94 onwards, emphasis was laid on construction of leach-pit-pour-flush-water household toilets under stage II of this programme. For this purpose, Government of India provides subsidy to the extent of 45 per cent of the cost of sanitary latrine upto plinth area and HUDCO provides 50 per cent as loan while the beneficiary has to contribute 5 per cent. For the superstructure of sanitary latrine, HUDCO provides 90 per cent of the cost as loan while the beneficiary should contribute the remaining 10 per cent. It has been observed that the progress of implementation of the scheme has been very poor.

Though the incidence of urban poverty is about 30 per cent, it is estimated that the poverty in small and medium towns is about four times that in metropolitan cities. The lack of economic development as well as the nature of development itself is causing poverty in India. The small towns are at a disadvantage in getting funds from the donor agencies since the latter are more interested in commercially viable projects in big cities. The allocation for anti-poverty programmes has gone down in recent years - the per capita figures in nineties being about 24 per cent less than in mid-eighties. Further, these allocations have a higher component of loans than grants compared to earlier years. With the government programmes emphasising on self-employment, economic viability and cost recovery, the most vulnerable groups among the urban poor are likely to be left out of the development process (Kundu, 2000).

Urban Transport - Road Length

The NCU (1988) had noted that the urban transportation continued to remain the single most neglected function of development that was coupled with incredible public apathy and governmental indifference. In this section, as a variable for urban transportation, the combined length of black-topped (BT), cement and metal roads has been considered as a ratio to population and area of the towns. The information for number of motor vehicles is not available at town level. On average, there is less than one kilometre of road length per thousand population in the state. Despite high density in Class I towns, the road length is also higher in them (1.03 km) compared to other towns. As the city size grows, more roads are also developed in them due to higher pressure of activities. There may be a certain bias also in favour of big towns.

At regional level the municipalities in Rayalaseema (R1) have less road length for population because of high density. In terms of area, Class I towns have high road length (8.75) and it declines steeply to 3.47 km in Class II and 2.15 km in Class III towns. The length of internal roads in the towns declining with size may create a situation in which the roads will be crowded in small towns even with less number of vehicles. The municipalities in Telangana (R2) have less roads in terms of area but have higher road length for population which indicates wider spatial spread of towns in this region. While analysing urban transportation in the metropolitan cities of India, it was observed that there is a general reduction in per capita road length as city size increases, with the exception of Chennai. Further, there is a general decrease in the ratio of road length to area as city size increases, with a few exceptions (Ramanathan, 1999). The experience shows that average trip distances lengthen when a city grows in population and size. Decreasing population density also increases trip length. Urban development and urban living will be influenced significantly by urban transportation (NCU, 1988).

5. RAINWATER HARVESTING (RWH)[8]

Urban centres may have to take up water conservation measures on a large scale to augment future supplies. This is essential to reduce dependence on long distance sources and avoid expensive schemes. RWH simply means harnessing local rainfall for local use. It means capturing runoff where it falls: runoff from rooftops, from local catchments, capturing floodwaters from local streams etc. It can take the forms of storing rainwater or allowing groundwater recharge by artificial methods. Artificial recharge is defined as the process of augmenting the underground water table by artificial infiltration of rainwater and surface runoff. Several developed countries like Germany, Japan, USA, Australia, France, Singapore etc., and developing countries like Israel, Egypt, Mexico etc., have adopted RWH methods on a large scale to augment their water resources. In urban areas, RWH would be useful for the following purposes:

- To allow recharge and improve the quality & quantity of groundwater;
- To improve water supply for potable needs;
- To improve water supply for certain uses like gardening, washing cloths and for sanitary needs;
- To provide water for institutional needs;
- To reduce storm water runoff and thus avoid flooding of urban areas; and overloading of urban drainage and sewerage treatment plants; and

- To prevent intrusion of saline water into aquifers in coastal areas etc.

There are several methods to implement RWH in urban areas like percolation (recharge) pits, recharge trenches along compound walls, using defunct wells and borewells for recharge, and construction of sumps to store water etc. In areas of slope, dwarf walls can be constructed to a height of one foot to reduce runoff, retain rainwater and allow recharge. The techniques to be used for RWH depend on the rooftop area of the building, open space available, use of the building etc. The percolation pits are filled with 40 mm metal/pebbles up to 50 per cent of the depth from below, followed by 20 mm metal/pebbles by 25 per cent and sand for the remaining 25 per cent (preferably coarse sand with fine sand on the top). Thus, a recharge pit is a three-layered structure with sand at the top, 20 mm metal/pebbles in the middle and 40 mm metal/pebbles at the bottom. The sand at the top acts as a filter to retain impurities. Trenches can be dug up along compound walls and filled in the same way as that of percolation pits.

The campaign for RWH in urban areas has been going on in Andhra Pradesh in the last four years with active participation of the government and also builders' associations. It has still not caught the imagination of the general public largely due to the excessive control of bureaucracy, and very little involvement of the beneficiaries in implementing RWH. The task of preserving rainwater should include protection of the existing lakes and other water bodies from encroachment and pollution. The water bodies act as natural reservoirs for storing rainwater and recharging groundwater in urban areas. The most urgent task in urban areas is to protect the existing water bodies and improve their ecology.

6. CONCLUSION

The state of Andhra Pradesh is witnessing a "top-heavy" growth of urbanisation with a few large urban centres comprising much of the urban population. Hyderabad's pre-eminence has been reinforced overtime as the highly urbanised region amidst the backward districts of Telangana. The level of urbanisation in the state has remained around 27 per cent only, and it has declined in several districts in nineties. The state has registered a low urban growth rate in nineties compared to the eighties. Part of this decline has been due to the declassification of 79 towns in the state in 2001. Of these, 46 towns had more than 30 per cent of their male workforce engaged in agriculture in 1991. This indicates that the 'urban' criterion was not applied rigorously in 1991 itself. When the 46 towns are excluded from the urban population of 1991, the growth rate during nineties works out to 20.5 per cent instead of 15.1 per cent as per the Census. With the adjusted figures, the Telangana region shows a slightly higher urban growth rate (25.2) than Rayalaseema (23.5) with Coastal Andhra (14.1) falling much behind. An analysis of the economic base of small and medium towns, and the issue of application of 'urban' criterion in Census should be given adequate importance, which is brought into focus with the declassification of as many as 79 towns in 2001 in the state.

The Class I towns are able to provide higher level of water supply which supports the hypothesis that larger urban centres will have financial capability to provide higher level of civic amenities. Small and medium towns suffer from a double disadvantage of low level of finances as well as amenities. It is interesting to note that the small towns (Class III) are generating more garbage per capita than bigger towns but the proportion of garbage lifted is higher in the latter. The efforts of the government in garbage clearing seem to have had a positive impact, which is reflected in clearing of about 88 per cent of garbage in municipalities. There is a lot to be done in the sanitation sector, as about 27 per cent (30.8 per cent as per NSSO 54th Round) of urban households do not have individual toilets. And this figure is increasing with declining size of towns. In transportation, bigger towns (Class I) have higher road length in terms of population as well as area. In view of the importance of urban centres in promoting employment and economic development, the situation in Andhra Pradesh calls for development of water supply, public health, sanitation and transportation infrastructure especially in small and medium towns for promoting a more sustainable and balanced urbanisation.

Notes

1 Information on such villages is not yet available for 2001.

2 Vizinagaram district was formed later out of Srikakulam and Visakhapatnam districts. Prakasam and Rangareddy districts were also formed in the state in course of time.

3 There are several urban centres which are not municipalities. Further, the municipal corporations of Hyderabad, Visakhapatnam, Vijayawada, Guntur, Rajahmundry, Kurnool, and Warangal are excluded in the analysis. That is why, 105 municipalities account for only about 52 per cent of the total urban population.

4 The population range adopted by the Census of India is 100,000 and above for Class I, 50,000-99,999 for Class II and 20,000-49,999 for Class III towns.

5 The National Commission on Urbanisation (NCU) in 1988 recommended 70 LPCD to be the bare minimum, level of water supply 90 LPCD as desirable and about 100-110 LPCD as sufficient to carry on human life with reasonable level of hygiene and this level of supply must be ensured to all the citizens.

6 The Census of India 2001 has adopted an "inclusive approach" to define slum areas as follows:

(a) All areas notified as 'Slum' by State/Local Government and UT Administration under any Act;

(b) All areas recognized as 'Slum' by State/Local Government and UT Administration which have not been formally notified as slum under any Act;

(c) A compact area of at least 300 population or about 60-70 households of poorly built congested tenements, in unhygienic environment usually with inadequate infrastructure and lacking in proper sanitary and drinking water facilities.

7 The data for these aspects was taken from a different source other than that for water supply. Therefore, there is some variation in the list of towns between these sources though the number is the same.

8 The discussion on RWH is based on the recommendations of the Conference on Potential of Water Harvesting: Traditions, Policies and Social Mobilisation in New Delhi organised by the Center for Science and Environment during 3-5 October, 1998; correspondence with K.R.G. Rainwater Harvesting Co., Chennai, and personal knowledge.

References

Alam, S.M. (1968), "A Note on the Realignment of the Urban System of Andhra Pradesh", cited in Alam, S.M. and W. Khan (1970), *Metropolitan Hyderabad and its Region-A Strategy for Development*, Asia, New Delhi.

Bose, Ashish (1994), *India's Urban Population: 1991 Census Data*, Wheeler, New Delhi.

Census of India (2001), *Provisional Population Totals, Paper 1 of 2001*, Series-29: Andhra Pradesh.

Chattopadhyay, B. and Moonis Raza (1975), "Regional Development: Analytical Framework and Indicators", *Indian Journal of Regional Science*, Vol. 7, No. 1.

Chen, Xiangming and William L. Parish (1996), "Urbanisation in China: Reassessing an Evolving Model", in Josef Gugler (ed.) *The Urban Transformation of the Developing World*, pp. 61-92, Oxford, New York.

CPCB (1997), *Parivesh (Newsletter)*, 4(1), June, Central Pollution Control Board, New Delhi.

IIHFW (1997), "Andhra Pradesh Vision 2020: Population Projections for State and Districts - 1995-2020", Indian Institute of Health and Family Welfare, (mimeo), Hyderabad.

Kundu, A. (2001), "Brakes on the Urban Sprawl", *Business Standard*, 28th August, Hyderabad,

Kundu, A. (2000), "Trends in Urban Poverty Alleviation Over the Past 10 years and Directions for the Future", Tenth Meeting of Urban Think Tank on Flow and Utilisation of Urban Poverty Funds, February 25, Hyderabad.

Kundu, A. (1993), *In the Name of the Urban Poor* (Access to Basic Amenities), Sage, New Delhi.

Nagarpalika Network (2002), "The Census 2001 – Urbanisation and Growth Dynamics in India: An Analysis of Trends and Processes", All India Institute of Local Self Government, (mimeo), New Delhi.

NCU (1988), *Report of National Commission on Urbanisation, Vol-II*, National Commission on Urbanisation, New Delhi.

NSSO (1999), *Drinking water, sanitation and hygiene in India*, National Sample Survey (54th Round), National Sample Survey Organisation, New Delhi, July.

Parikh, K.S. (ed.) (1999), *India Development Report 1999-2000*, Oxford-IGIDR, Mumbai.

Parikh, K.S., Jyothi Parik, and Tata L. Raghu Ram, (1999), "Air and Water Quality Management: New Initiatives Needed", in Parikh, K.S. (ed.): *op.cit.*

PHED (1995), "Status of Water Supply Schemes and Other Engineering Services in Andhra Pradesh", Office of the Engineer-in- Chief, Public Health and Municipal Engineering Department, (mimeo), Hyderabad.

Planning Commission (1997), *Approach Paper to the Ninth Five Year Plan 1997-2002,* Government of India, New Delhi.

Prakasa Rao, V.L.S. (1983), *Urbanisation in India – Spatial Dimensions,* Concept, New Delhi.

Ravindra Prasad, D. and K. Rajeswar Rao (2000), *Handbook of Municipal Statistics: Andhra Pradesh,* Regional Centre for Urban and Environmental Studies, Osmania University, Hyderabad.

Ramachandraiah, C. (1999), "Municipal Borrowings and Debts in Andhra Pradesh", Centre for Economic and Social Studies, (mimeo), Hyderabad.

Ramachandraiah, C. and V.K. Bawa (2000), "Hyderabad in the Changing Political Economy", *Journal of Contemporary Asia,* Vol. 30, No. 4.

Ramanathan, R. (1999), "Urban Transport", in Parikh, Kirit S. (ed.) *op.cit.*

Ratna Reddy, V. (2001), "Declining Social Consumption in India", *Economic and Political Weekly,* Vol. 36, No. 29.

Raza, Moonis (1991), "On the Nature of Rural Urban Interactions in the Indian Context", *IASSI Quarterly,* Vol. 10, No. 1.

Tewari, Vinod K. (1997), "Urbanisation in India: Patterns and Perspectives", *Urban India,* Vol. 17, Nos. 1&2.

World Resource Institute (1997), *World Resources 1996-97,* Oxford.

Wang, Gabe T. and Xiaobo Hu (1999), "Small Town Development and Rural Urbanisation in China", *Journal of Contemporary Asia,* Vol. 29, No. 1.

PART - VI

DECENTRALISATION

22

Decentralised Local Bodies: Post 73rd Amendment Scenario

M. Gopinath Reddy

1. INTRODUCTION

In recent times there is an increasing realization that genuine decentralization leads to development. It is also felt that decentralization of power to the local units of government and management is one of the best ways of empowering people, promoting public participation and increasing efficiency. According to Human Development Report, 1993 where decentralization has taken place, it has often been fairly successful in encouraging local participation, increasing accountability of local officials, reducing the costs and increasing the efficiency. Decentralisation can help to mobilize the resources, introduce locally and regionally diverse solutions and promote equitable growth by bringing the poor into the mainstream of development.

In this paper, it is attempted to dwell on the present status of rural local bodies (Panchayati Raj Institutions) in the State of Andhra Pradesh in the aftermath of 73rd Constitution Amendment. The focus would be on I) functional and financial devolution, ii) structural aspects of Andhra Pradesh Panchayati Raj System (APPR), iii) working of reservation system especially for Dalits and Women iv) interface between PRIs and `Janmabhoomi' programme, v) linkages with PRIs and Community Based Organisations (CBOs). On the whole, an overview will be presented on the current status of decentralization experience in Andhra Pradesh and identify the gray areas in the process. The issues raised in Vision 2020 document on local bodies are also addressed in the paper. The paper depends mainly on published literature and secondary sources. Some of the micro studies recently conducted also provided useful insights in the preparation of this paper.

The paper is organized in the following sections. Section II deals with functional devolution while financial devolution is dealt in Section III. Structural dimensions of APPR system are discussed in Section IV and Section V deals with the effectiveness of the reservation system especially for dalits and women. The discussion on PRIs versus `Janmabhoomi' programme and parallel bodies (CBOs) is presented in Section VI while section VII provides summary and conclusions.

Keeping in view the main objectives of the 73rd Constitutional Amendment Act, the A.P Government has passed the A.P Panchayat Raj Act 1994. The main features of the AP Act are the following:

i. The Act is aimed at promoting participatory democracy

ii. The Act seeks to ensure regular elections to the PRIs for a period of 5 years and prevent scandalous suppression of the local bodies;

iii. The Act aims to create institutions of self- government at the panchayat level by endowing them with the needed powers, authority and finances. It provides for revenue raising powers for the Panchayats;

iv. The Act specifically mandates the creation of an independent State Finance Commission (SFC) for the purpose of ensuring financial transfers to the PR bodies.

v. Lastly, it seeks to promote bottom- up planning process.

Vision 2020 of AP Government and The Role of Local Bodies

The Government of Andhra Pradesh articulates its commitment to strengthening local bodies in its vision 2020 Document in the following words: 'By 2020, the A.P Government will be an enabler of market based development by providing a growth conducive, deregulated policy environment. Decentralized decision –making will be the norm. local bodies encouraged and empowered to participate in administration. Andhra Pradesh Government will remain transparent, effective and responsive to the people, primarily by maintaining close contact with them and involving them in governance. In order to achieve this vision AP Govt. feels that decentralization is an essential part of the programme to make Government institutions more efficient and responsive. The state is therefore determined to strengthen its administration through responsible management by Panchayati Raj Institutions (PRI's) and Community organizations. To this end, it will enable local management devolving administrative and economic powers and responsibilities. To successfully implement this framework, change in administrative system will be carefully managed'. According to vision 2020 Document, local empowerment is already emphasized in the 73rd and 74th Constitutional Amendments. Accordingly, the state will devolve the administration of Government services mentioned in the 73rd to the appropriate Panchayati Raj Institutions. It will also provide Gram Panchayats control over local services such as sanitation and primary schools and mandals and zilla parishads control over 'shared' services, such as secondary schools and colleges. Directly involving people in the management of the services they use is another important initiative required. The people can play a major role in managing education, health and infrastructure services through Community Based Organization (CBOs) such as School Committees, or Development of Women and Children in Rural Areas (DWCRA) (Government of AP, 1999).

2. STATUS OF DEVOLUTION OF POWERS AND FUNCTIONS

When the authority and power in respect of certain activity is transferred from the state to the panchayats, the latter should have the prerogative of making "decisions", in respect of planning and implementation of such activity. In the sphere of devolution of responsibilities on lower level of governance, some important principles should be kept in view. In the first place the principle of ' subsidiarity' needs to be given adequate attention. The principle of subsidiarity postulates that any function which can be performed by a lower tier, should be handled by that tier alone and not by any higher tier of PRI. Second, the State Government should not unilaterally withdraw the responsibilities and powers already granted to the panchayat without adequate justification and prior consultation with the latter. Third, responsibilities, authorities and powers granted to the panchayats should be extremely specific, clear and simple in order to be comprehended by the panchayats. Lastly, whenever, functions and responsibilities are transferred to the panchayats, it should be ensured that the necessary funds, functionaries and freedom in decision-making also accompany such transfer (Report of Tenth Five Year Plan Working Group, 2001)

Article 243(G) of the constitution stipulates endowment by law and by the legislative of a state such powers and authority and functions as may be necessary to enable them to function as institutions of self-government. The states were supposed to study this article along with the 11th schedule and allocate the powers and functions among the three tiers of the panchayats.

The Amendment Act further directs that states should have provisions for the devolution of powers and responsibilities upon panchayats at appropriate level for the following purposes:

a) The preparation of plans for economic development and social justice and
b) The implementation of schemes for economic development and social justice as may be entrusted to them including those in relation to the matters listed in the Eleventh Schedule.

Under the new Act, PRIs are expected to perform all development functions as suggested in the 11th schedule, as mentioned above. For doing so, proper devolution of functions and powers to local bodies is necessary. In particular, devolution of functions and powers from the regular line departments to the PRIs is a necessary prerequisite for healthy functioning of local bodies. We discuss below how the functional devolution has taken place in Andhra Pradesh.

Before addressing the issue of actual decentralization /devolution that has taken place, an understanding of what each tier is expected to perform will be in order.

The AP act specifies that the zilla parishads (the highest tier located at district level) have been given powers of supervision and control of the Mandal Parishads including collection of data, consolidation of plans of the Mandal Parishads, distribution of funds allotted to the district further down to the Mandal Parishads, examining and appraising the budgets of the mandals.

The Mandal Parishad will be responsible for the implementation of rural development programmes in the mandal area in association with the panchayats, cooperatives, voluntary organization and other development institutions. The Act also specifies a number of development functions to be performed by the mandal parishad for stepping up agricultural production, for improving livestock and establishing minor veterinary dispensaries under animal husbandry and for expanding and monitoring medical and health services under rural health and sanitation.

The Act (Section 45) also specifies that Gram Panchayats (GPs) perform the duty of providing civic amenities, maintenance of GP roads, construction and maintenance of drains, cleaning streets etc. Besides usual functions, the Act specifies a long list of development functions. The development activities that GPs are supposed to perform are minor irrigation, watershed management, land reform measures including consolidation of holdings and cooperative management of community lands.

In order to perform the numerous functions enlisted in the Act, the extent of devolution required should be adequate. Coming to the actual devolution that has taken place, it needs to the stated that the ground reality in A.P is not satisfactory.

The various development departments, which are listed in Appendix I, need to be brought under the control of PR bodies for enabling them to discharge functions enshrined in the 11th schedule (29 items) as well as to become institutions of self government.

The ground reality existing in the AP state is that a majority of the line departments mentioned in the Appendix I exist separately and have not been brought under the control of PR bodies. A separate 'Panchayat Raj Cadre' has not been created.

Besides, the District Rural Development Agency (DRDA) which commands sizeable resources functions independently of PR bodies. Similarly, there are a few other development corporations like AP Scheduled Caste Corporation, AP Backward Caste Corporation, AP Women Development Corporation, which work independently of PR bodies in the state. Unless these bodies /agencies and their finances are brought under the PR bodies purview, it is difficult to call PR bodies as institutions of self-government.

In this context it may be mentioned that state government constituted an expert committee with the Principal Secretary, Panchayat Raj and Rural Development as the chairman and the secretaries and heads of concerned departments and a few MLAs as members to study the pattern of devolution of powers and functions. Based on the committee's recommendations, the state government has decided to transfer 16 out of the 29 subjects to the PRIs. It is believed that formal announcement of the devolution of 16 functions has been made due to the pressure mounted by the Association of the sarpanches of AP which carried a protracted struggle for the implementation of the various provisions of the Act.

The following is the list of functions that were transferred and those yet to be transferred.

<u>List of Subjects Already Transferred</u>

1. Agriculture, including Agricultural Extension.
2. Maintenance of Community Assets.
3. Social Forestry and Farm Forestry
4. Minor Irrigation, Water management and Watershed Development
5. Fuel and Fodder.
6. Khadi, Village and Cottage industry
7. Roads, Culverts, Bridges, Ferries, Waterways and other means of Communication
8. Non-conventional Energy Sources. including distribution of Electricity.
9. Education, including Primary and Secondary Schools.
10. Adult and non-formal Education
11. Libraries
12. Cultural activities
13. Women and Child Development
14. Social Welfare including welfare of handicapped and mentally retarded
15. Public Distribution System.
16. Drinking Water.

<u>List of Subjects yet to be Transferred</u>

1. Markets and Fairs
2. Land improvement, implementation of land reforms, land consolidation and soil conservation
3. Animal Husbandry, Dairying and Poultry
4. Fisheries
5. Minor Forest Produce..
6. Small Scale Industries including Food Processing
7. Rural Housing
8. Rural Electrification
9. Poverty Alleviation Programme.
10. Technical Training and Vocational Schools
11. Health Training and Sanitation including Hospitals, Primary Health Centers and Dispensaries
12. Family Welfare.
13. Welfare of the weaker sections, in particular of the SC & STs.

Out of the 16 functions that were transferred out of the 29 subjects, orders were issued for transfer of 14 subjects only. Regarding the balance two Subjects orders transferring them are to be issued by the government. With regard to transfer of other 13 subjects for devolution, the matter is under consideration.

The present status of functional devolution in AP shows that its position is lowest among a few important States listed in the table. It transferred functions in respect of sixteen (16) subjects of which five (05) subjects are with funds (Agriculture, Drinking Water Supply, Minor Irrigation Tanks, Social Forestry, Primary and Secondary Education and Khadi and Village Industries) and only two subjects are with functionaries (Drinking Water Supply and Minor Irrigation Tanks). Number of functions yet to be transferred remain thirteen (13); with funds twenty four (24) subjects; and with functionaries are twenty seven (27) subjects, whereas in Karnataka State all the 29 Subjects/ Departments have been transferred to panchayats with funds, functions and functionaries. Next comes Kerala followed by West Bengal and Madhya Pradesh as presented in Table 1.

Table 1. Status of Devolution of Departments/Subjects with Functions, Funds and Functionaries to Panchayat Raj Institutions in a Few Important States.

State	No. of Departments/Subjects transferred to Panchayats with			No. of Departments/Subjects yet to be transferred to Panchayats with		
	Funct-ions	Fun-ds	Functio-naries	Funct-ions	Funds	Functionaries
1 Andhra Pradesh	16	05	02	13	24	27
2 Karnataka	29	29	29	-	-	-
3 Kerala	29	15	15	-	14	14
4 West Bengal	29	12	12	-	17	17
5 Madhya Pradesh	23	10	09	06	19	20

Source: Ministry of Rural Development.

(Report of the Fifth Five Year Plan Working Group, 2001). National Commission to Review the Working of the Constitution comments on the functional and financial devolution in AP in these terms: In Andhra Pradesh, the gram panchayats and the mandal parishads are not required to plan for ' economic development and social Justice'. All the tiers of panchayat have been assigned with large number of functions. But none of them has financial or administrative resources under their control to execute them. The mandal parishad has no control over the staff of the Development blocks and zilla parishad has no control over the DRDA which controls huge funds under various poverty alleviation programmes (National Commission to Review the Working of the Constitution, 2001).

In the aftermath of the recent Assembly elections, the state government has also constituted a cabinet sub-committee headed by Minister for Panhayat Raj as chairman and Ministers of Municipal Administration and Urban Development, Endowments and Cooperation as members. It is known as Madhava Reddy Committee Report on Local Bodies. This exercise was carried out as a part of concretizing vision 2020 Document (Swarnandhra Pradesh) which has separate section on local bodies. This envisages empowerment of local bodies to manage services and create mechanisms for local communities to articulate their demands. The final report was submitted recently.

The present situation has forced some of the dedicated implementers of the various rural development programmes to comment that in Andhra Pradesh all the subjects of the Eleventh Schedule continue to be dealt with by the various departmental heads at the district level, except a few subjects which already had been over a long period under the control of zilla parishad. (Yugandhar, 2001). Similarly, yet another scholar who studied recent decentralization experience in Andhra Pradesh mentioned that the sector service delivery assigned to the PRIs in AP is negligible. The particular sectors studied are primary education, primary health, rural roads, water supply and rural roads. So far, the functions and responsibilities to the PRIs pertaining to agriculture extension are restricted to the selection of beneficiaries to various agricultural implements at the mandal. There are no funds devolved for this purpose (Sitaram, 2000). On similar lines, another study mentions that still a large number of subjects mentioned in Schedule I and three subjects under Schedule II of the Act have not been devolved to the PRIs so far. Only some residuary powers have been entrusted and as such the question of planning by decentralized bodies does not arise (Babu, 1997) In case transfer of functions, as listed in the schedule II, takes place in the form of real decentralization, the entire picture of local bodies will undergo drastic change for the very reason that the devolution of finances also will have to follow. However in A.P the identification of the programmes/ functions to be transferred to local bodies has not been finalized (AP SFC Report, 1997)

3. STATUS OF FINANCIAL DEVOLUTION

All along the history of local self government, the inadequate and unsound financial base has impaired the working of the local bodies. It is realized that any talk of the effectiveness of the local bodies in the absence of a strong financial base is of no use. Accordingly, 73rd Amendment Act has made it mandatory for all the State Governments to constitute State Finance Commissions to work out the proper allocation of devolution of state funds to the local bodies.

By and large in A.P the income of ZPs (Zilla Parishads) and MPs (Mandal Parishads) originate mainly from the grants. The contribution of non-tax revenue sources is either zero or negligible. In AP these two tiers do get some resources from assigned tax revenues such as land cess, surcharge on stamp duty, mineral cess etc. Mandal Parishads depend predominantly on grants from the state government which are mostly tied in nature. Another feature observed with mandal level finances is that MPs have to deposit 15 percent of their grant exclusively for the purpose of housing programmes implemented by state Housing Corporation.

In the case of ZPs there are four categories which constitute the revenue / income base of the zilla parishads i) ZPs can mobilize resources on their own through non tax avenues; ii) ZPs get revenue from assigned duties such as land cess, mineral cess, stamp duty etc. iii) Tied grants from the State and Center towards social sectors like education, drinking water supply and rural roads iv) grant.

In respect of Gram panchayats, the sources of finance are more diversified and are large in number. GPs derive their incomes from grants, tax and non-tax sources and property and peoples contribution and so on. They also overwhelmingly depend on government grants. Though in AP, GPs have been assigned many local taxes, duties and fees, they raise just about a third of their total resources from these sources. The important tax powers of GPs in the state are house tax, vehicles tax, land cess, surcharge on stamp duty, surcharge on seignorage fees (fees on materials other than minerals and minor minerals quarried in the village). However the fact remains that GPs, despite their larger tax base, depend overwhelmingly on government grants- development and general grants from the state governments and the JRY grants from the Union Government. While grants in general constitute the major sources of finance to GPs, the JRY grant constitutes the bigger slice in it and in the total income of the panchayat. Thus, it constitutes as much as 51% of the total income of the GPs in Andhra Pradesh (Aziz, 1998). What follows is an account of the resource flows to the local bodies since the beginning of late 80's in A.P.

It is seen that during the last decade the income of the State Government had gone up from Rupees 2199.02 crores to Rupees 8959. 49 crores while the grants released to the PR institutions have gone up from Rupees 663.98 crores to 2123.65 crores. However, as seen from the figures, the percentage of devolution of finances to PR institutions was 30.19 during 1987-88 but has gone down to 23. 70 during 1997-98. (Table. 2)

Income of the PR bodies from their own sources is only about 10 percent of their total receipts. For gram panchayats it is about 15 percent, for mandals it is about 0.5 percent and for zilla parishads it is about 5 percent of their total income and the rest of the money is obtained through grants released by the government and the revenues assigned by the state government. Government pays a variety of grants to the PR Institutions, some of which are for specific purposes while others are un-tied. As a part of these grants, gram panchayats receive per capita grant of rupee 1/- per head of population and salary grant for the provincialised panchayat employees which together amounts to 10 percent of the total revenues of the panchayats. The system of per capita grant to P.R Institutions was started in 1959-60 which is meant for general purposes and can be spent as per the felt needs of the gram panchayats. Per capita grant which was twenty five paise in 1959-60 was subsequently increased to rupee one to gram panchayats.

Table. 2 Grants Released to the PR Institutions During the Last Decade.

(Rs. In crores)

SL.No.	Year	Revenue of the State from taxes and non -taxes	Grants released to PRIs including share of grants from Govt. of India	Percentage of the grants to the Revenue of the state
1	2	3	4	5
1.	1987-88	2199.02	663.98	30.19
2.	1988-89	2464.74	761.52	30.89
3.	1989-90	2804.37	870.63	31.04
4.	1990-91	3101.62	812.26	26.18
5.	1991-92	3689.40	1111.20	30.11
6.	1992-93	4006.66	1412.72	35.25
7.	1993-94	4748.98	1447.28	30.47
8.	1994-95	5176.09	1373.51	26.53
9.	1995-96	6678.77	1545.41	23.14
10.	1996-97	7950.71	1712.05	21.53
11.	1997-98 (B.E)	8559.49	2123.65	23.70

B.E – Budget Estimates.
Source: SFC Report.

JYR grant is of the order rupees 110 crores. Salary grant towards the payment of salary to the provincialised staff of gram panchayat which is of the order of Rs.33 crores (1994-95) is the second largest grant. One rupee per capita grant is of the order of Rs.5.19 crores. Administrative grant for payment of honorarium to S.C and S.T sarpanches is of the order of rupees 0.52 crores (1994-95).

Since 1989, gram panchayats are receiving substantial money by way of plan grants under the head Jawahar Rojgar Yojana (JRY). The following tables (Tables 3&4) indicates the income of the gram panchayats from the JRY funds between 1989-94 and their percentage to the total income of the gram panchayats.

In A.P the first State Finance Commission under the chairmanship of M.V Lakshman Swamy submitted its report on 31-5-1997. The government appointed a committee of Secretaries to study the recommendations and suggest measures for implementation. In addition, a cabinet sub committee was also appointed to look into the recommendations of the SFC report.

Table 3. Grants Released to Gram Panchayats in A.P During Years 1989-94.

SL. No.	Year	Grants (in lakhs)
1	1989-90	1049.67
2	1990-91	746.82
3	1991-92	1420.75
4	1992-93	1507.25
5	1993-94	2751.33

Source: SFC Report.

Table 4. Share of JRY Grants in the Total Income of the Gram Panchayats 1989-95.

SL. No.	Year	Total income of gram panchayats (in crores)	JRY grants (in crores)	Share of JRY to total income (percentage)	Per capita income with JRY grants	Percapita income without JRY grants
1.	1989-90	230.91	115.28	62.91	56.59	20.98
2.	1990-91	191.28	111.55	58.32	46.88	19.54
3.	1991-92	213.29	114.62	49.55	44.56	22.47
4.	1992-93	220.77	111.79	50.63	42.53	20.99
5.	1994-95	242.81	115.81	47.63	46.78	24.44

Source: SFC Report.

According to first SFC Report, the annual devolution to local bodies for 97-98 was Rs. 2536.53 crores (which includes central and state grants). In addition to this, SFC has recommended an additional devolution of Rs. 979.16 crores. The total comes to Rs. 3515.69 crores (39.24 % of tax and non-tax revenue of the state) (1st SFC Report, 1997).

The above recommended total (39.24 % of the state revenue) includes both *central and state grants.* According to the Action taken Report of the SFC, the grant *exclusively given by the state government* to the local bodies is 11.09 % of the state revenue (Rs. 1087. 74 crores) in the year 1998-99. This amount is exclusive of salaries, pensions, establishment cost, allocations made as matching contribution to centrally sponsored schemes and central grants (NIRD, 1998).

Out of an additional devolution of Rs. 979.16 crores recommended by the State Finance Commission for devolution to Panchayati Raj and Municipal bodies, Government accepted devolution to an extent of Rs. 432.42 crores mainly relating to doubling the per capita grants, increase of R.W.S grants (rural water supply), rural sanitation, grants for construction of school buildings, construction and maintenance of rural roads etc.

It needs to be noted that the exact quantum of funds to be devolved will however need to be based on the extent to which personnel and functional responsibilities are proposed to be delegated to the local bodies.

According to SFC recommendations, local bodies receive three kinds of revenues i.e., i) Assigned revenues, ii) Grants –in – aid, iii) Revenue sharing.

Under assigned revenues the important sources are profession tax, surcharge on stamp duty and land/local cess. Under grants –in- aid two kinds of sources are important namely, a) untied per capita grant (varies for each tier- Rs four for the gram panchayats; rupees eight for the mandal panchayats and rupees four for zilla parishads) and b) capital grants, which are meant for rural water supply, minor irrigation, rural roads, school buildings, mandal parishad office buildings, rural sanitation etc. Capital grants are meant for creation of infrastructure as well as for the maintenance of existing infrastructure. Under revenue sharing, assignment of taxes levied by government to local bodies is not recommended. Revenue sharing between the state government and local bodies was preferred.

One important recommendation of the State Finance Commission that a sum of Rs. 229.15 crores towards civic and developmental functions be devolved to Gram Panchayats, has not been accepted by the state government (NIRD, 1998).

In addition to the State grants, Tenth Finance Commission (TFC) has recommended an amount of Rs. 351.00 crores for rural local bodies for four years from the year 1996-97 to 1999- 2000 to supplement resources of the panchayats in the state.

Based on this recommendation, Government has released an amount of Rs. 87. 75 crores during 1996-97 and 62.00 crores during 1997-98 (covering three instalments out of the four) for taking up schemes by the gram panchayats. There are certain conditions imposed by the TFC for utilizing the grants. These are the following:

i) The grant is not intended for expenditure on salaries and wages and should not be used for financing employment generating schemes.
ii) The funds released under the TFC grants shall be entirely released to the GPs only as per the existing norm of Rs. 16/- percapita so that concrete assets should be created in the gram panchayat areas.

Fiscal decentralization, along with functional decentralization is imperative in order to make local bodies vibrant and dynamic. The present system of providing per capita grant is not of much help. In fact whatever life the present PRIs enjoys in the state is due to the grants given under various centrally sponsored schemes. In particular, the reliance of zilla parishads and mandal parishads on state grants is too large and they receive more of tied grants which restrict their autonomy. Therefore, they should be more of untied grants so that they can plan and proritize to their own specific needs. Once the powers and functions enumerated in schedule I and II are transferred a commensurate amount of finances should be devolved to the panchayats so that they can plan and prioritize their own specific needs.

Another aspect which undermines the autonomy of the local bodies in the state is the phenomenon of reverse flow of funds from panchayats to other development organizations. It is mandatory that the MPs and ZPs have to transfer 15 percent and 6 percent of their funds to Scheduled Caste and Scheduled Tribes Development Corporations. Similarly grants meant for IAY (Indira Awas Yojana) and MWP (Millon Wells Programme) under JRY have to be transferred to the Z.P. Added to this, state government releases various types of grants to ZP and MPs for social welfare activities. However, the panchayats, inturn, have to transfer these grants to the social welfare department and other welfare units run by different departments. Thus, reverse flow of funds further erodes the fiscal powers of the local bodies (Rajiv Gandhi Task Force Report 2000).

4. STRUCTURAL DIMENSION OF APPR SYSTEM

There are a number of structural aspects of AP Panchayati Raj system that need to be discussed to get a comprehensive idea of various omissions and commissions in the Act as well its operational dimensions.

AP has introduced a three-tier system – zilla Parishad, Mandal Parishad and Gram Panchayat at district, intermediate and village levels. The Act also provides for the constitution of Gram Sabha where all the adult members (registered voters) of the village function as general body of the panchayat. The Gram Sabha shall meet atleast twice a year to consider matters such as annual statement of accounts and annual reports of Gram Panchayats, proposals for fresh taxation, programmes for works for the current year, selection of schemes, beneficiaries and locations. Another important function of gram sabha is to act as institution of 'social audit' and to ensure social justice.

A gram panchayat consists of 5 to 21 elected members inclusive of its sarpanch depending upon the size of its population. The members of gram panchayats are elected by all registered voters of gram panchayat from wards whereas the sarpanch of the gram panchayat is elected by all registered voters of the gram panchayat and continues in office for a period of five years unless otherwise removed from office. However, the upasarpanch of gram panchayat is elected by the elected members of the gram panchayat.

The other features of the gram panchayats in Andhra Pradesh are that they are classified into (a) notified gram panchayats and (b) non-notified gram panchayats on the basis of their annual income. The notified gram panchayat's are again classified into (a) Group I notified gram panchayats (with an annual income of over Rs.60,000 and (b) Group - II notified gram panchayats (with an annual income of more than 40,000 but less than Rs. 60,000). Administratively, the notified gram panchayats are headed by an Executive officer and assisted by clerks - cum - bill collectors, bill collectors, sanitary inspector etc. The staffing pattern of non-notified gram panchayats comprises part-time bill collectors and part-time sweepers only. They are controlled by the Group Executive Officer. The salaries of these staff are to be met by panchayats' own resources in the non-notified villages, whereas in the notified villages the salaries of these personnel are met by the government.

The Act provides for the formation of mandal parishad for each mandal. The nomenclature of this intermediary tier in the state earlier was mandala praja parishad which has been changed to mandal panchayat by the Act and finally coined as mandal parishad following the suggestions made by the select committee (Sastry, etal 1995).

For the purpose of election of members for mandal parishad from territorial constituencies, each constituency consists of population between 3000-4000. The elected members of mandal parishad only are eligible either to contest or vote in the election to the offices of president/ vice – president of the mandal parishad.

At district level, the Act provides for the constitution of zilla parishad consisting of i) Members elected from territorial constituencies which obviously is a mandal, ii) Members of the legislative assembly of the state representing constituencies which form part or whole of the district, iii) Member of the house of the people representing constituency iv) Member of the council of states who is a registered voter in the district, v) two members belonging to minorities and co-opted by the elected members of the zilla parishad.

The staff of the zilla parishad consists of Chief Executive Officer (CEO) to oversee the administration of the zilla parishad supported by the Deputy CEO, Parishad Education Officer, Executive Engineers, besides a few administrative personnel.

The staff at mandal parishad consists of the Mandal Parishad Development Officer (MPDO), who is the overall incharge of administration, supported by Mandal Engineering Officer, Mandal Education Officer, Extension Officer (Rural Development), Village Development Officer (Men), Village Development Officer (women) etc.

The striking feature in AP is that the administrative line of control of Gram panchayat is direct and is different from that exercised at the mandal parishad and zilla parishad level. The gram panchayats are under the control of District Panchayat Officer (DPO). The Executive Officer of the gram panchayat works under the Extension Officer (E.O), Divisional

Panchayat Officer and District Panchayat Officer who are answerable to the collector. The other two bodies i.e., mandal and zilla parishads are administered by the Chief Executive Officer (CEO). This arrangement is peculiar to the AP State alone.

The State Government, the Commissioner and the District Collector have been given powers to control the PR institutions at all the three levels. To be specific, as per the section 249 of the Act, the district collector in case of chairpersons of mandal parishads and zilla parishads have the powers to suspend the elected heads on the grounds of omission and commission. Under section 250 of the Act the state government is also empowered to dissolve the democratically elected bodies on grounds of incompetence, abuse of power etc. These provisions of the state Act erode the autonomy of the local bodies to a great extent.

At the district level, one of the features of the zilla parishad is that MPS and MLAs represented on it have been accorded voting rights. This unrestricted involvement of the MPs and MLAs in the PR bodies in the states will marginalize these democratically elected institutions. This is likely to inhabit local leadership.

Another instance of state control over local bodies is in the form of budget of the zilla parishads that needs to be approved by the state government which cuts into the autonomy of the institution of self government.

As already mentioned AP Act does not provide for the constitution of District Planning Committee (DPC) at district level which is very glaring omission. Same is the case with the institution of Nyaya panchayat.

According to the Act, the ZP will be having seven Standing Committees which have since been formed. The chairman of ZP will be the chairman of four Committees, the vice-chairman of ZP for one Committee and two women members for two Committees. In the present mandal system there is no provision for formation of standing Committees whereas under earlier PSs (Panchayati Samithies) there was provision for 7 standing Committees. The Act, at the gram panchayat level provides for the constitution of 'Beneficiary Committees' for the execution of works of the GP and 'Functional Committees' for agriculture, public health, water supply, sanitation, family planning, education and communication. However, in practice there is no evidence of such committees having been formed by the GPs.

Another important structural dimension of AP Panchayati Raj Systems is that it provides for an organic linkage among the three- tiers of PRIs. This is sought to be achieved in AP in the form of provision for the elected heads of the lower tier as permanent invitees to the meetings of the next higher tier body. Thus all the sarpanchs of the gram panchayats in a mandal will participate in the mandal parishad meetings and mandal parishad presidents in a district participate in the zilla parishad meetings.

These members do not enjoy voting right. This arrangement appears sound. However, in AP there exists a system of MPTCs (Mandal Parishad Territorial Constituencies) and ZPTCs (zilla Parishad Territorial Constituencies) who elect chairpersons of MPPs and ZPPs. This type of arrangement (5 functionary structure) is said to loosen the organic linkages. As one study mentions the territorial constituency members of both ZP (ZPTCMs) and MP (MPTCMs) are in utter confusion as to their respective roles in the schemes of PR system in AP (Sastry, 1996). Our interviews with ZPTc members also reveals that they do not have any substantive role to play other than participating in the elections of the chairpersons of MPPs and ZPPs. They are of the opinion that at present they carry the resolutions passed at gram panchayat to mandal and at mandal level to zilla parishad. They further mentioned that their position would have been better had they been vested with some financial and functional powers (Reddy, forthcoming). It is in this background that the central government is contemplating bringing in the constitution (Eighty Seventh Amendment) Bill, 1999 which was introduced in the Rajya Sabha in December 2001. This was done at the behest of Telugu Desam Government in Andhra Pradesh. This move of AP Govt. was seriously questioned by leading advocates of democratic decentralization (Mathew, 2000, Bandyopadhyaya, 2000; Natraj, 2000). Following the State Government directive, the Governor of Andhra pradesh has promulgated an ordinance seeking to postpone the elections to mandal parishads and zilla parishads and to appoint special officer-in- charge to replace the elected representatives of these institutions. However the supreme court had set aside the ordinance passed by AP Govt. to postpone the elections. Consequently recent local body elections were held to MPTC and ZPTC positions. So the issue of bringing perfect organic linkages is not resolved.

5. PARTICIPATION OF DISADVANTAGED GROUPS (SCs, STs, BCs AND WOMEN) IN PANCHAYATS.

It is a historical fact that traditionally local bodies have been dominated by the powerful castes/ classes. In order to broaden the participation by the larger critical mass in the local bodies, in particular, the disadvantaged sections, reservations for leadership and membership to these sections is a first step. In the context of meager representation of women in the national and state legislatures vis-a vis their population, reservation of not less than one-third of the total number of seats and posts of chairpersons of panchayats for them should be considered a land mark in the process of political empowerment of women.

The social hierarchies and inequalities that exist in the society deter the marginalized to come and participate in the local bodies. Women in particular face multiple disadvantages on account of patriarchial value system which never allowed them for centuries to play active role in the societal functions including participation in political institutions.

The available data in respect of post 73rd Amendment panchayat elections in the states show that of the total number of 29.2 lakh elected representatives of panchayats at various levels, about 10 lakh are women. A large majority of them were elected for the first time for any political representation. 9.2 lakh of these women representatives were elected to the village panchayats. Similarly, schedule caste and schedule tribe members accounted for 3.65 lakh and 2.5 lakh respectively (Govt. of India, 2001).

The 73rd Amendment has greatly contributed to the political empowerment of the women and marginalized communities in the rural society. It has thrown open political opportunities in the panchayats to these disadvantaged sections. However, mere representation in terms of numbers does not add much to the quality of governance unless this is reflected in the efficient delivery of the services to the poor and needy.

In the state of Andhra Pradesh, as mentioned above, the visibility of the vulnerable sections in the positions of decision making was ensured by the protective discrimination measures (There are about 73513 women members at GP level, 4776 at MP level and 361 at ZP level; 38764 SC members at GP level, 789 MPTCs and 126 ZPTCs; 15304 ST members at GP level, 803 MPTCs and 66 ZPTCs). What is more important is the performance level of these sections in the service of the poor and needy. There are only few studies which examined the role of disadvantaged sections in decision making and their effectiveness in delivering public goods. One such study mentions that the post amendment phase proved beyond doubt that the women in Panchayati Raj moved from peripheral to leadership roles. The study which covered 14 mandal women Presidents says: "A high proportion of these women are young, educated and new entrants in respect of political involvement. Six of them have a clear perception of their role and six have a reasonably good view. Of the remaining two women, one is ignorant and the other has a very limited perception of her role. Male domination in case of three women and male interference in the performance of seven women were noticed. The remaining four women presidents have been independently performing their roles" (Manikyamba, 2000).

The positive outcome of the induction of women in the panchayats is also felt in the pro-poor, especially pro-women welfare programmes pursued by women chairpersons. In places where young and energetic women assumed chair positions, special attention is paid to promote income generating activities to rural women. In one such case a woman Mandal chairperson motivated a begging community (nomads) to take up self employment and engage in small business (Manikyamba, 2000).

However, certain negative facets have been observed in the working of PR bodies headed by women. The most common observation is 'proxy rule' by the family members (husbands in particular). This was observed in a mandal close to the capital of A.P where a woman was nominally placed in the role of president and functionally it is the husband who is the defacto president. He goes through all the records and puts his initials on the official papers. No one including Mandal Development Officer objected to this practice (Manikyamba, 2000).

Yet another study which investigated into a few case studies covering the performance of women chairpersons at mandal as well as panchayat level (both pre and post 73rd Amendment periods) mentions that the experience is not altogether unsatisfactory. Certain case studies proved that women leaders had shown great degree of dedication and honesty in their activities and performed a number of welfare programmes benefiting community. The political background of the family from which these women leaders have emerged is a major contributory factor for their success. The same study mentions that there are proxy panchayats where husbands and sons of the women sarpanchs played a prominent role in running the panchayats. In their case the failure for the women sarpanchs to assert themselves and break free is probably due to the subordination of women for several years. The degree of control by men is such that women are unable to break free and take advantage of the position of power offered to them. Willy nilly, they become pawns in the game of power, played by a majority of men who do not want to dilute their power base (Har Anand, 1995).

One other study that is being conducted in CESS (Reddy, forthcoming) in the two districts of Andhra Pradesh observed that there are a few cases where women, although inducted by men into panchayats, did perform reasonably well in terms of implementing certain developmental programmes. At the same time, there are cases where women sarpanches totally surrendered to proxy rulers. On similar lines, a Ford Foundation-sponsored study in the district of Kurnool in AP mentions that a large number of elected members of the local bodies especially women, SC/ST and backward caste members are not actively participating in the meetings of the panchayats. In large cases, husbands of women members attend meeting on their behalf (Babu, 1998).

On the whole, it would be too optimistic to expect an overnight change in gender relations because of the 73rd amendment. The effect of reservation cannot be viewed in the narrow corridor of time to guage the level of empowerment women can achieve. Reservation is not an end itself but an enabling tool to support and help create a critical mass of women to enter the political arena to bring about gender equality and social justice.

6. PANCHAYATS, JANMABHOOMI AND PARALLEL BODIES

A lot has been said and debated in A.P about non- involvement of panchayats in the State sponsored 'Janmabhoomi' programme and the creation of parallel bodies in the form of a number of Community Based Organizations (CBOs) for managing various sectors like natural resource management (water users' associations, watershed committees, Vana Samrakshana Samithiees) and social sectors (school education committees, mothers ' Committees) etc.

Essentially, there are two schools of thought prevalent today that put forward arguments for and against panchayats and parallel bodies. Those on the side of panchayats would argue that benefits from user committees managed natural resource projects, such as forest, watershed management, are not sustainable in the long run. After the source of funds from the projects dries up, committees are disbanded or abandoned and the livelihoods base of the poor remains only marginally improved. Those who argue for stakeholders' approach (managing the programmes directly by CBOs) feel that multiplicity of Committees is a means of getting more benefits from the government. The villagers see this as an opportunity to ensure the development of their villages through involvement of large number of government departments. The bureaucracy too favors these committees as it is able to have a greater say in the implementation of the programmes through these committees. Committees also create a broader leadership base and provide an opportunity for more people to be involved in decision making through membership. The protagonists of the stakeholders' approach feel that the panchayats have to address several issues at the same time making their work onerous. Committees focusing on specific issues, be it education, health or forest management would be able to take note of the specific objectives of the programme and deliver better results. It is expected that in the long-run members of these committees would also get elected as members of the panchayats. In other words, though the link between these committees and the panchayats is somewhat tenuous, these parallel institutions are imperative for ensuring greater peoples' participation in the development process. Overtime, the relationship between these people's institutions and the panchayats will become stronger (Mid-Tern Appraisal of the Ninth Plan, 1999). In this context it is apt to note the Chief Minister of AP, Shri Chandra Babu Naidu thinks that empowering Committees by way of people's direct participation in governance is different from representative democracy (Naidu, 2000).

Janmabhoomi was launched by Government of AP on January, 1997 as a "people centered development process aimed at establishing an ideal society. It embodies and cherishes the principles of people participation, equality, transparency and accountability leading to sustained economic development and excellence in all walks of life. The goal is an enhanced quality of life of every man and woman and child in the State". This programme has drawn experiences from earlier programmes namely, Prajala Vaddaku Palana (taking administration to door steps of the people), Shramadanam (contribution of free labor for development) and micro-level planning from November 1995 to 1996 in the state.

The Janmabhoomi as per official document is a peoples movement for reconstruction and revitalization of the society. People's participation and self-help are the two principles enunciated for achieving the goals while empowerment of people with knowledge and skills is part of the process.

One of the objectives of the programme is to eliminate the contractor system in the government under this programme. Under this programme the State government sanctions directly to the village Communities, who are willing to take up the works on their own and ready to contribute a part (minimum of 25%) of investment. In order to ensure more professionalism in project implementation, a number of sector specific Community Based Organization (CBOs) have been formed in almost all the development sectors. Such CBOs include:

- Water User Associations for irrigation works
- Watershed Development Committees
- Joint Forest Management Committees
- Education Committees
- DWCRA Groups
- CMEY
- Village level Committees for Janmabhoomi work

The state government argues that these CBOs will eventually form the technical wings of the village panchayat and the panchayats will get strengthened in course of time (Rao, 2000).

Each round of Janmabhoomi would have thrust areas like 'Mahila Janmabhoomi' (women welfare); clean and green (environmental) social forestry, social Justice etc. The important activities taken up for the programme include: white washing of school buildings, cleaning streets, laying down of roads, sanitation, desilting the tanks, watershed programmes etc. (Reddy, 2000). Till date, 17 rounds of this programme have been completed covering above core areas.

One important feature of Janmabhoomi Programme is that gram Sabhas would play an important role, as Janmabhoomi Programme would build up the mechanism for active and vibrant gram sabha.

The above initiatives in AP evoked keen interest all over the country for its experiments in direct democracy. A brief review of the few assessments done is in the order. Contrary to what is stated, there is heavy dose of bureaucratic involvement in running Janmabhoomi Programme. The reliance on nodal officer for implementing the programme is clearly evident. The bureaucratic nodal agency has the authority to disburse the funds. Apparently, Janmabhoomi denounces the bureaucracy for its failures, but bestows a crucial position to it in the form of nodal agency. Further, it is mentioned that various user committees have systematically usurped the functions constitutionally entrusted to panchayats (Reddy, 2002).

According to another study, Sarpanches are unhappy that Janmbhoomi programme, which should rightly be implemented by PRIs, is being implemented by State Government departments. (Rajiv Gandhi Task Force Report, 2000). It is also observed that parallel institutions and panchayats are working at cross purposes (Reddy, 1999). Even the performance of CBOs was said to be positive initially, but the net contribution of the CBOs in the State is not very significant (Rao, 2000).

7. CONCLUSION

Consequent to the 73rd Constitution Amendment Act, AP has brought out AP Conformity Act, 1994 incorporating the salient features of the Central Act. However, the progress on fiscal and functional decentralization has not made much headway in the State. AP is also experimenting with direct democracy in the form of number of CBOs for various sectors. In the realm of administrative decentralization also, a number of initiatives were taken. The State Government's 'Janmabhoomi' Programme mainly through State bureaucracy goes against the spirit of the 73rd Constitution Amendment Act. The State Government's claim of integrating CBOs with Panchayats has not been made so far a reality. It is in this context, a recent proposal made by the few eminent practionaries of development administration for the convergence of SHGs and PRIs needs to be given serious thought.

Their proposal/model is as follows:

'APPR Act, 1994, provides for six functional standing committees at the Gram Panchayat (GP) level. The seven to ten Self Help Groups operating at the village level also represent more or less the same or similar types of activities. The Gram Sabhas shall co-opt one or more representatives of the SHGs into the respective Standing Committees of the Gram Panchayat. For instance members of the Village Education Committee will be co-opted as members of the Standing Committee on Education at the Gram Panchayat level. From amongst the co-opted members on the Standing Committees on Education in all the Gram Panchayats, in a Mandal, the Mandal Panchayat will co-opt in an open meeting of the Mandal Panchayat Simithi, a member/ members onto the

Standing Committee on Education of the Mandal Panchayat. The zilla parishad in turn will co-opt, in an open meeting of the zilla parishad from amongst the co-opted members of Standing Committees on Education of all the Mandal Panchayats in the district. The mechanism for selecting members in the other Standing Committees from the SHGs will be similar, starting from the Gram Panchayat level to the zilla parishad level'. (Bandhyopadhyay *et al,* 2002; see Appendix –II in this paper).

The goals enunciated in Vision 2020 Document regarding strengthening PRIs have not been met satisfactorily so far. According to James Manor (Manor, 1999) four crucial conditions required for democratic decentralization to succeed are:

i) Sufficient powers to exercise substantial influence within the political system and over significant development activities.
ii) Sufficient financial resources to accomplish important tasks;
iii) Adequate administrative capacity to accomplish those tasks and iv) reliable accountability mechanisms to ensure both the accountability of elected politicians to citizens and the accountability of bureaucracy to elected politicians.

Looking at these four crucial conditions set by Manor, one can conclude that AP has to travel a long way towards achieving genuine decentralization.

References

Aziz, Abdul (1998), "Financial Devolution to the Panchayats", Paper presented in a workshop held at NIRD, Hyderabad.

Babu, Devendra M (1998), "Status and Working of Decentralized Bodies in Andhra Pradesh: An Analysis", *Working Paper* presented at a one-day seminar, organized by Institute for Social and Economic Change, Bangalore.

Bandyopadhyay, D (2000), "Constitution Eighty-seventh Amendment Bill 1999", *Economic and Political Weekly,* Vol. 35, No. 18.

Bandhyopadhyay, D etal, (2002), "Convergence of Programmes by Empowering SHGs and PRIs", *Economic and Political weekly,* Vol. 37, No. 26.

Naidu, Chandrababu and Sevanti Ninan (2000), *Plain Speaking,* Viking by Penguin Books, New Delhi.

Government of Andhra Pradesh (1997), *Report of the First state Finance Commission,* Hyderabad.

Government of Andhra Pradesh (1999), People Centered, Growth Oriented Governance, In *Andhra Pradesh Vision 2020,* Hyderabad.

Government Of India (1999), *Mid Term Appraisal of the Ninth Five-Year Plan,* Planning Commission New Delhi.

Government of India (2001), *Report of the Working Group on Decentralized Planning and Panchayati Raj Institutions* for the Tenth Five year Plan, Ministry of Rural Development Government of India, New Delhi.

Government of India (2001), *National Commission to Review The Working of The Constitution,* A Consultation Paper on Review of the Working of the Constitutional Provisions for Decentralization (Panchayats), Vigyan Bhavan Annexe, New Delhi.

Har-Anand (1995), "Case Studies Andhra Pradesh- Gender and Caste Bias", downloaded from the Web Site.

Manikyamba, P (2000), "*Women in Local Governance Experience in Andhra Pradesh*", Paper presented at the seminar held on 1st and 2nd June, the Institute of Social Studies Trust, Bangalore.

Manor, James (1999), *The Political Economy of Democratic Decentralization,* The World Bank, Washington, D.C.

Mathew, George (2000), *The Hindu,* February. 16.

Natraj, V.K (2000), "Political Decentralization and Development Models", *Economic Political Weekly,* Vol. 35, No. 26.

National Institute of Rural Development (1998), *State Finance Commission Recommendations and Action Taken Reports of State Governments,* State Finance Commission Cell, Hyderabad.

Rajiv Gandhi Foundation (2000), *Panchayati Raj in India Status Report 1999,* Rajiv Gandhi Task Force on Panchayati Raj, New Delhi.

Rao, Bhaskara. G (2000), "Strengthening of Panchayats: Beyond Contractors Role'. A Note on Andhra Pradesh Experience", in Proceedings and Compilation of papers of the workshop on *Role of PRI's in Natural Resource Management,* organized by Society for Promotion of Wasteland Development, New Delhi.

Reddy, M Gopinath (1999), "Local Bodies and Community Based Organisations in Vision 2020: An Analysis" in D. Narasimha Reddy (ed), *Vision 2020 Myths and Realities,* Sundarayya Vignana Kendram, Hyderabad.

Reddy, M Gopinath (Forthcoming), *The Role of Local Bodies in Rural Development: The Impact on Rural Poor,* Center for Economic and Social Studies (CESS), Hyderagbad,

Reddy, G Krishana (2002), "New Populism and Liberalization Regime shift under Chandra Babu Naidu in AP", *Economic and Political Weekly,* vol. 37, No. 9.

Sastry, K.R, C.P Vithal and G. Ramachanraiah (1995), *Panchayati Raj in Andhra Pradesh. An Analytical Study,* NIRD, Rajendranagar, Hyderabad.

Sitaram, S (2000), *Decentralization in Andhra Pradesh (Draft)* World Bank Working Paper, New Delhi

Yugandhar (Forthcoming), *India Social Development Report,* New Delhi.

Appendix – I

1) District Agricultural Officer
2) District Horticultural Officer
3) District Officer for Land Reforms
4) District Soil Conservation Officer
5) District Officer for Animal Husbandry and
6) District Fisheries Officer
7) Deputy Conservatory of Forests incharge of social Forestry
8) District Industries Officer
9) District Officer for Khadi and Village Industries
10) Executive Engineer of Rural Housing
11) Executive Engineer of Public Health
12) Executive Engineer, PWD
13) Executive Engineer of State Electricity Board
14) Project Officer, Bio-Gas
15) All Block/ Mandal Development Officers
16) District Education Officer
17) District Adult Education Officer
18) District Education Officer incharge of Regulated Markets
19) District Health Officer
20) District Family Welfare Officer
21) District Officer for Women and Child Welfare
22) District Social Welfare Officer
23) District Officer for Backward Classes and Minorities
24) District Food and Civil Supplies Officer.

Category 2

1. District Rural Development Agency (DRDA)
2. District Industries Centre (DIC)
3. District Informatics Officer (of NIC)

Appendix –II

Diagram

Diagrammatic Representation of the Proposed Relationship Between Self Help Groups And Panchayati Raj Institutions in Andhra Pradesh

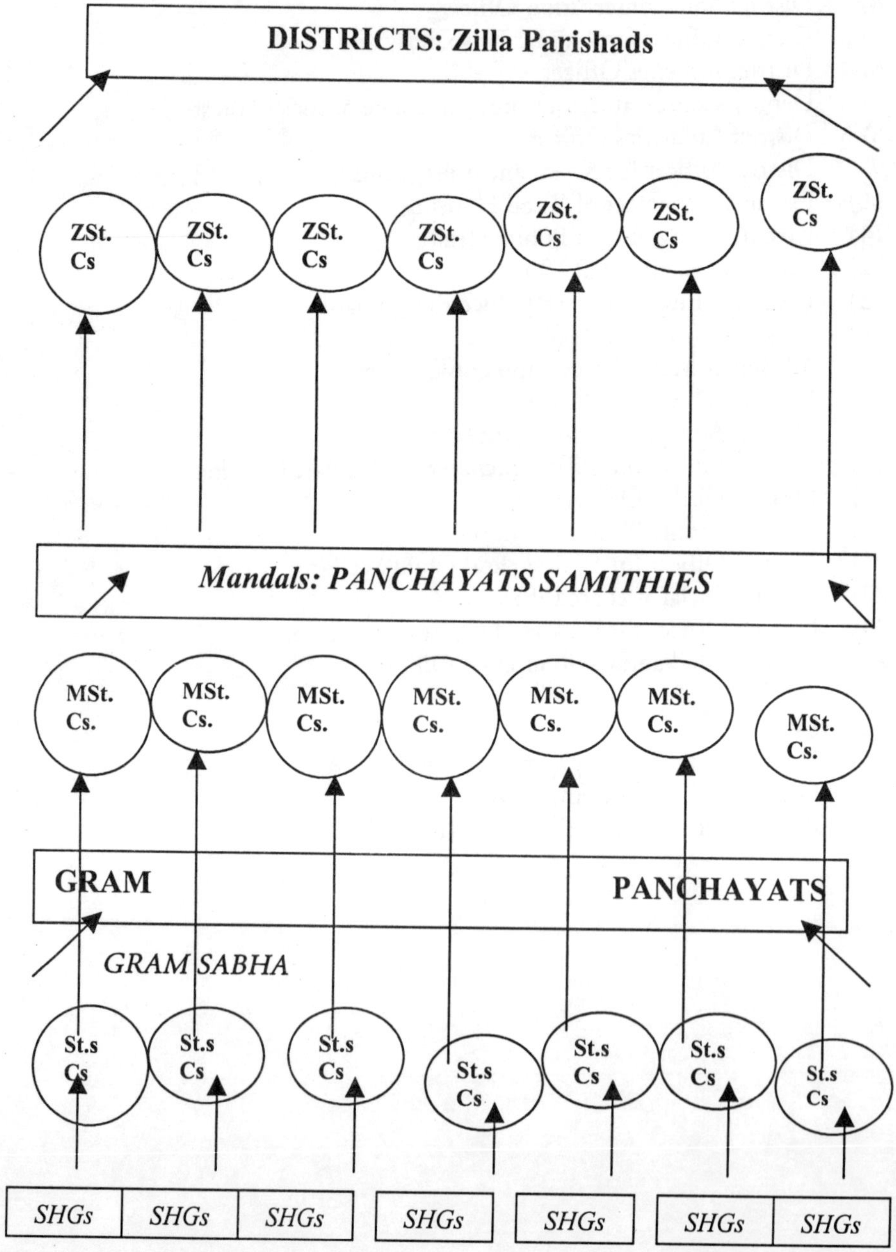

St.s = Standing Committees
SHGs = Self Help Groups
MSt.Cs = Mandal Level Standing Committees
ZSt. Cs = Zilla Parishad Level Standing Committees

Source: Draft Report of the Task Force Committee on Convergence of Programmes by Empowering the Self-Help groups and Panchayati Raj Institutions.

Map of Andhra Pradesh

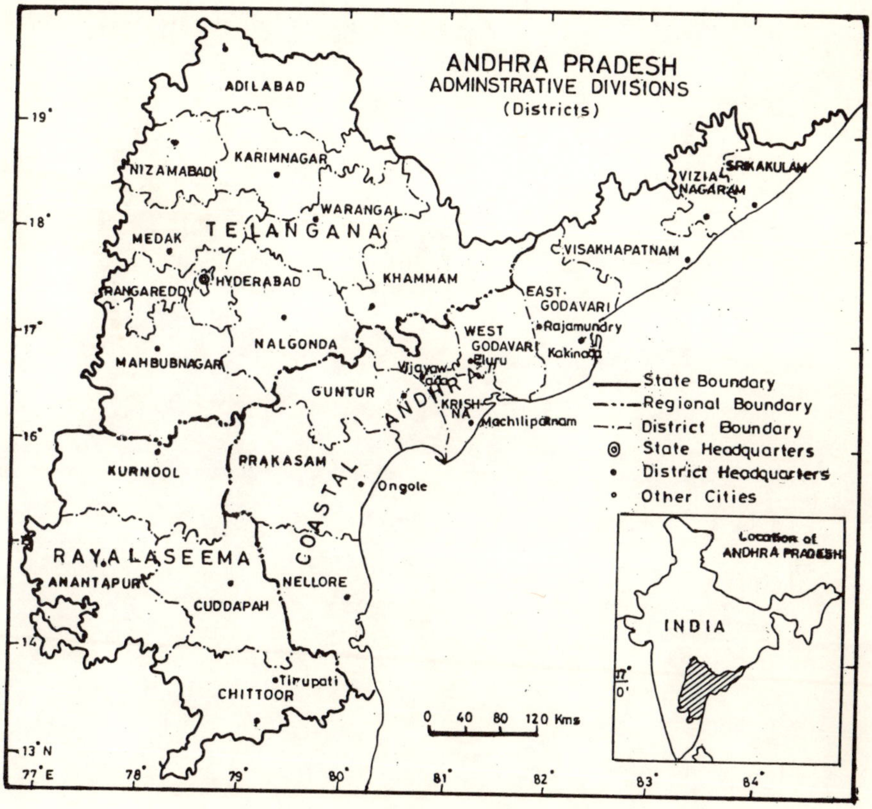

Subject Index

Author Index